Human Resource Management

Seventh Edition

HUMAN RESOURCE MANAGEMENT

SEVENTH EDITION

ROBERT L. MATHIS
University of Nebraska at Omaha

JOHN H. JACKSON
University of Wyoming

WEST PUBLISHING CORPORATION
Minneapolis/St. Paul▲ New York▲ Los Angeles▲ San Francisco

Copyediting and Indexing: Maggie Jarpey
Composition: The Clarinda Company

WEST'S COMMITMENT TO THE ENVIRONMENT

In 1906, West Publishing Company began recycling materials left over from the production of books. This began a tradition of efficient and responsible use of resources. Today, up to 95 percent of our legal books and 70 percent of our college and school texts are printed on recycled, acid-free stock. West also recycles nearly 22 million pounds of scrap paper annually – the equivalent of 181,717 trees. Since the 1960s, West has devised ways to capture and recycle waste inks, solvents, oils, and vapors created in the printing process. We also recycle plastics of all kinds, wood, glass, corrugated cardboard, and batteries, and have eliminated the use of styrofoam book packaging. We at West are proud of the longevity and the scope of our commitment to the environment.

Production, Prepress, Printing and Binding by West Publishing Corporation.

01 00 99 98 97 96 95 94   8 7 6 5 4 3 2 1 0

Library of Congress Cataloging-in-Publication Data

Mathis, Robert L., 1944-
      Human resource management / Robert L Mathis, John H. Jackson. — 7th ed.
           p. cm.
      Updated ed. of: Personnel/human resource management. 6th ed. © 1991
      Includes bibliographical references and indexes.
      ISBN 0-314-02529-4 (hard)
      1. Personnel management. I. Jackson, John Harold. II. Mathis, Robert L., 1944-
Personnel/human resource management. III. Title.
HF5549.M3349 1994
658.3—dc20   93-4430
                                           CIP

CONTENTS IN BRIEF

CONTENTS

Section 6: Employee and Labor Relations   443

16   Health and Safety   445

PREFACE

Too often we face the past and back into the future
George Schultz

Managers of human resources in organizations today face a rapidly changing world, and many of their past practices are being challenged because of changes in many areas. Every week numerous newspaper articles, television special reports, and seminars describe such issues as changing workforce demographics, labor shortages, family/work balancing, and equal employment concerns. The thrust of this book is to cover the relevant ideas and developments in the field of human resource (HR) management that managers will face into the next century.

The seventh edition of this book continues an established tradition, but the authors have made many changes in this edition in order to address newly emerging issues and to reflect changes in the way traditional HR activities are being practiced. Every line and word of content from the previous edition has been reviewed and major revisions made in many areas. Therefore, we believe that this edition again provides an excellent text which is both readable—and up-to-date.

There are a number of reasons for studying this book. Certainly not everyone who reads it will become an HR manager. In fact, many students who take HR courses will not become HR generalists or specialists. But everyone who works in any organization will come in contact with HR management—both good and bad. Those who become operating managers must be able to manage HR activities because every manager's HR actions can have major consequences for their organizations. A feature continued in the book specifies the typical areas of contact between operating managers and the HR unit. These "interfaces" throughout the book describe typical divisions of HR responsibilities, even though some variations will occur depending on the site of the organization, its technology, history, and other factors.

Organization of the Book

Each chapter begins with an example of an HR problem, situation, or practice in an actual organization to illustrate a facet of the content that follows in the chapter. Within each chapter, vignettes entitled "HR Perspectives" highlight specific practices by employers, research studies on HR topics, global HR issues and practices, and/or ethical issues in HR management. All of the cases at the end of chapters are "real-life" problems and situations using actual organizations as examples. Some of the section cases which were considered valuable by reviewers have been retained, but several new cases have been provided, including one on diversity management at Motorola.

A special feature in this edition is a completely new comprehensive case on HR activities at Federal Express, a company known as a leader in effective management of its human resources. Prepared specifically for this text, the case shows how integral HR management has been to Federal Express as it has built its "absolutely, positively" culture and operations.

The seventh edition opens with an overview of HR as a field of study, with Chapter 1 stressing both the strategic and administrative roles of HR management. Chapter 2 discusses the impact of changes in economic and employment patterns, demographic and workforce composition, work patterns and contingent workers, social values, and family/work issues. Significant new content on managing workforce diversity has been added to this edition. The second chapter also discusses HR management in global settings, in smaller entrepreneurial organizations, and in public-sector entities. Chapter 3 examines the strategic role of HR management and why it is growing in importance. Chapter 4 has been revised to focus on HR issues as they relate to organizational productivity and quality. The chapter specifically addresses the major part HR management plays in quality improvement efforts in organizations, including Total Quality Management (TQM).

Major revisions have been made in Chapters 5 and 6, (Section 2), on equal employment opportunity to ensure that content coverage of changes in legislation and recent court decisions is accurate and current. Specific coverage of the Civil Rights Act of 1991 and the Americans with Disabilities Act of 1990 (ADA) has been included.

Section 3 on analyzing and staffing jobs begins with Chapter 7, which covers job analysis and provides details on preparation and use of job descriptions and job specifications. New content has been added on identifying essential job functions as required by the ADA. Chapter 8 on recruiting has been revised, and it includes more on recruiting planning and evaluation. The ninth chapter contains solid coverage of the employment process and selection activities.

Chapter 10 on training contains comprehensive coverage on employee orientation and various other facets of training. Specific content addresses the topic of educational and skill deficiencies among U.S. workers and how employers are addressing those deficiencies. Chapter 11 discusses employee development and career planning and the importance of HR activities in these areas. The final chapter of Section 4 on performance appraisal includes both research and practice information.

Section 5 on compensating human resources covers pay administration, incentives, and benefits. More information has been included on pay-for-performance, gainsharing, and other incentive programs that are presented in Chapters 13 and 14. Major changes in content have been made in Chapter 15 on benefits in order to highlight the growing cost concerns facing managers and organizations. Special coverage of mandated benefits, health-care cost management, and family-related benefits highlight current changes, while discussion of flexible benefits systems identifies one response of employers to those challenges.

Employee and labor relations activities are covered in Section 6. In Chapter 16, Health and Safety, additional coverage has been included on hazard communications, fetal protection, and other evolving issues. Chapter 17 discusses the various issues associated with employee rights and discipline, such as employment-at-will, privacy rights, and substance abuse. The coverage of union/management relations in Chapters 18 and 19 highlights the legal framework for unionism, emerging trends in unionism, collective bargaining, and effective grievance management.

The text concludes with a chapter on assessing HR effectiveness. Significant revisions have been made in this chapter in order to incorporate coverage of human resource information systems. The focus of the final chapter is on assessing the effectiveness of HR activities in organizations.

The instructor's manual, prepared by Jack A. Hill (University of Nebraska at Omaha), represents one of the most exciting, professionally-useful instructor's aids available. The test bank contains approximately 2,000 test questions prepared by Ellen Frank (Southern Connecticut State University) and Roger Dean (Washington and Lee University). The same test bank also is available in computerized form from West Publishing. Over 60 color transparencies are available in a separate package. An excellent student resource guide prepared by Sally A. Coltrin (University of North Florida) and Roger Dean contains sample test questions, cases, and exercises to enhance the learning potential of this text.

Acknowledgments

Producing any book requires assistance from many others. The authors are especially grateful to those individuals who provided reviews and numerous helpful comments for this edition, including the following who did comprehensive reviews:

Reviewers

Ellen J. Frank
Southern Connecticut State University

Walter E. Greene
University of Texas-Pan American

David S. Hames
University of Nevada, Las Vegas

D. Lynn Hoffman
University of Northern Colorado

Vicki S. Kaman
Colorado State University

Daniel J. Koys
DePaul University

Mark L. Lengnick-Hall
Wichita State University

Nancy G. Lynch
Canisius College

Michael T. Roberson
Eastern Kentucky University

Ted Valvoda
Lakeland Community College

Charles White
Florida A & M University

In addition, specific suggestions from Larry Brandt (Nova University) and Carl Thornton (General Motors Institute) were appreciated.

Finally, some leading HR professionals provided ideas and assistance. Appreciation is expressed to Raymond B. Weinberg, SPHR; Jerry L. Sellentin, SPHR; William L. Kelly, SPHR; Michael R. Losey, SPHR; and Herbert E. Gerson, J.D. Special thanks go to James A. Perkins, SPHR of Federal Express, for his willingness to describe the evolution of the HR function at this firm, and to Gail Majors, SPHR, for describing Diversity Management efforts at Motorola.

Those involved in changing messy scrawls into printed ideas deserve special recognition. At the top of that list is JoAnn Mathis whose guidance and prodding made this book better. Others who assisted with many miscellaneous but necessary details included Nancy Hess and Carolyn Foster. Special thanks for their support and encouragement throughout the production process go to Carole Balach, Denise Simon, and Bridget Neumayr of West Publishing.

The authors are confident that this edition will continue to fill the need for a relevant and interesting text for those learning more about HR management. We are optimistic that those who use the book will agree.

Robert L. Mathis, SPHR   **John H. Jackson**
Omaha, Nebraska   Laramie, Wyoming

Perspectives on Human Resource Management

In order to compete in the 1990s, organizations of all types are focusing on improving productivity, quality, and service. Key to each of these areas is tapping the talents of the human resources available to the organization. New challenges in many areas are stretching the capabilities of managers, employees, and organizations. This text provides perspectives on current and emerging issues and activities, focusing on the management of human resources between now and the year 2000. Section 1 examines the nature of human resource management, diversity, and global issues as a prelude to discussing strategic human resource planning and productivity. Practical, realistic, and contemporary views of the field are essential for all who study the management of human resources today.

The first chapter introduces human resource (HR) management as a field of study and practice. The chapter stresses that for HR activities to be performed effectively in an organization, both professionals and staff in the special unit, called either the personnel department or human resource department, and managers throughout the organization must interact and interface effectively. Both the strategic and administrative aspects of HR management are identified as being important. A growing concern is the need for HR activities to be practiced in an ethical manner, and the chapter discusses the ethical dimension of HR management. Finally, the chapter examines HR management as a career field.

Chapter 2 examines the two overriding issues confronting organizations and managers from now until the end of the century: the increasing diversity of the workforce and the globalization of HR management. The nature of diversity and its effects must be understood if HR management is to help organizations deal effectively with all employees, regardless of their differentiating characteristics. The diverse workforce includes a growing number of older workers, women, individuals from racial and minority groups, persons with disabilities, and people with differing lifestyles. The diversity of family situations creates more pressures on employees to balance family and work, at the same time that shifts in work patterns and employment are occurring. A critical concern is the increasing number of current and future workers with educational deficiencies, particularly because of the increasing knowledge and skills required due to technological advances. The globalization of commerce and technology means that internationalization is occurring in more and more organizations. Because an increasing number of employees and managers live and work in a variety of countries and cultures, the second chapter concludes by highlighting some special international HR management considerations.

Chapter 3 focuses on the strategic side of HR management and the importance of strategic HR planning. External environmental scanning of a wide range of forces affecting HR management is necessary if organizations are to be able to forecast the supply and demand for human resources of all types. Particularly challenging is dealing with human resource shortages and surpluses. Downsizing and restructuring have occurred in many organizations, and the third chapter concludes by discussing how workforce adjustments are being made.

Chapter 4 focuses on individual performance and motivation within organizations as they affect productivity and quality. After discussing several approaches to motivation, the chapter emphasizes that analyzing human behavior helps organizations improve existing working environments and jobs. The interrelationships among job satisfaction, turnover, absenteeism, and job loyalty are discussed from a managerial perspective. How jobs are designed is examined in light of motivation theory to conclude the chapter.

CHAPTER 1

NATURE OF HUMAN RESOURCE MANAGEMENT

After you have read this chapter, you should be able to:

1. Identify the major HR challenges currently facing organizations and managers.

2. Define and clarify the two roles of HR management.

3. Explain why HR professionals and managers must share HR responsibilities.

4. List and define each of the six major categories of HR activities.

5. Explain why HR management must be adapted for smaller, family, public-sector, and international organizations.

6. Discuss why ethical issues permeate HR management.

7. Discuss HR management as a career field, including job levels, career outlooks, and preparation.

HR Today and Tomorrow:

HR Management Excellence at Hewlett-Packard

The role of the human resources (HR) function at Hewlett-Packard is changing. No longer the solvers of "people" problems, HR professionals have become "management enhancers"—that is, they help the managers themselves solve the people problems. Rather than being a catch-all for everything management wishes to delegate in this regard, the HR unit now facilitates, measures, and improves the quality of the management process. It has meant a complete change in functional perspective.

The firm was founded in 1939 by Bill Hewlett and David Packard—two Stanford electrical engineers from Palo Alto whose efforts in technology gave birth to California's Silicon Valley. Early on, the growing company became known for innovation in people-oriented practices and values, embodied later in a set of organizational values called *The HP Way.*

It was not until 1956, 17 years after the company was founded, that Hewlett and Packard agreed to have an HR function. Their earlier reluctance had been founded in their strong belief that managers should be responsible for the people-related aspects of the business. The creation of a separate department, they feared, might lead to diminished managerial effectiveness in these areas. "The pendulum within our company swung in the direction that Dave and Bill feared," says Pete Peterson, Vice-President of Personnel. "Now we're moving it back a little bit in the other direction." Hewlett-Packard's HR department is becoming a complement to management, not a substitute for it.

Overall, the revised strategic intent of the HR function is to *create an environment* conducive to increasing human value, providing higher quality, and utilizing resources more efficiently. Along with the senior managers of the HR function at Hewlett-Packard, Peterson formulated a revised vision for the department:

▲ Facilitate, measure, and improve the quality of management and teamwork.
▲ Contribute to business decision making and facilitate changes consistent with the basic values of Hewlett-Packard.
▲ Manage people-related processes, which are defined as those processes for which the HR department is directly responsible.

One HR goal that Peterson has set to help meet company goals is to achieve a ratio of one HR professional to every 75 employees. When the department embarked on the goal, the ratio was 1:56. About two years later, it was 1:68, which represented a 26% improvement in two years—and departmental savings of more than $25 million.

Goals already achieved include the following impressive list:

1. An accelerated 12-month development program aimed at advancing high-potential women and minorities, each of whom has a senior management mentor.
2. A Technical Women's Conference that showcased the achievements of female engineers and scientists.
3. Benefits for part-time employees working at least 20 hours a week.
4. A video on the company's management-development efforts.
5. Procedures for measuring the connection between general managers' performance appraisals and the results of their management, such as employee-morale surveys, marketing plans, profitability, growth, and new-product success.
6. An action plan to increase the hiring and promotion of women, people with disabilities, and older workers in Japan, Taiwan, Germany, and other countries in which Hewlett-Packard operates.
7. An on-line database called the *Practices Hotline,* which links HR professionals in the organization worldwide.
8. A workforce balancing plan that helps the company avoid layoffs and achieve its no-layoff goal.
9. A flex-force program, which gives the company more flexibility in redistributing personnel to various areas of the organization as needed.

These changes have reinforced the importance of HR management to the organizational success of HP. The revitalizing of HR management is a continuing challenge for all organizations including Hewlett-Packard.[1]

66 ————————————

The changes are so deep and far reaching that there are no simple
descriptions or answers as to the real nature of work and employment in
the 21st century.

Jeffrey J. Hallett ————————— 99

T he management of people at work is one of the primary keys to organizational success. Just as Hewlett-Packard did, many employers have discovered that better management of human resources can enhance productivity,
quality, and service.

Productivity Improving productivity becomes more challenging as global
competition increases, particularly when technology keeps changing. Firms are
discovering that the traditional approach of cutting costs, specifically labor costs,
may be counterproductive because employees (human resources) often are the
ones holding the keys to productivity improvement.

Quality and Service Likewise, quality and service depend primarily on organizational human resources. Organizations have rediscovered that being competitive requires continual improvement or maintenance of product/service
quality and attention to customers. Because the human resources (employees) are
the ones delivering the services, they must be included in identifying quality and
service blockages and redesigning operational processes. Such involvement in
problem solving by all employees, not just managers, often requires a change in
corporate culture, leadership styles, and HR policies and practices. Enhanced
results often are obtained when both managers and employees are trained in new
technology and interpersonal skills.

But as more and more organizations and managers have discovered, the availability and composition of the human resources today are dramatically different
from those in previous decades. Likewise, various shifts in the economies of the
United States and other countries are forcing changes in many industries as a result of global competitive processes. Finally, a wide range of political forces and
social trends are forcing changes in employment policies and practices. With all
of these changes affecting organizations at the same time, managers must be prepared for many challenges in obtaining, retaining, and developing their human
resources.

▲ TO THE YEAR 2000

For managers and organizations, the decade leading up to the year 2000 is best
characterized as turbulent. Those managers who try to operate as if their organizations are still facing the problems of the 1970s and 1980s are as obsolete as the
horse-drawn carriage in an era of cars and jet air travel. It has become evident in
the past few years that the "modern" world demands different strategies, policies, and practices from those in the past. Briefly, consider the following as chal-

lenges related to the management of human resources in organizations of all types:

▲ **Economic and employment shifts.** Some industries are declining (e.g., steel, rubber), while others are expanding rapidly (e.g., health care, computer processing). Service industry jobs are growing, while U.S.–based manufacturing jobs shrink.

▲ **Global competition.** Firms today compete in a global economy. Competition is increasing from firms in China, Taiwan, South Korea, Japan, the European Economic Community, Eastern Europe, and Latin America. Also, more foreign-owned firms are buying U.S. companies or starting up new operations in the United States.

▲ **Organizational restructuring.** Many organizations have "right-sized" either by: (1) eliminating layers of managers, (2) closing facilities, (3) merging with other organizations, or (4) outplacing millions of workers.

▲ **Demographic/workforce diversity.** Employees of today are more diverse in term of age, racial/ethnic heritage, gender, abilities, and lifestyles.

▲ **Family/work balancing.** For many workers in the United States, such as dual-career couples and single parents, balancing family responsibilities and work requirements is a significant challenge. Organizations are having to develop more "family friendly" policies and support systems for their employees by adopting flexible work schedules, assisting with child- and elder-care arrangements, revising maternity and family leave policies, and permitting more work-at-home and telecommuting options.

▲ **Education and training.** Changing patterns in many occupations and industries require better educated and trained workers. But the educational performance of those recently entering the workforce generally is deficient when compared with that of many other developed countries. Technology shifts and computerization also require continual training and updating of employees in many organizations.

▲ **Employee rights.** With more diversity of employees, organizations are having to adapt to ensure that all employees are treated appropriately and with dignity. Part of this treatment is creating a cultural environment in the organization in which individual rights are respected, while recognizing the legitimate rights of managers. Issues include drug testing, smoking restrictions, employee privacy, and employee due-process systems.

All of these challenges are discussed in more detail in later chapters of the text. The purpose here is to stress that the management of human resources in the future will require major changes in the way organizations are managed, so that the people working in them truly are viewed as *human resources,* whose value can be managed, not just viewed as labor costs.

▲ TRANSITIONAL NATURE OF HUMAN RESOURCE (HR) MANAGEMENT

The field of human resource (HR) management is in the throes of several major transitions because organizations themselves are changing. As a result, the terminology used in the field is in transition. What traditionally were called "personnel departments" often are termed "human resource departments." But more than the name has changed. The focus of such departments has shifted and their responsibilities have expanded.

Evolution of HR Management

Figure 1–1 highlights the major shifts that have occurred in the field. Before 1900, improving the working life of individuals was a major concern of reformers. Some employees attempted to start unions or strike for improved conditions. As far back as 1786, the Philadelphia Cordwainers (shoemakers) went on strike to obtain a $6 per week minimum wage.

▲ **Figure 1–1**   Changing Concerns of HR Management

TIME PERIOD	SUBJECT OF PRIMARY CONCERN TO MANAGEMENT	MANAGERIAL PERCEPTIONS OF EMPLOYEES	HR ACTIVITIES
Before 1890	Production technologies	Indifference to needs	Discipline systems
1890 to 1910	Employee welfare	Employees need safe conditions and opportunity	Safety programs, English-language classes, inspirational programs
1910 to 1920	Task efficiency	Employees need high earnings made possible with higher productivity	Motion and time studies
1920 to 1930	Individual differences	Employees' individual differences considered	Psychological testing, employee counseling
1930 to 1940	Unionization	Employees as management adversaries	Employee communication programs, anti-unionization techniques
1940 to 1950	Economic security	Employees need economic protection	Employee pension plans, health plans, benefits
1950 to 1960	Human relations	Employees need considerate supervision	Supervisor training (role-playing, sensitivity training)
1960 to 1970	Participation	Employees need involvement in task decisions	Participative management techniques (MBO, etc.)
1970 to 1980	Task challenge	Employees need work that is challenging and congruent with abilities	Job enrichment, integrated task teams, etc.
1980 to 1990	Employee displacement	Employees need jobs—lost through economic downturns, international competition, and technology changes	Outplacement, retraining, restructuring
1990 to 2000	Workforce changes and shortages	Employees need more flexibility in schedules, benefits, policies	Strategic HR planning, employee rights, training, flexible benefits, computerization, etc.

SOURCE: Adapted from Stephen J. Carroll and Randall S. Schuler, "Professional HRM: Changing Functions and Problems," in *Human Resources Management in the 1980s,* edited by Stephen J. Carroll and Randall S. Schuler (Washington D.C.: Bureau of National Affairs, 1983), 8–10. Used with permission.

HR management as a specialized function in organizations began its formal emergence shortly before 1900. Before that time most hiring, firing, training, and pay-adjustment decisions were made by individual supervisors. Some organizations adopted programs to benefit some employees, such as American Express, which established a pension plan in 1875. Also, the Scientific Management studies conducted by Frederick W. Taylor and others, beginning in 1885, helped management identify ways to make work more efficient and less fatiguing, thus increasing worker productivity.

As organizations grew larger, many managerial functions such as purchasing and personnel began to be performed by specialists. The first employment agents were hired by B. F. Goodrich Company in 1900. Some firms offered English-language classes to their many immigrant workers. Also, because many employees lived in tenements in crowded, unsanitary conditions, health and social workers were hired to help and instruct employees in good hygiene practices.[2] Concerns about unsafe working conditions and child labor led to the enactment of some state laws protecting workers beginning in 1908. Some corporations hired specialists to interpret the laws and ensure compliance.

The growth of organizations also led to the establishment of the first personnel departments about 1910. Work by individuals such as Frank and Lillian Gilbreth dealt with task design and efficiency. The Hawthorne Studies, conducted by Elton Mayo in the mid-1920s, revealed the impact of work groups on individual workers. Ultimately, these studies led to the development and use of employee counseling and testing in industry.

In the 1930s the passage of several major labor laws, such as the National Labor Relations Act of 1935, led to the growth of unions. The importance of collective bargaining and union/management relations following the labor unions' rise to power in the 1940s and 1950s expanded the responsibilities of the personnel area in many organizations, especially those in manufacturing, utilities, and transportation. Such work as keeping payroll and retirement records, arranging stockholder visits, managing school relations, and organizing company picnics were often the major tasks of personnel departments. The role of the HR department in the organization as a staff function to support operational (line) departments expanded during this period, and line-staff issues grew to influence HR departments in the following decades.

Increased legal requirements and constraints arising from the social legislation of the 1960s and 1970s forced dramatic changes in the HR departments of most organizations. HR departments had to become much more professional and more concerned about the legal ramifications of policies and practices. Also, organizations took a new look at employee involvement and quality of work as a result of concerns about the impact of automation and job design on worker productivity.

During the 1980s, the strategic role of HR management became essential as organizations reduced staff, closed plants, or "restructured." The ability of foreign firms from Japan, Korea, and other countries to outperform U.S.–based manufacturing companies forced U.S. organizations to become more productive. Outplacement of employees and retraining of those kept became prime concerns of HR departments. Also, containment of health-care benefits costs became more important.

For the 1990s, it appears that one major area of emphasis in HR management will be dealing with workforce diversity. Also, computerization of HR activities, even in small firms, will continue to receive attention. Finally, the growth of employee-rights issues such as drug testing and smoking restrictions will affect how HR activities are managed. All these changes and others reflect the evolving nature of the field.

Strategic and Operational Roles of HR Management

At the heart of the transition and terminology shifts is the fact that there are two major roles associated with the management of human resources in organizations. Figure 1–2 shows those roles as:

▲ **Strategic**
▲ **Operational**

Strategic Role of HR Management   The strategic role of HR emphasizes that the people in an organization are valuable resources representing a significant investment of organizational efforts. These human resources can be a source of competitive strength if they are managed effectively.

Strategically then, human resources must be viewed in the same context as the financial, technological, and other resources that are managed in organizations. At the same time that jobs are eliminated and experienced workers become unemployed in some industries, shortages of qualified people in other industries and occupations have occurred. Therefore, HR supply and demand must be viewed from a strategic standpoint. At a computer software firm growth is being limited by shortages of programmers and systems analysts. Therefore, the HR director heads up a site-selection team for opening up a new facility in another state, so that a different labor market can be tapped.

One study by the Conference Board identified that top HR managers in larger companies are key members of the business management teams and serve as a

Role	Focus	Most Often Reports to	Typical Activities
Strategic	Global, long-run, innovative	CEO/ President	• Human resource planning • Evolving legal issues • Workforce trends and issues • Community economic development • Organizational restructuring and downsizing • Merger/acquisition advising • Compensation planning and strategies
Operational	Administrative, short-term, maintenance	Corporate Vice President of Administration	• Recruiting and selecting for current openings • Conducting employee orientation • Reviewing safety and accident reports • Resolving employee complaints/ grievances • Administering employee-benefits programs

▲ **Figure 1–2**

HR Management Roles

catalyst for strategic planning in these organizations.[3] Their role as catalyst would be beneficial to organizations of all different sizes. Consider these two examples:

▲ In a firm with 100 employees, the HR Director is developing career plans and succession charts to determine if the firm has sufficient human resources to operate and manage the 70% growth it expects over the upcoming four years.

▲ In a firm with 1,000 employees, the Vice-President of Human Resources spends one week in any firm that is proposed for merger or acquisition to determine if the "corporate cultures" of the two entities are compatible. Two potential acquisitions that were viable financially were discontinued because he determined that the organizations would not mesh well and that some talented employees in both organizations probably would quit.

As Donna Goya, Senior Vice-President of Human Resources at Levi Strauss, says, "People issues *are* business issues."[4] Note, too, that the strategic focus of HR must be long term for effective planning to occur. More on the strategic role of HR is discussed in Chapter 3.

Operational Role of HR Management   Operational activities are both tactical and administrative in nature. Compliance with equal employment opportunity and other laws must be ensured, applicants must be interviewed, new employees must be oriented to the organization, supervisors must be trained, safety problems must be resolved, and wages and salaries must be administered. In short, a wide variety of activities typically associated with the day-to-day management of people in organizations must be performed efficiently and appropriately. It is this collection of activities that often has been referred to as "the personnel function," and the newer strategic focus of HR management has not eliminated it. However, instead of encompassing both roles, many HR practitioners are, unfortunately, continuing to perform only the operational role of HR management. This emphasis occurs in some organizations because of individual limitations and partly because of top management's resistance to an expanded HR role.

Defining the Field   Both roles are captured in the following definition of the field. **Human resource (HR) management** is the strategic and operational management of activities to enhance the performance of the human resources in an organization. Throughout this text the acronym HR will be used. Designations such as HR department, HR professionals, and HR management all reflect the dual roles.

Managing HR Activities

Managers and supervisors throughout organizations are responsible for the effective use of all of the resources available to them.[5] Therefore, effective management of the human resources is integral to any manager's job, whether as a hospital head nurse, assistant manager in a retail store, director of engineering, or president of a nonprofit agency.

Moreover, cooperation among people who specialize in HR management and other managers is critical to organizational success. This cooperation requires contact, or **interface,** between the HR unit and managers within the organization. These points of contact represent the "boundaries" that determine who

---

HUMAN RESOURCE (HR) MANAGEMENT

is the strategic and operational management of activities related to the performance of the human resources in an organization.

INTERFACES

are areas of contact between the HR unit and managers within the organization.

HR Unit	Managers
• Develops legal, effective interviewing techniques • Trains managers in selection interviewing • Conducts interviews and testing • Sends top three applicants to managers for final interview • Checks references • Does final interviewing and hiring for certain job classifications	• Advise HR of job openings • Decide whether to do own final interviewing • Receive interview training from HR unit • Do final interviewing and hiring where appropriate • Review reference information • Provide feedback to HR unit on hiring/rejection decisions

Figure 1–3

Typical Selection Interviewing Interface between HR Unit and Other Managers

does what in the various HR activities. In all organizations, decisions must be made to manage the "people-related" activities; they cannot be left to chance. For example, Figure 1–3 illustrates how some of the responsibilities in the process of selection interviewing might be divided between the HR unit and other managers.

A possible division of various HR responsibilities is outlined in each chapter, illustrating HR responsibilities in an area and who typically performs what portion of them. However, these illustrations are not attempts to indicate "the one way" all organizations should perform HR activities, but only how these activities can be divided. For example, in one medium-sized bank, all new nonmanagement employees are hired by the HR department. In another equally successful company, applicants are screened by the HR department, but the new employees actually are selected by the supervisors for whom they will work.

Clearly HR management is a concern of *both* the managers *and* the HR unit in an organization. Also, the HR managers must train other managers to perform HR activities effectively. In both large and small organizations, ensuring coordination and cooperation between HR managers and other managers can be a problem. To counter such concerns, Texas Instruments has established a Human Resources Policy Committee composed of both HR managers and operating managers to review HR policy issues and to resolve issues in which HR and operating decisions may conflict.[6]

In smaller organizations without a separate HR department, the cooperation of managers at different levels and in different departments also is essential if HR activities are to be performed well. For instance, in a small distribution firm hiring a new sales representative, the sales manager coordinates with the office supervisor, who may place a recruiting ad in a local newspaper, respond to telephone inquiries about the job from interested applicants, and conduct a telephone screening interview.

HR Management Costs

As an organization grows, so does the need for a separate HR department, especially in today's climate of increasing HR emphasis. One survey of 600 organizations revealed the following differences in the number of HR unit employees by industry:[7] The average bank/finance industry organizations have more HR unit employees per 100 workers than nonbusiness or health-care organizations. Organizations with fewer than 250 employees have a higher average of HR unit em-

▲ **Figure 1–4**

Costs of HR Function

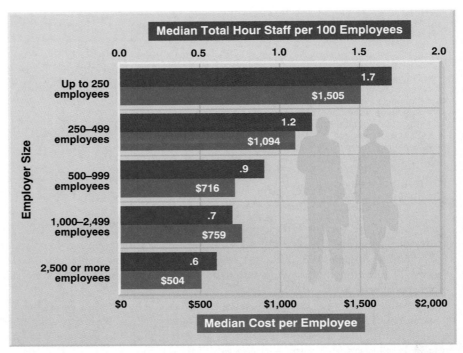

SOURCE: Adapted from SHRM-BNA Survey #58, "Human Resources Activities, Budgets, and Staffs: 1992–1993," *Bulletin to Management,* May 27, 1993.

ployees per worker (1.6 per 100 workers) than larger organizations. As might be expected, the number of HR unit employees needed to serve 200 employees is not significantly different from the number needed to serve 300 or 400 employees. The same activities simply must be provided for more people. Consequently, the cost of having an HR department is greater in organizations with fewer than 250 employees, as Figure 1–4 shows.

In a growing number of organizations, some specialty HR activities are being contracted to outside providers and consultants. For example, one firm with 1,500 employees has many processing activities related to employee benefits performed by a service bureau instead of hiring two full-time benefits technicians.

▲ HUMAN RESOURCE MANAGEMENT ACTIVITIES

As Figure 1–5 depicts, HR management is composed of several groups of interrelated activities. All managers with HR responsibilities must consider legal, political, economic, social, cultural, and technological forces when performing HR activities. The myriad of pressures from the environment affect the following groupings of HR activities:

▲ HR Planning and Analysis
▲ Equal Employment Opportunity Compliance
▲ Staffing
▲ HR Development
▲ Compensation and Benefits
▲ Employee and Labor/Management Relations

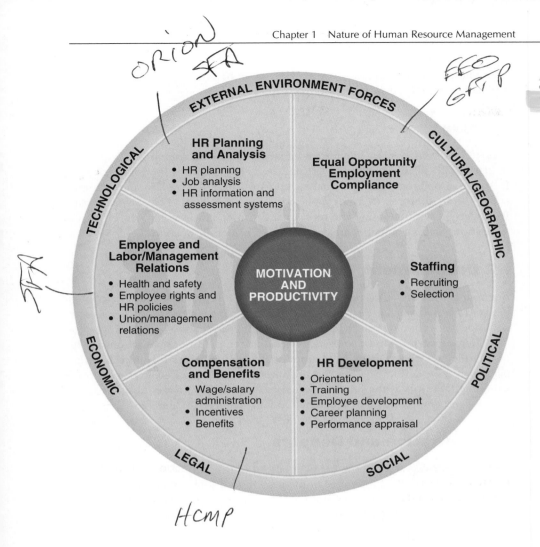

ORION SFA

EEO GFTP

SFA

HCMP

The environmental forces and their effects are discussed in Chapter 2, and the importance of motivation and productivity are discussed in Chapter 4. The nature of each of the activities is highlighted next.

HR Planning and Analysis

HR planning and analysis activities have several facets. Through *HR planning*, managers attempt to anticipate forces that will influence the future supply of and demands for employees. *HR analysis* comprises information, communications, and assessment systems that are vital to the coordination of HR activities. These topics are examined in Chapters 3 and 20.

Equal Employment Opportunity Compliance

Compliance with Equal Employment Opportunity (EEO) laws and regulations affects all other HR activities. For instance, strategic HR plans must ensure sufficient availability of a diversity of individuals to meet *affirmative action* requirements. In addition, when recruiting, selecting, and training individuals, all managers must be aware of EEO requirements. The nature of EEO and equal employment compliance are discussed in Chapters 5 and 6.

Staffing

The aim of staffing is to provide an adequate supply of appropriately qualified individuals to fill the jobs in an organization. *Job analysis* is the foundation for the staffing function. From job analysis information, *job descriptions* and *job specifications* can be prepared to *recruit* applicants for job openings. The *selection* process is concerned with choosing the most qualified individuals to fill jobs in the organization. Staffing activities are discussed in Chapters 7, 8, and 9.

HR Development

Beginning with the *orientation* of new employees, HR training and development includes *job-skill training*. As jobs evolve and change, *retraining* is necessary to accommodate technological changes. Encouraging *development* of all employees, including supervisors and managers, is necessary to prepare organizations for future challenges. *Career planning* identifies paths and activities for individual employees as they develop within the organization. Assessing how well employees are doing their jobs is the focus of *performance appraisal.* Activities associated with training and development are examined in Chapters 10, 11, and 12.

Compensation and Benefits

Compensation rewards people for performing organizational work through *pay, incentives,* and *benefits.* Employers must develop and refine their basic *wage and salary* systems. Also, *incentive programs* such as gainsharing and productivity rewards are growing in usage. The rapid increase in the costs of *benefits,* especially for health-care benefits, will continue to be a major issue. Compensation and benefits activities are discussed in Chapters 13, 14, and 15.

Employee and Labor/Management Relations

The relationship between managers and their employees must be handled effectively if both the employees and the organization are going to prosper together. Whether or not some of the employees are represented by a union, activities associated with employee *health and safety* and *employee rights* must be addressed in all organizations. To facilitate good employee relations, it is important to develop, communicate, and update HR *policies and rules* so that managers and employees alike know what is expected. In some organizations, *union/management relations* must be addressed as well. Activities associated with employee and labor/management relations are discussed in Chapters 16, 17, 18, and 19.

▲ HR MANAGEMENT IN SPECIAL SETTINGS

HR management for large private-sector corporations differs somewhat from that in small organizations, public-sector organizations, and international corporations. This section will consider the adaptations necessary to reflect the limited financial resources and workforce of smaller organizations, the unique environmental pressures and characteristics in the public sector, and the multifaceted requirements of firms that operate internationally.

HR Management in Small and Entrepreneurial Organizations

HR management is critical in small and entrepreneurial organizations. "People problems" are among the most frustrating ones faced by small-business owners and entrepreneurs. At the beginning of a small business, only basic HR activities must be performed. As the organization evolves, a few employees must be recruited and selected, and compensation and government-required benefits must be paid. Also, some orientation and on-the-job training, usually haphazardly done, is necessary.

The evolution proceeds through several stages. The focus of each stage reflects the needs of the organization at the time. In the initial stage, the organization first hires an HR clerk, then possibly an HR administrator. As the organization grows, it adds more HR professionals, often including an employment or benefits specialist. With further growth, other specialists, such as trainers, may be needed. From this point, additional clerical and specialist employees can be added, and separate functional departments (employment, compensation, benefits, and training) can evolve.

Family Relationships and HR Management   One factor often affecting the management of HR activities in small firms is family relationships. Particular difficulties arise when a growing business is passed on from one generation to another, resulting in a mix of family and nonfamily employees. Some family members may use employees as "pawns" in disagreements with other employed family members. Also, nonfamily employees may see different policies and rules being used for family members than for them. Key to a successful transition of a business from one generation to another is having a clearly identified succession plan, along with an estate financial plan.[8]

Public-Sector HR Management

Effective HR management is as necessary in public-sector organizations as it is in private-sector ones, even though the necessity of making a profit may be absent. Government employment in the United States has been climbing. The total for federal, state, and local government units was 18.7 million employees in 1993, which exceeded by 600,000 the number of employees in manufacturing.[9]

Although many similarities exist in the HR practices of private- and public-sector organizations, there are several notable differences stemming from their distinctly different environments. The U.S. Federal Civil Service System, established in the 1880s to reduce political patronage and favoritism in the selection of government employees, operates somewhat differently than HR systems in private-sector organizations. Many state and local government bodies have established merit systems and formal HR policies and procedures patterned after the federal system.

Privatization   One practice that is growing in usage in the public sector is **privatization,** wherein services formerly performed by public employees are

▼ **PRIVATIZATION**

occurs when services formerly performed by public employees are contracted to private-sector firms.

contracted to private-sector firms. Privatization has occurred in in such city services as operation of municipal golf courses, city trash collection, bus company operations, tree trimming, and data processing. A survey of large U.S. cities revealed that the major reason for privatization is to save money, particularly on employee wages and benefits. Naturally, resistance from public-sector unions has been fierce. But, when tried, just the threat of privatization has led to greater negotiating flexibility by public-employee unions.[10]

International HR Management

An organization that operates internationally must adapt its HR activities to reflect the cultural, social, political, and other forces present in other countries. Many U.S. firms have operations in other countries; likewise, a growing number of foreign firms are establishing operations in the United States. As a result, HR managers in all types of organizations and industries are having to think globally and monitor HR developments and practices internationally.

Ineffective international HR management can be quite costly. As an example, the actual annual costs of an executive located outside the United States who is paid $100,000 in salary is more likely to be $250,000 when housing costs, school subsidies, and tax-equalization payments are considered. If an executive quits prematurely or insists on a transfer home, costs can equal or exceed the person's annual salary. Consequently, international HR management practices focus heavily on staffing and selection, training and development, compensation, and safety. More on international HR management is discussed in Chapter 2, which deals with the globalization of HR management. Also, international facets of HR management are integrated throughout other chapters in the text.

▲ ETHICS AND HR MANAGEMENT

As the issues faced by HR managers have increased in number and complexity, so have the pressures and challenges of acting ethically. Ethical issues in HR management pose fundamental questions about fairness, justice, truthfulness, and social responsibility. Concerns have been raised about the ethical standards used by managers, particularly those in business organizations.

Ethical Issues in HR Management

Ethical issues and choices arise for HR decision makers in a variety of areas, as the "HR Perspective" indicates. Other ethical issues that are more specific include

- ▲ How much information on a problem employee should be given or withheld from another potential employer?
- ▲ Should an employment manager check credit agency or law enforcement records on applicants without informing them?
- ▲ What obligations are owed a long-term employee who has become an ineffective performer because of changes in the job skills required?
- ▲ What impact should an employee's off-the-job lifestyle have on promotion decisions if on-the-job work performance has been satisfactory?
- ▲ Should employees who smoke be forced to stop smoking on the job when new no-smoking restrictions are implemented by the employer? Should an

HR Perspectives:
Research on HR Ethical Issues

A survey to identify HR ethical issues and how to respond to them was sponsored by Commerce Clearing House and the Society for Human Resource Management. Conducted by Professors Danley, Harrick, Strickland, and Sullivan, questionnaires were received from more than 1,000 practicing HR professionals. The items on the questionnaires asked respondents to identify HR ethical situations and how those and other situations should be handled.

The study found that the ten *most serious* ethical situations reported by HR managers were those summarized in the box below.

One positive result was that about 70% of the HR respondents felt that their top managements were committed to ethical conduct and 65% said that their organizations were serious about uncovering unethical conduct and disciplining those involved. The study also found that 95% of the respondents felt that HR professionals should be responsible for ethical leadership in organizations.[11]

SITUATION	*PERCENT*
Hiring, training, or promotion based on favoritism (friendships or relatives)	30.7
Allowing differences in pay, discipline, promotion, etc., because of friendships with top management	30.7
Sexual harassment	28.4
Sex discrimination in promotion	26.9
Using discipline for managerial and nonmanagerial personnel inconsistently	26.9
Not maintaining confidentiality	26.4
Sex discrimination in compensation	25.8
Nonperformance factors used in appraisals	23.5
Arrangements with vendors or consulting agencies leading to personal gain	23.1
Sex discrimination in recruitment or hiring	22.6

*Those responding with 4 or 5 on five-point scale measuring "degree of seriousness." Number of respondents = 1,078.

employer be allowed to reject a job applicant on the basis of off-the-job smoking?

▲ Should an otherwise qualified applicant be refused employment because a dependent child has major health problems that would raise the employer's insurance costs?

▲ How should co-workers' "right to know" be balanced with individual privacy rights when a worker discloses he or she has AIDS?

These and many other situations pose both ethical and legal questions in which there may be a variety of conflicting facts, concerns, and options. With HR management in an international environment, other ethical pressures arise. Such practices as gift giving and hiring customs vary in other countries, and some of those practices would not be accepted as ethical in the United States. Consequently, all managers, including HR managers, must deal with ethical issues and be sensitive to how they interplay with HR activities.

What Is Ethical Behavior?

Ethics deals with what "ought" to be done. For the HR manager, there are ethical ways in which the manager "ought" to act relative to a given human resource issue. Determining specific actions, however, is not always easy. Ethical issues in management, including HR issues, often have five dimensions:[12]

1. **Extended consequences.** Ethical decisions have consequences beyond the decisions themselves. Closing a plant and moving it to another location to avoid unionization of a workforce has impact on the affected workers, their families, the community, and other businesses.

2. **Multiple alternatives.** Various alternatives exist in most decision situations, so the issue may be how far to "bend" principles. How much flexibility should be offered employees with family problems, while denying other employees similar flexibility, may require considering various alternatives.

3. **Mixed outcomes.** Decisions with ethical dimensions often involve weighing some beneficial outcomes against some negative ones. For example, preserving the jobs of some workers in a plant might require eliminating the jobs of others. The result would be a mix of both negative and positive outcomes for the organization and the affected employees.

4. **Uncertain consequences.** The consequences of making decisions with ethical dimensions often are not known. Should employees' personal lifestyles or family situations eliminate them from promotion even though they clearly are the most qualified candidates?

5. **Personal effects.** Ethical decisions often affect the personal lives of employees, their families, and others. Allowing foreign customers to dictate that they will not have a female or minority sales representative call on them may help with the business relationship short term, but what are the impacts on the employees denied career opportunities?

Responding to Ethical Situations

A growing number of organizations have established codes of ethics and training programs in ethical conduct for all employees. For instance, following several scandals, NYNEX Corporation, a large telecommunications firm, developed a written code of ethics and then conducted a full-day seminar for about 1,500 managers. NYNEX also established a hotline for employees to report unethical behavior.[13] Other firms have similar training, as shown in one survey that reported 44% of the firms had conducted ethical training.[14]

To respond in situations with ethical dimensions, the following standards have been suggested:[15]

1. Does the behavior or result achieved comply with all *applicable laws, regulations,* or *government codes?*
2. Does the behavior or result achieved comply with all *organizational standards* of ethical behavior?
3. Does the behavior or result achieved comply with *professional standards* of ethical behavior?

The complete study of ethics is philosophical, complex, and beyond the scope of this book. The intent here is to highlight the ethical aspects of HR management. Various ethical issues are highlighted throughout the text.

▲ HR MANAGEMENT AS A CAREER FIELD

As HR activities become more and more complex, the demands placed on individuals who make the HR field their career specialty are increasing. Although many of the readers of this book will not become HR managers, it is important that they know about HR as a career field so that they can appreciate the professional preparation required.

Types of HR Jobs

There are a variety of jobs within the HR field, ranging from executive to clerical. Here are some examples of each level:

▲ *Executive:* Vice-president of human resources, personnel director
▲ *Managerial:* Employment manager, HR manager
▲ *Technical/specialist:* Job analyst, employment interviewer, benefits specialist
▲ *Clerical:* Personnel clerk, HR secretary

A wide variety of jobs can be performed in HR departments, as the examples listed in Figure 1–6 illustrate. As a firm grows large enough to need someone to focus primarily on HR activities, the role of the **HR generalist** emerges—that is, a person who has responsibility for performing a variety of HR activities. Further growth leads to adding **HR specialists** who are individuals who have in-depth knowledge and expertise in a limited area. Intensive knowledge of an activity such as benefits, testing, training, or affirmative action compliance typifies the work of HR specialists. One study of 151 larger companies found that in HR departments 51% of the staff were generalists and 49% were specialists.[16]

▼ HR GENERALIST
is a person with responsibility for performing a variety of HR activities.

▼ HR SPECIALIST
is a person with in-depth knowledge and expertise in a limited area of HR.

Salaries

HR salary levels, as in other fields, vary by geographic area, educational level, and experience. Top HR jobs in manufacturing organizations generally pay more than those in nonmanufacturing organizations. As would be expected, HR practitioners in small organizations generally are paid less than their counterparts in large organizations.[17] Figure 1–6 shows typical salaries for a variety of HR jobs.

Career Outlook

The number of HR jobs has increased as the field has grown in importance. Projections made by the U.S. Bureau of Labor Statistics indicate that HR jobs

▲ **Figure 1–6**   HR Jobs and Salaries

TITLE OF JOB	ANNUAL BASE COMPENSATION (IN THOUSANDS)	ANNUAL TOTAL COMPENSATION (INCLUDING INCENTIVES, IN THOUSANDS)
GENERALISTS		
Vice-President of HR (with Industrial Relations)	$135.7	$173.7
Vice-President of HR (without Industrial Relations)	115.2	139.4
Director of Human Resources (small organization)	63.3	67.9
Employee Relations Manager	76.3	84.3
Plant HR Manager (nonunion)	52.1	54.3
Personnel Generalist	43.8	44.7
Personnel Assistant	24.4	24.6
SPECIALISTS		
Human Resource Planning Manager	68.6	73.2
Compensation and Benefits Administrator	39.9	40.0
Training Manager	55.1	56.9
Safety Specialist	45.6	46.3
Compensation Analyst	33.6	33.8
Employee Assistance Counselor	41.4	41.9
HR Information Specialist	38.5	38.9
Recruiter	32.7	33.0
Benefits Clerk	24.4	24.5

SOURCE: *1993 Human Resource Management Compensation Survey* (Kansas City: William M. Mercer, Inc.), 1993.

will grow through the mid-1990s about as fast as the average for all occupations.[18] Most HR job needs will be in the private sector. Even though the number of jobs in the field will increase some, most job openings will be for replacements. An abundant supply of candidates is foreseen. Consequently, entry into the field will be very competitive and salary levels likely will not increase significantly because of a plentiful supply of qualified experienced workers and the growing number of college-trained graduates.

Career Factors

The idea that "liking to work with people" is the major qualification necessary for success in HR is one of the greatest myths about the field. It ignores the technical knowledge and education needed. Depending on the job, HR professionals may need considerable knowledge about tax laws, finance, statistics, or computers. In all cases, they need extensive knowledge about equal employment opportunity regulations and wage/hour regulations. In sum, the specialized terminology of HR must be learned.[19] Additionally, those who want to succeed in the field must update their knowledge continually. Reading HR publications, such as those listed in Appendix A, is one way to do this.

The breadth of issues and activities faced by professionals in the field requires competence in a broad range of business and other topics. One study identified the following basic sets of competencies that HR professionals must have:[20]

HR Perspectives:

HR Certification

Professional in Human Resources (PHR) Requirements[a]

▲ A minimum of four years of HR professional experience,

▲ *or* an HR-related bachelor's degree and two years of HR professional experience,

▲ *or* an HR-related master's degree and one year of HR professional experience.

[a]For information regarding the above HR certification, contact the Human Resource Certification Institute, 606 North Washington St., Alexandria, VA 22314 (703-548-3440).

▲ **Students:** Special provisions for the PHR allow students to take the PHR exam within one year of graduation, even though they do not have the required experience. If they pass the examination, they receive a letter certifying examination results. Then they have four years in which to complete the specific experience requirements to earn certification. Full certification is granted as soon as they submit evidence of meeting the work experience requirements.

Senior Professional in Human Resources (SPHR) Requirements[a]

▲ Eight years of professional HR experience,

▲ *or* an HR-related bachelor's degree and six years of HR professional experience,

▲ *or* an HR-related master's degree and five years of HR professional experience.

▲ *Knowledge of the business.* Knowledge of financial, strategic, and technological capabilities in organizations.

▲ *HR processes and practices.* Expertise in fundamental HR activities (e.g., staffing, compensation, etc.).

▲ *Organizational change management.* Abilities in managing organizational change, including problem diagnoses, relationship building, leadership, and implementing change.

Certification   One of the characteristics of a professional field is having a means to certify the knowledge and competence of members of the profession. The C.P.A. for accountants and the C.L.U. for life insurance underwriters are well-known examples. The most well-known certification program for HR generalists is administered by the Human Resource Certification Institute (HRCI), which is affiliated with SHRM. Over 15,000 HR professionals have been certified by HRCI. The program has seen significant growth in those certified in the 1990s. Increasingly, employers hiring or promoting HR professionals are requesting certification as a "plus." A study of 280 HRCI-certified individuals revealed that their primary reasons for being certified were (in order): *professional accomplishment, personal satisfaction, demonstrating test knowledge, providing career advancement possibilities,* and *increasing peer recognition.*[21]

To become certified by HRCI, individuals must meet experience and/or educational requirements. Also, they must pass a comprehensive four-hour exam. Certification by HRCI is available at two levels; and both levels have education and experience requirements, as noted in the "HR Perspective." All individuals certified by HRCI must demonstrate that they have continued their professional learning and competence by meeting recertification requirements every three years.

Additional certification programs exist for both specialists and generalists sponsored by other organizations. For specialists, the most well-known programs include the following:

▲ Certified Compensation Professional (CCP), sponsored by the American Compensation Association.

▲ Certified Employee Benefits Specialist (CEBS), sponsored by the International Foundation of Employee Benefits Plans.

▲ Certified Benefits Professional, sponsored by the American Compensation Association.

▲ Certified Safety Professional, sponsored by the Board of Certified Safety Professionals.

▲ Occupational Health and Safety Technologist, given by the American Board of Industrial Hygiene and the Board of Certified Safety Professionals.

Regardless of the certification attained, those individuals who are certified demonstrate their professional commitment and competence. Also, certification may enhance job and career prospects.

▲ SUMMARY

▲ Productivity, quality, and service are driving forces in organizations today.

▲ Successful HR management is essential to organizational success. HR management has both strategic and operational dimensions.

▲ Challenges faced by managers and organizations include economic and employment shifts, demographic and workforce diversity, global competition, organizational restructuring, family/work balancing, education and training, and employee rights.

▲ Transitions in HR management over the past 100 years have paralleled general social changes, and the field has become increasingly complex and multifaceted.

▲ HR management is the strategic and operational management of activities to enhance the performance of the human resources in an organization.

▲ A sharing of HR responsibilities between the HR unit and operating managers creates an interface on HR activities.

▲ HR management activities can be grouped as follows: *HR planning and analysis, equal employment opportunity compliance, staffing, HR development, compensation and benefits, and employee and labor/management relations.*

▲ Special considerations are involved in managing HR activities in smaller or family businesses, in the public sector, and internationally.

▲ Ethical issues in HR management have proliferated for all types and sizes of organizations.

▲ HR departments are composed of generalists and specialists. A generalist has broad knowledge of a number of HR activities, whereas a specialist has intensive knowledge of a limited set of activities.

▲ Salaries in the HR field differ by job level and type, industry and size of organization, regional area, educational background, and experience.

▲ Preparation for a career in HR management includes broad and specialized education, experience, professional involvement, and certification.

◣ REVIEW AND DISCUSSION QUESTIONS

1. How have some of the HR challenges listed in the book affected organizations at which you or a family member has worked?
2. Why are both the strategic and operational roles of HR management necessary in organizations today?
3. Discuss the following statement: "In many ways all managers are HR managers."
4. What are the six major sets of HR activities, and what activities fall within each set?
5. Discuss the following statement: "The same HR management activities must be performed in every organization, but special adaptations may be necessary in the public sector, in smaller businesses, and internationally."
6. Identify two HR management situations with ethical dilemmas that you have observed, then discuss how those situations should have been (and were) handled.
7. Would HR management be a possible career field for you? Why or why not?

 REVITALIZING THE HR DEPARTMENT AT CALCOMP

Several years ago, it was apparent that changing the role and activities of the human resources (HR) function at CalComp was essential for the firm's future. CalComp, a worldwide wholly owned subsidiary of Lockheed Corporation, produces and sells computer graphics equipment. The company had 2,700 employees working in offices located in 14 countries. Consequently, the firm and its HR department faced problems on both the domestic and international fronts.

Employee morale was low and the HR department was viewed simply as a "traffic cop" that told employees and managers why they could not do something. It was difficult to recruit workers at corporate headquarters, located in Orange County in the Los Angeles area, which was a highly competitive labor market.

To lead the change, Charles Furniss was hired as Vice-President of Human Resources. Furniss first called the 22-person HR staff together to develop a strategic plan for the HR department. He conducted interviews with the HR staff and all top-level managers in the firm to determine what the HR department needed to do to become more "customer focused" internally. Following the interviews, a strategic plan for the HR future for a two-year period was prepared. The plan was titled "World-Class Human Resources." Once the plan was developed and endorsed by top management, the HR staff marketed it by making presentations to employees, managers, and local professional associations in order to communicate that CalComp was going to have a progressive and responsive HR department.

Some of the initial activities taken to implement the plan included redesigning the employee publications and publishing them more frequently. Also, motivation and training services were offered to all employees in the headquarters office. One program was so successful that it was duplicated at the CalComp plant in Scottsdale, Arizona, by closing the plant for a full day so that all 250 employees could participate. Shortly after, the HR department sponsored an open house for employees to show off newly refurbished department offices and to encourage employees to meet with HR staff members. Also, management development training was expanded; over 300 managers and supervisors attended programs over a six-month period of time.

While a more active and responsive image of the HR department was being established, Furniss and his staff members moved to implement some of the other components of the World-Class Human Resources Plan by setting specific strategies, goals, and timetables for various HR activities. For instance, one goal was to reduce turnover 4% and recruiting costs 20% in one year, both of which were accomplished. In addition, measures for assessing the performance of the HR department were set, and a regular reporting process was established for five major HR areas: staffing, compensation, benefits, training and development, and employee relations. Key indicators are tracked on a monthly basis.

After five years, the HR Department at CalComp is seen as a viable business unit. Today, the HR department at CalComp has a different image with employees and managers. More importantly, the HR department is playing a vital role for the corporation as it faces the challenges of the future.[22]

▲ QUESTIONS

1. Discuss how Charles Furniss and his HR staff played both strategic and operational roles at CalComp.

2. Which of the six major HR management activities were mentioned in the case as part of changing the HR focus in CalComp?

▲ NOTES

1. Adapted from Jennifer J. Laabs, "HR at Hewlett-Packard Marries the Best of Old and New Approaches," *Personnel Journal,* January 1993, 52–53. Reprinted with the permission of *Personnel Journal,* ACC Communications, Inc., Costa Mesa, CA; all rights reserved.

2. Peter B. Petersen, "A Pioneer in Personnel," *Personnel Administrator,* June 1988, 60–64.

3. Audrey Freedman, *The Changing Human Resources Function* (New York: The Conference Board, 1990).

4. Jennifer J. Laabs, "HR's Vital Role at Levi Strauss," *Personnel Journal,* December 1992, 34–46.

5. Barbara W. Shimko, "All Managers Are HR Managers," *HR Magazine,* January 1990, 67–70.

6. Peggy Stuart, "HR and Operations Work Together at Texas Instruments," *Personnel Journal,* April 1992, 64–68.

7. Adapted from SHRM-BNA Survey #58, "Human Resource Activities, Budgets, and Staffs: 1992–1993," *Bulletin to Management,* May 27, 1993.

8. Joan Warner, "Nothing Succeeds Like a Succession Plan," *Business Week,* September 30, 1991, 126–127.

9. "Government Workforce Outpaces Manufacturing," *USA Today,* February 18, 1993, B1.

10. Albert G. Holzinger, "Entrepreneurs to the Rescue," *Nation's Business,* August 1992, 20–28.

11. Adapted from "HR Professionals Agree: Workplace Ethics Require People to Be Judged Solely on Performance," 1991 SHRM/CCH Survey, *CCH Human Resources Management* (Chicago: Commerce Clearing House, 1991).

12. The authors acknowledge the contribution to the discussion of ethics by Larue T. Hosmer, *The Ethics of Management,* (Homewood, IL: Richard D. Irwin, 1987), 12–14.

13. Bruce Hager, "What's Behind Business' Sudden Fervor for Ethics," *Business Week,* September 23, 1991, 65.

14. Susan J. Harrington, "What Corporate America Is Teaching About Ethics," *Academy of Management EXECUTIVE,* February 1991, 21–30.

15. Robert D. Gatewood and Archie B. Carroll, "Assessment of Ethical Performance of Organization Members: A Conceptual Framework," *Academy of Management Review* 16 (1991), 667–690.

16. *HR's Strategic Role in Building Competitiveness,* (Lincolnshire, IL: Hewitt Associates, 1992), 42.

17. L. Kate Beatty, "The 1992 HR Pay Picture," *HR Magazine,* June 1992, 62–64.

18. Bureau of Labor Statistics, U.S. Department of Labor, *Occupational Outlook Handbook,* Bulletin No. 2250 (Washington, DC: U.S. Government Printing Office, April 1990), 46–58.

19. See William R. Tracy, *The Human Resources Glossary: A Complete Desk Reference for HR Professionals* (New York: AMACOM, 1991).

20. David Ulrich, Wayne Brockbank, and Arthur Young, "HR Competencies in the 1990's," *Personnel Administrator,* November 1989, 91–93.

21. Carolyn Wiley, "The Certified HR Professional," *HR Magazine,* August 1992, 77–84.

22. Adapted from Larry K. Kromling, "CalComp Considers HR a Business Unit," *Personnel Journal,* February 1993, 36–41; and Larry K. Kromling, "CalComp Reshapes HR for the Future," *Personnel Journal,* January 1990, 57–63.

CHAPTER 2

HUMAN RESOURCE MANAGEMENT: DIVERSITY AND GLOBAL ISSUES

When you finish this chapter you should be able to:

1. Explain management of diversity and why it is important.

2. Identify how the demographic and workforce shifts in four groups will affect organizations during the 1990s.

3. Describe how organizations are assisting employees in balancing family and work responsibilities.

4. Discuss why growth has occurred in the use of contingent workers and alternative work schedules.

5. Identify the changes in occupation and employment patterns that are occurring and why education and training needs will increase.

6. Explain how four HR activities are altered to serve expatriate employees.

HR Today and Tomorrow:
Tailoring HR Management to Fit at Levi Strauss & Co.

Just as Levi Strauss & Co. tailors its products to fit a variety of markets, it also has tailored its HR management activities to fit a variety of employee and corporate needs. Several years ago the company redefined the role of HR management, as well as the company as a whole. The senior management of the firm met to identify the basic values and mission for the company. Part of the *mission statement,* and an *aspiration statement* flowing from it, follows:

> We all want a Company that our people are proud of and committed to, where all employees have an opportunity to contribute, learn, grow and advance based on merit, not politics or background. We want our people to feel respected, treated fairly, listened to and involved. Above all, we want satisfaction from accomplishments and friendships, balanced personal and professional lives, and to have fun in our endeavors.

Then they specified the principles of the type of leadership necessary to fulfill these aspirations:

▲ New leadership behavior
▲ Value diversity of people in Levi's workforce
▲ Greater recognition for individual and team contributions
▲ Ethical management practices
▲ Timely communications with employees
▲ Empowerment of employees to act

Fulfilling these lofty aspirations in a company of 31,000, of whom 8,000 are located outside the United States (with 78 facilities worldwide), has been the challenge of the HR professionals at Levi's, headed by Donna Goya, Senior Vice-President of Human Resources. She says her job is made easier because, "I really think that our senior directors do understand now that people can give you the competitive edge."

One critical focus of Levi's HR management is to become a truly global company. Accordingly, HR programs are adapted or revised to fit local cultural differences in the European, Asian, and Latin American countries where Levi's operates. Cross-country movement of managers and professionals has aided the career development of employees while also expanding the company's global perspectives. International jobs are posted throughout Levi's. The firm does not have specifically targeted career tracks for individuals, but expects them and their managers to develop their abilities in the directions they desire.

Extensive investment in training has been required. A core curriculum of classes was started in which every employee participates. Topics in the core focus on the key dimensions of the aspiration statement. Extensive time is spent on values, diversity, and ethics. Understanding people with different backgrounds and lifestyles is explored through a variety of exercises.

Another area of concern at Levi's is aiding employees to balance their personal/family and professional/work responsibilities. A Work/Family Taskforce identified the major individual issues and developed surveys of employees throughout the United States. Over 17,000 employees (representing 73% of Levi's workforce) completed the 27-page survey. As a result of the surveys, the following programs were implemented:

▲ Training to make managers and supervisors aware of work and family issues
▲ "Time-off with Pay" program that replaces vacation, sick leave, and floating holidays
▲ Expanded child-care and elder-care leaves for individuals with family problems
▲ Financial support to improve existing child-care programs in communities where Levi's operates

One result of this expanded view of HR is that the corporate personnel policy manual decreased from 300 to 24 pages. The idea is to allow managers, HR professionals, and employees to adapt policies to fit individual and local needs. Also, Levi's does not have a dress code, but expects employees to dress professionally and appropriately for their jobs. Naturally, many employees wear Levi's products. At Halloween many people (including executives) dress in costume. Behind the fun and flexibility is the solid business reality expressed by Donna Goya, "HR is here to make the workforce effective and productive."[1]

66

The world hates change, yet it is the only thing that has brought progress.

C. F. Kettering ——————— *99*

The way Levi Strauss is managing its HR activities is only one illustration of how employers currently are facing a wider range of pressures and problems than those faced in the 1970s and 1980s. Organizations are a microcosm of the society in which they exist. Therefore, the changes and problems in society ultimately will be faced internally by managers. Until the mid-1980s, employers rarely were confronted with such issues as AIDS policies, smoke-free workplaces, employee drug testing, employer-sponsored child-care assistance, workplace violence, and workforce diversity training. Yet, today all of these issues and many others must be addressed in organizations of all sizes and industries by all managers, including HR managers. The purpose of this chapter is to scan the strategic issues in HR management that must be considered continually as individual HR activities are discussed.

▲ MANAGEMENT OF DIVERSITY AND CHANGE

The two words that best describe the challenges of HR management are *change* and *diversity.* Change and diversity are seen in the following major areas:
- ▲ An increasingly diverse workforce
- ▲ Balancing of family and work responsibilities by employees
- ▲ Changing work patterns and more contingent workers
- ▲ Industry and occupation employment shifts
- ▲ Education and training needed by a diverse workforce
- ▲ Economic changes resulting from global competition and the growing internationalization of U.S. organizations

Each of these issues is examined in detail later in the chapter. As a prelude, an overview of the management of diversity is appropriate.

Nature of Diversity

Managers must provide an environment that encourages the performances of individuals of differing races, ages, cultural and geographic origins, abilities and disabilities, and genders. In addition, varied lifestyles, personalities, family arrangements, and other factors affect each individual's performance. Job functions, work patterns, training, and HR management practices must be flexible enough to accommodate these diverse individuals.[2]

Approaches to Diversity   According to Roosevelt Thomas of the American Institute for Managing Diversity, there are three approaches to diversity.[3] The *traditional* approach requires that diverse individuals be assimilated into the workforce, using affirmative action programs, so that an employee "melting pot" is achieved. Another approach focuses on *understanding diversity.* Here the objective is to expand the abilities of employees to understand, accept, and value differences among co-workers. A third approach is *managing diversity,* meaning a

▲ **Figure 2–1**   Spheres of Activity in Management of Cultural Diversity

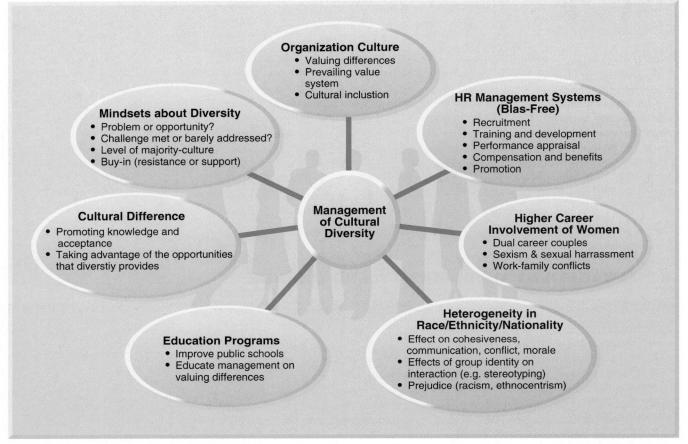

SOURCE: Taylor H. Cox and Stacey Blake, "Managing Cultural Diversity: Implications for Organizational Competitiveness," *The Academy of Management EXECUTIVE,* August 1991, 46.

continuing process that requires a variety of proactive efforts by employers, managers, and employees. Figure 2–1 indicates the wide range of areas that require attention when managing diversity.

HR Management and Diversity

A growing number of employers have taken steps to manage diversity through HR activities. Training often is at the heart of these efforts. The goal is to sensitize all employees to diversity issues and the needs of co-workers who are dissimilar in some ways. Colgate-Palmolive, Corning, Quaker Oats, Union Pacific, U.S. West, and Pacific Gas and Electric are among those organizations that have established diversity-management activities. Even smaller organizations have had to deal with this issue. Umanoff and Parsons, a small bakery in New York City, has 35 employees, 90% of whom are foreign born. Trader Publications in San Diego has made special efforts to enhance teamwork among its 230 employees, who have diverse backgrounds.[4] Some companies are establishing *workforce-diversity*

HR Perspectives:
Research on Managing Diversity

With the management of diversity at the forefront of HR challenges, it is important to know how HR professionals identify what is involved in managing diversity and how HR management and organizations are affected by it. Research conducted by Rosen and Rynes was sponsored by the Society for Human Resource Management (SHRM) and Commerce Clearing House, Inc.

To conduct the research a survey was used, which was returned by 785 SHRM members. Inconsistencies in defining the management of diversity were found, but the definition that ultimately was developed in the study is as follows:

Managing diversity is the management of organizational culture and systems to ensure that all people are given the opportunity to contribute to the goals of the organization.

However, the importance of managing diversity is not the highest priority in organizations. As might be expected, diversity was rated by a majority of responding HR professionals as being lower in priority than profitability, market share, capital investments, health-care costs, total quality management, and restructuring and downsizing.

Other key findings from the study were:

▲ Diversity management is a necessity, not a choice for their organizations, according to 61% of the respondents.
▲ Legal concerns still dominate diversity efforts, with sexual harassment policies, providing physical access for individuals with disabilities, and EEO/affirmative action policies and programs being cited frequently as diversity efforts.
▲ Approximately one-third of the respondents were in organizations in which diversity training had been conducted, with awareness of and sensitivity to individuals of diverse backgrounds being the most frequent topics covered.[5]

managers in their HR departments to elevate the importance of diversity management and to ensure that someone focuses specifically on diversity issues and implements appropriate training. The "HR Perspective" describes what HR professionals report that their organizations are doing to respond to the need for diversity in management.

▲ DEMOGRAPHIC SHIFTS AND WORKFORCE DIVERSITY

The shifting makeup of the U.S. population accounts for today's increased workforce diversity. A major study by the Hudson Institute entitled *Workforce 2000* brought management's attention to these multifaceted shifts.[6] Upon its release, the report received extensive media attention, which helped many organizations recognize the following facts (confirmed by projections of the U.S. Labor Department):[7]

▲ Total workforce growth will be slower during the 1990s than in previous decades.
▲ Only 32% of the entrants to the workforce between 1990 and 2005 will be white males.
▲ Women will constitute a greater proportion of the labor force than in the past, and 63% of all U.S. women will be in the workforce by 2005.
▲ Minority racial and ethnic groups will account for a growing percentage of the overall labor force. Immigrants will expand this growth.

▲ Average age of the U.S. population will increase, and full-time workforce participation rates for workers over 55 will decline. The total number of individuals aged 16 to 24 available to enter the workforce will decrease.

▲ As a result of these shifts, employers in a variety of industries will face shortages of qualified workers.

Organizations today are already seeing the effects of these trends. A more detailed look at some of the key changes follows.

Aging of the Workforce

Most of the developed countries are experiencing an aging of their populations—Australia, Japan, most European countries, and the United States.[8] For instance, the Japanese population over age 65 will double in just 26 years. In the United States the median age will increase from 31.5 in 1986, to 39 by the year 2000. This increase is due to people living longer and a decrease in the number of children, particularly those in the 16–24 age bracket. Little growth in this "teen" age group is projected until at least 2000.

One of the major implications of the age shift is that employers who in the 1980s filled large numbers of entry-level jobs with younger workers will have to look for other labor sources. In particular, service-sector employers, such as hotels, fast-food chains, retailers, and military branches of the government will face significant staffing difficulties. Some employers are trying new approaches to this problem. To generate additional applicants, McDonald's hired a home delivery service to distribute the mini-application form pictured in Figure 2–2, placing it on door handles in neighborhoods near local McDonald's restaurants. It had some success and illustrates the creativity being used by service industries to obtain workers.

Employers also are attracting more senior citizens to return to the workforce through the use of part-time and other work-scheduling options. According to the U.S. Bureau of Labor Statistics, the proportion of workers aged 55 to 64 holding part-time jobs has been increasing. Many are those who lost their jobs in organizational restructurings or who took early retirement buyout packages.

Implications   Implications of the shifting age of the U.S. workforce include the following:

▲ Retirement will change character as organizations and older workers choose phased retirements, early retirement buyouts, and part time work.

▲ Service industries actively will recruit senior workers for many jobs.

▲ Retirement benefits will increase in importance, particularly pension and health-care coverage for retirees.

▲ Fewer promotion opportunities will exist for midcareer baby boomers and the baby busters below them in experience.

▲ Baby boomers will have more "multiple" careers as they leave organizations (voluntarily or through organizational restructurings) and/or they start their own businesses.

Women in the Workforce

The influx of women into the workforce has major social and economic consequences. As Figure 2–3 shows, from 1970 to 1990 the percentage of women of

▲ **Figure 2–2**   McDonald's Mini-Application

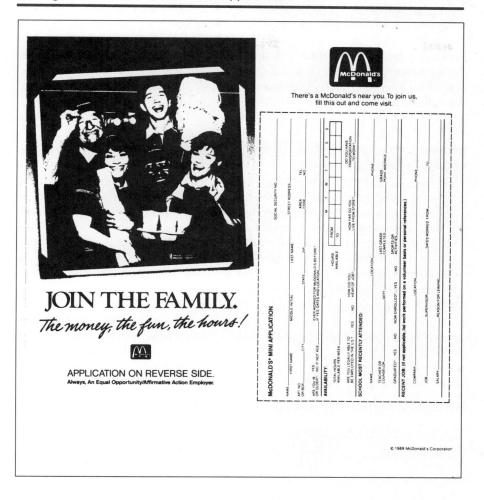

working age in the workforce rose from 43.3% to 57.5%, and that pattern of increase is expected to continue. As a result, it is projected that 62.6% of all women of working age and over 80% of women from 25 to 40 years old will be working or looking for work by the year 2000. This increase will mean that women will make up 47% of the total workforce by 2005. Further, about half of all working women are single, separated, divorced, widowed, or otherwise single

Sex	1970	1980	1990	Projected 2000
Women	43.3	51.5	57.5	62.6
Men	79.7	77.4	76.1	75.9

▲ **Figure 2–3**

Percentages of Working-Age Men and Women in the Workforce

SOURCE: U.S. Labor Department, Bureau of Labor Statistics, 1993.

heads of households. Consequently, they are "primary" income earners, not co-income providers.

As more women work, earning and employment patterns will continue to change. A growing number of women are entering jobs traditionally held by men. Earnings patterns for women will improve as more women shift into higher-paying professional and technical fields. However, women's average pay still is only 69% of men's (although in about 20% of all working couples, women earn more than their husbands).

Implications   Some of the implications for HR activities of more women working include the following:

▲ Greater flexibility in work patterns and schedules to accommodate women with family responsibilities, part-time work interests, or other pressures.

▲ More variety in benefits programs and HR policies, including child-care assistance and parental-leave programs.

▲ Job placement assistance for working spouses if their mates are offered re-location transfers.

▲ Greater employer awareness of gender-related legal issues such as sexual harassment and sex discrimination.

Additional implications are discussed later in the chapter when balancing of work and family issues is examined. But it is important to recognize that as more women enter the workforce, greater diversity will be found in organizations.

Racial/Ethnic Diversity in the Workforce

The fastest-growing segments of the U.S. population are minority racial and ethnic groups, especially Hispanics, African Americans, and Asian Americans. By the year 2000, about 30% of the U.S. population will be from such groups. Already nonwhite individuals are a majority in 51 cities of at least 100,000 population. Most of these cities are located in California, Texas, and Florida.[9] Some of the changes in racial/ethnic groups are as follows:

▲ The population of Asian Americans increased 108% from 1980 to 1990 and is expected to jump fivefold from 1990 to 2050, with half of these people being foreign born.

▲ The number of African Americans in the labor force is projected to grow twice as fast as the white labor force from 1990 to 2000.

▲ Hispanics will be the largest nonwhite group by 2010. Projections are that about 20% of the U.S. population will be Hispanic by 2020, the number of Hispanics having tripled by then. Also, the percentage of Hispanics in the workforce will double in 20 years.

Much of the growth in the various racial and ethnic groups is due to immigrants coming from other countries. Approximately 700,000 immigrants are arriving annually to the United States. About three-fourths come from Asian, Latin American, and Caribbean countries.[10] About one-third of immigrants have less than a high school education, while about one-fourth are college graduates. Increasingly, people with advanced degrees in science and engineering being hired by U.S. firms are foreign born.

Implications Implications of the increase in racial and ethnic cultural diversity are as follows:

▲ The potential for work-related conflicts between racial/ethnic groups and whites will increase, which may result in more workplace violence.

▲ Extensive employer-sponsored cultural awareness training will be required to defuse conflicts and promote multicultural understanding.

▲ Training in communication skills for those with English as a second language will increase, and job training will have to accommodate the different language abilities of a multicultural workforce.

▲ Employees with dual-language skills will be essential, particularly in service industries in certain geographic locales.

▲ Greater cultural diversity in dress, customs, and lifestyles will be permitted by employers.

Individuals with Disabilities in the Workforce

Another group adding diversity to the workforce is composed of individuals with differing abilities and disabling conditions. With the passage of the Americans with Disabilities Act (ADA) in 1990, employers were reminded of their responsibilities for employing individuals with different disabilities. There are at least 43 million Americans with disabilities covered by the ADA. The disabilities of this group are shown in Figure 2–4. Estimates are that up to 10 million of these individuals could be added to the workforce with appropriate accommodations being made. More discussion of the ADA is in Chapter 5.

The number of individuals with disabilities is anticipated to continue growing as the workforce ages. Also, those with AIDS or other life-threatening illnesses are considered disabled, and their numbers are expected to increase.

▲ **Figure 2–4**   Disabled Population in the United States

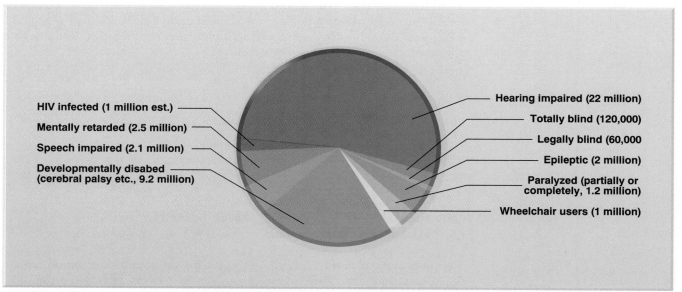

HIV infected (1 million est.)
Mentally retarded (2.5 million)
Speech impaired (2.1 million)
Developmentally disabed (cerebral palsy etc., 9.2 million)

Hearing impaired (22 million)
Totally blind (120,000)
Legally blind (60,000
Epileptic (2 million)
Paralyzed (partially or completely, 1.2 million)
Wheelchair users (1 million)

SOURCE: Office of Special Education and Rehabilitative Services, Centers for Disease Control, as reported in *USA Today*, January 24, 1992, 6A.

Implications   Implications of greater employment of individuals with disabilities include the following:

▲ Employers must define more precisely what are the essential tasks in jobs, and what knowledge, skills, and abilities are needed to perform each job.

▲ Accommodating disabled workers through more flexible work schedules, altering facilities, and purchasing special equipment will become more common.

▲ Nondisabled workers will be trained on ways to work with co-workers with disabilities.

▲ Health and medical examination requirements will be revised to avoid discriminating against individuals with disabilities.

Individuals with Differing Lifestyles in the Workforce

As if all of the demographic diversity is not pressure enough on managers and organizations, individuals in the workforce today have widely varying lifestyles that have work-related consequences. These range from conflicts between smokers and nonsmokers in offices to individuals with differing sexual orientations. Add to these issues growing concerns about balancing employee privacy rights with legitimate employer requirements, and the challenges involved with the management of human resources are expanded.

Implications   Some of the implications of these issues include the following:

▲ Policies on smoking must be developed and implemented that comply with relevant state and local laws, while recognizing the rights of both smokers and nonsmokers.

▲ Policies and procedures for preemployment screening and after-hire use of drug tests must be developed and implemented.

▲ Employee assistance programs must be established to help individuals with substance-abuse problems.

▲ The potential for workplace violence and conflicts is heightened as people with different lifestyles and sexual orientations work together. Training to reduce such conflicts will be necessary.

▲ Access to employee records will be limited and the types of information kept must be reviewed.

▲ Balancing of employee rights and employer quality and productivity needs must address such concerns as electronic and telephone monitoring of workers and searching of employees' desks and lockers.

▲ Generally, managers must recognize they should not attempt to "control" off-the-job behavior of employees unless it has a direct negative effect on the organization.

▲ FAMILY DIVERSITY AND WORK RESPONSIBILITIES

For many workers in the United States, balancing family and work demands is a significant challenge. While always a concern in the past, the decade of the 1980s saw major growth in the number of working women and dual-career couples. Family composition also is changing.

Family Composition

Just as the workforce and population have become more diverse, so too have the living patterns and household composition of families. According to data from the U.S. Census Bureau, the following describes families and households:

▲ The number of married couples who are childless or without children living at home exceeds couples with children at home by 3 million.

▲ A majority of all U.S. households have no children at home.

▲ 58% of all married couples are dual-career couples, representing 30.3 million couples.

▲ Households headed by a single parent make up 27% of all families, with women heading most of these households.

▲ Single-parent households are less prevalent among whites than among other racial/ethnic groups.

▲ About two-thirds of all women with children under age 6 are in the workforce, and 55% of all women with children under age 3 are working.

▲ Both men and women are marrying at later ages, with the median age of first marriage for men about age 27 and for women about age 24.

▲ A majority of both men and women aged 18 to 24 still live with their parents or are considered dependents.

These statistics reveal that the traditional family (the father worked, the mother stayed home, and there were several children) exists only in some families and in the misperceptions of some managers who think that it is widely prevalent. Actually, the "traditional family" represents only about 10% of the modern American households.

Dependent Care

To respond to the changes in the composition of families, employers are facing growing pressures to provide "family friendly" policies and benefits. The assistance given by employers ranges from maintaining references on child-care providers to establishing on-site child-care and elder-care facilities.

One study of over 1,006 companies found that 66% of the firms provide some type of child-care assistance and 36% provide elder-care assistance.[11] Also, surveys of workers in large companies have found that about one-third of all workers have significant responsibilities for caring for elderly relatives, and these responsibilities can detract from job performance and increase absenteeism. In recognition of this problem, some employers offer elder-care benefits.

Despite the protestations of some employers about parental-leave laws, a study done of organizations in four states found that such laws formalized practices that many employers already were following.[12] Legislation requiring employers with at least 50 workers to provide up to 12 weeks of unpaid parental/family leave was enacted in the Family and Medical Leave Act of 1993. Additional requirements of the act are described in Chapter 15.

Balancing Family and Work Roles

The decline of the traditional family and the increase in dual-career couples and working single parents places more stress on employees to balance family and work responsibilities. Increasingly, HR managers are having to deal with the organizational consequences of the family/work conflicts faced by employees.[13] For instance, many employees are less willing than in the past to accept relocations and transfers if it means sacrificing family or leisure time. Those firms that do get employees to relocate often must offer spouse employment assistance. Such assistance can include contacting other employers, providing counseling and resume-development assistance, or hiring employment-search firms to assist the relocated spouse.

Balancing work/family concerns also has particular career implications for women, because they tend to interrupt careers for childrearing to a greater degree than do men. According to Felice Schwartz, employers should recognize that there are two groups of women managers and professionals:

▲ *Career-primary women*—those who forgo or subsume family responsibilities to be executives
▲ *Career-and-family women*—those who stay in middle management and professional jobs and accept less pay in exchange for more family time and flexibility

It is this second group that gave rise to the "mommy track," a name given by critics to a subtle classification in the business world of women who were paid less and offered fewer opportunities because they had chosen to have families.[14] As would be expected, this dual-track view continues to be controversial. The balancing of work/family issues is sure to affect the management of human resources throughout the 1990s.

▲ CHANGING WORK PATTERNS AND CONTINGENT WORKERS

Other important changes in the workforce are the result of changing lifestyles and work patterns. Many of today's employees require temporary or part-time employment at certain stages in their work lives, and many firms find they are able to cut costs by employing such workers. Consequently, employers are offering greater variety in work patterns and schedules.

▼ **CONTINGENT WORKERS** are employed on a temporary or part-time basis.

Individuals are classified as **contingent workers** when they are employed on a temporary or part-time basis. Estimates are that about 25% of the total U.S. civilian workforce is composed of contingent workers.

Temporary Workers

Temporary employees can be obtained by an employer hiring its own temporary staff or by using a temporary-worker agency. Such agencies supply workers on a rate-per-day or per-week basis. Originally developed to provide clerical and office workers to employers, agencies now provide temporary accountants, lawyers, systems analysts, nurses, and many other professionals. Because employee benefits generally are not provided to temporary workers, employers can lower their overall labor costs by using them.

▼ **INDEPENDENT CONTRACTORS** perform specific services on a contract basis.

Independent Contractors   Other firms employ **independent contractors** to perform specific services on a contract basis. However, those contractors must be independent and meet a 20-item test identified by the U.S. Internal

Revenue Service and the U.S. Department of Labor.[15] Estimates are that up to 40% savings occur by using independent contractors because benefits do not have to be provided.

Part-Time Workers

U.S. workers who work fewer than 35 hours per week are considered part-timers. Although part-time employment is concentrated mainly in the retail trade and service industries, many part-timers hold professional or technical positions. Many employers increasingly are using part-time workers on a regular basis, but usually not for managerial positions.

Types of Part-Time Workers   There are two groups of part-time workers: voluntary and involuntary. **Voluntary part-time workers** are individuals who work less than 35 hours per week by choice. They represent an important segment of the U.S. labor force. According to the U.S. Bureau of Labor Statistics, about 15% of all employed people in the United States are voluntary part-time workers.

Involuntary part-time workers are persons who work less than 35 hours per week because of: (1) their inability to find full-time employment, or (2) an accepted reduction in full-time hours because of unfavorable conditions faced by their employers.

To prevent layoffs, organizations can use **work sharing,** in which an employer reduces work hours and total pay for all or a segment of the employees. This alternative permits individual employees to maintain their jobs, although with reduced hours and wages.

Job Sharing   A different part-time work pattern is **job sharing,** whereby two part-timers share one full-time job by choice. The potential advantages of job sharing include reduced turnover, increased efficiency, greater continuity, and higher productivity. A survey of 412 firms found that 28% have job sharing arrangements in use.[16] Many times a full-time job does not suit workers' personal needs. Job sharing offers one way of recruiting and maintaining highly capable employees who might otherwise choose different employment. This attraction has been particularly strong for working women who want more time to spend with their children. For example, two women may have a job and perform their childrearing duties by splitting one position.

Alternative Work Schedules

The regular full-time, 8-hour-a-day, 5-day-workweek schedule is in transition. Organizations have been experimenting with many different possibilities for change: the 4-day, 40-hour week; the 4-day, 32-hour week; the 3-day week; and flexible scheduling. According to the Bureau of Labor Statistics, about 60% of all employers have adopted some flexibility in work schedules. Changes of this nature require some major adjustments for organizations, but in some cases they have been very useful. They allow organizations to make better use of workers by matching work demands to work hours. Ultimately, everyone benefits by helping workers to balance their work and family responsibilities—the employer, the employee, and society at large.[17]

VOLUNTARY PART-TIME WORKERS

are individuals who by choice work less than 35 hours per week.

INVOLUNTARY PART-TIME WORKERS

are individuals who work less than 35 hours per week, but would be working full time if they could.

WORK SHARING

occurs when an employer reduces work hours and total pay for all or a segment of the employees.

JOB SHARING

is where two part-timers share one full-time job by choice.

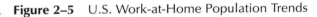

FLEXTIME

occurs when employees work a set
number of hours per day but vary
starting and ending times.

A COMPRESSED WORKWEEK

is one in which a full week's work is
accomplished in fewer than five days.

Flextime   In a type of schedule redesign called **flextime,** employees work a set number of hours per day but vary starting and ending times. The traditional starting and ending times of the 8-hour work shift can vary up to one or more hours at the beginning and end of the normal workday. Flextime allows management to relax some of the traditional "time clock" control of employees.

Compressed Workweeks   Another way to change work patterns is with the **compressed workweek,** in which a full week's work is accomplished in fewer than five days. Compression simply alters the number of hours per day per employee, usually resulting in longer working times each day and a decreased number of days worked per week.

Working at Home and Telecommuting

A growing number of workers in the United States do not leave home to go to work. One estimate is that about 40 million U.S. workers work at home on job-related work at least part time, including corporate after-hours home workers. But as Figure 2–5 shows, about 12 million workers earn all of their income at home.[18]

▲   **Figure 2–5**   U.S. Work-at-Home Population Trends

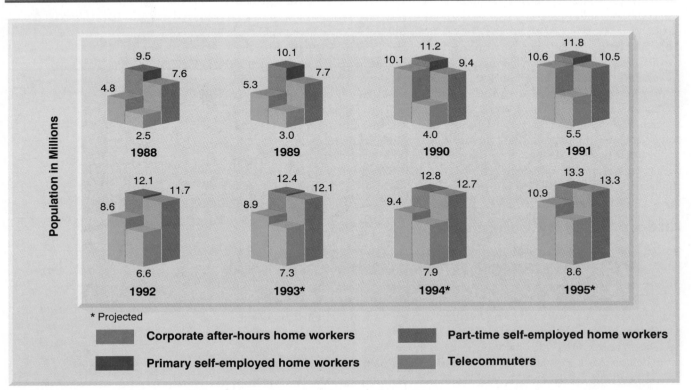

SOURCE: Data obtained from *INC.,* December 1992, 16.

Telecommuting   **Telecommuting** is the process of going to work via electronic computing and telecommunications equipment. Over 300 U.S. employers have telecommuting employees or are experimenting with them, including such firms as American Express, Travelers Insurance, and J.C. Penney Co.

One reason for offering telecommuting jobs is to attract workers who might otherwise be restricted from working, such as those with small children or aging relatives with health problems. Also, telecommuting allows individuals with disabilities, who might not otherwise be able to hold jobs, to work at home.

But not all the news about at-home work and telecommuting is positive.[19] The difficulties in restructuring jobs and tasks to make them suitable for such work have discouraged some employers. Also, problems about supervision and compensation of at-home workers, particularly those performing clerical tasks, must be worked out. Some at-home workers report they miss the social interactions associated with working in an office. Additionally, labor unions are adamantly opposed to telecommuting on the grounds that employers will use it as a way to avoid paying benefits.

> ▼ **TELECOMMUTING**
>
> is the process of going to work via electronic computing and telecommunications equipment.

▲ EMPLOYMENT SHIFTS

Several economic changes have occurred that have changed employment and occupational patterns in the United States. A major one is the shift of jobs from manufacturing and agriculture to service industries and telecommunications. Additionally, pressures from global competitors have forced many U.S. firms to close facilities, adapt their management practices, increase productivity and decrease labor costs to be competitive. For instance, in a 2-year period of time during 1991–1993, over 3.7 million jobs were eliminated by major U.S. firms. Over half of the jobs cut were in manufacturing, indicating that significant shifts in industries and occupations continue to occur.

The U.S. economy increasingly has become a service economy, and that shift is expected to continue. Over 80% of U.S. jobs are in service industries, and most new jobs created by the year 2005 also will be in services. It is estimated that manufacturing jobs will represent only 12% to 15% of all U.S. jobs by that date. From 1990 to 2005, the number of service jobs will increase 35%, while the number of manufacturing jobs will decrease 3%.[20]

Occupational Projections to 2005

Service-sector jobs generally include industries such as financial services, health care, transportation, retail, fast food and restaurants, legal and social services, education, and computer systems. As Figure 2–6 indicates, the fastest-growing occupations (percentage) are predominately in the computer and health-care fields. Actual numbers of jobs will be added the most in retail sales, nursing, office/clerical, and trucking. Another facet of change is the pattern of job growth or shrinkage in firms of varying sizes. Whereas many large firms have cut jobs by reducing their workforces, many smaller firms have continued to create jobs.

Education and "Knowledge Jobs"

Many occupational groups and industries will require more educated workers. The number of jobs requiring advanced knowledge is expected to grow at a much more rapid rate than other jobs. This growth means that people without high school diplomas or appropriate college degrees increasingly will be at a disadvantage, as their employment opportunities are confined to the lowest-paying service jobs. Therefore, there is a growing gap between the knowledge and skills required by many jobs and those possessed by employees and applicants. Several different studies and projections all point to employers in many industries having difficulties obtaining sufficiently educated and trained workers.

▲ **Figure 2–6**   Occupations That Will Grow the Fastest and the Most

OCCUPATIONS THAT WILL GROW THE FASTEST (PERCENTAGE)

OCCUPATION	EMPLOYMENT (IN THOUSANDS)		PERCENT CHANGE
	1990	2005	
Home health aids	287	550	92%
Paralegals	90	167	85%
Systems analysts and computer scientists	463	829	79%
Personal and home care aides	103	183	77%
Physical therapists	88	155	76%
Medical assistants	165	287	74%
Operations research analysts	57	100	73%
Human services workers	145	249	71%
Radiologic technologists and technicians	149	252	70%
Medical secretaries	232	390	68%

OCCUPATIONS THAT WILL GROW THE MOST (NUMBERS)

OCCUPATION	EMPLOYMENT (IN THOUSANDS)		NUMBER CHANGE
	1990	2005	
Retail salespersons	3,619	4,506	887
Registered nurses	1,727	2,494	767
Cashiers	2,633	3,318	685
Office clerks	2,737	3,407	670
Truck drivers	2,362	2,979	617
General managers and top executives	3,086	3,684	598
Janitors, cleaners, and housekeepers	3,007	3,562	555
Nursing aides, orderlies, and attendants	1,274	1,826	552
Food-counter, fountain, and related workers	1,607	2,158	551
Waiters and waitresses	1,747	2,196	449

SOURCE: U.S. Bureau of Labor Statistics, *Occupational Outlook Handbook* (Washington, DC: U.S. Government Printing Office, 1992).

▲ EDUCATION AND TRAINING AND THE WORKFORCE

Quite simply, there is an education and training crisis in the United States that increasingly will affect the quality of the human resources available to employers. One estimate by the American Society for Training and Development (ASTD) is that approximately 42% of the U.S. workforce (about 50 million workers) need or will need new or enhanced workplace training to adapt to the myriad of job and technological changes.[21]

A special taskforce set up through the U.S. Department of Labor, the Secretary's Commission Achieving Necessary Skills (SCANS) found that effective job performance is defined by workplace know-how, which is built upon a foundation of skills and competencies, as well as certain personal characteristics. In a harsh commentary, the SCANS report identified that many persons entering the U.S. workforce or already in it are deficient in one or more of the foundation skills.[22] Unless major efforts are made to improve educational systems, especially those serving minorities, employers will be unable to find enough qualified workers for the growing number of "knowledge jobs." The "HR Perspective" highlights ways that employers are addressing the deficiencies many employees have in basic literacy and mathematics skills.

Implications of Education and Training Trends

Increased emphasis on remedial education and job training for employees will be a continuing HR management concern. Implications are as follows:

▲ New training methods, such as interactive videos and individualized computerized training, will grow in usage.

▲ Training for future jobs and skills must be available for all levels of employees, not just managers and professionals.

▲ More accurate skills assessment for existing employees and jobs will be critical. Screening applicants for specific skills will be necessary.

▲ Remedial and literacy training programs will be offered by more employers.

▲ Employers increasingly will become active partners with public school systems to aid in the upgrading of the skills of high school graduates.

▲ GLOBAL HUMAN RESOURCE MANAGEMENT

Unprecedented political realignments and a changing world economic order guarantee a new era for international business in the 1990s. The reunification of Germany, the transformation of the Soviet bloc, the consolidation of the Eastern European countries, the growing economic might of Asian countries, and the new opportunities in Latin America and Africa create a markedly distinct world from that of the past.[24]

Global Competition

Truly the world has become a global economy. Many U.S. firms receive a substantial portion of their profits and sales from outside the United States. Estimates are that the largest 100 U.S. multinational firms have foreign sales of more than $500 billion in one year. For firms such as Colgate and Coca-Cola, foreign

HR Perspectives:
Employer Responses to Employee Basic Skills Deficiencies

Approximately 23 million Americans cannot read well enough to comprehend the daily newspaper. A study of 360 companies done by the National Association of Manufacturers found that a third of the employers consistently reject job applicants for not having sufficient reading and/or writing skills. Also, over half of the firms said that there were major deficiencies in basic skills within their existing workforces. For example, a paper company in Georgia installed automated equipment that required the use of tenth-grade math and reading skills by operators. But when the firm surveyed its workers, most of whom had high school diplomas, one-third did not have the necessary skills.

Consequently, the company established a math and reading center on site, spending $200,000. After three years, virtually all of the employees had obtained the necessary skills.

Many companies have had similar experiences:

▲ Motorola has spent over $50 million teaching seventh-grade math and English to its thousands of workers.

▲ Adolph Coors established a learning center for employees and families to aid them in obtaining general equivalency diplomas.

▲ Loxcreen in West Columbia, South Carolina, participates in a state-sponsored program to teach employees basic skills after work

hours. Loxcreen pays workers 50% of their wage rates for the time spent in class.

▲ Valmont Corporation, a manufacturer of steel and aluminum lighting and irrigation systems, based in Valley, Nebraska, conducted a year-long program to train 350 employees in math, English, and science skills. Employees participating in the program work as machine operators, welders, material handlers, and other plant jobs.

Given the demographic trends and the declining educational skills seen in the U.S., it is likely that basic skills training will grow in importance.[23]

---

sales and profits account for over 60% of total sales and profits. Other U.S. firms have substantial operations in other countries as well.[25]

Worldwide economic forces have affected the competitiveness of U.S. firms. As a result, the number and types of jobs in those firms have changed. The impact of global competition can be seen in many industries. The automobile, steel, and electronics industries have closed unproductive facilities or reduced employment because of competition from firms in Japan, Taiwan, Korea, Germany, and other countries.

At the same time, foreign-owned firms have been investing in plants and creating jobs in the United States. Over 3 million Americans are employed in foreign-owned firms.[26] The growth in employment resulting from foreign investments has helped to replace some of the jobs lost at U.S. firms. Global competition is occurring throughout the world on an ever-increasing scale. Numerous examples can be cited, but a brief look internationally illustrates the world economic linkages.

North American Trade   The United States, Canada, and Mexico have recognized the importance of world trade by eliminating barriers and working more closely together, starting in North America. U.S. firms and those from other nations such as Japan, South Korea, and Taiwan have taken advantage of the lower Mexican wage rates to establish *maquiladoras,* Mexican plants where parts are received from outside of Mexico and are assembled at low labor costs for shipment back to the other country. Such diverse corporations as Outboard Marine, RCA, General Motors, Zenith, Sunbeam, and R. G. Barry have established *maquiladoras*. One estimate is that over 1,700 such plants employing approximately 500,000 Mexican workers have been established in Mexican border towns.[27]

Europe   Consider the events in Europe, including the disintegration of the USSR into 14 independent states. The opening of Eastern European countries such as Poland and Romania, gives U.S.–based and other firms dramatically expanded opportunities to sell products and services. Also, the ample supply of workers available in those countries, whose wage rates are relatively low, means that labor-intensive manufacturing facilities can be started up to tap the available labor pools. In Europe, efforts to create a unified European economic market have led to cross-country mergers of firms and greater cooperation by European governments. At the same time, those efforts may have the effect of limiting the import of U.S. and Japanese-made goods to the participating European countries. Therefore, U.S. and Japanese firms have added offices and production facilities in Europe to avoid potential trade restrictions.

Asia and Japan   On the other side of the world, in Asia, Japan's economy has been maturing, and Japanese society has been changing because of a rapidly aging population. Also, younger Japanese are becoming more "westernized" and they are buying more imported goods. Gradually, the Japanese government has had to open up its markets and make changes in its economy in response to pressure from the United States and other countries. Economic relations between U.S. firms and those in countries such as Taiwan, South Korea, Singapore, and Malaysia have become more complex as the latter's exports to the United States have increased, while U.S. firms have established production operations in those countries.

Internationalization of HR Management

All of these examples emphasize that success within the global environment requires the flow of corporate capital, technology, and human resources. Thus HR management has become more global in nature. HR practices in one country are being adopted in other countries. For example, the national health insurance program in Canada has been examined as the basis for U.S. health insurance practices. Worker-involvement programs in Sweden and total quality programs in Japan have been adopted by U.S. manufacturers. Training and retraining programs at German companies are being emulated by a growing number of U.S. firms to deal with the shortage of qualified, trained technical workers.

International Staffing and Selection

As individual firms develop and expand their international operations, they typically employ individuals from both inside and outside the country in which the operations occur. One group of employees are called **expatriates**, individuals who are not citizens of the countries in which they work. Companies headquartered in countries other than the U.S. also make extensive use of expatriates.

AN EXPATRIATE

is a person working in a country who is not a citizen of that country.

International and staffing selection activities must be tailored to ensure that those sent to other countries will function effectively and complete their assignments. Research by the Employee Relocation Council indicates that the average annual cost to send an employee overseas for a year or two is $200,000 to $250,000.[28] The costs may rise to $1 million depending on the employee's salary, the location, and whether a family transfer is involved. However, improvement in selection is needed, especially when considering that the expatriate failure rate is 18% in London, 27% in Brussels, 35% in Tokyo, and 68% in Saudi Arabia.[29]

Many companies have the misguided notion that a good employee in a domestic operation will make a good expatriate. Poor staffing for international assignments occurs for several reasons. A study by Tung suggests the following:[30]

▲ Inability of spouse to adapt to international environment or other family related problems.
▲ Inappropriate personality or maturity of selected individual.
▲ Inability of international manager to handle the expanded responsibilities faced overseas.
▲ Lack of technical competence and/or motivation to work overseas.

Selection Process for Global Assignments   The selection process for international assignment should provide the candidate with a realistic picture of the life, work, and culture to which he or she might be sent, because most expatriate failure occurs because of cultural adjustment problems, not difficulties with job or technical skills.[31] Throughout the selection process, especially in the selection interviews, it is crucial to assess the potential employee's ability to accept and adapt to different customs, management practices, laws, religious values, and infrastructure conditions.

Communication Skills   One of the most basic skills needed by expatriate employees is oral and written communication capabilities in the host-country language. Inability to communicate adequately in the language may significantly inhibit the success of an expatriate. Numerous firms with international operations select individuals based on their technical and managerial capabilities, and then have the selected individual take foreign language training. Intensive ten-day courses offered through Berlitz or other schools can teach basic foreign language skills.

Family Factors   The preferences and attitudes of a spouse and other family members also are major staffing considerations. The availability of good schooling opportunities, the roles of men and women in the foreign country, and the availability of employment opportunities for the spouse must be considered by the potential expatriate. The expatriate employee may have an easier adjustment than a spouse or other family members because of involvement in work activities. The "HR Perspective" highlights a study on ways to improve the adjustment of spouses to international assignments.

EEO and International Selection Practices   For years in many U.S. firms, women were not considered for overseas jobs. Because of cultural values and historical traditions in some foreign countries, women who worked as professionals were a rarity, if such employment was allowed at all. Unaccompanied women still have some difficulty obtaining visas to enter some countries, particularly those in the Middle East and Orient. Also, the male-dominated culture of

HR Perspectives:

Global Assignments and Spouse Adjustment

The importance of spouse acceptance of and adjustment to international assignments by expatriates has been well documented. Black and Gregersen conducted a research study to identify the effectiveness of various HR actions in aiding such adjustment. Questionnaires were mailed to expatriates located in France, Great Britain, Hong Kong, Japan, Korea, the Netherlands, and Taiwan. A total of 321 were returned. The questionnaire asked the expatriates and spouses to evaluate international adjustment, pre-departure training, pre-move visit, desire to move prior to departure, social support in the host country, family support, living conditions, and

culture. Data also were obtained on previous international experience and how long they had been in the host countries.

The study found that spouse adjustment was positively related to pre-move visits, an attempt by the firm to seek spouse input about the assignment, and pre-departure cross-cultural training. Favorable living conditions, host-country social support, and family support related also positively to the adjustment of spouses. However, there was not a significant relationship between previous international experience and spouse adjustment.

One interesting result was that the

more a spouse, on his or her own initiative, sought cross-cultural training, the greater the eventual adjustment. Therefore, the authors recommend providing self-study materials and cross-cultural materials to augment formal training. The study generally suggests if the employer ignores the spouse in the pre-departure planning, the probability of expatriate failure increases. Black and Gregersen said, "U.S. firms would likely have more adjusted and committed spouses and expatriates by providing rigorous pre-departure training, especially when individuals are being sent to novel cultures."[32]

Japan has posed significant problems for women who attempt to represent U.S. firms to top-level Japanese executives or to obtain executive positions in Japanese-owned firms in the U.S.

When given the opportunity, women appear to function effectively in foreign countries. Those women who do obtain overseas assignments are expected to be more qualified professionally and personally than men in similar positions, according to many observers. Nevertheless, a growing number of women are interested in international assignments.

International Training and Development

Employees working internationally face special situations and pressures, for which special training and development programs are required. For the firms that have them, formal training programs have been found to have a positive effect on the cross-cultural adjustment of individuals. Training activities are of three types, as shown in Figure 2–7.

▲ *Pre-departure orientation and training of expatriate employees and their families.* Foreign language and culture-familiarization training are the two most important areas affecting expatriate successes.[33]

▲ *Continuing employee development.* Career planning and corporate development programs must consider expatriates.

▲ *Readjustment training for a return to the home country.* This training prepares the expatriate and family members to readjust upon their return to the home country. The expatriate's new subordinates and supervisors at home must be trained for the return of the expatriate also.[34]

▲ **Figure 2–7** International Training and Development

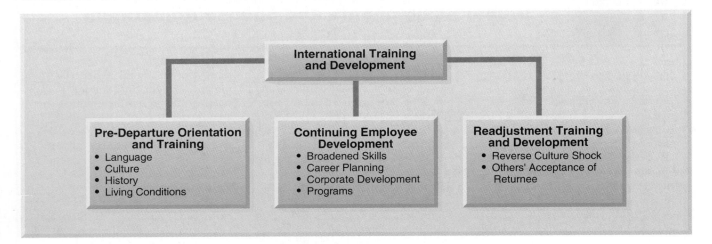

International Compensation

The major focus of most international compensation programs is to keep international employees at a sufficient financial level during their international assignments so that they do not lose ground economically. Components of an international compensation package, in addition to the normal salary and benefits offered in the home country, frequently include the following:

▲ Foreign service premium
▲ Hardship allowance
▲ Cost-of-living adjustment
▲ Housing and utilities allowance
▲ Educational allowances for children
▲ Relocation and moving allowances
▲ Home leave and travel allowances
▲ Tax equalization payments

Many multinational firms have compensation programs that use the "balance sheet" approach for expatriates. The heart of this concept is that international employees receive a compensation and benefits package that equalizes cost differences between an international assignment and one in the U.S.

▼ **A TAX EQUALIZATION PLAN**

is used to protect expatriates from negative tax consequences.

Tax Concerns Many international compensation plans attempt to protect an expatriate from negative tax consequences by using a **tax equalization plan.** Under this plan, the company adjusts an employee's base income downward by the amount of estimated U.S. tax to be paid for the year. Thus the employee pays only the foreign-country tax. The intent of the tax equalization plan is to ensure that expatriates will not pay any more or less taxes than if they had stayed in the United States.[35]

International Safety and Terrorism

With more and more U.S. firms operating internationally, the threat of terrorist actions against those firms and the employees working for them has increased.

U.S. citizens are especially vulnerable to extortion, kidnapping, bombing, physical harassment, and other terrorist activities. For instance, in a three-month period in a recent year, several hundred terrorist acts were aimed at businesses and businesspeople. While many of these acts targeted company facilities and offices, individual employees and their families living internationally constantly must be aware of security issues.[36]

Many firms provide bodyguards who escort executives everywhere. Different routes of travel are used, so that "normal" patterns of movement are difficult for terrorists to identify. Family members of employees also receive training in security. Children are told to avoid wearing U.S. logo sweatshirts and to be discreet when meeting friends. Schools for American children have instituted tight security procedures, including sign-in procedures for visitors, guards for the grounds, and improved security fences and surveillance equipment.

International HR professionals play a crucial role in providing security and protecting expatriates. Employees and their families must be made aware of these concerns before accepting international assignments. Training for all family members is essential and must be part of the pre-departure orientation process.[37] In especially dangerous environments, hazard pay must be offered.

 ## SUMMARY

▲ The management of diversity increasingly is affecting HR management.

▲ Effective management of diversity requires that organizations offer training to all employees on diversity issues.

▲ A demographically more diverse workforce will affect all managers and organizations.

▲ Some of the major demographic shifts include the aging of the population and workforce, the increasing number and percentage of women workers, growth in nonwhite racial and ethnic groups, accommodations for individuals with disabilities, and adapting to differing lifestyles.

▲ Organizations are addressing family/work balancing by offering dependent care, family leaves, dual-career couples, and spouse relocation assistance.

▲ Contingent workers include temporary workers, independent contractors, and part-time workers.

▲ Work patterns and schedules have become more varied. Growing use is being made of flextime, compressed workweeks, and telecommuting.

▲ Economic and employment changes include the increase in global competition, shifts in employment from manufacturing to service industries, and the growth of jobs requiring higher knowledge and education levels.

▲ Significant education and training needs must be addressed by employers in order to remedy deficiencies in worker skills and prepare for changes in occupational demands.

▲ Global competition means that international HR activities must be expanded in many organizations.

▲ Expatriates are persons who are working in a country other than their countries of citizenship.

▲ Staffing international jobs can be costly, and selection criteria for them must consider a wide range of skills, abilities, and family factors in addition to the required business knowledge and experience.

▲ Training and development activities for international employees focus on pre-departure orientation and training, continued employee development, and readjustment training for repatriates.

▲ Compensation practices for international employees are much more complex because many more factors must be considered.

▲ International employees must be concerned about their safety and the potential for terrorism.

▲ REVIEW AND DISCUSSION QUESTIONS

1. Discuss the following statement: "Adjusting to diversity must occur if U.S. organizations are to manage the workforce of the present and future."

2. What major demographic shifts will have an impact on organizations and their workforces between now and the year 2010?

3. Discuss how balancing work and family responsibilities has caused difficulties for you and/or others that you know. What have employers done to assist you or others?

4. What advantages and disadvantages of using contingent workers and alternative work schedules can you identify?

5. Discuss the following statement: "Shifts in the types of jobs and the industries in which jobs are gained or lost reflect global competition and other economic shifts that are occurring in the United States."

6. Assume you have been asked to consider a job in a foreign country with a U.S.–based corporation. Develop a list of questions/issues that the corporation should address with you before making a decision.

 WANTED: TELEMARKETING WORKERS

One illustration of the shift in jobs from manufacturing to service industries in the U.S. is the rapid growth of the telemarketing industry. From 1983 to 1993 employment in the telemarketing industry rose from 175,000 workers to over 5 million. It is projected that almost another 5 million workers will be added between 1993 and the year 2000.

The industry includes both firms that receive inbound calls on 800 numbers and those whose employees call out to businesses and individual consumers to sell products and services. Inbound telemarketing includes catalog orders, hotel and other travel industry reservations, product orders from cable television commercials, and many others. Outbound telemarketing often is done by service bureaus, which are firms hired to call customers to market such products as credit cards, auto club memberships, photography services, and financial investments. Legal restrictions exist on calling hours for outbound telemarketing, and these firms have had more difficulty hiring and retaining workers than inbound firms because calling consumers to sell products or services is less appealing than taking calls from customers who wish to order goods or services.

In addition to small- and medium-sized local firms, major corporations such as American Express, Marriott, and Hyatt have reservation and telemarketing centers. Most of the workers in the industry are part-timers working fewer than 25 hours per week. The wage rates have risen over the last few years so that starting rates of $5.50 per hour for inbound telemarketing are common, and the starting wage rates for employees whose jobs require outbound calling have increased to over $7.00 per hour.

Among the first cities to develop telemarketing as an industry is Omaha, Nebraska. Beginning in the early 1970s, several firms started in Omaha, and those firms have grown and spread throughout the country. In Omaha, a city of about 350,000, approximately 12,000 to 15,000 people are employed in the telemarketing industry. Some of the reasons for the growth of this industry in Omaha are:

▲ Central time zone location of the city
▲ Good telephone communications systems with ample room for additional lines for expansion
▲ Midwestern work ethic in a relatively union-free state
▲ Neutral speaking accent by most residents
▲ Lower cost of living and wage structures, when compared with larger cities in the Midwest and East

The problem faced by the telemarketing industry in Omaha is simple: a shortage of workers willing to do telemarketing part time. The telemarketing companies in Omaha are finding the competition for the same labor pool becoming severe. Some companies are adding jobs in other cities instead of Omaha. Others are considering relocating to smaller cities to find an untapped pool of part-time workers. Those located in Omaha are having to become more aggressive in attracting and retaining workers. Some firms are paying hiring bonuses of $100 if employees complete training successfully. Others are offering tuition and up to $1,000 if employees stay with the firm for a year.

The most extreme illustration of the pressure to find workers was seen when an Omaha-based firm, Sitel Corporation, had to hire 3,000 workers within a three-week period in order to fulfill a contract to introduce a credit card program for a major corporation. Employment for the 3,000 ran nine to twelve weeks. John Gajewski, Director of Human Resources for Sitel, resorted to "Sitel Man," a member of the HR staff who lived on a billboard for 12 days at the busiest intersection in Omaha. Live radio broadcasts were made by Sitel Man during radio time purchased by Sitel, exhorting potential workers from the Omaha area to stop by and complete applications. On the ground below the billboard Sitel HR representatives distributed application blanks or directed potential applicants to a circus tent set up at the company's operational center where interviews were held. Fortunately for Sitel and its HR staff, sufficient workers were enticed to enable the firm to meet its contract commitment to its customer.

The shortage of telemarketing workers is not limited to Omaha. As the industry has grown in other cities, similar shortages have appeared. At telemarketing industry meetings it is common for more than 70% of the telemarketing executives and managers to indicate that they could increase their sales by at least 25% if they had enough workers.[38]

▲ QUESTIONS

1. How have the economic and workforce changes discussed in the chapter contributed to the worker shortage in the telemarketing industry?
2. What specific suggestions to telemarketing executives would you make to aid them in locating and attracting additional workers?

▲ NOTES

1. Adapted from Jennifer J. Laabs, "HR's Vital Role at Levi Strauss," *Personnel Journal,* December 1992, 34–46. Reprinted with the permission of *Personnel Journal,* ACC Communications, Inc., Costa Mesa, CA; all rights reserved.

2. Marilyn Loden and Judy B. Rosener, *Workforce America: Managing Employee Diversity as a Vital Resource* (Homewood, IL: Business One Irwin, 1991), 19–21.

3. R. Roosevelt Thomas, *Beyond Race and Gender: Unleashing the Power of Your Total Workforce by Managing Diversity* (New York: AMACOM, 1991).

4. Sharon Nelton, "Winning with Diversity," *Nation's Business,* September 1992, 18–24.

5. Adapted from "Diversity Management Is a Cultural Change, Not Just Training." 1993 SHRM/CCH Survey, May 26, 1993, *CCH Human Resources Management* (Chicago: Commerce Clearing House, 1993).

6. W. B. Johnston and A. E. Parker, *Workforce 2000: Work and Workers for the 21st Century* (Indianapolis: The Hudson Institute, 1987).

7. Throughout the following section, various statistics on workforce composition and trends are taken from U.S. Department of Labor, Bureau of Labor Statistics, and Census Bureau data widely reported in various reference and news media reports. For additional details, pertinent issues of the *Monthly Labor Review* can be consulted, but specific reference sources are not presented.

8. U.S. Bureau of the Census, *An Aging World* (Washington DC: Superintendent of Documents, 1991).

9. "Minorities in Majority," *USA Today,* December 4, 1992, 8A.

10. "The Immigrants," *Business Week,* July 13, 1992, 114–122; and Diane Filipowski, "Coming to America," *Personnel Journal,* February 1993, 26.

11. *Work and Family Benefits Provided by Major U.S. Employers* (Lincolnshire, IL: Hewitt Associates, 1991).

12. Aaron Bernstein, "Family Leave May Not Be That Big a Hardship for Business," *Business Week,* June 3, 1991, 28.

13. M. N. Martinez, "Family Support Makes Business Sense," *HR Magazine,* January 1993, 38–43.

14. Felice Schwartz, "The Mommy Track," *Harvard Business Review,* January–February 1989.

15. Peter A. Gold and Michael D. Esposito, "Are Your Workers Independent Contractors or Employees?" *Compensation and Benefits Review,* July–August, 1992, 30–36.

16. Carol Kleiman, "Job-Sharing Benefits Appeal to More Workers," *Omaha World-Herald,* September 15, 1991, 11G.

17. Jennifer McEnroe, "Split-Shift Parenting," *American Demographics,* February 1991, 50–53.

18. Alessandra Bianchi, "U.S. Work-At-Home Population Trends," *INC.,* December 1992, 17.

19. "Telecommuting Grows Despite Bosses' Doubts," *Omaha World-Herald,* April 5, 1992, G1.

20. George Silvestri and John Lukusiewcz, "Occupational Employment Projections," *Monthly Labor Review,* November 1991, 81.

21. "ASTD Effort Pushes for Better Training of America's Workforce," *Personnel,* March 1991, 18.

22. The Secretary's Commission on Achieving Necessary Skills, U.S. Department of Labor, *What Work Requires of Schools: a SCANS Report for American 2000* (Washington DC: U.S. Department of Labor, 1991).

23. Adapted from "When Johnny's Whole Family Can't Read," *Business Week,* July 20, 1992, 68–70; Joan C. Szabo, "Boosting Workers' Basic Skills," *Nation's Business,* January 1992, 38–40; and R. Ruggles, "Grant Offers Valmont Workers Math, English, and Science Classes," *Omaha World-Herald,* March 16, 1993, A11.

24. Petro Belli, "Globalizing the Rest of the World," *Harvard Business Review,* July–August, 1991, 54.

25. "The 100 Largest U.S. Multinationals," *Forbes,* July 19, 1993, 182–186.

26. "Foreign Role in U.S. Business is Detailed," *Omaha World-Herald,* June 25, 1992, 2D.

27. "The Mexican American Border: Hi, Amigo," *The Economist,* December 12, 1992, 21–23.

28. Mike Fergus, "Employees on the Move," *HR Magazine,* May 1990, 45.

29. Shari Caudron, "Training Ensures Success Overseas," *Personnel Journal,* December 1991, 27.

30. Rosalie L. Tung, *The New Expatriates: Managing Human Resources Abroad* (Cambridge, Mass.: Ballinger Publishing Co., 1988), 14–15.

31. Caudron, "Training Ensures Success Overseas," 27.

32. Adapted from J. Stewart Black and Hal B. Gregersen, "The Other Half of the Picture: Antecedents of Spouse Cultural Adjustment," *Journal of International Business Studies* 22 (1991): 461–477.

33. Shari Caudron, "Surviving Cross-Cultural Shock," *Industry Week,* July 6, 1992, 35–38.

34. Marvina Shilling, "How to Win at Repatriation," Personnel Journal, September, 1993, 40–46.

35. David W. Ellis, "The Impact of Income Tax Treaties on Executive Transfers," *Journal of International Compensation & Benefits,* July–August 1992, 7–12.

36. Patricia Digh Howard, "Circle of Impact: HR Professionals Respond to War, Riot, Terrorism," *Employment Relations Today,* Spring 1991, 29–38.

37. Robert C. Maddox, "Terrorism: The Current Corporate Response," *SAM Advanced Management Journal,* Summer 1991, 18–21.

38. Adapted from John Greenwald, "Sorry, Right Number," *Time,* September 13, 1993, and personal interviews with telemarketing executives in Omaha.

CHAPTER 3

STRATEGIC HUMAN RESOURCE PLANNING

After you have read this chapter, you should be able to:

1. Define HR planning and discuss management and HR–unit responsibilities for it.

2. Outline the strategic HR planning process.

3. Define organizational culture and explain how it affects HR planning.

4. Discuss why external environmental scanning is an important part of HR planning.

5. Explain how auditing current jobs and skills relates to HR planning.

6. Identify factors to be considered when forecasting the supply and demand for human resources in an organization.

7. Discuss several ways to manage both a surplus and a shortage of human resources.

Planning in a Changing Competitive Environment

Projections from *Workforce 2000* forecast that for certain industries and jobs there will be shortages of competent employees by the turn of the century. However, like all projections, this one is based on the assumption that relationships from the past will hold in the future. But will they?

Traditionally, when the economy turns down, businesses lay off workers as the demand for the company's product becomes less. When the economy picks up again, companies increase overtime work until it is clear that the corner is indeed turned, and then permanent employees are hired. But as the recession of the early 1990s ended, it was clear the old relationships were no longer holding. Overtime increased—but it was not always followed by the hiring of full-time employees. Instead of replacing the regular full-time employees they had laid off, many employers hired part-time, temporary, consultant, and independent-contractor workers when overtime became insufficient to meet workloads. As pointed out in Chapter 2, as much as 30% of the country's entire workforce is now considered "contingent."

More and more organizations are taking out layers of reporting systems and structures. Many now view administrative overhead as a "dragging anchor" that keeps employers from adapting to changing markets and intense international competition. They want a "flatter" structure that can respond more quickly to change. For the first time since the Great Depression of the 1930s, white-collar workers, not just blue-collar ones, are being trimmed and not replaced. When workers are hired, they often are contingent workers. In order to save money, temporaries usually can be hired without providing them health insurance, retirement, or even the assurance of a job tomorrow. The effect on society is felt as they respond to the temporary status of their jobs by spending less. Meanwhile, regular, full-time workers are working significant amounts of overtime before any additional workers are hired. Ironically, while the underemployed would like more hours of work, those who are employed and are working overtime regularly would like more free time—even at the expense of a smaller paycheck.

Federal Reserve Chairman Alan Greenspan told the Senate Finance Committee that employers are burdened with health care, workers' compensation, and other government mandated costs that have created "a disincentive for full-time permanent employment." Indeed, with usual benefits, employer costs to keep employees are estimated to average 140% of a person's gross pay.

As employers struggle to control costs to be competitive in world markets, the cost of capital, raw materials, and technology are relatively *fixed* to the business. The cost of the workforce—total payroll—is often the only major opportunity for making costs more flexible. Indeed, it may be the greatest opportunity for flexibility. Total payroll costs can be cut by hiring individuals or groups on a contingent basis for a specified task for a limited period. Maintenance services, engineering design, and public relations can be contracted out, eliminating corporate staffs. For many companies, change and adaptive structuring has been the only ways to survive. An additional benefit to paying only for the time needed from a contractor is that performance and standards must be specified in order to contract with someone. A drawback may be that loyalty and shared values do not develop on contract. The question is, what price tag should be placed on loyalty and shared values? Does their importance outweigh the financial blessings of eliminating worker benefits? For a growing number of employers, the answer appears to be no.

This phenomenon is not confined to the U.S. German businesses, with the highest wage costs in the world, are making investments abroad in more cost-effective countries. Companies that cannot move abroad are trimming staff to reduce production costs. Other European countries are moving to reduce production costs as well.

All of these changes in the basic relationships in an economy make HR planning both difficult and critical. Without planning, employers are sure to suffer more problems with surpluses or shortages of employees.[1]

Plan ahead: It wasn't raining when Noah built the ark.

Richard Cushing

This chapter deals with planning for the human resources the organization will need in the future. But any description of HR planning must begin on a level one step higher—with the overall strategic plan of the organization. **Strategic planning** can be defined as the process of identifying organizational objectives and the actions needed to achieve those objectives. It involves analyzing such areas as finance, marketing, and human resources to determine the capacities of the organization to meet its objectives.

Strategic planning must include planning for human resources to carry out the rest of the plans. Figure 3–1 shows the relationship among the variables that ultimately determine the HR plans an organization will develop. Overall strategy affects the strategies and activities in the HR area. For example, several years ago First Chicago Bank began planning to become one of the top financial institutions in the country. Two parts of its strategic plan were: (1) a global focus and (2) service improvement. HR plans to support global goals included integrating compensation and benefits systems and hiring policies for international operations and domestic operations. Service improvement plans hinged on well-trained, capable first-level employees. But an HR diagnosis turned up basic skills deficiencies in employees. Therefore, as a result of HR planning, a series of programs designed to remedy those basic skills problems in the workforce was developed. The plan, which evidently was used effectively, resulted in First Chicago being given the Optimas Award for excellence.[2] The coordination of companywide strategic planning and strategic HR planning was successful in this case, because HR plans supported corporate strategic plans.

To understand the interaction of strategic planning and HR planning, two underlying concepts should be explored before discussing the specifics of plan-

▼ **STRATEGIC PLANNING**

is the process of identifying organizational objectives and the actions needed to achieve those objectives.

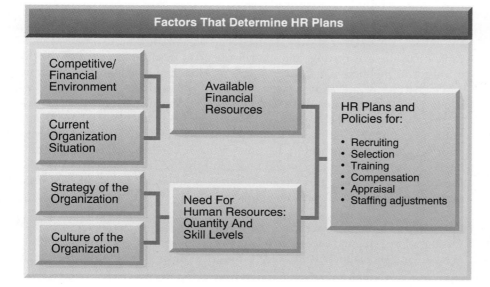

▲ **Figure 3–1**

Factors That Determine HR Plans

ning. Those concepts are the position of an organization in its *life cycle* and its *culture*. These are important because just as the organization is affected by the strategic plans that are made, so are its plans limited by what the human organization can reasonably be expected to do.

▲ ORGANIZATIONAL LIFE CYCLE AND HR PLANNING

Most organizations have a *life cycle* of four stages: *introduction, growth, maturity,* and *decline.* An organization needs different human resource strategies at different times in this cycle, and the plans flowing from these strategies reflect those differences.[3] For example, a small, three-year-old high-tech software firm will have differing HR needs than a large computer company. Apple Computer is a good illustration. At one time Apple, founded by Steven Jobs and Stephen Wozniak, was a laid-back, entrepreneurial organization. But as the company grew, the need for more structure and formalization of plans and policies became evident. A new president, John Scully, was hired from PepsiCo, and within two years the founders left Apple. Scully reduced staff to eliminate duplicate jobs and instituted more formalized policies throughout the company. Apple had passed from the growth to the maturity stage of its life cycle. In 1993, Scully left Apple as the evolution in the company continued.[4]

Life Cycle Stages

The relationships between the life cycle of an organization and related HR activities are capsuled in Figure 3–2. A discussion of each follows.

Introduction   At the introduction stage, a high-risk and entrepreneurial spirit pervades the organization. The founders often operate with limited financial resources; consequently, HR activities are handled reactively and training seems less important. When skills are needed, the organization recruits and hires individuals who are already trained.

Growth   During the growth stage, the organization continues to take risks and invest in marketing and operations. The organization needs investments to expand facilities, marketing, and human resources to take advantage of the demand for its products and services. Often backlogs and scheduling problems indicate that the organization has grown faster than its ability to handle the demand. One study revealed that the decisions made during the growth stage have a critical impact on the organization as it moves into maturity. Consequently, just as in the Apple Computer situation, some formalization of policies and rules must occur. Inadequate staffing becomes a major concern, so the organization begins to focus on recruitment and selection of workers. It recognizes the need for some HR planning, not just for reacting to immediate pressures, and institutes some simplified HR planning procedures.[5]

Maturity   In the maturity stage, the organization and its culture are stabilized. Organizational size and success enable it to develop even more formalized plans, policies, and procedures. It now reaps the fruits of its past risky labors. Often,

▲ **Figure 3–2**   Organizational Life-Cycle Stages and HR Activities

LIFE-CYCLE STAGE	STAFFING	COMPENSATION	TRAINING AND DEVELOPMENT	LABOR/EMPLOYEE RELATIONS
Introduction	Attract best technical and professional talent.	Meet or exceed labor market rates to attract needed talent.	Define future skill requirements and begin establishing career ladders.	Set basic employee-relations philosophy of organization.
Growth	Recruit adequate numbers and mix of qualified workers. Plan management succession. Manage rapid internal labor market movements.	Meet external market but consider internal equity effects. Establish formal compensation structures.	Mold effective management team through management development and organizational development.	Maintain labor peace, employee motivation, and morale.
Maturity	Encourage sufficient turnover to minimize layoffs and provide new openings. Encourage mobility as reorganizations shift jobs around.	Control compensation costs.	Maintain flexibility and skills of an aging workforce.	Control labor costs and maintain labor peace. Improve productivity.
Decline	Plan and implement workforce reductions and reallocations, downsizing and outplacement may occur during this stage.	Implement tighter cost control.	Implement retraining and career consulting services.	Improve productivity and achieve flexibility in work rules. Negotiate job security and employment-adjustment policies.

SOURCE: Thomas A. Kochan and Thomas A. Barocci, *Human Resource Management and Industrial Relations: Text, Readings, and Cases,* 105. Copyright © 1985 by Thomas A. Kochan and Thomas A. Barocci. Adapted by permission of Scott, Foresman and Company.

organizational politics flourish and HR activities expand. At the same time, managers are concerned about keeping costs under control. Compensation programs become a major focus for HR efforts. HR planning becomes vital, especially for workforce shifts, as demand for some products and services slows.

Decline The organization in the decline stage experiences resistance to change: rules and policies have hardened into a structure. Numerous examples can be cited in the manufacturing sectors of the U.S. economy. Manufacturing firms have had to reduce their workforces, close plants, and use their accumulated profits from the past to diversify into other industries. During the decline stage, employers try certain HR practices such as productivity-enhancement, and cost-reduction programs. Unionized workers resist the decline by demanding no pay cuts and greater job-security provisions in their contracts. Nevertheless, employers are compelled to reduce their workforces through attrition, early retirement incentives, and major facility closings.

Rogers Corporation moved manufacturing operations to a *maquiladora* plant in Mexico like hundreds of other U.S. companies. But the savings were not what had been expected by the Connecticut-based manufacturer of electronic and automotive products. Unacceptably high costs were the culprit. Quality was so bad that the scrap rate was running 25%, on-time delivery was 40%, and employee turnover was 20% in a *good* week.

The new manager spent three weeks talking with operating-level employees to understand the culture in the plant and the problems. The culture included no focus on the customer at all, no real recognition of the poor results by the employees, and absolutely no loyalty to the company from employees with the most advanced technical skills.

To bring about cultural changes, the new manager focused on increasing quality, training, and communication. By restructuring the plant along customer-oriented product lines, more time was devoted to training employees on quality standards and recognizing the difference between a good and bad job. A certification program allowed employees (who averaged a sixth-grade education) to earn extra pay by passing exams showing they had gained higher levels of knowledge about their jobs. An employee-suggestion plan and other communications activities were used to change the culture of the plant to a more participative one.

These techniques *worked*. The changed culture of the plant enhanced its operating results, and quality became so good that a new way to measure it had to be devised. On-time performance was 96%, and turnover dropped to only 9%. The climate changed to one that values knowledge, quality, and loyalty.[7]

▲ ORGANIZATIONAL CULTURE AND HR PLANNING

ORGANIZATIONAL CULTURE is a pattern of shared values and beliefs giving members of an organization meaning and providing them with rules for behavior.

Just as nations and regions have unique cultural characteristics, so do organizations.[6] **Organizational culture** is a pattern of shared values and beliefs giving members of an organization meaning and providing them with rules for behavior. These values are inherent in the ways organizations and their members view themselves, define opportunities, and plan strategies. Much like the way personality shapes an individual, organizational culture shapes its members' responses and defines what an organization can or is willing to do.

The culture of an organization is seen in the norms of expected behaviors, values, philosophies, rituals, and symbols used by its employees. Culture evolves over a period of time. Only if an organization has a history in which people have shared experiences for years does a culture stabilize. A relatively new firm, such as a business existing for less than two years, probably will not have developed a stabilized culture.

Culture is important because it tells people how to behave (or not to behave). It is relatively constant and enduring over time. Newcomers learn the culture from the senior employees, and so the rules of behavior are perpetuated. These rules may or may not be beneficial. In other words, the culture can either facilitate or limit change. The "HR Perspective" shows how changing the culture in a plant south of the border paid off for one company.

Effect of Organizational Culture on Strategy

When engaging in both strategic and HR planning, managers must consider the culture of the organization because excellent strategies can be negated by an incompatible culture.[8] For example, both AT&T and IBM have had to try to shift from a process culture to a results-oriented culture in the aftermath of company restructuring in an attempt to change an incompatible culture.

For another example, consider the case of an insurance firm whose culture was highly stable, resistant to innovation, and low on customer service and marketing. The firm wanted to start a financial-services unit and modified its strategic plan accordingly. To be successful, an extensive number of service contracts and rapid financial marketing adjustments were necessary. Unfortunately, because of the mismatch between culture and strategy, the firm decided it could not implement this strategy, even though it was a viable possibility from a business standpoint.

The culture of an organization also affects the way external forces are viewed. In one culture, external events are seen as threatening, whereas another culture views risks and changes as challenges requiring immediate responses. The latter type of culture can be a source of competitive advantage, especially if it is unique and hard to duplicate.[9]

▲ STRATEGY AND HR PLANNING

The strategic planning process can be thought of as a circular process. As Figure 3–3 shows, the process begins with identification and recognition of the philoso-

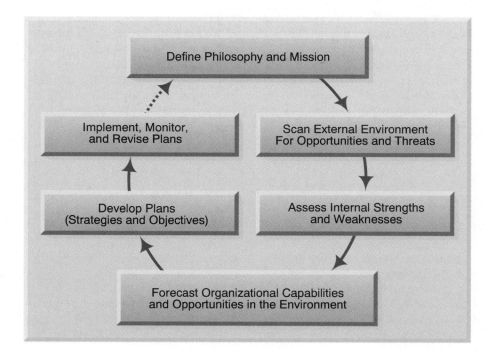

▲ **Figure 3–3**

Strategic Planning Process

phy and mission of an organization. This first step addresses the most fundamental questions about an organization:

▲ Why does the organization exist?

▲ What is the unique contribution it makes?

▲ What are the underlying values and motivations of key managers and owners?

Once the philosophy and mission of the organization are identified, the next requirement is to scan the environment. **Environmental scanning** is the process of studying the environment to pinpoint opportunities and threats. Environmental scanning for HR concerns provides information about the external forces and pressures that affect the organization and the people in it. Workforce patterns, economic conditions, social values and lifestyles, and technological developments are some of the external factors.[10]

After external forces are examined, an internal assessment is made of what the organization *can* do before deciding on what it *should* do. Internal strengths and weaknesses must be identified in light of the philosophy and culture of the organization. Factors such as current workforce skills, retirement patterns, and demographic profiles of current employees are items that relate to human resource capabilities.

Next comes forecasting organizational capabilities and future opportunities in the environment to match organizational objectives and strategies. Finally, specific plans are developed to identify how strategies will be implemented. Details of the plans become the basis for implementation and later adjustments. As with all plans, they must be monitored, adjusted, and updated continually. The strategic planning process is circular, since the environment is always changing and the steps in the process must be repeated over and over again.[11]

HR Planning Responsibilities

In most organizations that do HR planning, the top HR executive and subordinate staff specialists have most of the responsibilities for this planning. However, as Figure 3–4 indicates, other managers must provide data for the HR specialists to analyze. In turn, those managers need to receive data from the HR unit. Because top managers are responsible for overall strategic planning, they usually ask the HR unit to project the necessary human resources needed to implement overall organizational goals. The "HR Perspective" shows how business-level planning and HR planning were linked at one organization.

▼ **ENVIRONMENTAL SCANNING**

is the process of studying the environment of the organization to pinpoint opportunities and threats.

▲ **Figure 3–4**

Typical HR Planning Responsibilities

HR UNIT	MANAGERS
▲ Prepares objectives for HR planning ▲ Participates in strategic planning process for overall organization ▲ Designs HR planning data systems ▲ Compiles and analyzes data from managers on staffing needs ▲ Identifies HR strategies ▲ Implements HR plan as approved by top management	▲ Identify supply-and-demand needs for each division/department ▲ Review/discuss HR planning information with HR specialists ▲ Integrate HR plans with departmental plans ▲ Monitor HR plan to identify changes needed ▲ Review employee-succession plans and career paths in line with HR plan

HR Perspectives:

HR Planning at People's Bank

In the mid-1980s, changes in the environment of regional banks had shaken the industry to the core. Deregulation, growing competition, and large increases in expenses led one of these—People's Bank—to alter its strategic direction to minimize risks in its new environment and take advantage of new opportunities. Headquartered in Connecticut, the bank has over $4 billion in assets and 60 branches. The bank's objectives, growth and a market orientation, required aligning all of its human resources.

First, the bank analyzed its current situation to decide what changes were needed. Growth would require new jobs and a new structure for the organization. A market orientation required a diversified product portfolio of services. As areas of the bank expanded or contracted, there would be shifts in the numbers and kinds of people needed.

Following the analysis, the bank generated a series of action plans to address the specific needs that were identified. New positions were first filled with internal management talent. The company found it had outgrown its own HR data system and few people were being transferred across divisions. The bank's talent pool was "inventoried," and a new internal recruitment strategy was implemented. The inventory pinpointed needs for more people with skills in marketing, sales, and general management.

The audit revealed much more as well, but the primary interest was the plan the bank used to link HR planning with business planning from that time forward. People's Bank now conducts HR planning in conjunction with its business-planning process. Both HR and department managers are responsible for various parts of the process, as the following chart shows.[12] This approach helped refocus many of the bank's efforts and address its HR requirements in an ongoing way.

Accountability		*Component*
HR	**Mgmt**	
		I. Situation Analysis
		A. External:
X		1. Labor market pool/availability of key skills
		2. Industry trends (compensation, benefits, etc.)
		B. Internal:
		1. Organizational implications of business plans:
		a. Required changes in structure
	X	b. Number/types of key positions
		2. Human resources implications of business plans:
		a. Demand (number and kinds of skills required)
	X	b. Supply (turnover, skill levels and productivity of current workforce)
		c. Actions to assure supply meets demand (recruitment, training, etc.)
		3. Management process implications of business plans:
		a. Compensation/other reward systems
	X	b. Communication process
		4. Culture implication of business plans:
	X	a. Current attitudes and behavior compared to desired culture
		II. Plan Development
X	X	A. Objectives and strategies to ensure that organizations, people, process, and culture support business plans
		B. Actions to ensure human resources supply meets demand (recruitment, training, downsizing, productivity programs, etc.)
		III. Evaluation
X	X	A. Costs and expected payoffs associated with human resource strategies

HR Planning Process

**HUMAN RESOURCE (HR)
PLANNING**

consists of analyzing and identifying the
need for and availability of human
resources required for an organization to
meet its objectives.

The competitive organizational strategy of the firm as a whole becomes the basis
for **human resource (HR) planning,** which is the process of analyzing and
identifying the need for and availability of human resources required for an organization to meet its objectives. Figure 3–5 shows the steps in the HR planning
process, each of which will be considered separately.

Effective HR planning cannot take place in a void. It must be guided by and
coordinated with top management plans. For example, in planning for human
resources, an organization must consider the allocation of people to jobs over
long periods of time—not just for the next month or even the next year. This
allocation requires knowledge of any foreseen expansions or reductions in operations and/or technological changes that may affect the organization. On the
basis of such analyses, plans can be made for shifting employees within the organization, laying off or otherwise cutting back the number of employees, or re-

▲ **Figure 3–5**

Steps in HR Planning

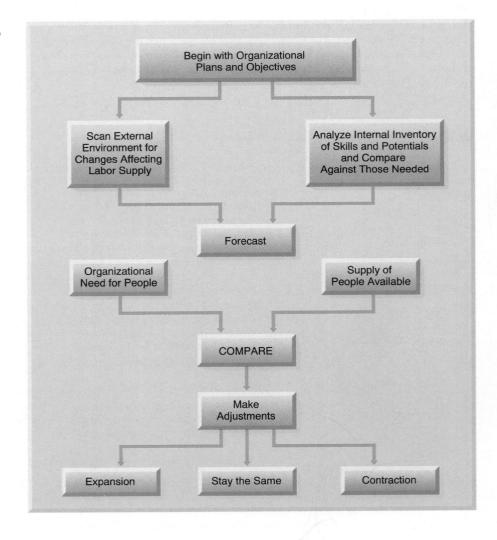

training present employees. Factors to consider include the current level of employee knowledge, skills, and abilities in an organization and the expected vacancies due to retirement, promotion, transfer, sick leave, or discharge.

Further, the pay system has to fit with the performance appraisal system, which must fit with selection decisions, and so on. The different activities in the HR area must be in tune with the general business strategy, as well as the overall HR strategy, in order to provide support for business goals.

▲ SCANNING THE EXTERNAL ENVIRONMENT

At the heart of strategic planning is the knowledge gained from scanning the external environment for changes. Scanning especially affects HR planning because every organization must draw from the same labor market that supplies all other employers. Indeed, one measure of organizational effectiveness is the ability of an organization to compete for critical human resources. Many factors can influence the supply of labor available to an employer and to the general economy. The reputation of the organization is one factor, but labor market conditions and the HR plan also must be considered. Some of the more significant environmental factors are identified in Figure 3–6. Factors for scanning include workforce composition, work patterns and schedules, government influences, and economic, geographic, and competitive conditions.

Workforce Composition and Work Patterns

Chapter 2 dealt with the major changes in the composition of the workforce in the U.S. Racial, gender, and educational changes in the composition of the workforce combine with the use of contingent workers, alternative work schedules, and family/work balancing to create a very different workplace than that of a generation ago. HR planners need up-to-date information on these changes. Such information is available in libraries through sources such as *Monthly Labor Review,* a publication put out by the U.S. Bureau of Labor Statistics.[13]

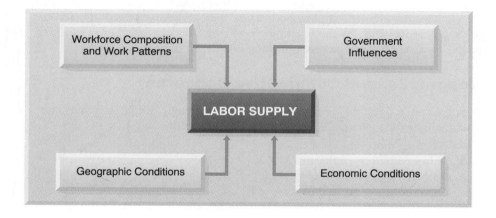

▲ **Figure 3–6**

External Environmental Factors Affecting Labor Supply

Government Influences

Another major element that affects labor supply is the government. Today managers are confronted with an expanding and often bewildering array of government rules as government regulation of HR activities has steadily increased.[14] The Equal Employment Opportunity Commission (EEOC) is a major influence because it can require employers to alter their hiring and promotion practices to assure that certain groups of people, such as women, are provided equal chances for employment and advancement. As a result, HR planning must be done by individuals who understand the legal requirements of various EEOC regulations.

Government trade policies and restrictions also can affect HR planning in other ways. For example, government policies on importing Japanese cars affect the plans of automakers like General Motors, Ford, and Chrysler because under a *closed-import policy,* foreign firms may establish more American-based manufacturing operations using American labor. An *open-import policy,* on the other hand, creates an entirely different economic labor environment.

Tax legislation at local, state, and federal levels also affects HR planning. Pension provisions and Social Security legislation may change retirement patterns and funding options. Elimination or expansion of tax benefits for job-training expenses might alter some job-training activities associated with workforce expansions. Employee benefits may be affected significantly by tax law changes. Tax credits for employee day care and financial aid for education may affect employer practices when recruiting and retaining workers. In summary, an organization must consider a wide variety of government policies, regulations, and laws when doing HR planning.[15]

Economic Conditions

The general business cycle of recessions and booms also affects HR planning.[16] Such factors as interest rates, inflation, and economic growth help determine the availability of workers and figure into organizational plans and objectives. Decisions on wages, the need for overtime, and whether to hire or lay off workers all hinge on economic conditions. For example, suppose economic conditions lead to a decrease in the unemployment rate. There is a considerable difference between finding qualified applicants in a 5% unemployment market and in a 9% unemployment market. In the 5% unemployment market, significantly fewer qualified applicants are likely to be available for any kind of position. Those who are available may be less employable because they are less educated, less skilled, or unwilling to work. As the unemployment rate rises, the number of qualified people looking for work increases, making it easier to fill jobs.

Geographic and Competitive Concerns

A global competition for labor appears to be developing.[17] Employers must consider the following geographic and competitive concerns:

- ▲ Net migration into the area
- ▲ Other employers in the area
- ▲ Employee resistance to geographic relocation
- ▲ Direct competitors in the area
- ▲ Impact of international competition on the area

The *net migration* into a particular region is important. For example, after World War II, the population of northern U.S. cities grew rapidly and provided a ready source of labor. Recently there has been a shift to the Sunbelt.

Other employers in a geographic region can greatly expand or diminish the labor supply. If, for example, a large military facility is closing or moving to another geographic location, a large supply of good civilian labor, previously employed by the military, may be available for a while. On the other hand, the opening of a new plant may decrease the supply of potential employees in a labor market for some time.

Within the last decade, there has been a growing reluctance on the part of many workers, especially those with working spouses, to accept *geographic relocation* as a precondition of moving up in the organization. This trend has forced organizations to change their employee development policies and practices and their HR plans.

Direct competitors are another important external force in staffing. Failure to consider the competitive labor market and to offer pay scales and benefits competitive with organizations in the same general industry and geographic location may cost a company dearly in the long run. Underpaying or "undercompeting" may result in a much lower-quality workforce. Finally, the impact of *international competition,* as well as numerous other external factors, must be considered as part of environmental scanning.[18] For an example, see the "HR Perspective" on how diversity in the European workforce influences HR planning.

▲ INTERNAL ANALYSIS OF JOBS AND PEOPLE

Analyzing the jobs that will need to be done and the skills of people currently available to do them is the next part of HR planning after scanning the external environment (refer again to Figure 3–5). The needs of the organization must be compared against the labor supply available.

Auditing Jobs

The starting point for evaluating internal strengths and weaknesses is an audit of jobs currently being done in the organization. A comprehensive analysis of all current jobs provides a basis for forecasting jobs that will need to be done in the future. A planner should examine the following questions:

▲ What jobs now exist?
▲ How many individuals are performing each job?
▲ What are the reporting relationships of jobs?
▲ How essential is each job?
▲ What jobs will be needed to implement the organizational strategy?
▲ What are the characteristics of anticipated jobs?

Much of the data to answer these questions should be available from existing organization charts. However, determining the essential nature of each job may require some judgment on the part of planners.[20]

HR Perspectives:
Diversity in the European Workforce

In Europe the labor market now contains people from *at least* 12 nations each with its own language, culture, and traditions. The goal for many European companies and American multinationals has been to create organizations where the full cultural diversity present in Europe is reflected in the professionals employed.

However, HR planning might need to consider some additional issues that suggest possible problems. Not only is the population in Europe aging but it will begin to decrease in numbers—much like that in the U.S.

To keep pace with the need for skilled people a company planning for human resources in Europe will need to assure not only that a Greek and a Danish engineer can work together effectively, but that a young Turkish employee will be able to fit into the company without prejudice. Such multicultural hiring raises issues of comparable credentials and training, and of cultural differences in the styles of interviewing, communication, and management. Yet competition for the best people will require that such problems be solved.

During the 1990s workers who have the skills and education most in demand will be valuable in world labor markets. If opportunities are poor in their native countries, better jobs will available elsewhere. This will put yet more pressure on immigration, already a sore spot in most European countries. Patterns of immigration will vary depending on what skills the local markets demand.[19]

	% Workers Under 34 yrs		% Population Over 65 yrs		% Workers Over 65 Still Working
	1985	*2000*	*1985*	*2000*	*1985*
USA	50.4	39.5	12.3	12.9	9
Germany	45.7	37.4	14.2	16.0	3.2
United Kingdom	43.6	38.8	15.5	15.4	4.6
France	47	41.5	13.6	15.6	3.0
Italy	48	44.6	14.0	16.7	3.9
Spain	49.9	49.0	9.1	11.5	3.8
Sweden	38.7	36.3	16.9	17.2	5.4
WORLD	57.1	51.7	5.9	6.8	32.8

Auditing Skills

Once planners obtain an understanding of current jobs and the new jobs that will be necessary to carry out the organization's plans, they can make a detailed audit of current employees and their skills. The basic source of data on employees and their skills is the HR records of the organization. Increasingly, employers are making use of computerized human resource information systems (HRISs) to compile such records.[21] The specifics of developing and using an HRIS are discussed in Chapter 20.

Individual Employee Data   For conducting HR planning, personal data on individual employees should include the following:

▲ Individual employee demographics (age, length of service in organization, time in present job)
▲ Individual career progression (jobs held, time in each job, promotions or other job changes, pay rates)
▲ Individual performance data (work accomplishment, growth in skills)

These three types of information form an **employee skills inventory,** which is defined as a compilation of data on the skills and characteristics of employees, including:

▲ Education and training
▲ Mobility and geographic preferences
▲ Specific aptitudes, abilities, and interests
▲ Areas of interest and internal promotion ladders
▲ Promotability ratings
▲ Anticipated retirement

All the information that goes into an employee skills inventory affects a person's promotability. Therefore the data and their use must meet the same standards of job-relatedness and nondiscrimination as those used when the employee was initially hired. Furthermore, security of such information is important to ensure that sensitive information is available only to those who have specific use for it. The skills inventory can be used by planners to determine long-range needs for recruiting, selection, and training, as well as the feasibility of making bids for new work.

Aggregate Workforce Profiles   The data on individual employees can be aggregated into a profile of the organization's current workforce. This profile will reveal many of the organization's strengths and weaknesses. The absence of some skills, such as computer skills, may affect the ability of an organization to take advantage of new technological developments. If a large group of skilled employees are all in the same age bracket, their retirement plans or group turnover rate may leave a major void in the organization. For example, consider the case where eight skilled line workers of a small rural electric utility were due to retire within a three-year period of time. Yet it takes seven years of apprenticeship and on-the-job training for a person to be qualified for a senior skilled job within the utility.

Other areas often profiled include turnover, mobility restrictions of current workers, and specialization of workers by group. A number of these factors are ones over which the organization has little control. Some employees will die, leave the firm, retire, or otherwise contribute to a reduction in the current employee force. It can be helpful to plot charts giving an overview of the employee situation for each department in an organization, suggesting where external candidates might be needed to fill future positions. Likewise, the chart may indicate where there is a reservoir of trained people that the employer can tap to meet future conditions.[22]

▲ **FORECASTING**

The information gathered from external environmental scanning and assessment of internal strengths and weaknesses is used to predict, or *forecast,* HR supply and

> **EMPLOYEE SKILLS INVENTORY**
>
> is a compilation of data on the skills and characteristics of employees.

FORECASTING

uses information from the past and present to identify expected future conditions.

demand in light of organizational objectives and strategies. **Forecasting** uses information from the past and present to identify expected future conditions. Projections for the future are, of course, subject to errors. Changes in conditions upon which the projections are based might even completely invalidate them,[23] which is the chance forecasters take. Usually, though, experienced people are able to forecast with enough accuracy to benefit an organization's long-range plans.

Approaches to forecasting human resources range from a manager's best guess to a rigorous and complex computer simulation. Simple models may be quite sufficient in certain instances, but complex models may be necessary for others. It is beyond the scope of this text to discuss in detail the numerous methods of forecasting available, but a few of the more prominent ones will be highlighted.

Despite the availability of sophisticated mathematical models and techniques, forecasting is still a combination of quantitative method and subjective judgment. The facts must be evaluated and weighed by knowledgeable individuals, such as managers and HR experts who use the mathematical models as a tool rather than relying blindly on them.

Forecasting Periods

HR forecasting should be done over three planning periods: short range, intermediate, and long range. The most commonly used planning period is *short-range,* usually a period of six months to one year. This level of planning is routine in many organizations because very few assumptions about the future are necessary for such short-range plans. These short-range forecasts offer the best estimates of the immediate HR needs of an organization. Intermediate and long-range forecasting are much more difficult processes. *Intermediate* plans usually project one to five years into the future, and *long-range* plans extend beyond five years.

Forecasting the Need for Human Resources (Demand)

The main emphasis to date has been on forecasting organizational need for human resources, or HR demand. Forecasts of demand may be either judgmental or mathematical. As mentioned before, mathematical methods usually still require some judgmental human input. Purely judgmental methods include:

1. *Estimates.* These forecasts can be either *top-down* or *bottom-up,* but essentially people who are in a position to know are asked, "How many people will you need next year?"
2. *Rules of Thumb.* These forecasts rely on general guidelines applied to a specific situation within the organization. For example, a guideline of "one operations manager per five reporting supervisors" aids in forecasting the number of supervisors needed in a division. However, it is important to adapt the guidelines in order to recognize widely varying departmental needs.
3. *Delphi Technique.* Here input from a group of experts is sought by administering them separate questionnaires to be filled out anonymously on what forecasted situations will be. These expert opinions are then aggregated, and returned to the experts for a second anonymous opinion. The process continues through several rounds until the experts essentially agree on a judgement.

4. *Nominal-Group Technique.* Unlike the Delphi method, the nominal-group technique requires people to meet face to face. Their ideas are usually generated independently at first and then discussed as a group.

There are various mathematical approaches used in forecasting demand. Some of the more common ones are:

1. *Statistical Regression Analysis* makes a statistical comparison of past relationships among various factors. For example, a statistical relationship between gross sales and number of employees in a retail chain may be useful in forecasting the number of employees needed in the future if the retailer's sales increase 30%.

2. *Simulation Models* are representations of real situations in abstract form. They may include available economic models. Numerous other methods and techniques are available also, but surveys reveal that the more complex simulation techniques are used by relatively few firms.

3. *Productivity Ratios* calculate the average number of units produced per employee. These can then be applied to sales forecasts to determine the number of employees needed.

4. *Staffing Ratios* can be used to estimate indirect labor. For example, if the company usually used one clerical person for every 25 production employees, that ratio can be used to help estimate the need for clerical people.

The demand for employees can be calculated on an organizationwide basis and/or calculated based upon the needs of individual units in the organization. For example, to forecast that the firm needs 125 new employees next year might mean less than to forecast that it needs 25 new people in sales, 45 in production, 20 in accounting, 5 in HR, and 30 in the warehouse. This unit breakdown obviously allows for more consideration of the specific skills needed than the aggregate method does.

A *demand-pull approach* to forecasting (as contrasted with a *supply-push approach,* covered later) considers specific openings that are likely to occur and uses that as the basis for planning. The openings (or demands) are created when employees leave a position because of promotions, transfers, and terminations. The analysis always begins with the top positions in the organization, because from those there can be no promotions to a higher level. Consider the example of loaders and drivers on the loading dock.[24] The loading dock has two basic job classifications, loaders and drivers, and there are two levels of each. Currently the staffing situation is

	Loaders	Drivers	
Level II	50	30	
Level I	90	60	
			Total
			230

Decision rules (or "fill rates") are developed for each position or level. (For example, 50% of loaders Level II will come through promotions from loader Level I, 25% from promoting drivers Level I, and 25% will be filled with new hires). Then anticipated openings are estimated to be:

　　　　　+ 8 Openings due to predicted turnover
　　　　　<u>+ 6</u> Added loaders due to expansion
　　　　　 14 openings

Since 50% of loader (Level II) jobs are to be filled by promotions from loader Level I, it is forecasted that 7 will come from that source, and so on. Forecasters must be aware of chain effects throughout, because as people are promoted, their previous positions become available.

Unfortunately, the accuracy of forecasts for human resources demand has been relatively weak. In one survey of 5,000 firms, only 35% of the forecasts were correct within 1%, whereas about one-third were off by more than 25%. The troubling part of this survey is that the forecasts were only for one year, not the three years commonly projected in HR planning.[25]

Forecasting Availability of Human Resources (Supply)

Forecasting the availability of human resources considers both *external* and *internal* supplies. Although internal supply is easier to calculate, it is important to calculate the external supply also.

External Supply The external supply of potential employees available to the organization can be estimated by considering the following factors:

▲ Net migration in/out of area
▲ Individuals entering/leaving workforce
▲ Individuals graduating from schools and college
▲ Changing workforce composition and patterns
▲ Economic forecasts for the next few years
▲ Technological developments and shifts
▲ Actions of competing employers
▲ Government regulations and pressures
▲ Factors affecting persons entering/leaving the workforce

Internal Supply Figure 3–7 shows in general terms how the internal supply can be calculated. The internal supply is influenced by training and development programs, transfer and promotion policies, and retirement policies, among other factors.

A supply-push approach considers that employees move from their current jobs into others through promotions, lateral moves, and terminations. Again, if a loading dock has two basic job classifications—loaders and drivers—and there are two levels of each, the following situation exists:

Level II	15 Loaders + Drivers	21
Level I	25 Loaders + 10 Drivers	35
TOTAL	Loaders and Drivers	56

Now suppose that to the 25 loaders in Level I the following happens:

25 (Beginning number)
−8 (Promoted to Level II)
−1 (Promoted to Driver Level II)
−1 (Fired)
+1 (Transferred in from Driver Level I)
+5 (New hires)
21 Loaders Remaining

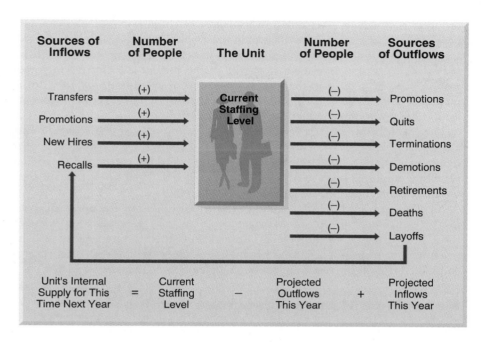

The proportion of the beginning pool of 25 loaders (Level I) that were promoted, fired, or transferred can be estimated from these historical data for next year.

Internally *succession analysis* is a widely used method to forecast the supply of people for certain positions. It relies on *replacement charts,* which are succession plans developed to identify potential personnel changes, select backup candidates, promote individuals, and keep track of attrition (resignations, retirements) for each department in an organization. Replacement charts are the most widely used forecasting technique in HR planning.

A *transition matrix,* or *Markov Matrix,* can be used to model the flow internally of human resources. These matrices simply show as probabilities the average rate of historical movement from one job to another. Figure 3–8 presents a very simple transition matrix. A line worker, for example, has 20% probability that he or she will be gone in 12 months, 0% probability of promotion to manager, 15% probability of promotion to supervisor, and a 65% probability of being a line worker this time next year. Such transition matrices are the bases for computer simulations of the internal flow of people through a large organization over time.

▲ MAKING WORKFORCE ADJUSTMENTS

With all the data collected and forecasts done, an organization has the information it needs to develop an HR plan. Such a plan can be extremely sophisticated

	EXIT	MANAGER	SUPERVISOR	LINE WORKER
Manager	.15	.85	.00	.00
Supervisor	.10	.15	.70	.05
Line Worker	.20	.00	.15	.65

▲ **Figure 3–8**

Transition Matrix for 12-Month Period

or rather rudimentary. Regardless of its degree of complexity, the ultimate purpose of the plan is to enable managers in the organization to match the available supply of labor with the forecasted demands in light of the strategies of the firm. If the necessary skill level does not exist in the present workforce, employees may need to be trained in the new skill, or outside recruiting may need to be undertaken. Likewise, if the plan reveals that the firm employs too many people for its needs, workforce reductions may be necessary.

The HR plan provides a "road map" for the future, identifying where employees are likely to be obtained, when employees will be needed, and what training and development employees must have. Through career and succession planning, employee *career paths* can be tailored to individual needs that are consistent with organizational requirements.

All efforts involved in HR planning will be futile unless management takes action to implement the plans. Managerial actions vary depending on whether there is a surplus or a shortage of workers forecasted. Consideration will be given here to managing a surplus of employees, since dealing with a shortage is considered later in the recruiting and training chapters (Chapters 8 and 10).

Managing a Human Resources Surplus

There are a variety of ways that a surplus of workers can be managed within an HR plan. But regardless of the means, the actions are difficult because they require that some employees be removed from the organization.

Downsizing

DOWNSIZING

is reducing the size of an organizational workforce.

The 1980s saw the introduction of the trend toward downsizing, which likely will continue through the 1990s. **Downsizing** is reducing the size of an organizational workforce. A wave of merger and acquisition activity in the U.S. has often left the new, combined companies with redundant departments, plants, and people. Another cause for downsizing is the need to meet foreign competition and cut costs.

Downsizing has inspired a variety of innovative ways of removing people from the payroll, some on a massive scale. For example, at one major company more than 40,000 employees were given the option of leaving the company voluntarily or taking a chance that their jobs would be among the ones retained. To encourage volunteers, an early retirement buyout plan was offered to anyone over 50 years of age who had at least 15 years' service. Improved pensions were offered to people who took retirement. For those not eligible for the early retirement buyout, a lump-sum settlement of approximately two weeks' pay for each year of service was offered. Further, those entitled to regular pensions could still get them when they became eligible later in life. For both the volunteers who chose to leave and the employees laid off, employee relations specialists developed retirement-counseling seminars, outplacement assistance to aid former employees in finding other jobs, and stress counseling. Ultimately over 6,000 employees elected to leave under the program.

This first major *reduction-in-force (RIF)* of workers ever undertaken gave a major jolt to the way in which employees viewed the company. Bitterness, anger, disbelief, and shock were common reactions. For those who survived the cuts, The paternalistic culture and image of the firm as a "lifetime" employer were gone forever.

Studies of the effects of downsizing show mixed results. Cost control is most often the reason given for downsizing, but the relationship between downsizing and increases in profitability appears questionable.[26] Some studies even show a negative or at best indifferent effect on quality, productivity, and morale.[27]

Another large study that looked at the lessons learned from downsizing made these recommendations:[28]

▲ *Investigate alternatives to downsizing.* Given the potential problems of downsizing, alternatives should be seriously considered first.

▲ *Involve those people necessary for success in the planning for downsizing.* The study found this frequently was not done; those who had to make the downsizing operation work were not involved in its planning.

▲ *Develop a comprehensive communications plan.* Employees are entitled to advance notice so they can make plans.

▲ *Nurture the survivors.* Remaining employees may be confused about their future careers and other concerns obviously can have negative effects.

▲ *Outplacement pays off.* Helping separated employees find new work is good both for the people and the reputation of the firm.

Alternatives to Downsizing

There are several alternatives to immediate downsizing. Attrition, early retirement/buyouts, and layoffs are the ones most frequently used.

Attrition and Hiring Freeze   Through *attrition,* individuals who quit, die, or retire are not replaced. With this approach, no one is cut out of a job, but those who remain must handle the same workload with fewer people. Unless turnover is high, attrition will eliminate only a relatively small number of employees. Therefore, attrition may be supplemented by freezing hiring. This method is usually received with better employee understanding than many of the other methods.

Early Retirement/Buyouts   Early retirement is a means of encouraging more senior workers to leave the organization early. To provide this voluntary incentive, employers make additional payments to employees so that they will not be penalized too much economically until their pensions and Social Security benefits take effect. Such voluntary termination programs or buyouts entice an employee to quit with financial incentives. They are widely viewed as ways to accomplish workforce reduction without the general ugliness of layoffs and individual firings.

Buyouts appeal to employers because they can reduce payroll costs significantly over time.[29] Although there are some up-front costs, the organization does not incur the continuing payroll costs. One hospital saved $2 for every $1 spent on early retirees. Early retirement buyouts are a more humane way to reduce staff than just terminating long-service, loyal employees. In addition, as long as buyouts are truly voluntary, the organization is less exposed to age discrimination suits.[30]

Most early retirement buyout programs usually offer a one-time "window." Employees must decide on early retirement during that window, typically 60 to 90 days, or take their chances that their jobs will not be eliminated in future restructuring efforts. Both employees whom the company wishes would stay and those it wishes would leave can take advantage of the buyout. Consequently, some individuals whom the employer would rather have retained often take the buyout.

Layoffs Layoffs occur when employees are put on unpaid leaves of absence. If business improves for the employer, then employees can be called back to work. Careful planning of layoffs is essential. Managers must consider the following questions:

▲ How are decisions made about whom to lay off (seniority, performance records)?

▲ How will call-backs be made if all workers cannot be recalled at the same time?

▲ Will any benefits coverage be given workers laid off?

▲ If workers take other jobs, do they forfeit their call-back rights?

Layoffs may be an appropriate downsizing strategy if there is a temporary downturn in an industry. Companies have no legal obligation to provide a financial cushion to laid-off employees; however, many do. When a provision exists for severance pay, the most common formula is one week's pay for every year of employment. Larger companies tend to be more generous. Loss of medical benefits are a major problem for laid-off employees. But under a federal law (COBRA) displaced workers can retain their medical group coverage for up to 18 months and 36 months for dependents if they pay the premiums themselves.

Surplus Created by Mergers/Acquisitions

During the 1980s in the United States, a large number of firms acquired or merged with other firms. Some of these mergers were large while others were smaller, such as the merger of two local hospitals. But a common result of most mergers and acquisitions is an excess of employees once the firms have been combined. Because much of the rationale for combinations is financial, elimination of employees with overlapping responsibilities in both entities is a primary concern. The natural response of employees is anxiety about their futures: Who will be eliminated? What operations will be closed? Who will be required to relocate or lose employment? Stress follows anxiety because the climate and culture of the organization are strained.

HR experts can help employees with these adjustments. At the same time, HR specialists must be involved in identifying and planning how the combined firms will operate. They must evaluate surplus-reduction options and implement the selected options. Different HR policies, benefit programs, compensation plans, and human resource information systems must be integrated. In sum, many of top factors to be considered after a merger are related directly to human resources.[31]

Managing Survivors of Downsizing

The corporate myth is that those who are still around after downsizing in any of its many forms are so glad to have a job that they pose no problems to the company. However, some observers draw an analogy between those who survive downsizing and to those who survive wartime with the guilt that they feel because they were spared while their friends were not.[32] The result is that the performance of the survivors may be affected.

Survivors need information as to why the actions had to be taken and what the future holds for them personally. The more that employees are involved in the regrouping, the more likely the transition will be smooth.[33] One employer set aside some of the money saved from downsizing to reward employee suggestions for getting more work done with fewer employees, thereby involving and rewarding the survivors.

Outplacement

Outplacement is a group of services provided to displaced employees to give them support and assistance. It most often is used with those involuntarily removed because of plant closings or elimination of departments. Outplacement services typically include personal career counseling, resume preparation and typing services, interviewing workshops, and referral assistance. There are several reasons why a company should consider such a seemingly costly and time-consuming program even though employees are terminated because of financial burdens:[34]

1. *Cost.* It may not be as great as it seems. For example, helping workers find jobs more quickly can cut down on unemployment benefits.
2. *Company image.* Outplacement efforts typically project the image of the company as a caring employer.[35]
3. *Legal issues.* The longer employees are out of work, the more likely they are to consider suing for damages.
4. *Social responsibility.* Some believe that employers have a moral or ethical obligation to former employees.

A variety of services may be available to displaced employees. Typically, outplacement is done using outside firms that specialize in providing such assistance. Additionally, special severance pay arrangements may be used. Also firms commonly continue medical benefit coverage for a period of time at the same company-paid level as before. Other aids include retraining for different jobs, establishing on-site career centers, and contacting other employers for job placement possibilities.

> **▼ OUTPLACEMENT**
>
> is a group of services provided to displaced employees to give them support and assistance.

▲ EVALUATING HR PLANNING

HR planning is a critical part of managing human resources in an organization. If it is poorly done, there may be no one to staff the company or, conversely, massive layoffs may be necessary—with all the attendant problems. If HR planning is well done, the following benefits should result:

- ▲ Upper management has a better view of the human resource dimensions of business decisions.
- ▲ HR costs may be less because management can anticipate imbalances before they become unmanageable and expensive.
- ▲ More time is provided to locate talent because needs are anticipated and identified before the actual staffing is required.
- ▲ Better opportunities exist to include women and minority groups in future growth plans.
- ▲ Development of managers can be better planned.

To the extent that these results can be measured, they can form the basis for evaluating the success of HR planning. Another approach is to measure projected levels of demand against actual levels at some point in the future. But the most telling evidence of successful HR planning is an organization in which the human resources are consistently aligned with the needs of the business over a period of time.

 ## SUMMARY

▲ HR planning involves analyzing and identifying the future needs for and availability of human resources for the organization.

▲ In developing an HR plan, strategists must consider the stage in the organizational life cycle: introduction, growth, maturity, or decline.

▲ Organizational culture is a pattern of shared values and beliefs giving members meaning and providing them with rules for behavior.

▲ HR planning is tied to the broader process of strategic planning, beginning with identification of the philosophy and mission of the organization. The HR unit has major responsibilities in HR planning, but managers must provide supportive information and input.

▲ Assessment of internal strengths and weaknesses as a part of HR planning requires that current jobs and employee skills be audited and aggregate workforce profiles be developed.

▲ Using information on past and present conditions to identify expected future conditions and forecast the supply and demand for human resources can be done with a variety of methods for differing periods of time.

▲ Supply-push and demand-pull approaches to forecasting help identify specific needs.

▲ Management of HR surpluses may require downsizing and outplacement.

REVIEW AND DISCUSSION QUESTIONS

1. What is HR planning and what differences exist in the responsibilities of managers compared with HR specialists?
2. Discuss how organizational culture, organizational life cycle, and HR activities are interrelated.
3. Why must HR planning be seen as a process flowing from the organizational strategic plan?
4. Assume you have to develop an HR plan for a local bank. What specific external factors would be important for you to consider? Why?
5. At a computer software firm, how would you audit the current jobs and skills of employees?
6. Why are the time frame and methods used to forecast supply and demand for human resources so important?
7. Assume that as a result of HR planning, a hospital identifies a shortage of physical therapists, but a surplus of administrative workers. Discuss what actions might be taken to address these problems and why they must be approached carefully.

CASE | **CULTURE CLASH AND CHANGE AT GENERAL MOTORS**

For many years General Motors Corporation (GM) had been one of the largest and most successful firms in the United States. However, the 1980s and early 1990s were not outstanding years for GM. For example, from 1980 to 1986, GM dropped almost 5% in its share of the U.S. auto market. In some years, earnings dropped as much as 15% from the previous year.

To address GM's long-term survival, changes were needed in its organizational structure, products, and corporate culture. The Saturn project represented one such attempt. By targeting a new automobile slated for production in a new factory in Tennessee, GM hoped to use advanced production methods, including robotics, and Saturn employees were to use significantly different staffing and work methods. Results have been good to date.

Additionally, to enhance its technological capabilities, GM spent billions to buy Hughes Aircraft Company. Another costly purchase was Electronic Data Systems (EDS), a Dallas-based computer service and information-processing firm founded by H. Ross Perot. Each of these firms had its own unique corporate culture; blending them has represented a major challenge. Perot captured the essence of the cultural differences when he commented, "Revitalizing GM is like teaching an elephant to tap dance. You find the sensitive spots and start poking."

The culture clashes between GM and EDS employees are legendary. For example, EDS had a required dress code and made rules against employees drinking alcohol at lunch. When 10,000 data-processing employees were transferred from GM to EDS, dissatisfaction was rampant. Over 600 GM data-processing employees quit, and others filed for union elections. At the same time, the EDS employees became frustrated with some GM managers' efforts to use a bureaucratic approach. Perot commented, "The first EDSer to see a snake kills it. At GM the first thing you do is organize a committee on snakes. Then you bring in a consultant who knows about snakes. Third thing you do is talk about it for a year." Perot was later bought out and removed from the scene. To reduce culture clashes between Hughes and GM, divisions in each were insulated by setting up independent subsidiaries.

But the change did not happen quickly enough for the GM board of directors who replaced Roger Smith with Robert Stempel, a career employee. However, he too, couldn't "break" the GM culture. Finally, the GM Board of Directors forced changes and removed Stempel. The new president, John F. Smith, was installed in 1992 and he immediately faced formidable problems, beginning with downsizing. Meanwhile GM has continued to lose market share and money. John Smith told analysts that GM's traditional culture was his greatest challenge. The bloated bureaucratic organization simply has not responded to the changes in the competitive environment. For the future, Vice-President William Hogland says, "We have learned from our predecessors, and we are driving in a different direction."[36] Time will tell if GM is really capable of the changes necessary to compete.

▲ **QUESTIONS**

1. What are the implications of the differences in cultures that were merged at GM?
2. What external and internal factors do you believe have contributed to the latest determination to change many facets of GM?
3. If you had to blend two totally separate organizations with different cultures, life-cycle stages, and strategies, what general approaches would you use?

▲ **NOTES**

1. Adapted from Mike Fernsilber, "Factory Overtime Mounts," *Denver Post,* March 18, 1993, 1C; C. Skrzycki, "Employers Adapt to Lean Times," *Denver Post,* September 27, 1992, 38A; M. Osborn, "Companies May Slash 700,000 Jobs this Year," *USA Today,* January 22, 1992, 1; "Greenspan Bashes Clinton," *The Wall Street Journal,* March 30, 1993, 4; "The Changing Human Resources Function," *The Conference Board* (Report No. 950), 1990, 18; T. Roth, "German Firms Bemoan Production Costs," *The Wall Street Journal,* January 24, 1992, A8.

2. Shari Caudron, "Strategic HR at First Chicago," *Personnel Journal,* November 1991, 50–56.

3. Therse R. Welter, "The Source of Strength: Roots and Reach," *Industry Week,* October 21, 1991, 10–17.

4. "Apple's Future," *Business Week,* July 5, 1993, 22–28.

5. See D. Jarrell, *Human Resource Planning* (Englewood Cliffs, NJ: Prentice-Hall), 1993.

6. C. A. O'Reilly IV et al, "People and Organizational Culture: A Profile Comparison Approach to Assessing Person-Organization Fit," *Academy of Management Journal* 34 (1991), 487–516.

7. Adapted from William Miller, "Textbook Turnaround," *Industry Week,* April 20, 1992, 11–14.

8. T. Mack, "Eager Lions and Reluctant Lions," *Forbes,* February 17, 1992, 98–101.

9. K. Golden, "The Individual and Organizational Cultures," *Journal of Management Studies* 29, (1991): 1–21; and John Sheridan, "Organizational Culture and Employer Retention," *Academy of Management Journal,* 35 (1992), 1036–1056.

10. Peg Anthony and Lincoln A. Norton, "Link HR to Corporate Strategy," *Personnel Journal,* April 1991, 75–78.

11. P. Herriot and R. Pinder, "HR Strategy in a Changing World," *Personnel Management,* August 1992, 56–59; and G. Chowanec et al, "The Strategic Management of International Human Resources," *Business Quarterly,* (Fall 1991), 65–70.

12. Adapted from S. M. Coleman, M. Leshner, and C. Hewes, "HRP: A Tool for Strategic Change," *The Banker's Magazine,* November–December 1986, 39–44.

13. For example, see "Current Labor Statistics," *Monthly Labor Review,* January 1992, 71–96.

14. A. D. Vinokur et al, "Long Term Follow-up and Benefit-Cost Analysis of the Jobs Program. . .", *Journal of Applied Psychology* 76 (1991), 213–219.

15. C. T. Kydd and L. Oppenheim, "Using HRM to Enhance Competitiveness: Lessons from Four Excellent Companies," *Human Resource Management* 29, 145–166.

16. D. Mitchell and M. Zaidi, "Macroeconomic Conditions and HRM-IR Practice," *Industrial Relations,* 29 (1990), 164–188.

17. W. B. Johnston, "Global Work Force 2000," *Harvard Business Review,* March–April 1991, 115–127.

18. R. C. DeMoss, "New Rules on Immigration," *Nation's Business,* September 1991, 35.

19. Barry Rubin, "Europeans Value Diversity," *HR Magazine,* January 1991, 38; and Jim Kennedy and Anna Everest, "Put Diversity in Context," *Personnel Journal,* September 1991, 50–54. Statistics from International Labour Office, *Economically Active Population, 1950–2025* and *Yearbook of Labour Statistics, 1988.*

20. T. E. Weinberger, "The Strategic Centrality of Jobs: A Measure of Value," *Compensation and Benefits Review,* January–February 1992, 61–68.

21. V. J. Bush and Ren Nardoni, "Integrated Data Supports AT&T's Succession Planning," *Personnel Journal,* September 1992, 103–108.

22. Paul Miller, "A Strategic Look at Management Development," *Personnel Management,* August 1991, 37–41.

23. Phyllis Barnum, "Misconception about the Future U.S. Work Force: Implications for Strategic Planning," *Human Resource Planning* 14, (1991), 209–219.

24. The following examples of supply-push and demand-pull analysis were adapted from

T. Bechet and W. Maki, "Modeling and Forecasting Focusing on People as a Strategic Resource," *Human Resource Planning* 10 (1987), 214–217.

25. "Businesses Are Naive Forecasters," *Dun's Business Month,* October 1985, 82.

26. M. Greller and J. Dory, "Staff Reduction and the Bottom Line: Less Is Not Always More," in *Bottom Line Results from Strategic HRP,* R. J. Niehaus and K. F. Price, (eds) (New York: Plenum Press, 1992), 149–159.

27. L. Baggerman, "The Futility of Downsizing," *Industry Week,* January 18, 1993, 27–29, and J. Gutknecht and J. Keys, "Mergers, Acquisitions and Takeovers: Maintaining Morale of Survivors" *Academy of Management Executive,* August, 1993, 26.

28. *Lessons Learned: Dispelling the Myths of Downsizing* (Philadelphia, PA: Right Associates, 1992).

29. "Early Retirement," *The Wall Street Journal,* August 25, 1992, 1.

30. Julia Lawlor, "Some Offers Aren't So Voluntary," *USA Today,* October 29, 1992, B1–B2.

31. S. Marcus and A. Saunier, "Filling the Void on the M + A Team," *Perspectives* III (1990), 9–14.

32. B. S. Moskal, "Managing Survivors," *Industry Week,* August 3, 1992, 15.

33. "Successful Downsizers Consider Those Who Stay On," *Personnel* (April 1991).

34. V. M. Gibson, "In the Outplacement Door," *Personnel* 68, October 1991, 3.

35. "Displaced Workers Enter Land of 'Outplacement'," *Sunday World-Herald,* April 5, 1992, 20–26.

36. Adapted from "Roger Smith's Campaign to Change the GM Culture," *Business Week,* April 7, 1986, 84–85; "Ross Perot's Crusade," *Business Week,* October 6, 1986, 60–65; and J. B. White, "GM Is Overhauling Corporate Culture in an Effort to Regain Competitiveness," *The Wall Street Journal,* January 13, 1993, A3.

CHAPTER 4

HUMAN RESOURCE ISSUES IN PRODUCTIVITY AND QUALITY

After you have read this chapter, you should be able to:

1. Explain how human resources contribute to productivity.

2. Discuss how productivity, innovation, and loyalty are interrelated.

3. Describe four views of why people behave as they do.

4. Diagram and discuss the relationship between job satisfaction to turnover and to absenteeism.

5. Identify three alternatives for absenteeism and turnover control.

6. Define job design and discuss its dimensions.

7. Explain the difference between job enrichment and job enlargement.

8. Identify the five components of the job–characteristics model.

9. Describe how employee involvement relates to productivity.

HR Today and Tomorrow:
Productivity through "Reengineering" and Automation

Productivity, quality, job design, and individual performance are all interrelated. In trying to improve productivity, one fact driven home to U.S. managers in the last several years is that people cost money, and there are some jobs that machines (which generally cost less than people) can do just as well as people. As a result, the shift toward automation (replacing people with machines) has accelerated, especially in those jobs that are routine.

"*Reengineering*" of work may have just as big an impact as automating it. Xerox, Ford, and Banc One Corporation have already achieved stunning gains in productivity through reengineering. The term includes such techniques as work teams, training employees in multiple skills so they can do multiple jobs, pushing decision making as far down the organizational hierarchy as possible, and reorganizing operations and offices to simplify and speed work.

Unions, understandably, have been concerned about losing jobs to such reengineering and automation efforts. Even white-collar jobs are being affected. *Lexicons,* machines that type directly from speech, are growing in use and ultimately may eliminate 50% of all clerical and stenographic jobs.

Automation is essentially a substitute for human labor, but some robots do more than substitute—they perform certain tasks better than humans. A Japanese engineer notes that they provide a level of precision, quality, and cleanliness that humans cannot. Robots also work at precise speeds and do not make mistakes.

There has been much speculation about how people will cope with the loss of work resulting from increased automation and reengineering in the future. But researchers who have examined the kinds of jobs generated after automation and reengineering have been implemented suggest that more interesting jobs are a likely result, which should increase employee motivation. At Ford Motor Company's Livonia, Michigan, transmission plant, computers on the lines summon unmanned vehicles that glide across the factory floor bringing parts as needed. Unskilled labor is history in this 80% automated factory, and unskilled workers have been replaced with better-educated employees who have stronger voices in decision making.

Job shrinkage is not new, of course. U.S. manufacturers have increased productivity over the years since 1946, so that they employ virtually the same number of employees they did then, producing five times as many goods. However, as the field of manufacturing has lost jobs, other fields have gained. New jobs are being created by new technology. Many managers have been slow to realize that workers can learn the new skills associated with new equipment. One observer pointed out that in the 1880s it was thought that only mechanics could drive cars—but the average person soon learned to operate an automobile.

Previous waves of change, mostly from automation, have caused unemployment in the short term, but they have been accompanied with corresponding changes in the workforce that have softened the initial effect. Increased education, shorter workweeks and workdays, longer training, earlier retirement, child labor laws, and welfare and unemployment payments all have had roles in easing our adjustments to new technologies. Americans have been successful in translating productivity gains from less human labor into higher levels of competitiveness.

However, the increasing productivity of today brings requirements for organizations that are somewhat different from those of the past. It requires a greater investment in human capabilities than ever before. In the wake of technological advances comes a need for higher levels of skill and motivation on the part of employees, proving the inseparability of technology and human resources.[1]

> The perception used to be that Human Resources thought about the happiness of employees. . . . Now we realize the overriding concern is the yield from employees.
>
> *Jean Coyle*

Productivity is a major competitive issue for business firms and for countries alike. **Productivity** is a measure of the quantity and quality of work done, considering the cost of the resources it took to do the work.

$$\text{Productivity} = \frac{\text{quantity of work} + \text{quality of work}}{\text{cost of resources needed to do the work}}$$

Perhaps none of the resources for productivity are so closely scrutinized as human resources. Many of the activities undertaken in an HR system deal with individual or organizational productivity. Pay and appraisal systems, training, selection, job design, and incentives are HR issues concerned with productivity very directly.

Productivity at the level of the organization ultimately affects profitability and competitiveness in a for-profit organization and total costs in a not-for-profit organization. Decisions to close (or open) plants often are the result of productivity concerns. A useful way to measure organizational HR productivity is by **unit labor cost,** or the total labor cost per unit of output, which is computed by dividing the average wages of workers by their levels of productivity. Using the unit labor cost, it can be seen that a company paying relatively high wages still can be economically competitive if it can also achieve an offsetting high productivity level. Figure 4–1 shows the trend in productivity figures for several major producing nations.

▼ **PRODUCTIVITY**

is a measure of the quantity and quality of work done, considering the cost of the resources it took to do the work.

▼ **UNIT LABOR COST**

is the total labor cost per unit of output which is the average wage's of workers divided by their levels of productivity.

▲ **Figure 4–1**

Trends in Productivity

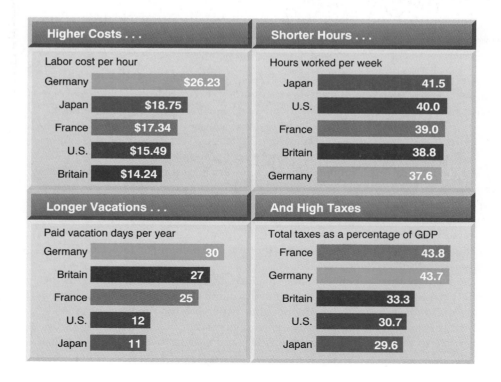

Higher Costs . . .

Labor cost per hour

Germany	$26.23
Japan	$18.75
France	$17.34
U.S.	$15.49
Britain	$14.24

Shorter Hours . . .

Hours worked per week

Japan	41.5
U.S.	40.0
France	39.0
Britain	38.8
Germany	37.6

Longer Vacations . . .

Paid vacation days per year

Germany	30
Britain	27
France	25
U.S.	12
Japan	11

And High Taxes

Total taxes as a percentage of GDP

France	43.8
Germany	43.7
Britain	33.3
U.S.	30.7
Japan	29.6

HR Perspectives:
Productivity in the Auto Industry

In the early 1980s productivity became a major concern of U.S. automakers. Japanese automobile imports were priced well below American products. The U.S. auto companies, feeling the crunch of foreign competition, looked closely at output per employee. Then a wide variety of techniques to improve productivity, ranging from automation and work redesign to "motivation programs" and attempts at psychological "involvement," were tried, but the results were mixed.

One successful example is the General Motors assembly plant in Fremont, California. In the early 1980s, the absenteeism rate was about 20%. There were 5,000 outstanding grievances, frequent wildcat strikes, and constant feuds between management and labor. Finally, General Motors shut the plant down and turned it over to Toyota Motor Corporation as part of a joint venture

called New Unit Motor Manufacturing, Inc. (NUMMI). Adding little new technology, Toyota implemented a typical Toyota production system with just-in-time delivery of parts and components and flexible assembly lines run by teams of workers in charge of their own jobs. The firm hired back the United Auto Workers (UAW) members who wanted to work, including their militant leaders. As a result, 2,500 employees assemble what it formerly took 5,000 people to produce with GM. Significantly, absenteeism decreased to about 2%, and outstanding grievances averaged only about two at a time.

Productivity (including quality) in U.S.–owned plants in the United States still is below that of Japanese plants (both in Japan and in the U.S.) but is better than that in 17 European-owned plants in Europe.[17]

More recently, GM's Saturn division has utilized employee-involvement and quality-improvement techniques to make a success of its Saturn autos. But Saturn has not been able to produce enough cars to meet demand, so customers have long waits for cars. GM could "lean on" Saturn for an improvement in productivity. But when employees and equipment are pushed too far, quality suffers. Saturn employee pay is tied to quality targets, and they already have demonstrated they will not compromise quality. When management pushed through a production increase that raised the number of defects, employees staged a work slowdown until management eased off those production goals.[4] Saturn is a case in point for how productivity, quality, and employee involvement are interrelated.

Germany's concern about its lower rates of productivity and therefore higher costs is shown rather graphically in the Figure 4–1. It has had the highest labor costs for several years. This is based on very short workweeks, long vacations, short careers, students in school for many years, and rampant holidays. High wage costs and restrictive union work rules keep German machines running 20% fewer hours than those of the western economies shown in Figure 4–1.

At the national level, productivity is of concern for several reasons. First, high productivity leads to high standards of living, as symbolized by a greater ability of a country to pay for what its citizens want. Next, increases in national wage levels without increases in national productivity lead to inflation. This means an increase in costs and a decrease in purchasing power. Finally, lower rates of productivity make for higher unit labor costs and a less competitive position for a nation's products in the world marketplace.

Productivity, then, is a concern of individuals, organizations, and nations. As the "HR Perspective" indicates, the automobile industry worldwide is an interesting study in how one industry has attempted to cope with the problems of individual and organizational productivity. This chapter will examine major HR issues that relate to productivity at both individual and organizational level: individual productivity variables, employee-involvement efforts, quality improvement and control, innovation, employee loyalty and motivation, job satisfaction, job design, and absenteeism and turnover control. Other HR practices that relate to productivity also will be considered in the chapters discussing selection, training, and incentives.

▲ WHAT ORGANIZATIONS NEED FROM EMPLOYEES TO SUCCEED

In a competitive environment, not all organizations succeed. Those that do need certain ongoing contributions from the human resources in the organization to remain successful as Figure 4–2 shows.[3]

▲ *Individual productivity.* If a company's individual employees are significantly less productive than a competitor's, it will ultimately incur higher costs and be unable to compete.

▲ *Innovation.* An organization changes constantly. Dealing with the changes requires innovations in design of work, production, service, and every other phase of operations. Innovations do not come solely from research and development (R&D) or management. Intelligence and ideas are widely distributed among the people (the human resources) of the organization.

▲ *Loyalty.* To be successful an organization needs continuity in the form of loyalty from employees. Without it, the collective memory is lost and the "wheel continually reinvented" without a continuing core of employees. However, loyalty is clearly reciprocal. An organization cannot expect to receive loyalty if it does not manifest the same to its employees.

All three—productivity, innovation, and loyalty—are necessary for competitive organizations to succeed. In the wave of downsizing through the 1980s and early 1990s, many firms sought to increase economic productivity by cutting people to cut costs. Anticipated financial results were lower expenses, higher profits, increased returns on investments, and boosted stock prices. Better communications, more entrepreneurship, more effort expended, and lower overhead were seen as potential operational benefits. Yet research suggests that in many firms these benefits failed to materialize. HR problems developed as a result of the downsizing that adversely affected productivity. Motivation and loyalty were reduced and employee mobility increased[5]. Although not directly studied, it seems likely innovative behavior did not fare well in many cases.

A senior manager at a Fortune 100 company explained how a bookkeeper making $9 an hour was let go in a downsizing. The company later discovered

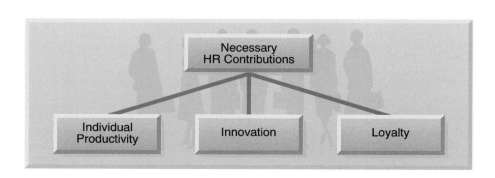

▲ **Figure 4–2**

Human Resource Contributions Needed for Competitive Organizations to Succeed

that this bookkeeper knew how and why activities were done that *no one else did*. Because critical institutional memory had been lost, the bookkeeper was hired back as a consultant at $42 per hour.[6] This example does not argue against downsizing when necessary; rather, it argues for an understanding of how all three human contributions (productivity, loyalty, and innovation) are necessary for success. Each of these qualities is discussed separately.

Individual Productivity

Individual productivity depends upon: (1) a person's innate ability to do the job, (2) the level of effort he or she is willing to exert, and (3) the support given that person.[7] Figure 4–3 shows the relationship of these factors. HR management has a role in each. Recruiting and selection are directly involved with the first aspect, choosing the person with the right talents and interests for a given job. Then, the effort expended by an individual (the second aspect) is influenced by many HR issues, such as compensation, incentives, and job design.[8] Support (the third aspect) includes training, equipment provided, and knowledge of expectations. HR functions involved here include training and development and performance appraisal.[9]

Quality in the Productivity Equation   Quality must be considered part of productivity. The alternative may be to trade off quality of production for quantity of production. Currently, some American goods suffer from an image of poor quality as a result of this very trade-off. Some observers blame the problem on the failure of U.S. manufacturers to make quality a first priority. W. Edwards Deming, American quality expert, has argued that, "Fifteen to forty percent of the cost of almost any American product you buy is for the waste embedded in it."[10] He advocates "getting the job done right the first time"

▲ **Figure 4–3**

Components of Individual Productivity

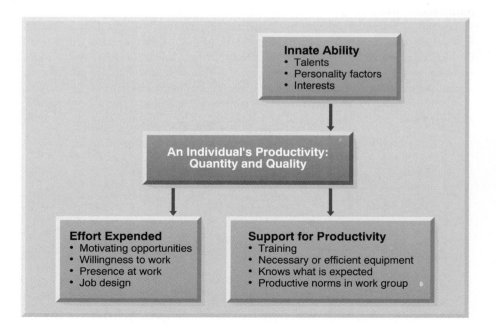

through individual pride in craftsmanship, vigorous training, and an unwilling-ness to tolerate delays, defects, and mistakes.

U.S. companies are proceeding on the quality front in many different ways, ranging from general training of workers on improving and maintaining quality to better engineering of products prior to manufacturing. The consensus seems to be that organization-wide dedication is required. Productivity without quality has proved costly. The "HR Perspective" shows how the European community is attempting to deal with quality issues.

Baldrige Awards   The U.S. Department of Commerce gives the Malcolm Baldrige Awards annually for quality improvement in American companies. These awards require that companies examine their operations to identify ways to improve quality. For quality improvements, they must make necessary changes and describe them in the Baldrige applications. Before Tramex Travel of Austin, Texas, entered the contest, is spent a year developing internal logs to help mea-sure quality. It tracked how many incoming telephone calls were answered with-in three rings and the time if took to deliver tickets. It started **quality circles**— small groups of employees who monitor productivity and quality and suggest solutions to problems. The president of the small company notes that although Tramex did not win a Baldrige award, it gained competitive leverage by taking part in the competition for it. In contending for the award, the company estab-lished the kind of quality improvement program that customers value.[11]

The link between human resources and quality is very strong in the judging of the Baldrige awards.[12] A combination of the Baldrige criteria and other sources indicates the following guidelines for improving quality:[13]

▲ Emphasize a team approach to quality.
▲ Provide continuous training in customer relations.
▲ Emphasize quality and team performance in performance evaluations.
▲ Give more authority to employees who deal with customers.
▲ Focus innovative efforts on products and services.
▲ Support employee development through cross training and succession.

Note that the suggestions recommend employee involvement in the efforts through a team approach. More will be presented on employee involvement later in this chapter.

Total Quality Management   Total Quality Management (TQM) is a comprehensive management process focusing on the continuous improvement of organizational activities to enhance the quality of the goods and services sup-plied. TQM programs have become quite popular as companies try to improve their productivity and quality.[14] The results are mixed, though. A comprehensive study of 584 organizations concluded that some companies do not benefit from all of the TQM tools. In such organizations TQM programs may achieve signifi-cant results initially as problems are solved; however, as higher standards are achieved, the results of the programs may diminish and it is important that the organization does not lose sight of broader issues as quality improves.[15]

Innovation

Organizations require innovation in order to adjust to changes and to continue to be productive. **Innovation** is the introduction of new or creative methods, products, or services. For example, American Express, the financial services or-

HR Perspectives:

European Quality and ISO 9000

The European Community (EC) has adopted a set of quality standards for its marketplace called ISO 9000, derived from the International Standards Organization in Geneva. These standards cover everything from training to purchasing. To do business with the EC, a company must be certified as complying with ISO 9000.

This approach has its supporters and detractors. On the plus side, it is argued that if the standards become universal, there will be one set of audit standards recognized by all to measure quality of operations. On the minus side, ISO has ignored customer input. A company might meet all ISO requirements for "quality" and still produce something no one wants.

Much of the world sees these standards as an attempt to keep competition out of the EC. Also, ISO certification may be confusing—each of the 55 countries that has adopted it interprets it differently, so certificates awarded by auditors in one country may not be accepted elsewhere. Meanwhile, failure to get ISO approval could keep a company's products out of the EC.

Companies seeking ISO approval begin with a 100-page, 5-part ISO guidebook that asks them to document how employees perform every function that affects quality. There are standards for 20 different functions including: design, process control, purchasing, service, inspection and testing, and training practices.

Because the focus here is on HR issues, following is the training standard ISO 901, 1987E that states:

"4.18 Training
The supplier shall establish and maintain procedures for identifying the training needs and provide for the training of all personnel performing activities affecting quality. Personnel performing specific assigned tasks shall be qualified on the basis of appropriate education, training, and/or experience, as required. Appropriate records of training shall be maintained."[16]

Some of the questions provoked by ISO 9000 include: Can quality be legislated given the changing nature of the environments in which people operate? How can standards for training be specified without excluding innovative but yet unproven training methods?

ganization, used taskforces to develop an innovative method that reduced the time needed to process applications for personal credit cards. The company was concerned because delays in approving credit applications led to lost revenue and unhappy clients in the competitive credit card industry. The firm asked members of the taskforce to describe and measure each step of the application-review process. By carefully identifying each step, the task force was able to target and remove unnecessary ones. Average application-review time was cut 60% (from 35 to 14 days). Thus, this innovation improved productivity, customer satisfaction, employee involvement, and overall organizational performance.

Implementation of innovation is often stymied by the universal human tendency to resist change—even beneficial change. Employees and customers are both prone to such resistance, which must be overcome for innovation to be successful. Some innovative efforts may prove to be unproductive or costly—an unavoidable risk. But people who do not take risks cannot innovate.[17] Innovation requires interaction between the characteristics of the individual (knowledge, motivation, etc.), the characteristics of the work group (diversity, norms) and the characteristics of the organization (rewards for innovation, climate), as Figure 4–4 illustrates.

Certain companies seem to be more adept at innovation than others. Merck, 3M, Hewlett-Packard, and Rubbermaid are considered among the best currently. 3M spins out new products better than almost anyone. In a recent year 32 % of 3M's $10.6 billion in sales came from products introduced in the previous five years.[18] The simple rules that 3M relies on are similar to those used in other in-

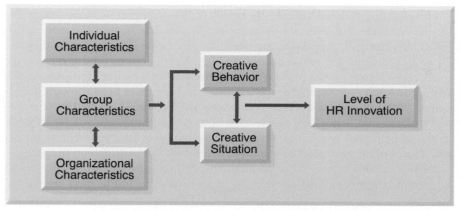

Figure 4–4

Innovation/Creativity from Human Resources

SOURCE: Adapted from R. Woodman, J. Sawyer, and R. Griffin, "Toward a Theory of Organizational Creativity," *Academy of Management Review* 18, (1993), 309.

novative companies. The Vice-President for Human Resources summarizes employees' feelings this way:

> Our studies have shown that the biggest reward they can receive is to be given the opportunity to be innovative many times during their careers. We have never paid our technical people on the basis of what they actually invented. It might get reflected in a merit increase but we don't give them a specific bonus.[19]

Loyalty

The long-term economic health of most organizations depends on the continuity of a stable, skilled core of employees. **Loyalty,** defined here as a commitment to and allegiance with an organization, must be an ingredient in that stable workforce. It is safe to say that loyalty has diminished in U.S. companies. In many ways loyalty appears to be an exchange.[20] The employee supplies effort, loyalty, and productivity to the organization and in return *expects* loyalty from the organization. As organizational mergers and employment cutbacks have swept the country, resulting in layoffs and restructuring, more employees seem convinced that organizations will not return their loyalty, so they do not offer it. A quote from one employee illustrates this fact: "If I am expendable, I owe the company nothing more than a fair day's work."[21]

Higher-than-normal turnover is one possible result where loyalty is missing. Others are less effort expended by employees, high rates of absenteeism—and even sabotage and theft. In high-tech work and professional occupations, loyalty is more likely to be to the profession or to the technology used than to one's employer.[22] In Central California's Silicon Valley, turnover rates at 231 electronics companies at one point averaged more than five times the rate for all U.S. manufacturing companies.

Downsizing, reengineering, and "delayering" of hierarchical levels have done recognizable damage to loyalty. The older hierarchical approach offered career progression in a single firm. Job security allowed large firms to demand sacrifices such as moving families regularly. It also allowed the companies to invest in training and development of their employees, confident they would not immediately go to another firm.

LOYALTY

is commitment to and allegiance with an organization.

However, as can be seen from the Silicon Valley example, the "one-company-for-life" attitude that prevailed from before World War II until the early 1970s has indeed changed. Employees are changing jobs twice as frequently as they did 20 or 30 years ago. Job tenure in the 1960s averaged 20 years. Today the average is below 8.75 years.[23] A recent survey of American workers depicted a workforce with little loyalty to employers: 42% of those surveyed had been through downsizing, 28% had seen management cutbacks at their companies, and 20% said they personally feared being fired. Only 28% agreed that they were willing to work harder to help their employers succeed. Those who saw little opportunity for career advancement tended to be less loyal, committed, and satisfied on the job.[24]

One management researcher predicts that in the future big firms will have to offer their best professional workers the opportunities to add to their knowledge and skills in order to recruit or retain them. However, this will also increase the likelihood that they will leave for another firm. Managers and in-demand professionals can then use their options to leave as leverage for regular increases in salary.[25]

Increased mobility and changing societal values have further diminished loyalty in employees. Yet it is a quality very valuable to organizations, providing them with advantages in productivity, stability, and knowledge. The "HR Perspective" on retaining cultural diversity shows how some companies are trying to instill loyalty in some employees.

In summary, human resources are the obvious ones to consider when attempting to reduce organizational costs. But organizations need individual productivity, innovation, and loyalty from employees in order to succeed in the long term. Employers can foster those qualities by providing employees with jobs that motivate them, offer job satisfaction, and encourage employee involvement. The results should be reduced absenteeism and turnover. Understanding a person's willingness to exert effort requires knowledge of the interrelationships among motivation, job satisfaction, and job design.

▲ MOTIVATION

Motivation is an emotion or desire within a person causing that person to act. People usually act for one reason: to obtain a goal. Thus, motivation is a goal-directed drive and, as such, it seldom occurs in a void. The words *need, want, desire,* and *drive* are all similar to *motive.*

Approaches to understanding motivation differ because many individual theorists have developed their own views and theories of motivation. They approach motivation from different starting points, with different ideas in mind, and from different backgrounds. No one approach is considered to be the "correct" one. Each has contributed to the understanding of human behavior.

Motivation underlies the productive behavior employers look for in individuals. Further, HR professionals are interested in the topic of motivation because many of their responsibilities (compensation, incentives, discipline, job design, career planning, and appraisal, to name a few) require assumptions about what motivates people.

Many managers' views of motivation are based on assumptions about what goals they expect people to achieve as employees. For example, if a manager says he wants to "motivate" employees, he is really saying he wants his employees to select goals with which he agrees. His employees undoubtedly are motivated, but perhaps not toward doing what he would have them do. Figure 4–5 illus-

HR Perspectives:
Trying to Retain Cultural Diversity

Major companies are changing their last-hired, first-fired rules to preserve their cultural diversity with newly hired women and minorities who are typically the newest hires. They do not want to risk job-bias suits from such protected-class individuals or the loss of government contracts.

Unions have traditionally argued for the use of seniority in determining who will be laid off, but some firms that have used that criterion previously now reduce their workforces differently to protect women and minorities. For example, the four large companies listed below had the following proportions of women and minority supervisors before and after major cuts.[26]

However, court decisions on the relationship between seniority and discrimination have been very mixed.

In some cases, the courts have held that a valid seniority system does *not* violate rights based on sex or race. In other cases gender and racial considerations were given precedence over seniority. Another concern is how employers' attempts to retain diversity will affect the loyalty of minority and female employees.

	AT&T BEFORE—AFTER	DUPONT BEFORE—AFTER	NYNEX BEFORE—AFTER	HONEYWELL BEFORE—AFTER
Minority supervisors	3%—9%	11%—12%	22%—22%	13.5%—14%
Women supervisors	2.5%—9%	16%—17%	47%—47%	37.6%—36.7%

trates such a manager's model of motivation. This view, although widely held by managers, is too restrictive because it does not consider the needs of employees.

The study of motivation over the last century has been focused partly on answering the question, "What is the basic goal of humans?" Managers have operated with their own preconceived ideas about these goals. Over time, five major assumptions about human nature and the mainsprings of motivation have emerged. These assumptions have been translated into various managerial philosophies.

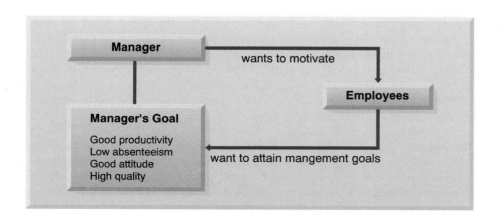

▲ **Figure 4–5**

Managerial Model of Motivation

Rational-Economic View

One long-lived approach to motivation is based on the assumption that people are rational-economic beings, so they reasonably, logically, and rationally make decisions that will result in the most economic gain for themselves. Therefore, it is assumed that employees are motivated by the opportunity to make as much money as possible and will act rationally to maximize their earnings. The assumption is that money, because of what it can buy, is the most important motivator of all people.

This explanation of human motivation fails to explain a great deal of behavior. For example, if employees are primarily interested in maximizing their economic return, why do some turn away from the potential profits of piece-rate production and others refuse to take overtime? Obviously, the rational-economic view has some limitations.

Social View

The social view of human nature suggests that all people can be motivated to perform by satisfying their social needs. Expressions of this viewpoint are, "Happiness and harmony in the group lead to productivity," or "A happy worker is a productive worker."

Self-Actualizing View

During the late 1950s and early 1960s, the ideas of another group of management thinkers, many of whom were trained in the behavioral sciences, became very popular. They assumed that each person strives to reach self-actualization; that is, to reach his or her full potential, and implicitly that productivity will be a by-product of self-actualization. Included in the discussions that follow are the theories of Maslow, McGregor, and Herzberg.

Maslow   The concept of self-actualization was developed by a clinical psychologist, Abraham Maslow, whose theory of human motivation continues to receive a great deal of exposure in management literature. Maslow classified human needs into five categories that ascend in a definite order. Until the more basic needs are adequately fulfilled, a person will not strive to meet higher needs. Maslow's well-known hierarchy is composed of: (1) physiological needs, (2) safety and security needs, (3) belonging and love needs, (4) self-esteem needs, and (5) self-actualization needs.[27]

An assumption often made by those using Maslow's hierarchy is that workers in modern, technologically advanced societies basically have satisfied their physiological, safety, and belonging needs. Therefore, they will be motivated by the needs for self-esteem, esteem of others, and self-actualization. Consequently, conditions to satisfy these needs should be present at work; the job itself should be internally meaningful and motivating.

McGregor   Douglas McGregor, using the self-actualization view as a point of departure, presented two opposite sets of assumptions about people's work motivations that he believed were held by most managers. Summarized in Figure 4–6, one set (which is negative) was labeled Theory X and the other (which is positive) was labeled Theory Y.[28] McGregor felt that managers typically held

THEORY X	THEORY Y
▲ People dislike work and will attempt to avoid it. ▲ People have to be coerced and threatened with punishment for organizational goals to be met. ▲ Most workers like direction and will avoid responsibility. ▲ People want security above all in their work.	▲ People do not inherently dislike work. ▲ People do not like rigid control and threats. ▲ Under proper conditions, people do not avoid responsibility. ▲ People want security but also have other needs, such as self-actualization and esteem.

SOURCE: Douglas McGregor, *The Human Side of Enterprise* (New York: McGraw-Hill, 1960), 33–45.

▲ **Figure 4–6**

A Summary of Theory X and Theory Y (McGregor)

one of these sets of assumptions about human nature and acted in keeping with those assumptions. However, McGregor argued that people are really more like Theory Y than Theory X. A key point in McGregor's Theory Y is that work itself is a motivator for most people.

Herzberg   In the late 1950s Frederick Herzberg and his research associates conducted interviews with 200 engineers and accountants who worked in different organizations. The result of this research was a theory that, like Maslow's, has been widely discussed in the management literature.[29] Maslow identifies basic human needs, while Herzberg's work relates factors in the job to a person's motivation.

Herzberg's motivation/hygiene theory assumes that one group of factors, *motivators,* accounts for high levels of motivation to work. Another group of factors, *hygiene,* or maintenance, factors can cause discontent with work. Figure 4–7 compares Herzberg's motivators and hygiene factors with Maslow's needs hierarchy.

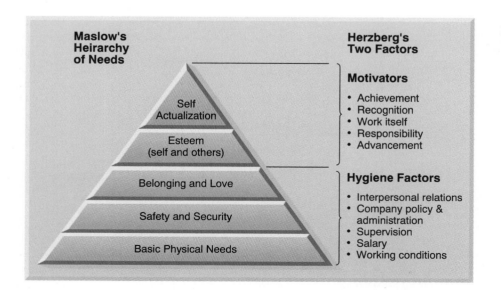

▲ **Figure 4–7**

Maslow's and Herzberg's Ideas Compared

The implication of Herzberg's research for management and HR practices is that although managers must carefully consider hygiene factors in order to avoid employee dissatisfaction, even if all these maintenance needs are addressed, people may not necessarily be motivated to work harder. Only motivators cause employees to exert more effort and thereby attain more productivity.

The self-actualizing schools of thought, with their sometimes moralistic requests to improve the job and let the individual achieve self-actualization, have given way to the recognition that people differ and that job situations vary. To understand motivation and human behavior, one must understand the interactions between individual characteristics and the characteristics of the situation. This fourth approach to motivation and human behavior recognizes this complexity.

Complex View

A complex view suggests that a variety of factors may prove to be motivating, depending on the needs of the individual, the situation that the individual is in, and the rewards that the individual expects for the work done. Theorists who hold to this view do not attempt to fit people into a single category, but rather accept human differences.

Porter and Lawler Model of Motivation   An approach by Lyman Porter and E. E. Lawler focuses on the value a person places on a goal as well as the person's perceptions of workplace *equity,* or fairness, as factors that influence his or her job behavior. In a work situation, *perception* is the way an individual views the job. Figure 4–8 contains a simplified Porter and Lawler model which indicates that motivation is influenced by people's expectations. If expectations are not met, people may feel that they have been unfairly treated and consequently become dissatisfied.[30]

Using the Porter and Lawler model, suppose that a salesclerk is motivated to expend effort on her job. From this job she expects to receive two types of re-

▲ **Figure 4–8**

Porter and Lawler Motivation Model

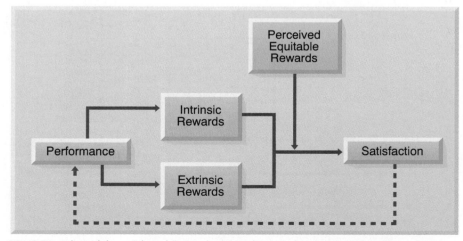

SOURCE: Adapted from Edward E. Lawler III and Lyman W. Porter, "The Effect of Performance on Job Satisfaction," *Industrial Relations 7* (1966).

wards: intrinsic (internal) and extrinsic (external). For this salesclerk, intrinsic rewards could include a feeling of accomplishment, a feeling of recognition, or other motivators. Extrinsic rewards might be such items as pay, benefits, good working conditions, and other hygiene factors. The salesclerk compares her performance with what she expected and evaluates it in light of both types of rewards she receives. She then reaches some level of job satisfaction or dissatisfaction. Once this level is reached, it is difficult to determine what she will do. If she is dissatisfied, she might put forth less effort in the future, she might work harder to get the rewards she wants, or she might just accept her dissatisfaction. If she is highly satisfied, it does not always mean she will work harder. She may even slack off a bit, saying, "I got what I wanted."

The essence of the Porter and Lawler view of motivation is perception. In addition, as the feedback loop in Figure 4–8 indicates, performance leads to satisfaction rather than satisfaction leading to performance.

Equity as a Motivator   People want to be treated fairly, not just in the rewards they receive, but also in such areas as vacations, work assignments, and penalties assessed. This is the concept of **equity,** which is the perceived fairness of what the person does (inputs) compared with what the person receives (outcomes). *Inputs* are what a person brings to the organization and include educational level, age, experience, productivity, and other skills or efforts. The items received by a person, or the *outcomes,* are the rewards obtained in exchange for inputs. Outcomes include pay, benefits, recognition, achievement, prestige, and any other rewards received. Note that an outcome can be either tangible (extrinsic rewards such as pay or economic benefits) or intangible (internal rewards such as recognition or achievement).

The individual's view of fair value is critical to the relationship between performance and job satisfaction because one's sense of equity is an exchange-and-comparison process. Assume you are a laboratory technician in a hospital. You exchange talents and efforts for the tangible and intangible rewards the hospital gives. Then you compare your inputs (what you did) and your outcomes (what you received) with those of others to determine the equity of your compensation. As Figure 4–9 shows, the comparison process includes the individual's comparison of inputs/outcomes to the inputs/outcomes of other individuals. Thus, you also will compare your talents, skills, and efforts to those of other laboratory technicians or other hospital employees. Your perception—correct or incorrect—significantly affects your valuation of your inputs and outcomes. A

▼ **EQUITY**

is the perceived fairness of what the person does (inputs) compared with what the person receives (outcomes).

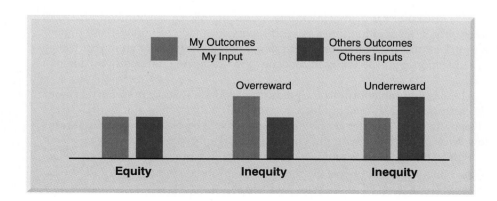

▲ **Figure 4–9**

Equity Evaluations

sense of inequity occurs when the comparison process results in an imbalance between inputs and outcomes.

If Inputs Exceed Outcomes   One view of equity theory research suggests that if an employee is underrewarded (more inputs than outcomes), then the employee will tend to reduce his or her inputs. If, in your job as a lab technician, you feel that your rewards have been fewer than your inputs, you will attempt to resolve the inequity. Your reactions can include some or all of the following: increasing dissatisfaction, attempting to get compensation raised, quitting the job for a more equitable one, changing your perceptual comparison, or reducing your productivity. All these actions are attempts to reduce the inequity.

If Outcomes Exceed Inputs   One way a person may attempt to resolve being overrewarded is by putting forth more effort. If you feel that you receive more rewards than you deserve, you might work harder to justify the "overpayment." Or you might process the same number of laboratory samples, but do so more accurately and produce higher-quality results. Another action could include a recomparison, whereby you might decide that you evaluated your efforts inaccurately and that you really were not overpaid.

Regardless of what action you take, you will make some attempt to relieve the inequity tension. Research evidence on the type of action you are most likely to take is mixed. Because perceptions of inequity can affect motivation, they have important implications for the design and administration of compensation programs, staffing, training, and performance appraisal.

▲ JOB SATISFACTION

▼ JOB SATISFACTION

is a positive emotional state resulting from the appraisal of one's job experiences.

In its most basic sense, **job satisfaction** is a positive emotional state resulting from the appraisal of one's job experiences. Job *dissatisfaction* occurs when these expectations are not met. For instance, if you expect clean and safe working conditions on the job, you are likely to be dissatisfied if your workplace is dirty and dangerous.

Job satisfaction is determined by an individual's evaluation of his or her work experiences. The evaluation may be personal and internal or it may be partly external, influenced by managers, co-workers, or the like; but the individual is the final determinant of the positive (or negative) feeling that results.

Job satisfaction has many dimensions. Some include satisfaction with the work itself, wages, recognition, rapport with supervisors and co-workers, and organizational culture and philosophy. Each dimension contributes to an overall feeling of satisfaction with the job itself, but the "job" is defined differently by different people.

There is no simple formula for predicting a worker's satisfaction. Furthermore, the relationship between productivity and job satisfaction is not entirely clear. "Happy workers" are not always more productive workers. For example, at times low levels of productivity in the United States have been coupled with a generally high level of job satisfaction. In nationwide polls, common findings are:

▲ Nine out of ten people say they like their jobs.
▲ More than 60 % say they are paid fairly.

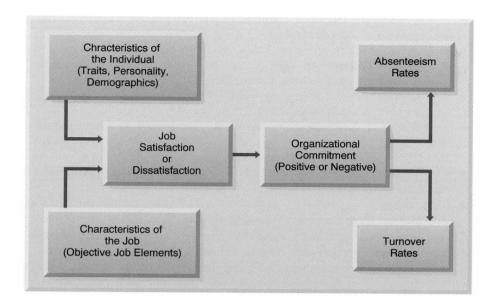

Causal Model: Job Satisfaction, Absenteeism, and Turnover

- ▲ Of those who like their jobs, about one-third like the work best, a quarter like their co-workers best, and around 10% like the money best.
- ▲ White-collar workers like their jobs better than blue-collar workers like their jobs.
- ▲ Older workers like their jobs better than younger workers like their jobs.

Research indicates that job satisfaction affects organizational commitment which affects the rates of absenteeism and turnover as Figure 4-10 shows. Although job satisfaction itself is interesting and important, perhaps the "bottom line" is the impact job satisfaction has on employee absenteeism and turnover.

▲ ABSENTEEISM

Being absent from work may seem like a small matter to an employee. But if a manager needs 12 people to work in a unit to get the work done, and 4 of the 12 are absent most of the time, the unit's work will probably not get done, or additional workers will have to be hired.

Some absenteeism is unavoidable. People do get sick or encounter other circumstances that make it impossible for them to attend work. This is usually referred to as *involuntary* absenteeism. However, much absenteeism is avoidable, called *voluntary,* and a relatively small percentage of individuals in the workplace is responsible for a disproportionate share of the total absence.

Cost of Absenteeism

Absenteeism is expensive. Nationally, absenteeism is estimated to cost $40 billion per year in reduced productivity.[31] Certain elements of labor costs continue for an employer even though an employee is absent. For example:[32]

▲ *Benefits.* Most organizations continue to pay benefits for employees who are absent on a long-term basis.

▲ *Workers' compensation premiums.* Employers who use a private insurer for workers' compensation are likely to face an increase in premiums as a result of long-term work-related absenteeism.

▲ *Lost productivity.* With both short- and long-term absenteeism, a certain amount of productivity will be lost.

▲ *Supervisory time.* Supervisors must make decisions regarding the delegation of the absent employee's work and sometimes spend extra time instructing those filling in for the absent employee.

▲ *Overtime pay.* Other employees may have to be paid overtime to do the absent employee's work.

▲ *Temporary help.* If a temporary worker is hired to fill in, there is the cost of those services plus the time spent in instruction.

Organizations consistently have noted that there are more absences on Fridays and Mondays than on other days because some employees like to stretch the weekend to three or four days. Employees with higher job satisfaction will probably be absent less often than those who are dissatisfied with their jobs. (See the "HR Perspective" for creative reasons for being late or absent.)

Absenteeism Control

Controlling voluntary absenteeism is easier if managers understand its causes more clearly, but a solid theory of voluntary absenteeism has not yet emerged. One concept that has some support is that such absence occurs when people do not cope well with certain aspects of their jobs, so absenteeism is a way of *avoiding* such a situation.[34]

Controlling or reducing absenteeism must begin with continuous monitoring of the absenteeism statistics in work units. Such monitoring helps managers pinpoint employees who are frequently absent and departments that have excessive absenteeism. A formula for computing absenteeism rates, suggested by the U.S. Department of Labor, is as follows:

$$\frac{\text{Number of person-days lost through job absence during period}}{(\text{Average number of employees}) \times (\text{Number of work days})} \times 100$$

(Note: Rate can be based on number of hours instead of number of days.)

Organizational policies on absenteeism should be clearly stated in an employee handbook and stressed by supervisors and managers. Counseling employees may correct some problems that make people reluctant to come to work. Positive actions to avoid being absent should be suggested. Absenteeism control options fall into three categories: (1) discipline, (2) positive reinforcement, or (3) a combination of both.

Disciplinary Approach Many employers use a disciplinary approach. People who are absent the first time receive an oral warning, but subsequent absences bring written warnings, suspension, and finally dismissal.

Absenteeism often varies from 2% to 12% per month. Employees can be absent from work for several reasons. Illness, death in the family, or other personal reasons are unavoidable and understandable. Consequently, many employers have

HR Perspectives:
Creative Reasons for Being Late or Absent

From time to time, "creative" excuses for tardiness or absence from work are used. Here are some that are hard to believe:

"My pet chicken froze to the driveway and I had to wait around to thaw it loose."

"My six-year-old son set all the clocks in the house back an hour as a joke."

"I thought Halloween *was* a national holiday."

"The dog hid my toupee."

"I fell asleep over breakfast and the waitress didn't wake me up till 9:30."

"I thought I saw a flying saucer and followed it 50 miles down the road."

"Someone stole one of my shoes on the bus."

"A spider cornered me in the bathroom."

"I was up half the night looking for Halley's Comet."

"When you work as hard as I do, you're entitled."

"My dog carried away the car keys."

"The wind was blowing against me."

"A plane landed on the highway and blocked cars."

"I thought Monday was Sunday."

"My husband's pet spider died and I had to console him."[33]

---

sick-leave policies that allow employees a certain number of paid absent days per year. Employees who miss fewer days are reimbursed with sick pay.

Positive Reinforcement   Positive reinforcement includes such methods as giving employees cash, recognition, time off, or other rewards for meeting attendance standards. In one firm, employees with perfect attendance records were given the opportunity to participate in a lottery with a cash reward. The program helped reduce absenteeism. Offering rewards for good attendance, giving bonuses for missing fewer than a certain number of days, and "buying back" unused sick leave are all positive methods of reducing absenteeism. Further, flexible scheduling has been shown to have a positive impact on absence rates.[35] If absenteeism is excessive, the problem employees can be dismissed.

Combination Approach   Combination approaches ideally reward desired behavior and punish undesired behavior. At some firms, including some hospitals, each employee gets a time-off "account," against which vacations, holidays, and sick days are drawn. If employees run out of days in their accounts, they are not paid for additional days missed.

Impact of Absence Policies

The policies and rules an organization uses to govern absenteeism may provide a clue to the effectiveness of that control. Studies indicate that absence rates are highly related to the control policies used for absenteeism. Policies can encourage attendance or absence. For example, one examination concluded:[36]

▲ Organizations that pay more have higher absence rates because employees can afford to "buy" leisure.

▲ Companies that require employees to present a doctor's certificate when ill have lower absence rates.

▲ Organizations that allow employees to accrue sick leave faster have higher absenteeism (some people feel sick leave is to be used).

▲ Organizations that do not reimburse employees for unused sick leave have higher absenteeism rates.

▲ TURNOVER

Turnover occurs when employees leave an organization and have to be replaced. It can be a very costly problem, one with a major impact on productivity. One firm had a turnover rate of more than 120% per year! It cost the company $1.5 million a year in lost productivity, increased training time, increased employee selection time, lost work efficiency, and other indirect costs.

It is the cost that makes turnover a common indicator of the HR performance of a company. But cost is not the only reason turnover is important. Lengthy training times, interrupted schedules, overtime for others, mistakes, and not having knowledgeable employees in place are some of the frustrations associated with excessive turnover.

The turnover rate for an organization can be computed in a number of different ways.[37] The following formula from the U.S. Department of Labor is widely used. (*Separations* are people who left the organization.)

$$\frac{\text{Number of employee separations during the month}}{\text{Total number of employees at midmonth}} \times 100$$

Common turnover figures range from 2% to 35% per year and normal turnover rates vary among industries. Organizations that require entry-level employees to have few skills are likely to have higher turnover rates among those employees than among managerial personnel. As a result, it is important that turnover rates be computed by work units. For instance, one organization had a companywide turnover rate that was not severe—but 80% of the turnover occurred within one department. This imbalance indicated that some action was needed to resolve problems in that unit.

Causes of turnover are varied: lack of challenge, better opportunity, pay, supervision, geography, and pressure. Certainly, not all turnover is negative. Some workforce losses are quite desirable, especially if those workers who leave are lower-performing, less reliable individuals.

Turnover often is classified as voluntary or involuntary, meaning avoidable or unavoidable, just as absenteeism is. *Involuntary turnover* occurs when an employee is fired. *Voluntary turnover* occurs when an employee leaves by his or her own choice, and can be caused by many factors. The obvious ones are those that cause job dissatisfaction.

Figure 4–11 shows the results of a comparison of 120 different turnover studies. Three classes of variables (external factors, work-related factors, and personal characteristics) were considered. In each classification, certain items were related to a person's likelihood of leaving the organization.

▲ **Figure 4–11**   Factors Associated with Higher Turnover

EXTERNAL FACTORS	WORK-RELATED FACTORS	PERSONAL CHARACTERISTICS
▲ Other job alternatives available ▲ No union present ▲ Low unemployment rate	▲ Low pay ▲ Low job satisfaction ▲ Low job performance ▲ Unclear job responsibilities	▲ Young age ▲ New employee ▲ High education level ▲ Few dependents ▲ Female ▲ Expectations not met

SOURCE: Adapted from J. Colton and J. M. Tuttle, "Employee Turnover: A Meta-Analysis and Review with Implications for Research," *Academy of Management Review* (1986), 55–70.

New employees are more likely to leave than employees who have been on the job longer. One estimate is that a company is likely to lose 16% to 20% of its employees during the first year, 8% to 9% during the second year, and only 1% of those remaining after ten years.[38] Studies of new employee turnover suggest that if people view job performance as based on unstable factors such as luck, they are more likely to leave.[39] If luck is the explanation for one's early performance, it may not give the employee enough feeling of achievement to persist through the anxious first few months of work. Turnover also shows something of a "snowball" effect—that is, turnover itself causes more turnover.

Turnover Control

Turnover can be controlled in several ways. Because it is related to job satisfaction, matching an employee's expectations of rewards and satisfaction to what is actually provided by the job may help reduce turnover problems. A good way to eliminate turnover is to *improve selection* and to better match applicants to jobs. By fine-tuning the selection process and hiring people who are more likely to stay, managers can decrease the chances that employees will leave.[40]

Good *employee orientation* also will help reduce turnover. Employees who are properly inducted into the company and are well trained tend to be less likely to leave. If people receive some basic information about the company and the job to be performed, they can determine early whether they want to stay. If individuals believe that they have no opportunities for career advancement, they may leave the organization. Consequently, *career planning* and *internal promotion* can help an organization keep career employees.

In addition, a fair and equitable *pay system* can help prevent turnover. An employee who is underpaid relative to employees in other jobs with similar skills may leave if there is an inviting alternative job available. An awareness of employee problems and dissatisfaction may provide a manager with opportunities to resolve them before they become so severe that employees leave.

In extreme cases in which there is a shortage of qualified workers, companies may spend heavily on training only to have competitors "pirate" away employees. Such situations have led to "payback agreements" whereby an employee must repay training, relocation, and even some salary costs if he or she leaves within a certain time.[41] But people are less likely to add to the turnover rate

▼ **JOB DESIGN**

refers to organizing tasks, duties, and responsibilities into a unit of work.

▼ **A POSITION**

is a collection of tasks, duties, and responsibilities performed by one person.

▼ **A JOB**

is a grouping of similar positions having common tasks, duties, and responsibilities.

▼ **A TASK**

is a distinct identifiable work activity composed of motions.

▼ **A DUTY**

is a larger work segment composed of several tasks that are performed by an individual.

▼ **RESPONSIBILITIES**

are obligations to perform certain tasks and duties.

when they like the work they are doing. Designing jobs with that in mind is the next topic.

▲ JOB DESIGN

Job design refers to organizing tasks, duties, and responsibilities into a productive unit of work. It involves the content and the effect of jobs on employees. Today more attention is being paid to job design for three major reasons:

1. Job design can influence *performance* in certain jobs, especially those where employee motivation can make a substantial difference.[42] Lower costs through reduced turnover and absenteeism also are related to good job design.
2. Job design can affect *job satisfaction*. Because people are more satisfied with certain job configurations than with others, it is important to be able to identify what makes a "good" job.
3. Job design can affect both *physical and mental health*. Problems such as hearing loss, backache, and leg pain sometimes can be traced directly to job design, as can stress and related high blood pressure and heart disease.

What Is a Job?

Although the terms *position* and *job* are often used interchangeably, there is a slight difference in emphasis. A **position** is a collection of tasks, duties, and responsibilities performed by one person. A **job** is a grouping of similar positions having common tasks, duties, and responsibilities and may include more than one position. Thus, if there are two persons operating postage meters in a mailroom, there are two positions (one for each person) but just one job (postage meter operator).

A **task** is composed of motions and is a distinct identifiable work activity, whereas a **duty** is composed of a number of tasks and is a work segment performed by an individual. Because both tasks and duties describe activities, it is not always easy or necessary to distinguish between the two. If one of the employment supervisor's duties is to "interview applicants," one task associated with that duty would be "asking questions."

Responsibilities are obligations to perform certain tasks and duties. Because managerial jobs carry greater responsibilities, they are usually more highly paid.

Person/Job Fit

Not everyone would be happy as a physician, as an engineer, or as a dishwasher. But certain people like and do well at each of those jobs. The person/job fit is a simple but important concept that involves matching characteristics of people with characteristics of jobs. Figure 4–12 depicts the person/job fit. Obviously, if a person does not fit a job, either the person can be changed or replaced, or the job can be altered. In the past, it was much more common to make the round person fit the square job. Titles such as farmhand or factory hand suggested that *hands* were hired, not whole people. However, successfully "reshaping" people is not easy to do. By redesigning jobs, the person/job fit can be improved more easily. Jobs may be designed properly when they are first established or redesigned later.

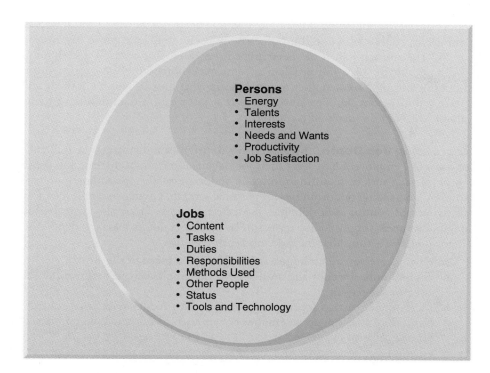

Nature of Job Design

Identifying the components of a given job is an integral part of job design. Designing or redesigning jobs encompasses many factors, and a number of different techniques are available to the manager. Job design has been equated with job enrichment, a technique developed by Frederick Herzberg, but job design is much broader than job enrichment alone.

Job Enlargement/Job Enrichment

Attempts to alleviate some of the problems encountered in excessive job simplification fall under the general headings of job enlargement and job enrichment. **Job enlargement** involves broadening the scope of a job by expanding the number of different tasks to be performed. **Job enrichment** is increasing the depth of a job by adding responsibility for planning, organizing, controlling, and evaluating the job.[43]

An assembly-line worker is very restricted in choosing what is done and when it is done, and therefore has very little *depth* in the job. A purchasing manager has a wide **job scope** because the job has a greater variety of duties than the assembly line job. Enlarging job scope means adding similar operations to a job.

Job Rotation   The technique known as **job rotation** can be a way to break the monotony of an otherwise routine job with little scope by shifting a person from job to job. For example, one week on the auto assembly line, John Williams attaches doors to the rest of the body assembly. The next week he attaches bumpers. The third week he puts in seat assemblies, then rotates back to

▼ **JOB ENLARGEMENT**

is broadening the scope of a job by expanding the number of different tasks to be performed.

▼ **JOB ENRICHMENT**

is increasing the depth of a job by adding employee responsibility for planning, organizing, controlling, and evaluating the job.

▼ **JOB SCOPE**

refers to the number of similar operations of a job.

▼ **JOB ROTATION**

is the process of shifting a person from job to job.

doors again the following week. Job rotation need not be done on a weekly basis. John could spend one-third of a day on each job or one entire day, instead of a week, on each job. It has been argued, however, that rotation does little in the long run to solve the problem of employee boredom. Rotating a person from one boring job to another may help somewhat initially, but the jobs are still perceived to be boring. The advantage is that job rotation does develop an employee who can do many different jobs.

▼ **JOB DEPTH**

refers to the amount of influence and control that employees have over their jobs.

Increasing Job Depth   Increasing **job depth** means increasing the influence and control employees have over their jobs. A manager might increase job depth by promoting variety, requiring more skill and responsibility, providing more autonomy, and adding opportunities for personal growth. Giving an employee more planning and control responsibilities over the tasks to be done also increases job depth. However, simply adding more similar tasks does not increase job depth.

Examples of actions that increase job depth include

▲ Giving a person an entire job rather than just a piece of the work.
▲ Giving more freedom and authority so the employee can perform the job as he or she sees fit.
▲ Increasing a person's accountability for work by reducing external control.
▲ Expanding assignments so employees can learn to do new tasks and develop new areas of expertise.
▲ Giving feedback reports directly to employees rather than to management only.

Supporters of increased job depth contend that the additional challenge and responsibility lead to higher productivity, lower absenteeism, and increased motivation. However, while job enrichment may result in substantial improvements in employee attitudes, it may not necessarily lead to greater productivity.

Job Characteristics and Job Design

Individual responses to jobs vary. A job may be fascinating to one person but not to someone else. It is useful for a manager to know what effect a job has on different people.

Depending on how jobs are designed, they may provide more or less opportunity for employees to satisfy their job-related needs. For example, a sales job may furnish a good opportunity to satisfy social needs, whereas a training assignment may satisfy a person's need to be an expert in a certain area. A job that gives little latitude may not satisfy an individual's creative or innovative needs.

The job-characteristics model developed by Hackman and Oldham identifies five important design characteristics of jobs. Figure 4–13 shows that *skill variety, task identity,* and *task significance* stimulate meaningfulness of work. *Autonomy* stimulates responsibility, and *feedback* provides knowledge of results. Following is a description of each characteristic:[44]

▲ *Skill variety.* The extent to which the work requires several different activities for successful completion. The more skills involved, the more meaningful is the work.
▲ *Task identity.* The extent to which the job includes a "whole" identifiable unit of work, carried out from start to finish, with a visible outcome. It is more meaningful to make a pair of shoes from start to finish than simply to nail on the heels, even though the skills may be equal in difficulty.

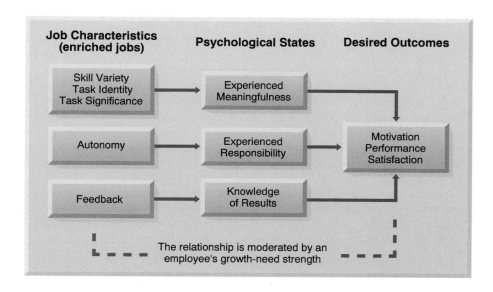

▲ **Figure 4–13**

Job-Characteristics Model

▲ *Task significance.* The amount of impact the job has on other people. A job is more meaningful if it is important to other people for some reason. For instance, a soldier may experience more fulfillment when defending his or her country from a real threat than when merely training to stay ready in case such a threat arises.

▲ *Autonomy.* The extent of individual freedom and discretion in the work and its scheduling. More autonomy leads to a greater feeling of personal responsibility for the work.

▲ *Feedback.* The amount of clear information received about how well or poorly one has performed. Feedback leads to a greater understanding of the effectiveness of one's performance and contributes to the overall knowledge an employee has about the work.

Jobs designed to take advantage of these important job characteristics are more likely to be positively received by employees. Such characteristics help distinguish between "good" and "bad" jobs.[45]

▲ EMPLOYEE INVOLVEMENT

In an attempt to make jobs more meaningful and to take advantage of the increased productivity and commitment that can follow, more organizations are turning to employee involvement as a basic part of modern jobs. Quality circles, self-directed/autonomous work groups, and production teams all share a common philosophy: employees are more likely to be productive and innovative if they have a say in how the work is to be done.

Typically, employee involvement means that a team of employees replaces some of the boss's authority by controlling matters from scheduling to hiring and sometimes firing. About one in five U.S. firms operate with self-managed teams today, and predictions are that by 2000, 40% to 50% of the U.S. workforce could be managing themselves through such teams.[46] The push for better quality, and the need to reduce management layers and costs have led to an emphasis on employee involvement, because it seems to help in all these areas.[47]

As some other countries discovered earlier, people tend to be more productive, innovative, and motivated when they have the opportunity to participate in designing their jobs. The impact of the group dynamics of employee-involvement teams on the individuals seems beneficial as well.[48]

But there are drawbacks to the team approach. A manager at Honeywell, where work teams in the United States have been used for at least ten years, reflects that while media and research attention is focused on what is being done in team-oriented companies, it is "very hard to notice what *doesn't* happen." The strength of many world-class companies, he points out, is built on the leadership skills of one person. He wonders whether an environment focused exclusively on teams might lose the edge provided by individual leadership.[49]

In conclusion, there is no formula guaranteeing productivity with human resources, not even employee involvement. However, like many other HR approaches, it has its uses. In time, research will point where employee involvement and work teams are most appropriate.

▲ Summary

- ▲ Productivity at individual, organizational, and national levels has important implications for organizational ability to compete.
- ▲ Employers want "motivated" employees, which usually means employees who are productive, innovative, and loyal to the organization.
- ▲ Motivation deals with the "whys" of human behavior.
- ▲ Four major views of human nature are rational-economic, social, self-actualizing, and complex.
- ▲ The complex view of motivation includes the expectancy and equity theories and recognizes the current situations people in organizations face.
- ▲ Job satisfaction affects commitment to the organization which, in turn, affects the rates of absenteeism and turnover.
- ▲ Absenteeism is expensive, but it can be controlled by discipline, positive reinforcement, or some combination of the two.
- ▲ Turnover has been studied extensively and appears to be strongly related to certain external, work-related, and personal factors.
- ▲ A job is a grouping of similar positions.
- ▲ Job design affects the performance, satisfaction, and health of the job holder.
- ▲ When people and jobs are mismatched, jobs are sometimes more easily changed than are people.
- ▲ Job enlargement, job enrichment, and job rotation all have been used to redesign jobs.
- ▲ The job-characteristics model suggests that five different characteristics of jobs (skill variety, task identity, task significance, autonomy, and feedback from the organization) affect motivation, performance, and satisfaction.
- ▲ Employee involvement is increasing in popularity as a way to foster innovation and commitment.

▲ REVIEW AND DISCUSSION QUESTIONS

1. Explain why managers often are not willing to look at the effort portion of the performance model to explain performance.
2. How is productivity in organizations affected by the absence of innovation and a lack of loyalty by employees?
3. Why is it difficult to identify what motive is operating in a person at a given time?
4. Of the four views about human behavior, which one/ones are most compatible with your own values and beliefs? Why?
5. "Increasing job satisfaction is a prime way to reduce absenteeism and turnover." Discuss.
6. Contrast the use of control and discipline with rewards and positive reinforcement as ways to reduce absenteeism and turnover.
7. Why is job design important to productivity and loyalty?
8. Compare and contrast job enlargement with job enrichment.
9. Use the job-characteristics model (Figure 4-13) to analyze a job you have had.

 CASE | **I WON'T GIVE AT THE OFFICE**

The Cigna Corporation employee had not "given at the office" for 20 years. Early in his career his boss had *insisted* that he give his "fair share." He did, but vowed when the manager changed departments that he never would give again—and he did not.

In a different organization, an employee got a message from the boss: "Give to the United Way, or else." She refused, so she was fired from her part-time job as a bank teller. The president of the company said, "I've had 100% participation from my employees for years and I'll be damned if one person is going to come along and change that." He offered her the job back only after the firing received publicity. This incident may not be unusual.

Employees cannot be legally dismissed over fundraising conflicts, but they can be subjected to more subtle forms of pressure. At one bank many employees fill out their contribution cards in front of a supervisor who reads the donation amounts in the employees' presence. At another firm workers are rewarded if the desired levels are reached.

At the bank "team captains" call meetings to give employees payroll-deduction cards. One participant watched as his supervisor read every card turned in. The supervisor called several people to the front to "correct" their cards when they indicated they were not giving.

Some workers rebel. One worker said, "Last year I gave money because they called me into a meeting and gave me the pitch and then handed me the card. This year I just skipped the meeting, and I won't give, either."

Although many workers resent the United Way, the organization actually evolved to protect them. Its nearly exclusive right to collect money at the workplace was meant to protect workers from an onslaught of outstretched hands. Instead, one hand—the United Way—collects and distributes money. The United Way says it discourages coercion, but acknowledges it has no control over how the money is raised. It hired a pollster who studied donor attitudes and found that 15% of workers felt coerced into giving.

Experts say image promotion is behind the emphasis on giving at most companies. "Companies want to look good in comparison with their competitors in the industry. It just looks better to say that all the employees gave."

At Cigna the drive chairman notes that the program had been basically a management program. The company discovered that the employees' resentment against the pressure has changed, as the nature of the program has changed. Employees are now simply sent pledge cards, not pressured, and the variety of charities to which one might contribute has been expanded.[50]

▲ QUESTIONS

1. Describe the motives of management and the motives of different employees in situations such as those described in the case.
2. How might the treatment employees receive affect the organizational commitment of other employees?

▲ NOTES

1. Adapted from A. Ehrbar, "Price of Progress," *The Wall Street Journal,* March 16, 1993, 1, and D. Woodruff; et al., "Saturn," *Business Week,* August 17, 1992, 89–91.

2. "Productivity in '92 Posts 20-Year High," *Omaha World-Herald,* February 4, 1993, A15.

3. Dun and Bradstreet Survey, reported in *The Wall Street Journal,* November 12, 1986, 35.

4. D. Woodruff, "Saturn," *Business Week,* August 17, 1992, 87–88.

5. Wayne F. Cascio, "Downsizing: What Do We Know? What Have We Learned?" *The Academy of Management Executive,* February 1993, 95–104.

6. Ibid., 99.

7. John R. Schermerhorn et al., "Management Dialogues: Turning on the Marginal Performer," *Organizational Dynamics,* 1989, 47–59.

8. C. Snow and M. Alexander, "Effort: The Illusive Variable in a Productivity Problem," *Industrial Management,* May–June 1992, 31–32.

9. D. Kosteva, "Managing Performance: How Do You Measure Up?" *NAPM Insights,* November 1992, 14.

10. K.R. Sheets, "Showdown on the Dollar," *U.S. News and World Report,* February 2, 1989, 20.

11. E. Carlson, "Enterprise," *The Wall Street Journal,* March 9, 1993, B1.

12. L. Dobyns and C. Crawford-Mason, *Quality or Use* (Boston: Houghton-Mifflin, 1991), 181.

13. M. Barnier, "Small Firms Put Quality First," *Nation's Business* May 1992, 22–32; and T. E. Benson, "Quality Is Not What You Think It Is," *Industry Week,* October 5, 1992, 21–39.

14. Tracy E. Benson, "TQM," *Industry Week,* April 5, 1993, 16.

15. G. Fuchsberg,"Total Quality Is Termed Only Partial Success," *The Wall Street Journal,* October 1, 1992, B1.

16. Jonathan Levine, "Want EC Business? You Have 2 Choices," *Business Week,* October 19, 1992, 57–58.

17. L. Lewis and D. Serbold, "Innovation Modification during Intraorganizational Adoption," *Academy of Management Review* 18, (1993), 322–354.

18. R. Mitchell, "Masters of Innovation," *Business Week,* April 10, 1989, 58.

19. S. Vittolino, "3M Stuck on Creativity," *Human Resource Executive,* April 1989, 26.

20. "The Checkoff," *The Wall Street Journal,* March 31, 1992, 1.

21. "Loyalty Up to a Point," *Business Month,* November 1990, 9.

22. M. Osborn, "90's Workers Turning Page on Loyalty," *USA Today,* September 17, 1991, B1–2.

23. P. Sherrod, "Workers Now Seminomadic, Ethic of Loyalty to Firms Ebbs," *Arizona Republic,* November 16, 1986, E9.

24. C. J. Mottaz, "An Analysis of the Relationship between Education and Organizational Commitment in a Variety of Occupational Groups," *Journal of Vocational Behavior* 28 (1986), 214–228.

25. "The Death of Corporate Loyalty," *The Economist,* April 3, 1993, 64.

26. Julia H. Lopez, "Companies Alter Layoff Policies to Keep Recently Hired Women and Minorities," *The Wall Street Journal,* September 18, 1992, B1.

27. A. H. Maslow, *The Motivation and Personality* (New York: Harper & Row, 1954).

28. Douglas McGregor, *The Human Side of Enterprise* (New York: McGraw-Hill, 1960), 33–45.

29. F. Herzberg, B. Mausner, and B. Snyderman, *The Motivation to Work* (New York: John Wiley & Sons, 1959).

30. Edward E. Lawler, III, and Lyman W. Porter, "The Effect of Performance on Job Satisfaction," *Industrial Relations* 7 (1966).

31. Wayne F. Cascio, *Costing Human Resources: The Financial Impact of Behavior in Organizations* (Boston: Kent Publishing, 1991), p. 58.

32. "CCH Absence Survey," *Ideas and Trends in Personnel,* February 20, 1991, 2.

33. D. Dalton and D. Mesch, "On the Extent and Reduction of Avoidable Absenteeism: An Assessment of Absence Policy Provisions," *Journal of Applied Psychology,* 76, (1991), 810–817.

34. G. P. Lathan and C. A. Frayore, "Self-Management Training for Increasing Job Attendance," *Journal of Applied Psychology* 74 (1989), 411–416; and D. A. Harrison and C. L. Hulin, "Investigations of Absenteeism: Using Event History Models," *Journal of Applied Psychology* 74 (1989), 300–316.

35. D. Dalton and D. Mesch, "The Impact of Flexible Scheduling on Employee Attendance and Turnover," *Administrative Science Quarterly* 35 (1990): 370–387.

36. Jeff Stinson, "Company Policy Attends to Chronic Absentees," *Personnel Journal,* August 1991, 82–85.

37. Robert P. Steel, Guy S. Shane, and Rodger W. Griffeth, "Correcting Turnover Statistics for Comparative Analysis," *Academy of Management Journal* 33 (1990), 179–187.

38. M. J. Major, "Turning Over the Odds to Your Favor," *Modern Office Technologies,* October 1986, 112.

39. Donald P. Schwab, "Contextual Variables in Employee Performance—Turnover Relationships," *Academy of Management Journal* 34, (1991), 966–975.

40. Cascio, 41.

41. C. Jones and W. Crandall, "Determining the Sources of Voluntary Employee Turnover," *SAM Advanced Management Journal,* Spring 1991, 16–20.

42. Michael Campion and Chris Berger, "Conceptual Integration and Test of Job Design . . .," *Personnel Psychology* 43,(1990), 525.

43. J. B. Cunningham and T. Eberle, "A Guide to Job Enrichment and Redesign," *Personnel,* February 1990, 56.

44. T. Schellhardt, "Few Employers Give Job Rotation a Whirl," *The Wall Street Journal,* July 22, 1992, B1; B. Posner, "Role Changes," *INC.,* February 1990, 95; and L. Hazzard et al. "Job Rotation Cuts Cumulative Trauma Cases," *Personnel Journal,* February 1992, 29.

45. P. Spector and S. Jex, "Relations of Job Characteristics from Multiple Data Sources with Employee Affect . . .," *Journal of Applied Psychology* 76, 1(1991), 46–53; and J. Kelley, "Does Job Redesign Theory Explain Job Redesign Outcomes?" *Human Relations* 45 (1992), 753.

46. JoAnn S. Lublin, "Trying to Increase Worker Productivity," *The Wall Street Journal,* February 13, 1992, B1.

47. T. O'Brien, "Self-Directed Work Groups Gain Popularity," *The Wall Street Journal,* February 12, 1993, B1.

48. M. H. Safizadeh, "The Case of Workgroups in Manufacturing Operations," *California Management Review,* Summer 1991, 61–79.

49. Tracy E. Benson, "A Braver New World?" *Industry Week,* August 3, 1992, 54.

50. Adapted from "Pressures Altering Office Drives," *Omaha World-Herald,* December 20, 1992, 10.

The increasing diversity of the U.S. workforce is focusing even greater attention than before on Equal Employment Opportunity (EEO). From both legal and managerial perspectives, organizations, managers, and employees of all types are recognizing that EEO considerations permeate all facets of an organization and its operations. A variety of groups have been identified for special protection against discrimination by various laws. Therefore, HR professionals and managers throughout organizations must be aware of EEO considerations and their effects on other HR management activities. For example, recruiting advertisements often contain notations that employers are "equal opportunity employers." Employment processes, including application blanks, interviews, and tests, must be free of discriminatory references and effects. Training programs and performance appraisal practices also can be impacted by equal employment concerns and regulations. Throughout all of the discussions the emphasis is on EEO as effective management, not just as a legal requirement.

Chapter 5 examines the legal constraints that EEO introduces onto the staffing process of an organization. There are a variety of terms and concepts that are used in EEO laws, regulations, and court cases. The chapter begins by explaining these terms and concepts before discussing the Civil Rights Act of 1991 and Title VII of the Civil Rights Act of 1964. To enforce these laws several different agencies have been established, the most important one being the federal Equal Employment Opportunity Commission. The two major strategies for complying with EEO regulations, identified in the 1978 Uniform Selection Guidelines, are covered. The chapter concludes with a discussion of several types of validity.

Chapter 6 looks at issues associated with implementing EEO in an organization. Concerns about discrimination on the basis of gender have led enforcement agencies and employers to address a variety of issues relating to sex discrimination. A particularly prominent concern is sexual harassment and how organizations and managers should deal with such situations. Other sex discrimination issues include the "glass ceiling," restrictive job conditions, and pregnancy discrimination. Another area of discrimination that is visibly increasing due to the aging of the U.S. workforce and organizational downsizing is age discrimination.

The greatest area of EEO concern for HR managers during the last few years has been adapting to, and complying with, the Americans with Disabilities Act (ADA). Following an extensive discussion of the ADA, other bases of discrimination are examined. The chapter then discusses the legal requirements, dictated by the Equal Employment Opportunity Commission and the Office of Contract Compliance Programs, that often require affirmative action programs be established. The nature of affirmative action and EEO record-keeping requirements are addressed as well, and the chapter concludes by outlining the EEO investigative process.

CHAPTER 5

Equal Employment

After you have read this chapter, you should be able to:

1. Define equal employment opportunity (EEO) and discuss the two reasons that it is part of effective management.

2. Explain how to identify when illegal discrimination occurs and define five basic EEO concepts.

3. Discuss the key provisions of the Civil Rights Act of 1964, Title VII, and the Civil Rights Act of 1991.

4. Identify the two primary EEO enforcement agencies.

5. Discuss the two general approaches that can be used to comply with the 1978 Uniform Selection Guidelines.

6. Define validity and reliability, and explain three approaches to validating employment requirements.

HR Today and Tomorrow:
Costs of Discrimination

A number of employers have discovered that engaging in illegal employment discrimination is costly. Whether based on age, sex, race, disability, or other factors, both large and small employers have paid for their illegal discriminatory actions. OFCCP, a federal compliance agency that enforces equal employment regulations, collected about $105 million over a two-year period from various firms that were found to have discriminated against various protected-class individuals. A Philadelphia bank paid $175,000 in back pay for race discrimination in hiring tellers. A computer company in Fremont, California, paid $436,687 to African Americans denied employment. Additional examples follow:

▲ *Shoney's, Inc.,* based in Nashville, Tennessee, paid legal fees, court costs, and expenses totaling $132.5 million to settle racial discrimination cases brought by African Americans. About 30,000 employees, former employees, and applicants received payments from the settlement fund. (See case at end of chapter.)

▲ *AT&T* agreed to a $66 million settlement for 13,000 women who experienced pregnancy discrimination. The settlement covered women who worked for the Western Electric portions of AT&T (prior to the breakup of AT&T into separate companies) between 1965 and 1977. The firm had forced women to take unpaid maternity leaves, had discounted seniority for those on maternity leaves, and had not allowed those returning from maternity leaves to resume their jobs.

▲ *State Farm Insurance* agreed to settle 814 sex discrimination suits by paying $157 million. For the period 1974 to 1987, the company was found to have discouraged about 85,000 women from applying for insurance sales jobs in California. Similar suits were settled in Texas for $14 million.

▲ *Stites Concrete, Inc.* in Florida was found to have discriminated against a 75-year-old man who injured himself while working on a company truck. The man was not allowed to return to work following surgery and claimed age discrimination. As a result of the company being found guilty, the man was awarded $38,500 in damages and $28,089 in attorney's fees.

▲ *Tempel Steel Co.,* based in Niles, Illinois, settled a race bias case on behalf of African Americans who had applied for or who could show that they would have applied for jobs at the firm. Only 70 of the firm's 1,000 workers were African Americans. The case involved Tempel's recruiting practices, in which job advertisements were placed in Polish- and German-language newspapers where few African Americans would see them. Therefore, the recruiting continued a past pattern of discrimination. In addition to paying $4 million total to the victims of past discrimination, the firm was required to file reports on its hiring practices for four years, and pay $500,000 to set up a training program to aid African-American employees to qualify for the higher-skilled, higher-paying jobs in the two factories in the Chicago area.

▲ *Interplace,* a Los Angeles employment agency, agreed to pay $1.6 million to over 3,000 people who had applied for jobs between 1987 and 1990. Interplace interviewers used codes on job orders submitted by employers who had indicated that some protected-class individuals would not be acceptable to them. The settlement reinforced the principle that employment agencies cannot discriminate even if employers ask them to do so.[1]

66————————————————

Injustice anywhere is a threat to justice everywhere.

Martin Luther King ——————— *99*

A s the examples in "HR Today and Tomorrow" indicate, the days are past when employers can manage their workforces in any manner they wish. Federal, state, and local laws prohibit unfair discrimination against individuals on a variety of bases.

▲ NATURE OF EQUAL EMPLOYMENT OPPORTUNITY

Equal employment opportunity (EEO) is a broad concept that states that individuals should have equal treatment in all employment-related actions. Individuals who are covered under equal employment laws are protected from illegal discrimination.

EQUAL EMPLOYMENT OPPORTUNITY (EEO)

states that individuals should have equal treatment in all employment-related actions.

EEO as Effective Management

Many employers have discovered that equal employment opportunity (EEO) is good business, resulting in the full use of the talents present in the widely diverse workforce of today. Practicing EEO is important for two reasons. First and most important, effective management of human resources requires understanding that all people have knowledge, skills, and abilities that can be used by organizations today. For instance, the necessary level of manual dexterity or creative reasoning required by a job is not limited to certain race, gender, or age groups. Nor are mathematical aptitudes or computer skills factors that are genetically exclusive to some "classes" and not to others.

EEO is basic to HR management, which focuses on tapping the potential of all individuals in order to achieve organizational goals and objectives. One study found that more EEO charges were brought involving actions by HR managers during recruitment, selection, or disciplinary termination situations.[2] People should be hired, promoted, appraised, compensated, disciplined, and trained based on how well they can or do perform their jobs. That is the primary reason that EEO is important.

Second, even if an employer has no regard for the principles of EEO, it must follow federal, state, and local EEO laws and regulations to avoid costly penalties such as those listed in "HR Today and Tomorrow." Whether violations of such laws occur intentionally, accidently, or through ignorance, many employers have learned the hard way that they may be required to pay back wages, reinstate individuals to their jobs, reimburse attorneys' fees, and possibly pay punitive damages. Even if not guilty, the employer still will have considerable costs in HR staff and managerial time involved and legal fees. Therefore it is financially prudent to establish a management culture in which it is expected that compliance with EEO laws and regulations will occur.

Laws establishing the legal basis for equal employment opportunity generally have been written in a broad manner. Consequently, only through application to specific organizational situations can one see how the laws affect employers. The broad nature of the laws has led enforcement agencies to develop guidelines and to enforce the acts as they deem appropriate. However, agency rulings and the language of those rulings have caused confusing and differing interpretations by employers. Interpretation of the ambiguous provisions in the laws also changes as the membership of the agencies change.

The court system is left to resolve the disputes and issue interpretations of the laws. The courts, especially the lower courts, have issued conflicting rulings and interpretations. The ultimate interpretation often has rested on decisions by the U.S. Supreme Court, although Supreme Court rulings, too, have been interpreted differently. Thus, equal employment opportunity is an evolving concept that often appears confusing because of conflicting decisions and rulings by courts and agencies.

When Does Illegal Discrimination Occur?

The term *discrimination* simply means the ability to recognize differences among items or people. Thus, discrimination involves choosing among alternatives. For example, employers must discriminate (choose) among applicants for a job on the basis of job requirements and each candidate's qualifications. However, discrimination can become illegal in employment-related situations in which either: (1) two different standards are used to judge different individuals, or (2) the same standard is used but it is not related to the jobs of individuals.

When deciding if and when illegal discrimination has occurred, courts and regulatory agencies have had to consider the following issues:

▲ Protected-Class Membership
▲ Employer Intentions
▲ Disparate Treatment
▲ Disparate Impact
▲ Business Necessity and Job-Relatedness
▲ Bona Fide Occupational Qualifications
▲ Burden of Proof
▲ Retaliation

Protected Class   Illegal discrimination occurs when individuals all having a common characteristic are discriminated against based on that characteristic. Therefore, various laws have been passed to protect individuals who share certain characteristics such as race, age, or gender. Those having the designated characteristics are referred to as a protected class or "members of a protected group." A **protected class** is composed of individuals who fall within a group identified for protection under equal employment laws and regulations. Many of the protected classes historically have been subjected to illegal discrimination. The following protected classes have been identified by various federal laws:

▲ *Race, ethnic origin, color* (African Americans, Hispanics, Native Americans, Asian Americans)
▲ *Gender* (women, including those who are pregnant)
▲ *Age* (individuals over 40)
▲ *Individuals with disabilities* (physical or mental)
▲ *Military experience* (Vietnam-era veterans)
▲ *Religion* (special beliefs and practices)

▼ **A PROTECTED CLASS**

is composed of individuals who fall within a group identified for protection under equal employment laws and regulations.

Disparate Treatment and Disparate Impact   It would seem that when considering whether discrimination has occurred, the motives or intentions of employers might enter into the determination—but they do not. It is the outcome of the employer's actions, not the intent, that will be considered by the regulatory agencies or courts when deciding if illegal discrimination occurred. The outcome of **disparate treatment** means that protected-class members are treated differently from others. For example, if female applicants must take a special skills test not given to male applicants, then disparate treatment may be occurring. If disparate treatment has occurred, the courts generally have said that intentional discrimination exists.

Disparate impact occurs when there is a substantial underrepresentation of protected-class members as a result of employment decisions that work to their disadvantages. The landmark case that established the importance of disparate impact as a legal foundation of EEO law is *Griggs v. Duke Power* (1971). The decision of the U.S. Supreme Court established two major points:

1. It is not enough to show a lack of discriminatory intent if the employment tool results in a disparate impact that discriminates against one group more than another or continues a past pattern of discrimination.
2. The employer has the burden of proving that an employment requirement is directly job related as a "business necessity." Consequently, the intelligence test and high school diploma requirements were ruled to be not related to the job.

Business Necessity and Job-Relatedness   A **business necessity** is a practice necessary for safe and efficient organizational operations and has been the subject of numerous court decisions. Educational requirements often are based on business necessity. However, an employer who requires a minimum level of education, such as a high school diploma, must be able to defend the requirement as essential to the performance of each job. For instance, equating a degree or diploma with the possession of math or reading abilities is considered questionable. Having the general requirement of a degree cannot always be justified on the basis of the need for a certain level of ability. All requirements must be *job related,* or proven necessary for job performance. Determining and defending the job-relatedness of employment requirements through validation procedures is discussed later in this chapter.

Bona Fide Occupational Qualification (BFOQ)   Title VII of the 1964 Civil Rights Act specifically states that employers may discriminate on the basis of sex, religion, or national origin if the characteristic can be justified as a "bona fide occupational qualification reasonably necessary to the normal operation of the particular business or enterprise."[3] Thus, a **bona fide occupational qualification (BFOQ)** is a legitimate reason why an employer can exclude persons on otherwise illegal bases of consideration. What constitutes a BFOQ has been subject to different interpretations in various courts across the country. Some examples include:

▲ Women can be excluded from jobs as prison guards in an all-male, maximum-security prison because of the assault possibilities and the security risks posed for other guards and inmates.[4]
▲ Loyola University of Chicago can use a Jesuit-only policy for selecting individuals for certain teaching positions in the philosophy department.[5]

▼ **DISPARATE TREATMENT**

occurs when protected-class members are treated differently from others.

▼ **DISPARATE IMPACT**

occurs when there is a substantial underrepresentation of protected-class members as a result of employment decisions that work to their disadvantages.

▼ **A BUSINESS NECESSITY**

is a practice necessary for safe and efficient organizational operations.

▼ **BONA FIDE OCCUPATIONAL QUALIFICATION (BFOQ)**

is a legitimate reason why an employer can exclude persons on otherwise illegal bases of consideration.

▲ Age is not a legal BFOQ in the case of construction workers, because individuals above an age limit vary in their physical capabilities.[6]

Burden of Proof   Another legal issue when discrimination is alleged is the determination of which party has the *burden of proof.* At issue is what the individuals who are filing suit against employers must prove in order to establish that illegal discrimination has occurred.

Based on the evolution of court decisions, current laws and regulations state that the plaintiff charging discrimination first must be a protected-class member and, second, must prove that disparate impact or disparate treatment existed. For instance, in *McDonnell Douglas v. Green* (1973), the U.S. Supreme Court ruled that a preliminary *(prima facie)* case of discrimination existed by showing that: (1) the person (Green) was a member of a protected class, (2) the person applied for and was qualified for a job but was rejected, and (3) the employer (McDonnell Douglas) continued to seek other applicants after the rejection occurred.[7]

This case indicates that once a court rules that a *prima facie* case has been made, the burden of proof shifts to the employer. The employer then must show that the bases for making employment-related decisions were specifically job related for the position and consistent with "business-necessity" considerations.

In *Texas Department of Community Affairs v. Burdine* in 1981, the Supreme Court, in ruling against Burdine, decided that the employer needs only to establish a business-related nondiscriminatory reason for not hiring or promoting a member of a protected group. The employer does not have to prove that the hired individual was more qualified than the protected-class person. Thus, the individual charging illegal discrimination has the burden of establishing that illegal discrimination occurred.[8]

▼ **RETALIATION**

occurs when an employer takes punitive actions against individuals who exercise their legal rights.

Retaliation   Employers are prohibited by EEO laws from retaliating against individuals who file discrimination charges with government agencies. **Retaliation** occurs when an employer takes punitive actions against individuals who exercise their legal rights. For example, an employer was ruled to have engaged in retaliation when an employee who filed a discrimination charge was assigned undesirable hours and his work schedule was changed frequently.[9] Various laws, including Title VII of the Civil Rights Act of 1964, protect individuals who have: (1) "made a charge, testified, assisted, or participated in any investigation, proceeding, or hearing"; or (2) "opposed any practice made unlawful."[10]

▲ CIVIL RIGHTS ACTS OF 1964 AND 1991

Numerous federal, state, and local laws address equal employment opportunity concerns. As the chart in Figure 5–1 indicates, some laws have a general civil rights emphasis, while others address specific EEO issues and concerns. At this point, it is important to discuss the two major broad-based civil rights acts that encompass many areas. In the next chapter specific acts and priorities will be discussed.

Civil Rights Act of 1964, Title VII

Although the first Civil Rights Act was passed in 1866, it was not until the passage of the Civil Rights Act of 1964 that the keystone of antidiscrimination legislation was put into place. Title VII, Section 703(a) of the act states:

It shall be unlawful employment practice for an employer: (1) to fail or refuse to hire or to discharge any individual, or otherwise to discriminate against any individual with respect to his compensation, terms, conditions, or privileges of employment, because of such individual's race, color, religion, sex, or national origin; or (2) to limit, segregate, or classify his employees in any way which would deprive or tend to deprive any individual of employment opportunities or otherwise adversely affect his status as an employee because of such individual's race, color, religion, sex, or national origin.[11]

The Civil Rights Act was passed by Congress to bring about equality in all employment-related decisions. As is often the case, the law contains ambiguous provisions giving considerable leeway to agencies that enforce the law. The

Figure 5–1   Major Federal Equal Employment Opportunity Laws

ACT	YEAR	PROVISIONS
Equal Pay Act	1963	Requires equal pay for men and women performing substantially the same work
Title VII, Civil Rights Act	1964	Prohibits discrimination in employment on basis of race, religion, color, sex, or national origin
Executive Orders 11246 and 11375	1965 1967	Requires federal contractors and subcontractors to elimi nate employment discrimination and prior discrimination through affirmative action
Age Discrimination in Employment Act (as amended in 1978 and 1986)	1967	Prohibits discrimination against persons over age 40 and restricts mandatory retirement requirements, except where age is a bona fide occupational qualification
Executive Order 11478	1969	Prohibits discrimination in the U.S. Postal Service and in the various government agencies on the basis of race, color, religion, sex, national origin, handicap, or age
Vocational Rehabilitation Act, Rehabilitation Act of 1974	1973 1974	Prohibits employers with federal contracts over $2,500 from discriminating against handicapped individuals
Vietnam-Era Veterans Readjustment Act	1974	Prohibits discrimination against Vietnam-era veterans by federal contractors and the U.S. government and requires affirmative action
Pregnancy Discrimination Act	1978	Prohibits discrimination against women affected by pregnancy, childbirth, or related medical conditions; requires that they be treated as all other employees for employment-related purposes, including benefits
Immigration Reform & Control Act	1986 1990	Establishes penalties for employers who knowingly hire illegal aliens; prohibits employment discrimination on the basis of national origin or citizenship
Americans with Disabilities Act	1990	Requires employer accommodation of disabled individuals
Older Workers Benefit Protection Act of 1990	1990	Prohibits age-based discrimination in early retirement and other benefits plans
Civil Rights Act of 1991	1991	Overturned several past Supreme Court decisions and changed damage claims provisions

Equal Employment Opportunity Commission (EEOC) was established to enforce the provisions of Title VII.

Who Is Covered?   Title VII, as amended by the Equal Employment Opportunity Act of 1972, covers most employers in the United States. Any organization meeting one of the criteria listed below is subject to rules and regulations that specific government agencies set up to administer the act:

- ▲ All private employers of 15 or more persons who are employed 20 or more weeks per year
- ▲ All educational institutions, public and private
- ▲ State and local governments
- ▲ Public and private employment agencies
- ▲ Labor unions with 15 or more members
- ▲ Joint (labor/management) committees for apprenticeships and training[12]

Civil Rights Act of 1991

The major purpose for the passage of the Civil Rights Act of 1991 was to overturn or modify seven U.S. Supreme Court decisions handed down during the 1988–1990 period. Those decisions made it more difficult for individuals filing discrimination charges to win their cases. Also, the 1991 act amended other federal laws, including Title VII of the 1964 Civil Rights Act, Section 1981 of the Civil Rights Act of 1866, and others. The major effects of the 1991 Act are discussed below.

Disparate Impact   The major decision that was overturned had been issued in the *Ward's Cove Packing v. Atonio* (1989) case.[13] In that case the Supreme Court, by a five-to-four vote, ruled that the statistical imbalance between job groups was not a sufficient basis for establishing a *prima facie* case of illegal discrimination. Instead, the appropriate statistical comparisons should be made between the racial percentage of jobs in question and the racial composition of the local labor market. The end result of that decision was that the ruling made it more difficult for protected-class individuals to use statistics to show that illegal discrimination occurred. The 1991 act reversed that ruling, relying on earlier reasoning in the *Griggs v. Duke Power* decision.

The Civil Rights Act of 1991 requires that employers show that an employment practice is *job related for the position* and is consistent with *business necessity* if *disparate impact* occurs. The act did clarify that the plaintiffs bringing the discrimination charges had to identify the particular employer practice being challenged as causing disparate impact. However, according to one study, disparate-impact cases were less than 2% of all discrimination suits filed in a two-year period. Most were filed on the basis of *discriminatory intent*.[14]

Discriminatory Intent   The Civil Rights Act of 1991 overturned several court decisions that had made it more difficult for plaintiffs to bring suits based on intentional discrimination. In one of those cases, *Price Waterhouse v. Hopkins* (1989),[15] the U.S. Supreme Court ordered a lower court to rehear Ann Hopkins's charges that the large accounting firm for which she worked had been guilty of sex discrimination. Hopkins charged that she was denied a partnership at Price Waterhouse because of "sexual stereotyping" in which she was viewed as being too macho and aggressive. The Supreme Court ruled that when an employment decision is based on both legitimate and impermissible factors, the employer can avoid liability if the same decision would have been reached without the "impermissible factor" (in this case, gender) being considered.

The 1991 act says that an employer is liable if the protected-class status of an individual was a *motivating factor* that caused discriminatory action to occur. The act does not define clearly what a motivating factor is, though. Therefore, a plaintiff charging intentional discrimination must show only that protected-class status played *some* factor. For employers, it means that "an individual's race, color, religion, sex, or national origin *must play no factor* in the challenged employment practice."[16] However, the act limits the damages given to complainants if the employer can demonstrate that the same decision would have been made without the impermissible consideration.

Compensatory and Punitive Damages and Jury Trials   The 1991 act allows victims of discrimination on the bases of sex, religion, and disabilities to receive both compensatory and punitive damages in the cases of intentional discrimination. Under the 1991 act, compensatory damages do not include back pay and interest on it, front pay, or other damages authorized by Title VII of the 1964 Civil Rights Act. Such damages typically include payments for emotional pain and suffering, loss of enjoyment of life, mental anguish, or inconvenience.[17] However, limits were set on the amount of compensatory and punitive damages, beginning with a cap of $50,000 on employers with 100 or fewer employees, to a cap of $300,000 for those with over 500 employees.

Additionally, the 1991 act allows jury trials to determine the liability for and the amount of compensatory and punitive damages, subject to the caps just mentioned. Prior to this act, decisions in these cases were made by judges. Generally, this provision is viewed as a victory for those who bring discrimination suits against employers, because juries tend to be more sympathetic to individuals than to employers.

Other Provisions of 1991 Act   The Civil Rights Act of 1991 contained a number of sections that addressed a variety of other issues. A more detailed discussion on most issues is contained later in this or the next chapter. But, briefly, some of the issues and the provisions of the act are as follows:[18]

▲ *Race Norming.* The 1991 act prohibited the adjusting of employment test scores or using alternative scoring mechanisms on the basis of race or gender of test-takers. The concern addressed by this provision is using different passing or cut-off scores for protected-class members than for nonprotected-class individuals.

▲ *International Employees.* The act extended coverage of U.S. EEO laws to U.S. citizens working internationally, except where local laws conflict (see the "HR Perspective").

▲ *Employment Contracts.* The act overturned a Supreme Court decision so that EEO laws will apply to employment contracts.[19]

▲ *"Right to Sue" Notification.* The act amends other acts dealing with age discrimination to require the EEOC to notify age discrimination complainants when the agency is terminating action of their cases. The individuals then can file civil suits if they wish.

▲ *Seniority Systems.* The act overturned a Supreme Court decision and allows for protected-class members to challenge the discriminatory operation of seniority systems.[20]

HR Perspectives:

Global Employees and EEO

Many U.S. firms operating internationally have had to adapt their employment practices to reflect the culture and customs of the the countries in which they operate. Specifically, assignments of women and protected-class race/ethnic individuals were limited in deference to cultural concerns. In a case brought by a Lebanese American working in Saudi Arabia who was fired by Aramco Oil Company,[21] the U.S. Supreme Court ruled that the EEO regulations of Title VII did not cover U.S. employees working for U.S. firms internationally.

The Civil Rights Act of 1991 overturned this decision and extended coverage of EEO laws and regulations to U.S. citizens working internationally for U.S.–controlled companies. However, the act states that if laws in a foreign country require actions in conflict with U.S. EEO laws, the foreign laws will apply. If no laws exist, only customs or cultural considerations, then the U.S. EEO laws will apply.[22]

In a related area, some foreign firms, particularly Japanese-owned ones, have "reserved" top-level positions for those from the home country. Consequently, EEO charges have been brought against these firms. A circuit court decision ruled that because of a treaty between Japan and the United States, Japanese subsidiaries can give preference to Japanese over U.S. citizens.[23] However, it should be noted that most of the other EEO regulations and laws apply to foreign-owned firms.

Women have brought sexual harassment charges against foreign managers, and other protected-class individuals have brought EEO charges for refusal to hire or promote them. In those cases, courts have treated the foreign-owned firms just as they would U.S.–owned employers. Interestingly, a survey of Japanese firms found that training on U.S. EEO laws was one of the most important topics for Japanese nationals being assigned to the United States.

▲ *Consent Decrees.* The act modified a Supreme Court decision and limited challenges to court-ordered consent decrees designed to remedy past discriminatory actions. The effect is to restrict nonprotected-class members from challenging the consent decrees.

▲ *Glass Ceiling Initiative.* Associated with the 1991 act, the Glass Ceiling Act of 1991 established a commission to study and make recommendations on how to eliminate the barriers to the advancement of women and other protected-class members to management and executive positions.

▲ *Government Employee Rights.* Responding to criticism that some government employees were being excluded from EEO law coverage, Congress extended such coverage to employees of the Senate, presidential appointments, and previously excluded state government employees.

Effects of the Civil Rights Act of 1991   By overturning certain Supreme Court decisions, the 1991 act negated many of the more "employer friendly" decisions made by the Supreme Court from 1988 to 1990. Allowing jury trials and compensatory and punitive damages when intentional discrimination is alleged means that the costs of being found guilty of illegal discrimination increased significantly. It is projected that the number of EEO complaints filed will increase because of some of the provisions of the 1991 act. Consequently, more than ever before, employers must make sure their actions are job related, based upon business necessity.

▲ ENFORCEMENT AGENCIES

Government agencies at several levels have powers to investigate illegal discriminatory practices. At the state and local levels, various commissions have enforcement authority. At the federal level, the two most prominent agencies are the Equal Employment Opportunity Commission (EEOC) and the Office of Federal Contract Compliance Programs (OFCCP).

Equal Employment Opportunity Commission (EEOC)

The EEOC, created by the Civil Rights Act of 1964, is responsible for enforcing the employment-related provisions of the act. The agency initiates investigations, responds to complaints, and develops guidelines to enforce various laws. The EEOC has enforcement authority for charges brought under the following federal laws:

▲ Civil Rights Act of 1964, Title VII
▲ Civil Rights Act of 1991
▲ Equal Pay Act of 1963
▲ Pregnancy Discrimination Act
▲ Age Discrimination in Employment Act
▲ Americans with Disabilities Act
▲ Vocational Rehabilitation Act

The EEOC has been given expanded powers several times since 1964 and is the major agency involved with employment discrimination. Over the years, the EEOC has been given the responsibility to investigate equal pay violations, age discrimination, and handicapped discrimination, in addition to areas identified by Title VII of the Civil Rights Act.

As an independent regulatory agency, the EEOC is composed of five members appointed by the President and confirmed by the Senate. No more than three members of the commission can be from the same political party. Members serve for seven years. In addition, the EEOC has a staff of lawyers and investigators who do investigative and follow-up work for the commission.

Office of Federal Contract Compliance Programs (OFCCP)

Whereas the EEOC is an independent agency, the OFCCP is part of the Department of Labor, established by executive order to ensure that federal contractors and subcontractors have nondiscriminatory practices. A major thrust of OFCCP efforts is to require that federal contractors and subcontractors take affirmative action to overcome the effects of prior discriminatory practices. Affirmative action plans are discussed in detail in the next chapter.

Enforcement Philosophies and Efforts

Since 1964 the various U.S. presidential administrations have viewed EEO and affirmative action enforcement efforts from different philosophical perspectives. Often, the thrust and aggressiveness of enforcement efforts vary depending on whether a Republican or Democratic President and Congress are in office. For example, under the Carter administration (1977–1980) the appointees to the EEOC tended to be activists who believed strongly that protected-class members should be given opportunities to move ahead through affirmative action programs. Enforcement efforts from both the EEOC and the OFCCP were wide and varied. However, under the Reagan/Bush administrations (1980–1992), philosophical disagreements with affirmative action efforts led to appointees who had differing views from those appointed by Carter.

The purpose of this discussion is not to suggest who is right or wrong, but rather to emphasize that laws are enforced by agencies staffed by presidential appointees. Differing degrees of activism and emphasis result, depending on the philosophical beliefs and priorities held by a particular administration.

State and Local Enforcement Agencies

In addition to federal laws and orders, many states and municipalities have passed their own laws prohibiting discrimination on a variety of bases. Often these laws are modeled after federal laws; however, the state and local laws sometimes provide greater remedies, require different actions, or prohibit discrimination in areas beyond those addressed by federal law. As a result, state and local enforcement bodies have been established to enforce EEO compliance also. Fortunately, the three levels of agencies generally coordinate their activities to avoid multiple investigations of the same EEO complaints.

To implement the provisions of the Civil Rights Act of 1964 and the interpretations of it based on court decisions, the EEOC and other federal agencies developed their own compliance guidelines and regulations, each having a slightly different set of rules and expectations. Finally, in 1978 the major government agencies involved agreed upon a set of uniform guidelines.

▲ UNIFORM GUIDELINES ON EMPLOYEE-SELECTION PROCEDURES

The Uniform Guidelines for employee-selection procedures apply to the EEOC, the Department of Labor's OFCCP, the Department of Justice, and the Office of Personnel Management. The guidelines provide a framework used to determine if employers are adhering to federal laws on discrimination.

These guidelines affect virtually all phases of HR management because they apply to employment procedures, including but not limited to the following:

- ▲ Hiring (qualifications required, application blanks, interviews, tests)
- ▲ Promotions (qualifications, selection process)
- ▲ Recruiting (advertising, availability of announcements)
- ▲ Demotion (why made, punishments given)
- ▲ Performance appraisals (methods used, how used for promotions and pay increases)
- ▲ Training (access to training programs, development efforts)
- ▲ Labor union membership requirements (apprenticeship programs, work assignments)
- ▲ Licensing and certification requirements (job requirements tied to job qualifications)

The guidelines apply to most employment-related decisions, not just to the initial hiring process. There are two major means of compliance identified by the guidelines: (1) no disparate impact; or (2) job-related validation.

No Disparate Impact Approach

Generally, when courts have found discrimination within organizations, the most important issue concerns the *effect* of employment policies and procedures, regardless of the *intent*. Remember, *disparate impact* occurs when there is a substantial underrepresentation of protected-class members in employment decisions. The Uniform Guidelines identify this strategy in the following statement: "These guidelines do not require a user to conduct validity studies of selection procedures where no adverse impact results.[24]

Under the guidelines, disparate impact is determined with the **4/5ths rule.** If the selection rate for any protected group is less than 80% (4/5ths of the selection rate of the majority groups) or if there is proportional underrepresentation in relation to the relevant labor market, discrimination exists. Thus the guidelines have attempted to define discrimination in statistical terms. Disparate impact can be checked both internally and externally.

Internal   Checking for disparate impact internally requires that employers compare the treatment received by protected-class members to that received by nonprotected-group members. Assume, for example, that Standard Company interviewed both men and women for manufacturing assembly jobs. Of the men who applied, 40% were hired; of the women who applied, 25% were hired. As shown in Figure 5–2, the selection rate for women is less than 80% (4/5ths) of the selection rate for men (40% × 4/5 = 32%). Consequently, Standard Company does have "disparate impact" in its employment process. HR activities for which internal disparate impact can be checked by comparing the treatment and results of protected and nonprotected-class members include:

▲ Candidates selected for interviews of those recruited
▲ Performance-appraisal ratings as they affect pay increases

▼ **THE 4/5THS RULE**

states that discrimination generally occurs if the selection rate for a protected group is less than 80% of their representation in the relevant labor market or 80% less than the majority group.

▲ **Figure 5–2**   Internal Disparate Impact at Standard Company

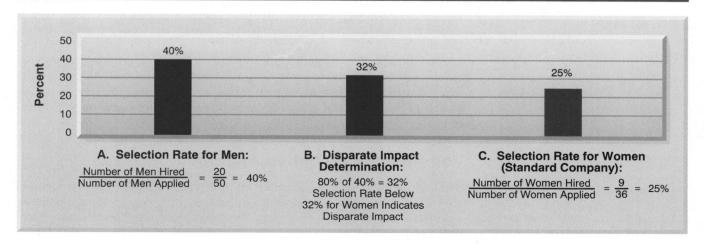

A. Selection Rate for Men:

$$\frac{\text{Number of Men Hired}}{\text{Number of Men Applied}} = \frac{20}{50} = 40\%$$

B. Disparate Impact Determination:

80% of 40% = 32%
Selection Rate Below
32% for Women Indicates
Disparate Impact

C. Selection Rate for Women (Standard Company):

$$\frac{\text{Number of Women Hired}}{\text{Number of Women Applied}} = \frac{9}{36} = 25\%$$

▲ Promotions, demotions, or terminations
▲ Pass rates for various selection tests.

External   Disparate impact is checked externally by comparing the percentage of employed workers in a protected class in the organization to the percentage of protected-class members in the relevant labor market. External comparisons also are made on the percentage of protected-class members who are recruited and who apply for jobs to ensure that the employer has drawn a "representative sample" from the relevant labor market. Although employers do not have to have exact proportionate equality, they must be "close." Courts have applied statistical analyses to determine if any disparities that exist are too much.

To illustrate, assume the following situation. In the Valleyville area, Hispanics are 15% of those in the job market. RJ Company is a firm with 500 employees, 50 of whom are Hispanic. Determining disparate impact is done as follows if the 4/5ths rule is applied:

Percent of Hispanics in the labor market   15%
× 4/5ths rule   ×.8
Disparate-impact level   12%

Comparison:
RJ Co. has 50/500 = 10% Hispanics.
Disparate-impact level = 12% Hispanics.
Therefore, disparate impact exists because the firm has fewer than 12% Hispanics.

In reality, statistical comparisons for disparate-impact determination may use more complex statistical methods. The preceding example illustrates one way external disparate impact can be determined. However, external disparate-impact charges make up a very small number of EEOC cases. Instead most cases deal with the disparate impact of internal employment practices.

Effect of the No Disparate Impact Strategy   The 4/5ths rule is a yardstick that employers can use to determine if there is disparate impact on protected-class members. However, to meet the 4/5ths compliance requirement, employers must have no disparate impact at all levels and in all jobs for each protected class.

Some skeptics have suggested that this approach comes down to "getting your numbers in line." Consequently, using this strategy is not really as easy or risk free as it may appear. Instead, employers may want to turn to the compliance approach of validating that their employment decisions are based on job-related factors.

Job-Related Validation Approach

The idea that employment practices must be valid includes such practices and tests as job descriptions, educational requirements, experience requirements, work skills, application forms, interviews, paper-and-pencil tests, and performance appraisals. Virtually every factor used to make employment-related decisions—recruiting, selection, promotion, termination, discipline, and performance appraisal—must be shown to be specifically job related. Hence, the concept of validity affects many of the common tools used to make HR decisions.

Validity simply means that a "test" actually measures what it says it measures and refers to inferences about tests. It may be valid to infer that college admission test scores predict college academic performance. However, it is probably invalid to infer that those same test scores predict athletic performance. As applied to employment settings, a test is any employment procedure used as the basis for making an employment-related decision. For a general intelligence test to be valid, it must actually measure intelligence, not just a person's vocabulary. An employment test that is valid must measure the person's ability to perform the job for which he or she is being hired. Validity will be discussed in detail later in this chapter.

The ideal condition for employment-related tests is to be both valid and reliable. **Reliability** refers to the consistency with which a test measures an item. For a test to be reliable, an individual's score should be about the same every time the individual takes it (allowing for the effects of practice). Unless a test measures a trait consistently (or reliably), it is of little value in predicting job performance.

Reliability can be measured by several different statistical methodologies. The most frequent ones are test-retest, alternate forms, and internal-consistency estimates. A more detailed methodological discussion is beyond the scope of this text; those interested can consult appropriate statistical references.[25]

▼ **VALIDITY**

means that a "test" actually measures what it says it measures.

▼ **RELIABILITY**

refers to the consistency with which a test measures an item.

▲ VALIDITY AND EQUAL EMPLOYMENT

If a charge of discrimination is brought against an employer on the basis of disparate impact, the employer must be able to demonstrate that its employment procedures are valid. That is, they relate to the job and the requirements of the job. Key to establishing job-relatedness is to conduct a *job analysis* to identify the *knowledge, skills, abilities* (KSAs), and other characteristics needed in order to perform a job satisfactorily. A detailed examination of the job provides the foundation for linking the KSAs to job requirements and job performance. Chapter 7 discusses job analysis in more detail. Both the Civil Rights Act of 1964, as interpreted by the *Griggs v. Duke Power* decision, and the Civil Rights Act of 1991 emphasize the importance of job-relatedness in establishing validity.

The legislation and court decisions mentioned in this chapter are forcing employers to make changes that probably should have been made earlier. Using an invalid instrument to select, place, or promote an employee has never been a good management practice, regardless of its legality. Management also should be concerned with using valid instruments from the standpoint of operational efficiency. Invalid tests may result in screening out individuals who might have been satisfactory performers and hiring less satisfactory workers instead.

Many organizations are increasing the use of instruments that have been demonstrated to be valid. In one sense, the current requirements have done management a favor because they force employers to do what they should have been doing previously—using job-related employment procedures.

The 1978 uniform selection guidelines recognize the three validation strategies discussed next.

▲ **Content validity**
▲ **Criterion-related (concurrent and predictive) validity**
▲ **Construct validity**

Content Validity

▼ **CONTENT VALIDITY**

is a logical, nonstatistical method used to identify the KSAs and other characteristics necessary to perform a job.

Content validity is a logical, nonstatistical method used to identify the KSAs and other characteristics necessary to perform a job. Thus the test is content valid if it reflects an actual sample of the work done on the job in question. For example, an arithmetic test for a retail cashier should contain problems that typically would be faced by cashiers on the job. Content validity is especially useful if the workforce is not large enough to allow the other, more statistical approaches.

A content-validity study begins with a comprehensive job analysis to identify what is done on a job and what KSAs are used. Then managers, supervisors, and HR specialists must use their judgments to identify the most important KSAs needed for the job. Finally, a "test" is devised to determine if individuals have the necessary KSAs. The test may be an interview question about previous supervisory experience, or an ability test in which someone types a letter using a word-processing software program, or a knowledge test about consumer credit regulations.

Many practitioners and specialists see content validity as a commonsense way to validate staffing requirements that is more realistic than statistically oriented methods. In the *Washington v. Davis* case, the Supreme Court also appeared to support the content-validity approach in that its decision implied approval of a reading comprehension test given to potential police officers that represented actual materials used by police officers in the training academy and on the job.[26] Content-validity approaches are growing in use.

Criterion-Related Validity

▼ **CRITERION-RELATED VALIDITY**

assumes that a test is the predictor of how well an individual will perform on the job.

Employment tests of any kind attempt to predict how well an individual will perform on the job. In **criterion–related validity** a test is the *predictor* and the desired job knowledge, skills, abilities (KSAs), and measures of job performance the *criterion variables.* Job analysis determines as exactly as possible what KSAs and behaviors are needed for each task in the job. Tests (predictors) are then devised and used to measure different dimensions of the criterion-related variables. Examples of "tests" are: (1) requiring a college degree, (2) scoring a required number of words per minute on a typing test, or (3) having five years of banking experience. These predictors are then validated against the criteria used to measure job performance, such as performance appraisals, sales records, or absenteeism rates. Some court cases, such as *Albermarle Paper v. Moody,* have pointed out the difficulty in using subjective performance appraisals by supervisors as the criteria against which the tests are validated. However, if the predictors satisfactorily predict job performance behavior, they are legally acceptable and useful.[27]

A simple analogy is to think of two circles, one labeled the *predictor* and the other the *criterion variable.* The criterion-related approaches to validity attempt to see how well the two circles overlap. The more overlap, the better is the performance of the predictor. The degree of overlap is described by a **correlation coefficient,** which is an index number giving the relationship between a predictor and a criterion variable. These coefficients can range from −1.0 to +1.0. If a correlation coefficient is +.99, it is almost an exact predictor, whereas a +.02 correlation coefficient indicates that the test is a very poor predictor.

▼ **A CORRELATION COEFFICIENT**

is an index number giving the relationship between a predictor and a criterion variable.

▲ **Figure 5–3**   Concurrent Validity

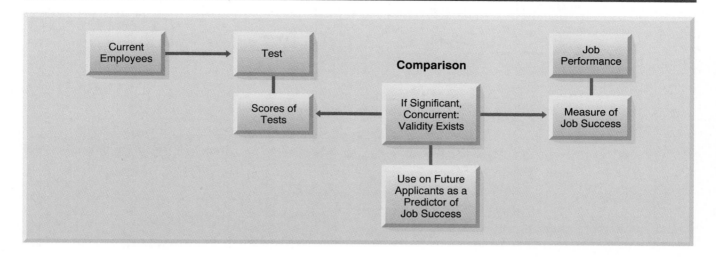

Within criterion-related validity there are two different approaches. *Concurrent validity* represents an "at-the-same-time" approach to validity, while *predictive validity* is a "before-the-fact" approach.

Concurrent Validity   *Concurrent* means "at the same time." As shown in Figure 5–3, when an employer uses **concurrent validity,** a test is given to current employees and the scores are correlated with their performance ratings. The test is given to these employees and the scores are correlated with their performance ratings, determined by such measures as accident rates, absenteeism records, or supervisory performance appraisals. A high correlation suggests that the test is able to differentiate between the better-performing employees and those with poor performance records.

A drawback of concurrent validity is that those employees who did not perform satisfactorily are probably no longer with the firm and therefore cannot be tested, and the extremely good employees may have been promoted or may have left the organization for better jobs. Thus, the firm does not really have a representative range of people to test. Also, the test-takers may not be as motivated to perform well on the test because they already have jobs. Any learning that has taken place on the job may influence the test score, presenting another problem. Therefore, applicants taking the test without the benefit of on-the-job experience might score low on the test, but might be able to learn to do the job well.

As a result of these problems, a researcher might conclude that a test is valid when it is not, or discard a test because the data indicated that it is invalid when, in fact, it was valid. In either case, the organization has lost because of poor research.

Predictive Validity   To measure **predictive validity,** test results of applicants are compared with their subsequent job performance (Figure 5–4). The following example illustrates how a predictive-validity study might be designed. A retail chain, Eastern Discount, wants to establish the predictive validity of requiring one year of cashiering experience, a "test" it plans to use in hiring cashiers. Obviously, the retail outlet wants a test that will do the best job of sepa-

▼ **CONCURRENT VALIDITY**

tests current employees and correlates the scores with their performance ratings.

▼ **PREDICTIVE VALIDITY**

uses test results of applicants to compare subsequent performance.

▲   **Figure 5–4**   Predictive Validity

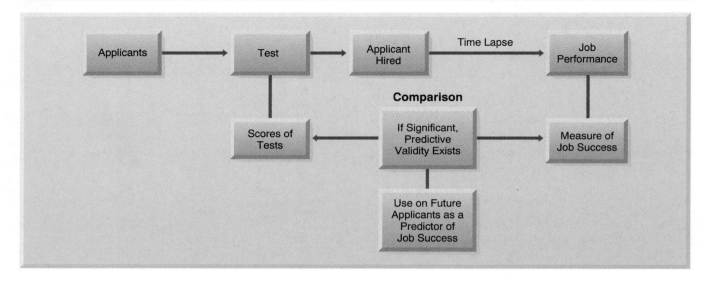

rating those who will do well from those who will not. Eastern Discount first hires 30 people, regardless of their cashiering experience or other criteria that might be directly related to their experience. Sometime later (perhaps one year) the performance of these same employees who joined the company with and without cashiering experience is compared. Success on the job is measured by such yardsticks as absenteeism, accidents, errors, and performance appraisals. If those employees who had one year of experience demonstrate better performance, as statistically compared with those without such experience, then the experience requirement is considered a valid predictor of performance and may be used in hiring future employees.

In the past, predictive validity has been preferred by EEOC because it is presumed to give the strongest tie to job performance. However, predictive validity requires: (1) a fairly large number of people (usually at least 30), and (2) a time gap between the test and the performance (usually one year). As a result, it is not useful in many situations. Because of these and other problems, other types of validity often are used.

Construct Validity

▼ **CONSTRUCT VALIDITY**

involves the relationship between an abstract characteristic and job performance.

Construct validity shows a relationship between an abstract characteristic inferred from research and job performance. Researchers who study behavior have given various personality characteristics names such as introversion, aggression, or dominance. These are called *constructs*. When a test measures an intangible or abstract construct such as intelligence quotient (IQ), it has construct validity. Other common constructs for which tests have been devised are creativity, leadership potential, and interpersonal sensitivity. Because a hypothetical construct is used as a predictor in establishing this type of validity, personality tests and other such constructs are more likely to be questioned for their legality and usefulness than other measures of validity. Consequently, construct validity is used less frequently in employment selection than the other types of validity.

Validity Generalization

Validity generalization means that the validity of a test extends to different groups, similar jobs, and in other organizations. Rather than viewing the validity of a test as being limited to a specific situation and usage, the test may be a valid predictor in other situations. Therefore, if a test is found to be valid, it can be valid across diverse groups and diverse organizational settings. Those advocating validity generalization believe that variances in the validity of a test are attributable to the statistical and research methods used.[28]

The importance of validity generalization is that a separate validation study does not have to be done for every usage of an employment test. Instead, the results can be generalized to other situations.[29] Proponents particularly believe validity generalization exists for general-abilities tests.

Although the approach is controversial, it has been adopted by the U.S. Employment Service, a federal agency, for the General Aptitude Test Battery (GATB). Also, it has been adopted for use throughout the United States in many state and local job service offices. As more and more such job services adopt the approach, more detailed records of results will be available. Anyone interested in learning more about the GATB and validity generalization should contact the job service office in a specific locale to find out how it is used.[30]

▼ **VALIDITY GENERALIZATION**

means that the validity of a test extends to different groups, similar jobs, and in other organizations.

 SUMMARY

▲ Equal Employment Opportunity (EEO) states that individuals shall have equal treatment in all employment-related actions.

▲ EEO is part of effective management for two reasons: a) it focuses on using the talents of all human resources; b) the costs of being found guilty of illegal discrimination can be substantial.

▲ Protected classes are composed of individuals identified for protection under equal employment laws and regulations.

▲ Disparate treatment occurs when protected-class members are treated differently from others, whether or not there is discriminatory intent.

▲ Disparate impact occurs when employment decisions work to the disadvantage of members of protected classes, whether or not there is discriminatory intent.

▲ Employers must be able to defend their management practices based on bona fide occupational qualifications (BFOQ), as a business necessity, and as job related.

▲ Once a *prima facie* case of illegal discrimination is shown, the burden of proof shifts to the employer to demonstrate that the bases for employment-related decisions were job related.

▲ Retaliation occurs when an employer takes punitive actions against individuals who exercise their legal rights, and it is illegal under various laws.

▲ The 1964 Civil Rights Act, Title VII, was the first significant equal employment law, but the Civil Rights Act of 1991 altered or expanded upon the 1964 provisions by overturning several U.S. Supreme Court decisions.

▲ The Civil Rights Act of 1991 addressed a variety of issues such as disparate impact, discriminatory intent, compensatory and punitive damages, jury trials, and EEO rights of international employees.

▲ The Equal Employment Opportunity Commission (EEOC) and the Office of Federal Contract Compliance Programs (OFCCP) are the major federal equal employment enforcement agencies.

▲ The 1978 Uniform Guidelines are used by enforcement agencies to examine recruiting, hiring, promotion, and many other employment practices.

▲ Under the 1978 Guidelines, two alternative compliance approaches are identified: (1) no disparate impact; and (2) job-related validation.

▲ Disparate impact is determined through use of the 4/5ths rule.

▲ Job-related validation requires that tests measure what they are supposed to measure (validity) in a consistent manner (reliability).

▲ There are three types of validity: content, criterion-related, and construct.

▲ The content-validity approach is growing in use because it shows the job-relatedness of a measure, by using a sample of the actual work to be performed.

▲ The two criterion-related strategies are concurrent validity and predictive validity. Whereas predictive validity is a "before-the-fact" measure, concurrent validity compares tests and criteria measures available at the same time.

▲ Construct validity involves the relationship between a measure of an abstract characteristic, such as intelligence, and job performance.

▲ REVIEW AND DISCUSSION QUESTIONS

1. Discuss the following statement: "By not providing equal employment opportunity for all employees, an employer really is not managing effectively."
2. If you were asked by an employer to review an employment decision to determine if discrimination had occurred, what factors would you consider and how would you evaluate them?
3. Why is the Civil Rights Act of 1991 such a significant law?
4. What are the differences in enforcement responsibilities of the EEOC and the OFCCP?
5. Why is validation considered to be a more business-oriented approach than the no-disparate-impact approach in complying with the 1978 Uniform Guidelines on Selection Procedures?
6. Explain what validity is and why the content validity approach is growing in use compared with the criterion-related and construct validity approaches.

RACE DISCRIMINATION AT SHONEY'S

One of the largest class-action suits based on race discrimination involved Shoney's, Inc., headquartered in Nashville, Tennessee. At the time the suit concluded, Shoney's had approximately 30,000 employees and more than 1,800 restaurants in 36 states. As a result of its discriminatory practices over the previous 15 years, the firm agreed to settle the case in 1992 by paying $105 million to employees and job applicants who were discriminated against in employment actions. Also, Shoney's agreed to spend more than $92 million to establish minority-owned franchise restaurants. What led to this settlement illustrates how racist practices encouraged by top management created illegal race discrimination throughout Shoney's.

Raymond Danner bought franchises to some Shoney's Big Boy Restaurants in Tennessee in 1959, and for the next 15 plus years, he and his partner increased the size of the chain by adding restaurants. They sold the Big Boy trademark, using only Shoney's as the name for most of the restaurants. However, throughout the history of the company, there were allegations of race discrimination against Shoney's. Finally in 1989, a class-action suit was brought by nine African-American employees in Pensacola, Florida. During the investigation for that suit, numerous examples of racial bias and discrimination were cited, such as the following:

▲ Until the late 1980s Shoney's headquarters had no African Americans in white-collar jobs such as secretaries or data processors.

▲ Prior to 1987, no African American had been promoted to the division-director level, even though there were 90 of those positions.

▲ Restaurant managers were told to "hide" nonwhite employees when Danner or other executives came to inspect individual restaurants. One manager testified that she hid two African-American waitresses in a restroom when an unexpected visitation occurred.

▲ Some restaurant managers and assistant managers were told to "fill in the letter *o*" in Shoney's on application blanks to indicate that the applicants were African Americans. That way they would not receive calls for follow-up interviews.

▲ Employees referred to the "Danner Way" as meaning that only Shoney's restaurants in predominantly African-American neighborhoods could hire African Americans.

Finally, in 1988 so many complaints were being filed with the EEOC against Shoney's that the firm asked a civil rights group to help develop a plan for improving the opportunities for racial minorities. It recommended that Shoney's spend $30 million to recruit more racial minorities and help African Americans and other minorities acquire Shoney's franchises.

About this same time Shoney's new chairman, Leonard Roberts, who had significant fast-food industry experience, arrived from outside Shoney's. According to others in Shoney's, Roberts was committed fully to improving the equal employment compliance at Shoney's. He hired an African-American woman as a vice-president and named an African-American franchisee to the Shoney's Board of Directors. Also, all middle managers were required to attend diversity training sessions. Finally, Roberts spent time negotiating a settlement without admitting guilt. The following settlements were involved:

▲ Payment of $105 million to up to 10,000 workers and applicants if they could show they were discriminated against in employment or promotions.

▲ A commitment that approximately 20% of Shoney's management positions will be filled by African Americans by 1997 and 3 African Americans will be among the 25 regional directors.

▲ Use of tests to ensure that individuals of different races will be treated equally as applicants.

▲ Veto power for attorneys for the African-American plaintiffs over those named to executive jobs in human resources.

Getting the Board to agree to that settlement required that Roberts ask Danner to pay for some of the costs of the settlement by contributing some of his stock to the company. That action, plus other conflicts with some Board members, led Roberts to resign in late 1992. The new chairman, Taylor Henry, Jr., had been with Shoney's for 18 years, most recently as chief financial officer. He said that Shoney's commitment to diversity would continue in the future.[31]

▲ QUESTIONS

1. Discuss why the absence of equal employment opportunity at Shoney's showed ineffective management of human resources.
2. How likely is it that Shoney's treatment of African Americans would have changed without legal intervention? Support your answer.
3. What are some actions that you would recommend to Shoney's to establish a new culture that practices EEO and values diversity?

▲ NOTES

1. Adapted from *HR News,* March 1992, A11; *Omaha World-Herald,* January 26, 1993, 3; *Human Resource Executive,* June 1992, 14; *Labor & Employment Update,* November 1992, 1; *Omaha World-Herald,* August 20, 1992, 5; *The Wall Street Journal,* March 27, 1992, B2; *The Wall Street Journal,* November 5, 1991, B1; and *USA Today,* October 7, 1992, B1.

2. Ann C. Wendt and William M. Slonaker, "Discrimination Reflects on You," *HR Magazine,* May 1992, 44–47.

3. Civil Rights Act of 1964, Title VII, Sec. 703e.

4. *Dothard v. Rawlinson,* 433 U.S. 321 (1977).

5. *Prime v. Loyola University of Chicago,* 42 FEP Cases I (1986).

6. Michael D. Levin-Epstein, *Primer of Equal Employment,* 4th ed. (Washington, DC: Bureau of National Affairs, 1987), 64–65.

7. *McDonnell Douglas v. Green,* 411 U.S. 972 (1973).

8. *Texas Department of Community Affairs v. Burdine,* 25 FEP Cases 113 (1981).

9. EEOC Decision #72-0455, 4 FEP Cases 306.

10. Mark A. Player, *Federal Law of Employment Discrimination,* (St. Paul, MN: West Publishing Co., 1992), 166–170.

11. Civil Rights Act of 1964, Title VII, Sec. 103a.

12. U.S. Equal Employment Opportunity Commission, *Affirmative Action and Equal Employment* (Washington, DC: U.S. Government Printing Office, 1974), 12–13.

13. *Ward's Cove Packing Co. v. Antonio,* 87-1937 (1989).

14. John J. Donohue III and Peter Siegleman, "The Changing Nature of Employment Discrimination," *Stanford Law Review* 43(1991), 983–998.

15. *Price Waterhouse v. Hopkins,* 87-1167 (1989).

16. Timothy D. Loudon, "The Civil Rights Act of 1991: What Does It Mean and What Is Its Likely Impact?" *Nebraska Law Review* 71 (1992), 304–322.

17. The EEOC enforcement guidelines are identified in Equal Employment Opportunity Commission, "Enforcement Guidance: Compensatory and Punitive Damages Available Under Section 102 of the Civil Rights Act of 1991," *Bureau of National Affairs Daily Labor Reporter,* #131, E-1, July 8, 1992.

18. For a discussion of the legal issues of each of the issues, see Niall A. Paul, "The Civil Rights Act of 1991: What Does It Really Accomplish?" *Employee Relations Law Journal* 17 (1992), 567–591.

19. *Patterson v. McLean Credit Union,* 491 U.S. 164 (1989).

20. *Lorance v. AT&T Technologies, Inc.,* 490 U.S. 900 (1989).

21. *EEOC and Boureslan v. Aramco,* 111 SCt 1227 (1991).

22. Joy Cherian, "Enforcement of American Workers' Rights Abroad," *Labor Law Journal* 43 (1992), 563–566.

23. *Fortino v. Quasar Co.* 950 F. 2d 389 (7th Cir. 1991).

24. "Adoption by Four Agencies of Uniform Guidelines on Employee Selection Procedures (1978)," *Federal Register,* August 15, 1978, Part IV, 38295-38309.

25. For a discussion in the context of employment selection, see Robert D. Gatewood and Hubert S. Feild, *Human Resource Selection,* 2d ed. (Chicago: Dryden Press, 1990), 117–196.

26. *Washington, Mayor of Washington D.C. v. Davis,* 74-1492 (1976).

27. *Albermarle Paper Co. v. Moody,* 74-389 (1975).

28. See *Personnel Psychology* 38 (1985), 697–801, for questions, commentary, and discussion on validity generalization and meta-analysis.

29. F. L. Schmidt, J. E. Hunter, and N. S. Rau, "Validity Generalization and Situational Specificity," *Journal of Applied Psychology* 73 (1988), 665–672.

30. The authors express their appreciation to Professor Carl Thornton, GMI Engineering and Management Institute, for his assistance on this section.

31. Adapted from information in Julia Lawlor, "Shoney's Settles Race-Bias Lawsuit," *USA Today,* November 6, 1992, B2; and Brett Pulley, "Culture of Race Bias at Shoney's Underlies Chairman's Departure," *The Wall Street Journal,* December 21, 1992, A1, 4.

CHAPTER 6

IMPLEMENTING EQUAL EMPLOYMENT

After you have read this chapter, you should be able to:

1. Discuss the two types of sexual harassment and employer responses to complaints.

2. Give examples of three sex-based discrimination issues besides sexual harassment.

3. Identify two age discrimination issues.

4. Discuss the major requirements of the Americans with Disabilities Act.

5. Describe two other bases of EEO discrimination in addition to those listed above.

6. Define affirmative action and what is contained in an affirmative action plan (AAP).

7. Identify typical equal employment opportunity (EEO) record-keeping requirements and those records used in the EEO investigative process.

HR Today and Tomorrow:
Men and Women at Work: Sexual Harassment and Workplace Relationships?

Even prior to the 1990s, sexual harassment in the workplace had been a major issue addressed by equal employment regulations and court decisions. But in the fall of 1991, the problem of sexual harassment exploded on the nation's conscience during the Senate confirmation hearings for Judge Clarence Thomas's appointment to the U.S. Supreme Court. Allegations of sexual harassment by Thomas were made by a former associate of his, Anita Hill, a law professor at the University of Oklahoma. Ultimately, Thomas was confirmed to be a U.S. Supreme Court Justice. But even after the hearings, debate by politicians, media reporters, and citizens on which one should have been believed continued.

One effect of the Thomas confirmation hearings was to heighten awareness of sexual harassment throughout U.S. workplaces. Nationally, over 7,400 sexual harassment complaints were filed in the first nine months following the Thomas-Hill hearings, compared with only 6,100 for the previous year.

Sexual harassment returned to national attention with the "Tailhook" scandal. During a convention of U.S. Navy aviators in Las Vegas, female naval officers were subjected to lewd remarks, fondling, being physically undressed, and other sexually inappropriate actions. Ultimately, some of the offenders were discharged from the services or disciplined, and the military services instituted mandatory training and improved policies on sexual harassment.

Apparently, the two situations receiving national exposure are representative of a widespread problem. In a survey of U.S. government workers, 42% of the women employees reported that they had been sexually harassed within the previous two years. The most frequent complaints involved included:

- ▲ Sexual teasing or telling of sexually explicit jokes.
- ▲ Sexually suggestive looks or gestures.
- ▲ Repeated requests for dates or meetings outside work.
- ▲ Actual touching, fondling, or pinching.
- ▲ Physical cornering, "trapping," or leaning over a worker.

To counter sexual harassment in the federal government, the Office of Personnel Management developed a training course for managers and supervisors. But because attendance at courses was not mandatory, relatively few managers have participated.

In the private sector, a survey of 495 companies found that 40% had provided training about sexual harassment. Some organizations have been more aggressive. Chase Manhattan Bank has a two-hour sexual harassment awareness program for all managers. Firms that offer specific mandatory training include Douglas Aircraft, AT&T, DuPont, and Digital Equipment.

As the percentage of women in the workforce grows and sexual harassment awareness is heightened, there is an increase in the number of both men and women in organizations who are becoming more concerned about sexual harassment. Anxiety about social and workplace interactions has led some males to become wary of telling any jokes that might be misinterpreted or making any comments about the appearance of women colleagues. They may even be hesitant to invite women to lunch or other social functions.

Workplace "romance" also poses problems for employees and employers alike. Because work consumes so much of many people's time, the workplace is a major meeting place for individuals of the opposite sex. One survey by *Working Women* magazine found that 76% of surveyed women executives had had or were having an office romance. If work-based friendships lead to romance and off-the-job sexual relationships, managers and employers then face the dilemma of "meddling" in the private, off-the-job lives of individuals versus monitoring for and protecting the firm from potential sex harassment complaints.

Some companies have attempted to prohibit dating and romances between superiors and subordinates, while others have tried to ignore such situations. Employment attorneys generally recommend that the HR manager remind both parties in workplace romances of the company policy on sexual harassment and encourage either party to contact the HR department should the relationship cool and become one in which the relationship becomes unwanted and unwelcome. Also, the HR manager should document that such conversations occurred.[1]

25

> There are, in every age, new errors to be rectified and new prejudices to be opposed.
>
> *Samuel Johnson*

Equal employment opportunity (EEO) regulations deal with more than the initial employment of individuals. As the opening discussion on sexual harassment illustrates, employers must take steps to implement equal employment opportunity in a variety of areas. But EEO is broader than many employers realize. One of the purposes of this chapter is to discuss the range of issues that have been addressed by EEO laws, regulations, and court decisions. The other purpose is to review what employers should do to comply with the regulations and requirements of various EEO enforcement agencies.

▲ SEX DISCRIMINATION

Title VII of the Civil Rights Act of 1964 prohibits discrimination in employment on the basis of sex. Other laws and regulations are aimed at eliminating sex discrimination in specific areas. The first area discussed is sexual harassment.

As the opening discussion of the chapter indicates, there is growing awareness of sexual harassment and less tolerance of it than before, both by employers and those individuals affected by it. As the cartoon shown here indicates, the victims of sexual harassment are more likely to bring charges and take legal actions against employers and the harassing individuals than they were in the past.

Sexual Harassment

The EEOC has issued guidelines designed to curtail sexual harassment. A variety of definitions of sexual harassment exist, but generally **sexual harassment** refers to actions that are sexually directed, unwanted, and subject the worker to adverse employment conditions or that create a hostile work environment. Sexual harassment can occur between a boss and subordinate, among co-wotkers, and among nonemployees who have business contracts with employees. A few

▼ **SEXUAL HARASSMENT**

refers to actions that are sexually directed, unwanted, and subject the worker to adverse employment conditions or that create a hostile work environment.

Reprinted with special permission of King Features Syndicate, Inc.

sexual harassment cases also have been filed involving a manager and an employee of the same sex. However, according to EEOC statistics, well over 90% of the situations have been harassment of women by men.

Two types of sexual harassment are defined as follows:

▲ *Quid pro quo* occurs when an employer or supervisor links specific employment outcomes to the individual's granting sexual favors.

▲ *Hostile environment* occurs when sexual harassment has the effect of unreasonably interfering with employee work performance or psychological well-being, or when intimidating or offensive working conditions are created.

Quid pro Quo   Any condition of employment that is linked to sexual harassment, including pay raises, promotions, assignments of work and work hours, performance appraisals, meetings, disciplinary actions, and many others, are included as quid pro quo harassment. Others have labeled this type of harassment as "sexual extortion,"[2] because it essentially is an abuse of power. Certainly, harassment by supervisors and managers who expect sexual favors as a condition for a raise or promotion is inappropriate behavior in a work environment. This view has been supported in a wide variety of cases.

Hostile Environment   The second type of sexual harassment involves the creation of a hostile work environment. A landmark case decided by the U.S. Supreme Court, *Meritor Savings Bank v. Vinson,* ruled that creation of a hostile work environment due to sexual harassment is illegal even if the complainant suffered no earnings or job loss. The case was brought by a former female employee who charged that a vice-president of the bank sexually harassed her.[3]

There are five basic phases in proving sexual harassment. It must be established that the employee was:[4]

1. A member of a protected class
2. Subjected to unwelcome sexual harassment
3. Harassed on the basis of sex
4. Harassed so that the conditions of employment were changed and a hostile working environment was created
5. Employer liability for the harassment established

What numerous cases in which sexual harassment has been found to illustrate is that harmless joking or teasing in the eyes of one person may be seen as offensive and hostile behavior in the eyes of another. Comments on dress or appearance, telling jokes that are suggestive or sexual in nature, allowing centerfold posters to be on display, or making continual requests for getting together after work all can lead to the creation of a hostile work environment.

Employer Responses to Sexual Harassment Complaints

Employers generally are held responsible for sexual harassment unless they take appropriate action in response to complaints. Employers also are held responsible if they knew (or should have known) of the conduct and failed to stop it. With the passage of the Civil Rights Act of 1991, the costs to employers of being found guilty of sexual harassment likely will increase as a result of jury trials with punitive damages being awarded. Therefore, employers must take positive action to eliminate sexual harassment from their workplaces (see the "HR Perspective").

HR Perspectives:
Research on Employer Responses to Sexual Harassment

A study by Terpstra and Baker of federal court cases on sexual harassment, as reported in the *Academy of Management Journal,* identified factors that related to whether court decisions were for or against employers. Using a total of 133 cases filed in federal courts, two research assistants, one male and one female, coded the cases to classify the case variables and factors. Actions examined were sexual assault, unwanted physical contact of a sexual nature, sexual propositions linked to employment consequences, and sexual propositions not linked to employment consequences. Also coded was who were the harassers.

Key factors identified were as follows:

▲ Severity of harassment behavior
▲ Presence of witnesses
▲ Notice to management of harassment
▲ Absence or presence of supporting documents by complainants
▲ Absence or presence of investigative or remedial action by employers

The researchers found that the complainant won virtually every case if the harassment was severe, if there were witnesses and additional documentation, and if management had been notified of the harassment but failed to take action. However, if management had taken action, then the employer tended to.

These findings reinforce that employers should have specific sexual harassment complaint procedures and policies that allow complainants to bypass a supervisor who may be the harasser. The researchers found that if such a complaint process existed and it was not used by the complainant, the employer was more likely to win the case. Finally, prompt action by the employer to investigate sexual harassment complaints and then to punish the identified harassers aided the employer's defense. In summary, the research revealed that if harassment is taken seriously by employers, the outcomes of cases are more likely to be favorable to them.[5]

Sexual Harassment Policy   Every employer should have a policy on sexual harassment. That policy should address such issues as the following:[6]

▲ Instructions on how to report complaints, including how to bypass a supervisor if he or she is involved in the harassment.
▲ Assurances of confidentiality and protection against retaliation from those against whom the complaint is filed.
▲ A guarantee of prompt investigation.
▲ A statement that disciplinary action will be taken against sexual harassers, up to and including termination of employment.

Court cases make it clear that employers have a duty to do more than publish a policy.[7] For example, in the *Bundy v. Jackson* case, a female vocational rehabilitation specialist (Bundy) suffered from sexual propositions and sexual intimidation and was passed over for a promotion. She filed a complaint within the agency, which had a policy against sexual harassment, but no organizational investigation followed. The court decision favored Bundy and found that a violation of Title VII occurred "where an employer created or condoned a substantially discriminatory work environment, regardless of whether the complaining employee lost any tangible job benefits."[8] By failing to investigate this employee's charges, the employer had "condoned" the harassment.

Communications and Training   All employees, but especially supervisors and managers, should be informed that sexual harassment will not be tolerated in an organization. To create such awareness, communications to all employees should highlight the employer's policy on sexual harassment and the importance of creating and maintaining a work environment free of sexual harassment.

In addition, training of all employees, especially supervisors and managers, is recommended. The training should identify what constitutes sexual harassment and alert employees to the types of behaviors that create problems. In the *Robinson v. Jacksonville Shipyards* case, the court ordered the employer to adopt a model policy requiring that all employees be reminded of the sexual harassment policy at safety meetings, and to conduct training at least once a year for supervisors and managers, and separate training for female employees.[9]

Investigation and Action   Once management gains knowledge of sexual harassment, then the investigation process should begin. Often an HR staff member and/or outside legal counsel will spearhead the investigation in order to provide objectivity. The procedures should be identified at the time the sexual harassment policy is promulgated, and all steps taken during the investigation should be documented. It is crucial to ensure that the complainant is not subjected to any further harassment or retaliation for filing the complaint.[10]

When determining if sexual harassment occurred, in legal cases there is growing use of the "reasonable woman" standard. In the *Ellison v. Brady* case, the court ruled that sexual harassment must be viewed from the perspective of a "reasonable woman," and not just people in general. Also, the court ruled that employers must take significant action to remedy sexual harassment situations in order to avoid liability. The remedial actions must be forceful, such as separating the two parties involved by job reassignment or discharging the harasser.[11]

Sex Discrimination in Selection

One result of the increasing number of women in the workforce is the movement of women into jobs traditionally held by men. More women are obtaining jobs such as welders, railroad engineers, utility repair specialists, farm equipment sales representatives, sheet metal workers, truck drivers, and carpenters. Yet, many kinds of discrimination in the assignment of women to jobs still exist.

▼ **GLASS CEILING**

refers to discriminatory practices that have prevented women and other protected-class members from advancing to executive-level jobs.

"Glass Ceiling" and Job Assignments   The concept alleged by women's groups for years of a **glass ceiling** refers to discriminatory practices that have prevented women and other protected-class members from advancing to executive-level jobs. A 1991 study by the U.S. Department of Labor revealed that top executive jobs rarely go to women and racial/ethnic minorities, even though they composed over 45% of the U.S. workforce. Of more than 6,500 jobs at the level of vice-president or above, women held only 175 (2.6%) in another study. Those women who were executives were concentrated in positions in the HR Department and Corporate Communications.[12]

All of these studies led to the passage of the Glass Ceiling Act of 1991 in conjunction with the Civil Rights Act of 1991. A Glass Ceiling Commission was established to conduct a study on how to shatter the glass ceiling for women and other protected-class members. The commission, composed of 21 members, terminates in 1995 following investigative hearings, after which a report containing recommendations will be released.

The selection or promotion criteria that employers use can discriminate against women. Some cases have found that women were not allowed to enter certain jobs or job fields because of sexual stereotyping. Particularly problematic is the use of marital or family status as a basis for not selecting women. The "HR Perspective" regarding ethical issues involved when women are interviewed shows some of the ways that discrimination in selection practices can occur.

Nepotism   Many employers have policies that restrict or prohibit *nepotism,* the practice of allowing relatives to work for the same employer. Other firms require only that relatives not work directly for or with each other or be placed in a position where potential collusion or conflicts could occur. The policies most frequently cover spouses, brothers, sisters, mothers, fathers, sons, and daughters. Generally, employer antinepotism policies have been upheld by courts, in spite of the concern that they discriminate against women more than men because women tend to be denied employment more often or leave employers more often if two employees marry.[13]

In a related area, inquiries about previous names (not maiden name) under which any applicant may have previously worked may be necessary in order to check reference information with former employers, educational institutions, or employers' own files, in the case of former employees. This kind of inquiry is not illegal.

Height/Weight Restrictions   Many times height/weight restrictions have been used to discriminate against women or other protected-member groups. For example, the state of Alabama violated Title VII in setting height and weight restrictions for correctional counselors. The restrictions (5 feet 2 inches and 120 pounds) would exclude 41.14% of the female population of the country but less than 1% of the men. The Supreme Court found that the state's attempt to justify the requirements as essential for job-related strength failed for lack of evidence. The Court suggested that if strength was the quality sought, the state should have adopted a strength requirement.[14]

Job Conditions and Restrictions

Having different job conditions for men and women usually is discriminatory. In one case, an EEO violation occurred when a retail firm allowed male sales clerks to wear slacks, shirts, and ties, but required women sales clerks to wear smocks.[15] Another retailer paid over $2,500 in back pay for firing a full-figured female employee because, according to the owner, her figure was too distracting, especially when she wore sweaters.[16]

Many states in the past had laws to "protect" women by requiring that they be restricted to a certain number of working hours a week or by specifying the maximum weight a woman was allowed to lift at work. The EEOC has disputed these laws in court, and in most cases, the restrictions have been ruled invalid because they conflict with federal law and are not reasonable grounds for denying jobs to women.

The right of employers to reassign women from hazardous jobs to others that may be lower paying because of health-related concerns is another issue. Employers' fears about higher health-insurance costs, and even possible lawsuits regarding such problems as birth defects sustained during pregnancy, have led to *reproductive and fetal protection policies.* But the U.S. Supreme Court ruled that such policies were illegal.[17]

HR Perspectives:
Ethical Issues in Interviewing Women

A faculty member at Memphis State University, Arthur Eliot Berkeley, wrote the following observations of the behavior and questioning techniques used in job interviews for *The Wall Street Journal*. He obtained his information from numerous conversations with personnel specialists, interviewers, and employees. What he said raises some ethical issues with equal employment implications.

It's the law: Interviews for such employment-related decisions as hiring, transfer, and promotion are supposed to be conducted in an objective fashion with no personal inquiries that aren't clearly job related. For example, an interviewer should not ask a young woman about her marital status, birth control, or plans for childbearing.

If a position involves extensive travel with frequent overnights away from home, an interviewer might legitimately ask whether any situation in the candidate's life would serve as a barrier to travel. Otherwise, for a typical officebound job involving regular business hours, no such inquiry would be permissible.

All personnel administrators and most, if not all, managers know the law. Yet what actually occurs in an interview frequently deviates dramatically from the legally permissible. For years the actual substance of interviews has been a dirty little secret with no one willing to own up to the sorts of illegal inquiries frequently made of candidates.

Most impermissible areas of inquiry appear to be directed at women. Most typically, the concern of the interviewer is a young woman's childbearing plans and child-care situation. Given managers' great curiosity about such matters, how is the information—unlawful if not clearly job related—obtained?

Sneaky Strategems: One large manufacturing firm (and a huge federal contractor) uses the simple expedient of having a low-level personnel clerk ask the candidate about her choice of health-insurance plans. An executive from the firm says: "During a lull in between interviews, I have a clerk ask whether the applicant wants individual, husband-and-wife, or family coverage, and in choosing an option, the candidate will usually tell the clerk everything we need to know."

Another effective technique is used by a large financial-service firm, which takes the job candidate to lunch at a nice restaurant. Given the informal atmosphere, the applicant is more easily caught off-guard by a personal inquiry. Typically the prospective supervisor and his assistant eat lunch with the candidate and begin to discuss their children.

One of the firm's supervisors says: "I'll say something like: 'Our car-pool arrangements got messed up this morning and I was almost late for work.' Then I ask the applicant if anything like that ever happens to her. And almost always, the information I want will just come pouring out. The candidate will say something like no, she has no children, isn't even married, or doesn't want children. Or she'll tell me how she's a single mother with two little girls and is always having a problem with car pools and sitters. This tells me what I need to know."

The Direct Approach: Most starkly, some employers—often in an informal or cocktail setting—will ask flat out about a woman's family situation, putting the candidate in an extremely delicate position. If the female applicant refuses to answer the question, citing its illegality, she runs a very real risk of alienating the interviewer and wrecking her chances of being hired. If she answers the question truthfully, the information may prove fatal to her candidacy.

Sneaky Responses: In what was the most startling revelation in this area, I learned that many women respond falsely to these illegal inquiries, rationalizing that since the questions are unlawful, they are morally entitled to offer untrue responses. Said one woman, the divorced mother of two children, one of whom is severely handicapped: "Even though I'm a very reliable worker, I knew if I told the truth, I wouldn't get the job, and I needed this job badly. So I said I wasn't married—which was true—and I had no intention of having children—which is sort of true because certainly I don't plan to have any more children . . . I got the job. I figured that my kids were none of their business, so it didn't matter what I told them. Once I was hired, what could they do?"

The Implications: When disobedience of any law becomes as widespread as it apparently has here, it seems clear that a new approach is necessary. Increased enforcement of the law with stiffer penalties is one approach, but this is almost bound to fail. Both interviewer and candidate probably would become even more skilled at evading the law—to everyone's detriment.

The best approach is to encourage discussion and education on the subject. If both interviewer and candidate can get beyond the gamesmanship and focus in on the optimum fit between the job and the person, everyone will benefit.

Interviewers should learn not merely the techniques for a lawful employment interview, but, even more important, the reasons for the restrictions. They need to be made to question and confront their underlying prejudicial assumptions and then to change them. Only then can candidates trust the interview process and end this unethical cycle.[18]

Pregnancy Discrimination

The major effect of the Pregnancy Discrimination Act (PDA) of 1978, passed as an amendment to the Civil Rights Act of 1964, was that any employer with 15 or more employees had to treat maternity leave the same as other personal or medical leaves. Closely related to the PDA is the Medical and Family Leave Act of 1993, which requires that individuals be given up to 12 weeks family leave without pay and also requires that those taking family leave be allowed to return to jobs. (See Chapter 15 for details.)

The greatest concern of employers is handling the work of employees on leave while they are gone and having to hold their jobs open until their return. But a survey of women who had taken maternity leave found that 20% returned to work within six weeks and another 66% in six weeks to six months. Of those, 80% returned to the same jobs, although many were critical of their employers for not allowing them to return to work on a part-time basis, at least for a while.[19]

Compensation Issues and Sex Discrimination

A number of concerns have been raised about employer compensation practices that discriminate on the basis of sex. At issue in several compensation practices is the extent to which men and women are treated differently, with women most frequently receiving less compensation or benefits. Equal pay, comparable worth, and benefits coverage are three prominent issues.

Equal Pay The Equal Pay Act enacted in 1963 forbids employers to pay lower wage rates to employees of one sex for equal work performed under similar working conditions. Tasks performed only intermittently or infrequently do not make jobs different enough to justify significantly different wages. But differences in pay may be allowed because of: (1) differences in seniority, (2) differences in performance, (3) differences in quality and/or quantity of production, and (4) factors other than sex, such as skill, effort, or working conditions.

Comparable Worth Issue The concept of **comparable worth** is that jobs with comparable levels of knowledge, skill, and ability should be paid similarly even if actual duties differ significantly. The Equal Pay Act applies to jobs that are substantially the same, whereas comparable worth applies to jobs that are *valued* similarly in the organization, whether or not they are the same.

A major reason for the development of the comparable worth idea is the continuing gap between the earnings of women and men. A study by the U.S. Census Bureau found that the salaries of younger, college-educated women average 92% of those of their male peers. However, the gap widens over time, such that by ages 55 to 64 women are making only 54% of what men earn.[20]

Whatever the merits of the concept, the U.S. Supreme Court has ruled that comparable worth is not required by law. Nevertheless a number of state and local government employers have mandated "pay equity" for public-sector employees through legislation.

Benefits Coverage A final area of sex-based differences in compensation relates to benefits coverage. One concern has been labeled "unisex" pension

▼ **COMPARABLE WORTH**

requires that jobs with comparable levels of knowledge, skill, and ability should be paid similarly even if actual duties differ significantly.

coverage. The *Arizona Governing Committee v. Norris* decision held that an employer's deferred compensation plan violated Title VII because female employees received lower monthly benefits payments than men upon retirement, despite the fact that women contributed equally to the plan.[21] Regardless of longevity differences, men and women who contribute equally to pension plans must receive equal monthly payments.

▲ AGE DISCRIMINATION

For many years, race and sex discrimination cases overshadowed age discrimination cases. However, starting with the 1978 amendments to the Age Discrimination in Employment Act (ADEA) of 1967, a dramatic increase in age discrimination suits occurred. For instance, in a recent year, about 30,000 age discrimination complaints were filed with the EEOC, almost equal to the number of sex discrimination complaints.

Age Discrimination in Employment Act (ADEA)

The Age Discrimination in Employment Act (ADEA) of 1967, amended in 1978 and 1986, makes it illegal for an employer to discriminate in compensation, terms, conditions, or privileges of employment because of an individual's age. The later amendments first raised the minimum mandatory retirement age to 70, and then eliminated it completely.[22] The ADEA applies to all individuals above the age of 40 working for employers having 20 or more workers. However, the act does not apply if age is a job-related occupational qualification.

Prohibitions against age discrimination do not apply when an individual is disciplined or discharged for good cause, such as poor job performance. Older workers who are poor performers can be terminated just as anyone else. However, numerous suits under the ADEA have been filed involving workers over 40 who were forced to take "voluntary retirement" when organizational restructuring or workforce reduction programs were implemented.

Workforce Reductions

In the 1990s early retirement programs and organizational downsizing have been used by many employers to reduce their employment costs. Illegal age discrimination sometimes occurs in the process. If disparate impact or treatment for those over 40 exists, age discrimination occurs, as the "HR Perspective" indicates. Age discrimination also occurs when an individual over the age of 40 is denied employment or promotion on the basis of age.[23]

Ensuring that age discrimination—or any kind of illegal discrimination—does not affect employment decisions requires that documentation of performance be completed by supervisors and managers. In the case of older employees, care must be taken that references to age ("good old Fred" or "need younger blood") in conversations with older employees are not used. Terminations based on documented performance deficiencies not related to age are perfectly legal. When a retail collection manager over age 40 was terminated by Sears, after receiving five negative performance-appraisal ratings from five different supervisors, the

HR Perspectives:

Forced Retirements and "Overqualified" Older Workers

Many employers have instituted early retirement programs as part of downsizing and restructuring efforts to encourage employees to leave their jobs. While often unstated, the design of these programs targets older individuals because the eligibility criteria for many programs includes a combination of age and experience. For instance, in one plan a combination of age and years of service had to add up to at least 70, and a minimum of 10 years service with the employer was required. By eliminating older workers, employers may be reducing the most costly portion of their employment budget because older workers tend to have higher salaries due to greater length of service and job progressions that have occurred.

However, those programs also have led to workers filing discrimination charges, claiming that the "voluntary" programs really are not truly voluntary. Instead, older workers allege that they are forced to take the retirement buyouts or lose their jobs and get little or no severance payments.

The wave of organizational downsizing has led to a jump in age discrimination claims. In one recent year the EEOC reported that the number of age discrimination claims rose 20%, to over 28,000. This pattern is typical when economic recessions occur, but the growth also may be due to the overall aging of the U.S. workforce. The age discrimination charges were about one-fourth of all charges filed with the EEOC.

A related problem is older employees who are not given appropriate consideration for other jobs in an organization when restructuring is done. In one case an older employee had his position eliminated. However, he claimed that there were several open positions that he was qualified for that were filled with younger employees. The company did not disagree with the older worker, but relied on a defense that the available jobs were not "appropriate" or "suitable" because they were at different pay grades and did not require his advanced technical skills. The issue of having someone "overqualified" also was raised when the employer indicated a concern about the older worker becoming frustrated because his knowledge,

skills, and abilities would be underutilized.

The court decision ruled against the employer, and said that the employer was relying on assumptions, not facts. Particularly significant was that the older worker had not been asked if he would be willing to take the lower-paying job. Similar decisions have been reached in other cases. Another court decision summarized the issue as follows:

> "Characterizing an applicant in an age discrimination case as overqualified has a connotation that defies common sense: How can a person overqualified by experience and training be turned down for a position given to a younger person deemed better qualified? Denying employment to an older job applicant because he or she has too much experience, training, or education is to employ a euphemism to mask the real reason for refusal, namely, in the eyes of an employer, the applicant is too old."

As a result, employers must evaluate older applicants and workers for their knowledge, skills, and abilities, instead of relying upon age stereotyping that may be erroneous when applied to specific older workers.[24]

termination was ruled to be performance based, not age discrimination.[25] As pointed out in Chapter 2, older people often are very diligent and productive workers.

Older Workers Benefit Protection Act (OWBPA)

The Older Workers Benefit Protection Act (OWBPA) of 1990 was passed to amend the ADEA and to overturn a 1989 decision by the U.S. Supreme Court in the *Public Employees Retirement System of Ohio v. Betts* case.[26] This act requires equal treatment for older workers in early retirement or severance situations. It sets forth some very specific criteria that must be met when older workers sign waivers promising not to sue for age discrimination. The effect of the OWBPA is that employers should have two separately worded severance agreements, one for employees under 40 and one for those over 40 years of age.[27]

▲ AMERICANS WITH DISABILITIES ACT (ADA)

The passage of the Americans with Disabilities Act (ADA) in 1990 represented an expansion in the scope and impact of laws and regulations on discrimination against individuals with disabilities. By July 1994 all employers with 15 or more employees are covered by the provisions of the ADA, which are enforced by the EEOC. The ADA was built upon the Vocational Rehabilitation Act of 1973 and the Rehabilitation Act of 1974, which applied only to federal contractors. The ADA affects more than just employment matters, as Figure 6–1 shows, and applies to private employers, employment agencies, labor unions, and state and local governments. Federal government and government-owned organizations, Native-American tribes, and tax-exempt private membership clubs are not covered by the employment-related provisions in Title I.

Specifically, the ADA contains the following requirements regarding employment:

▲ Discrimination is prohibited against individuals if they can perform the *essential job functions,* a standard that is somewhat vague.
▲ A covered employer must make *reasonable accommodation* for persons with disabilities, so that they can function as employees unless *undue hardships* would be placed on the employer.
▲ Preemployment medical examinations are prohibited except after an employment offer is made, conditional upon passing a physical examination.
▲ Federal contractors and subcontractors with contracts valued at more than $2,500 must take affirmative action to hire qualified disabled individuals.

Discrimination Against Individuals with Disabilities

Employers looking for workers with the knowledge, skills, and abilities to perform jobs often have neglected a significant source of good, dedicated people—those individuals with various physical or mental disabilities. According to U.S. government estimates, there are 43 million Americans with some sort of disability. Many of them between the ages of 16 and 64 are unemployed, but would like to work if given appropriate opportunities.[28]

When individuals with disabilities are hired and placed into jobs that match their capabilities, they often are very good workers. One firm, the Principal Financial Group, has saved over $1 million in disability claims and costs through its Mainstream Program to accommodate employees who develop disabilities, so that they can continue employment.[29]

Who Is Disabled?

▼ **A DISABLED PERSON**

is someone who has a physical or mental impairment that substantially limits that person in some major life activities, has a record of, or is regarded as having, such an impairment.

As defined by the ADA,[30] a **disabled person** is someone who has a physical or mental impairment that substantially limits that person in some major life activities, has a record of, or is regarded as having, such an impairment. Persons who qualify for protection under the act are those who have obvious disabilities such as the absence of a limb, sight or hearing impairment, and those with other

ADA SECTION	FOCUS OF SECTION
Title I	Prohibits employment discrimination against individuals with disabilities for employers with 15 or more employees (effective July 1994).
Title II	Prohibits discrimination against individuals with disabilities from participating in services, programs, or activities of "public entities" (i.e., state and local governments). All fixed bus routes and commuter rail services must be accessible to passengers with disabilities.
Title III	Requires that places of public accommodation and commercial facilities be accessible to individuals with disabilities. Any area of a business or organization open to the public is classified as a "public accommodation." Office buildings, warehouses, factories, and nonresidential buildings are covered if their operations affect commerce.
Title IV	Requires that telecommunications for hearing and speech-impaired individuals be provided. Also, closed-captioning of public-service announcements on television broadcasts is required.
Title V	Contains administration and enforcement provisions and lists individuals who are *not* considered disabled under the Act.

▲ **Figure 6–1**

Major Sections of Americans with Disabilities Act

physical or mental impairments. Individuals with less visible disabilities classified as disabled under the ADA include persons with life-threatening diseases (i.e., AIDS, cancer, leukemia), rehabilitated drug users or alcoholics, those with major muscular limitations or breathing difficulties, and people with various mental disorders. But regulations exclude current users of illegal drugs, people with sexual behavior disorders, and compulsive gamblers from being classified as disabled.

Some court decisions and laws have protected individuals who may be perceived as impaired to a degree that their employment is affected. Thus, even individuals with facial disfigurements may qualify as disabled. Other court decisions have found individuals who have high blood pressure, epilepsy, allergies, obesity, and color blindness to be disabled.

AIDS and Life-Threatening Illnesses

In recent years, the types of disabilities that are protected against discrimination by the various local, state, and federal acts have expanded. For example, a U.S. Supreme Court case held that an employer cannot discriminate against an individual whom the employer feels may have a contagious disease. The case involved an individual who had a relapse of tuberculosis and was discharged from her job as a schoolteacher because her employer feared she might be contagious.[31]

The most feared contagious disease is acquired immune deficiency syndrome (AIDS). The disease was almost unknown in 1980, but by the early 1990s estimates were that approximately 2 million people in the United States either had AIDS or were carrying the HIV virus.

Unfortunately, some employers and employees often react with fear about working with an AIDS victim. If an employer does have an employee with a life-threatening illness, educating other employees is more appropriate than terminating the victim's employment. A medical leave of absence (without pay if that is the general policy) can be used to assist the AIDS-afflicted employee during medical treatments. Employees who indicate they will not work with an AIDS victim should be told that their refusal to work is not protected by law and they could be subjected to disciplinary action up to and including discharge.[32]

Essential Job Functions

▼ **ESSENTIAL JOB FUNCTIONS**

are the fundamental job duties of the employment position that an individual with a disability holds or desires, but they do not include marginal functions of the position.

The ADA requires that employers identify for all jobs the **essential job functions**—the fundamental job duties of the employment position that an individual with a disability holds or desires, but they do not include marginal functions of the position.

The essential functions should be identified through written job descriptions that indicate the amount of time spent performing various functions and their criticality. Most employers have interpreted this provision to mean that they should develop and maintain current and comprehensive job descriptions for all jobs. These job descriptions should list the job functions in the order of "essentiality." Also, the job specification statements that identify the qualifications required of those in each job should specify the exact knowledge, skills, abilities, and physical demands involved. For example, hearing, speaking, climbing, lifting, or stooping should be mentioned if any of those actions are necessary in performing specific jobs.

"Reasonable Accommodation" for Disabled Individuals

▼ **REASONABLE ACCOMMODATION**

is a modification or adjustment to a job or work environment that enables a qualified individual with a disability to enjoy equal employment opportunity.

Reasonable accommodation is a modification or adjustment to a job or work environment that enables a qualified individual with a disability to enjoy equal employment opportunity. Employers are required to provide "reasonable accommodation" for disabled individuals to ensure that illegal discrimination does not occur.

There are several areas of reasonable accommodation. First, disabled individuals must have *access to work areas.* Steps, extremely narrow corridors, and/or absence of elevators may prevent an otherwise qualified person from applying for employment because of his or her inability to get to the employment office. Accessibility to rest rooms and equipment within them also are required so that architectural barriers do not result in discrimination.

A second area of reasonable accommodation is the assignment of work tasks. This requirement may mean modifying jobs, work schedules, equipment, or work area layouts. Some examples include teaching sign language to a supervisor so that a deaf person can be employed, modifying work schedules to assist disabled workers, buying special amplifiers for hearing-impaired employees, or having another worker perform minor duties. For example, one firm made reasonable accommodation for an employee in a wheelchair by moving some furniture to widen an aisle and having another employee file the correspondence typed by the physically impaired employee. Under the ADA, employers even may have to hire readers, interpreters, or personal attendants to assist disabled individuals during the workday. However, there are few specific rules on which an employer can rely because every situation is considered on its own merits by the courts.

Undue Hardship

Reasonable accommodation is restricted to actions that do not place an "undue hardship" on an employer. **Undue hardship** means an action requiring significant difficulty or expense for an employer. Initially, employers were very concerned about facing extensive costs for remodeling facilities or making other accommodations. However, a study found that 88% of the accommodations necessary can be done for less than $1,000, many for little or no cost.[33] Some examples follow:

▲ Placing a paper-cup dispenser by a recessed water fountain so that disabled individuals in wheelchairs can get drinks cost $4.95 for each dispenser plus continuing costs of cup refills.

▲ A one-handed person working in a kitchen could do all jobs except the opening of food cans. A one-handed electric can opener was purchased for a cost of $35.

▲ A housekeeper in a motel could not bend to inspect under beds. A mirror was placed on a cleaning wand device for her use. The cost was $11.[34]

Other accommodations can be more expensive. But the ADA offers only general guidelines on when an accommodation becomes unreasonable and places undue hardship on an employer.

▼ **UNDUE HARDSHIP**

means an action requiring significant difficulty or expense for an employer in making "reasonable accommodation" for disabled individuals.

▲ OTHER BASES OF DISCRIMINATION

The original purpose of the Civil Rights Act of 1964 was to address race discrimination. This area continues to be important today, and employers must be aware of potentially discriminating practices on the basis of race. Also, the requirements of the EEOC and the affirmative action requirements of the Office of Federal Contract Compliance Programs (OFCCP) specifically designate race as an area for investigation and reporting. Race is often a factor in discrimination on the basis of national origin. This topic is examined next, followed by discussions of religious discrimination and other types of discrimination.

Discrimination Based on National Origin and Citizenship

What rights do people from other countries, especially those illegally in the United States, have concerning employment and equality? Illegal aliens often are called *undocumented workers* because they do not have the appropriate permits and documents from the Immigration and Naturalization Service. The passage of the Immigration Reform and Control Acts (IRCA) in 1986 and 1990 clarified an issue that had confronted politicians, labor leaders, and employers for many years.

Immigration Reform and Control Acts (IRCA)   To deal with the problems arising from the continued flow of immigrants to the United States, the

Immigration Reform and Control Act (IRCA) was passed in 1986. Based upon complaints by employers and advocacy groups representing various immigrants and nationalities, the law was changed through a 1990 revision. The IRCA makes it illegal for an employer to discriminate in recruiting, hiring, or terminating based on an individual's national origin or citizenship. Many employers were avoiding the recruitment and hiring of individuals who were "foreign looking" or who spoke with an accent, presuming them possibly to be undocumented workers. Hispanic leaders voiced concern about the discriminatory effects of this practice on Hispanics who were U.S. citizens. The 1990 act attempted to address this issue. It also prohibits employers from requiring more documentation for some prospective employees than for others. But the IRCA requires that employers who knowingly hire illegal aliens be penalized.

Employer Documentation Required   Under these acts employers are required to examine applicants' identification documents; new employees also must sign verification forms about their eligibility to work legally in the United States. Employers must ask for proof of identity, such as driver's license with a picture, Social Security card, birth certificate, immigration permit, or other documents. Cases brought by the EEOC also have sought to extend Title VII protection against race discrimination to undocumented workers who are illegally working in the United States. Lower court decisions have been inconsistent, with some courts ruling one way and some the opposite. Until the U.S. Supreme Court makes a ruling, this issue likely will remain unresolved.

Immigration Visas   The 1990 revisions also eased restrictions on the entry of immigrants to work in U.S. organizations, particularly in "scarce-skill" areas. The number of immigrants who are allowed legal entry was increased, and several categories for entry visas were established.[35]

Foreign-Language Requirements   Questions about an applicant's language skills should be limited to those situations in which workers will have job-related reasons for using the language. The employer is restricted to making such inquiries only in regard to those specific jobs that warrant use of the foreign language. Court decisions in this area generally have rejected attempts by employers to ban employees from speaking foreign languages at all times in work areas.[36] However, some court decisions have supported the idea that some business operations require communications in a single language. For instance, a Honolulu court ruled that denying employment to a person because he could not communicate clearly due to a hard-to-understand accent was acceptable because the job he applied for required him to communicate with up to 300 individuals per day.[37]

Some states have recently passed laws making English the official language of the state. Therefore, employers should monitor developments at both the federal and state levels.

Religious Discrimination

Title VII of the Civil Rights Act also identifies discrimination on the basis of religion as illegal. However, religious schools and institutions can use religion as a BFOQ for employment practices on a limited scale. A major guide in this area was established by the U.S. Supreme Court, in *TWA v. Hardison*.

TWA v. Hardison   Hardison worked for TWA in Kansas City and was a member of the Worldwide Church of God, which forbids working on Saturday. However, under the terms of a union contract, workers with low seniority, such as Hardison, could be called to work special assignments on Saturdays. TWA offered to change the work assignment, but the union objected. Then TWA tried other alternatives, but none were acceptable to Hardison and the union. Ultimately, Hardison refused to work on Saturday, was discharged, and filed suit.

The ruling by the Supreme Court was that an employer is required to make *reasonable accommodation* of an employee's religious beliefs. Because TWA had done so, the ruling denied Hardison discrimination charges.[38] In summary, offering alternative work schedules, making use of compensatory time off, or otherwise adjusting to employees' religious beliefs are recommended to employers. But once reasonable accommodation efforts have been made, the employer is considered to have abided by the law.[39]

Sexual Orientation and Gay Rights

The battle over revising policies for nonheterosexuals in the U.S. military services in 1993 illustrates the depth of emotions that accompany discussions of "gay rights." Seven states and 100 cities have passed laws prohibiting discrimination based on sexual orientation or lifestyles.[40] However, at the federal level no laws have been passed of a similar nature.

Whether gay men and lesbians have rights under the equal protection amendment to the U.S. Constitution has not been decided by the U.S. Supreme Court. Regarding transsexuals, who are individuals who have had sex-change surgery, court cases and the EEOC have ruled that sex discrimination under Title VII refers to a person's gender at birth, not to those who have had gender-altering operations.[41] Transvestites and individuals with other sexual behavior disorders specifically are excluded from being considered disabled under the Americans with Disabilities Act of 1990.

Discrimination and Appearance

Several EEO cases have been filed concerning appearance of employees. Court decisions consistently have allowed employers to have dress codes as long as they are applied uniformly. But requiring a dress code for women but not for men has been ruled to be discriminatory. Most of the dress standards contested required workers to dress in a conservative manner.

Other individuals have brought cases of employment discrimination based on obesity or on unattractive appearance. Laws have been proposed but not adopted in some states to prohibit "sizism" discrimination.[42] A woman weighing over 300 pounds was rejected for employment as a clerical worker for an electric utility. In another case, an airline fired a woman flight attendant for being unattractive and overweight. Employers lost in both cases because of their inabilities to prove any direct job-related value in their requirements.[43] Now, under the Americans with Disabilities Act, obese individuals may qualify as having a covered disability when they are perceived and treated as if they have a disability.

Cases also have addressed the issue of beards, mustaches, and hair length and style. Because African-American men are more likely than white males to suffer from a skin disease that is worsened by shaving, they have filed suits challenging policies prohibiting beards or long sideburns. Generally, courts have ruled for employers in these cases.

Conviction and Arrest Records

Court decisions consistently have ruled that using records of arrests, rather than records of convictions, has a disparate impact on some groups protected by Title VII. An arrest, unlike a conviction, does not imply guilt. Statistics indicate that in some geographic areas, a greater number of racial-minority-group members are arrested than nonminorities. However, generally courts have held that conviction records may be used in determining employability if the offense is job related in nature. For example, a bank could use an applicant's conviction for forgery as a valid basis for rejection. Some courts have held that only job-related convictions occurring within the most recent five to seven years are allowed. Consequently, employers inquiring about convictions often add a phrase such as "indication of a conviction will not be an absolute bar to employment."

▲ AFFIRMATIVE ACTION

▼ **AN AFFIRMATIVE ACTION**

occurs when employers identify problem areas, set goals, and take positive steps to guarantee equal employment opportunities for people within a protected class.

Affirmative action occurs when employers identify problem areas, set goals, and take positive steps to guarantee equal employment opportunities for people within a protected class. Affirmative action focuses on hiring, training, and promoting of protected-class members where they are *underrepresented* in an organization. An **affirmative action plan (AAP)** is a formal document that the organization makes available for review by employees and enforcement officers.

▼ **AFFIRMATIVE ACTION PLAN (AAP)**

is a formal document that the organization makes available for review by employees and enforcement officers.

Quotas, Preferential Selection, and Reverse Discrimination

When equal employment opportunity regulations are discussed, probably the most volatile issues concern *quotas, preferential selection,* and *reverse discrimination.* At the heart of the conflict is the role that employers have in selecting, training, and promoting protected-class members when they are underrepresented in various jobs within an organization. Those who are not members of any protected class have claimed that they are being discriminated against in reverse.[44] **Reverse discrimination** is said to exist when a person is denied an opportunity because of preferences given to a member of a protected class who may be less qualified. Specifically, some charge that white males are at a disadvantage today, even though they traditionally have held many of the better jobs. They charge that they are having to "pay for the sins of their fathers."[45]

▼ **REVERSE DISCRIMINATION**

may exist when a person is denied an opportunity because of preferences given to protected-class individuals who may be less qualified.

It has been stated by some that the use of affirmative action to remedy underrepresentation of protected-class members is really a form of quotas, or "hiring by the numbers." However, the Civil Rights Act of 1991 specifically prohibits the use of quotas. It also sets limitations on when affirmative action plans can be challenged by nonprotected-class individuals. Some of the phrases that are used to convey that goals are not quotas include "relative numbers," "appropriately represented," and "balanced workforce."[46]

Along with the economic restructuring of many organizations has come a growing backlash against affirmative action. Some see it as an unfair quota system rather than sound HR management. Proponents of affirmative action maintain that it is a proactive way for employers to ensure that protected-class members have equal opportunity in all aspects of their employment, and that it is indeed sound management. The "HR Perspective" illustrates the conflicts.

HR Perspectives:
Backlash

Running a newspaper in an inflamed central city these days involves the proprietors and editors in all the problems of that city. During the Spring 1992 looting and rioting in Los Angeles, its racial overtones reverberated in the editorial department of the *Los Angeles Times.*

African-American and Hispanic reporters and photographers who worked in zoned editions in the Los Angeles suburbs claimed they were shipped downtown and dispatched to cover the mayhem because the paper felt it was unsafe for white reporters. Some felt they were cannon fodder. Maybe, but one of the strong arguments used to justify affirmative action hiring at the paper had been

that African Americans and Hispanics understood their own communities better than white reporters ever could.

The newspaper's reaction was to appease the minority staff members by promoting some of them and some women. This move, intended to placate minority staffers, caused yet another problem. White male reporters, passed over for promotion or shipped to regional editions, complained strongly that *they* were being discriminated against. Several white male *Times* staffers reported that they were promised promotions or better assignments only to have them later rescinded and awarded to women or minorities.

The *Times* is getting unwanted help in creating a more diverse staff. A number of its white male reporters have left voluntarily in spite of the tight job situation. The paper's job-cutting buyout offer, announced in November 1992, drew 668 takers, 33% more than the company projected. The departees included 88 editorial staffers.

Capitol Editor Coffey has formed a diversity committee to promote more minority hiring and resolve racial tensions. The staff in 1993 was 17% minority and about 30% female; not enough, said the paper. This example illustrates the issues and conflicts that can occur.[47]

Seniority and Discrimination

Conflict between EEO regulations and organizational practices that give preference to employees on the basis of seniority represent another problem area. Employers, especially those with union contracts, frequently make layoff, promotion, or internal transfer decisions by giving employees with longer service first consideration. However, the use of seniority often means that there is disparate impact on protected-class members, who may have been the most recent workers hired. The result of this system is that protected-class members who have obtained jobs through an affirmative action program are at a disadvantage because of their low levels of seniority. They may find themselves "last hired, first fired" or "last hired, last promoted."

Government Contractors and Affirmative Action Plans (AAPs)

Throughout the last 30 years, employers with federal contracts and other government entities have had to address additional areas of potential discrimination. Several acts and regulations have been issued that apply specifically to government contractors. One of these acts, the Rehabilitation Act of 1973, had many of its provisions incorporated into the Americans with Disabilities Act. Several federal acts and regulations specify a minimum number of employees and size of government contracts. These requirements primarily come from Executive Orders 11246, 11375, and 11478.

Vietnam-Era Veterans Readjustment Act of 1974   Concern about the readjustment and absorption of Vietnam-Era veterans into the workforce led to the passage of the Vietnam-Era Veterans Readjustment Act. The act requires that affirmative action in hiring and advancing Vietnam-Era veterans be undertaken by federal contractors and subcontractors having contracts of $10,000 or more.

Executive Orders 11246, 11375, and 11478   Beginning with President Franklin D. Roosevelt and continuing through the passage of the Civil Rights Act of 1964, numerous executive orders have been issued that require employers holding federal government contracts to be nondiscriminatory on the bases of race, color, religion, national origin, and sex. An **executive order** is issued by the President of the United States to provide direction to government departments on a specific issue or area.

> ▼ **AN EXECUTIVE ORDER**
>
> is an order issued by the President of the U.S. to provide direction to government departments on a specific issue or area.

During the 1960s, by executive order, the Office of Federal Contract Compliance Programs (OFCCP) in the U.S. Department of Labor was established and given responsibility for enforcing nondiscrimination in government contracts. Under Executive Order 11246 issued in 1965, amended by Executive order 11375 in 1967, and updated by Executive Order 11478 in 1979, the Secretary of Labor was given the power to:

▲ Publish the names of noncomplying contractors or unions

▲ Recommend suits by the Justice Department to compel compliance

▲ Recommend action by the Equal Employment Opportunity Commission (EEOC) or the Justice Department to file suit in federal district court

▲ Cancel the contract of a noncomplying contractor or blacklist a noncomplying employer from future government contracts

These orders have required employers to take *affirmative action* to overcome the effects of past discriminatory practices.

Who Must Have an Affirmative Action Plan (AAP)?   Generally, an employer with at least 50 employees and over $50,000 in government contracts must have a formal, written affirmative action plan. A government contractor with fewer than 50 employees who has contracts totaling more than $50,000 can be required to have an AAP if it has been found guilty of discrimination by the EEOC or other agencies. The contract size can vary depending on the protected group and the different laws on which the regulations rest.

Courts have noted that any employer that is not a government contractor may have a *voluntary* AAP, although the employer must have such a plan if it wishes to be a government contractor. A *required* AAP means that a court has ordered an employer to have an AAP as a result of past discriminatory practices and violations of laws.

Contents of an Affirmative Action Plan (AAP)

The contents of an AAP and the policies flowing from it must be available for review by managers and supervisors within the organization. Plans vary in length; some can be long and require extensive staff time to prepare. The table of contents of a plan as specified by the OFCCP is shown in Figure 6–2.

```
┌─────────────────────────────────────────────────────────────────┐
│                      TABLE OF CONTENTS                            │
├─────────────────────────────────────────────────────────────────┤
│                Statement of Confidentiality                       │
│           I. Purpose                                              │
│          II. Policy Statement                                     │
│         III. Dissemination of Policy                              │
│          IV. Responsibility for Implementation                    │
│           V. Utilization Analysis                                 │
│                 a) Organization Chart                             │
│                 b) Workforce Analysis                             │
│                 c) Job Group                                      │
│          VI. Availability Analysis                                │
│         VII. Goals and Timetables                                 │
│        VIII. Identification of Problem Areas                      │
│          IX. Development, Execution, and Support of Action-Oriented Programs │
│           X. Internal Audit and Reporting                         │
│          XI. Consideration of Minorities and Women not Currently in the Work- │
│              force                                                │
│         XII. Compliance with Religion and National Origin Guidelines │
│        XIII. Analysis of Previous Year Goal Accomplishment        │
│         XIV. Lines of Progression                                 │
│          XV. Compliance with Sex Discrimination Guidelines        │
│         XVI. EEO-1 Reports                                        │
│        XVII. New Hires and Terminations                           │
│       XVIII. Transfers and Promotions                             │
│ APPENDIX 1 Affirmative Action Program Covering Persons With Disabilities │
│              and Vietnam-Era Veterans.                            │
└─────────────────────────────────────────────────────────────────┘
```

▲ **Figure 6–2**

Sample Table of Contents for an Affirmative Action Plan

Utilization Analysis   One of the major sections of an AAP is the **utilization analysis,** which identifies the number of protected-class members employed and the types of jobs they hold. According to Executive Order 11246, employers who are government contractors meeting the required levels for contract size and number of employees must provide data on protected classes in the organization.

▼ **UTILIZATION ANALYSIS**

identifies the number of protected-class members employed and the types of jobs they hold in an organization.

Availability Analysis   As part of the utilization analysis, an **availability analysis** also must be conducted, identifying the number of protected-class members available to work in the appropriate labor market in given jobs. This analysis, which can be developed with data from a state labor department, the U.S. Census Bureau, and other sources, serves as a basis for determining if *underutilization* exists within an organization. The census data also must be matched to job titles and job groups used in the utilization analysis.

▼ **AVAILABILITY ANALYSIS**

identifies the number of protected-class members available to work in the appropriate labor market in given jobs.

Underutilization   As discussed in Chapter 5, the 4/5ths rule is a guide to calculating the underutilization of protected-class members. To calculate underutilization, the employer considers the following:

▲ Number of protected-class members in the surrounding area population
▲ Number of protected-class members in the surrounding area workforce compared with the total workforce in the organization

▲ Number of unemployed members of protected classes in the surrounding area

▲ General availability of protected-class members having requisite skills in the immediate area and in an area in which an employer reasonably could recruit

▲ Availability of promotable and transferable protected-class members within the organization

▲ Existence of training institutions that can train individuals in the requisite skills

▲ Realistic amount of training an employer can do to make all job classes available to protected-class members

Fortunately for many employers, much of the data on the population and workforce in the surrounding area is available in computerized form, so availability analysis and underutilization calculations can be done more easily. However, an employer still must maintain an accurate profile of the internal workforce. Also, the employer can determine the protected-class status of applicants by reviewing applicant flow data. An example of such a form is shown in Figure 6–3. Notice that this form is filled out voluntarily by the applicant and that the data must be maintained separately from all selection-related materials. These analyses may be useful in showing that the reason why an employer has underutilization of a protected class is because of an inadequate applicant flow of protected-class members, in spite of special efforts to recruit them.[48]

Implementation of an Affirmative Action Plan (AAP)

The implementation of an AAP must be built on a commitment to affirmative action. The commitment must begin at the top of the organization. The crucial factor is the appointment of an affirmative action officer to monitor the plan.

Once a plan is developed, it should be distributed and explained to all managers and supervisors. It is particularly important that everyone involved in the selection process review the plan and receive training on its content. Also, the AAP plan must be updated and reviewed each year to reflect changes in the utilization and availability of protected-class members. If an audit of an AAP is done by the OFCCP, employers must be prepared to provide additional details and documentation.[49]

▲ EEO COMPLIANCE

Employers must comply with all EEO regulations and guidelines. To do so, managers should be aware of what specific administrative steps are required and how charges of discrimination are investigated.

EEO Records

All employers with 20 or more employees are required to keep records that can be requested by the Equal Employment Opportunity Commission (EEOC). If the organization meets certain criteria, then reports and investigations by the Office of Federal Contract Compliance Programs (OFCCP) also must be addressed.

▲ **Figure 6–3**   Applicant Flow Data Form

THE C COMPANY

THE FOLLOWING STATISTICAL INFORMATION IS REQUIRED FOR COMPLIANCE WITH FEDERAL LAWS ASSURING EQUAL EMPLOYMENT OPPORTUNITY WITHOUT REGARD TO RACE, COLOR, SEX, NATIONAL ORIGIN, RELIGION, AGE OR HANDICAP AS WELL AS THE VIETNAM ERA READJUSTMENT ACT. THE INFORMATION REQUESTED IS VOLUNTARY AND WILL REMAIN SEPARATE FROM YOUR APPLICATION FOR EMPLOYMENT.

A MONTH DAY YEAR   APPLICATION DATE
   1   6

B [ ][ ][ ] — [ ][ ] — [ ][ ][ ] [A]   APPLICANT SOCIAL SECURITY NUMBER
   7   16

C [ ] FIRST INITIAL   D [ ] MIDDLE INITIAL
   17   18

E [ ][ ][ ][ ][ ][ ][ ][ ][ ][ ][ ][ ][ ] LAST NAME
   19   32

F STREET
   [ ]...[ ]   ADDRESS
   33   58

G CITY   STATE (first 2 letters)   ZIP
   59   71   72 73   74   78

H [ ] 1/ EEO CODES   EEO CODES 1/   A—White Male   F—Hispanic Female (Spanish Origin)
                                           B—White Female   G—American Indian/Alaskan Native Male
   MONTH DAY YEAR   C—Black Male   H—American Indian/Alaskan Native Female
I [ ][ ] [ ][ ] [ ][ ] BIRTH DATE   D—Black Female   I —Asian or Pacific Islander Male
   80 81 82 83 84 85   E—Hispanic Male   J —Asian or Pacific Islander Female
                                             (Spanish Origin)

J [ ] ARE YOU HANDICAPPED—Impairment which substantially limits one   NO —LEAVE BLANK
   86   or more of a person's life activities   YES—ENTER 'Y' Ask for Form 2

K [ ] ARE YOU A DISABLED VETERAN—   30% V.A. Compensation or   NO —LEAVE BLANK
   87   discharged because of disability YES—ENTER 'Y'
                                      incurred in line of duty   Ask for Form 2

L [ ] ARE YOU A VIETNAM ERA VETERAN— 180 days Active Duty between NO —LEAVE BLANK
   88   Aug. 15, 1964 & May 7, 1975   YES—ENTER 'Y'
                                                                      Ask for Form 2

JOB YOU HAVE APPLIED FOR (see reverse side) _____

LOCATION APPLICATION IS MADE FOR _____
                    (City or Town)   State

TO BE COMPLETED BY OFFICE ACCEPTING APPLICATION
[ ] DIVISION

DEPT. APPLICATION IS MADE FOR

_____

EEO STAFF USE ONLY

[ ][ ][ ][ ][ ][ ][ ][ ][ ][ ]
90   99

[ ][ ][ ][ ]   [ ]

M [ ]   REFERRAL SOURCE
   89   A—Walk in/Write in
         B—Ad Response
         C—State Employment Agency
         D—College Placement Office
         E—Minority Referral Agency
         F—CETA Referral
         G—Private Employment Agency

Applicant's Signature

Under various laws, employers also are required to post an "officially approved notice" in a prominent place where employees can see it. This notice states that the employer is an equal opportunity employer and does not discriminate.

EEO Records Retention   All employment records must be maintained as required by the EEOC, and *employer information reports* must be filed with the federal government. Further, any personnel or employment record made or kept by the employer must be maintained for review by the EEOC. Such records include application forms and records concerning hiring, promotion, demotion, transfer, layoff, termination, rates of pay or other terms of compensation, and selection for training and apprenticeship. Even application forms or test papers completed by unsuccessful applicants may be requested. The length of time documents must be kept varies, but generally three years is recommended as a minimum time period.

Keeping good records, whether required by the government or not, is simply a good HR practice. Complete records are necessary for an employer to respond when a charge of discrimination is made and a compliance investigation begins.

Annual Reporting Form   The basic report that must be filed with the EEOC is the annual report form EEO-1 (Figure 6–4). All employers with 100 or more employees (except state and local governments) or subsidiaries of another company that would total 100 employees must file this report. Also, federal contractors who have at least 50 employees and contracts of $50,000 or more and financial institutions in which government funds are held or savings bonds are issued must file the annual report. The annual report must be filed by March 31 for the preceding year. The form requires employment data by job category, classified according to various protected classes.

Applicant Flow Data   Under EEO laws and regulations, employers may be required to show that they do not discriminate in the recruiting and selection of members of protected classes. For instance, the number of women who applied and the number hired may be compared with the selection rate for men to determine if adverse impact exists. The fact that protected-class identification is not available in employer records is not considered a valid excuse for failure to provide the data required.

Because racial data are not permitted on application blanks or other preemployment records, the EEOC allows a "visual" survey or a separate *applicant flow form* that is not used in the selection process.

EEO Compliance Investigation

When a discrimination complaint is received by the EEOC or a similar agency, it must be processed. The process outlined here is the one used by the EEOC.

In a typical situation, a complaint goes through several stages before the compliance process is completed.[50] First, the charges are filed by an individual, a group of individuals, or their representative. A charge must be filed within 180 days of when the alleged discriminatory action occurred. Then the EEOC staff reviews the specifics of the charges to determine if it has *jurisdiction,* which means that the agency is authorized to investigate that type of charge. If jurisdiction exists, a notice of the charge must be served on the employer within 10

▲ **Figure 6–4**   Annual Report Form EEO-1

Standard Form 100
(Rev. 12-76)
Approved GAO B-180541 (R0077)
Expires 12-31-78

EQUAL EMPLOYMENT OPPORTUNITY
EMPLOYER INFORMATION REPORT EEO-1

Joint Reporting Committee

- Equal Employment Opportunity Commission
- Office of Federal Contract Compliance Programs

Section A— TYPE OF REPORT
Refer to instructions for number and types of reports to be filed.

1. Indicate by marking in the appropriate box the type of reporting unit for which this copy of the form is submitted (MARK ONLY ONE BOX).

(1) ☐ Single-establishment Employer Report

Multi-establishment Employer:
(2) ☐ Consolidated Report
(3) ☐ Headquarters Unit Report
(4) ☐ Individual Establishment Report (submit one for each establishment with 25 or more employees)
(5) ☐ Special Report

2. Total number of reports being filed by this Company (Answer on Consolidated Report only)_____

Section B— COMPANY IDENTIFICATION *(To be answered by all employers)*

OFFICE USE ONLY

1. Parent Company
   a. Name of parent company (owns or controls establishment in item 2) omit if same as label

a.

Name of receiving office | Address (Number and street)

City or town | County | State | ZIP code | b. Employer Identification No.

b.

2. Establishment for which this report is filed. (Omit if same as label)
   a. Name of establishment

c.

Address (Number and street) | City or town | County | State | ZIP code

b. Employer Identification No. | (If same as label, skip.)

d.

3. Parent company affiliation
   (Multi-establishment Employers: Answer on Consolidated Report only)
   a. Name of parent—affiliated company | b. Employer Identification No.

Address (Number and street) | City or town | County | State | ZIP code

Section C— EMPLOYERS WHO ARE REQUIRED TO FILE *(To be answered by all employers)*

☐ Yes ☐ No 1. Does the entire company have at least 100 employees in the payroll period for which you are reporting?

☐ Yes ☐ No 2. Is your company affiliated through common ownership and/or centralized management with other entities in an enterprise with a total employment of 100 or more?

☐ Yes ☐ No 3. Does the company or any of its establishments (a) have 50 or more employees AND (b) is not exempt as provided by 41 CFR 60-1.5, AND either (1) is a prime government contractor or first-tier subcontractor, and has a contract, subcontract, or purchase order amounting to $50,000 or more, or (2) serves as a depository of Government funds in any amount or is a financial institution which is an issuing and paying agent for U.S. Savings Bonds and Savings Notes?

NOTE: If the answer is yes to ANY of these questions, complete the entire form; otherwise skip to Section G.

▲ **Figure 6–4**   Continued

Section D — EMPLOYMENT DATA

Employment at this establishment--Report all permanent, temporary, or part-time employees including apprentices and on-the-job trainees unless specifically excluded as set forth in the instructions. Enter the appropriate figures on all lines and in all columns. Blank spaces will be considered as zeros.

JOB CATEGORIES	OVERALL TOTALS (SUM OF COL B THRU K)	MALE						FEMALE				
		WHITE (NOT OF HISPANIC ORIGIN)	BLACK (NOT OF HISPANIC ORIGIN)	HISPANIC	ASIAN OR PACIFIC ISLANDER	AMERICAN INDIAN OR ALASKAN NATIVE		WHITE (NOT OF HISPANIC ORIGIN)	BLACK (NOT OF HISPANIC ORIGIN)	HISPANIC	ASIAN OR PACIFIC ISLANDER	AMERICAN INDIAN OR ALASKAN NATIVE
	A	B	C	D	E	F		G	H	I	J	K
Officials and Managers												
Professionals												
Technicians												
Sales Workers												
Office and Clerical												
Craft Workers (Skilled)												
Operatives (Semi-Skilled)												
Laborers (Unskilled)												
Service Workers												
TOTAL												
Total employment reported in previous EEO-1 report												

(The trainees below should also be included in the figures for the appropriate occupational categories above)

Formal On-the-job trainees	White collar											
	Production											

1. NOTE: On consolidated report, skip questions 2-5 and Section E.
2. How was information as to race or ethnic group in Section D obtained?
   1 ☐ Visual Survey   3 ☐ Other — Specify ....
   2 ☐ Employment Record
3. Dates of payroll period used –

4. Pay period of last report submitted for this establishment

5. Does this establishment employ apprentices?
   This year? 1 ☐ Yes   2 ☐ No
   Last year? 1 ☐ Yes   2 ☐ No

Section E — ESTABLISHMENT INFORMATION

1. Is the location of the establishment the same as that reported last year?
   1 ☐ Yes   2 ☐ No   3 ☐ Did not report last year   4 ☐ Reported on combined basis

2. Is the major business activity at this establishment the same as that reported last year?
   1 ☐ Yes   2 ☐ No   3 ☐ No report last year   4 ☐ Reported on combined basis

OFFICE USE ONLY

3. What is the major activity of this establishment? (Be specific, i.e., manufacturing steel castings, retail grocer, wholesale plumbing supplies, title insurance, etc. Include the specific type of product or type of service provided, as well as the principal business or industrial activity.

Section F — REMARKS

Use this item to give any identification data appearing on last report which differs from that given above, explain major changes in composition or reporting units, and other pertinent information.

Section G — CERTIFICATION (See Instructions G)

Check one
1. ☐ All reports are accurate and were prepared in accordance with the instructions (check on consolidated only)
2. ☐ This report is accurate and was prepared in accordance with the instructions.

Name of Certifying Official	Title	Signature		Date
Name of person to contact regarding this report (Type or print)	Address (Number and street)			
Title	City and State	ZIP code	Telephone Area Code	Number Extension

All reports and information obtained from individual reports will be kept confidential as required by Section 709 (e) of Title VII.

days after the filing, and the employer is asked to respond. Following the charge notification, the EEOC's major thrust turns to investigating the complaint.

The next stage involves conciliation efforts by the agency and the employer if the charge is found to be valid. If the employer agrees that discrimination has occurred, and the employer accepts the proposed settlement, then the employer posts a notice of relief within the company and takes the agreed-on actions. This notice indicates that the employer has reached a conciliation agreement on a discrimination charge and reiterates the employer's commitment to avoid future discriminatory actions.

Individual Right to Sue   If the employer objects to the charge and rejects conciliation, the EEOC can file suit or issue a **right-to-sue letter** to the complainant, which notifies the person that he or she has 90 days in which to file a personal suit in federal court. Thus, if the EEOC decides that it will not bring suit on behalf of the complainant, the individual has the right to bring suit. The suit usually is brought in the U.S. District Court having jurisdiction in the area.

> **A RIGHT-TO-SUE LETTER** is a letter issued by the EEOC that notifies a complainant that he/she has 90 days in which to file a personal suit in federal court.

Litigation   In the court litigation stage, a legal trial takes place in the appropriate state or federal court. At that point both sides retain lawyers and rely on the court to render a decision. The Civil Rights Act of 1991 provides for jury trials in most EEO cases. If either party disagrees with the court ruling, either can file appeals with a higher court. The U.S. Supreme Court becomes the ultimate adjudication body.

Internal Employer Investigation   Many problems and expenses associated with EEO complaints can be controlled by employers who vigorously investigate their employees' discrimination complaints before they are taken to outside agencies. An internal employee complaint system and prompt, thorough responses to problem situations are essential tools in reducing EEO charges and in remedying illegal discriminatory actions.[51] More on protecting employee rights is contained in Chapter 17.

Use of "Testers"   A controversial policy involves the use of "testers" to see if employers are discriminating illegally or not. A **tester** is a protected-class member who poses as an applicant to determine if employers discriminate in their hiring practices. The purpose, according to the EEOC, is to use testers to identify employers who discriminate illegally. The testers can file charges with the EEOC if they are treated differently from other applicants or believe that they have been discriminated against.

> **A TESTER** is a protected-class member who poses as an applicant to determine if employers discriminate in their hiring practices.

Naturally, employers generally are outraged at this practice. Their argument is that because the testers are not truly applicants, they should not be able to file charges. Also, employers view the use of testers as "entrapment" or "trickery," which is not permitted in criminal law cases.[52]

After-Hire Inquiries

Once an employer tells an applicant he or she is hired (the "point of hire"), inquiries that were prohibited earlier may be made. After hiring, medical examination forms, group insurance, and other enrollment cards containing inquiries related directly or indirectly to sex, age, or other bases may be requested. Photographs or evidence of race, religion, or national origin also may be requested after hire for legal and necessary purposes, but not before. Such data should be maintained in a separate personnel records system in order to avoid their use when making appraisals, discipline, termination, or promotion decisions.

Figure 6–5 contains a list of preemployment inquiries that may or may not be discriminatory. All those preemployment inquiries labeled in the figure as "may be discriminatory" have been so designated because of findings in a variety of court cases. Likewise, those labeled as "may not be discriminatory" are practices that are legal, but only if they reflect a "business necessity" or are job related for the specific job under review.

▲ **Figure 6–5**   Guidelines to Lawful and Unlawful Preemployment Inquiries

SUBJECT OF INQUIRY	IT MAY NOT BE DISCRIMINATORY TO INQUIRE ABOUT:	IT MAY BE DISCRIMINATORY TO INQUIRE ABOUT:
1. Name	a. Whether applicant had ever worked under a different name	a. The original name of an applicant whose name had been legally changed b. The ethnic association of applicant's name
2. Age	a. If applicant is over the age of 18 b. If applicant is under the age of 18, or 21 if job related (i.e., selling liquor in retail store)	a. Date of birth b. Date of high school graduation
3. Residence	a. Applicant's place of residence, length of applicant's residence in state and/or city where employer is located	a. Previous addresses b. Birthplace of applicant or applicant's parents
4. Race or Color		a. Applicant's race or color of applicant's skin
5. National Origin & Ancestry		a. Applicant's lineage, ancestry, national origin, parentage, or nationality b. Nationality of applicant's parents or spouse
6. Sex & Family Composition		a. Sex of applicant b. Dependents of applicant c. Marital status d. Child-care arrangements
7. Creed or Religion		a. Applicant's religious affiliation b. Church, parish, or holidays observed
8. Citizenship	a. Whether the applicant is a citizen of the U.S. b. Whether the applicant is in the country on a visa which permits him to work, or is a citizen	a. Whether applicant is a citizen of a country other than the United States

▲ **Figure 6–5**   Guidelines to Lawful and Unlawful Preemployment Inquiries, continued

SUBJECT OF INQUIRY	IT MAY NOT BE DISCRIMINATORY TO INQUIRE ABOUT:	IT MAY BE DISCRIMINATORY TO INQUIRE ABOUT:
9. Language	a. Language applicant speaks and/or writes fluently, only if job related	a. Applicant's native tongue, language commonly used at home
10. References	a. Names of persons willing to provide professional and/or character references for the applicant	a. Name of applicant's pastor or religious leader
11. Relatives	a. Names of relatives already employed by the employer	a. Name and/or address of any relative of applicant b. Whom to contact in case of emergency
12. Organizations	a. Applicant's membership in any union, professional, service, or trade organization	a. All clubs or social organizations to which applicant belongs
13. Arrest Record & Convictions	a. Convictions, if related to job performance (disclaimer should accompany)	a. Number and kinds of arrests b. Convictions unless related to job performance
14. Photographs		a. Photographs with application, resume, or before hiring
15. Height & Weight		a. Any inquiry into height and weight of applicant except where a BFOQ
16. Physical Limitations	a. Whether applicant has the ability to perform job-related functions with or without accommodation	a. The nature or severity of an illness or the individual's physical condition b. Whether applicant has ever filed workers' compensation claim c. Any recent or past operations or surgery and dates
17. Education	a. Training applicant has received if related to the job under consideration b. Highest level of education attained, if validated that having certain educational background (i.e., high school diploma or college degree) is necessary to perform the specific job	
18. Military	a. What branch of the military served in b. Type of education or training received in military c. Rank at discharge	a. Type of military discharge
19. Financial Status		a. Applicant's debts or assets b. Garnishments

SOURCE: Employee Relations-Management Services, Inc., 1429 N. 131st Ave. Circle; Omaha, NE 68154. May not be used without permission.

SUMMARY

▲ Sexual harassment occurs under two conditions: (a) *quid pro quo*; (b) hostile environment.

▲ Employers should have policies on sexual harassment, have identifiable complaint procedures, train all employees on what constitutes sexual harassment, promptly investigate complaints, and take action when sexual harassment is found to have occurred.

▲ Sex discrimination exists when the following occurs: unequal job assignments, sexual harassment, pregnancy discrimination, and unequal compensation for similar jobs.

▲ Age discrimination, especially in the form of forced retirements and terminations, is a growing problem.

▲ The definition of who is disabled has been expanding in recent years.

▲ The Americans with Disabilities Act requires that most employers identify the essential functions of jobs and make reasonable accommodation for individuals with disabilities unless undue hardships result.

▲ Discrimination on the basis of national origin still is illegal, but the Immigration Reform and Control Act has affected how employers inquire about and verify citizenship.

▲ Reasonable accommodation is a strategy that can be used to deal with religious discrimination situations.

▲ Affirmative action requires employers to identify problem areas in the employment of protected-class members and to set goals and take steps to overcome those problems.

▲ The question of whether or not affirmative action requires quotas and reverse discrimination has been intensely discussed and litigated.

▲ Many employers are required to develop affirmative action plans that identify problem areas in the employment of protected-class members and initiate goals and steps to overcome those problems.

▲ Implementation of equal employment opportunity requires appropriate record keeping, such as completing the annual report (EEO-1) and keeping applicant flow data.

 REVIEW AND DISCUSSION QUESTIONS

1. Give examples that you have experienced or observed of the two types of sexual harassment in employment situations.
2. Based on your past experiences, identify examples of sex discrimination in job conditions, sexual stereotyping, and pregnancy discrimination.
3. Why are age discrimination issues growing in importance?
4. The Americans with Disabilities Act contains several key terms. Define each: (a) essential job function, (b) reasonable accommodation and, (c) undue hardship.
5. Respond to the following comment made by the president of a company: "It's getting so you can't ask anybody anything personal, because there are so many protected classes."

6. Explain your personal views on the debate over whether preferential selection as a part of affirmative action leads to reverse discrimination.

7. Discuss: "How can I report protected–class statistics to the EEOC when I cannot ask about them on my application blank?"

 CASE | **WILLFUL AGE DISCRIMINATION?**

One of the growing EEO issues facing employers is age discrimination. Following are the details of one case that has been heard by the U.S. Supreme Court.

Walter Biggins worked for Hazen Paper Company in Holyoke, Massachusetts, as Technical Director. Using his educational experience as a chemist, Biggins had worked to develop new technical processes for paper coating. He had a history of frequent job changes during his 25-year career as a chemist in the paper industry. In 1976, at age 52 he joined Hazen Paper and worked there until 1986. However, his relationship with the company deteriorated, beginning in 1984 when he asked for a raise from $44,000 to $100,000. He felt that the company's growth and profitability had been affected positively by his technical contributions. The top managers of Hazen Paper Co., Thomas and Robert Hazen, refused his request, but offered him stock in the company; however, over time the stock offer never materialized. In 1986, just a few weeks short of his becoming vested in the company pension plan with 10 years service, Biggins was fired. Two years later, in 1988, Biggins filed a suit charging age discrimination. His attorneys agreed to take his case for a contingency fee of one-third of any monies awarded Biggins.

The Hazens stated that Biggins was fired because he refused to sign a noncompete agreement with the firm. Testimony in court revealed that Biggins's son Tim had started a company that provided consulting services to some of Hazen's clients and competitors. The senior Biggins had "moonlighted" by helping his son on a consulting basis. The Hazens stated that if Biggins had signed the agreement, he could still be working at Hazen Paper. Biggins countered that the Hazens knew of his moonlighting and had approved of it.

By 1993, when the case reached the U.S. Supreme Court on appeal, the Hazens had over $500,000 in attorneys' fees. The question before the Supreme Court was whether or not Biggins's dismissal was "willful" age discrimination, in which case any damages awarded Biggins would be doubled. In lower courts juries had ruled for Biggins that age discrimination had occurred and that it was willful. However, in spite of agreeing to pay $600,000 in damages to Biggins, the Hazens chose to fight the "willful" issue.

The U.S. Supreme Court ruled against Biggins in 1993 when it said that to be guilty of willful discrimination, employers must violate the Age Discrimination in Employment Act knowingly or recklessly. The impact of the decision was that interfering with an older worker's retirement benefits is not sufficient to get a determination of willful discrimination, thus doubling the damages. Therefore, Hazen Paper was guilty of age discrimination, but it did not have to pay the double damages.[53]

▲ **QUESTIONS**

1. Identify the applicable laws and EEO issues that are relevant in this case.

2. Assuming you had to argue for Hazen Paper, what would be your key points? For Biggins?

3. If you had been the HR Director at Hazen Paper in 1986, what would you have recommended to the Hazens as a way to address company concerns without creating age discrimination liabilities?

▲ NOTES

1. Adapted from "Sex Harassment Charges Rise," *USA Today,* October 2, 1992, 6A; Ellen Rapp, "Dangerous Liaisons," *Working Women,* February 1992, 56–61; Jo Ann S. Lublin, "Sexual Harassment Moves Atop Agenda in Many Executive Education Programs," *The Wall Street Journal,* December 29, 1992, B1, 4; and J. H. Foegen, "The Double Jeopardy of Sexual Harassment," *Business and Society Review,* Summer 1992, 31-35.

2. Sheryl A. Greene, "Reevaluation of Title VII Abusive Environment Claims Based on Sexual Harassment after *Meritor Savings Bank v. Vinson,*" *T. Marshal Law Review,* Spring 1987–1988, 29–65.

3. *Meritor Savings Bank (FBS) v. Vinson,* 106 S.Ct. 57 aff. and remanded 106 S.Ct. 2399 (1986).

4. Paul S. Greenlaw and John P. Kohl, "Proving Title VII Sexual Harassment: The Court's View," *Labor Law Journal* 431 (1992), 164–171.

5. David E. Terpstra and Douglas D. Baker, "Outcomes of Federal Court Decisions on Sexual Harassment," *Academy of Management Journal* 35 (1992), 181–190.

6. Jonathan A. Segal, "Seven Ways to Reduce Harassment Claims," *HR Magazine,* January 1992, 84–85.

7. Charles S. Miskind, "Sexual Harassment Hostile Work Environment Class Actions," *Employee Relations Law Journal* 18 (1992), 141–147.

8. *Bundy v. Jackson,* 641 F.2d 934 (D.C.Dir. 1981).

9. Dana S. Cornell, "Effective Sexual Harassment Policies: Unexpected Lessons from *Jacksonville Shipyards,*" *Employee Relations Law Journal* 17 (1991), 191–206.

10. Mark L. Legnick-Hall, "Checking Out Sexual Harassment Claims," *HR Magazine,* March 1992, 77–79.

11. Howard A. Simon, *"Ellison v. Brady:* A 'Reasonable Woman' Standard for Sexual Harassment," *Employee Relations Law Journal* 17 (1991), 71–80.

12. "Corporate Women," *Business Week,* June 8, 1992, 74–83; and "The Glass Ceiling," *Omaha World-Herald,* September 15, 1991, G1.

13. "Nepotism Rules Under Fire," *Omaha World-Herald,* October 11, 1992, G1.

14. *Dothard v. Rawlinson,* 433 U.S. 321 (1977).

15. *Donald v. Burlington Coat Factory,* No. C-1-86-0069 (S.D. Ohio 1987).

16. *Omaha World-Herald,* September 29, 1986. 3B.

17. *United Auto Workers v. Johnson Controls,* 111 S.Ct. 1196 (1991).

18. Adapted from Arthur Eliot Berkeley, "Job Interviewers' Dirty Little Secret," *The Wall Street Journal,* March 20, 1989, A13. Reprinted with permission of Arthur E. Berkeley, Memphis TN; and The Wall Street Journal © 1989 Dow Jones & Company, Inc. All rights reserved.

19. Julia Lawlor, "Survey: Good Maternity Leave Plans Hard to Find," *USA Today,* April 22, 1992, B1.

20. U.S. Census Bureau, November 1991.

21. *Arizona Governing Committee v. Norris,* 103 S.Ct. 3492 (1983).

22. *U.S. News & World Report,* November 3, 1986, 60.

23. John R. Hurdley, "Age Discrimination Cannot Continue," *HR Magazine,* October 1992, 74–76.

24. Adapted from Cathy Ventrell-Monsees, "Too Much of a Good Thing: Overqualified Older Workers," *Textbook Authors Conference Presentation* (Washington, D.C.: American Association of Retired Persons, 1992), 34–38.

25. *Sherrod v. Sears, Roebuck & Co.,* 36 EDP 36, 073 (1986).

26. *Public Employees Retirement System of Ohio v. Betts,* 109 S.Ct. 256 (1989).

27. For details, see Jonathan A. Segal, "New Rules for Waivers by Older Workers," *HR Magazine,* April 1991, 84–88.

28. U.S. Office of Special Education and Rehabilitative Services, Centers for Disease Control, as reprinted in *USA Today,* January 24, 1992, 6A.

29. Sue Tucker, "Mainstreaming Employees Who Have Disabilities," *Personnel Journal,* August 1992, 43–49.

30. All of the definitions used in the discussion of the Americans with Disabilities Act are those used in the act itself or in the *Technical Assistance Manual* issued by the EEOC.

31. *School Board on Nassau County, Florida v. Airline,* 107 S.C. 1123 (1987).

32. Ralph S. Berger and Gregory L. Lewis, "AIDS and Employment: Judicial and Arbitral Responses," *Labor Law Journal* 43 (1992), 259–280.

33. Lura K. Romei, "No Handicap to Hiring," *Modern Office Technology,* September 1991, 87–89.

34. For other examples, see James G. Frierson, *Employer's Guide to the Americans with Disabilities Act* (Washington, DC: The Bureau of National Affairs, 1992), 104–105.

35. For more details on the categories, see Robert S. Groban, Jr., "The Immigration Act of 1990: An Employer's Primer of Its New Provisions," *Employee Relations Law Journal* 17 (1992), 357–387.

36. C. Yang, "In Any Language, Its Unfair," Business Week, June 21, 1993, 110–111.

37. *Fragante v. Honolulu,* 87-2921, 9th Cir. (1989).

38. *Trans World Airlines v. Hardison,* 432 U.S. 63 (1977).

39. Robert M. Preer, Jr., "Reasonable Accommodation of Religious Practices: The Conflict Between the Courts and the EEOC," *Employee Relations Law Journal* 15 (1989), 86–91.

40. Julie Lawlor, "Employers Outshine Military Brass on Gay Rights," *USA Today,* February 9, 1993, B1.

41. Eric Matusewitch, "The Legal Status of Transsexuals in the Workplace," *Personnel Journal,* August 1988, 74–78.

42. Christine D. Keen, "Anti-Discrimination Laws May Begin to Broaden," *HR News,* August 1991, 8.

43. Lynn D. Mapes-Riordan, "Sex Discrimination and Employer Weight and Appearance Standards," *Employee Relations Law Journal* 16 (1991), 493–505.

44. John A. Gray, "Preferential Affirmative Action in Employment," *Labor Law Journal,* 43 (1992), 23–30.

45. Charlene Marmer Solomon, "Are White Males Being Left Out?" *Personnel Journal,* November 1991, 88–94.

46. Peter Brimelow and Leslie Spencer, "When Quotas Replace Merit, Everybody Suffers," *Forbes,* February 15, 1993, 80–102.

47. Adapted from John H. Taylor, "Backlash," *Forbes,* April 12, 1993, 48. Used with permission.

48. David Ankeny and David Israel, "Preparing for an OFCCP Audit," *HR Magazine,* September 1992, 99–102.

49. Michael D. Esposito, "Update Your Affirmative Action Plan," *HR Magazine,* July 1991, 59–61.

50. For more details on the process, *How to Respond to an EEOC Complaint* (Chicago: Commerce Clearing House, Inc., 1992).

51. James A. Burns, Jr., "EEO and Employer/Employee Rights," *Employee Relations Law Journal* 17 (1992), 521–529.

52. John F. Wymer and Deborah A. Sudbury, "Employment Discrimination 'Testers': Will Your Hiring Practices 'Pass'?" *Employee Relations Law Journal* 17 (1992), 623–633.

53. Adapted from information in Tony Mauro, "Age Bias Case Hinges on 'Wilfulness' Issue," *USA Today,* January 13, 1993, 9A; Paul M. Barrett, "How One Man's Fight For a Raise Became a Major Age Bias Case," *The Wall Street Journal,* January 7, 1993, A1+; and Paul M. Barrett, "Age Bias Law Can't Be Used in Suits Charging Pension Violations in Layoffs," *The Wall Street Journal,* April 21, 1993, B2.

Analyzing and Staffing Jobs

The first phase of staffing any organization is understanding the jobs to be done. What do people do in a given job? Is there a better way to do it? What specific qualifications must a candidate have to be able to do the job? When a person is hired, both management and the employee must have a clear understanding of the job to be performed. A job is the basic organizational unit of work.

Chapter 7 considers job analysis—the process of getting information about jobs performed in the organization. Various job analysis techniques are described, and the effect of jobs on human behavior is considered.

A recent development has greatly affected job analysis and the job descriptions and job specifications that come from it. As the Americans with Disabilities Act has been implemented, it has become important for employers to review their job analysis processes. The ADA requires employers to identify "essential functions" in each job to show whether persons with disabilities can do the job. The job analysis process will be critical to ADA compliance.

Chapter 8 examines the process involving organizational recruiting of a pool of possible employees. They may come from internal or external sources. College recruiting and executive search are two special means discussed. Recruiting takes on a special significance for many organizations when there is a tight labor market in an area. The goal of a good recruiting program is to generate a sufficient pool of applicants from which to make a choice.

A special set of problems is involved with recruiting international employees as many U.S.-based companies are discovering. Electronic databases are growing in usefulness. Such databases can provide more potential applicants that an employer might contact in different geographical areas. The chapter goes on to evaluate the costs and benefits of various courses of recruits for the potential employer.

Chapter 9 considers selecting the right employees. Once a pool of applicants has been generated, the actual selection for employment takes place. A variety of data sources can be used for selection decisions. Application blanks, interviews, tests, physical examinations, references, and assessment centers all can be used. However, regardless of the methods chosen, the goal is to choose the person most likely to do a good job for the organization. The method of offering employment to an applicant is examined. An area in the news today that elicits mixed feelings from people is personality and honesty testing.

The selection interview is familiar to virtually all who have had a job. Yet they are often poorly done and not good predictors of success on the job. The chapter deals with ways to improve the predictability of the selection interview. The chapter concludes by discussing reference checking and using medical exams in the selection process.

CHAPTER 7

JOB ANALYSIS

After you have read this chapter, you should be able to:

1. Define job analysis, job descriptions, and job specifications.

2. Identify how job analysis information is used in four other HR activities.

3. Explain how job analysis is used to comply with the Americans with Disabilities Act and other legal requirements.

4. Identify the five steps in conducting a job analysis.

5. Discuss three behavioral aspects common with job analysis.

6. List and explain four job analysis methods.

7. Write a job description and the job specifications for it.

HR Today and Tomorrow:
Computerized Job Analysis

The process of determining what is done on a job through job analysis traditionally has relied upon paper-and-pencil forms, personal interviews, and observations by trained analysts. However, just as the computer has changed many others areas of management, so has it enhanced the job analysis process. A variety of software programs now exist to guide the writing of job descriptions. Blending the administrative convenience of paper and pencil with the power of computerization, one of the new approaches is the Common-Metric Questionnaire: A Job Analysis System (CMQ). The CMQ System consists of a computer-scannable document that is fed into computer-based scoring and reporting services that are capable of recording, analyzing, and reporting thousands of pieces of information about any job.

The CMQ measures jobs on four major dimensions:

▲ Interpersonal   ▲ Decision making
▲ Mechanical and   ▲ Work context
   physical activities

For example, the interpersonal dimension examines the human resource responsibility, employee supervision, internal and external contact, and level and impact of interpersonal decisions in each job. There are a total of 242 core questions that comprise the CMQ; by pairing these questions with specially designed common-metric rating scales, the CMQ can collect 2,077 different pieces of work activity data.

The CMQ is written at an eighth-grade reading level to ensure its readability by employees with widely varying jobs and skills. Employees and/or their supervisors provide answers to CMQ questions, although some organizations opt to employ trained job analysts to complete the questionnaires on behalf of employees. Typically, it takes less than two hours for a CMQ administration.

An important feature of the CMQ is its behavioral specificity which allows for the objective verification of job analysis ratings and makes the basis for human resource decisions clear and understandable. This feature facilitates both management and employee acceptance of the job analysis process.

Following collection of the data, the CMQ System performs a variety of statistical analyses and produces a number of different reports. For job descriptions, the CMQ System produces Profile Description Reports that detail the work activities and environment of each job. Information on essentiality and frequency of activities is included. Empirically-derived dimension scores also are presented, providing a summary picture of each job. These dimension scores are actually percentage scores that reflect the degree to which a set of related work behaviors is present in a job.

The same data generated and presented in the Profile Description Reports is used to evaluate jobs for compensation purposes, produce performance-appraisal forms, and provide criteria for validating employment test results. The dimension scores for a set of jobs are used to identify the internal pay policies of an organization. Also, the CMQ System is capable of examining the external market value of the job. Using external pay survey data, the CMQ System calculates the current dollar value of each job or position. This information shows whether certain employees are underpaid or overpaid, or whether the entire compensation system is above market, at market, or below market.

For performance appraisal, the CMQ System uses behaviorally-based rating scales to measure performance of relevant work activities for a job. Performance thus is reviewed on job-related dimensions, rather than the personality traits found on many appraisal forms. These same performance measures can serve as criteria for selection test validation.

As is evident, the melding of computer technology with psychological methodology allows firms to develop more accurate and comprehensive job descriptions, more equitable compensation programs, and performance-appraisal systems that are more closely job related. In addition, these processes can provide better data for legal defensibility than once was available.[1]

T he most basic building block of HR management, **job analysis,** is the systematic way to gather and analyze information about the content of jobs, the human requirements, and the context in which jobs are performed. This information is essential to other HR management activities. It must be known what the exact tasks, duties, and responsibilities of a job are, and what type of knowledge, skills, and abilities are needed to perform the job.

Before discussing job analysis further, some clarification of terms is useful. A **job** is a grouping of similar positions having common tasks, duties, and responsibilities. Although the terms *job* and *position* often are used interchangeably, there is a difference in meaning. A **position** is a collection of tasks, duties, and responsibilities performed by one person. Thus, if a food store has seven individuals working as cashiers, there are seven positions associated with the one job of cashier.

Job analysis usually involves collecting information on the characteristics of a job that differentiate it from other jobs. Information that can be helpful in making the distinction includes the following:

- ▲ Work activities and behaviors
- ▲ Interactions with others
- ▲ Performance standards
- ▲ Machines and equipment used
- ▲ Working conditions
- ▲ Supervision given and received
- ▲ Knowledge, skills, and abilities needed

▲ NATURE OF JOB ANALYSIS

Job analysis provides the information necessary to develop job descriptions and specifications. In most cases, the job description and job specifications are combined into one document that contains several different sections.

Job Descriptions   A **job description** indicates the tasks, duties, and responsibilities of a job. It identifies what is done, why it is done, where it is done, and, briefly, how it is done. **Performance standards** should flow directly from a job description, telling what the job accomplishes and what performance is considered satisfactory in each area of the job description. The reason is clear. If employees know what is expected and what constitutes good or poor performance, they have a much better chance of performing satisfactorily. Unfortunately, performance standards often are omitted from job descriptions.

Job Specifications   The job description describes activities to be done in the job, while **job specifications** list the knowledge, skills, and abilities (KSAs) an individual needs to perform the job satisfactorily.

▼ **JOB ANALYSIS**

is a systematic way to gather and analyze information about the content of jobs, human requirements, and the context in which jobs are performed.

▼ **A JOB**

is a grouping of similar positions having common tasks, duties, and responsibilities.

▼

is a collection of tasks, duties, and responsibilities performed by one person.

▼ **A JOB DESCRIPTION**

specifies in written form the tasks, duties, and responsibilities of a job.

▼ **PERFORMANCE STANDARDS**

tell what the job accomplishes and what performance is considered satisfactory in each area of the job description.

▼ **JOB SPECIFICATIONS**

list the knowledge, skills, and abilities an individual needs to do the job satisfactorily.

KNOWLEDGE, SKILLS, AND ABILITIES (KSAs)

include education, experience, work skill requirements, personal requirements, mental and physical requirements, and working conditions and hazards.

Knowledge skills and abilities (KSAs) include education, experience, work skill requirements, personal requirements, mental and physical requirements, and working conditions and hazards. Job specifications for a remote visual display terminal operator might include a required education level, a certain number of months of experience, a typing ability of 60 wpm, a high degree of visual concentration, and ability to work under time pressure. An example of job specifications for a clerk-typist might be: "Types 50 words per minute with no more than two errors; successful completion of one year of high school English or passing of an English proficiency test." It is important to note that accurate job specifications are the KSAs a person needs to do the job, not necessarily what qualifications the current employee possesses.

Job Analysis Responsibilities

Most methods of job analysis require that a knowledgeable person describe what goes on in the job or make a series of judgments about specific activities required to do the job. Such information can be provided by the employee doing the job, the supervisor, and/or a trained job analyst. Each source is useful, but each has drawbacks. The supervisor seems to be the best source of information on what *should be* done, but the employee knows most about what actually *is* done. However, both may lack the knowledge needed to complete all sections of a job analysis questionnaire and draw the appropriate conclusions from it. Thus, job analysis requires a high degree of coordination and cooperation between the HR unit and operating managers.

The responsibility for job analysis depends on who can best perform various aspects of the process. Figure 7–1 is a typical division of responsibilities in organizations that have an HR unit. In small organizations, managers have to perform all the work activities in Figure 7–1. In larger companies, the HR unit supervises the process to maintain its integrity and writes the job descriptions and specifications for uniformity. The managers review the efforts of the HR unit to ensure accuracy and completeness. They also may request reanalysis when jobs change significantly.

Figure 7–1

Typical Job Analysis Responsibilities

HR UNIT	*MANAGERS*
▲ Prepares and coordinates job analysis procedures ▲ Writes job descriptions and specifications for review by managers ▲ Revises and periodically reviews job descriptions and specifications ▲ Checks on managerial input to ensure accuracy ▲ May seek assistance from outside experts for difficult or unusual analyses	▲ Complete or assist in completing job analysis ▲ Review and maintain accuracy of job descriptions and job specifications ▲ May request reanalysis ▲ Identify performance standards based on analysis information

Job Analysis and Productivity

Done properly, job analysis can be used to improve the productivity of an organization. By analyzing of a group of jobs, managers can provide the foundation for a strategic assessment of the jobs and the organization structure.[2] This way, they can identify how jobs must be adjusted or what jobs can be combined or eliminated. Specifically, job analysis is useful in answering such questions as the following:

▲ What are the jobs in the organization?

▲ How do each of the jobs relate to organizational objectives and strategic plans?

▲ How are the tasks, duties, and responsibilities grouped into jobs and functions?

▲ What are the reporting relationships of jobs in the organization structure?

▲ What knowledge, skills, and abilities (KSAs) are needed to perform various tasks, duties, and responsibilities in jobs?

▲ To what extent are employees with higher KSAs being paid to perform lower-level tasks, duties, and responsibilities?

▲ How should tasks, duties, and responsibilities be restructured so that jobs can be redesigned or eliminated?

Such usage of job analysis is beneficial to organizations of all sizes. For example, a small communications firm with 28 employees did an analysis of all jobs. When reviewing the information provided by both employees and supervisors, the director of administration and an outside consultant noted that several duties associated with maintaining customer service records were divided among three different employees, which often led to delays in recording customer payments and scheduling repair services. Therefore, the various customer service duties were regrouped so that two of the employees performed complete but different functions, and filing activities were concentrated with the third employee, who also served as backup for the other two.

Another use of job analysis is to audit jobs in the organization. By identifying what functions are being performed and how much time is being spent to perform them, managers and HR specialists can redesign jobs to eliminate unnecessary tasks and combine responsibilities where desirable. For example, in the sales department of a distribution firm, the sales representatives spent considerable time performing clerical tasks in the office instead of calling on customers. Job analysis revealed the situation, which was remedied by hiring specific clerical support employees. Consequently, the higher-paid sales representatives were able to spend more time actually selling.

Job Analysis and Other HR Activities

The completion of job descriptions and job specifications, based upon a job analysis, is at the heart of many other HR activities, as Figure 7–2 indicates. Job analysis is especially critical for compliance with a wide range of laws and government regulations, and these aspects are discussed later in the chapter. But even if the legal requirements did not force employers do job analysis, effective HR management would demand it.

Figure 7–2

Job Analysis and other HR Activities

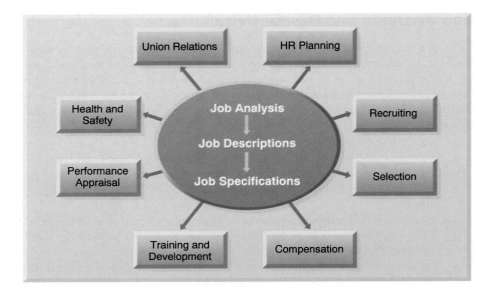

HR Planning   A key part of HR planning is the auditing of current jobs. A current job description provides the basic details necessary for this internal assessment, including such items as what jobs exist, what are the reporting relationships of jobs, and how many positions and jobs are currently present. Job analysis information also is one component considered in productivity analyses and organizational restructuring efforts.

Recruiting and Selection   Choosing a qualified person for an opening requires thorough knowledge of the work to be done and the KSAs that will be needed. Thus, before a clerk in a retail store can be hired, the manager must know if the person hired should be able to lift boxes, run a cash register, or keep the accounting books.

Job analysis is used to identify job specifications in order to plan how and where to obtain employees for anticipated job openings, whether recruited internally or externally. Internal selection decisions made through promotions and transfers of current employees to new jobs also must be based on required qualifications. For example, a job analysis in a small manufacturer of electric equipment showed that the Accountant II job, which traditionally had required a college-trained person, really could be handled by someone with high school training in bookkeeping and several years of experience. As a result, the company could select from within and promote a current accounting clerk. In addition to saving on recruiting costs, promotion can have a positive impact on employee commitment and career-planning efforts.

Compensation   Job analysis information is very useful in determining compensation. People should be paid more for doing more difficult jobs. Information from job analysis can be used to give more weight, and therefore more pay, to jobs with more difficult tasks, duties, and responsibilities.

Job analysis also can aid in the management of various employee benefits programs. For instance, a job analysis can be used to determine what functions can be performed by workers who have been on workers' compensation disability leave.[3]

Training and Development By providing a definition of what activities comprise a job, a job analysis helps the supervisor explain that job to a new employee. In addition, information from job descriptions and job specifications can be helpful in career planning by showing employees what is expected in jobs that they may choose to move to in the future. Job specification information can point out areas in which employees might need to develop in order to further their careers. Employee development efforts by organizations depend on the job descriptions and job specifications generated from job analyses.

Performance Appraisal By comparing what an employee is supposed to be doing to what the person actually has done, a supervisor can determine the level of the employee's performance and competency. Many organizations publicly state the ideal of "pay for performance," meaning that pay should reflect how well a person is performing a job, not just the level of his or her position. To do this, it is necessary to base comparisons on performance standards. Performance standards give the employee a clear idea of what is expected in each area of the job. The development of clear and realistic performance standards can reduce communication problems related to performance appraisals.

Safety and Health Job analysis information is useful in identifying possible job hazards and working conditions associated with jobs. From the information gathered, managers and HR specialists can work together to identify health and safety equipment needed, specify work methods, and train workers.

Union Relations In situations where workers are represented by a labor union, job analysis is used in several ways. First, job analysis information may be needed to determine if the job is one that should be covered by the union agreements. Specifically, if someone is a supervisor, management may be able to exclude the job and its incumbents from the bargaining unit. Also, it is common in unionized environments for job descriptions to be very specific about what tasks are and are not covered in a job. Where two unions exist, the union agreements between the two may specify which union has jurisdiction over certain tasks. For example, in the construction of one large office building, the plumbers' union had jurisdiction over all bathroom fixtures, except the installation of toilet stall dividers and doors. Those tasks were designated for members of the carpenters' union to perform.

Finally, well-written and specific job descriptions can reduce the number of grievances filed by workers. In one manufacturing plant, a worker refused to sweep up his work area and was disciplined. He filed a grievance and won, because cleaning his work area was not mentioned in the job description.

▲ LEGAL ASPECTS OF JOB ANALYSIS

Job analysis is especially critical for legal compliance with equal employment opportunity and other government regulations. Only by tying HR requirements to specific job factors can an employer defend HR practices as job related and a business necessity. Likewise, whether individuals must be paid overtime rates depends on their meeting specific conditions about the type, nature, and frequency of the tasks they perform.

Job Analysis and Americans with Disabilities Act (ADA)

The passage of the Americans with Disabilities Act (ADA) dramatically increased the legal importance of job analysis, job descriptions, and job specifications. The ADA requires that organizations identify the *essential functions* of jobs. Specifically, the ADA indicates that:

> essential functions means "the fundamental job duties of the employment position that an individual with the disability holds or desires." The term "essential functions" does not include the marginal functions of the positions.[4]

Having identified the essential job functions through a job analysis, an employer must be prepared to make reasonable accommodations. Again, the "core" job duties and KSAs must be considered. One manufacturing company with multiple buildings identified that participation in design planning meetings was an essential job function. To accommodate a physically disabled individual, who was otherwise qualified, the firm purchased a motorized cart and required that all design team meetings be held in first-floor, accessible conference rooms.

Evidence of essential functions may include, but is not limited to, the following:[5]

▲ Employer's judgment about which functions are essential
▲ Job descriptions prepared *before* advertising for or interviewing applicants
▲ Amount of time on the job spent performing the function
▲ Consequences of not requiring the employee to perform the function
▲ Terms of a collective bargaining agreement
▲ Work experience of past incumbents in the job and/or incumbents in similar jobs

What is noticeable is that job analysis is at the heart of virtually all of the above means of identifying essential functions. Particularly important is the specific reference to job descriptions. One industrial analyst has said,

> The *defensibility* or *verifiability* of the job analysis process and results will be crucial in ADA compliance. . . . In the post-ADA era, organizations must document and be prepared to defend *every* step in the progression from the identification of job activities to the final job description.[6]

One result of the passage of the ADA is increased emphasis by employers on developing and maintaining current and accurate job descriptions.[7] Also, many employers have had to revise their job specifications to reflect the essential prerequisite KSAs, rather that the "puffed up" ones favored by some managers and employees. More on how the ADA influences the writing of job descriptions and job specifications is contained later in the chapter.

The ADA makes it even more important that selection criteria and performance appraisal standards be clearly job related. The identification of the essential job functions forms the base for:[8]

▲ Developing selection interview questions
▲ Determining what competencies are needed to perform jobs
▲ Developing any selection tests to determine ability to perform essential functions
▲ Identifying performance standards for approving employee performance of the essential functions

▲ Identifying to what extent, if any, job accommodation can be made for a particular disabled individual

▲ Evaluating whether such accommodation would be an unreasonable hardship on the employer

An important part of job analysis is to obtain information about what duties are performed and the percentage of time devoted to each duty. As the ADA suggests, it generally is true that the percentage of time spent on a duty indicates its relative importance.

Another aspect is to identify the physical demands and environmental condition of jobs. The HR Perspective contains a sample page from a job analysis questionnaire for office jobs that requests such information.

Job Analysis and Employment Practices

The current interest in job analysis results from the importance assigned to the activity by federal courts. The legal defensibility of an employer's recruiting and selection procedures, performance-appraisal system, employee disciplinary actions, and pay practices all should rest on the foundation of a job analysis. In a number of court cases, employers lost because their HR processes and practices were not viewed by judges or juries as sufficiently job related. For instance, in the *U.S. v. City of Chicago* case, the courts found that the performance-appraisal system used by the Chicago Police Department discriminated against persons of Hispanic and African-American descent. The court ruled that the performance-appraisal system used was not tied directly enough to job-related criteria. Also, the selection and promotion exams for officer and sergeant were found to be discriminatory.[9]

Equal employment opportunity guidelines clearly require a sound and comprehensive job analysis to validate selection criteria. Without a systematic investigation of a job, an employer may be using requirements that are not specifically job related. For example, if a trucking firm requires a high school diploma for a dispatcher's job, the firm must be able to indicate how such an educational requirement matches up to the tasks, duties, and responsibilities of a dispatcher. It must be able to show that the knowledge, skills, and abilities needed by the dispatcher could be obtained only through formal education.

Job Analysis and Wage/Hour Regulations

Typically a job analysis identifies the percentage of time spent on each duty in a job. This information helps determine whether someone should be classified as exempt or nonexempt under the wage/hour laws.

As will be noted in Chapter 13, the federal Fair Labor Standards Act (FLSA) and most state wage/hour laws indicate that the percentage of time employees spend on routine, manual, or clerical duties affects whether or not they must be paid overtime for hours over 40 per week. To be exempt from overtime, the employees must perform their *primary duties* as executives (managers), administrative, and professional employees. *Primary* has been interpreted to be at least 50% of the time. Additionally, the exemption regulations state that no more than 20% (40% in retail settings) of the time can be spent on manual, routine, or clerical duties.

Another compensation-related issue, *comparable worth,* is a difficult issue that job analysis does not fully address. Much controversy has revolved around the degree to which jobs traditionally held by men (for example, those that require

HR Perspectives:

Job Analysis Obtains Information for ADA Compliance Purposes

One result of the Americans with Disabilities Act is that job analysis information on the physical dimensions of jobs must be delineated. With this information, job descriptions and specifications can be written to include the essential functions and knowledge, skills, and abilities (KSAs). By identifying the critical and necessary KSAs, employers will be prepared to deal with current employees with disabilities who apply for job transfers and promotions, as well as external applicants with disabilities who apply for jobs. One mistaken idea that many managers have is that the ADA affects only jobs that are extremely physical, such as those requiring climbing, heavy lifting, or other physical acts. But, many office jobs require employees who must see well enough to read computer screens, reports, and data print-outs. Or, many customer service jobs require hearing capabilities.

Gathering the necessary ADA information through job analysis may be done using a job questionnaire to obtain ADA-related information from current employees and their supervisors and managers. Below is a sample page from a job analysis questionnaire that requests such information.

Sample Page from Job Analysis Questionnaire (for office jobs)

PHYSICAL ACTIVITIES AND CHARACTERISTICS:

Please identify the physical characteristics of this position. For each type of activity, be as specific as possible on how often the activity is performed.

ACTIVITY	% of TIME	FREQUENCY
a. Seeing and Hearing well enough to:		
b. Standing and Walking well enough to:		
c. Climbing and Balancing well enough to:		
d. Body Movement (kneeling, crawling, stooping, reaching)		
e. Lifting, Pulling, and Pushing (give typical weights/frequency of activity)		
f. Dexterity (fingering, grasping, feeling)		

WORKING CONDITIONS:

Please describe the typical work environment in terms of heat, cold, noise, dirt, confined spaces, fumes, or other conditions different than in a normal office setting.

extensive physical skills) can be compared to those traditionally held by women. How do you compare the physical danger of underground coal mining with the mental and emotional demands of nursing or teaching?

Other legal-compliance efforts, such as those on workplace safety and health, can be aided through the data provided by job analysis, too. In summary, it is extremely difficult for an employer to have a legal staffing system without performing job analysis. Truly, job analysis is the most basic HR activity.[10]

▲ JOB ANALYSIS PROCESS

The process of conducting a job analysis must be done in a logical manner that follows appropriate psychometric practices. Therefore, a multistep process usually is followed, regardless of the job analysis methods used. Additionally, HR specialists must be aware of the behavioral reactions of employees to an intensive examination of their jobs.

Conducting a Job Analysis

The steps outlined here for a typical job analysis will vary if different methods are used or the number of jobs changes. However, the basic process is that shown in Figure 7–3.

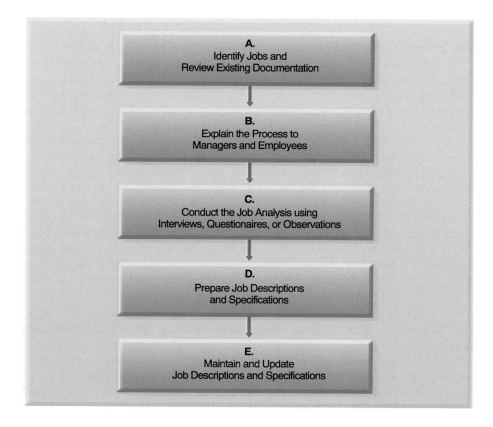

▲ **Figure 7–3**

Typical Job Analysis Process

A. Identify Jobs and Review Existing Documentation   The first step is to identify the jobs under review. For example, are the jobs to be analyzed hourly jobs, clerical jobs, all jobs in one division, or all jobs in the entire organization? Part of the identification phase is to review existing documentation, such as existing job descriptions, organization charts, previous job analysis information, and other industry-related resources. In this phase, those who will be involved in conducting the job analysis and what methods will be used are identified. Also specified is the way current incumbents and managers will participate in the process and how many employees' jobs will be considered.

B. Explain the Process to Managers and Employees   A crucial step is to explain the process to managers, affected employees, and other concerned people such as union stewards. Explanations should address the natural concerns and anxieties people have when someone puts jobs under close scrutiny. Items to be covered often include the purpose of the job analysis, the steps involved, the time schedule, how managers and employees will participate, who is doing the analysis, and whom to contact as questions arise.

C. Conduct the Job Analyses   The next step is actually gathering the job analysis information. Questionnaires might be distributed, interviews conducted, and/or observations made. Depending on the methods used, this phase often requires follow-up contacts to remind managers and employees to return questionnaires or to schedule interviews. As the job analysis information is received, analysts review it to ensure its completeness. Additional clarifying information can be gathered, usually in the form of interviews.

D. Prepare Job Descriptions and Specifications   All job analysis information must be sorted, sifted, and used when drafting the descriptions and specifications for each job. Usually, the drafts are prepared by members of the HR department, then they are sent to appropriate managers and employees for their review. Following the review, all necessary changes are made and the final job descriptions and specifications are prepared.

Once job descriptions and specifications are prepared, the manager should provide feedback to the current job holders, especially to those who assisted in the job analysis. One feedback technique is to give employees a copy of their own job descriptions and specifications for review. Giving the current employees the opportunity to make corrections, ask for clarification, and discuss their job duties with the appropriate manager or supervisor enhances manager/employee communications. Questions may arise about how work is done, why it is done that way, and how it can be changed. When employees are represented by a union, it is essential that union representatives be included in reviewing the job descriptions and specifications to lessen the possibility of future conflicts.

E. Maintain and Update Job Descriptions and Specifications   Once job descriptions and specifications are completed and reviewed with all appropriate individuals, a system must be developed for keeping them current. Otherwise the entire process, beginning with a job analysis, may have to be repeated in several years. Because organizations are dynamic and evolving entities, rarely do all jobs stay the same for years.

Someone in the HR department usually has responsibility for ensuring that job descriptions and specifications stay current. Employees performing the jobs and their managers play a crucial role because they are the ones closest to the jobs and know when changes occur. One effective way to ensure that appropriate reviews occur is to use job descriptions and job specifications in other HR activities. For example, each time a vacancy occurs, the job description and specifications should be reviewed and revised as appropriate *before* recruiting and selection efforts begin. Likewise, in some organizations managers review the job description during each performance-appraisal interview. This review enables the job holder and the supervisor to discuss whether the job description still describes the actual job adequately or whether it needs to be revised. In addition, a comprehensive and systematic review may be done during HR planning efforts. For many organizations, a complete review is made once every three years and more frequently when major organizational changes are made.

Behavioral Aspects of Job Analysis

A detailed examination of jobs, while necessary, can be demanding and threatening experiences for both managers and employees, depending on the situation. In one printing firm, two employees having different jobs in the production planning department refused to complete questionnaires. Through interviews it was learned that they were doing parts of each other's jobs, and they were concerned that management might discipline them or force them to change back to the way that the jobs had been designed by management.

Current Job Emphasis Job analysis can identify the difference between what is being performed in a job and what *should* be done. Because jobs may shift some due to the desires and skills of incumbent employees, determining what the "core" job is may require discussion with managers about the design of the job. For example, a woman promoted to office manager in one firm continued to spend considerable time opening and sorting the mail because she had done that duty in her old job. (Yet, she needed to be supervising the work of the eight clerical employees more and should have been delegating the mail duties to one of the clerks.) Her manager indicated that opening and sorting mail was not one of the top five tasks of her new job, and the job description was written to reflect this. The manager also met with the employee to discuss what it meant to be a supervisor and what duties should receive more emphasis.

Employees and managers also have some tendency to inflate the importance and significance of their jobs. Because job analysis information is used for compensation purposes, they hope that by puffing up their jobs, higher pay levels will result. Titles often get inflated also, as the "HR Perspective" illustrates.

The important point is that a job analysis and the resulting job description and specifications *should not describe just what the person currently doing the job does and what his or her qualifications are.* The person may have unique capabilities and the ability to expand the scope of the job to assume more responsibilities. The company would have difficulty finding someone exactly like that individual if he or she left. Consequently, it is useful to focus on the "core" jobs and needed KSAs by determining what the jobs would be if the current incumbents quit or were no longer available to do the jobs.

HR Perspectives:
Job Title Inflation

Inflation of job titles has been prevalent for years, but some HR specialists believe that it is becoming worse. Some firms give fancy titles in place of pay raises, while others do it to keep well-paid employees from leaving for "status" reasons. Some industries, such as banking and entertainment, are known for having more title inflation than others. For instance, banking and financial institutions use officer designations to enhance status. In one small midwestern bank, an employee who had three years' experience as a teller was "promoted" with no pay increase to "Second Vice-President and Senior Customer Service Coordinator." She

basically became the head teller when her supervisor was out of the bank and now could sign a few customer-account forms.

Other examples abound. Some secretarial employees are titled Administrative Assistants or Administrative Office Coordinators. Other examples include a car salesperson called a Vehicle Sales Consultant and a supply clerk called an Inventory Technician.

Even Japanese firms are becoming concerned about title inflation. Dai-Ichi Kangyo Bank ordered all of its employees to stop addressing each other differently based on rank. Terms such as *kacho* or *bucho* (Section Chief

or Department Head) generally had been used to follow such a person's name (i.e., Omura-bucho). Subordinates were called *kan* (i.e., Sakura-kan). However, the bank now wants all employees to use the *san* term (meaning Mr., Mrs., Miss) regardless of age, rank, or sex (i.e., Isicho-san). The purpose, according to the chairman of the bank, is "to get rid of a class system and treat people equally, imitating America." However, resistance is likely. One newly promoted *bucho* said, "We just got named *bucho* and we would like to be called *bucho* for a while."[11]

Employee Anxieties   One fear that some employees may have concerns the *purposes* of a detailed job investigation. The attitude behind such a fear might be, "As long as no one knows precisely what I am supposed to be doing, I am safe." Some employees may fear that an analysis of their jobs will put a "straight-jacket" on them, limiting their creativity and flexibility by formalizing their duties. However, it does not necessarily follow that analyzing a job will limit job scope or depth. In fact, having a well-written, well-communicated job description can assist employees by clarifying their roles and what is expected of them. Management should explain why the job analysis is being done, because some employees may be concerned that someone must feel they have done something wrong if such a searching look is being taken.

Resistance to Change   As jobs change, job descriptions and job specifications should be updated. Because people become used to working within defined boundaries, any attempt to change those "job fences" generates fear, resistance, and insecurity. Suggesting that it is time to revise job descriptions provokes anxiety because the employees' safe and secure job worlds are threatened. They may worry that they may have to take on new and difficult responsibilities. Also they may fear that change could have a negative impact on their pay. Because resistance to change is a natural reaction, managers should expect it and be prepared to deal with it. Perhaps the most effective way to handle this resistance is to involve employees in the revision process.

Managerial Straitjacket Through the information developed in a job analysis, the job description is supposed to capture the nature of a job. However, if it fails—if some portions of the job are mistakenly left out of the description—some employees may use that to limit managerial flexibility. The attitude, "It's not in my job description," puts a straitjacket on a manager. Such a situation is burdensome for management involved in changing jobs in response to changing economic or social conditions. Consequently, some nonunion employers refuse to show job descriptions to their employees. The idea is to make it difficult for an employee to say, "I don't have to do that because it is not in my job description." In some organizations with a unionized work force, very restrictive job descriptions exist.

Therefore, *miscellaneous clause* is the final statement in many job descriptions which consists of a phrase similar to "Performs other duties as needed upon request by immediate supervisor." This statement covers the unusual situations that may occur in an employee's job. However, duties covered by this phrase cannot be considered as essential functions under the ADA.

▲ JOB ANALYSIS METHODS

Information about jobs can be gathered in several ways. Four common methods are: (1) observation, (2) interviewing, (3) questionnaires, and (4) structured analysis. Combinations of these approaches frequently are used, depending on the situation and the organization.

Observation

Observation may be continuous or based on sampling. A manager, job analyst, or industrial engineer observes the individual performing the job and takes notes to describe the tasks and duties performed.

Use of the observation method is limited because many jobs do not have complete and easily observed job cycles. Observation may not be as useful for jobs that are "knowledge work" as it is for ones that are primarily physical work. For example, complete analysis of a pharmaceutical sales representative's job would demand that the observer follow the sales representative around for several days. Furthermore, many managers may not be skilled enough to know what to observe and how to analyze what they see. Thus, observation may be more useful in repetitive jobs and in conjunction with other methods. Managers or job analysts using other methods may watch parts of a job being performed to gain a general familiarity with the job and the conditions under which it is performed. Multiple observations on several occasions also will help them use some of the other job analysis methods more effectively.

Work Sampling The work sampling type of observation does not require attention to each detailed action throughout an entire work cycle. Instead, a manager can determine the content and pace of a typical workday through statistical sampling of certain actions rather than through continuous observation and timing of all actions. Work sampling is particularly useful for routine and repetitive jobs.

Employee Diary/Log   Another method requires that employees "observe" their own performances by keeping a diary/log of their job duties, noting how frequently they are performed and the time required for each duty. Although this approach sometimes generates useful information, it may be burdensome for employees to compile an accurate log. Also, employees sometimes perceive this approach as creating needless documentation that detracts from the performance of their work.

Interviewing

The interview method of gathering information requires that a manager or HR specialist visit each job site and talk with the employees performing each job. A structured interview form is used most often to record the information. Frequently, both the employee and the employee's supervisor must be interviewed to obtain a complete understanding of the job. During the job analysis interview, the interviewer must make judgments about the information to be included and its degree of importance.

Although research has shown that incumbents know their jobs best, their perceptions of their jobs can be affected by their most recent activities. If an incumbent is asked to describe his or her job at two different times during the year, the incumbent may use different words and focus on different duties. Further, the incumbent usually is aware that it may be beneficial to inflate the results because the analysis may be used in making pay decisions.[12]

Group interviews also can be used. Members of the group are usually experienced job incumbents and/or supervisors. The method is expensive because of the number of people involved, and it usually requires the presence of a representative from the HR department as a mediator. However, it does bring together a large body of experience concerning a particular job in one place at one time. For certain difficult-to-define jobs, group interviews are probably most appropriate.

The interview method can be quite time consuming, especially if the interviewer talks with two or three employees doing the same job. Professional and managerial jobs often are more complicated to analyze and usually require longer interviews. For these reasons, combining the interview with one of the other methods is suggested. For example, if a job analyst has observed an employee perform a job, a check on observation data can be made by also interviewing the employee. Likewise, the interview frequently is used as a follow-up to the questionnaire method.

Questionnaire

The questionnaire is a widely used method of gathering data on jobs. A survey instrument is developed and given to employees and managers to complete. The typical job questionnaire often includes questions on the following areas:

▲ Duties and percentage of time spent on each
▲ Special duties performed less frequently
▲ External and internal contacts
▲ Work coordination and supervisory responsibilities
▲ Materials and equipment used

▲ Decisions made and discretion exercised

▲ Records and reports prepared

▲ Knowledge, skills, and abilities used

▲ Training needed

▲ Physical activities and characteristics

▲ Working conditions

Sometimes it is beneficial for the employee and supervisor to complete the questionnaire independently. At least one employee per job should complete the questionnaire, which is then returned to the supervisor or manager for review before being used in preparing job descriptions.

The major advantage of the questionnaire method is that information on a large number of jobs can be collected inexpensively in a relatively short period of time. However, follow-up observations and discussions often are necessary to clarify questions arising from inadequately completed questionnaires and to deal with other interpretation problems.

The questionnaire method assumes that employees can accurately analyze and communicate information about their jobs. That may not be a valid assumption in all cases. Research shows that job analysis outcomes are affected by the employees selected to fill out the questionnaire. Different employees produce different job analysis outcomes.[13] Employees may vary in their perceptions of the job, and even in their literacy. The ability to read and write accurately could affect how employees use the questionnaire to describe their jobs. For these reasons, the questionnaire method is usually combined with interviews and observations to clarify and verify the questionnaire information.

One type of questionnaire sometimes used is a *checklist*. Differing from the open-ended questionnaire, the checklist offers a simplified way for employees to give information. An obvious difficulty with the checklist is its construction, which can be a complicated and detailed process.

Specialized Job Analysis Methods

Several job analysis methods are built on the questionnaire approach. The most prominent of these structured methods are described next.

Position Analysis Questionnaire (PAQ)

Position Analysis Questionnaire (PAQ) The PAQ is a specialized questionnaire method incorporating checklists. Each job is analyzed in terms of 27 dimensions composed of 187 "elements" of a job. A sample page is illustrated in Figure 7–4. The PAQ is divided into six divisions, each division containing numerous job elements. The divisions include:[14]

▲ *Information input.* Where and how does the worker get information to perform the job?

▲ *Mental process.* What levels of reasoning are necessary on the job?

▲ *Work output.* What physical activities are performed?

▲ *Relationships with others.* What relationships are required to perform the job?

▲ *Job context.* What working conditions and social contexts are involved?

▲ *Other.* What else is relevant to the job?

▲ **Figure 7–4**   Sample PAQ Item Mental Processes

INFORMATION PROCESSING ACTIVITIES

In this section are various human operations involving the "processing" of information or data. Rate each of the following items in terms of how *important* the activity is to the completion of the job.

Code	Importance to This Job (1)
N	Does not apply
1	Very minor
2	Low
3	Average
4	High
5	Extreme

— Combining information (*combining*, synthesizing, or integrating information or data from two or more sources to establish new facts, hypotheses, theories, or a more complete body of *related* information; for example, an economist using information from various sources to predict future economic conditions, a pilot flying an aircraft, a judge trying a case, etc.)

— Analyzing information or data (for the purpose of identifying *underlying* principles or facts by *breaking down* information into component parts; for example, interpreting financial reports, diagnosing mechanical disorders or medical symptoms, etc.)

— Compiling (gathering, grouping, classifying, or in some other way arranging information or data in some meaningful order or form; for example, preparing reports of various kinds, filing correspondence on the basis of content, selecting particular data to be gathered, etc.)

— Coding/decoding (coding information or converting coded information back to its original form; for example, "reading" Morse code, translating foreign languages, or using other coding systems such as shorthand, mathematical symbols, computer languages, drafting symbols, replacement part numbers, etc.)

— Transcribing (copying or posting data or information for later use; for example, copying meter readings in a record book, entering transactions in a ledger, etc.)

— Other information processing activities (specify)

SOURCE: E. J. McCormick, P. R. Jeanneret, and R. C. Mecham, *Position Analysis Questionnaire,* Occupational Research Center, Dept. of Psychological Sciences, Purdue University, West Lafayette, IN 47907. © 1969 by Purdue Research Foundation.

The PAQ focuses on "worker-oriented" elements that describe behaviors necessary to do the job, rather than on "job-oriented" elements that describe the technical aspects of the work. The assumption made in the PAQ is that comparing worker behaviors across jobs is more valid than trying to compare the technological similarities of different jobs in different work fields.

The PAQ can be completed by job analysts who interview workers and observe work as it is being done. It also can be completed by the worker. Although its complexity may deter many potential users, the PAQ is easily quantified and can be used to conduct validity studies on selection tests.[15] It also is useful in helping to ensure internal pay fairness because it considers the varying demands of different jobs.

Functional Job Analysis (FJA)   This method is a comprehensive approach to job analysis. FJA considers: (1) the goals of the organization, (2) what a worker does to achieve those goals in his job, (3) the level and orientation of what workers do, (4) performance standards, and (5) training content. A functional definition of what is done in a job can be generated by examining the three components of *data, people,* and *things.*[16] Identification of the levels of these components is used to identify and compare important elements of jobs given in the *Dictionary of Occupational Titles (DOT),* a standardized data source provided by the federal government.[17]

Dictionary of Occupational Titles (DOT)   Functional Job Analysis, as captured in the *DOT,* is a valuable source of job information, regardless of the job analysis method used. The *DOT* describes a wide range of jobs, samples of which are shown in Figure 7-5. A manager or HR specialist confronted with preparing a large number of job descriptions can use the *DOT* as a starting point. The job description from the *DOT* then can be modified to fit the particular organizational situation.

Computerized Job Analysis   As computer technology has expanded, efforts by researchers have led to the development of computerized job analysis systems. The opening discussion on the CMQ System illustrates one approach. Others also have been developed, and they all have several common characteristics. First, task statements are used that relate to all jobs. For example, the Occupational Measurement System (OMS) uses over 900 statements.[18] Second, individual employees indicate if and to what degree each task statement is present in their jobs. Figure 7–6 shows sample OMS statements.

A computerized job analysis system often can reduce much of the time and effort involved in writing job descriptions. These systems have banks of job duty statements that relate to each of the task and scope statements of the questionnaires, and the job questionnaire data is input into the computer using optical scan forms. Then the data from employees are used to generate behaviorally specific job descriptions. These descriptions categorize and identify the relative importance of various job tasks, duties, and responsibilities.

One advantage of these systems is that the results can be used to develop job evaluation weights and rankings that are tied into pay structures. As each job is scored, it is related to labor market pay data, so that jobs with higher scores are placed in higher pay grades. Also, any mismatches between job scores and pay survey data are highlighted, so that a more intensive job analysis using interviews or other methods can be conducted to resolve the discrepancies.

Another advantage of some of these systems is that because they are behaviorally based, they can identify the specific skills and abilities required in the job. Thus, job specifications that focus on specific KSAs for each job can be developed, which aids legal-compliance efforts and may improve recruiting, selection, training, and other HR efforts. Some of the skill-based approaches also define the proficiency levels for each job, so that performance appraisals can be made more job specific.[19]

Managerial Job Analysis   Because managerial jobs are different in character from jobs with clearly observable routines and procedures, some specialized methods have evolved for their analyses. One of the most well known was developed at Control Data Corporation and is labeled the *Management Position Description Questionnaire (MPDQ).* Composed of a listing of over 200 statements, the MPDQ examines a variety of managerial dimensions, including decision making and supervising.[20]

▲ **Figure 7–5**   Sample Job Titles from the *Dictionary of Occupational Titles*

SUPERVISOR (any industry) alternate titles: boss; chief; leader; manager; overseer; principal; section chief; section leader
Supervises and coordinates activities of workers engaged in one or more occupations: Studies production schedules and estimates worker-hour requirements for completion of job assignment. Interprets company policies to workers and enforces safety regulations. Interprets specifications, blueprints, and job orders to workers, and assigns duties. Establishes or adjusts work procedures to meet production schedules, using knowledge of capacities of machines and equipment. Recommends measures to improve production methods, equipment performance, and quality of product, and suggests changes in working conditions and use of equipment to increase efficiency of shop, department, or work crew. Analyzes and resolves work problems, or assists workers in solving work problems. Initiates or suggests plans to motivate workers to achieve work goals. Recommends or initiates personnel actions, such as promotions, transfers, discharges, and disciplinary measures. May train new workers. Maintains time and production records. May estimate, requisition, and inspect materials. May confer with other SUPERVISORS (any industry) to coordinate activities of individual departments. May confer with workers' representatives to resolve grievances. May set up machines and equipment. When supervising workers engaged chiefly in one occupation or craft, is required to be adept in the activities of the workers supervised. When supervising workers engaged in several occupations, is required to possess general knowledge of the activities involved. Classifications are made according to process involved, craft of workers supervised, product manufactured, or according to industry in which work occurs. Classifications are made according to workers supervised.

030.162-014 PROGRAMMER-ANALYST (profess. & kin.) alternate titles: applications analyst-programmer
Plans, develops, tests, and documents computer programs, applying knowledge of programming techniques and computer systems: Evaluates user request for new or modified program, such as for financial or human resource management system, clinical research trial results, statistical study of traffic patterns, or analyzing and developing specifications for bridge design, to determine feasibility, cost and time required, compatibility with current system, and computer capabilities. Consults with user to identify current operating procedures and clarify program objectives. Reads manuals, periodicals, and technical reports to learn ways to develop programs that meet user requirements. Formulates plan outlining steps required to develop program, using structured analysis and design. Submits plans to user for approval. Prepares flow charts and diagrams to illustrate sequence of steps program must follow and to describe logical operations involved. Designs computer terminal screen displays to accomplish goals of user request. Converts project specifications, using flowcharts and diagrams, into sequence of detailed instructions and logical steps for coding into language processable by computer, applying knowledge of computer programming techniques and computer languages. Enters program codes into computer system. Enters commands into computer to run and test program. Reads computer printouts or observes display screen to detect syntax or logic errors during program test, or uses diagnostic software to detect errors. Replaces, deletes, or modifies codes to correct errors. Analyzes, reviews, and alters program to increase operating efficiency or adapt to new requirements. Writes documentation to describe program development, logic, coding, and corrections. Writes manual for users to describe installation and operating procedures. Assists users to solve operating problems. Recreates steps taken by user to locate source of problem and rewrites program to correct errors. May use computer-aided software tools, such as flowchart design and code generation, in each stage of system development. May train users to use program. May oversee installation of hardware and software. May provide technical assistance to program users. May install and test program at user site. May monitor performance of program after implementation. May specialize in developing programs for business or technical applications.

166.117-018 MANAGER, PERSONNEL (profess. & kin.) alternate titles: manager, human resources
Plans and carries out policies relating to all phases of personnel activity: Recruits, interviews, and selects employees to fill vacant positions. Plans and conducts new employee orientation to foster positive attitude toward company goals. Keeps record of insurance coverage, pension plan, and personnel transactions, such as hires, promotions, transfers, and terminations. Investigates accidents and prepares reports for insurance carrier. Conducts wage survey within labor market to determine competitive wage rate. Prepares budget of personnel operations. Meets with shop stewards and supervisors to resolve grievances. Writes separation notices for employees separating with cause and conducts exit interviews to determine reasons behind separations. Prepares reports and recommends procedures to reduce absenteeism and turnover. Represents company at personnel-related hearings and investigations. Contracts with outside suppliers to provide employee services, such as canteen, transportation, or relocation service. May prepare budget of personnel operations, using computer terminal. May administer manual and dexterity tests to applicants. May supervise clerical workers. May keep records of hired employee characteristics for governmental reporting purposes. May negotiate collective bargaining agreement with BUSINESS REPRESENTATIVE LABOR UNION (profess. & kin.) 187.167-018

189.117-034 VICE PRESIDENT (any industry)
Directs and coordinates activities of one or more departments, such as engineering, operations, or sales, or major division of business organization, and aids chief administrative officer in formulating and administering organization policies: Participates in formulating and administering company policies and developing long range goals and objectives. Directs and coordinates activities of department or division for which responsibility is delegated to further attainment of goals and objectives. Reviews analyses of activities, costs, operations, and forecast data to determine department or division progress toward stated goals and objectives. Confers with chief administrative officer and other administrative personnel to review achievements and discuss required changes in goals or objectives resulting from current status and conditions. May perform duties of PRESIDENT (any industry) 189.117-026 during absence. May serve as member of management committees on special studies.

373.364-010 FIREFIGHTER (any industry)
Controls and extinguishes fires, protects life and property, and maintains equipment as volunteer or employee of city, township, or industrial plant: Responds to fire alarms and other emergency calls. Selects hose nozzle, depending on type of fire, and directs stream of water or chemicals onto fire. Positions and climbs ladders to gain access to upper levels of buildings or to assist individuals from burning structures. Creates openings in buildings for ventilation or entrance, using ax, chisel, crowbar, electric saw, core cutter, and other power equipment. Protects property from water and smoke by use of waterproof salvage covers, smoke ejectors, and deodorants. Administers first aid and artificial respiration to injured persons and those overcome by fire and smoke. Communicates with superior during fire, using portable two-way radio. Inspects buildings for fire hazards and compliance with fire prevention ordinances. marine division of fire department and be designated Firefighter, Marine (any industry). GOE: 04.02.04 STRENGTH: V GED: R4 M2 L3 SVP: 6 DLU: 81

SOURCE: U.S. Department of Labor, *Dictionary of Occupational Titles*, 4th ed., revised (Washington, DC: U.S. Government Printing Office, 1991).

SCOPE
▲ Do you have access to confidential agreements/contracts?   ▲ What foreign languages do you use (spoken/written) and the fluency required?   ▲ What is the total dollar value of customer accounts you represent or handle?   ▲ How much do you travel (%) as part of your job (foreign, domestic)?
TASK STATEMENTS
Include the time you spend *supervising* and *performing* each of the following: ▲ Analyzing training needs   ▲ Recommending purchase of computer software products   ▲ Entering data into computer system   ▲ Interviewing applicants for clerical openings   ▲ Administering disciplinary procedures   ▲ Developing methods for improving operations

▲ **Figure 7–6**

Sample Organizational Measurement System (OMS) Statements

SOURCE: Adapted from Organizational Measurement System, Technical Job Analysis Questionnaire.

Another approach is the *Executive Checklist (EXCEL)*. Closely related to the CMQ described earlier, approximately 250 statements are available on planning and decision making, product R&D, and sales, among others.[21] Notice that both of these methods focus on similar dimensions and make use of checklists completed by managers. If appropriate, these methods may be supplemented by use of interviews.

Combination Methods

There are indeed a number of different ways to obtain and analyze information about a job. No specific job analysis method has received the stamp of approval from the various courts in all situations. Therefore, when dealing with issues that may end up in court, care must be taken to document all of the steps taken. Each of the methods has strengths and weaknesses, and a combination of methods generally is preferred over one method alone.

▲ JOB DESCRIPTIONS AND JOB SPECIFICATIONS

The output from analysis of a job is usually a job description and job specifications. Together, they summarize job analysis information in a readable fashion. More than 100 managerial uses of job descriptions have been documented.[22] Primarily, they should permit defensible job-related actions. But in addition, they serve the individual employees by providing documentation from management that identifies their jobs.

Several events tend to prompt changes in job descriptions and job specifications. One is a change in organization size or structure (growth, restructuring, downsizing). Another is routine periodic review of jobs. The passage and implementation of the Americans for Disabilities Act (ADA) also caused many organizations to develop or update job descriptions.

▲ **Figure 7–7**   Job Descriptions and Specifications

JOB TITLE: Human Resource Assistant

REPORTS TO: Human Resource Manager

NO. _____
GRADE   OH 6
STATUS   Nonexempt
CLASS   Clerical

GENERAL SUMMARY:

Performs a variety of administrative support and clerical functions for human resource department personnel.

ESSENTIAL JOB FUNCTIONS:

1. Types correspondence utilizing a personal computer or typewriter.
2. Receives and directs telephone calls to appropriate departmental personnel.
3. Updates employee personnel records using information submitted by new or existing employees.
4. Prepares employee health-insurance claims for submission to insurance carriers, and discusses problem situations with carriers and employees to ensure timely payment of claims.
5. Prepares various reports such as benefit usage and employee turnover reports.
6. Performs other related duties as assigned by management.

KNOWLEDGE, SKILLS, AND ABILITIES:

1. Knowledge of general office practices and procedures.
2. Knowledge of written communication formats, business English, and composition.
3. Knowledge of medical insurance and employee benefit plans.
4. Knowledge of industry and employee benefit terminology.
5. Skill in operating personal computer.
6. Skill in operating various office equipment, such as adding machine, calculator, copy machine, facsimile machine, postage scale, typewriter, and telephone system.
7. Ability to type 60 wpm using computer word-processing software.
8. Ability to maintain confidentiality of classified information.
9. Ability to communicate with employees and other business contacts in a courteous and professional manner.
10. Ability to hear and speak well enough to converse over telephone up to 50% of the time.
11. Ability to see well enough to use computer efficiently and read computer reports and correspondence up to 80% of the time.
12. Ability to lift up to 20 lbs. on a frequent basis.

EDUCATION AND EXPERIENCE:

High school graduate or equivalent plus completion of several secretarial or general business courses. Experience in a secretarial office environment helpful.

The statements herein are intended to describe the general nature and level of work being performed by employees assigned to this classification. They are not intended to be construed as an exhaustive list of all responsibilities, duties, and skills required of personnel so classified.

Job Description Components

The typical job description, such as the one in Figure 7–7, contains three major parts: identification, general summary, and essential functions and duties.

Identification   The first part of the job description is the identification section, in which the job title, reporting relationships, department, location, and date of analysis may be given. Usually it is advisable to note other information that is useful in tracking jobs and employees through human resource information systems (HRIS), including the following:

▲ Job number
▲ Pay grade
▲ Fair Labor Standards Act (FLSA) status (exempt/nonexempt)
▲ EEOC Code (from EEO-1 Form)

General Summary   The second part, the general summary, is a concise summation of the general responsibilities and components that make the job different from others. One HR specialist has characterized the general summary statement as follows: "In thirty words or less, describe the essence of the job."

Essential Functions and Duties   The third part of the typical job description lists the essential functions and duties. It contains clear and precise statements on the major tasks, duties, and responsibilities performed. The most time-consuming aspect of preparing job descriptions is writing this section.

Preparing Job Descriptions

The ADA focused attention on the importance of well-written job descriptions. Legal compliance requires that they accurately represent the actual jobs. Some guidelines that grew out of the intensified effort to prepare legally satisfactory job descriptions are noted next.

Identifying Titles   Job titles should be descriptive of the job functions performed. For instance, one firm lumped all clerical jobs into four secretarial categories, even though the actual jobs were for such functions as payroll processor, marketing secretary, and receptionist. When the firm reviewed its descriptions, each job was given a function-related title. However, the jobs still were grouped for pay purposes into the same pay grades as before.

Such titles as Senior Worker or Lead Worker, Supervisor, Coordinator, Specialist, Manager, and Director are often misapplied. Titles should reflect the relative responsibilities in the organization and be tied to the pay grade system.

Writing the General Summary and Essential Functional Duties
Most experienced job analysts have found that it is easier to write the general summary *after* the essential functions and duties statements have been completed. Otherwise, there is a tendency for the general summary to be too long and to repeat some of the specific statements.

The general format for specific essential functions statements is shown in Figure 7–8. There is a real art to writing job descriptions that are sufficiently descriptive without being overly detailed. It is important to use precise action verbs

▲ **Figure 7–8**   Job Description Essential Functions Statements

JOB	ACTION VERB	TO WHAT APPLIES?	USING WHAT?	WHY/HOW/HOW OFTEN?
Payroll Clerk	Prepares	payroll reports	from time cards	on a biweekly basis
Benefits Manager	Conducts and analyzes	benefits usage	from claims reports	monthly to identify cost exceptions

that accurately describe the employee's tasks, duties, and responsibilities. For example, generally it is advisable to avoid the use of vague words such as *maintains, handles,* and *processes.* Compare the following statements: "Processes expense vouchers" to "Reviews employee expense reports, verifies expense documentation, and submits to accounting for payment." The second statement more clearly describes the scope and nature of the duty performed. However, it is just as important to avoid the trap of writing a motion analysis. The statement, "Walks to filing cabinet, opens drawer, pulls folder out, and inserts material in correct folder," is an extreme example of a motion statement. The specific duty statement, "Files correspondence and memoranda to maintain accurate customer policy records," is sufficiently descriptive without being overly detailed.

The language of the ADA has highlighted that the essential function statements should be organized in the order of importance or "essentiality." If a description has eight statements, it is likely that the last two or three are less essential than the first two or three. Therefore, it is important that job duties be arranged so that the most essential (in terms of criticality and amount of time spent) be listed first, and the supportive or marginal ones listed later. Within that framework, specific functional duties should be grouped and arranged in some logical pattern. If a job requires an accounting supervisor to prepare several reports, among other functions, statements relating to the preparation of reports should be grouped together. The *miscellaneous clause* mentioned earlier typically is included to assure some managerial flexibility.

Some job descriptions contain sections about materials or machines used, working conditions, or special tools used. This information is often included in the specific duty statements or in comment sections. Job descriptions of executive and upper-management jobs, because of the wide range of duties and responsibilities, often are written in more general terms than descriptions of jobs at lower levels in the organization.

Writing Job Specifications

Job specifications can be developed using a variety of information sources. Obviously, the job analysis process provides a primary starting point. Also, the analyst can obtain job specification information by talking with the current holders of the jobs and their supervisors and managers about the qualifications needed to perform the jobs satisfactorily. However, caution is needed here, because the characteristics of the current job occupant should not be the sole basis for the job specification statements. The current incumbent's job qualifications often exceed the minimum KSAs required to perform the job satisfactorily. Checking the job requirements of other organizations with similar jobs is another means of obtaining information for job specifications.

The ADA and Writing KSAs   In writing job specifications, it is important to list specifically those KSAs essential for satisfactory job performance. Only job-related items that are nondiscriminatory should be included. For example, a high school diploma should not be required for a job unless the manager can demonstrate that an individual with less education cannot perform the job as well. Because of this concern, some specification statements read, "High school diploma or equivalent acceptable experience."

In light of the ADA, it is crucial that the physical and mental dimensions of each job be clearly identified.[23] If lifting, stooping, standing, walking, climbing, or crawling is required, it should be noted. Also, weights to be lifted should be specified, along with specific visual and hearing requirements of jobs. Refer to Figure 7–7 for examples of KSA statements. Remember, these job specifications are the foundation for evaluating individuals with disabilities for employment.

Summary

▲ Job analysis is a systematic investigation of the tasks, duties, and responsibilities necessary to do a job.

▲ The end-products of job analysis are: (1) job descriptions, which identify the tasks, duties, and responsibilities in jobs; and (2) job specifications, which list the knowledge, skills, and abilities (KSAs) needed to perform a job satisfactorily.

▲ Job analysis information is useful in many HR activities: human resource planning, recruiting and selection, compensation, training and development, performance appraisal, safety and health, and union relations.

▲ Legal compliance in HR must be based upon job analysis. The Americans with Disabilities Act (ADA) increased the importance of job analysis and its components. Other legal requirements also can be based upon job analysis information.

▲ The process of conducting a job analysis is as follows:
  A. Identify jobs and review existing documentation.
  B. Explain the process to managers and employees.
  C. Conduct the job analyses.
  D. Prepare job descriptions and job specifications.
  E. Maintain and update job descriptions and job specifications.

▲ Job analysis, while seemingly straightforward, has several behavioral implications that managers should consider: employees' fears of the process and resistance to change, management's tendency to overemphasize the current job holder's qualifications, and the danger of job descriptions putting a straitjacket on managerial flexibility.

▲ Four general methods of gathering job analysis information are observation, interviews, questionnaires, and standardized methods. In practice, a combination of methods is often used.

▲ Writing job descriptions and job specifications can be challenging, and the essential functions and KSAs should be described clearly.

▲ REVIEW AND DISCUSSION QUESTIONS

1. Clearly define and differentiate among job analysis, job descriptions, and job specifications.
2. Job analysis is the most basic HR activity. Discuss why.
3. Discuss why the Americans with Disabilities Act (ADA) has heightened the importance of job analysis activities.
4. Explain how you would conduct a job analysis in a company that never had job descriptions.
5. How would you deal with behavioral reactions to job analysis by employees?
6. Describe the four general methods of analyzing jobs, devoting two sentences to each method.
7. Discuss how you would train someone to write job descriptions and job specifications for a small bank.

  JOB ANALYSIS FLIES AT DUNCAN AVIATION

Duncan Aviation, headquartered in Lincoln, Nebraska, provides flight service, private aircraft maintenance, and small jet airplane repair and renovation in Lincoln and seven other satellite locations in the United States. Duncan and its approximately 600 employees have established an industry reputation for outstanding customer service and technical quality. However, recently its Chief Executive Officer, J. Robert Duncan, recognized that the corporate culture in the firm needed to change if Duncan was to continue to develop and grow during the turbulent years ahead for the aviation industry. Consequently, with the assistance of an organizational consultant, a major restructuring was undertaken at Duncan Aviation. Particularly in the technical areas, the organization was restructured into a matrix format in which workers with different technical specialities working on the same aircraft could be grouped together in order to achieve greater coordination of activities. Even in administrative and support areas, the structure and reporting relationships of jobs were examined and changes made to allow for greater empowerment of nonmanagerial employees to take actions necessary to resolve customer and operational problems.

As if this undertaking were not ambitious enough, Duncan recognized that the firm's existing compensation and performance-appraisal systems had to be updated and redesigned to support the corporate culture and structural adjustments made. Finally, Duncan and the HR staff members recognized that the Americans with Disabilities Act, effective July 1992, meant that the firm should develop new and updated job descriptions and specifications to ensure compliance.

Upon the advice of the HR staff, it was decided that if the "new world" of Duncan Aviation was to become reality, the firm should start with a comprehensive look at all of the jobs in the firm, and a complete job analysis should be conducted for each. Duncan Aviation was fortunate to have a highly competent and professional HR staff, but like many similarly sized firms, that staff of five people was very busy with many other facets of HR work associated with the restructuring, in addition to expanding training efforts, implementing a flexible benefits program, and other ongoing HR activities. Consequently, the firm retained a team of consultants to assist with conducting the job analyses, preparing the job descriptions and specifications, and developing the new compensation and performance-appraisal systems.

The consultant team and Duncan's HR staff developed an extensive 12-page job analysis questionnaire tailored to the various job functions at the firm. The questionnaires were distributed to all employees, beginning in April, following training sessions held by the HR staff with all levels of managers and team leaders. In spite of the grumbling from some employees about the length of the questionnaire, over 90% of the questionnaires were returned within the allotted three-week period to the appropriate departmental and division managers for review, and then to the HR staff. At that point the job analyst from the consulting firm began the arduous task of writing approximately 200 job descriptions and specifications.

Throughout the drafting of the job descriptions and specifications, the consultants questioned Duncan managers and employees about the content and organization of the jobs in the new structure. A unique challenge was that in several of the technical areas the team leaders had been performing their newly redefined jobs for only one month. Consequently, it was common that follow-up interviews with team leaders and the managers above them had to be conducted. In addition, numerous organizational and work-flow issues were identified, and each of them had to be resolved before the job descriptions could be written correctly. Finally, a job-titling guide was developed so that the new job descriptions would contain appropriately descriptive titles without being too "puffed up."

Once draft descriptions were available, the HR staff coordinated the review of them by the appropriate managers and team leaders. Then the drafts were finalized and prepared for use in the development of the compensation system. The entire process of conducting the job analysis and developing finalized job descriptions and specifications took four months of intensive effort by all of the various participants. The process of developing the compensation and performance-appraisal systems took another three months, and the refinement and implementation of all of the components of the "new and improved" HR activities took a total of nine months. However, it was well worth all of the effort involved, because now Duncan Aviation has a comprehensive and well-designed foundation for managing its HR activities more effectively.[24]

▲ QUESTIONS

1. Discuss why job analysis was an essential part of the corporate change process at Duncan Aviation.
2. How does the process described in the case compare to the steps mentioned in the chapter?
3. Discuss how and why managerial and employee behavioral factors were important considerations in the case.

▲ NOTES

1. Robert J. Harvey, *CMQ: A Job Analysis System.* (San Antonio: The Psychological Corporation, 1991).

2. Lynda C. McDermatt, "Effective Use of a Job Analysis System in Strategic Planning," *Journal of Compensation and Benefits,* January–February 1987, 202–207.

3. Christopher K. Wood, "Job Analysis: A Powerful Tool for Managing Employee Disability," *Employee Benefit News,* February 1992, 43, 48.

4. "Equal Employment for Individuals with Disabilities." Federal Register 56(144), 35735.

5. Ibid.

6. Robert J. Harvey, "The Americans with Disabilities Act: Using Job Analysis to Meet New Challenges," Presented to IPMAAC Conference; Baltimore, MD, June 1992.

7. Pat Vacarro, "Review Job Descriptions," *Human Resource Executive,* June 1992, 20.

8. Susana R. Lozada-Larsen, "The Americans with Disabilities Act: Using Job Analysis to Meet New Challenges," (San Antonio: The Psychological Corporation, 1992).

9. *U.S. v. City of Chicago,* 549 F2d 415 (1977). *Cert denied* 434 US875 (1977).

10. *Guinn v. Bolger,* 36 FEP Cases 506 (D.D.C. 1984).

11. Adapted from Suzanne Scholsberg, "Is That a Job Title or Exercise in Adjectives?" *Omaha World-Herald,* May 12, 1991, 1G; and Urban C. Lehner, "Just Wait Until Your Young Teller-San tells Old-Chairman-San 'Get Lost'," *The Wall Street Journal,* April 23, 1992, B1.

12. H. Risher, "Job Evaluation: Validity and Reliability," *Compensation and Benefits Review,* January–February 1989, 24.

13. W. Mullins and W. Kimbrough, "Group Composition as a Determinant of Job Analysis Outcomes," *Journal of Applied Psychology* 73(1988), 657–664.

14. Ernest J. McCormick et al., *PAQ: Job Analysis Manual* (Logan, Utah: PAQ Services, 1977).

15. Michael Campion, "Ability Requirement Implications of Job Design: An Interdisciplinary Perspective," *Personnel Psychology* 42(1989), 9.

16. For more details, see Sidney A. Fine, *Functional Job Analysis Scales: A Disk Aid* (Milwaukee, WI: Sidney A. Fine, 1992).

17. U. S. Department of Labor, *Dictionary of Occupational Titles,* 4th ed., revised (Washington, DC: U.S. Government Printing Office, 1991).

18. For more details on the Organizational Measurement System, contact Steven Roop, Ph.D., College Station, Texas.

19. Kathleen K. Lundquist and David P. Jones, "Skill-Based Job Analysis," *Technical & Skills Training,* February–March 1992, 1–5.

20. W. W. Tornow and P. R. Pinto, "The Development of a Managerial Job Taxonomy: A System for Describing, Classifying, and Evaluating Executive Positions," *Journal of Applied Psychology* 61(1976), 410–418.

21. Susana R. Lozada-Larsen and Stephen B. Parker, "The Executive Checklist (EXCEL): A Common-Metric Questionnaire for Analyzing Supervisory, Managerial and Executive Jobs," presented to Sixth Annual Conference of the Society for Industrial and Organizational Psychology, St. Louis, MO, April 1991.

22. P. Grant, "What Use Is a Job Description?" *Personnel Journal,* February 1988, 45.

23. Matt Calker, "Tooling Up for ADA," *HR Magazine,* December 1991, 61–65.

24. Based on personal interviews with Duncan Aviation personnel, 1992–1993.

CHAPTER 8

RECRUITING HUMAN RESOURCES

After you read this chapter, you should be able to:

1. Define recruiting and outline a typical recruiting process.

2. Explain the basic recruiting concepts of labor force population, applicant population, and applicant pool.

3. Compare internal and external sources of candidates.

4. Identify three internal sources of candidates.

5. List and briefly discuss five external recruiting sources.

6. Discuss why the evaluation of recruiting efforts is important.

HR Today and Tomorrow:
Recruiting Retirees

Wait a minute! Look at that title again . . . recruiting retirees? Is that some kind of misprint? Didn't those people retire and leave the workforce on purpose? Weren't the companies pleased to replace them with younger employees? What's going on here?

As people with scarce skills retire, they are *not* always replaced with younger workers. In some cases their exact combinations of skills and experience may not be replaceable. In other cases, a lot of time and training are necessary to replace a retired worker. So sometimes a company tries to get its retirees back. Gruman Corporation of Bethpage, New York, rehires its skilled machinists, inspectors, and engineers after they have retired when it needs more help rather than seeking and training new people. To avoid pension dilemmas, it rehires its former employees through an outside agency as independent contractors for temporary jobs. A manager at Travelers, the Hartford, Connecticut insurance firm, notes, "Business is not going to be able to go back to the days when it overstaffed for peak needs."

Companies can recruit good retirees as an alternative form of staffing—one that requires little training time and expense. A manager at NCR Corporation, Dayton, Ohio, notes that "There are 10 million retirees sitting at home who want to work, but who are unable to get jobs." He believes that since the pool of young people entering the workforce is shrinking, and the demand for skilled workers is increasing, America cannot afford to fully retire educated, skilled workers.

That sounds reasonable, but companies like Gruman, Travelers, NCR, McDonald's, and Days Inn who use retirees extensively are in the minority. Part of the reason is a lingering belief in myths about older people—that they are clumsy, slow, set in their ways, ill prepared for promotion, and have more accidents. Research shows older workers to be more reliable, easier to train, more cooperative, and more competent than their younger counterparts. They are safer, too. They can be retrained in new technologies, have lower absenteeism, and are better salespeople.

Although some older people work to put food on the table, others work to supplement a very adequate retirement income to have extra luxuries, and still others work simply because they want to do so. Many enjoy the social aspects of working, as well as gaining a sense of accomplishment from using the skills they have spent a lifetime developing. But current Social Security rules, which create financial incentives to remain at work until age 62, also create disincentives to work after age 65. In addition, most corporate retirement policies encourage retirement at age 65 or before.

Days Inn never intended to be an advocate for hiring senior workers, but in the mid-1980s a labor shortage left the firm trying to grow without the employees it needed. Managers attended a job fair in Atlanta, hired some older people, and were extremely pleased with the results. Six years later, 25% of the 600 employees at Days Inn's national reservation centers are seniors. A Senior Vice-President says, "We did it because it made good business sense. We were not trying to be good corporate citizens. We were trying to run a business."

Employers can set up a "retiree job bank" by identifying those older employees they would like to reemploy after retirement, perhaps on a temporary basis whenever the work load requires it. Then they must keep track of those employees after they leave. Policy decisions about how long a temporary assignment can last must be made, and pensions must be written so that the retiree is not penalized for returning to work. The question of benefits must be thought through as well. Such efforts seem to be well worthwhile in view of the positive reports received thus far on returning retirees to the workplace.

In summary, a growing number of employers are recruiting retirees, both their own and those from other companies as well. Perhaps what will have to change is the idea that a person is either employed or not employed, retired or not retired. There are clearly points in between.[1]

If you can't staff your store, you can't operate your store.

Richard Pires

Recruiting is the process of generating a pool of qualified applicants for organizational jobs. If the number of available candidates only equals the number of people to be hired, there is no selection—the choice has already been made. The organization must either leave some openings unfilled or take all the candidates.

Recruiting efforts may be viewed as either continuous or intensive. *Continuous* efforts to recruit have the advantage of keeping the employer in the recruiting market. For example, with college recruiting, it appears to be advantageous for some organizations to have a recruiter on a given campus each year. Those employers that visit a campus only occasionally are less likely to build a following in that school over time.

Intensive recruiting may take the form of a vigorous recruiting campaign aimed at hiring a given number of employees, usually within a short period of time. Such efforts may be the result of failure in the HR planning system to identify needs in advance or to recognize drastic changes in workforce needs due to unexpected work loads.

> ▼ **RECRUITING**
>
> is the process of generating a pool of qualified applicants for organizational jobs.

▲ THE RECRUITING PROCESS

An HR plan helps determine the current and projected need for people in various job categories and any cultural-diversity goals the organization may have set. Then the recruiting and selection processes operationalize the HR plan. Thus, recruiting efforts translate human resource plans into action. They also fill openings when unexpected vacancies occur. Even during periods of reduced hiring, implementation of long-range plans means keeping in contact with outside recruiting sources to maintain visibility while also maintaining employee recruiting channels in the organization. These activities are essential for management to be able to step up recruiting activity on short notice. The steps in a typical recruiting process are identified in Figure 8–1.

Regardless of organization size, the following decisions about recruiting must be made:

▲ How many people does an organization need?
▲ Where will the organization get these people?
▲ What special skills and experience are *really* necessary?
▲ How will the organization spread its message of openings?
▲ How effective are the recruiting efforts?

In larger organizations, a manager notifies someone in the HR unit that an opening needs to be filled. Submission of a *requisition* to the HR unit, much as a supply requisition is submitted to the purchasing department, is a common way to trigger recruiting efforts. The HR representative and the manager must *review the job description and job specifications* so that both have clear and up-to-date information on the job duties and the specific qualifications desired of an applicant. For example, whether a job is for a computer programmer or for a

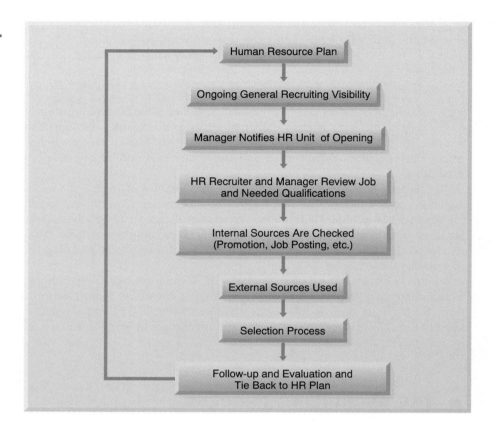

systems analyst would significantly affect the screening of applicants and the content of a recruiting advertisement. Familiarity with the job makes it easier to identify the minimum qualifications someone needs to perform the job satisfactorily.

Following this review, the actual recruiting effort begins. *Internal sources* of available recruits through transfers, promotions, and job posting usually are checked first. Then *external sources* are contacted as required, and all applicants are screened through the selection process. *Follow-up* is necessary to evaluate the effectiveness of the recruiting efforts and to tie those efforts back into the human resource plan and ongoing recruiting activities.

Organizational Recruiting Responsibilities

In small organizations the recruiting process is simplified. For many positions an advertisement in the local paper may be enough to tap the local labor market. In very small organizations the owner/manager often places the ad, determines the recruiting criteria, and makes the decision. However, for some specialist jobs, a regional or national search may be undertaken. Figure 8–2 shows a typical distribution of recruiting responsibilities between the HR department and managers in larger organizations.

HR UNIT	MANAGERS
▲ Forecasts recruiting needs ▲ Prepares copy for recruiting ads and campaigns ▲ Plans and conducts recruiting efforts ▲ Audits and evaluates recruiting activities	▲ Anticipate needs for employees to fill vacancies ▲ Determine KSAs needed from applicants ▲ Assist in recruiting effort with information about job requirements ▲ Review recruiting efforts

▲ **Figure 8–2**

Typical Recruiting Responsibilities

▲ RECRUITING AS PUBLIC RELATIONS

For many people the only contact they will have with an organization occurs when they apply for a job there. Of course, the chances are good they will not get the job. If 50 people apply for a job and one is hired, 49 were *not* hired and are potentially unhappy. It is at this point that recruiting can do real damage to the perceptions people have of that organization. Further, recent research shows that recruiting delays, recruiter competence, and other variables that can only be interpreted as commitment to doing a good job in recruiting affect job seekers' decisions.[2]

Realistic Job Previews   Most job seekers appear to have little information initially about the organizations to which they apply for jobs. But the information they receive from prospective employers in the recruiting/selection process is apparently given considerable weight in deciding whether or not to accept a job. Pay, nature of the work, geographic location, and opportunity for promotion are important to almost everyone. In addition, job security is particularly important to blue-collar applicants.

Some employers oversell their jobs in recruiting advertisements, making them appear better than they really are. A **realistic job preview (RJP)** is the process through which an interviewer provides a job applicant with an accurate picture of a job. RJPs have been linked to reduced turnover. Of course, they also may lead to an increase in candidates who refuse job offers. But realistic recruiting presentations are obviously the ethical choice regardless of the impact on the recruiting effort.

▼ **A REALISTIC JOB PREVIEW (RJP)**

is the process through which an interviewer provides a job applicant with an accurate picture of a job.

▲ BASIC RECRUITING CONCEPTS

Recruiting and selection are closely related. Recruiting determines the types of applicants from which selection will be made. Selection involves the actual choosing of a new employee based on predictive information obtained from that applicant. Both take place in a labor market environment. To understand the environment in which recruiting takes place, three different groups must be considered. Those three groups are *labor force population, applicant population,* and *applicant pool.*

The **labor force population** includes all individuals who are available for selection if all possible recruitment strategies are used. This vast array of possible

▼ **THE LABOR FORCE POPULATION**

includes all individuals who are available for selection if all possible recruitment strategies are used.

▼ THE APPLICANT POPULATION

is a subset of the labor force population that is available for selection using a particular recruiting approach.

applicants may be reached in very different ways. Different recruiting methods—for example, newspaper ads versus college recruiting—will reach different segments of the population.

The **applicant population** is a subset of the labor force population that is available for selection using a particular recruiting approach. For example, an organization might limit its recruiting for management trainees to MBA graduates from the top ten business schools. This recruiting method will result in a very different group of applicants from those who would have applied had the employer chosen to advertise openings for management trainees on a local radio station.

At least four recruiting decisions affect the nature of the applicant population:

1. *Recruiting method* (advertising medium chosen and use of employment agencies)
2. *Recruiting message* (what is said about the job and how it is said)
3. *Applicant qualifications required* (education level and amount of experience necessary)
4. *Administrative procedures* (time of year recruiting is done, follow-ups with applicants, and use of previous applicant files)

▼ THE APPLICANT POOL

consists of all persons who are actually evaluated for selection.

The **applicant pool** consists of all persons who are actually evaluated for selection. Many factors can affect the size of the applicant pool. For example, the organization mentioned previously is likely to interview only a small percentage of the MBA graduates at the top ten business schools because not all graduates will want to be interviewed. The applicant population at this step will depend on the reputation of the organization and industry as a place to work, the screening efforts of the organization, and the information available to the applicant population. Assuming a suitable candidate can be found, the final selection is made from the applicant pool.

Relevant Labor Markets

An organization will be most successful in finding the right applicants if it recruits in the relevant labor market, even globally as the "HR Perspective" indicates. There are many ways to define labor markets, including by geographical area, type of skill, and education level. For our purposes here, *labor market* will be defined as individuals with similar skills or experience. Some labor market segments might include managerial, clerical, professional and technical, and blue collar. Each can be further divided. Some markets are local, others regional, some national, and there are international labor markets as well. For example, an interesting labor market segment opened up with the demise of the old Soviet Union. A number of excellent Soviet scientists became available because of the absence of job opportunities in their own countries. Several research organizations around the world quickly recruited them in that labor market.

Recruiting locally for a job market that is really national will result in disappointing applicant rates. For example, attempting to recruit a senior accounting faculty member in a small town is likely not to be successful. Conversely, it may not be necessary to recruit nationally for workers in unskilled positions on the assembly line. The job qualifications needed and the distribution of the labor supply determine which labor market is relevant. Successful recruiting efforts depend on identifying and pursuing the relevant labor market.

HR Perspectives:
Global Issues in Recruiting

Much international talent exists in a global labor market, but identifying the exact talent needed is not always easy. Nor is it an easy task to train and place people properly.

Boston-based Gillette International is one of the companies that has been successful in recruiting and placing international talent. Foreign Gillette subsidiaries hire top business students from local universities and train them for six months in the home country. Then they are sent to Boston for an 18-month training session in two of the major disciplines such as marketing, manufacturing, or HR.

Each trainee is paired with an executive mentor. If trainees are successful (80% are), they are usually offered entry-level management positions in the division in the geographic area of the home country. Gillette's International Personnel Director says, "The person we're looking for is someone who says, 'Today it's Manila. Tomorrow it's the U.S., four years from now, it's Peru or Pakistan.' We work hard at finding people who aren't parochial, and who want international careers."

He also notes that the program brings in international human resources at the entry level and at a cost way below recruiting a senior-level foreign executive later. "I'd say total, including airfare, visa processing, and gross costs, it's probably running us around $20,000 to $25,000 per trainee per year. An expatriate will cost you five to ten times that. I'm amazed more companies don't do this—there are only a handful."[3] Because the program works well, Gillette may find that many more companies *will* follow their innovative lead.

▲ INTERNAL VERSUS EXTERNAL RECRUITING

Pros and cons are associated with both promotion from within (internal source for recruitment) and hiring outside the organization (external recruitment) to fill openings. Figure 8–3 summarizes some of the most commonly cited advantages and disadvantages of each type of source.

Promotion from within generally is thought to be a positive force in rewarding good work, and some organizations use it well indeed. However, if followed exclusively, it has the major disadvantage of perpetuating old ways of operating. Recruiting externally can infuse the organization with new ideas. Also, it may be cheaper to recruit professionals such as accountants or computer programmers from outside than to train less skilled people promoted from within the organization. But recruiting from outside the organization for any but entry-level positions presents the problem of adjustment time for the new persons. Another serious drawback to external recruiting is the negative impact on current employees that often results from selecting an outsider instead of promoting a current employee.

Most organizations combine the use of internal and external methods. Organizations that operate in rapidly changing environments and competitive conditions may need to place a heavier emphasis on external sources as well as developing internal sources. However, for those organizations existing in environments that change slowly, promotion from within may be more suitable. A look at both internal and external sources of employees follows.

▲ **Figure 8–3**

Advantages and Disadvantages of
Internal and External Sources

ADVANTAGES	DISADVANTAGES
Internal	
▲ Morale of promotee	▲ Inbreeding
▲ Better assessment of abilities	▲ Possible morale problems of those
▲ Lower cost for some jobs	not promoted
▲ Motivator for good performance	▲ "Political" infighting for promotions
▲ Causes a succession of promotions	▲ Need strong management-
▲ Have to hire only at entry level	development program
External	
▲ "New blood" bringing new	▲ May not select someone who will
perspectives	"fit" the job or organization
▲ Cheaper and faster than training	▲ May cause morale problems for
professionals	internal candidates not selected
▲ No group of political supporters in	▲ Longer "adjustment" or orientation
organization already	time
▲ May bring industry insights	

▲ INTERNAL RECRUITING SOURCES

Among internal recruiting sources are present employees, friends of present employees, former employees, and previous applicants. Promotions, demotions, and transfers also can provide additional people for an organizational unit, if not for the entire organization.

Among the ways in which internal recruiting sources have an advantage over external sources is that they allow management to observe the candidate for promotion (or transfer) over a period of time and to evaluate that person's potential and specific job performance. Second, an organization that promotes its own employees to fill job openings may give its employees added motivation to do a good job. Employees may see little reason to do more than just what the current job requires if management's policy is to hire externally. This concern is indeed the main reason why an organization generally considers internal sources of qualified applicants first.

Job Posting and Bidding

One procedure for recruiting employees for other jobs within the organization is a *job posting and bidding* system. Employees can be notified of all job vacancies by posting notices, circulating publications, or in some other way inviting employees to apply for jobs. In a unionized organization, job posting and bidding can be quite formal; the procedure often is spelled out in the labor agreement. Seniority lists may be used by organizations that make promotions based strictly on seniority.[4]

Answers to many potential questions must be anticipated: What happens if there are no qualified candidates on the payroll to fill new openings? Is it necessary for employees to inform their supervisors that they are bidding for another job? How much notice should an employee be required to give before transferring to a new department? When should job notices not be posted?

A job posting system gives each employee an opportunity to move to a better job within the organization. Without some sort of job posting and bidding, it is difficult to find out what jobs are open elsewhere in the organization. The most common method employers use to notify current employees of openings is to post notices on bulletin boards in locations such as employee lounges, cafeterias, and near elevators.

Job posting and bidding systems can be ineffective if handled improperly. Jobs should be posted *before* any external recruiting is done. The organization must allow a reasonable period of time for present employees to check notices of available jobs before it considers external applicants. When employees' bids are turned down, they should be informed of the reasons.

Internal Recruiting Database

Computerized internal talent banks, or *skills inventories,* are used to furnish a listing of the talents, abilities, and skills available for organizations. Travelers, the insurance giant, was probably the first to use such a listing for retirees willing to work part time, but Wells Fargo Bank in California also has used the idea. Retirees are but one possible source of input for the database. A listing of the skills and interests of current employees lends itself to many useful applications.

Current Employee Referrals

A reliable source of people to fill vacancies is composed of friends and/or family members of current employees. Employees can acquaint potential applicants with the advantages of a job with the company, furnish letters of introduction, and encourage them to apply. These are external applicants coming from an internal information source. This source is usually one of the most effective methods of recruiting because many qualified people can be reached at a low cost. In an organization with a large number of employees, this approach can develop quite a large pool of potential employees. For example, Fidelity Investments developed a program to recruit data-processing employees. Employees were offered $2,000 for each person they recruited who remained on the payroll over a year. The program brought in 73 workers in one year at a cost of $97,000—a fraction of the fees employment agencies would have charged.[5]

However, a word of caution is appropriate. When the organization has an underrepresentation of a particular protected class, word-of-mouth referral has been considered a violation of Title VII of the Civil Rights Act. An organization composed primarily of nonprotected-class individuals presumably would refer more of the same for consideration as employees.

Promotion and Transfers

Many organizations choose to fill vacancies through promotions or transfers from within whenever possible.[6] Although most often successful, promotions from within have some drawbacks as well. The person's performance on one job may not be a good predictor of performance on another, because different skills may be required on the new job. For example, every good worker does not make a good supervisor. In most supervisory jobs an ability to accomplish the work through others requires skills in influencing and dealing with people that may not have been a factor in nonsupervisory jobs.

It is clear that people in pyramidal organizations may have less frequent chances for promotion. Also, in most organizations, promotions may not be an effective way to speed the movement of protected-class individuals up through the organization if that is an organizational concern.

Recruiting Former Employees and Applicants

Former employees and former applicants are also good internal sources for recruitment. In both cases, there is a time-saving advantage, because something is already known about the potential employee.

Former Employees   Former employees are considered an internal source in the sense that they have ties to the company. Some retired employees may be willing to come back to work on a part-time basis or may recommend someone who would be interested in working for the company. Sometimes people who have left the company to raise a family or complete a college education are willing to come back to work after accomplishing those personal goals. Individuals who left for other jobs might be willing to return for a higher rate of pay. Job sharing and flextime programs may be useful in luring back retirees or others who previously worked for the organization.

The main advantage in hiring former employees is that their performance is known. But many managers are not willing to take back an employee. A more competitive business climate may change managers' attitudes toward a high-performing former employee. It depends on the reasons the employee left in the first place. If there were problems with the boss or company, it is unlikely that matters have improved in the employee's absence. Concerns that employers have in rehiring former employees include trade-secret infringements, vindictiveness, and fear of morale problems among those who stayed.

Former Applicants   Another source of applicants can be found in the organizational files. Although not entirely an internal source, those who have previously applied for jobs can be recontacted by mail, a quick and inexpensive way to fill an unexpected opening. Although "walk-ins" are likely to be suitable only for filling unskilled and semiskilled jobs, some professional openings can be filled by turning to the filed applications. One firm that needed two cost accountants immediately contacted qualified previous applicants and was able to hire two individuals who were disenchanted with their current jobs.

▲ EXTERNAL RECRUITING SOURCES

If internal sources do not produce an acceptable candidate, many external sources are available. These sources include schools, colleges and universities, employment agencies, temporary-help firms, labor unions, media sources, and trade and competitive sources.

School Recruiting

High schools or vocational/technical schools may be a good source of new employees for many organizations. A successful recruiting program with these insti-

HR Perspectives:

Research on Recruiting and Diversity

Susan Jackson and five colleagues at New York University studied interpersonal variables concerning recruiting. The study, reported in the *Journal of Applied Psychology,* looked at 93 executive teams in bank holding companies over a four-year period.[7]

They found that the amount of turnover in the groups could be predicted by the extent to which group members differed in regard to several demographic variables. Thus,

more heterogeneous (dissimilar) groups showed higher turnover. Further, the use of internal recruiting predicted subsequent team homogeneity (similarity)—which in turn led to less turnover. Thus, internal recruiting leads to less turnover and similarity group members.

Recruiting potentially can lead to a work group composed of members who all look about the same

demographically. There is little reason for people to leave such a comfortable situation. Unfortunately, there may be violation of Title VII of the Civil Rights Act. Often there is also an inability in the group to change to meet new circumstances. Alternatively, external recruiting can lead to a very diverse workforce that is less comfortable and more "messy"—but also more likely to be innovative.

tutions is the result of careful analysis and continuous contact with the individual schools. Major considerations for such a recruiting program are:

▲ School counselors and other faculty members concerned with job opportunities and business careers for their students should be contacted regularly.

▲ Good relations should be maintained with faculty and officials at all times, even when there is little or no need for new employees.

▲ Recruiting programs can serve these schools in ways other than the placement of students. For instance, the organization might supply educational films, provide speakers, or arrange for demonstrations and exhibits.

As many organizations compete for their shares of capable graduates, continuing contact and good relations provide better opportunities to secure the best graduates. The extent and scope of recruiting programs will depend on employer needs for employees. However, maintaining good relations even when there is no need for new employees makes sense from a long-range point of view. Obviously, a long-range view of recruiting is more desirable than a campaign approach.

Some larger schools have a centralized guidance or placement office. Contact can be established and maintained with the supervisors of these offices; they are in a good position to help plan and conduct recruiting activities. School counselors generally are interested in the employer's policies and working conditions and will cooperate with an organization that treats its employees fairly. Promotional brochures that acquaint students with starting jobs and career opportunities can be distributed to counselors, librarians, or others. Participating in career days and giving tours of the company to school groups are other ways of maintaining good contact with school sources. Cooperative programs in which students work part time and receive some school credits also may be useful in generating qualified applicants for full-time positions.

College Recruiting

At the college or university level, the recruitment of graduating students is a large-scale operation for many organizations. Most colleges and universities maintain placement offices in which employers and applicants can meet. However, college recruiting presents some interesting and unique problems.

The major determinants that affect the selection of colleges at which an employer conducts interviews are:

▲ Current position requirements
▲ Past experience with placement offices and previous graduates
▲ Organizational budget constraints
▲ Cost of available talent (typical salaries)
▲ Market competition

College recruiting can be expensive; therefore, an organization should determine if the positions it is trying to fill really require persons with college degrees. A great many positions do not; yet many employers insist on filling them with college graduates. The result may be employees who must be paid more and who are likely to leave if the jobs are not sufficiently challenging.

There is a great deal of competition for the top students in a college and much less competition for those farther down the ladder. Attributes that recruiters seem to value most highly in college graduates—poise, oral communication skills, personality, appearance, and written communication skills—all typically are mentioned ahead of grade point average (GPA). However, for many, a high GPA *is* a major criterion.

Research has shown that a candidate's impression of an organization often is important because it affects hire rates.[8] The impression of the individual recruiter also is important. Successful recruiters are those who are enthusiastic and informed, show an interest in the applicant, use interview time well, and avoid overly personal or deliberately stressful questions.

Miscommunication between applicants and recruiters may contribute to poor placement decisions and subsequent performance problems and turnover. College graduates often fail to meet organizational expectations of performance and commitment. For their part, recruiters may overestimate the importance of various job rewards to college graduates. The recruiter overestimates the importance of intrinsic rewards (such as challenge, responsibility, advancement) while underestimating extrinsic rewards (such as pay, benefits, and security). Students purposely may communicate preferences for instrinsic rewards in order to portray attitudes they feel interviewers wish to see. Recruiting efforts and materials that are targeted appropriately can help address problems of miscommunication.

Labor Unions

Labor unions are a source of certain types of workers. In some industries, such as construction, unions have traditionally supplied workers to employers. A labor pool is generally available through a union, and workers can be dispatched to particular jobs to meet the needs of the employers. The union hiring hall is usually the contact point.[9]

In some instances, the union can control or influence recruiting and staffing needs. An organization with a strong union may have less flexibility than a nonunion company in deciding who will be hired and where that person will be placed. Unions also can work to an employer's advantage through cooperative staffing programs, as they do in the building and printing industries.

Trade and Competitive Sources

Other sources for recruiting are *professional and trade associations, trade publications,* and *competitors.* Many professional societies and trade associations publish a newsletters or magazines containing job ads. Such publications may be a good source for specialized professionals needed in an industry. Ads in other specialized publications or listings at professional meetings also can be good sources of publicity about professional openings.

An employer may meet possible applicants who are currently employed by a competitor at professional associations and industry meetings. Some employers directly contact individuals working for competitors. Employees recruited from these sources spend less time in training because they already know the industry.

Temporary Help

Perhaps the most accessible and immediate source of certain types of help is the temporary-help agency. These agencies typically supply secretarial, clerical, or semiskilled labor on a day-rate basis. The use of temporary help may make sense for an organization if its work is subject to seasonal or other fluctuations. Hiring permanent employees to meet peak employment needs would require that the employer find some tasks to keep employees busy during less active periods or resort to layoffs.

More recently, "temp" opportunities are opening up for professional and executive-level jobs, such as chefs, accountants, nurses, and managers. Downsizing has taken layers of management out of many firms, so companies may be hesitant to begin adding them back for projects that are temporary. The same downsizing has made available "temporary executives" with experience that would not have been available in years past. Other professionals and executives have taken early retirement but want to continue working on a part-time basis.

Temporary workers can and often do accept regular staff positions. In effect, this "try before you buy" approach is potentially beneficial to both employer and employee. However, some temporary-help services bill the client company a placement charge if a temporary worker is hired full time within a certain time period—usually 90 days.

A "Temporary" Workforce Entirely?

There is some concern that the workforce of the future is likely to be made up almost entirely of temporaries.[10] The argument is that the cost of keeping a full-time regular workforce has become excessive and is getting worse because of government-mandated costs. But it is not just the money that is at issue. It is also the number of rules that define the employment relationship, making many employers reluctant to hire new employees even when the economy turns up after a recession. The various forms of temporary employment allow an employer to avoid such issues as well as the cost of full-time benefits such as vacation pay and pension plans.

Leasing Employees

One way to deal with the increasingly complex employment regulations and costs for some small businesses is to "lease" instead of "own" employees. Leasing works like this: a company "fires" its workers, who are then hired by a leasing firm. The original company then leases the employees from the leasing company for which they now officially work. The company pays the leasing company, and the leasing company handles such functions as hiring, payroll, and training.[11] For more on leasing, see the case at the end of this chapter.

Employment Agencies

Every state in the United States has its own state-sponsored employment agency. These agencies operate branch offices in many cities throughout the state and do not charge fees to applicants or employers.

Private employment agencies also are found in most cities. For a fee collected from either the employee or the employer, usually the employer, these agencies will do some preliminary screening for an organization and put the organization in touch with applicants. These agencies differ considerably in terms of the level of service, costs, policies, and types of applicants they provide. Employers can reduce the range of possible problems from these sources by giving them a precise definition of the position to be filled.

Executive Search Firms

Some employment agencies focus their efforts on executive, managerial, and professional positions. These executive search firms may work on either a retainer basis or a fee based on the pay level of the hired employee. Those fees may range as high as 33% of the employee's first-year salary. Most employers pay fees, but there are some circumstances in which employees will pay the fees. For placing someone in a high-level executive job, a search firm may receive $300,000 or more, counting travel expenses, the fee, and other compensation. The size of the fees and the aggressiveness with which some search firms pursue candidates for openings have led to such firms being called *headhunters.*[12]

Although many organizations prefer to fill top and upper-middle management jobs from within, when outside search for an executive is necessary, personal contact (the "old boy" or "old girl" network) is most often used. However, executive search firms may be used if other methods do not turn up a successful candidate.

The executive search field is split into two groups: (1) contingency firms that charge a fee only after a candidate has been hired by a client company, and (2) retainer firms that charge a client a set fee whether or not the contracted search is successful. Most of the larger firms work on a retainer basis.

Search firms are ethically bound not to approach employees of client companies in their search efforts for another client. As search firms are retained by more corporations, an increasing number of potential candidates become off-limits. At some point, the large search firms feel they may lose their effectiveness, because they will have to shun the best candidates for some jobs because of conflict-of-interest concerns.

HR Perspectives:
Recruitment of Minority Group Members

The three largest racial minority groups in the U.S. are African Americans, Asians, and Hispanics. Statistics on those three labor market segments suggest that all three will be growing as a proportion of the total workforce. Employers are using specialized media sources to recruit minority employees. Some specialized sources follow.

The African-American population grew to 12.1% of all Americans during the last decade. Most African Americans live in suburbs of centralized cities. The southern U.S. is home to 53% of African Americans, while the number living in the Midwest is decreasing. Major media

sources for recruiting African-American employees include publications such as *Black Careers, Black Enterprise, Black Collegian, Dawn Magazine, National Black Monitor,* and *Dollars and Sense.*

Asian Americans are fewer than 3% of the total U.S. population, but their numbers doubled in the last decade with immigration from the Philippines, Vietnam, China, Korea, Taiwan, Cambodia, and Laos. Almost two out of five Asian Americans live in California. In targeting Asian American groups for recruiting, language can be an issue as there are many different Asian languages. Chinese, for example, is considerably

different from Vietnamese. Only one newspaper (in California) attempts to target all Asian Americans. *Standard Rate* and *Data Service* can help locate the appropriate language publication for recruiting efforts.

Seventy-five percent of the nation's Hispanic Americans live in California, Texas, New York, Florida, and Illinois. As a result, there are many regional media sources targeted to Hispanics. In Miami there are ten Spanish language radio stations alone. The major Hispanic print media are *Hispanic Magazine, Hispanic Business, Hispanic USA Magazine,* and *Vista.*[13]

Media Sources

Media sources such as newspapers, magazines, television, radio, and billboards are widely used. Almost all newspapers carry "Help Wanted" sections, and so do many magazines. For example, *The Wall Street Journal* is a major source used to recruit managerial and professional employees nationally or regionally. Whatever medium is used, it should be tied to the relevant labor market. The "HR Perspective" discusses using specialized media to recruit minority employees.

Newspapers are convenient because there is a short lead time for placing an ad, usually two or three days at most. For positions that must be filled quickly, newspapers may be a good source. However, there can be a great deal of "wasted circulation" with newspaper advertising because most newspapers do not aim to reach any specialized employee markets. Often applicants are only marginally suitable, primarily because employers who compose the ads do not describe the jobs and the necessary qualifications very well.[14] Figure 8–4 shows the kind of information a good media advertisement should include. Many employers have found that it is not cost efficient to schedule newspaper ads on days other than Sunday, the only day many job seekers read them. When using recruitment advertisements, employers should ask five key questions:

1. What do we want to accomplish?
2. Who are the people we want to reach?
3. What should the advertising message convey?
4. How should the message be presented?
5. In which medium should it run?

Figure 8–4

What to Include in an Effective Recruiting Ad

INFORMATION ON THE CANDIDATE
▲ Years of experience ▲ Three to five key characteristics of the successful candidate ▲ Any "preferences" that aren't requirements
INFORMATION ON THE JOB AND PROCESS OF APPLICATION
▲ Job title and responsibilities ▲ Location of job ▲ Starting pay range ▲ Closing date for application ▲ Whether to submit a resume and cover letter ▲ Whether calls are invited or not ▲ Where to mail application or resume
INFORMATION ON THE COMPANY
▲ That it is an EEO employer ▲ Its primary business

In addition to newspapers, other media sources include general magazines, television and radio, and billboards. These sources are usually not suitable for frequent use, but may be used for one-time campaigns aimed at quickly finding specially skilled workers.[15]

Evalution of Media   Recruitment advertising is a form of direct-response marketing. That is, employers are placing ads to generate direct, measurable responses. The more ads they place and track, the better they will become at projecting what responses to expect. To track responses, an employer first must code the ads. The easiest way to do this is to use different contact names and addresses (for example, specify a department number).

Then the employer can note the source each time a response is received. It is best to have one person responsible for opening and coding mailing responses. More people may be needed to respond to call-ins, so they should have some easy and convenient method to record the original source. If one or two people are responsible for screening phone calls, they should ask applicants where they saw the ad. If there are several people regularly taking call-in messages, an organization might consider having a special memo pad just for such inquiries, with a "source" section indicated on the form.

Judging the success of an ad only by the total number of responses is a mistake. For example, it is better to have ten responses with two qualified applicants than 30 responses with only one qualified applicant.

External Databases

Computerized aids for recruiters are growing in usage and complexity. Some computerized aids include:

▲ Databases of resumes that are kept and accessed to identify potential candidates as openings arise

▲ "Personalized" computer-generated letters to respond to applicants

▲ Computerized matching services available through some employment agencies and search firms

Some of the external computer database systems available are offered by employment search firms. One system is Electronic Job Matching (EJM), available from Human Resource Management Center, a Tampa, Florida, firm. Employers who contact the firm and provide details about openings receive information on potential candidates from the EJM database. Specific biographical data on the candidates referred by EJM allow employers to identify whom they wish to consider. Another is available from Corporate Organizing and Research Service (CORS), which has assisted over 4,000 corporations in locating qualified applicants from its database. Databases offered by other firms are specialized by such occupational fields as engineering, banking, and health-care industries.

Another system is the Restrac Resume Reader available from Micro Trac systems. This software allows employers to enter resumes and then sort the resumes by occupational fields, skills, areas of interests, and previous work histories. For instance, if a firm has an opening for someone with an MBA and marketing experience, the key words *MBA* and *marketing* can be entered, and all resumes containing these two items will be identified.

The advantage of all of these computerized products and services is that they allow recruiters to identify potential candidates more quickly than manually sorting numerous stacks and files of resumes. Employers who have used both the internal and external systems indicate that computer databases reduce recruiting costs associated with advertising expenditures, search-firm fees, and internal processing and record retention expenses.[16] However, those who use a preemployment computerized information service should be familiar with the potential legal problems that might arise.[17]

Innovative Recruiting Methods

The standard approaches to recruiting just presented are appropriate most of the time. But when it is really difficult to recruit the people needed, some innovative alternatives are available. Figure 8-5 shows such alternatives.

Special problems sometimes surface in recruiting efforts. Certain firms, such as those in the fast-food and retailing industries, have had continuing difficulties in recruiting sufficient employees for lower-paying jobs. The "HR Perspective" discusses recruiting in the retail business. These industries have traditionally relied on younger employees in the 18 to 24 age group, which as a group, will continue to diminish in number for several more years. But jobs in those industries will continue to increase rapidly for the next ten years.

Small employers may have difficulties recruiting against larger ones because smaller organizations often cannot offer extensive training programs and as many benefits. Consequently, creative approaches may be needed. One small firm in California has successfully recruited salespeople from unusual sources. During earlier years the firm found that disenchanted schoolteachers were excellent prospects. More recently, newer college graduates working in well-managed

▲ **Figure 8–5**   Innovative Recruiting Approaches

▲ Hire more part-timers/temporaries	▲ Use point-of-sale recruiting messages
▲ Partner with an educational institution	▲ Put up posters in community centers, churches, etc.
▲ Raise the pay	▲ Recruit from businesses that are laying off or closing
▲ Retrain present employees	▲ Offer sign-on bonuses
▲ Change the job	▲ Install employment hot lines
▲ Offer cash bonuses for employee referrals	▲ Place want ads in other sections of the newspaper
▲ Recruit nontraditional employees	▲ Hold informational seminars
▲ Attend job fairs	▲ Contact realtors
▲ Recruit outside local area	▲ Contact vocational rehabilitation centers
▲ Offer a three-year warranty on the job	▲ Buy mailing lists of professionals
▲ Try telerecruiting	▲ Provide child care for employees and advertise the fact

restaurants have been a good source. Since they are young, they tend to adapt quickly, and their restaurant experience produces good customer skills.

▲ EVALUATING RECRUITING EFFORTS AND SOURCES

Evaluating the success of recruiting efforts is important because this is the only way to find out whether the time and money spent in recruiting are cost effective. General areas for proper evaluation of recruiting include:

▲ *Quantity of Applicants.* Because the goal of a good recruiting program is to generate a large pool of applicants from which to choose, quantity is a natural place to begin evaluation. Is it sufficient to fill job vacancies?

▲ *Quality of Applicants.* In addition to quantity, there is the issue of whether the qualifications of the applicant pool are sufficient to fill the job openings. Do the applicants meet job specifications and can they perform the jobs?

▲ *Cost per Applicant Hired.* Cost varies depending on the position being filled, but knowing how much it costs to fill an empty position puts turnover and salary in perspective. The greatest single expense in recruiting is the cost of having a recruiting staff. Is the cost for recruiting employees from any single source excessive?

▲ *EEO/AA Goals Met.* Especially when a company is engaged in affirmative action (AA) to meet required goals for hiring protected–class individuals, the recruiting program is the key activity used to meet those goals. Is recruiting providing qualified applicants with an appropriate mix of protected–class individuals?

HR Perspectives:
Tough Recruiting at Retail

Retail stores in certain parts of the country keep encountering a challenge in finding and keeping good store-level employees. The problem is especially pronounced in certain parts of the country with high per capita income or low unemployment. Discount retailers usually pay a lower hourly wage and are at an even greater disadvantage for obtaining hourly employees. Traditional methods, such as running ads in local newspapers, have failed, and some chains are turning to other, more flexible methods—ones that also are more costly.

In one community with a 2.3% unemployment rate, a retail chain responded with these recruiting innovations:
▲ Provided a bonus for employees who recruited others
▲ Placed recruiting flyers in stores circulars
▲ Recruited in depressed parts of the country and paid some moving expenses
▲ Used a night crew for stocking to attract moonlighters

Other organizations have done the following:
▲ Placed hiring booths in problem stores to speed up hiring
▲ Provided vans to take employees to and from central-city areas where they live
▲ Experimented with flexible work schedules
▲ Experimented with hiring more part-timers and senior citizens

But as more retailers adopt such innovative recruiting methods, the competition for retail workers likely will become even more intense.

Specific Recruiting Evaluation Methods

In addition to the basic goals just discussed, a recruiting program can be evaluated in terms of more specific goals as well. The purpose of such specific measures is to achieve continuous improvement of the recruiting process.

Selection Rates   The selection rate is the percentage hired from a given group of applicants; for example, 3/10 (or 30%) equals the number hired divided by the number of applicants. The percentage goes down as unemployment rates in the job market go down. The selection rate also is affected by the sophistication of the selection process. A relatively unsophisticated selection program might pick eight out of ten applicants for the job. Four of those might turn out to be good employees. A more valid selection process might pick five out of ten applicants and have only one mediocre employee in the five.

Base Rate   In the preceding example, the base rate of good employees in the population is four out of ten. That is to say, if ten people were hired at random, one would expect four of them to be good employees. A good recruiting program should be aimed at attracting the four in ten who are capable of doing well on this particular job. Realistically, no recruiting program will attract *only* the four in ten who will succeed. However, efforts to make the recruiting program attract the largest proportion of those in the base rate group can make recruiting efforts more effective.

Time Elapsed   Hiring needs occur within a time frame. If an organization needs a Vice President of Marketing *immediately,* having to wait four months to find the right person presents a problem. Generally speaking, it is useful to calculate the average amount of time it takes from contact to hire for each source of applicants, because some sources may be faster than others for a particular employer.

Yield Ratios   Yield ratios can be calculated for each step of the recruiting/selection process, and the result is a tool for approximating the necessary size of the initial applicant pool. Figure 8–6 shows that to end up with 25 hires for the job in question, the company must begin with 300 applicants in the pool, as long as yield ratios remain the same at each step.

A different approach to evaluating recruiting using ratios suggests that over time organizations can develop ranges for critical ratios. When a given indicator ratio falls outside that range, there may be problems in the recruiting process.[18] For example, in college recruiting the following ratios might be useful:

$$\frac{\text{College seniors given second interview}}{\text{total number of seniors interviewed}} = \text{range of .30 to .50}$$

$$\frac{\text{Number who accept offer}}{\text{number invited to the company for visit}} = \text{range of .50 to .70}$$

Long-Term Measures   Certain long-term measures of recruiting effectiveness are quite useful. Information on job performance, absenteeism, cost of training, and turnover by recruiting source helps to adjust future recruiting. For example, some companies find that recruiting at certain colleges or universities furnishes stable, high performers, whereas other schools provide employees who are more prone to turnover.

▲ **Figure 8–6**

Using Yield Ratios to Determine
Needed Applicants

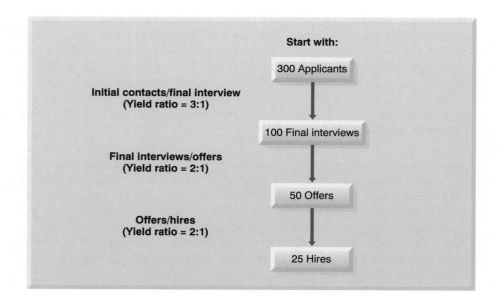

$$\frac{\text{Number who were hired}}{\text{number offered a job}} = \text{range of .70 to .80}$$

$$\frac{\text{Number finally hired}}{\text{total number interviewed on campus}} = \text{range of .10 to 20}$$

Recruiting Sources: Costs and Benefits

HR managers correctly regard recruiting as an important activity. Inability to generate enough or the appropriate type of applicants for jobs can be costly. When recruiting fails to bring in enough applicants, a common response is to raise starting salaries. This action initially may help recruiting, but often at the expense of others already in the organization. It also may create resentment in employees who started at much lower salaries than the new hires.

Cost/benefit information on each recruiting source can be calculated. Comparing the length of time applicants from each source stay in the organization with the cost of hiring from that source offers a useful perspective. Further, yield ratios from each source can help determine which sources generate the most employees. Figure 8–7 shows the cost per source for salespersons hired to open a new store. Fixed costs are not included here and the variable-cost figures shown are estimates made by experienced recruiters.

When making a cost/benefit analysis, costs may include both *direct costs* (advertising, recruiters' salaries, travel, agency fees, telephone) and *indirect costs* (involvement of operating managers, public relations, image). Benefits to consider include the following:

▲ Length of time from contact to hire
▲ Total size of applicant pool
▲ Proportion of acceptances to offers
▲ Percentage of qualified applicants in the pool

▲ **Figure 8–7**   Recruiting Source Cost Information for Salespersons

Source	NO. OF APPLICANTS Per Source	ESTIMATED COST ($) Per Source	COST PER APPLICANT ($) Per Source
Walk-ins	5	0	0
Internal posting	5	100	20
Weekly newspaper ad	50	2,000	40
Sunday newspaper ad	200	10,000	50
Expanded newspaper ad	25	3,000	120
Employee referrals	10	1,500	150
Job fairs	2	2,500	1,250
TOTAL	297	$19,100	$64.31 (Average)

SOURCE: Adapted from S. L. Martin and N. S. Raju, "Determining Cutoff Scores that Optimize Utility: A Recognition of Recruiting Costs," *Journal of Applied Psychology*, 77 (1992), 199. Used with permission.

In summary, the effectiveness of various recruiting sources will vary depending on the nature of the job being filled and the time available to fill it. But unless calculated, the effectiveness may not be entirely obvious.

▲ SUMMARY

- ▲ Recruiting is the process of generating a pool of qualified applicants for organizational jobs through a series of activities.
- ▲ The applicant population is affected by recruiting method, message, applicant qualification, and administrative procedures.
- ▲ Two general groups of recruiting sources exist: internal sources and external sources. An organization must decide whether it will look primarily within the organization or outside for new employees, or use some combination of each source.
- ▲ The decision to use internal or external sources should be based on the advantages and disadvantages associated with each.
- ▲ Current employees, former employees, and previous applicants are the most common internal sources available.
- ▲ External recruiting sources include schools, colleges and universities, employment agencies, temporary-help firms, labor unions, professional or trade organizations, and media sources.
- ▲ The costs and benefits of recruiting efforts should be evaluated to assess how well HR planning and recruiting responsibilities are being performed by the HR unit and operating managers.

▲ REVIEW AND DISCUSSION QUESTIONS

1. Design a recruiting process for a sales representative's job.
2. How does the applicant pool follow from labor force population and applicant population?
3. List two pros and two cons for internal sources versus external sources of recruits.
4. Which internal sources are least likely to present an EEO problem?
5. Why do organizations use college recruiting and executive search firms?
6. Discuss three ways to evaluate recruiting efforts.

 EMPLOYEE LEASING

Run a business without employees? Impossible! Yet today, there are an increasing number of professionals and small businesses that do just that through employee leasing.

Although not designed only as a substitute for recruiting, employee leasing is a concept that has grown rapidly in recent years. Approximately 1,400 employee leasing firms handle HR for over one million workers. Introduced in 1972, it is a means of solving HR problems, including paperwork, recruiting, and turnover for small- to medium-sized companies. The process is simple: a business signs an agreement with an employee leasing company, after which the existing staff is hired by the leasing firm and leased back to the company. The leasing firm then handles all paperwork, recruiting, and tax liabilities.

By pooling employees from many small businesses, the leasing company can usually get big-company benefits for its "employees" that are not available to employees of smaller firms. There is strength in large numbers. For example, when Wayne Mohle started his three-person accounting firm in Chico, California, he used employee leasing. As a small company, he could not get insurance for one employee whose son had diabetes, or dental insurance for the others. The leasing company provides both for the employees. In addition, offices with fewer than six employees can get maternity coverage only with a large deductible; some smaller offices can't get any coverage. Many business owners originally used employee leasing because it was good for their pensions. Internal Revenue Service regulations require that pension plans be the same for all employees. The leasing company took care of pensions for many of the employees, leaving business owners free to set up more generous plans for themselves. However, tax law changes now require organizations that lease more than 20% of their employees to treat them as their own employees in setting up pension plans.

The new law has forced the 300-plus leasing companies in the country to sell employers on the other services they can provide. For a fee, a small business owner or operator turns his or her staff over to the leasing company, which then writes the paychecks, pays the taxes, prepares and implements HR policies, and keeps all the required records.

All this service comes at a high cost. Leasing companies often charge between 4% and 6% of a monthly salary for their services. While leasing may save employers money on benefits, it can also increase payroll costs. For some organizations, it is well worth it. At Bartex, a Dallas construction company, the leasing company takes care of virtually all HR matters—no small task in the boom-and-bust construction business. Employees receive better benefits than they would have otherwise received and are generally satisfied with "being leased." In a Small Business Administration study of 21 companies leasing employees, all employers were found to be pleased with leasing. Their workers had more benefits, and paperwork had been reduced. Twelve of the 21 firms felt spending less time on HR matters was an advantage.[19]

▲ QUESTIONS

1. What are the potential disadvantages of employee leasing?
2. Which evaluation techniques discussed in the chapter could be used to assess the effectiveness of employee leasing?

▲ NOTES

1. Adapted from information in Michael A. Verespej, "Time for Open–door Employment Policies," *Industry Week*, May 6, 1991, 21–22; "Older Workers Still Encounter Stubborn Bias," *Omaha World-Herald*, October 20, 1991, 1G; "Older Workers: A Good Investment," *The Rotarian*, September 1991, 14; and "Playing Hero to Seniors Wasn't Plan," *Omaha World-Herald*, January 12, 1992, 1G.
2. Sara L. Rynes, et al., "The Importance of Recruiting in Job Choice: A Different Way of Looking," *Personnel Psychology*, 49, (1991), 44.

3. Jennifer J. Laabs, "The Global Talent Search," *Personnel Journal,* August 1991, 38–39.

4. "Job Posting Can Benefit Firms, Workers," *Omaha World-Herald,* September 22, 1991, 126.

5. "Recruiting—Hitting the Jackpot," *INC.,* March 1987, 88.

6. "Firms Promote from Within," *San Antonio Express News,* September 12, 1991, 1B.

7. S. E. Jackson et al., "Some Differences Make a Difference. . . .," *Journal of Applied Psychology,* 76, no. 5 (1991), 675–689.

8. Robert D. Gatewood, Mary A. Gowan, and Gary J. Lautenschlager, "Corporate Image, Recruitment Image, and Initial Job Choice," *Academy of Management Journal,* 36, (1993), 414–427.

9. B. S. Moskal, "Apprenticeships: Old Cure for New Labor Shortage," *Industry Week,* May 6, 1991, 30.

10. "The Jobs Market," *Laramie Daily,* February 10, 1993, p. 4.

11. Rosalind Resnick, "Leasing Workers," *Nation's Business,* November 1992, 20.

12. L. Brown and D. Martin, "What to Expect from an Executive Search Firm," *HR Magazine,* December 1991, 5G.

13. "Guide to Recruiting Markets," *Personnel Journal,* December 1991, 8–9.

14. Tracy E. Benson, "Ready, Aim, Hire," *Industry Week,* February 4, 1991, 16.

15. Jennifer J. Laabs, "Nurses Get Critical about Recruitment Ads," *Personnel Journal,* July 1991.

16. For several other databases for recruiting, see "High Tech Recruitment Solutions," *HR Magazine,* February 1992, 54.

17. Jeffrey Hahn, "Preemployment Information Services: Employers Beware?" *Employee Relations Law Journal,* 17, (1992), 45.

18. Personal communication from Dr. Carl Thorton, GMI Department of Management.

19. Adapted from T. Ulrich and C. Hollon, "A Guide to Employee Leasing," *Business,* October/December 1988, 44-47; S. Woolley, "Give Your Employees a Break—By Leasing Them," *Business Week,* August 14, 1989, 135; R. Schnapp, "Differentiate Between Employees and Independent Contractors," *Recruitment Today,* Fall 1989, 25; and "Employee Leasing on the Rise," Omaha World-Herald, May 16, 1993, G1, 5.

CHAPTER 9

SELECTING HUMAN RESOURCES

After you read this chapter, you should be able to:

1. Define selection and explain several reasons for having a specialized employment unit.

2. Diagram a typical selection process in sequential order.

3. Discuss the reception and application form phases of the selection process.

4. Identify two general and three controversial test types.

5. Discuss three types of interviews and six key considerations or problems in the selection interview.

6. Construct a guide for conducting a selection interview.

7. Explain how legal concerns affect background investigations of applicants.

8. Determine why medical examinations, including drug testing, may be useful in selection.

The manufacturing plant of tomorrow sits on a pothole-filled street across from a chicken-processing plant in Arkadelphia, Arkansas. It does not look like a plant—more like an insurance building: sleek, one-story, cleaner than most peoples' houses. Carrier Corporation makes compressors for air conditioners with its workforce of 150 in the Arkadelphia plant.

But what really differentiates this plant from yesterday's plants is its employees. If you want a job here, you go through a six-week course before even being considered for employment. The selection process weeds out 15 of every 16 applicants and provides Carrier Corporation with a top-quality workforce.

When they get the jobs, workers also get unusual authority with them. They order their own supplies (within reason) and can shut down the production line if they see a problem. One worker says that every day there are a hundred problems that management never even knows about. Management does not need to know about such problems because these "workers of the future" are able to take care of them. They save time, money, and productivity in the process. Flexibility is critical to this system of operation; each worker can do several jobs, so if someone is absent another can fill in quickly.

Getting a job with the plant is a bit like applying to college. High school graduates take a state test for job applicants first. Only one-third advance to the next step. References are closely checked, then the applicants are interviewed both by managers *and* the assembly-line workers with whom they will work. Those who have satisfactory interviews take a six-week course. It meets five nights a week for three hours, with some extra Saturdays. They learn to read blueprints, do math, including metric calculations and statistical process control, use a computer, and engage in problem solving with others. At this point the applicants have not been hired (or paid) and have no assurances they will be. Their performances to date are assessed by their instructors and by each other as well.

Does it work? The compressors produced at the Arkadelphia plant are less expensive and of higher quality than those produced by others in the industry. Carrier executives believe the plant will serve as a model for the future—small, flexible, and staffed with better-educated, better-motivated employees. The president of the compressor division says, "My goal is to sell compressors from Arkansas to Japan."[1]

25

> Selecting qualified employees is like putting money in the bank.
>
> *John Boudreau*

More than anything else, selection of human resources should be seen as a *matching process*. How well an employee is matched to a job affects the amount and quality of the employee's work. This matching also directly affects training and operating costs. Workers who are unable to produce the expected amount and quality of work can cost an organization a great deal of money and time.

Proper matching also is important to the individual applying for a job. The wrong choice of a vocation or improper job placement can result in wasted time for the employee, who could be getting useful experience elsewhere. The mismatched individual either will be unhappy in the job or perhaps dismissed from it if he or she proves too inept.

To put selection in perspective, consider that organizations on average reject about five out of six applicants for jobs they need to fill, usually because of gaps between employment skills and requirements of the job.[2] Figure 9–1 details the reasons why employers reject applicants.

▲ NATURE OF SELECTION

Selection is the process of choosing individuals who have relevant qualifications to fill jobs in an organization. The selection process begins when a manager or supervisor requests an individual to fill a certain vacancy. In large organizations

▼ **SELECTION**

is the process of choosing individuals who have relevant qualifications to fill jobs in an organization.

▲ **Figure 9–1** Reasons Applicants Are Not Selected

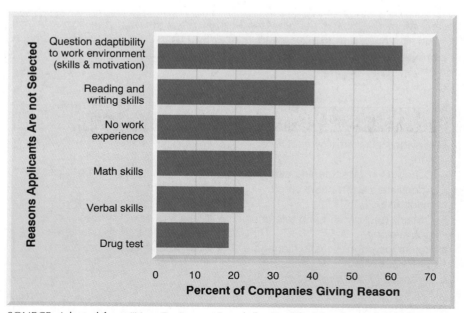

SOURCE: Adapted from "How Businesses Search for Qualified Applicants," Supplement to *Personnel Journal,* June 1992, 1.

a requisition is sent to the in-house employment office or an HR staff member. A *job description,* based on *job analysis,* identifies the vacancy. A *job specifications* statement, which may also accompany the request, describes the knowledge, skills, and abilities a person needs to fill the vacancy. HR specialists use the job description and specifications to begin the recruiting process. From the pool of applicants generated by recruiting activities, one person is selected to fill the job. In small organizations the manager often handles the whole process.

The process for selecting managers is a bit different. Managers selected from outside the organization often are chosen by upper management on the basis of reference checks, word of mouth, and interviews. The difficulty of specifying *exactly* the behaviors needed to be a successful manager makes management selection more difficult than selection of a good typist. Middle- and upper-level management selection may be handled outside the customary selection responsibilities detailed in the following section.

Selection Responsibilities

In different organizations, selection activities are done to a greater or lesser degree by HR specialists or managers. Until the impact of equal employment opportunity (EEO) regulations became widespread, selection often was carried out in a rather unplanned manner in many organizations. The need to meet EEO requirements has forced them to plan better in this regard. Still, in some organizations, each department screens and hires its own employees. Many managers insist on selecting their own people because they are sure no one else can choose employees for them as well as they can themselves. This practice is particularly prevalent in smaller firms. But the validity and fairness of such an approach may be questionable.

Other organizations maintain the traditional practice of having the HR unit do the initial screening of the candidates, while the appropriate managers or supervisors make the final selection. As a rule, the higher the position within the organization, the greater the likelihood is that the ultimate hiring decisions will be made by operating managers rather than by HR specialists. Typical selection responsibilities are shown in Figure 9–2.

▲ **Figure 9–2**

Typical Selection Responsibilities

HR UNIT	MANAGERS
▲ Provides initial employment reception	▲ Requisition employees with specific qualifications to fill jobs
▲ Conducts initial screening interview	▲ Participate in selection process as appropriate
▲ Administers appropriate employment tests	▲ Interview final candidates
▲ Obtains background and reference information	▲ Make final selection decision, subject to advice of HR specialists
▲ Refers top candidates to managers for final selection	▲ Provide follow-up information on the suitability of selected individuals
▲ Arranges for the employment physical examination, if used	
▲ Evaluates success of selection process	

Centralized Employment Office   Selection duties may be centralized into a specialized organizational unit that is part of an HR department. This specialization often depends on the size of the organization. In smaller organizations, especially in those with fewer than 100 employees, a full-time employment specialist or unit may be impractical.

The employment function in any organization may be concerned with some or all of the following operations: (1) receiving applications, (2) interviewing applicants, (3) administering tests to applicants, (4) conducting background investigations, (5) arranging for physical examinations, (6) placing and assigning new employees, (7) coordinating follow-up of these employees, (8) termination interviewing, and (9) maintaining adequate records and reports.

Some reasons generally voiced for conducting the employment function within one unit are as follows:

▲ It is easier for the applicant because there is only one place to apply for a job.

▲ Coordinating contact with outside applicant sources is easier because issues pertaining to employment can be cleared through one central location.

▲ It allows operating managers to concentrate on their operating responsibilities. This release is especially helpful during peak periods.

▲ Better selection may occur because it is done by a specialist trained in staffing.

▲ The applicant is assured of consideration for a greater variety of jobs.

▲ Selection costs may be cut because duplication of effort is avoided.

▲ With increased government regulations affecting the selection process, it is important that people most knowledgeable about these rules handle a major part of the selection process.

Selection and Employer Image

In addition to matching qualified people to jobs, the selection process has an important public-relations dimension. Discriminatory hiring practices, impolite interviewers, unnecessarily long waits, inappropriate testing procedures, and lack of follow-up letters can produce unfavorable impressions of an employer.[3] Providing courteous, professional treatment to all candidates during the selection process is important because for most applicants a job contact of any kind is an extremely personal event.[4] Sometimes the process is complicated by job seeker strategies and attitudes on the part of the applicant that may be less than ideal, as the "HR Perspective" indicates.

Legal Concerns with Selection

Selection is subject to all the EEO concerns that were covered in previous chapters. The interview itself is becoming a mine field; one major problem is that there is no standard list of taboo questions, but only general areas about which one cannot ask. Small businesses are the worst offenders, and their most common error is to ask a woman about child-care arrangements, an inquiry that assumes women are always the ones responsible for child-rearing.[6]

As noted in Chapter 6, the EEOC has recently endorsed the use of employment discrimination **testers,** protected-class members who pose as applicants to

▼ **TESTERS**

are protected-class members who pose as applicants to determine if employers discriminate in their hiring practices.

HR Perspectives:

Dysfunctional Job Seeker Strategies and Attitudes

People who are in the business of finding jobs for other people (outplacement counselors) see every kind of job hunter, including these:[5]

▲ *Heaven-Sent*—the egocentric applicant who thinks *everyone* wants to hire him/her.
▲ *Rootbound*—the applicant who refuses to leave his or her present geographical job market.

▲ *Nester*—the applicant who "hibernates" at home or office rather than actively pursuing job interviews.
▲ *Mailer*—the person whose strategy is to rely on mailing out resumes rather than applying in person.
▲ *Midnighter*—the one who waits until the last minute, just before resources run out, to start looking for a job.

▲ *Don Quixote*—the job hunter who holds out for a job for which he or she is simply not qualified.

The labels are not meant to be demeaning, but rather to reveal common mistaken strategies and attitudes in the job search process. As students look for jobs, they should see if they fit one of the above categories.

determine if employers discriminate in their hiring practices. Testers observe how employer representatives conduct themselves in the selection process. Then they file lawsuits if they feel their legal rights as a representative job applicant were ignored.[7]

It may be increasingly important for companies to define more carefully exactly who is an *applicant,* given the legal issues involved. If there is no written policy defining conditions that make a person an applicant, any person who calls or sends an unsolicited resume might later claim he/she was not hired because of illegal discrimination. A policy defining *applicant* might include the following:

▲ Applications are accepted only when there is an opening.
▲ Only persons filling out application blanks are considered applicants.
▲ A person's application ceases after a certain date.
▲ Only a certain number of applications will be accepted.
▲ People must apply for a specific job, not "any job."

It is wise for an organization to retain all applications for three years. Applicant flow data should be calculated if the organization has at least 50 employees, as discussed in Chapter 6.

▲ THE SELECTION PROCESS

Most organizations take certain common steps to process applicants for jobs. Variations on this basic process depend on organizational size, nature of the jobs to be filled, number of people to be selected, and pressure of outside forces such as EEO considerations. This process can take place in a day or over a much longer period of time. If the applicant is processed in one day, the employer usually checks references after selection. Often one or more phases of the process are omitted or the order changed, depending on the employer.

The selection process shown in Figure 9–3 is typical of a large organization. The applicant, perhaps a woman, comes to the organization, is directed to the

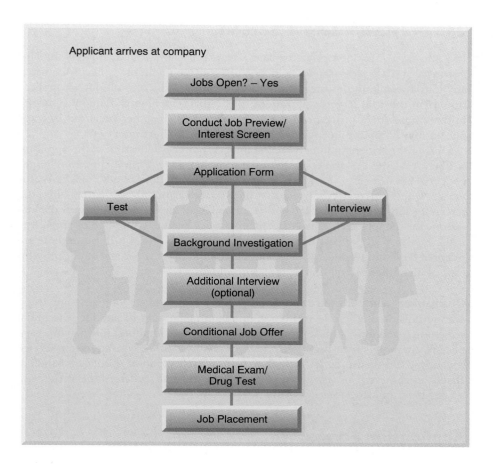

Selection Process Flowchart

employment office, and received by a receptionist. Some firms conduct a job preview/interest screen to determine if an applicant is or is not qualified for open jobs before giving out an application form. In this case, the receptionist gives the woman an application form to complete. The completed application form serves as the basis for an interview or a test, after which the applicant may be told that she does not fit any position the company has available. However, if she does appear to have appropriate qualifications, the applicant's background and previous employment history may be checked and/or an additional, more in-depth interview may be conducted. If responses are favorable, the applicant may be made a conditional offer of a job, based on her passing a medical and/or drug test.[8]

Reception

The job applicant's attitudes about the organization, and even about the products or services it offers, will be influenced by the reception stage of the selection process. Whoever meets the applicant initially should be tactful and able to offer assistance in a courteous, friendly manner. If no jobs are available, applicants can be informed at this point. Any employment possibilities must be presented honestly and clearly.

Job Preview/Interest Screen

In some cases, it is appropriate to have a brief interview, called an *initial screening interview,* or a *job preview/interest screen,* to see if the applicant is likely to match any jobs available in the organization before letting someone fill out an application form. In most large organizations, this initial screening is done by someone in the employment office or in the HR department. In other situations, the applicant may complete an application form before the short interview.

During the screening interview, the interviewer can determine if the applicant is likely to have the ability to perform available jobs. Typical questions might concern job interests, location desired, pay expectations, and availability for work. One firm that hires security guards and armored-car drivers uses the screening interview to verify whether an applicant meets the minimum qualifications for the job, such as having a valid driver's license, being free of any criminal conviction in the past five years, and having used a pistol. Because these are required minimum standards, it would be a waste of time for any applicant who cannot meet them to fill out an application form.

Computer and Electronic Interviews   A number of firms are using computerized or other electronic interviewing techniques to conduct the initial screening interview.[9] One example comes from a major hotel chain where applicants for hotel front-desk jobs view a videotape of certain customer-service situations, and then indicate how they believe each situation should be handled. Based on those responses, the applicants are evaluated to determine if they are acceptable candidates for employment.

Application Forms

Application forms are a widely used selection device. Properly prepared, like the one in Figure 9–4, the application form serves four purposes:

▲ It is a record of the applicant's desire to obtain a position.
▲ It provides the interviewer with a profile of the applicant that can be used in the interview.
▲ It is a basic employee record for applicants who are hired.
▲ It can be used for research on the effectiveness of the selection process.

EEO Considerations and Application Forms   Although application forms may not usually be thought of as "tests," the Uniform Guidelines of the EEOC and court decisions define them as employment tests. Consequently, the data requested on application forms must be job related. Illegal questions typically found on application forms ask for the following:

▲ Marital status
▲ Height/weight
▲ Number and ages of dependents
▲ Information on spouse
▲ Date of high school graduation
▲ Whom to contact in case of emergency and that person's relationship to applicant

The reason for concern about such questions is that they can have adverse impact on some protected groups. For example, the question about dependents can be

▲ **Figure 9–4**   Sample Application Blank

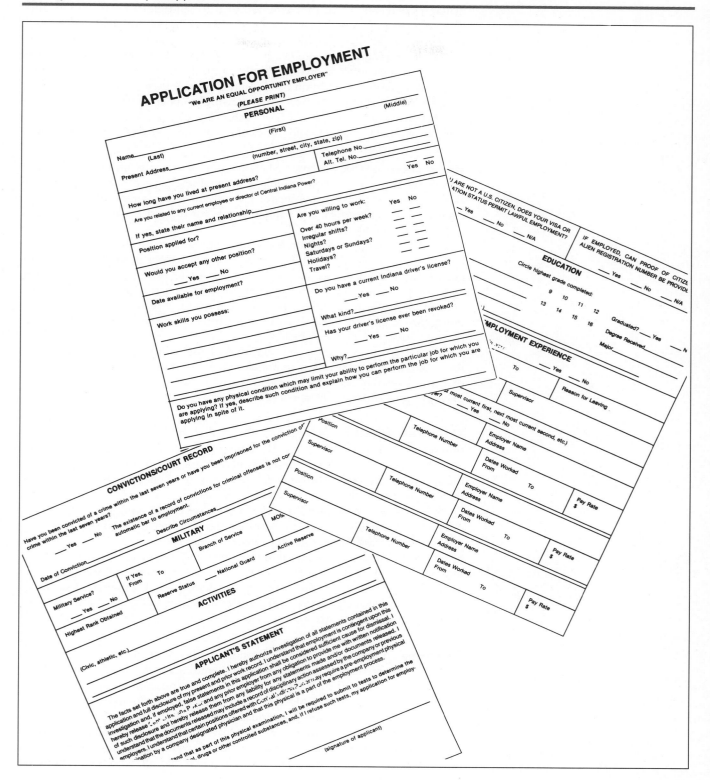

used to pinpoint women with small children who may not be hired because of a manager's perception that they will not be as dependable as those without small children. The high school graduation date gives a close identification of a person's age, which could be used to discriminate against individuals over age 40.

One interesting point to remember is that many employers must collect data on the race and sex of those who apply to fulfill requirements for reporting to the EEOC, but the application blank cannot contain these items. As discussed in Chapter 6, the solution picked by a growing number of employers is one in which the applicant provides EEOC reporting data on a separate form. This form is then filed separately and not used in any other HR selection activities.

Using Application Forms   Many employers use only one application form but others need several. For example, a hospital might need one form for nurses and medical technicians, another for clerical and office employees, another for managers and supervisors, and a different one for support persons in housekeeping and food service areas.

The information received on application forms or resumes may not always be completely accurate. This problem is discussed in greater detail later, but an important point must be made here. In an attempt to prevent inaccuracies, many application forms carry a statement that the applicant is required to sign, at the bottom of the form. In effect, the statement reads: "I realize that falsification of this record is grounds for dismissal if I am hired." The statement has been used by employers to terminate people.

Application forms traditionally have asked for references and requested that the applicant give permission to contact them. Rather than asking for personal or general references, though, it may be more useful to request the names of previous supervisors on the application form.

Weighted Application Forms   One way employers can make the application form more job related is by developing a weighted application blank. A job analysis is used to determine the KSAs needed for the job. Then *weights,* or numeric values, are placed on different responses to application blank items, and the responses of an applicant are scored and totaled.

There are several problems associated with weighted application forms. One difficulty is the time and effort required to develop such a form. For many small employers and for jobs that do not require numerous employees, the cost of developing the weights can be prohibitive. Also, the blank must be updated every few years to ensure that the factors previously identified are still valid predictors of job success. However, the concept can allow a valid, job-related set of inquiries to be evaluated relative to specific experiences and skills—and then compared with other applications numerically.

Resumes   One of the most common methods applicants use to provide background information is the resume. Resumes, also called *vitae* by some, vary in style and length. Technically, a resume used in place of an application form must be treated by an employer as an application form for EEO purposes. Consequently, even though an applicant may furnish some "illegal information" voluntarily on a resume, the employer should not use that information during the selection process. Because resumes contain only information applicants want to present, some employers require that all who submit resumes complete an application form as well, so similar information will be available on all applicants. Individuals who mail in resumes may be sent thank-you letters and application forms to be completed and returned. Appendix D contains some suggestions on resume preparation and getting a job.

Immigration Requirements

The Immigration Reform and Control Act (IRCA) of 1986, as revised in 1990, requires that within 24 hours of hiring, an employer must determine whether a job applicant is a U.S. citizen, registered alien, or illegal alien. Those not eligible to work in this country must not be hired. Figure 9–5 shows the *I-9 form* that employers must use to identify the status of potential employees. Many employers have applicants complete this form during the application process. Others have individuals submit the documents on the first day of employment. Employers do have a responsibility to make sure that the documents such as U.S. passports, birth certificates, original Social Security cards, driver's licenses, or other documents that are submitted by new employees "reasonably appear on their face to be genuine."

▲ SELECTION TESTING

Many people claim that formal tests can be of great benefit in the selection process when properly used and administered. Considerable evidence supports this claim. However, because of EEO concerns, many employers reduced or eliminated the use of tests beginning in the early 1970s, fearing that they might be judged discriminatory in some way. But test usage appears to be increasing again. A survey of 720 companies that recently had implemented testing programs found that 77% felt it had improved their selection processes. About two-thirds of the companies using applications, plus interviews, plus tests reported satisfaction with their selection procedures. That was a 50% increase over the satisfaction of those that did not use formalized approaches such as testing.[10]

Test Validity and Test Usage

Any use of a test must be shown to be valid. As described in Chapter 5, *validity* is the extent to which a test actually measures what it says it measures. A high score on a test supposed to measure "ability to learn" should translate to high performance in training if the test is valid. Calculating validity in psychological testing, in particular, should be done if the test is to be used for selection.[11]

Validity *coefficients* measure the strength of relationships between the test and performance. While the coefficient can theoretically range from zero to 1, coefficients of .3 and above are considered good. Above .5 is a truly outstanding predictor. The results from one study regarding validity coefficients found the following predictors:[12]

Method	Validity Coefficient	Method	Validity Coefficient
Ability testing	.53	Experience	.18
Skill testing	.44	Interview	.14
Reference checks	.26	Education	.10
Class rank or GPA★	.21	Interest measures	.10
★Grade point average.			

▲ **Figure 9–5** Employment Eligibility Verification Form I-9

EMPLOYMENT ELIGIBILITY VERIFICATION (Form I-9)

1 **EMPLOYEE INFORMATION AND VERIFICATION:** (To be completed and signed by employee.)

Name: (Print or Type) Last	First	Middle	Birth Name

Address: Street Name and Number	City	State	ZIP Code

Date of Birth (Month/Day/Year)	Social Security Number

I attest, under penalty of perjury, that I am (check a box):

☐ 1. A citizen or national of the United States.

☐ 2. An alien lawfully admitted for permanent residence (Alien Number A _____) .

☐ 3. An alien authorized by the Immigration and Naturalization Service to work in the United States (Alien Number A _____ ,
or Admission Number _____ , expiration of employment authorization, if any _____) .

I attest, under penalty of perjury, the documents that I have presented as evidence of identity and employment eligibility are genuine and relate to me. I am aware that federal law provides for imprisonment and/or fine for any false statements or use of false documents in connection with this certificate.

Signature	Date (Month/Day/Year)

PREPARER/TRANSLATOR CERTIFICATION (To be completed if prepared by person other than the employee). I attest, under penalty of perjury, that the above was prepared by me at the request of the named individual and is based on all information of which I have any knowledge.

Signature	Name (Print or Type)		
Address (Street Name and Number)	City	State	Zip Code

2 **EMPLOYER REVIEW AND VERIFICATION:** (To be completed and signed by employer.)

Instructions:
Examine one document from List A and check the appropriate box, **OR** examine one document from List B **and** one from List C and check the appropriate boxes.
Provide the *Document Identification Number* and *Expiration Date* for the document checked.

List A Documents that Establish Identity and Employment Eligibility	List B Documents that Establish Identity	**and**	List C Documents that Establish Employment Eligibility

☐ 1. United States Passport

☐ 2. Certificate of United States Citizenship

☐ 3. Certificate of Naturalization

☐ 4. Unexpired foreign passport with attached Employment Authorization

☐ 5. Alien Registration Card with photograph

☐ 1. A State-issued driver's license or a State-issued I.D. card with a photograph, or information, including name, sex, date of birth, height, weight, and color of eyes.
(Specify State)_____)

☐ 2. U.S. Military Card

☐ 3. Other (Specify document and issuing authority)

_____

☐ 1. Original Social Security Number Card (other than a card stating it is not valid for employment)

☐ 2. A birth certificate issued by State, county, or municipal authority bearing a seal or other certification

☐ 3. Unexpired INS Employment Authorization
Specify form
_____

Document Identification

_____

Document Identification

_____

Document Identification

_____

Expiration Date (if any)

_____

Expiration Date (if any)

_____

Expiration Date (if any)

_____

CERTIFICATION: I attest, under penalty of perjury, that I have examined the documents presented by the above individual, that they appear to be genuine and to relate to the individual named, and that the individual, to the best of my knowledge, is eligible to work in the United States.

Signature	Name (Print or Type)	Title
Employer Name	Address	Date

Form I-9 (05/07/87)
OMB No. 1115-0136

U.S. Department of Justice
Immigration and Naturalization Service

Interpreting test results is not always straightforward, either, even if the test is valid. Individuals trained in testing and test interpretation should be involved in establishing and maintaining a testing system. Finally, the role of tests in the overall selection process must be kept in perspective: tests represent only one possible data source.

However, a California court case raises issues relative to testing and privacy that are as yet unresolved. The court found that a psychological test violated the right to privacy afforded all California citizens. The other states with similar guarantees to privacy include Alaska, Arizona, Florida, Hawaii, Illinois, Louisiana, Montana, South Carolina, and Washington.[13]

Ability and Aptitude Tests

According to the Uniform Guidelines of the EEOC, any employment requirement is a "test." The focus in this section is on formal tests. As Figure 9–6 shows, a variety of types of tests are used. Notice that most of them focus on specific job-related aptitudes and skills. Some are paper-and-pencil tests (such as a math test), others are motor-skill tests, and still others use machines (polygraphs, for instance). Some employers purchase prepared tests, whereas others develop their own.

Ability tests assess the skills that individuals have already learned. **Aptitude tests** are used to measure general ability to learn or acquire a skill. The typing tests given at many firms to secretarial applicants are examples of a commonly

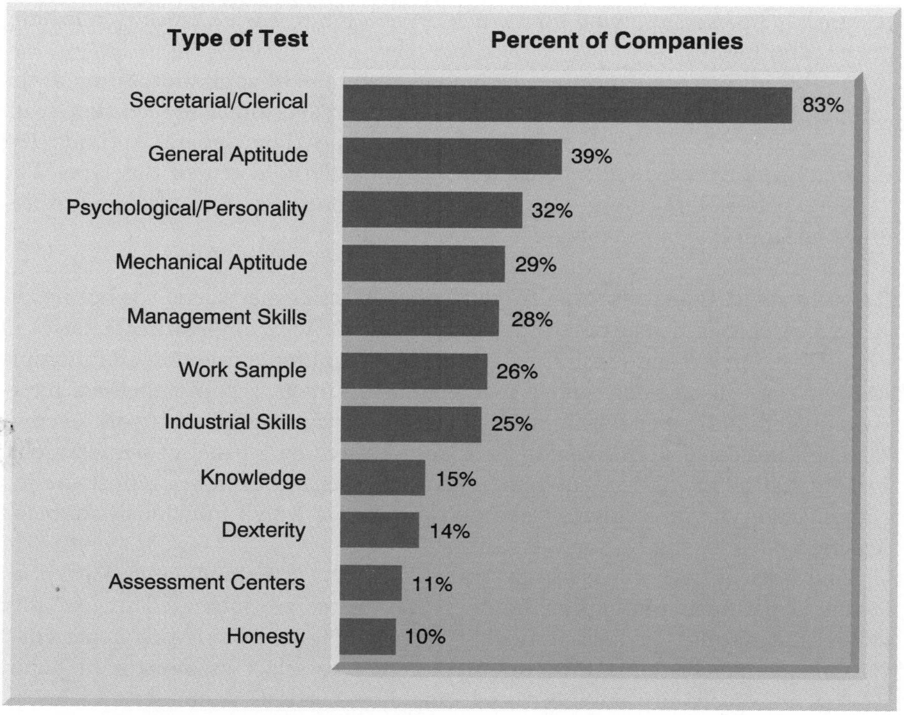

▼ **ABILITY TESTS**

assess the skills that individuals have learned.

▼ **APTITUDE TESTS**

measure general ability to learn or acquire a skill.

▲ **Figure 9–6**

Tests used for Selection

Type of Test	Percent of Companies
Secretarial/Clerical	83%
General Aptitude	39%
Psychological/Personality	32%
Mechanical Aptitude	29%
Management Skills	28%
Work Sample	26%
Industrial Skills	25%
Knowledge	15%
Dexterity	14%
Assessment Centers	11%
Honesty	10%

SOURCE: "Most Employers Test New Job Candidates, ASPA Survey Shows," *Resource,* June 1988, 2. Published by the Society for Human Resource Management. Used with permission.

HR Perspectives:
A Valid Battery of Tests

Manpower Temporary Services provides temporary employees to employers throughout the world. To make sure the employees have the skills and desire to do well, the company has designed a battery of tests they call Ultradex.

Applicants take tests that measure common skill necessities: speed, ability to follow instructions, attention to detail, and desire to do quality work.

They also can take specific skill tests as well. Four tests include oral instructions—sorting and checking, tool-related assembly, small-parts assembly, and coordinated rapid movement. Three pencil-and-paper tests—inspection, aiming, and logging production—measure hand-eye coordination and ability to do calculations.

The tests were validated by using longer-term workers and those who were the best performers scored highest on the tests. The valid tests evaluate knowledge, skills, abilities, and personal characteristics with a high accuracy rate. They are very useful for matching people to the right jobs.[14]

▼ **WORK SAMPLE TESTS**

require an applicant to perform a simulated job task.

▼ **MENTAL ABILITY TESTS**

measure reasoning capabilities of applicants.

used abilities test. Other widely used tests include ones testing mechanical abilities and manual dexterity.

Another type of abilities test used at many organizations simulates job tasks. These **work sample tests,** which require an applicant to perform a simulated job task which is part of the job being applied for, are especially useful. Having an applicant for a financial analyst's job prepare a computer spreadsheet is one. Requiring a person applying for a truck driver's job to back a truck to a loading dock is another.

Mental ability tests measure reasoning capabilities of applicants. Some of the abilities tested include spatial orientation, comprehension and retention span, and general and conceptual reasoning, among others. The General Aptitude Test Battery (GATB) discussed in Chapter 5 is a widely used test of this type. The "HR Perspective" regarding tests shows how a group of tests can be used to improve selection.

Assessment Centers and Selection   An assessment center is not necessarily a place, but a selection and development device composed of a series of evaluative exercises and tests. The assessment uses multiple exercises and multiple raters. In one assessment center, candidates go through a comprehensive interview, pencil-and-paper test, individual and group simulation, and work exercises. The candidates' performances are then evaluated by a panel of trained raters. It is crucial to any assessment center that the tests and exercises reflect the job content and type of problems faced on the jobs for which individuals are being screened.[15]

A number of state and local governments use the assessment center when selecting department or division heads, because they are interested in extensive job-related testing for skills difficult to evaluate from prior work experience. One major city has used the assessment center to select its director of public works, fire chief, city engineer, and employee-relations administrator. Assessment centers are especially useful in determining promotable employees and in helping to develop them.

Personality Tests

Personality is a unique blend of individual characteristics that affect interaction with the environment and help define a person. Historically, predictive validities have tended to be lower for personality tests when used as a predictor of performance on the job. However, some studies have shown that carefully chosen personality tests that logically connect to work requirements can help predict the interpersonal aspects of job success.[16] For example, a person's ability to tolerate stress might be a valid concern for a police officer, emotional stability for a nuclear plant operator, or a "people" orientation in a social worker.

Polygraph and Honesty Testing

The polygraph, more generally and incorrectly referred to as the "lie detector," is a mechanical device that measures a person's galvanic skin response, heart rate, and breathing rate. The theory behind the polygraph is that if a person answers incorrectly, the body's physiological response will "reveal" the falsification through the polygraph's recording mechanisms.

Employee Polygraph Protection Act Before 1989, thousands of employers used polygraph results to screen potential employees. The biggest users were in service industries such as retail, fast food, and health care. The purpose of polygraph use was to reduce employee theft. Individuals whose answers revealed a potential pattern of dishonesty were eliminated from employment consideration. However, serious questions were raised about polygraph use in employment settings, especially about its reliability and the invasion of the privacy of those tested.

As a result of those concerns, Congress passed the Employee Polygraph Protection Act of 1988. Effective in 1989, the act bars polygraph use for preemployment screening purposes by most employers. However, federal, state, and local governmental agencies are exempt from the act. Also exempted from the law are certain private-sector employers such as security companies and pharmaceutical companies. The act does allow employers to continue to use polygraphs as part of an internal investigation for theft or losses. But the polygraph must be administered voluntarily and the employee can end the test at any time. More on the use of polygraphs for internal investigations is contained in Chapter 17.

Honesty Tests Another controversial test is one that purports to measure employee honesty. The Reid Report and the Stanton Survey are the two most widely used of these pencil-and-paper tests. Individuals who take honesty tests answer yes or no to a list of questions. Sample questions include:[17]

- ▲ Would you tell your boss if you knew of another employee stealing from the company?
- ▲ Is it all right to borrow company equipment to use at home if the property is always returned?
- ▲ Have you ever told a lie?
- ▲ Have you ever wished you were physically more attractive?

Firms use honesty tests to help reduce losses due to employee theft. With preemployment polygraph testing no longer allowed, a growing number of firms have turned to such tests. In addition to being able to screen out potentially dis-

HR Perspectives:

Ethical Issues in Using Graphology and Blood Type for Employment Selection

Graphology is a type of "test" in which an "analysis" is made of an individual's handwriting. Such items as how people dot an "i," cross a "t," or write with a left or right slant, and the size and boldness of the letters they form supposedly tell graphologists about individuals' personalities and their suitability for employment.

With the restrictions on polygraph tests, a number of companies, including some large corporations, have used graphology to screen employees. One graphology firm has over 200 corporate clients, including Renault USA. The cost of an analysis ranges from $175 to $500, and includes an examination of about 300 personality traits.

Formal scientific evaluations of graphology are not easily found. It is an accepted criminal investigation tool, but its value as a personality predictor is much more controversial. In fact, many graphologists recommend that results should be used as an additional source of information about applicants, not as a screening device by themselves.

A problem in addition to validity is that so much depends on the graphologist who interprets the results. Also, as with many personality tests, an employer might have difficulty identifying the relationship between a series of personality traits and job performance.

Graphology may seem a bit

outlandish, but how about blood type as a predictor of personality? In Japan people think blood type is an excellent predictor. Forget the horoscope. Type O blood indicates a person who is generous and bold, Type A one who is industrious, and Type B one who is impulsive and flexible. The Type AB person is thought to be both rational and creative. A manager at Mitsubishi Electric chose ABs to dream up the next generation of fax machines. One nursery school divides children based on their blood types.[20]

Given the lack of formal validity evidence of handwriting or blood type as performance predictors, is there an ethical problem using them in selection?

honest individuals, these firms believe that giving honesty tests sends a message to applicants and employees alike that dishonesty will not be tolerated.[18]

Concerns about the validity of honesty tests continue to be raised, and many firms using them do not do validation studies on their experiences. Instead, they rely on the general validation results given by the test developers, even though that practice is not consistent with the EEOC's Uniform Guidelines. A review of research on the validity of honesty tests by independent researchers found that honesty tests may be useful as broad screening devices for organizations, but the tests may not be as good at predicting that a single individual will steal.[19] Also, the use of these tests can have a negative public relations impact on applicants. A final concern is the invasion of individual privacy through the types of questions asked.

Using tests that may not measure what they purport to measure raises not only legal questions, but ethical ones as well, such as the issue addressed in the "HR Perspective" on graphology and blood type.

▲ SELECTION INTERVIEWING

▼ **A SELECTION INTERVIEW**

is designed to assess job-related knowledge, skills, and abilities (KSAs) and clarify information from other sources.

A **selection interview** is designed to assess job-related knowledge, skills, and abilities (KSAs) and clarify information from other sources. This in-depth interview is designed to integrate all the information from application forms, tests, and reference checks so that a selection decision can be made. Because of the integration required and the desirability of face-to-face contact, the interview is the most important phase of the selection process in many situations. Conflicting information may have emerged from the tests, application forms, or references. As a result, the interviewer must obtain as much pertinent information about the applicant as possible during the limited interview time, evaluate this information against job standards, and make a decision.

The interview is not an especially valid predictor of job performance, but it has high "face validity"—that is, it *seems* valid to employers. Virtually no employers are likely to hire individuals without interviewing them.

Some interviewers may be better than others at selecting individuals who will perform better. Studies have found that there is very high *intra*rater (the same interviewer) reliability but only moderate-to-low *inter*rater (different interviewers) reliability.[21] Many factors affect the accuracy of the interview, from stereotypes carried by interviewers to the order in which interviewees are seen. The important point to remember is that the validity of the interview depends on the type of interview used and the capabilities of the individual interviewers.

Equal Employment and Interviewing

The interview, like a pencil-and-paper test and an application form, is a type of predictor and must meet the standards of job-relatedness and nondiscrimination. Some court decisions and EEOC rulings have attacked the interviewing practices of some organizations as discriminatory.

An interviewer making hiring recommendations must be able to identify the factors that shaped the decision. If that decision is challenged, the organization must be able to show justification. Everything written or said can be probed for evidence in a lawsuit. Lawyers recommend the following to minimize EEO concerns with interviewing:

▲ Identify objective criteria related to the job to be looked for in the interview.
▲ Put criteria in writing.
▲ Provide multiple levels of review for difficult or controversial decisions.
▲ Use structured interviews with the same questions asked of all interviewees.

FRANK AND ERNEST® by Bob Thaves

Reprinted by permission of NEA, Inc.

Types of Interviews

There are five types of interviews: structured, situational, behavioral description, nondirective, and stress interviews. Each type is discussed next.

Structured Interview   The **structured interview** uses a set of standardized questions that are asked of all applicants. Every applicant is asked the same basic questions so comparisons among applicants can more easily be made.

This type of interview allows an interviewer to prepare job-related questions in advance and then complete a standardized interviewee evaluation form. Completion of such a form provides documentation if anyone, including an EEO enforcement body, should question why one applicant was selected over another.[22] Sample questions that might be asked of all applicants for a production maintenance management opening are:

- ▲ Tell me about how you trained workers for their jobs.
- ▲ How do you decide the amount of work you and the maintenance crew will have to do during a day?
- ▲ How does the production schedule of the plant affect what a mechanic ought to repair first?
- ▲ How do you know what the needs of the plant are at any given time and what mechanics ought to be doing?
- ▲ How did you or would you go about planning a preventive maintenance program in the plant?

As is evident, the structured interview is almost like an oral questionnaire and offers greater consistency and accuracy than some other kinds of interviews. The structured interview is especially useful in the initial screening because of the large number of applicants in this step of the selection process. Obviously, it is less flexible than more traditional interview formats, and therefore may be less appropriate for second or later interviews.

Even though a series of patterned questions are asked, the structured interview does not have to be rigid. The predetermined questions should be asked in a logical manner, but the interviewer can avoid reading the questions word for word down the list. The applicant should be allowed adequate opportunity to explain answers clearly. The interviewer should probe until he or she fully understands the applicant's responses.

Research on interviews consistently has found the structured interview to be more reliable and valid than other approaches.[23] The format for the interview ensures that the same interviewer has similar information on each candidate, so there is higher intrarater reliability. Also, the fact that several interviewers ask the same questions of applicants has led to better interrater reliability.

Situational Interview   The **situational interview** is a highly structured interview that is limited strictly to job-related questions. With experienced applicants the format is essentially one of a job knowledge or work sample test.[25]

Interview questions are based on job analysis and checked by experts in the job so they will be content valid. There are three types of questions:[26]

1. *Hypothetical*—where an applicant is asked what he or she might do in a certain job situation.
2. *Related to knowledge*—which might entail explaining a method or demonstrating a skill.
3. *Related to requirements*—where areas such as willingness to work the hours required and travel demands are explored.

▼ **A STRUCTURED INTERVIEW**

uses a set of standardized questions that are asked of all job applicants.

▼ **SITUATIONAL INTERVIEW**

is a highly structured interview limited strictly to job-related questions.

Job experts also write "good," "average," and "poor" responses to the questions to facilitate rating the answers of the applicant. The interviewer can code the suitability of the answer, assign point values, and add up the total number of points the interview received.

Behavioral Description Interview   In **behavioral description interviews,** applicants are required to give specific examples of how they have performed a certain procedure or handled a problem in the past. For example, applicants might be asked the following:

- ▲ How did you handle a situation where there were no rules or guidelines on employee discipline?
- ▲ Why did you choose that approach?
- ▲ How did your supervisor react?
- ▲ How was the issue finally resolved?

Like other structured methods, behavioral descriptions provide better validity than unstructured interviews.

> **BEHAVIORAL DESCRIPTION INTERVIEWS**
>
> require applicants to give specific examples of how they have performed or handled a problem in the past.

Nondirective Interview   The **nondirective interview** uses general questions from which other questions are developed. It should be used mainly in psychological counseling, but it is also used in selection. The interviewer asks general questions designed to prompt the applicant to discuss herself or himself. The interviewer then picks up on an idea in the applicant's response to shape the next question. For example, if the applicant says, "One aspect that I enjoyed in my last job was my supervisor," the interviewer might ask, "What type of supervisor do you most enjoy working with?"

Difficulties with a nondirective interview include keeping it job related and obtaining comparable data on each applicant. Many nondirective interviews are only semiorganized; the result is a combination of general and specific questions that are asked in no set order, and different questions are asked of different applicants for the same job.

> **A NONDIRECTIVE INTERVIEW**
>
> uses general questions, from which other questions are developed.

Stress Interview   The **stress interview** is a special type of interview designed to create anxiety and put pressure on the applicant to see how the person responds. In the stress interview, the interviewer assumes an extremely aggressive and insulting posture. Those who use this approach often justify its use with individuals who will encounter high degrees of stress on the job, such as a consumer-complaint clerk in a department store or an air traffic controller.

The stress interview is a high-risk approach for a company. The typical applicant is already somewhat anxious in any interview, and the stress interview can easily generate a very poor image of the interviewer and the employer. Consequently, an applicant that the organization desires to hire might turn down the job offer. Even so, one study found that many interviewers deliberately put college seniors under stress. Less than 30% said they did it "*rarely.*"[24]

> **A STRESS INTERVIEW**
>
> is used to create pressure and stress on an applicant to see how the person responds.

Interviewing Basics

Many people think that the ability to interview is an innate talent, but this contention is difficult to support. Just because someone is personable and likes to talk, there is no guarantee that the person will be a good interviewer. Interviewing skills are developed through training. Some suggestions for good interviewing follow.

Planning the Interview   Effective interviews do not just happen; they are planned. Pre-interview planning is essential to a well-conducted in-depth selection interview. This planning begins with selecting the time and place for the interview. Sufficient time should be allotted so that neither the interviewer nor interviewee feel rushed. Also, a private location is important so that both parties can concentrate on the interview content. The interviewer should review the application form for completeness and accuracy before beginning the interview, and also should make notes to identify specific areas for questioning the applicant about during the interview.

Control   An important aspect of the interview is control. If the interviewer does not control the interview, the applicant usually will. Control includes knowing in advance what information must be collected, systematically collecting it, and stopping when that information has been collected.

Having control of the interview does not mean doing a lot of talking. The interviewer should talk no more than about 25% of the time in an in-depth interview. If the interviewer talks more than that, the interviewer is being interviewed.

▼ **A REALISTIC JOB PREVIEW (RJP)**

is the process through which an interviewer provides a job applicant with an accurate picture of a job.

Realistic Job Preview   Although the interviewer should limit the amount of time he or she spends talking, a key part of the interview is to offer information about the job for which the interviewee is applying. One approach that has been widely researched is the **realistic job preview (RJP),** the process through which an interviewer provides a job applicant with an accurate picture of a job.

The purpose of an RJP is to inform job candidates of the "organizational realities" of a job so that they can more accurately evaluate their own job expectations. By presenting applicants with a clear picture of the job, the organization hopes to reduce employee disenchantment or unrealistic expectations, and thereby to experience less turnover and employee dissatisfaction. A review of research on RJPs found that they do tend to result in applicants having lower job expectations.[27]

A recent court case is of interest here. A federal appeals court in Manhattan upheld an argument that a woman who was fraudulently lured into her job had her career derailed by the employer. The employee (a lawyer) claimed she left the environmental law department of one law firm to head the startup environmental department of another firm. That department never materialized.[28] Attorneys say the ruling should serve as a warning to companies not to exaggerate opportunities at their firms.

Questioning Techniques

The questioning techniques that an interviewer uses can and do significantly affect the type and quality of the information obtained. Some specific suggestions follow.

Good Questions   Many questions an interviewer asks assume that the past is the best predictor of the future, and it usually is. An interviewer is less likely to have difficulty when questioning the applicant's demonstrated past performance than when asking vague questions about the future.

Some types of questions provide more meaningful answers than others. Good interviewing technique depends on the use of open-ended questions directed toward a particular goal. An open-ended question is one that cannot be answered yes or no. *Who, what, when, why, tell me, how, which* are all good ways to begin questions that will produce longer and more informative answers. "What was your attendance record on your last job?" is a better question than, "Did you have good attendance on your last job?" because the latter question can be answered simply, "Yes," which elicits less information.

Poor Questions   Certain kinds of questions should be avoided:

1. *Questions that rarely produce a true answer.* An example is, "How did you get along with your co-workers?" This question is almost inevitably going to be answered, "Just fine."
2. *Leading questions.* A leading question is one in which the answer is obvious from the way in which the question is asked. For example, "You do like to talk to people, don't you?" Answer: "Of course."
3. *Illegal questions.* Questions that involve information such as race, creed, sex, national origin, marital status, and number of children, are illegal. They are just as inappropriate in the interview as they are on the application form.
4. *Obvious questions.* An obvious question is one for which the interviewer already has the answer, and the applicant knows it. Questions already answered on the application blank should be probed, not asked again. If an interviewer asks, "What high school did you attend?" the applicant is likely to answer, "As I wrote on my application form, South High School in Caveton." Instead, questions should be asked that probe the information given: "What were your favorite subjects at South High, and why?"
5. *Questions that are not job related.* All questions asked should be directly related to the job for which the applicant has applied. Some people believe discussion about the weather, sports, or politics helps a candidate relax and become at ease. However, those questions consume interview time that could be more appropriately used in other ways. Also, many times the interviewee does not relax and the interviewer may not listen to the responses because he or she is using the "chit-chat" time to review the candidate's application form or to otherwise make up for a lack of planning and preparation.

There are certain question areas that an interviewer probably should minimize. These areas can be referred to as the "egad" factors, which are questions the interviewer asks about the applicant's expectations, goals, aspirations, and desires. Although the answers to an egad question may be meaningful, usually the applicant will respond with a prepared "pat" answer. For example, in answer to the question, "What are your aspirations?" the college graduate will often respond that he or she wants to become a company vice-president. The person settles for vice-president instead of president in order not to appear egotistical. Because it is considered culturally desirable in our society to demonstrate a certain amount of ambition, the vice-presidential level appears to be appropriate.

Listening Responses   The good interviewer avoids *listening responses* such as nodding, pausing, casual remarks, echoing, and mirroring. Listening responses are an essential part of everyday, normal conversation, but they may unintentionally provide feedback to the applicant. Applicants may try to please the interviewer and look to the interviewer's listening responses for cues. Even though the listening responses may be subtle, they do provide information to applicants.

Problems in the Interview

There are a number of pitfalls that interviewers should avoid. Operating managers and supervisors most often use poor interviewing techniques because they do not interview often or have not been trained to interview. Some common problems encountered in the interview are highlighted next.

Snap Judgments   Ideally, the interviewer should collect all the information possible on an applicant before making a judgment. Reserving judgment is much easier to recommend than to do because it is difficult not to form an early impression. Too often, interviewers form an early impression and spend the balance of the interview looking for evidence to support it. This impression may be based on a review of an individual's application blank or on more subjective factors such as dress or appearance. Consequently, many interviewers make a decision on the job suitability of applicants within the first four or five minutes of the interview.

Negative Emphasis   As might be expected, unfavorable information about an applicant is the biggest factor considered in interviewers' decisions about overall suitability. Unfavorable information is given roughly twice the weight of favorable information. Often a single negative characteristic may bar an individual from being accepted, whereas no amount of positive characteristics will guarantee a candidate's acceptance.

Halo Effect   Interviewers should try to avoid the *halo effect,* which occurs when an interviewer allows a prominent characteristic to overshadow other evidence. The halo effect is present if an interviewer lets a candidate's accomplishments in athletics overshadow other aspects, which leads the interviewer to hire the applicant because "athletes make good salespeople." *Devil's horns* (a reverse halo effect), such as being inappropriately dressed or a low grade point average, may affect an interviewer as well.

Biases   An interviewer must be able to recognize his/her personal biases. For example, studies on the interview process indicate that women are rated lower by both female and male interviewers.[29] Other studies have found that interviewers tend to favor or select people who are perceived to be similar to the interviewer. This similarity can be on age, race, sex, previous work experiences, personal background, or other factors. As the workforce demographics shift and become more diverse, interviewers will have to be even more aware of this "similarity bias."

The selection of an applicant who falls below standards or the rejection of an applicant who meets standards is an indication that personal bias may have influenced a selection decision. An interviewer should be honest and write down the reasons for selecting a particular applicant. The solution to the problem of bias lies not in claiming that a person has no biases, but in demonstrating that they can be controlled.

Cultural Noise   The interviewer must learn to recognize and handle *cultural noise*—responses the applicant believes are socially acceptable rather than facts. Applicants want jobs; to be hired they know they must impress the interviewer. They may feel that if they divulge any unacceptable facts about themselves, they may not get the job. Consequently, applicants may be reluctant to tell an interviewer some details about themselves. Instead, they may try to give the interviewer responses that are socially acceptable but not very revealing.

An interviewer can handle cultural noise by not encouraging it. If the interviewer supports cultural noise, the applicant will take the cue and continue those kinds of answers. Instead, the applicant can be made aware that the interviewer is not being taken in. An interviewer can say, "The fact that you are the best pitcher on your softball team is interesting, but tell me about your performance on your last job."

What Interviewers Evaluate

Overall, interviewers look for evidence that an applicant is well rounded, competent, and successful. The factors found in one study, shown in order of importance, are presented in Figure 9–7. Notice that work experience is rated eighth, and grade point average and outside activities were rated last. These variables are not inclusive of all possible criteria that may be considered. Other studies have shown that a wide variety of other variables are considered as well.[30]

▲ **Figure 9–7**

Employment Variables Considered During an In-House Interview

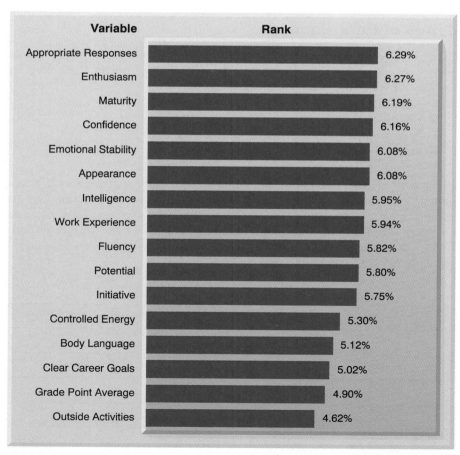

Variable	Rank
Appropriate Responses	6.29%
Enthusiasm	6.27%
Maturity	6.19%
Confidence	6.16%
Emotional Stability	6.08%
Appearance	6.08%
Intelligence	5.95%
Work Experience	5.94%
Fluency	5.82%
Potential	5.80%
Initiative	5.75%
Controlled Energy	5.30%
Body Language	5.12%
Clear Career Goals	5.02%
Grade Point Average	4.90%
Outside Activities	4.62%

SOURCE: Joe A. Cox et al., "A Look Behind Corporate Doors," *Personnel Administrator*, March 1989, 58. Published by the Society for Human Resource Management Used with permission.

▲ BACKGROUND INVESTIGATION

Background investigation may take place either before or after the in-depth interview. It costs the organization some time and money, but it is generally well worth the effort. Unfortunately, applicants frequently misrepresent their qualifications and backgrounds.

Many universities report that inquiries on graduates and former students often reveal that the individuals never graduated or may never have attended the university! Another type of credential fraud uses the mail-order "degree mill." To enhance their chances of employment, individuals purchase unaccredited degrees from organizations that grant them for a fee—as one advertisement puts it, "with no exams, no studying, no classes."

Estimates are that many resumes contain at least one lie or "factual misstatement" (see Figure 9–8). The only way for employers to protect themselves from resume fraud and false credentials is to request verification or proof from applicants either before or after hire. If hired, the employee can be terminated for falsifying employment information. Therefore, it is unwise for employers to assume that "someone else has already checked." Too often, no one took the trouble to check.[31]

Types of References

Background references can be obtained from several sources. Some of the following references may be more useful and relevant than others, depending on the jobs for which applicants are being considered:

- ▲ Academic references
- ▲ Prior work references
- ▲ Financial references
- ▲ Law enforcement records
- ▲ Personal references

Personal references often are of little value; they probably should not even be required. No applicant will ask somebody to write a recommendation who is going to give a negative response. Therefore, personal references from relatives, clergy, or family friends are likely to be a weak source of selection information. Instead, greater reliance should be placed on work-related references from previous employers and supervisors.

 Figure 9–8

Misrepresentations on Resumes
(n = 1,200)

INFORMATION MISREPRESENTED	PERCENT MISREPRESENTED
Expertise	22%
Salary, Job Title	12
Employment History	11
Educational Background	9
Self-Employment	4

SOURCE: Adapted from "Human Resource Measurements," Supplement to *Personnel Journal,* April 1992, 2.

HR Perspectives:
Ethics of Using Credit Histories in Selection

The use of an individual's credit history during the employment-selection process raises some ethical issues. Some firms that use credit histories as part of their reference-checking process do so for job-related purposes. For example, an individual's financial history may be very relevant to a bank hiring loan officers. However, other firms that are not justified in asking for such information deliberately violate the federal Fair Credit Reporting Act (FCRA) by doing so.

Many such employers check credit histories on applicants without their notification or approval, particularly in the retail and financial industries. Some examples of misuse by both employers and credit-reporting agencies include these:

▲ A medium-sized retailer checks credit histories on every applicant after the screening interview in order to decide who to invite back for second interviews.
▲ A financial firm always checks credit histories on all racial-minority applicants, but checks credit records of white applicants only for certain jobs.
▲ A reporter (as a test) told a credit bureau that he would be hiring one or two employees and needed credit reports on applicants. He then gave the name, address, and Social Security numbers of two of his fellow reporters (with their permission) to two credit-reporting firms. One firm charged $20 per report and the other a $500 signup fee and $15 per report.

▲ As another test, the same reporter requested a credit history on former Vice-President Dan Quayle. He received a complete listing, including the fact that Quayle had a big mortgage and more charges at Sears than at some luxury men's stores.

As would be expected, the credit-reporting firms say that the blame for misuse of credit records should be placed on those requesting the information, not the credit bureaus. Yet the easy access to those records raises disturbing privacy concerns. As our society becomes more computerized and information-intensive, the ethics of credit-reference checking during employment will continue to be an issue.[33]

Legal Constraints on Background Investigations

Various federal and state laws have been passed to protect the rights of individuals whose backgrounds may be investigated during preemployment screening. Depending on the state, employers may be able to request information from law enforcement agencies on any applicant, or they may be prohibited from getting certain credit information.

Impact of Privacy Legislation   Of the laws passed to protect the privacy of personal information, the most important is the Federal Privacy Act of 1974, which applies primarily to government agencies and units. However, bills to extend the provisions of the Privacy Act to other employers have been introduced in Congress at various times. Under the 1974 act, a government entity must have a signed written release from a person before information can be given to someone else. Under some legislation proposed in the past, either a copy of the obtained information would be given to the individual or the person would be given the right to inspect the personnel file.[32] The "HR Perspective" on the ethics of using credit information without notification to applicants illustrates why privacy concerns have affected reference-checking practices.

References on Former Employees   In a number of court cases, individuals have sued their former employers for slander, libel, or defamation of character as a result of what the employer said to other potential employers that prevented the individuals from obtaining jobs. Two examples illustrate why employers should be careful when giving reference information:[34]

▲ An executive at one firm remarked that a former employee was a "sociopath." The former employee sued and won $1.9 million in a judgment against the employer and the executive.

▲ Over $500,000 was paid by both Pan Am World Airways and Equitable Life to settle lawsuits on references given on former employees.

Consequently, many organizations have adopted policies restricting the release of reference information. Figure 9–9 lists some specific suggestions that employers should follow for releasing such information.

Negligent Hiring   The costs of a failure to check references may be high. A number of organizations have found themselves targets of lawsuits that charge negligence in hiring workers who commit violent acts on the job. Lawyers say

▲ **Figure 9–9**

Guidelines for Defensible References

1. Do not volunteer information. Respond only to specific company or institutional inquiries and requests. Before responding, telephone the inquirer to check on the validity of the request.
2. Direct all communication only to persons who have a specific interest in that information.
3. State that the information you are providing is confidential and should be treated as such. Use qualifying statements such as "providing information that was requested"; "relating this information only because it was requested"; or "providing information that is to be used for professional purposes only."
4. Provide only reference data that relates and pertains to the job and job performance in question.
5. Avoid vague statements such as: "He was an average student"; "She was careless at times"; "He displayed an inability to work with others."
6. Document all released information. Use specific statements such as: "Mr. _____ received a grade of C, an average grade"; "Ms. _____ made an average of two bookkeeping errors each week"; or "This spring, four members of the work team wrote letters asking not to be placed on the shift with Mr. _____".
7. Clearly label all subjective statements based on personal opinions and feelings. Say "I believe . . ." whenever making a statement that is not fact.
8. When providing a negative or potentially negative statement, add the reason or reasons why, or specify the incidents that led you to this opinion.
9. Do not answer trap questions such as "Would you rehire this person?"
10. Avoid answering questions that are asked "off the record."

SOURCE: "Employment References: Do You Know the Law?" by James D. Bell, James Castagnera, and Jane Patterson Young, © February 1984. Reprinted with the permission of *Personnel Journal,* Costa Mesa, California, all rights reserved.

that an employer's liability hinges on how well it investigates an applicant's fitness. Prior convictions and frequent moves or gaps in employment should be a cue for further inquiry. Yet lawyers also advise organizations who are asked about former employers to give out only name, employment date, and title. This restriction places employers in the position of needing information on those it may hire, but being unwilling to give out information in return.[35]

Details on the application form provided by the applicant should be investigated to the greatest extent possible, so the employer can show that due diligence efforts were undertaken. Also, applicants should be asked to sign releases authorizing the employer to check references, and those releases should contain a statement releasing the reference givers from any future liability actions.[36]

Reference-Checking Methods

Several methods of obtaining reference information are available to an employer. Telephoning a reference is the most-used method, although many firms prefer written responses.

Telephone Reference Checking Many experts recommend using a structured telephone reference-check form. Typically, questions asked on such a form focus on factual verification of information given by the applicant, such as employment dates, salary history, type of job responsibilities, and attendance record. Other questions often include reasons for leaving the previous job, the individual's manner of working with supervisors and other employees, and other less factual information. Naturally, many firms will provide only the factual information. But the use of the form can provide evidence that a diligent effort was made.

Written Methods of Reference Checking Some organizations have preprinted reference forms that they send to individuals who are giving references for applicants. These forms often contain a release statement signed by the applicant, so that those giving references can see that they have been released from liability on the information they furnish. Specific or general letters of reference also are requested by some employers or provided by applicants.

Medical Examinations

The Americans with Disabilities Act (ADA) prohibits a company from rejecting an individual because of a disability and from asking job applicants any question relative to current or past medical history until a conditional job offer is made. It also prohibits the use of preemployment medical exams except for drug tests until a job has been conditionally offered. Figure 9–10 shows proper and improper ways to ask questions about disabilities.

Drug Testing Drug testing also may be a part of a medical exam, or it may be done separately if a medical examination is not a part of the selection process. As a part of the selection process, drug testing has increased in the past few years, not without controversy. Employers should remember that such tests are not infallible—for a variety of reasons. The accuracy of drug tests varies according to the type of test used, the item tested, and the quality of the laboratory where the test samples are sent. If an individual tests positive for drug use, then a second,

▲ **Figure 9–10**

Questioning an Applicant about Disabilities

DO NOT ASK:	DO ASK:
▲ Do you have any physical or other limitations? ▲ Do you have any disabilities? ▲ Have you ever filed for or collected workers' compensation? ▲ How many times were you absent due to illness in the past two years? ▲ Have you been treated for any of the following medical conditions? ▲ Do you have any family members with health problems or history of illness or disabilities? ▲ Why are you using crutches, and how did you become injured?	▲ Have you ever consulted a psychiatrist or psychologist? ▲ Can you perform the essential functions of the job for which you are applying with or without accommodation? Please describe any accommodations needed. ▲ How would you perform the essential tasks of the job for which you have applied? ▲ If hired, discuss how you would perform the tasks outlined in the job description that you have reviewed. ▲ Describe your attendance record on your last job. ▲ Describe any problems you would have reaching the top of a six-foot filing cabinet? Lifting 50-pound boxes up to 25% of the time? Climbing 20-foot ladders up to 50% of the workday? ▲ What did your prior job duties consist of, and which ones were the most challenging?

more detailed analysis should be administered by an independent medical laboratory. Because of the potential impact of prescription drugs on test results, applicants should complete a detailed questionnaire before the drug test. Whether urine, blood, or hair samples are used, the process of obtaining, labeling, and transferring the sample to the testing lab should be outlined clearly and definite policies and procedures established.

Drug testing also has legal implications. In a number of cases, courts have ruled that individuals with previous substance-abuse problems who have received rehabilitation are disabled, and thus covered by the Americans with Disabilities Act. Also, preemployment drug testing must be administered in a nondiscriminatory manner, instead of being used selectively with certain groups. The results of the drug tests also must be used in a consistent manner, so that all individuals testing positive are treated uniformly. If a production worker applicant tests positive, he/she should be rejected for employment, just as an applicant to be vice-president of marketing would be.

Genetic Testing   Another controversial area of medical testing is genetic testing. One survey of large companies revealed that a few firms were using genetic tests, and many more were considering their use in the future. However, the general public disapproves strongly of their use.[37]

Employers that use genetic screening tests do so for several reasons. The tests may link workplace health hazards and individuals with certain genetic characteristics. Also, genetic testing may be used to make workers aware of genetic problems that could occur in certain work situations. The third use is the most controversial: to exclude individuals from certain jobs if they have genetic conditions that increase their health risks. Because someone cannot change his or her genes, the potential for discrimination based, for example, on race or sex, is very real. For instance, sickle-cell anemia is a condition found only in African Americans. If chemicals in a particular work environment can cause health problems for individuals with sickle-cell anemia, African Americans might be screened out on that basis. The question is whether that decision should be left to the individual or the employer.

▲ SUMMARY

- ▲ Selection is a process that matches individuals and their qualifications to jobs in an organization.

- ▲ Because of government regulations and the need for better coordination between the HR unit and other managers, many organizations have established a centralized employment office as part of the HR department.

- ▲ From the reception of an applicant, through the application and initial screening process, testing, in-depth selection interview, and background investigation, to the physical examination, the entire process must be handled by trained, knowledgeable individuals.

- ▲ Application forms must meet EEO guidelines and ask only for job-related information.

- ▲ All tests used in the selection process must be valid and reliable.

- ▲ Selection tests include: (1) ability and aptitude tests, (2) general personality and psychological tests, and (3) assessment centers. Tests should relate directly to the jobs for which individuals apply.

- ▲ Controversial psychological tests used to select employees are polygraphs, honesty tests, and graphology.

- ▲ From the standpoints of effectiveness and EEO compliance, the most useful interviews are structured, situational, and behavioral description, although nondirective and stress interviews are also used.

- ▲ Sound interviewing requires planning and control. Applicants should be provided a realistic picture of the jobs for which they are applying. Good questioning techniques can reduce problems.

- ▲ Background investigations can be conducted in a variety of areas, but concerns about individual privacy must be addressed.

- ▲ Care must be taken when either getting or giving reference information to avoid the potential legal problems of defamation, libel, slander, and negligent hiring.

- ▲ Medical examinations may be an appropriate part of the selection process for some employers but only after a conditional job offer has been made.

- ▲ Drug testing has grown in use as a preemployment screening device, in spite of some problems and concerns associated with its accuracy and potential for discrimination on the part of employers.

REVIEW AND DISCUSSION QUESTIONS

1. Why do many employers have a specialized employment office?
2. You are starting a new manufacturing company. What phases would you go through to select your employees?
3. Agree or disagree with the following statement: "A good application form is fundamental to a good selection process." Explain your conclusion.
4. Discuss the following statement: "We stopped giving tests altogether and rely exclusively on the interview for hiring."
5. Make two lists. On one list indicate what information you would want to obtain from the screening interview; on the other indicate what information you would want to obtain from the in-depth interview.
6. Develop a structured interview guide for a 20-minute interview with a retail sales clerk applicant.
7. How would you go about investigating a new college graduate's background? Why would this information be useful in making a selection decision?
8. Discuss how the Americans with Disabilities Act has modified the use of medical exams in the selection process.

 SELECTION FOR TEMPORARY EMPLOYEES

Manpower, Inc., the largest worldwide supplier of temporary help, identified a need for a better system of selecting and training office employees. Manpower employees are assigned on a temporary basis to companies, filling in for permanent employees who are absent and helping companies get through heavy workloads or special projects. Office workers supplied by Manpower include word-processing operators, data-entry operators, computer operators, typists, secretaries, transcriptionists, accounting clerks, and customer service representatives.

In a typical year, Manpower employs one million people worldwide. Like any business that hires and places its workers, Manpower needed effective selection tools and training techniques. It was essential that Manpower's selection and training systems be highly accurate, as well as time and cost-effective. Further, those systems needed to be flexible enough to expand along with new developments in office technology.

The company developed solutions on two fronts: selection and training. Tests were developed specifically for the selection of temporary workers for automated offices. And computer training was developed to equip temporary employees with skills for hundreds of popular software programs.

Manpower's two-pronged approach to assessment, using one set of tests for knowledge and another for skills, results in the most complete evaluation of workers for the automated office. Ultraskill, the firm's hands-on test for operators, requires them to prove their ability to produce a document in a reasonable period of time on the actual hardware and software they will use on the job. Ultraskill also tests for skills critical to document production such as spelling, punctuation, editing, and proofreading. In addition, a series of proficiency tests assesses knowledge of specific word-processing systems.

Manpower also developed tests to assess workers' abilities to perform general office tasks including proofreading, customer service, and order entry. By measuring competencies such as problem solving, decision-making, resource-fulness, and the ability to follow directions, Manpower's General Office Test Battery helps the company identify people with the skills and personal characteristics needed to be productive in general office jobs.

All of Manpower's tests are professionally developed and validated in accordance with EEOC standards and American Psychological Association guidelines. Test validation is not only important for the purpose of meeting EEO requirements but also to ensure that the test measures the skills and abilities most relevant to the job being filled.

The basis of Manpower's entire selection system, called the Predictable Performance System, is job analysis. Thorough analysis of office positions was the first step in the development of the tools that enable Manpower to make the best possible match of employee to assignment. Manpower's selection system also includes a structured interview that draws information about an applicant's experience, abilities, and interests. Information on customer needs and preferences is obtained through detailed assignment orders, surveys of customers' work environments, and temporary-worker peformance appraisals. The same sophisticated assessment tools and procedures apply to the selection of workers for light industrial assignments.

The development of Manpower's Performance System warranted a major investment of research, time, and money. However, all those involved in the process benefit, especially Manpower's temporary employees and customers.[38]

▲ QUESTIONS

1. What are the components of the selection process that are used by Manpower?
2. Discuss how the testing process and types of test used are job related.
3. Compare the sophistication of Manpower's selection process with that you have experienced when applying for jobs.

▲ NOTES

1. Adapted from Earle Norton, "Future Factories," *The Wall Street Journal,* January 13, 1993, A1, A8.

2. "How Businesses Search for Qualified Applicants: Trying to Bridge the Skills Gap," Supplement to *Personnel Journal,* June 1992, 1.

3. G. Powell, "Applicant Reactions to the Initial Employment Interview: Exploring Theoretical and Methodological Issues," *Personnel Psychology,* 44 (1991), 67; and Ivan T. Robertson et al., "The Impact of Personnel Selection and Assessment Methods on Candidates," *Human Relations* 44 (1991), 963.

4. C. L. Greathouse, "Ten Common Hiring Mistakes," *Industry Week,* January 20, 1992, 22–25.

5. "Working," reprinted from the *Washington Post* in *Omaha World-Herald,* July 19, 1992, 6G.

6. Junda Woo, "Job Interviews Pose Rising Risk to Employers," *The Wall Street Journal,* March 11, 1992, B1.

7. J. Wymer and Deborah A. Sudbury, "Employment Discrimination 'Testers'—Will Your Hiring Practices 'Pass?'," *Employee Relations Law Journal* 17 (1992), 623.

8. "In Tough Times Applicants Face More Job Testing," *Omaha World-Herald,* March 15, 1992, 10G.

9. Julia Lawlor, "Job Candidates Screened on Video," *USA Today,* June 16, 1993, 5B.

10. "Satisfaction with the Quality of New Hires," *Personnel Journal,* April 1992, 2.

11. M. Zeidner and M. Most (eds.), *Psychological Testing: An Inside View* (Baltimore: Consulting Psychologists Press Inc., 1992); and T. Maurer et al., "Methodological and Psychometric Issues in Setting Cutoff Scores.", *Personnel Psychology* 44 (1991), 235.

12. "Is This Test Valid?," Supplement to *Personnel Journal,* April 1992, 5.

13. John F. Meyers, *"Soroka vs. Dayton Hudson Corp.—Is the Door Closing on Pre-employment Testing of Applicants?,"* *Employee Relations Law Journal* 17 (1992), 645–653.

14. "Skill Tests Maximize Productivity, Quality," *Quality in Manufacturing,* May–June 1992, 10.

15. B. Crawley et al., "Assessment Center Dimensions, Personality and Aptitudes," *Journal of Occupational Psychology* 63 (1990), 211–216.

16. L. M. Hough et al., "Criterion-Related Validities of Personality Constructs and the Effect of Response Distortion on those Validities," *Journal of Applied Psychology,* 74 (1990), 581–595.

17. "Saint or Sinner? Score Yourself Honestly," *Omaha World-Herald,* October 18, 1981, 7A.

18. John W. Jones and William Terris, "After the Polygraph Ban," *Recruitment Today,* May–June 1989, 25–31; and J. Martin and K. Slora, "Employee Selection by Testing," *HR Magazine,* June 1991, 68–70.

19. Paul R. Sackett, Laura R. Burris, and Christine Callahan, "Integrity Testing for Personnel Selection: An Update," *Personnel Psychology* 42 (1989), 491–529; and J. Jones et al., "Employment Privacy Rights and Honesty Tests," *Employee Relations Law Journal,* 15 (1990), 561.

20. Adapted from "Handwriting and Business," *Omaha World-Herald,* May 5, 1992, G1; and "Sushi, a Show and a Quick Transfusion," *Business Week,* April 29, 1991, 40.

21. R. D. Arvey and J. E. Campion, "The Employment Interview: A Summary of Recent Research," *Personnel Psychology* 35 (1986), 570–578.

22. P. C. Sawyers, "Structured Interviewing: Your Key to the Best Hires," Supplement to *Personnel Journal,* December 1992.

23. Patrick M. Wright, Philip A. Lichtenfels, and Elliot D. Pursell, "The Structured Interview: Additional Studies and a Meta-Analysis," *Journal of Occupational Psychology* 62 (1989), 191–199.

24 C. Fletcher, "Ethics and the Job Interview," *Personnel Management,* March 1992, 39.

25. I. Robertson et al., "The Validity of Situational Interviews for Administrative Jobs," *Journal of Organizational Behavior* 11 (1990), 69–76.

26. For an example of such questions, see R. Rose, "Guerrilla Interviewing," *INC.,* December 1992, 145–147.

27. John P. Wanous, "Installing a Realistic Job Preview: Ten Tough Choices," *Personnel Psychology* 42 (1989), 117–134.

28. E. J. Pollock, "Ruling Frowns on Employer's False Promises," *The Wall Street Journal,* October 7, 1992, B1.

29. "Women Said to Be More Modest in Interviews," *Omaha World-Herald,* June 28, 1992, 11G.

30. J. Chatman, "Matching People and Organizations: Selection and Socialization in Public Accounting Firms," *Administrative Science Quarterly* 36 (1991), 459–484; N. Anderson and V. Shackleton, "Decision Making in the Grad Selection Interview" *Journal of Occupational Psychology* (1990), 63–76; T. Macan and Robert L. Dipboye, "The Relationship of Interviewers' Preinterview Impressions to Selection and Recruitment Outcomes," *Personnel Psychology* 43 (1990), 745–768; and Sara L. Rynes and B. Gebhart, "Interviewing Assessments of Applicant 'Fit': an Exploratory Investigation," *Personnel Psychology* 43 (1990), 13–35.

31. J. Rigdon, "Deceptive Resumes Can Be Door-Openers but Can Become an Employees' Undoing," *The Wall Street Journal,* June 17, 1992, B1.

32. J. Rothfeder, "Looking for a Job? You May Be Out Before You Go In," *Business Week,* September 24, 1990, 128.

33. Based on information in John R. Erickson, "Defamatory Employment References and the Fair Credit Reporting Act," *Labor Law Journal* 40 (1989), 150–157; and "Is Nothing Private?" *Business Week,* September 4, 1989, 74–83.

34. Donald F. Dvorak, "References, Resumes, and Other Lies," *Industry Week,* October 17, 1988, 14.

35. G. Munchus III, "Check References for Safer Selection," *HR Magazine,* June 1992, 74–77; J. W. Fenton, "Negligent Hiring," *Personnel Journal,* April 1990, 62; and A. Ryan and M. Lasek, "Negligent Hiring and Defamation," *Personnel Psychology,* 44 (1991), 293.

36. Paul W. Barada, "Check References with Care," *Nation's Business,* May 1993, 54–56.

37. "Genetic Testing Finds Little Support," *The Wall Street Journal,* January 28, 1992, B1.

38. Used with permission. May not be reproduced without the permission of Manpower Inc., Milwaukee, Wisconsin, 1993.

Section 4 — Training and Developing Human Resources

In any organization, employees must receive training to perform their jobs and to grow in their knowledge, skills, and abilities. Training provides employees with opportunities to learn new skills. The organization thus develops its internal talent for the future.

Training and orientation are the topics of Chapter 10. Orientation is the first organizational training an employee receives. Before a person can perform well on the job, he or she must be properly introduced, or oriented, to the organization. Determining training needs and evaluating the effectiveness of training are two important aspects of HR management, but two that are seldom done well. Training is most effective when it is specifically aimed at the individual needs of employees. An ideal training evaluation consists of checking to see if a newly-trained employee can now do something he or she could not do before training.

While on-the-job (OJT) training is the most common training method, it is often done in a haphazard fashion. Suggestions for more successful OJT are provided in Chapter 11 which examines on-the-job and off-the-job methods for developing employees. Development is more broad, and long-range than training. By developing employees, especially managers, an organization prepares itself for the future. Yet there is more to development than just sending someone off to take a course or get a degree since development also often has a large element of experience associated with it. Methods to provide this experience as well as more formal knowledge acquisition are important. Managerial modeling and mentoring are but two of the ways experience can be guided.

This chapter also considers careers. Careers can be viewed from the perspective of the individual who is having a career or from the perspective of the employer who provides career opportunity. However, careers are affected also as dual-career couples have become the norm rather than the exception. The problems presented to both the company and the couple by transfer, for example, are real and complex.

Chapter 12 considers performance appraisal. Once an employee has been trained to perform a job, a manager must review his or her performance. This review is a vital part of ongoing development because it provides feedback on what an employee is doing well and on what areas are needing improvement.

Appraisals examine employee performance, and are useful in solving some performance problems, but they can create other problems. This chapter examines behavioral reactions to appraisals, common mistakes made in appraising performance, and different methods that can be used to arrive at an acceptable Performance-Appraisal system. Peer ratings and subordinates' ratings of superiors have both received much attention recently. Certainly with the emphasis on teams, peer ratings take on a new importance. But self ratings and ratings by outsiders have a place in appraisal as well. Regardless of the method chosen the rater must watch for rater errors. There are many potential appraisal problems and the best defense against them seems to be an awareness of the potential each rater has to make these errors.

CHAPTER 10

ORIENTATION AND TRAINING

After you have read this chapter, you should be able to:

1. Define training and discuss its legal aspects.

2. Describe four characteristics of an effective orientation system.

3. Discuss at least four learning principles that relate to training.

4. Discuss the major phases of a training system.

5. Identify three ways to determine training needs.

6. List and discuss at least four training methods.

7. Give an example of each of the levels of training evaluation.

8. Identify three designs used in evaluating training.

U.S. employers have serious concerns about both applicants and employees. It has less to do with *quantity* of
applicants available than with their *quality.* The concern
is that a large and growing segment of the population
does not have the basic educational skills to do today's
jobs. The ability to read, write, and do arithmetic are
genuine BFOQs (bona fide occupational qualifications)
in a job market dominated by technology. Yet 20 to 30
million adults in the workforce have serious problems
with these basic skills. More than half of the Fortune
500 companies report they have to conduct remedial
training to bring employees to a minimal level. It costs
those firms over $300 million each year. A survey of
small and medium sized companies found that one-
third of their employees are deficient in basic educational skills as well.

Over the next decade the mismatch between job skill
requirements and the available pool of workers will get
worse. Trends unfavorable for employers were noted
earlier in this book, including a decline in population
growth, scarcity of educated immigrants, changing employee values, and the need for more job flexibility.

Faced with these challenges, U.S. employers have
begun to explore three avenues:

1. Forging partnerships with public school districts and
   community colleges.
2. Establishing advocacy groups to promote better
   schools and funding.
3. Establishing in-house basic skills training.

Beginning with the 1994 seniors, the Los Angeles
Unified School District (the nation's second largest) will
offer a *warranty* on the basic skills of reading, math,
communication, problem solving, reasoning, integrity,
self-management, initiative, and responsibility. Perhaps,

such efforts eventually will pay dividends, but they are
clearly a long-term solution, not an immediate one. In
the meantime in-house programs are growing, such as
the agreement between General Motors (GM) and the
United Auto Workers Union that commits funds and
manpower to a formal literacy program. Ford and
Chrysler established similar programs in 1983 and 1987,
respectively. So far GM operates classrooms in 30 of its
facilities and plans to put classrooms in all 150 of them
soon.

An example of how this program affects individual
people is Ed Castor, age 50, a former GM plant worker
with a third-grade reading level. He passed up several
promotions because he did not want people to know he
could not read well. He had friends fill out his reports
when necessary. Finally, his fear of failure led him to ask
for a demotion because he was frustrated about being
semiliterate, but his supervisor found him a tutor instead. He passed the GED and now works for GM in
the education program.

Smaller companies are getting into the act as well.
The Hach Company in Loveland, Colorado, offers its
820 employees basic math and writing—42 courses in
all. Kathryn Hach, Chairman and CEO, notes, "This is
the future. If people are educated, it makes running a
business that much easier."

Unfortunately, in-house programs are not a guarantee
and many programs fail. Students drop out of even successful programs. One study found that 25% of employees drop out of such programs. However, this very basic
element of training will have to be done *somewhere* by
someone. Employers cannot have high-tech complex
jobs if their human resources cannot read and write.[1]

> We are forced to rely on people, which is why we put so much emphasis on training them.
>
> *Henry Block*

Training has both current and future implications for the success of organizations. As the opening discussion indicates, remedial training is a major issue confronting employers for the 1990s. Employers also are aware that the training or retraining of individuals for the jobs of the future may determine the success of many U.S. firms.[2] Many types of training exist. Job-skill training, supervisory training, management development, and employee development, are a few.

The official figure for training expense in the United States is $44 billion, or about 1.5% of payroll for companies with more than 100 employees. Traditionally about two-thirds of that has been devoted to developing professional managers and one third to front-line workers. But that proportion is changing.[3] Organizations are realizing that they need to develop the skills of their front-line workers as much as those of their managers.

Something else is changing as well. An old axiom in HR management was, "When things get tough, training is the first expenditure cut." Accordingly, in the 1982 recession, training was cut disproportionately because it was little valued by the executives. In the 1992 recession, though, a survey done by the American Society for Training and Development found that 40% of companies described as "very hard hit" by the recession made no change in their training budgets, 30% increased them, and 30% decreased them. The biggest increases went to fund quality management, management development, and computer training.[4]

▲ THE CONTEXT OF TRAINING

Training is a learning process whereby people acquire skills or knowledge to aid in the achievement of goals. Because learning processes are tied to a variety of organizational purposes, training can be viewed either narrowly or broadly. In a limited sense, training provides employees with specific, identifiable knowledge and skills for use on their present jobs. Sometimes a distinction is drawn between *training* and *development,* with development being broader in scope and focusing on individuals gaining *new* knowledge and skills useful for both present and future jobs.

▼ **TRAINING**

is a learning process whereby people acquire skills or knowledge to aid in the achievement of goals.

Legal Aspects of Training

Because training has both current and future consequences for job success, it is an area targeted by equal employment opportunity (EEO) laws and regulations. One area of concern is the practice used to select individuals for inclusion in training programs. The criteria used must be job related and not unfairly restrict the participation of protected-class individuals. Another concern is differences in pay based on training to which protected-class members have not had equal access. A third is the use of training as a criterion for selecting individuals for promotions. In summary, fair employment laws and regulations definitely do apply to training, and employers must be aware of them.

Training is a cost, and some employers have gone to court to try and require individuals who leave their firms after training to repay the cost. For instance, Electronic Data Systems (EDS) sued a worker who signed a "promissory note" to repay the firm $9,000 if he left the firm voluntarily or was fired for cause within 24 months of starting a special training program. The employee contested the suit by saying that he did not learn anything he did not already know and thus received no benefits from the training.[5]

Training Responsibilities

A typical division of training responsibilities is shown in Figure 10–1. The HR unit serves as a source of expert training assistance and coordination. The unit often has a more long-range view of employee careers and development of the entire organization than do individual operating managers. This difference is especially true at lower levels in the organization.

On the other hand, managers are likely to be the best source of technical information used in skill training. They also are in a better position to decide when employees need training or retraining. Because of the close and continual interaction they have with their employees, managers are the appropriate ones to determine and discuss employee career potentials and plans.

Total Quality Management (TQM) Training

The pioneers in total quality management (TQM) believe that it takes a great deal of training to create and maintain a quality company. Building an environment that is "friendly" to TQM requires changed behaviors and much understanding by management of the leadership skills necessary.[6] In small firms managers may do much of the training themselves. For example, at Grand Rapids Spring and Wire Products, Jim Zawacki, who owns the firm, taught his employees the basic math skills needed to use statistical quality control (SQC). Zawacki believes the amount of time spent on this training has paid off. In five years on-time delivery has gone from 60% to over 95%, inventory has gone down 30%, and sales have doubled, thanks to SQC.[7] This example shows that focus on quality can pay off but it is training intensive.

▲ **Figure 10–1**

Typical Training Responsibilities

HR UNIT	MANAGERS
▲ Prepares skill-training materials ▲ Coordinates training efforts ▲ Conducts or arranges for off-the-job training ▲ Coordinates career plans and employee development efforts ▲ Provides input and expertise for organizational development	▲ Provide technical information ▲ Monitor training needs ▲ Conduct the on-the-job training ▲ Continually discuss employees' growth and future potential ▲ Participate in organizational change efforts

Cross-Cultural Training and Diversity

For many years certain companies have used training to familiarize their employees going overseas (and their families) with the new culture in which they will be living. General Motors believes its intensive cross-cultural training explains why very few of the firm's international employees return before completing their assignments. Contrast that to the 25% return rate reported by firms that do not conduct such training.[8]

Here at home the increasing cultural diversity of the workforce presents similar problems for some companies. Language differences can affect both productivity and safety, for example.[9] Living and working overseas or in a multicultural context in one's home country both require some cross-cultural awareness and interpersonal skills. A research study on such training concluded that in general it can be effective in helping people adjust successfully to both overseas assignments and culturally diverse situations in the U.S.[10]

▲ ORIENTATION

Orientation is the planned introduction of new employees to their jobs, co-workers, and the organization. However, orientation should not be a mechanical process. Because all employees are different, a sensitive awareness to anxieties, uncertainties, and needs is important.

▼ **ORIENTATION**

is the planned introduction of new employees to their jobs, co-workers, and the organization.

Purposes of Orientation

The overall goal of orientation is to help new employees learn about their new work environments and get their performances up to acceptable levels as soon as possible. The orientation process has several specific purposes: to create a favorable impression, to enhance interpersonal acceptance, and to reduce turnover.

To Create an Initial Favorable Impression   A good orientation program creates a favorable impression of the organization and its work. This impression begins even before the new employees report to work. Providing sufficient information about when and where to report the first day, handling all relevant paperwork efficiently, and having personable and efficient people assist the new hire all contribute to creating a favorable impression of the organization.

To Enhance Interpersonal Acceptance   Another purpose of orientation is to ease the employee's entry into the work group. New employees often are concerned about meeting the people in their work units. The expectations of a group of employees may not always parallel what was presented at management's formal orientation. However, if a well-planned formal orientation is lacking, the new employee may be oriented solely by the group, and thus possibly in ways not beneficial to the organization. For example, at a steel company the work group in the furnace section delighted in telling new employees the way "it really works here." Some of their views were not entirely accurate. Therefore, orientation was essential for management to make certain new employees knew what their supervisors wanted.

Many organizations use a "buddy" system whereby an existing employee is paired with a new employee as part of the orientation process. One research study found that this kind of socialization of newcomers is advantageous.[11]

▲ **Figure 10–2**

Orientation and Turnover at
Corning Inc.

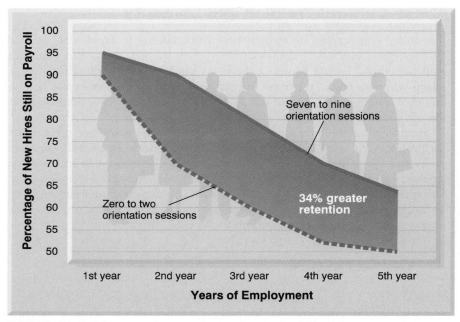

SOURCE: Adapted from Joseph McKenna, "Welcome Aboard," *Industry Week,* November 6, 1992, 34.

To Reduce Turnover   As many as 60% of all new hires may leave their jobs within the first seven months according to one study.[12] But, Corning, Inc. found that individuals who had been through more orientation sessions had a lower turnover rate than those who had less orientation (see Figure 10–2). At one time, Texas Instruments was able to reduce annual turnover rates 40%, and much of the decline was attributed to more effective orientation of new employees. Some other reported benefits of better employee orientation are:

▲ Stronger loyalty and greater commitment to organizational values and goals
▲ Lower absenteeism
▲ Higher job satisfaction

Orientation Responsibilities

Orientation requires cooperation between individuals in the HR unit and other managers and supervisors. In a small organization without an HR department, such as a machine shop, the new employee's supervisor or manager has the total orientation responsibility. In large organizations managers and supervisors, as well as the HR department, should work as a team in employee orientation.

Figure 10–3 illustrates a common division of orientation responsibilities in which managers work with HR specialists to orient a new employee. Together they must develop an orientation process that will communicate what the employee needs to learn. A supervisor may not know all the details about health insurance or benefit options, for example, but he/she usually can best present information on safety rules, allowing the HR department to explain benefits.

HR UNIT	MANAGERS
▲ Places employee on payroll ▲ Designs formal orientation program ▲ Explains benefits and company organization ▲ Develops orientation checklist ▲ Evaluates orientation activities	▲ Prepare co-workers for new employee ▲ Introduce new employee to co-workers ▲ Provide overview of job setting and work rules

▲ **Figure 10–3**

Typical Orientation Responsibilities

Establishing an Effective Orientation System

A systematic approach to orientation requires attention to attitudes, behaviors, and information that new employees need. Unfortunately, orientation often is conducted rather haphazardly. The general ideas that follow highlight the major components of an effective orientation system: preparing for new employees, providing them with needed information, presenting orientation information effectively, and conducting evaluation and follow-up on the initial orientation.

Prepare for New Employees   New employees must feel that they belong and are important to the organization. Both the supervisor and the HR unit should be prepared to give each new employee this perception. It is very uncomfortable for an employee to arrive at work and have a manager say, "Oh, I didn't realize you were coming to work today," or, "Who are you?" This type of depersonalization must be avoided.

Further, co-workers as well as the supervisor should be prepared for a new employee's arrival. This preparation is especially important if the new employee will be assuming certain duties that might be interpreted as threatening a current employee's job status and security. The manager or supervisor should discuss the purpose for hiring the new worker with all current employees.

Some organizations use co-workers or peers to conduct part of the new employees' orientation.[13] It is particularly useful to involve more experienced and higher-performing individuals who can serve as role models for new employees. One study found that the influence of information sources tended to change as the employee gained experience. The importance of co-workers as sources of information increased over time.[14]

Provide New Employees Needed Information   The guiding question in the establishment of an orientation system is, "What does the new employee need to know *now?*" Often new employees receive a large amount of information they do not immediately need, and they fail to get the information they really need the first day of a new job.

Some organizations systematize this process by developing an orientation checklist. Figure 10–4 indicates the items to be covered by the HR department representative and/or the new employee's supervisor. Using a checklist, one can ensure that all necessary items have been covered at some point, perhaps during the first week. Many employers have employees sign the checklist to verify that they have been told of pertinent rules and procedures.

Often, employees are asked to sign a form indicating that they have received the handbook and have read it. This requirement gives legal protection for em-

▲ **Figure 10–4**

Orientation Checklist

Name of Employee _____
Starting Date _____
Department _____

HR DEPARTMENT
Prior to Orientation
___ Complete Form A and give or
    mail to new employee
___ Complete Form B
___ Attach Form B to "Orientation
    Checklist—Supervisor" and
    give to the supervisor
Employee's First Day
Organization and Employee Poli-
cies and Procedures
___ History of XYZ Inc.
___ Organization chart
___ Purpose of the company
___ Employee classifications
Insurance Benefits
___ Group health plan
___ Disability insurance
___ Life Insurance
___ Workers' Compensation
Other Benefits
___ Holidays
___ Vacation
___ Jury and election duty
___ Funeral leave
___ Health services
___ Professional discounts
___ Child care
End of Orientation—First Day
___ Make appointment for second
    day
___ Introduce supervisor
Other Items
___ Job posting
___ Bulletin board—location and
    use
___ Safety
___ Alcohol/drug usage
___ Where to get supplies
___ Employee's records—updating

_____
Employee Signature

_____
Date

Name of Employee _____
Starting Date _____
Department _____
Position _____

SUPERVISOR
Employee's First Day
___ Introduction to co-workers
___ Tour of department
___ Tour of company
Location of
___ Coat closet
___ Restroom
___ Telephone for personal use and
    rules concerning it
Working Hours
___ Starting and leaving
___ Lunch
___ Breaks
___ Overtime
___ Early departures
___ Time clock
Pay Policy
___ Pay period
___ Deposit system
Other Items
___ Parking
___ Dress
Employee's Second Day
___ Pension retirement plan
___ Sick leave
___ Personal leave
___ Job posting
___ Confidentiality
___ Complaints and concerns
___ Termination
___ Equal Employment Opportunity
During Employee's First Two Weeks
Emergencies
___ Medical
___ Power failure
___ Fire

At the end of the employee's first
two weeks, the supervisor will ask if
the employee has any questions
concerning any items. After all
questions have been discussed,
both the employee and the supervisor
will sign and date this form and return
it to the HR Department.

_____
Orientation Conducted By

ployers who may have to enforce policies and rules later. Having signed forms, employees cannot deny that they were informed about policies and rules.

Several types of information usually are included in the orientation process. The information ranges from the nature of the organization and its culture to the specifics of a normal workday. A general organizational overview might include a brief review of the organization, its history, its structure, who the key executives are, what its purpose is, its products and/or services, how the employee's job fits into the big picture, and any other general information. If the employer prepares an annual report, giving a copy to a new employee may be beneficial. Also, some organizations have developed a list of terms that are used in the industry to help new employees learn regularly used vocabulary and terms.

To understand the organization fully, new employees also should be oriented to the culture of the organization. Giving informal information on such factors as typical dress habits, lunch practices, and what executives are called will aid the adjustment of new employees.

Another important type of initial information to give employees is the policies, work rules, and benefits. Policies about sick leave, tardiness, absenteeism, vacations, benefits, hospitalization, parking, and safety rules must be made known to every new employee immediately. Also, the employee's supervisor or manager should outline a normal workday for the employee on the first morning, covering the daily routine in detail. This information will include such essentials as introducing the new employee to other employees, showing him or her the work area, explaining when and where to take coffee breaks and lunch, what time work begins and ends, where to park, and where the restrooms are. Perhaps some of these explanations can be delegated to a co-worker.

Presenting Orientation Information Effectively   Managers and HR representatives should determine the most appropriate ways to present orientation information. For example, rather than telling an employee about company sick leave and vacation policies, an employee handbook might be presented on the first day. The manager or HR representative then can review this information a few days later to answer any of the employee's questions. Some companies present certain information on videotapes or computer.[15]

One common failing of many orientation programs is *information overload*. When too many facts are presented to new employees, they may ignore important details or inaccurately recall much of the information. If given an employee handbook, the new employee can refer to information when needed.

Employees will retain more of the orientation information if it is presented in a manner that encourages them to learn. Some organizations have successfully used filmstrips, movies, slides, charts, and computers. However, the emphasis should be on presenting information, not on "entertaining" the new employee. Materials such as handbooks and information leaflets should be reviewed periodically for updates and corrections.

Evaluation and Follow-Up   A systematic orientation program should have an evaluation and/or reorientation phase at some point after the initial orientation. An HR representative or a manager can evaluate the effectiveness of the orientation by conducting follow-up interviews with new employees a few weeks or months after the orientation. Employee questionnaires also can be used. Some organizations even give new employees a written test on the company handbook two weeks after orientation.

Too often, typical orientation efforts assume that, once oriented, employees are familiar with everything they need to know about the organization forever. Instead, orientation should be viewed as a never-ending process of introducing both old and new employees to the current state of the organization. To be assets to their organizations, employees must know current organizational policies and procedures, and these may be altered from time to time.

▲ LEARNING PRINCIPLES: THE PSYCHOLOGY OF LEARNING

Working in organizations is a continual learning process, and learning is at the heart of all training activities. However, different learning approaches are possible, some apparently more effective than others.[16] Learning is a complex psychological process that is not fully understood by practitioners or research psychologists.

Often, trainers or supervisors present information and assume that merely by presenting it they have ensured that it will be learned. But learning takes place only when information is received, understood, and internalized in such a way that some change or conscious effort has been made to use the information. Managers can use the research on learning to make their training efforts more effective. Some major learning principles that guide training efforts are presented next.

Intention to Learn

People learn at different rates and are able to apply what they learn differently. *Ability* to learn must be accompanied by motivation, or *intention,* to learn. Motivation to learn is determined by the answers to questions like, "How important is my job to me?" "How important is it that I learn that information?" "Will learning this help me in any way?" "What's in it for me?"[17]

People are more willing to learn when the material is important to them. Some of the following goals may encourage intention to learn in certain people:

- ▲ Achievement
- ▲ Advancement
- ▲ Authority
- ▲ Co-workers' influence
- ▲ Comprehension
- ▲ Creativity
- ▲ Curiosity
- ▲ Fear of failure
- ▲ Recognition
- ▲ Responsibility
- ▲ Status
- ▲ Variety

Whole Learning

It is usually better to give an overall view of what a trainee will be doing than to deal immediately with the specifics. This concept is referred to as *whole learning* or *Gestalt learning.* As applied to job training, this means that instructions should be divided into small elements *after* employees have had an opportunity to see how all the elements fit together. For example, in a plastics manufacturing operation, it would be desirable to explain to trainees how the raw chemical material comes to the plant and what is done with the plastic moldings after they are used in the manufacturing process before explaining the trainees' specific jobs. The information is presented as an entire, logical process, so that trainees can see how

HR Perspectives:
Seeing the "Big Picture" *First* Helps Learning

Read this passage and be prepared to recall the details when you have finished. Is it easy to understand and learn?

The procedure is actually quite simple. First you arrange items into different groups. Of course one pile may be sufficient, depending on how much there is to do. If you have to go somewhere else due to a lack of facilities, then that is the next step; otherwise, you are pretty well

set. It is important not to overdo things. That is, it is better to do too few things at once than too many. In the short run this may not seem important but complications can easily arise. A mistake can be expensive as well.

At first, the whole procedure will seem complicated. Soon, however, it will become just another facet of life. It is difficult to foresee any end to the necessity for this task in the immediate future, but

then, one never can tell. After the procedure is completed, one arranges the materials into different groups again. Then they can be put into their appropriate places. Eventually they will be used once more; then the whole cycle will have to be repeated. However, that is part of life.[19]

Now read the upside down sentences below.

The preceding passage is written about washing clothes. Reread it with that in mind. Does it make more sense when you have that "big picture"?

---

the various actions fit together into the big picture.[18] Then the supervisor can break the information into the specifics with which the trainees must deal. See the "HR Perspective" for a good illustration.

Reinforcement

The concept of **reinforcement** is based on the *law of effect,* which states that people tend to repeat responses that give them some type of positive reward and avoid actions associated with negative consequences. (This subject will be explored in more depth later in this chapter in connection with behavior modification.) The rewards (reinforcements) an individual receives can be either external or internal. For example, a registered nurse receives an external reward for learning how to use a new electrocardiogram machine by receiving a certificate of completion. Her internal reward may be a feeling of pride in having learned something new. Consider also a machinist who learns to use a new lathe in the machine shop. At first he makes many mistakes. With time and practice he begins to do better and better. One day he knows he has mastered the lathe. His feeling of accomplishment is a type of internal reward.

Many training situations provide both internal and external rewards. If a new salesclerk answers her supervisor's question correctly and is complimented for giving the correct answer, she may receive both an external reward (the compliment) and an internal reward (a feeling of pride). If a person is positively reinforced for learning, he or she will continue to learn.

▼ **REINFORCEMENT**

is based on the law of effect that states that people tend to repeat responses that give them some type of positive reward and avoid actions that are associated with negative consequences.

Immediate Confirmation

Another learning concept is **immediate confirmation,** which indicates that people learn best if reinforcement is given as soon as possible after training.

▼ **IMMEDIATE CONFIRMATION**

indicates that people learn best if reinforcement is given as soon as possible after training.

Feedback on whether a learner's response was right or wrong should be given as soon as possible after the response. To illustrate, suppose a corporate purchasing department has developed a new system for reporting inventory information. The new system is much more complex than the old one and requires the use of a new form that is longer and more difficult to complete. However, it does give computerized information much more quickly and helps eliminate errors in the recording process that delay the total inventory report. The purchasing manager who trains inventory processors may not have the trainees fill out the entire inventory form when teaching them the new procedure. Instead, the manager may explain the total process, then break it into smaller segments and have each trainee complete the form a section at a time. By checking each individual's form for errors immediately after each section is complete, the purchasing manager can give immediate feedback, or confirmation, before the trainees fill out the next section. This immediate confirmation corrects errors that, if made throughout the whole form, might establish a pattern that will need to be unlearned.

Practice

Learning new skills requires practice. Research and experience show that the following considerations must be addressed when designing training practice applications: active practice, reality of the practice, and spaced versus massed practice.

▼ **ACTIVE PRACTICE**
occurs when trainees perform job-related tasks and duties during training.

Active Practice   **Active practice** occurs when trainees perform job-related tasks and duties during training. It is more effective than simply reading or passively listening. Once some basic instructions have been given, active practice should be built into every learning situation. It is one of the advantages of good on-the-job training. Assume a person is being trained as a customer service representative. After being given some basic selling instructions and product details, the trainee should be allowed to call on a customer to use the knowledge received.

▼ **SPACED PRACTICE**
occurs when several practice sessions are spaced over a period of hours or days.

Spaced versus Massed Practice   Active practice can be structured in two ways. The first one, **spaced practice,** occurs when several practice sessions are spaced over a period of hours or days. It works better for some kinds of learning, whereas massed practice is better for others. If the trainee is learning physical skills (like learning to ski), several practice sessions spaced over a period of hours or days result in greater learning than the same amount of practice in one long period. Training cashiers to operate a new machine could be alternated with having the individuals do tasks they already know how to do. Thus, the training is distributed instead of being concentrated into one period. For this reason, some organizations spread their orientation of new employees over an entire week by devoting an hour or two daily to orientation, instead of covering it all in one day. This incremental approach to skill acquisition minimizes the physical fatigue that deters learning.

▼ **MASSED PRACTICE**
occurs when a person does all of the practice at once.

Massed practice occurs when a person does all of the practice at once. For memorizing tasks, massed practice is usually more effective. Can you imagine trying to memorize the list of model options for a dishwasher one model per day for 20 days as an appliance distribution salesperson? By the time you learned the last option you would have forgotten the first one.

Learning Curves

People learn in different patterns in different training situations. These patterns are called *learning curves*. The kind of learning curve typical of a given task has implications for the way the training program is designed. Figure 10–5 shows the learning curves mentioned. In the *decreasing returns* (Curve 1) pattern, the amount of learning and/or the skill level increases rapidly at first, then the rate of improvement slows. For example, when an employee first learns to operate a stamping machine, the rate of production increases rapidly at first, then slows as the normal rate is approached. Learning to perform most routine jobs follows such a curve.

The *increasing returns* (Curve 2) pattern is much less common. It occurs most often when a person is learning a completely unfamiliar task. Starting a completely new job with little formal orientation or training might require a slow beginning while the important vocabulary and relationships are learned. Then the learner begins to pick up expertise quickly.

A third pattern, the *S-shaped curve* (Curve 3), is a combination of the decreasing return and increasing return curves. S-curves usually result when a person tries to learn an unfamiliar, difficult task that also requires insight into the basics of the job. In this pattern, learning occurs slowly at first, then increases rapidly for a while, and then flattens out. Learning to debug computer systems is one example, especially if the learner has little previous contact with computers.

The *plateau* (Curve 4) in a learning curve indicates that as knowledge, skill, or speed is being acquired, the learner often reaches a point when there is no apparent progress. At this point, trainees should be encouraged and advised that these plateaus are expected, common, understandable, and usually are followed by new surges in learning.

Transfer of Training

The training from the class must be transferred to the job.[20] For effective *transfer of training* to occur, two conditions must be met:

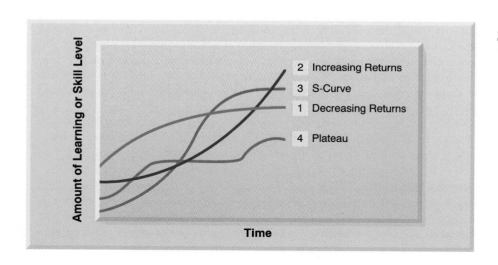

▲ **Figure 10–5**

Common Learning Curves

1. The trainees must be able to take the material learned in training and apply it to the job context in which they work.
2. Use of the learned material must be maintained over time on the job.

To aid transfer of training to the job situations, the training should be as much like the jobs as possible. In the training situation, trainees should be able to experience the types of situations they can expect on the job. For example, training managers to be better interviewers should include role-playing with "applicants" who can respond in the same way that real applicants would.

Two Processes Underlying Learning

Behavior modification and behavior modeling are two ways people learn, both on and off the job. They can be incorporated into the design of training programs and are based on the learning principles just described.

Behavior Modification   A comprehensive approach to training has been developed based on the concept of reinforcement. This approach is *behavior modification*. Using the theories of psychologist B. F. Skinner, behavior modification has become increasingly popular. Skinner states that "learning is not doing; it is changing what we do."[21]

Behavior modification makes use of four means of changing behavior, labeled *intervention strategies*. The four strategies are positive reinforcement, negative reinforcement, punishment, and extinction.

A person who receives a desired reward receives **positive reinforcement.** If an employee is on time every day during a week and, as a result, receives extra pay equivalent to one hour of normal work, the employee has received positive reinforcement of his or her good attendance by receiving a desired reward.

Negative reinforcement occurs when an individual works to avoid an undesirable consequence. An employee who arrives at work on time every day may do so to avoid a supervisor's criticism. Thus, the potential for criticism leads to the employee's taking the desired action.

Action taken to repel a person from undesirable action is **punishment.** A grocery manager may punish a stock clerk for leaving the stockroom dirty by forcing him or her to stay after work and clean it up.

Behavior can also be modified through a technique known as **extinction,** which is the absence of a response to a situation. Assume that an employee dresses in a new style to attract the attention of her superior. The supervisor just ignores the new type of dress. There is no reinforcement, positive or negative, and no punishment given. With no reinforcement of any kind, it is likely that the employee will quit dressing in that fashion. The hope is that unreinforced behavior will not be repeated.

All four strategies can work to change behavior. In fact, combinations may be called for in certain situations. But research suggests that for most training situations, positive reinforcement of the desired behavior is most effective.

Behavior Modeling   The most elementary way in which people learn—and one of the best—is **behavior modeling,** or copying someone else's behavior. A variation of modeling occurs when people avoid making mistakes they see others make. The use of behavior modeling is particularly appropriate for skill

▼ **POSITIVE REINFORCEMENT**

occurs when a person receives a desired reward.

▼ **NEGATIVE REINFORCEMENT**

occurs when an individual works to avoid an undesirable consequence.

▼ **PUNISHMENT**

is action taken to repel the person from the undesired action.

▼ **EXTINCTION**

is the absence of a response to a situation.

▼ **BEHAVIOR MODELING**

is copying someone else's behavior.

HR Perspectives:
Research on Training Methods for Acquiring Computer Skills

An increasing number of jobs require workers to have computer knowledge and skills. At the same time, workforce changes mean that employers will have to train or retrain many workers in computer knowledge and skills. To do this training, a variety of methods can be used. As described in *Personnel Psychology*, Gist, Rosen, and Schwoerer conducted a study to examine the impact of training methods and trainee age on learning computer software skills.[22]

The study was conducted with individuals recruited through newsletters who volunteered to receive three hours of training using a computer software spreadsheet program. The 146 individuals who volunteered for the program averaged 40 years of age, with almost half below and half above age 40. The three-hour program consisted of an introduction to microcomputing, the skills needed

to use a spreadsheet program, and an applications problem requiring the use of spreadsheets. Before the training, the participants filled out questionnaires giving demographic information and previous computer experience.

The class was divided into two groups, with each group having both younger and older workers. Each group was taught by a different training method. Trainers in one group used a tutorial approach, in which step-by-step instructions were given on computer diskettes. The trainees paced themselves, and if they gave incorrect responses at any step, they had to correct their mistakes before proceeding. The other group was taught by a modeling approach. The trainees first viewed a videotape that showed someone using the spreadsheet software; at each step the result was shown on the videotape. The videotape was stopped after each

demonstration and the trainees did the procedure just shown. If mistakes were made, the trainees had to correct them before proceeding further.

Following the training, the trainees were asked to perform 25 specific tasks using the spreadsheet software, and then their performance results were scored as correct or incorrect.

The authors found that the trainees using the modeling approach scored somewhat better than those using the tutorial approach. However, the older trainees scored significantly lower in both groups. Results indicated that the modeling method of training appears to be a superior approach when teaching computer software skills, although more research is needed in other settings. But the other finding about older individuals having more difficulty acquiring computer skills has important implications as employers train and retrain older individuals.

training in which the trainees must use both knowledge and practice. In such training situations, individuals must learn specific information and then apply it. For example, a workshop that trains managers to conduct job interviews might include presenting information on equal employment regulations and the types of questions to ask and not ask. Next, the trainees can be shown a videotape of an interview in which the interviewers use information previously presented. Then the trainees can apply their knowledge to interviews in role-playing situations. By videotaping the role-play interviews, the managers can receive feedback and reinforce their performances.

Most training programs are not structured adequately to take advantage of modeling. Passive classroom training whereby individuals listen to lectures allows little modeling, while videotapes of people showing the desired behavior allows much more. The importance of such modeling is seen in the "HR Perspective." When modeling is used, it is important to select a model who can and will exhibit the desired behaviors. An informal group leader who shares management's values often is a good choice. Likewise, a longer-service employee can become a newer one's mentor by using modeling and other psychological processes.

▲ SYSTEMS APPROACH TO TRAINING

The success of any training can be gauged by the amount of learning that occurs and is transferred to the job. Too often, unplanned, uncoordinated, and haphazard training efforts significantly reduce the learning that could have occurred.[23] Training and learning will take place, especially through informal workgroups, whether an organization has a coordinated training effort or not. Employees learn from other employees. But without a well-designed systematic approach to training, what is learned may not be what is best for the organization. Figure 10–6 shows the relevant components of the three major phases in a training system: (1) the assessment phase, (2) the implementation phase, and (3) the evaluation phase.[24]

In the *assessment* phase, planners determine the need for training and specify the objectives of the training effort. Looking at the performance of clerks in a billing department, a manager might find that their data-entry and keyboard abilities are weak and that they would profit by having specific instruction. An objective of increasing the clerks' keyboard entry speed to 60 words per minute without errors might be established. The number of words per minute without

▲ **Figure 10–6**   Model of Training System

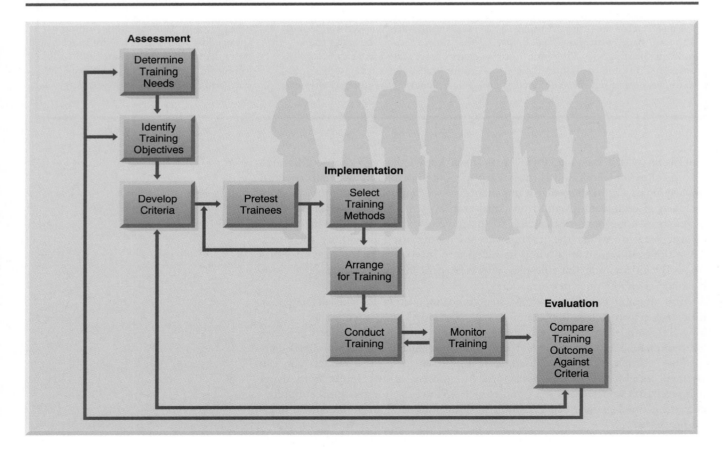

errors is the criterion against which training success can be measured and represents the way in which the objective is made specific. To make the bridge between assessment and implementation, the clerks would be given a keyboard data-entry test.

Using these results, *implementation* then can begin. For instance, the billing supervisor and an HR training specialist could work together to determine how to train the clerks to increase their speeds. Arrangements for instructors, classrooms, materials, and so on are made at this point. A programmed instruction manual might be used in conjunction with a special data-entry class set up at the company. Then training is actually conducted.

The *evaluation* phase is crucial and focuses on measuring how well the training accomplished what its originators expected. Monitoring the training serves as a bridge between the implementation and evaluation phases.

▲ TRAINING NEEDS ASSESSMENT

Training is designed to help the organization accomplish its objectives. Determining organizational training needs is the diagnostic phase of setting training objectives. Just as a patient must be examined before a physician can prescribe medication to deal with an ailment, an organization or an individual employee must be studied before a course of action can be planned to make the "patient" function better. Managers can identify training needs through three types of analyses:

▲ Organizational analyses
▲ Task analyses
▲ Individual analyses

Organizational Analyses of Training Needs

The first way of diagnosing training needs is through organizational analysis, which considers the organization as a system. As part of the company's strategic human resource planning, it is important to identify the knowledge, skills, and abilities that will be needed by employees in the future as both jobs and the organization change. For example, assume that in its five-year business plan, a manufacturer of mechanical equipment identifies the need to shift production to computer-based electronic equipment. As the organization implements its plans, current employees will need to be retrained so that they can do electronic instead of mechanical assembly work.

Both internal and external forces that will influence the training of workers must be considered. As the chapter-opening discussion of remedial training illustrates, the problems posed by the technical obsolescence of current employees and an insufficiently educated labor pool from which to draw new workers should be confronted before those training needs become critical.

Organizational analyses also can be done using various operational measures of organizational performance. On a continuing basis, detailed analysis of HR data can show training weaknesses. Departments or areas with high turnover, high absenteeism, low performance, or other deficiencies can be pinpointed. After such problems are analyzed, training objectives can be developed. Specific sources of information for an organizational-level needs analysis may include:

▲ Grievances   ▲ Complaints from customers
▲ Accident records   ▲ Equipment utilization figures
▲ Observations   ▲ Training committee observations
▲ Exit interviews   ▲ Waste/scrap/quality control data

Task Analyses

The second way to diagnose training needs is through analyses of the tasks performed in the organization. To do this, it is necessary to know what are the job
requirements in the organization. Job descriptions and job specifications provide
information on the performances expected and skills necessary for employees to
accomplish the required work. By comparing the requirements of jobs with the
knowledge, skills, and abilities of employees, training needs can be identified.[25]

One firm used task analyses to identify the tasks to be performed by engineers
who were to be trained as instructors to train other employees. By listing the
tasks required of a technical instructor, management established a program to
teach specific skills needed by the engineers to become successful instructors.

Individual Analyses

The third means of diagnosing training needs focuses on individuals and how
they perform their jobs. The use of performance-appraisal data in making these
individual analyses is the most common approach. To assess training needs
through the performance-appraisal process, an employee's performance inade-
quacies first must be determined in a formal review. Then some type of training
is designed to help the employee overcome the weakness. Figure 10–7 shows
how analyses of the job and the person mesh to identify training needs.

Another way to assess individual training needs is by asking employees. Both
managerial and nonmanagerial employees can be surveyed, interviewed, and/or
tested.[26] The results can give managers insight into what employees believe their
problems are and what actions they recommend. In one example, 110
city/county public administrators were questioned to see what training they felt
they needed. The survey revealed that the administrators' top needs were learning how to make more effective decisions, how to use their time better, and
how to set goals properly.

A survey can take the form of questionnaires or interviews with supervisors
and employees on an individual or group basis. The purpose is to gather information on problems, as perceived by the individuals involved.[27] Sources of information for surveys include:

▲ Questionnaires   ▲ Records of critical incidents
▲ Job knowledge tools   ▲ Data from assessment centers
▲ Skill tests   ▲ Role-playing results
▲ Attitude surveys

Determining Training Priorities

Because training seldom is an unlimited budget item and there are multiple
training needs in an organization, it is necessary to prioritize needs. Ideally,
training needs are ranked in importance on the basis of organizational objectives,

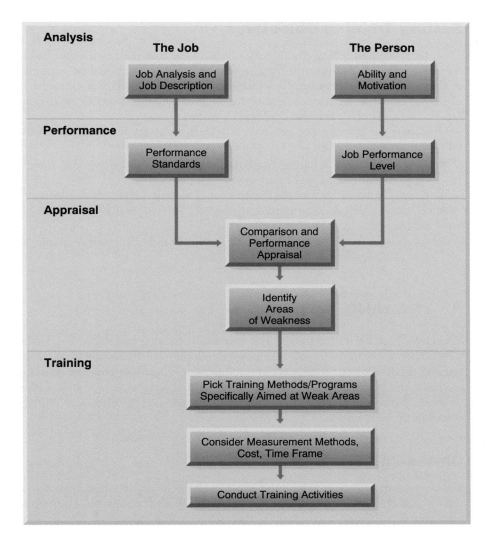

Using Job Performance to Analyze Training Needs

with the training most needed to improve the health of the organization done first. However, other considerations may enter into the decision:

- ▲ Upper management choices
- ▲ Money
- ▲ Time
- ▲ Likelihood of tangible results
- ▲ Trainers' abilities and motivations

An example of successful needs analysis was undertaken by a middle-sized wholesaler in Denver, Colorado. The company was experiencing a high error rate in its shipping records, which were prepared by a group of 23 clerical employees. The needs assessment consisted of checking all shipping records for one week and tabulating errors for each clerk. Five people accounted for 90% of the errors. These five then were observed for four hours each until a clear pattern emerged and the sources of the errors were identified. The company discovered that these people did not understand 4 of the 25 basic shipping transactions. A two-hour training session for those five employees was presented, reducing the error rate by 95%.

Setting Training Objectives

Objectives for the training should relate back to the training needs identified in the needs analysis. Evaluation of the success of the training should be measured in terms of the objectives set. Good objectives are measurable. For example, an objective for a new salesclerk might be to "demonstrate the ability to explain the function of each product in his department within two weeks."

Objectives for training can be set in any areas necessary by using one of the following four dimensions:

▲ *Quantity of work* resulting from training (number of words per minute typed or number of applications processed per day)
▲ *Quality of work* after training (dollar cost of rework, scrap loss, or errors)
▲ *Timeliness of work* after training (schedules met or budget reports in on time)
▲ *Cost savings* as a result of training (deviation from budget, sales expense, or cost of downtime)

▲ TRAINING METHODS

Objectives have been determined, and now actual training can begin. Regardless of whether the training is job related or developmental in nature, a particular training method must be chosen. The following overview of common training methods and techniques classifies methods into several major groups. Other methods that are used more frequently for management development are discussed in the next chapter.

On-the-Job Training

The most common type of training at all levels in an organization is *on-the-job training (OJT)*. Whether or not the training is planned, people do learn from their job experiences, particularly if these experiences change over time. On-the-job training usually is done by the manager and/or other employees. A manager or supervisor who trains an employee must be able to teach, as well as show, the employee. The problem with OJT is that it often is haphazardly done. Trainers may have no experience in training, no time to do it, and no desire to participate. Under such conditions, learners essentially are on their own, and training likely will not be effective.[28]

A special, guided form of on-the-job training is *job instructional training (JIT)*. Developed during World War II, JIT was used to prepare civilians with little experience for jobs in the industrial sector producing military equipment. Because of its success, JIT is still used. Figure 10–8 shows the steps in the JIT process.

On-the-job training is by far the most commonly used form of training because it is flexible and relevant to what the employee is doing. However, OJT has some problems as well. It can disrupt regular work, and the person doing the training may not be an effective trainer. Unfortunately, OJT can amount to no training in some circumstances, especially if the trainee simply is abandoned to learn the job alone.

▲ **Figure 10–8**   Job Instruction Training (JIT) Process

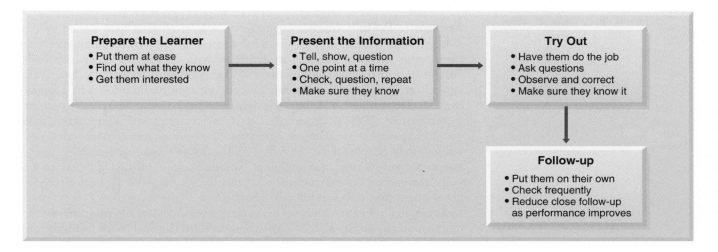

Simulation Training

Simulation training uses a duplicate work operation that is set up independently of the worksite. In this setting, trainees can learn under realistic conditions but away from the pressures of the production schedule. Having a receptionist practice on a switchboard in a simulated setting before taking over as a telephone receptionist allows the person to learn the job more easily and without stress. Consequently, there may be fewer mistakes in handling actual incoming calls. Airlines use simulators to train pilots and cabin attendants, astronauts train in mock-up space capsules, and nuclear power plant operators use model operations control rooms and consoles.

One caution about simulated training is that it must be realistic.[29] The equipment should be similar to the type the trainee actually will use so transfer of learning can be made easily. *Behavioral simulations* and computer-generated *virtual reality* hold promise for training simulators in the future.[30]

Cooperative Training

There are two widely used cooperative training methods: internships and apprentice training. Both mix classroom training and on-the-job experiences.

Internship   An internship is a form of on-the-job training that usually combines job training with classroom instruction in trade schools, high schools, colleges, or universities. According to one study, over 200,000 college students per year worked full or part time in cooperative programs and internships. Many fields were represented, including accounting, engineering, newspaper reporting, and HR management.[31]

Internships are advantageous to both employers and interns. Interns get "real world" exposure, a line on the *vita* (resume), and a chance to examine a possible employer closely. Employers who hire from campuses get a cost-effective selection tool that includes a chance to see an intern at work before a final hiring decision is made.[32]

Apprenticeship   Another form of cooperative training that is used by employers, trade unions, and government agencies is apprentice training. An apprenticeship program provides an employee with on-the-job experience under the guidance of a skilled and certified worker. Certain requirements for training, equipment, time length, and proficiency levels may be monitored by a unit of the U.S. Department of Labor. According to government sources, in one year approximately 280,000 apprentices were in training, and there were about 44,000 apprentice programs in operation.[33] Apprentice training is used most often to train people for jobs in skilled crafts, such as carpentry, plumbing, photoengraving, typesetting, and welding. Apprenticeships usually last two to five years, depending on the occupation. During this time the apprentice receives lower wages than the certified individual.

Apprentice programs seem to be experiencing a revival for students who are not planning to go to college.[34] They are much more widely used in Europe, especially Germany. In the U.S. about 1% of the workforce learns the job through apprenticeships. In Germany about 60% of the high school graduates who do not go to college enroll in apprenticeship programs.[35]

Behaviorally Experienced Training

Some training efforts focus on emotional and behavioral learning. Employees can learn about behavior by *role-playing,* in which individuals assume identities in a certain situation and act it out. *Business games, case studies,* other cases called *incidents,* and short work assignments called *in-baskets* are other behaviorally experienced learning methods. *Sensitivity training* or *laboratory training* is an example of a method used for emotional learning.

The critical issue in any situation using these methods is the purpose of the exercise. Employees may perceive role playing as fun or annoying, but they should understand clearly what the exercise is attempting to teach. Also, they must be able to transfer the learning back to their jobs. In addition, some behavioral methods are controversial and raise ethical issues, as shown in the "HR Perspective" on "New Age" training.

Classroom and Conference Training

Training seminars, courses, and presentations can be used in both job-related and developmental training. Lectures and discussions are a major part of this training. The numerous management development courses offered by trade associations and educational institutions are examples of conference training.

Company-conducted short courses, lectures, and meetings usually consist of classroom training, while company sales meetings are a common type of conference training. This type of training frequently makes use of training techniques such as case discussions, films, and tapes to enhance the learning experience.

Training methods of this kind are familiar to trainees because they have experienced them in school. However, they are essentially one-way communications. Although they may be good for knowledge enhancement, they probably are not appropriate for motor skill acquisition without some practice also being included.

HR Perspectives:
Ethical Issues in Training

One of the more controversial training methods that some firms have used is "New Age" (NA) training. This training was developed by Werner Erhard, also known for founding the *est* human potential movement. During the NA sessions, trainees are required to reveal intimate and personal episodes in their lives. The training uses meditation, yoga, self-hypnosis, and other behavioral techniques to change employee attitudes, values, and beliefs. According to some critics, trainees are pressured to make a total commitment to their employers and to believe that people create their own realities and determine what their world will be.

Some employers that have required workers to participate in NA training include car dealerships, farmer's cooperatives, and others. Some individuals who refused to participate in NA training or who objected to the training methods used and values espoused during training have been fired. Several have filed lawsuits charging their employers and the NA training firms with violating their privacy and requiring them to change their religious beliefs. For example, the sales manager of a car dealership in Pierce County, Washington, said he was fired because his Christian beliefs were not consistent with the NA training materials and content. In another case, a group of employees for a produce market cooperative in Atlanta, Georgia, filed suit, saying that the NA training used hypnosis to try

to change their religious beliefs and to make them discuss intimate details of their relationships with spouses and parents.

As would be expected, the NA training firm of Transformational Technologies (Greenbrae, California) and its affiliate, Consulting Technologies (Miami, Florida), dispute the accusations of assaults on religious beliefs and invasion of privacy. Nevertheless, the use of NA training raises profound and disturbing ethical issues about what the rights of employees and employers are when individuals are requested to participate in training by their employers, particularly when changes in values, beliefs, and behaviors are the focus of the training.[36]

▲ TRAINING MEDIA

Several aids are available to trainers presenting information. Some aids can be used in many settings and with a variety of training methods. The most common ones are computer-assisted instruction and audiovisual aids.

Computer-Assisted Instruction

Computer-assisted instruction (CAI) allows trainees to learn by interacting with a computer. Application of CAI technology is driven by the need to improve the efficiency or effectiveness of a training situation and to enhance the transfer of learning to improve job performance. Computers lend themselves well to instruction, testing, drill and practice, and application through simulation.

Audiovisual Aids

Other technical training aids are audio and visual in nature, including audio and video tapes, films, closed-circuit television, and interactive video teleconferencing. All but interactive video are one-way communications. They may allow presentation of information that cannot be recreated in a classroom. Demonstrations of machines, experiments, and examinations of behavior are examples.

Interactive video capability simply adds audio and video capability to CAI, but uses a touch-screen input instead of typing on a keyboard. These aids also can be tied into satellite communications systems to convey the same information, such as new product details, to sales personnel in several states.[37]

Trainers must avoid becoming dazzled with the machine gadgetry and remember that the real emphasis is on learning and training. The effectiveness of the technologies and media needs to be examined as a part of the evaluation.

▲ EVALUATION OF TRAINING

Evaluation of training compares the posttraining results to the objectives expected by managers, trainers, and trainees. Too often, training is done without any thought of measuring and evaluating it later to see how well it worked. Because training is both time consuming and costly, such evaluation should be an integral part of the program. Research examining the success of training programs has produced mixed results. People usually like the training and learn the material taught, but behavior and performance do not always reflect the extent of training delivered and supposedly learned.[38]

One management axiom that "nothing will improve until it is measured" may have some application to training assessment.[39] In fact at Federal Express, what an employee learns is directly related to what he or she earns, putting this principle of measurement into direct practice. Knowledge is measured every six months and compared against performance measures.[40]

One way to evaluate training is to examine the costs associated with the training and the benefits received through **cost/benefit analysis.** Comparing costs and benefits is easy until one has to assign an actual dollar value to some of the benefits. The best way is to measure the value of the output before and after training. Any increase represents the benefit resulting from training. Careful measurement of both the costs and the benefits may be difficult in some cases. Figure 10–9 shows some costs and benefits that may result. Some benefits (such as attitude change) also are hard to quantify. However, a cost/benefit comparison remains the best way to determine if training is cost effective. For example, one firm evaluated a traditional safety training program and found the program did not lead to a reduction in accidents. Therefore, the program was redesigned so that better safety practices resulted.

▼ **COST/BENEFIT ANALYSIS**

is comparing costs of training with the benefits received to see which is greater.

▲ **Figure 10–9**

Costs and Benefits of Training Evaluation

COSTS	BENEFITS
▲ Trainer's salary	▲ Increase in production
▲ Materials for training	▲ Reduction in errors
▲ Living expenses for trainer and trainees	▲ Reduction in turnover
▲ Cost of facilities	▲ Less supervision necessary
▲ Equipment	▲ Ability to advance
▲ Transportation	▲ New skills lead to ability to do more jobs
▲ Trainee's salary	▲ Attitude changes
▲ Lost production (opportunity cost)	
▲ Preparation time	

1. Reaction	How well did the trainees like the training?
2. Learning	To what extent did the trainees learn the facts, principles, and approaches that were included in the training?
3. Behavior	To what extent did their job behavior change because of the program?
4. Results	What final results were achieved (reduction in cost, reduction in turnover, improvement in production, etc.)?

Figure 10–10

Levels of Training Evaluation

SOURCE: Ralph F. Catalnello and Donald L. Kirkpatrick, "Evaluating Training Programs—The State of the Art," *Training and Development Journal,* May 1968, 2–3. Reproduced by special permission from the May 1968 *Training and Development Journal.* © 1968 by the American Society for Training and Development, Inc.

Levels of Evaluation

It is best to consider how training is to be evaluated *before* it begins. Kirkpatrick identified four levels at which training can be evaluated.[41] According to him, training becomes more rigorous and specific as the levels advance. Later research has examined this schematic and raised questions about how independent each level is from the others,[42] but the four levels described in Figure 10–10 are used to focus on the importance of evaluating training.

Reaction   Organizations evaluate the reaction level of trainees by conducting interviews or by administering questionnaires to the trainees. However, the immediate reaction may measure only how much the people liked the training, rather than how it benefited them.

Learning   Organizations evaluate learning levels by measuring how well trainees have learned facts, ideas, concepts, theories, and attitudes. Tests on the training material are commonly used for evaluating learning and can be given both before and after training to compare scores. In evaluating training courses at some firms, test results are used to determine how well the courses have provided employees with the desired content. If test scores indicate learning problems, then instructors get feedback and the courses are redesigned so that the content can be delivered more effectively. Of course, learning enough to pass a test does not guarantee that the trainee can *do* anything with what was learned.

Behavior   Evaluating training at the behavioral level measures the effect of training on job performance through interviews of trainees and their co-workers and observations of job performance. But behavior is more difficult to measure than reaction and learning. Even if behaviors do change, the results that management desires may not occur.

Results   Employers evaluate results by measuring the effect of training on the achievement of organizational objectives. Because results such as productivity, turnover, quality, time, sales, and costs are relatively concrete, this type of evaluation can be done by comparing records before and after training.

The difficulty with this measurement is pinpointing whether it was training that caused the changes in results. Other factors may have had a major impact as well. For example, a department manager who has completed a supervisory training program on controlling turnover can be measured on turnover before and after the training. But turnover is also dependent on the current economic situation, the demand for product, and the quality of employees being hired. Therefore, when evaluating results, managers should be aware of all issues involved in determining the exact effect of the training.[43]

Evaluation Designs

There are many ways to design and evaluate training programs to determine their effects. The three most common are shown in Figure 10–11. The level of rigor of the designs increases with each.

Post-Measure   The most obvious way to evaluate training effectiveness is to determine after the training whether the individuals can perform the way management wants them to perform after they have received training. Assume that a manager has 20 typists that need to improve their typing speeds. They are given

▲ **Figure 10–11**

Training Evaluation Designs

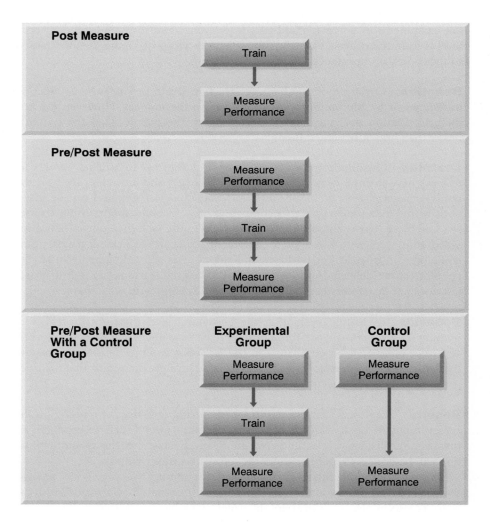

a one-day training session and then given a typing test to measure their speeds. If the typists can all type the required speed after training, was the training good? It is difficult to say; perhaps they could have done as well before training. It is difficult to know whether the typing speed is a result of the training or could have been achieved without training.

Pre-Post-Measure By designing the evaluation differently, the issue of pre-test skill levels could have been considered. If the manager had measured the typing speed before and after training, he or she could have known whether the training made any difference. However, a question remains. If there was a change in typing speed, was the training responsible for the change, or did these people simply type faster because they knew they were being tested? People often perform better when they know they are being tested on the results.

Pre-Post-Measure with Control Group Another evaluation design can address this problem. In addition to the 20 typists who will be trained, a manager can test another group of typists who will not be trained to see if they do as well as those who are to be trained. This second group is called a *control group*. If, after training, the trained typists can type significantly faster than those who were not trained, the manager can be reasonably sure that the training was effective. The final portion of Figure 10–11 shows the pre-post-measure design with a control group.

Other designs also can be used, but these three are the most common. When possible, the pre-post-measure or pre-post-measure with control group designs should be used because they provide much stronger measurement than the post-measurement alone.

SUMMARY

- ▲ Remedial training and retraining of existing workers are two of the major challenges facing employers in the 1990s.

- ▲ Training is a learning process whereby people acquire skills or knowledge to aid in the achievement of goals.

- ▲ Training has legal implications, such as who is selected for training, the criteria used for the selection, pay differences based on training, and use of training when making promotion decisions.

- ▲ Orientation is a special kind of training designed to help new employees learn about their jobs, co-workers, and the organization.

- ▲ Components of an effective orientation system include preparing for new employees; determining what information is needed and when it is needed by the employees; presenting information about the workday, the organization, and policies, rules, and benefits; and doing evaluation and follow-up.

- ▲ Basic learning principles that guide training efforts include intention to learn, whole learning, reinforcement, immediate confirmation, practice, learning curves, transfer, behavior modification, and modeling.

- ▲ A training system includes assessment, implementation, and evaluation.

▲ Of the many training methods, on-the-job training (OJT) is the most often used (and abused) method.

▲ Two widely used cooperative training methods include internships and apprenticeships.

▲ Training media such as computer-assisted instruction and other audiovisual aids each have advantages and disadvantages. They should be matched with training situations where they best apply because they will not all work in all situations.

▲ Evaluation of training success is important because if the training does not return as much in benefits as it costs, there is no reason to train. Training can be evaluated at four levels: reaction, learning, behavior, and results.

▲ A pre-post-measure with control group design is the most rigorous training evaluation design but others can be used as well.

▲ REVIEW AND DISCUSSION QUESTIONS

1. Why must employers be concerned about complying with equal employment requirements when selecting people for training?
2. Discuss the importance of orientation, and tell how you would orient a new management trainee.
3. Describe how you would use some of the learning concepts discussed in the chapter to train someone to operate a fax machine.
4. What are the three major phases in a training system? Identify the processes within each phase.
5. Assume that you want to identify the training needs of a group of sales employees in a luxury-oriented jewelry store. What would you do?
6. You are training someone to use a computer word-processing software program. What training methods would you use?
7. You want to evaluate the training received by some data-input operators:
   (a) Give examples of how to evaluate the training at four different levels.
   (b) What type of training design would you use, and why?

 EVALUATING POLICE TRAINING

Boulder, Colorado police chief Tom Koby said he wasn't surprised when an audit of the department's $50,000 training budget showed money was being wasted. When he had arrived from Houston the previous year, Koby said, "I saw a lot of training—twice the national average. But I'm not sure it was being focused. I wanted to know what the correlation was between training and product."

A recent report on training effectiveness over the past five years concluded that advanced training in work such as homicide investigation was worthwhile. But about 26% of the training was spent on seminars, such as "how to handle diversity in the workplace." Also, sometimes officers sent to the costly sessions weren't asked to identify how their new education was being used upon their return.

"One thing it pointed out was the need to research the classes before investing in them," said Tom Kilpatrick, commander of the detective division. "Like all departments, from time to time, we're somewhat vulnerable to trendy kinds of training." The conclusions, compiled by training commander Jerry Hoover, have spurred Koby and his staff to take a hard look at how training dollars should be spent.

Several solutions surfaced. For one, the Boulder County Regional Police Academy, known as the Boulder Police Academy until last year, likely will close. "Nobody in the country is hiring enough people to make running our own academy cost effective," Hoover said, so Boulder police officers will train at other area academies. Once trained, an officer's education will be tailored to the Boulder model. Koby also is promoting exchange programs with other departments nationwide, perhaps even in another country.

Ron McCarthy of the International Association of Chiefs of Police in Arlington, Virginia, believes it is wise of Boulder police to evaluate how they're spending tax dollars. "But when you wish to evaluate training, it's important not to separate Boulder from the rest of the human race. Police problems—as different and dissimilar as they may be—are also the same."[44]

▲ QUESTIONS

1. How would you assess the training needs of law enforcement officers?
2. What criteria could be used to evaluate the effectiveness of the training used by the Boulder Police Department?

▲ NOTES

1. Adapted from R. Zalman, "The 'Basics' of In-House Skills Training," *HR Magazine,* February 1991, 74–78; E. Jeanings, "Helping to Educate Small Firms Workers," *The Wall Street Journal,* June 26, 1992, B1; L. Armstrong and G. Smith, "Productivity Assured or We'll Fix Them Free," *Business Week,* November 25, 1991, 34; K. Miller, "A+ GM, The Three R's Are the Big Three," *The Wall Street Journal,* July 3, 1992, B1; and D. Machan, "Eager Pupils," *Forbes,* September 16, 1991, 188.

2. Joan C. Szabo, "Training Workers for Tomorrow," *Nation's Business,* March 1993, 22–32.

3. R. Hickox, "Employee Training," *Employee Benefits News,* December 1992, 63.

4. "Budget for Training Weathering Recession," *Omaha World-Herald,* October 11, 1992, 11G and B. Geber, "The Recession Squeezes Training," *Training,* April 1991, 27.

5. "Making Employees Repay Training Costs Called Trend," *Omaha World-Herald,* November 12, 1989, 1G.

6. T. Cocheu, "Training with Quality," *Training and Development,* May 1992, 23–32.

7. P. Galagan, "How to Get your TQM Training on Track," *Nation's Business,* October 1992, 26.

8. JoAnn S. Lublin, "Companies Use Cross Cultural Training," *The Wall Street Journal,* August 4, 1992, B1.

9. G. Rimalower, "Translation Please," *Training and Development,* February 1992, 71; and Peggy Stuart "New Directions in Training Individuals," *Personnel Journal,* September 1992, 86–91.

10. J. Stewart Black and Hal B. Gregersen, "Antecedents to Cross-Cultural Adjustment for Expatriates in Pacific Rim Assignments," *Human Relations* 44 (1991), 497–515.

11. D. Nelson and J. Quick, "Social Support and Newcomer Adjustment in Organizations," *Journal of Organizational Behavior* 12 (1991), 543–554.

12. Z. Leibowitz et al., "Stopping the Revolving Door," *Training and Development Journal,* February 1991, 43.

13. R. Federico, "Six Ways to Solve the Orientation Blues," *HR Magazine,* May 1991, 69–70.

14. J. G. Thomas, "Sources of Social Information: A Longitudinal Analysis," *Human Relations* 39 (1986), 885–870.

15. J. Brechlin and A. Rossett, "Orienting New Employees," *Training,* April, 1991, 45–51.

16. For a review, see Robert Glaser and Miriam Bassok, "Learning Theory and the Study of Instruction" *Annual Review of Psychology* 40 (1989), 631–666.

17. T. Baldwin et al.,"The Perils of Participation: Effects of Choice of Training on Trainee Motivation and Learning," *Personnel Psychology* 44 (1991), 51–65.

18. V. Humphrey, "Training the Total Organization," *Training and Development Journal,* October 1990, 57–64.

19. D. Lavitt, "Framework for Learning," *Training and Development Journal,* June 1992, 17.

20. For example, see J. Kevin Ford et al., "Factors Affecting the Opportunity to Perform Trained Tasks on the Job," *Personnel Psychology* 45 (1992), 511–527; and Marilyn Gist et al., "Transferring Training Method," *Personnel Psychology* 43 (1990), 501–523.

21. B. F. Skinner, "The Origins of Cognitive Thought," *American Psychologist* 44 (1989), 13–18.

22. Adapted from Marilyn Gist, Benson Rosen, and Catherine Schwoerer, "The Influence of Training Method and Trainee Age on the Acquisition of Computer Skills," *Personnel Psychology* 41 (1988), 225–265.

23. "Company Illustrates Power of Investing in Human Beings," *Omaha World-Herald,* January 3, 1993, 12G.

24. Adapted from I. L. Goldstein, *Training in Organizations* (Monterey CA: Brooks Cole, 1986).

25. K. Nowack, "A True Training Needs Analysis," *Training and Development Journal,* April 1991, 69–73.

26. J. Hazucha and K. Holt, "Starting Right," *Training and Development Journal,* January 1991, 71–72.

27. B. Darraugh, "Six Step, Two Step for Needs Analysis," *Training and Development Journal,* March 1991, 21–27.

28. J. Altonji and J. Spletzer, "Worker Characteristics, Job Characteristics and the Receipt of On-the-Job Training," *Industrial and Labor Relations Review,* 45 (1991), 58–79.

29. Charlene Solomon, "Simulation Training Builds Teams Through Experience," *Personnel Journal,* June 1993, 100–108.

30. P. McAteer, "Almost Like On-the-Job Training," *Training and Development,* October 1991, 19-24; and J. Hamilton et al., "Virtual Reality," *Business Week,* October 5, 1992, 97–105.

31. "Co-Op Programs Goal: Earn While You Learn," *Omaha World-Herald,* November 6, 1988, 16G.

32. Mary E. Scott, "Internships Add Value to College Recruiting," *Personnel Journal,* April 1992, 51.

33. William Miller, "New Life for an Old Idea," *Industry Week,* October 2, 1989, 78.

34. R. Wartzman, "Learning by Doing," *The Wall Street Journal,* May 19, 1992, 1.

35. J. Meister, "Employee Training," *Employee Benefit News,* December 1992, 63.

36. Adapted from "Workers Challenging 'New Age' Training," *Omaha World-Herald,* April 2, 1989, 1G.

37. R. Boser, "Learning Technology and Change: The Case for Interactive Video," *Performance and Instruction,* August 1991, 24.

38. C. Ostroff, "Training Effectiveness Measures and Scoring Schemes: A Comparison," *Personnel Psychology* 44 (1991), 353–374.

39. K. Ludeman, "Measuring Skills and Behavior," *Training and Development,* November 1991, 61–66.

40. P. Galagan, "Training Delivers Results to Federal Express," *Training and Development,* December 1991, 29–30.

41. Donald L. Kirkpatrick, "Four Steps to Measuring Training Effectiveness," *Personnel Administrator,* November 1983, 19–25.

42. George M. Alliger and Elizabeth Hanak, "Kirpatrick's Levels of Training Criteria: Thirty Years Later," *Personnel Psychology* 42 (1989), 331–342.

43. H. Schneider et al., "Training Function Accountability How to Really Measure Return on Investment," *Performance and Instruction,* March 1992, 12.

44. Adapted from Tracy Seipel, "Report: Much Boulder Police Training Is 'Trendy,'" *Denver Post,* August 17, 1992, B1, 5.

CHAPTER 11

HUMAN RESOURCE DEVELOPMENT AND CAREERS

After you have read this chapter, you should be able to:

1. Define human resource development, and identify two conditions for its success.

2. List and describe at least four on-the-job and off-the-job development methods.

3. Discuss specific advantages and problems associated with assessment centers.

4. Differentiate between organization-centered and individual-centered career planning.

5. Explain how dual-career ladders for engineers and scientists function.

6. Identify how dual-career marriages affect career paths and strategies by individuals and organizations.

7. Discuss moonlighting as a career strategy.

The federal Family and Medical Leave Act passed in 1993 may not solve the contemporary career problems facing many professionals who may have conflicts between career and family needs. Management employees traditionally have avoided family leave even when it was voluntarily offered for fear of hurting their careers. Furthermore, family and career inevitably clash when relocation, overseas assignment, increasing out-of-town travel, or demand for overtime or weekend work escalates.

However, relocation has been a cornerstone of management development, and employee development is certainly as much an issue as ever—especially with the flattened structures that follow downsizing and the need to push decision making down in the organization. A study sponsored by Xerox found that companies are experimenting with solutions such as moving jobs instead of people, assigning employees to temporary task forces, moving within "hub" locations rather than between locations, and making six-month assignments overseas instead of two- or three-year ones.

Employers are concerned about balancing the needs of families and employee development because high performing managers are difficult to recruit and to keep. Further, there is evidence that MBA candidates at top schools are giving higher priority to the quality of family and personal life when choosing a company. Another study found that the single biggest factor in an employee's relocation decision is the spouse's willingness to move. A significant part of the workforce, male and fe-

male, reports avoiding jobs involving travel and relocation. In one study, 25% of the men and 50% of the women said they have considered finding other jobs which might offer more flexibility in family matters. Other studies show that up to one-third of all relocation "opportunities" are being turned down because of family considerations—perhaps more so by women than by men.

The conflict between family and work is not new, but it has greatly intensified with the trend toward two working parents in many families. In view of the predicted shortage of certain high-demand workers, employers may find the interplay of careers and family responsibilities one of the most pressing issues of the mid- and late 1990s.

At Corning Glass, a very comprehensive program to help individuals develop and grow as managers has been designed. The company has focused on four employment categories for its development efforts: the newcomer functional specialist, the team leader, the functional leader, and the strategic leader. The first level deals with fundamental knowledge such as formal presentation skills and project management. At the next levels "competencies" such as networking, developing subordinates, self-assessment, quality orientation, and "visioning" are important.

Corning believes that to develop its future leaders without creating family/work conflicts, it must provide flexibility. The alternative is to become obsolete.[1]

Information is pretty thin stuff, unless mixed with experience.

Clarence Day ——————— "

Development is different from simple training in that it is the result of experience and the maturity that comes with it. It is possible to train most people to ride a bicycle, drive a truck, operate a computer, or assemble a radio. However, development in such areas as judgment, responsibility, compassion, or empathy is much more difficult. Such factors may or may not develop over time with the experiences of life, or as part of a planned program. Managers, particularly, need a variety of experiences to enhance their development; but a planned system of developmental experiences for all employees can help expand the overall level of abilities in an organization and increase its productivity, quality, and flexibility.

▲ HUMAN RESOURCE (HR) DEVELOPMENT

The purpose of **human resource (HR) development** is to increase the capabilities of employees for continuing growth and advancement. It usually is concerned with improving the intellectual or emotional capabilities of employees at all organizational levels. Training aimed at certain skills can be a part of development, of course. But HR development is a broader, less tangible concept than merely "training." It often includes such diverse aims as:

▲ Changing attitudes about involvement of employees in decision making

▲ Improving abilities to communicate

▲ Using better judgment on innovative decisions

Currently more jobs are taking on the characteristics of *knowledge work,* meaning that people must combine their mastery of some kind of technical expertise with the ability to work in teams with other employees, form relationships with customers, and analyze their own practices in order to improve. The practice of management increasingly is the guiding and integrating of autonomous, highly skilled people.[2] This is the subject matter of *management development.*

Conditions for Successful HR Development

Two conditions are critical for successful employee development: top management support and understanding the interrelated nature of development.

Top Management Support   Top management must believe strongly in the importance of HR development, or the process will become only a staff function made up of external courses and seminars. Also top management must be willing to delegate some decision-making authority to lower-level managers in the organization in order to develop them. These efforts must continue even if some of them fail. If top management is afraid or unwilling to relinquish control and authority to a younger manager for learning purposes, little development is likely to result.

Top management reveals its support of development activities—or its lack of support—through its promotion decisions and rewards. Management develop-

▼ **HUMAN RESOURCE (HR) DEVELOPMENT**

focuses on increasing the capabilities of employees for continuing growth and advancement.

ment can be the "glue" of common values and experiences that hold diverse autonomous subsidiaries together,[3] but only with top management's enthusiastic support.

Appropriate Relationship of Development to Other HR Activities

Important relationships exist between HR development efforts and selection, placement, compensation, and appraisal activities. Development is no substitute for good selection. If a person chosen for a job does not have the capacity to do the work, no amount of development will change that. Likewise, improper placement of a person within the organization can seldom be rectified by development. Expecting one set of behaviors from an employee but rewarding that person through pay raises for another set of behaviors also will not lead to the desired development. Here is an example: Managers in one firm are expected to meet quarterly with each employee in their departments to discuss performance issues. However, one manager consistently has refused to do so. In spite of his refusal, the manager has continued to receive excellent ratings and above-average salary increases. Consequently, this manager continues to ignore his developmental responsibilities.

Planning for HR Development

Planning for career paths and the development needed to move people along those paths must begin with the overall strategic plan of the organization. The demand for specific specialties depends on the overall strategy and technology to be used. However, to make planning for HR development effective, the following must be included:

- ▲ Performance appraisals of key players to identify the areas in which they need development.
- ▲ Evaluation of the capabilities that the organization needs in the future.
- ▲ Succession planning to identify replacements and provide management continuity.
- ▲ Career-management programs that reflect the future needs of the organization.

Succession Planning   Succession planning can be an important part of development. For example, it has been linked to "turning around" a plant acquired by Scott Paper Company when linked with skills training, management development, and promotion from within. The general result for the plant was a large increase in capacity over four years with virtually no infusion of new managers or employees.[4] Existing talent was developed instead. Succession planning can be especially important in small- and medium-sized firms, but studies show that firms of this size comprise the group that has done the least in this area. Only 24% of firms with reported earnings from $2 million to $100 million have formal succession plans.[5]

Replacement Charts   Standard career paths include a range of possible moves from any position, laterally across departments, vertically within a department, or others. But each possible path represents *actual* positions, the experience needed to fill the positions, and the relationship of positions to each other. Replacement charts (similar to depth charts used by football teams that show the backup players at each position) give a simple model of the process. The purpose of replacement charts is to ensure that the right individual is available at the right time and has had sufficient experience to handle the job. In Figure 11–1, a replacement chart for the APLO Manufacturing Company is shown.

Replacement charts can be part of the development planning process. Note that the chart specifies the kind of development each individual needs for promotion. Ms. Wilson needs exposure to manufacturing to be promotable to superintendent. Her job as office manager has not given her much exposure to the production side of the company. Ms. Paul needs exposure to plant operations and HR activities. Mr. French needs to learn how to handle young, aggressive managers. However, Mr. French's appraiser felt French would not be promotable to superintendent, even with additional training. Such information can be used to identify "career paths" and "promotion ladders" for people.

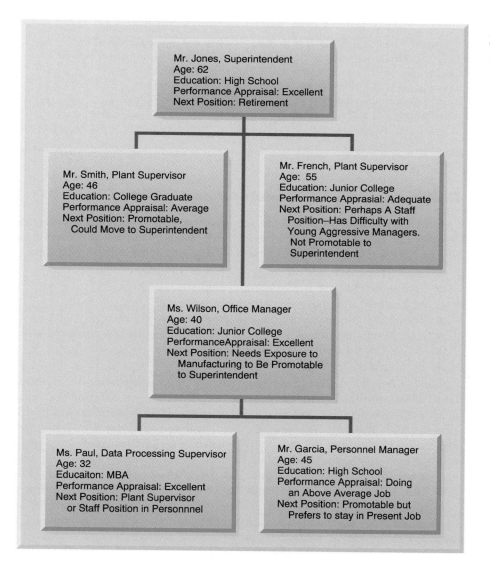

▲ **Figure 11–1**

Replacement Chart for APLO Manufacturing Company

HR Perspectives:
Developing Global Managers

It has become almost a cliché that management in the future will require global knowledge and experience. Indeed, U.S. companies are giving their fast-track managers a global orientation much sooner in their careers. Proctor & Gamble has begun a "P&G College" for new and midlevel managers that focuses heavily on global issues. General Electric teaches language and cross-cultural issues to people who may never go overseas. Other companies are moving foreigners to the U.S. and Americans abroad when they have only a few years experience—a major change in historical policy.

A Conference Board study of 130 multinational companies found a "certain sense of urgency" among American companies to build an internationally experienced cadre of executives. There are, however, problems inherent in the effort. 3M noted that there is a high risk associated with sending a young person abroad. Cost is a big factor, as it can cost four times as much to keep an employee overseas as in the U.S.

Generally speaking, the effort is thought to be worth the risk in that cultural blinders are removed by the experience of living abroad, and people gain an understanding of the global customer—and thus the company gains a competitive edge.

Inadequate planning for HR Development occurs, though. Several years ago, American-born Catherine Speldon, working for Colgate-Palmolive, had a rude shock during a business trip to a former Communist country in Eastern Europe. She quizzed shoppers about characteristics of their favorite soap brands. Their puzzled responses were explained when she discovered there was only one kind of soap available (when there was *any* available). The marketing situation there was far different from that in the U.S. and called for different approaches than those used at home.[6]

Problems With HR Development Efforts

Development efforts are subject to certain common mistakes and problems. Most of the problems result from inadequate planning and a lack of coordination of HR development efforts. Common problems include the following:

▲ Inadequate needs analysis
▲ Trying out fad programs or training methods
▲ Abdicating responsibility for development to staff
▲ Trying to substitute training for selection
▲ Lack of training among those who lead the development activities
▲ Using only "courses" as the road to development
▲ Encapsulated development

▼ **ENCAPSULATED DEVELOPMENT**

occurs when an individual learns new methods and ideas in a development course and returns to a work unit that is still bound by old attitudes and methods.

The last item on the list may require some additional explanation. **Encapsulated development** occurs when an individual learns new methods and ideas in a development course and returns to a work unit that is still bound by old attitudes and methods. The reward system and the working conditions have not changed. Although the trainee has learned new ways to handle certain situations, these methods cannot be applied because of resistance from those having an investment in the status quo and the unchanged work situation. The new knowledge remains encapsulated in the classroom setting. Encapsulated development is an obvious waste of time and money. In some organizations, diversity training efforts have been wasted because follow-up and reinforcement were not done.

▲ CHOOSING A DEVELOPMENT PROGRAM

Many HR development methods are available. Before describing several of these, it is important to identify some criteria for their use. Goals of development efforts can be: (1) people oriented, (2) job specific (technical), or (3) oriented toward planning and conceptual learning. Different techniques serve these different goals. Figure 11–2 shows the extent to which each method is suited to each goal.

It is estimated that over $40 billion a year is spent in the United States on formal training and development. Unfortunately, many of the development efforts suffer because programs are often very broad based and not developed with specific individuals in mind. Individual development needs always should be considered in designing development programs.

As with training, development methods can be classified as on the job or off the job. On-the-job methods generally are directly job related, so that effective development can be tailored to fit each trainee's background, attitudes, needs,

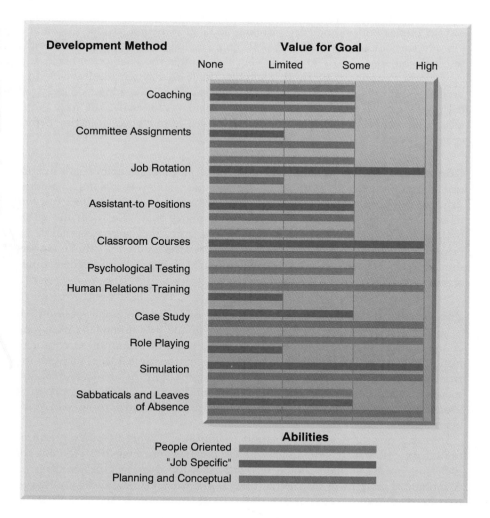

▲ **Figure 11–2**

Matching Development Goals and Methods

expectations, goals, and future assignments. However, off-the-job methods usually cannot be tailored as well to the exact needs of each trainee. Also, employee development is influenced to a large extent by the immediate supervisor. Employees are likely to accept supervisory expectations in on-the-job situations.

On-the-Job Methods

A major difficulty with on-the-job methods is that often too many unplanned activities are regarded as development. It is imperative that managers plan and coordinate development efforts so that the desired learning actually occurs.

▼ **COACHING**

is the daily training and feedback given to employees by immediate supervisors.

Coaching   The oldest on-the-job development technique is **coaching,** which is the daily training and feedback given to employees by immediate supervisors. It is a continual process of learning by doing. For effective coaching, a healthy and open relationship must exist between employees and their supervisors or managers. Many firms conduct formal training courses to improve the coaching skills of their managers.

Unfortunately, as with other on-the-job methods, coaching can be temptingly easy to implement without any planning at all. If someone has been good at a job or a particular part of a job, there is no guarantee that he or she will be able to coach someone else to do it well—but that is often the assumption made. It is easy for the "coach" to fall short in guiding the learner systematically, even if he or she knows which systematic experiences are best.[7] Sometimes doing a full day's work gets priority over learning and coaching. Also, many skills have an intellectual component that might be better learned from a book or lecture before coaching occurs.

Committee Assignments   Assignment of promising employees to important committees can be a broadening experience, and very helpful in understanding the personalities, issues, and processes governing an organization. For instance, assigning employees to a safety committee may give them the safety background they need to become supervisors. Also, they may experience the problems involved with maintaining employee safety awareness. But managers should be aware that it is possible for committee assignments to become time-wasting activities, too.

▼ **JOB ROTATION**

is the process of shifting an employee from job to job.

Job Rotation   **Job rotation** is the process of shifting an employee from job to job. It is widely used as a development technique. For example, a promising young manager may spend three months in the plant, three months in corporate planning, and three months in purchasing. When properly handled, such job rotation fosters a greater understanding of the organization. At one large firm, job rotation is used during a 15-month sales training program. Trainees work in at least three areas, such as industrial sales, retail sales, credit, advertising, and product training.

In some organizations, job rotation is unplanned, whereas other organizations have elaborate charts and schedules precisely planning the program for each employee. Managers should recognize that job rotation can be expensive. A substantial amount of managerial time is lost when trainees change positions because they must become acquainted with different people and techniques in each new unit.

Especially when the opportunities for promotion are scarce, job rotation through lateral transfers may be beneficial in rekindling enthusiasm and developing new talents. The best lateral moves do one or more of the following:[8]

▲ Move the person into the core business
▲ Provide closer contact with the customer
▲ Teach new skills or perspectives

"Assistant-to" Positions   The assistant-to position is a staff position immediately under a manager. Through this job, trainees can work with outstanding managers they may not otherwise meet. Some organizations have "junior boards of directors" or "management cabinets" to which trainees may be appointed. Assignments such as these are useful if trainees have the opportunity to deal with challenging or interesting assignments.

Off-the-Job Techniques

Off-the-job development techniques can be effective because an individual has an opportunity to get away from the job and concentrate solely on what is to be learned. Moreover, meeting with other people who are concerned with somewhat different problems and different organizations may provide an employee with new perspectives on old problems. A variety of methods may be used.

Classroom Courses and Degrees   Many off-the-job development programs include some classroom instruction. The advantage of classroom training is that it is widely accepted because most people are familiar with it. Specialists, either organization employees or outside experts, can conduct such training.

A disadvantage of classroom instruction is the lecture system, which encourages passive listening and reduced learner participation. Sometimes trainees have little opportunity to question, clarify, and discuss the lecture material. Classroom effectiveness depends on the size of the group, the ability of the instructor, and the subject matter.

Many organizations encourage continuing education by paying for employees to take college courses. A total of 91% of the organizations in one survey indicated that they would reimburse employees for school tuition.[9] Some employers encourage employees to study for advanced degrees, such as an MBA, in the same manner. Employees often earn these degrees at night, after their regular workday ends.

Organizations also may send employees to externally sponsored seminars or public short courses. These programs are offered by many colleges and universities and by professional associations such as the American Management Association. Some larger organizations have established training centers exclusively for their own employees.

Many universities and their business schools are more than willing to accommodate corporate customers also. Of the leading graduate business programs, many have developed "custom programs" where development courses are designed expressly for the needs of a given organization. For example, the Kellogg Graduate School of Management at Northwestern University's Evanston, Illinois campus, offers several custom programs.[10]

There are several common complaints about external classroom programs. Too many times, a high percentage of the participants simply are not ready for the courses they take. Some individuals attend at the wrong time in their careers, for example, near retirement. Many participants sent by their employers have not had the preliminary training that the programs assume. However, these problems can be overcome with some planning.

Interestingly, more education does not always lead to a better worker if pay differences reflect performance differences. One study showed that workers with substantially more schooling than others in the same occupation "often earn less than their adequately educated counterparts."[11] However, more education clearly does pay off for the degree holder when it qualifies people for more sophisticated jobs.

Psychological Testing   Psychological pencil-and-paper tests have been used for several years to determine an employee's developmental potential. Intelligence tests, verbal and mathematical reasoning tests, and personality tests are often used. Such testing can furnish useful information to employers about such factors as motivation, reasoning difficulties, leadership styles, interpersonal response traits, and job preferences. It is then up to the employee to take steps to address each area.

The biggest problem with psychological testing lies in interpreting the results. An untrained manager, supervisor, or worker usually cannot accurately interpret test results. After a professional reports the scores to someone in the organization, the interpretation often is left to untrained employees who may attach their own meanings to the results. It also should be recognized that some psychological tests are of limited validity and desirable responses can be faked easily by the test taker. Thus psychological testing is appropriate only when closely supervised by a qualified professional throughout the testing and feedback process.

Human Relations Training   Human relations training originated with the well-known Hawthorne studies. Initially, the purpose of the training was to prepare supervisors for "people problems" brought to them by their employees. This type of training focuses on the development of the human relations skills a person needs to work well with others. Many human relations training programs are aimed at new or relatively inexperienced first-line supervisors and middle managers. Human relations programs typically have sessions on motivation, leadership, employee communication, and humanizing the workplace.

No one questions the importance of human relations skills in successful management. In fact, again and again they are cited as the major difference between successful and unsuccessful managers. The problem with such programs is the difficulty in measuring their effectiveness. The development of human relations skills is a long-range goal; tangible results are hard to identify over the span of several years. Consequently, such programs often are measured only by participants' reactions to them. As mentioned in the previous chapter, reaction-level measurement is the weakest form of evaluating the effectiveness of training.

Case Study   The case study is a classroom-oriented development technique that has been widely used. Cases provide a medium through which the trainee can study the application of management or behavioral concepts. The emphasis is on application and analysis, not mere memorization of concepts.

One common complaint is that cases sometimes are not sufficiently realistic to be useful. Also, cases may contain information inappropriate to the kinds of decisions that trainees would make in a real situation. This also can be one of the values of case studies, though, if the focus is to test whether or not students can select appropriate information.

Role-Playing   Role-playing is a development technique requiring the trainee to assume a role in a given situation and act out behaviors associated with that role. Participants gain an appreciation of the many behavioral factors influencing on-the-job situations. For instance, a labor relations director may be asked to play the role of a union vice-president in a negotiating situation in order to give the director insight into the constraints and problems facing union bargaining representatives. Role-playing is a useful tool in some situations, but a word of caution applies: Trainees are often uncomfortable in role-playing situations, and trainers must introduce the situations well so that learning can occur.

▼ **ROLE-PLAYING**

is a development technique requiring the trainee to assume a role in a given situation and act out behaviors associated with that role.

Simulation (Business Games)   Several business games or simulations are available commercially. A simulation requires the participant to analyze a situation and decide the best course of action based on the data given. Some are computer-interactive games in which individuals or teams draw up a set of marketing plans for an organization to determine such factors as the amount of resources to allocate for advertising, product design, selling, and sales effort. The participants make a variety of decisions, then the computer tells them how well they did in relation to competing individuals or teams.

Simulations have been used to diagnose organizational problems as well.[12] When properly done, a simulation can be a useful management development tool. However, simulation receives the same criticism as role-playing: realism is sometimes lacking, so the learning experience is diminished. Learning must be the focus, not just "playing the game."

▼ **SIMULATION**

requires the participant to analyze a situation and decide the best course of action based on the data given.

Sabbaticals and Leaves of Absence   A sabbatical leave is paid time off the job to develop and rejuvenate oneself. Popular for many years in the academic world, where professors take a leave to sharpen their skills and advance their education or conduct research, similar sorts of plans have been adopted in the business community. Approximately 13% of U.S. corporations offer sabbaticals. For example, Xerox Corporation gives some of its employees six months or more off with pay to work on "socially desirable" projects. Projects include training people in urban ghettos or providing technical assistance to overseas countries. Companies offering sabbaticals speak well of the results. They say sabbaticals help prevent burnout, offer advantages in recruiting and retention, boost morale, and enable people to carry heavier workloads upon their return.[13] Sabbaticals are most commonly given to executives and in high-tech businesses with around-the-clock projects. They are becoming popular in other countries, including the United Kingdom, as well.[14]

The value of sabbaticals is seen in the case of an American Express systems manager who had worked for the company over 20 years. She took a year off to recruit local high school students for volunteer jobs. Commenting on her experience, she said "I worked for American Express for so long, I wanted to give something back to the community." She also indicated that American Express would benefit when she returned from the enhanced leadership and networking skills she gained.[15]

One of the disadvantages of paid sabbaticals is the cost. Also, the nature of the learning experience is not within the control of the organization and is left somewhat to chance.

▼ **A SABBATICAL LEAVE**

is paid time off the job to develop and rejuvenate oneself.

Outdoor Training   Many organizations send executives off to ordeals in the wilderness, called outdoor training, as a development tool. General Foods, Xerox, GE, Honeywell, Burger King, AMEX, Sears, and other organizations have sent executives and managers to the outdoors for stays of several days or even weeks. The rationale for these wilderness excursions is as follows: For individuals, such experiences can increase self-confidence and help them reevaluate personal goals and efforts. For work units, a shared risk outside the office environment can create a sense of teamwork. The challenges may include rock climbing in the California desert, white-water rafting on the Rogue River, backpacking in the Rocky Mountains, or handling a longboat off the coast of Maine.

John Temple of Touche Ross's New Jersey operation took several other partners in the consulting practice on an eight-day compass expedition in the Adirondacks and saw beneficial results six months later. "Our meetings go much smoother now," he says. "It has made a dramatic difference." The survival-type management development course may have more impact than many other management seminars.[16] There are perils, however, and some participants have not been able to handle the physical and emotional challenges associated with rappeling down a cliff or climbing a 40-foot tower. The decision on whether to sponsor such programs should depend on the personalities of the employees who will be involved.

Assessment Centers

▼ **ASSESSMENT CENTERS**
are a collection of instruments and exercises designed to diagnose a person's development needs.

Assessment centers are not places as much as they are collections of instruments and exercises designed to diagnose a person's development needs. They are used both for developing and for selecting managers. Typically, in an assessment-center experience, a potential manager spends two or three days away from the job performing many activities. These activities may include role-playing, pencil-and-paper tests, cases, leaderless group discussions, management games, peer evaluations, and in-basket exercises, where the trainee handles typical problems coming across a manager's desk. A study of fire departments in major cities revealed that the most commonly used exercises for firefighters are in-baskets (90.6%), leaderless groups (84.4%), structured interviews (71.9%), problem solving (68.8%), written assignments (68.8%), and fire-scene incident command situations (59.4%).[17] Police departments and many other types of large organizations also use assessment centers.

Operation of Assessment Centers   During the exercises, the participants are observed by several specially trained judges. For the most part, the exercises are samples of managerial situations that require the use of managerial skills and behaviors.

One major company has made large-scale use of assessment centers in which trained observers watch the candidates' behaviors in detail and record impressions. Each assessor writes a report on each candidate and gives it to the candidate's superior to use in selection and promotion decisions. The reports often identify guidelines for further development of the assessed employee.

Advantages of Assessment Centers   Assessment centers are praised because they are thought to overcome the biases inherent with interview situations, supervisor ratings, and written tests. Experience has shown that such key variables as leadership, initiative, and supervisory skills are almost impossible to measure with paper-and-pencil tests alone. Another advantage of assessment centers is that they help identify employees with potential in a large organization. Supervisors may nominate people for the assessment center, or employees may volunteer. The opportunity to volunteer especially is valuable for talented people who may not be recognized as such by their supervisors.[18]

Problems with Assessment Centers   Assessment centers are an excellent means for determining management potential. However, some managers may use the assessment center as a way to avoid difficult promotion decisions. Suppose a plant supervisor has personally decided that an employee is not a qualified candidate for promotion. Rather than stick by the decision and tell the employee, the supervisor may send the employee to the assessment center, hoping that the report will show that the employee is not qualified for promotion. Problems between the employee and the supervisor will be worse if the employee earns a positive report. If the report is negative, the supervisor's views are validated, but using the assessment center in this way is not recommended.

Two difficulties often encountered with assessment centers are: (1) making sure the exercises in the assessment center are valid predictors of management performance, and (2) properly selecting and training the assessors. Also, assessment centers are expensive. The actual cost varies from organization to organization, but it ranges from $600 to $6,000 for each candidate who goes through a center. Of course, the cost of making a mistake in management selection is great, too. Some estimates far exceed $20,000 worth of legal, salary, and benefit payments to terminate a department head. Many major firms that have created assessment centers, including General Electric, Union Carbide, AT&T, and IBM, have decided they are worth the cost.

Validity of Assessment Centers   The validity of assessment centers for selection has been studied extensively. Studies generally have suggested that assessment centers predict management success much better than other methods of assessing managerial skills. However, some researchers have been concerned with the very positive statistical results in these studies. They question whether the use of salary growth and advancement is appropriate to measure the success of assessment centers. It can be argued that these items may not be related to competence, effectiveness, or superior performance.

Recently, some researchers have argued that performance ratings at assessment centers are influenced by the way assessors deal with the information derived from the assessment center and by the methods used.[19] Further, there is the difficulty in defining the effective manager. Managerial jobs are broadly defined, yet tests to pick managers must be precisely defined. This dilemma reduces the generalizability of any battery of exercises and suggests that assessment-center exercises should be validated for each organization.

▲ MANAGEMENT DEVELOPMENT

Employee development is important for all employees, but especially so for managers. Unless managers are appropriately developed, resources (including employees) throughout the organization may not be managed well. Management development should be seen as a way of imparting the skills and knowledge needed by managers to meet the strategic objectives of the organization.[20] Among these skills are leadership, dealing with change, helping (coaching and advising) subordinates, controlling when necessary, and providing feedback.[21]

Common management success factors (as shown in Figure 11–3) have been harvested from many job analyses. The information in this figure demonstrates how difficult it is to define—much less teach—many of these development areas. The challenge for many management development programs, especially those aimed at executives, is to cultivate *articulative reflection* in the trainees—the ability to stand back from the work they direct or perform and articulate what is being done, form ideas about it, and evaluate those ideas.[22]

Managerial Modeling

A common adage in management development says managers tend to manage as they were managed. Another way of saying this is that managers learn by **behavior modeling,** or copying someone else's behavior. This is not surprising because a great deal of human behavior is learned by modeling others. Children learn by modeling parents and older children; they are quite comfortable with the process by the time they grow up. Management development efforts can take advantage of natural human behavior by matching young or developing managers with appropriate models and then reinforcing the desirable behaviors exhibited.

Modeling is less a straightforward imitation, or copying, process than is commonly believed, though. But the modeling process is considerably more complex, and exposure to both positive and negative models can be beneficial to a new manager.

▼ **BEHAVIOR MODELING**

is copying someone else's behavior.

▲ **Figure 11–3**

Examples of Some Common Managerial Success Factors

FACTOR	*THE SUCCESSFUL MANAGER:*
Analytical Thought	Can choose between important and unimportant details; finds inconsistencies; draws correct conclusions from data.
Forecasting	Accurately anticipates changes internally and externally.
Multiple Focus	Effectively manages many conflicting objectives at once.
Organizational Knowledge	Understands thoroughly all policies, procedures, and people involved in relevant jobs.
Priority Setting	Clearly sees the larger picture and maintains a clear sense of priorities in helping to attain the goals of that view.
Risk Taking	Takes risks when appropriate, even when upper management may disagree or personal image may suffer.

SOURCE: Adapted from R. J. Mirabile, "Pinpointing Development Needs," *Training and Development,* December 1991, 20.

Mentoring is a relationship in which managers at midpoints in careers aid individuals in the first stages of careers. Technical, interpersonal, and political skills can be conveyed in such a relationship from the older to the younger person. Not only does the younger one benefit, but the older one may enjoy the challenge of sharing his or her wisdom. The four stages in most successful mentor/learner relationships are shown in Figure 11–4.[23] Mentoring has been studied enough now to allowing some conclusions to be drawn. First, it apparently works. Women with mentors were found in one study to move up faster than those without mentors. As they moved to the top, they in turn became mentors. Mentoring may be a useful way to attack the "glass ceiling" phenomenon, in which an unspoken agreement keeps women and minorities from progressing past a certain point.[24]

Clearly, mentoring is not without its problems. Young minority managers report difficulty finding white mentors. Men are less willing than women to be mentors. Further, mentors who are dissatisfied with their jobs and those who teach a narrow or distorted view of events may not help the young manager's development.[25] However, since most managers have a series of advisors/mentors during a career, they may find advantages in learning from many perspectives. Further, they can use the networking that results from many having previous mentors to identify key behaviors in management success and failure.

▲ **CAREERS**

A **career** is the sequence of work-related positions occupied throughout a person's life. In the past, career guidance was considered a service for high school or college students. Today, as the employee work role becomes more complex,

▼ **MENTORING**

is a relationship in which managers at midpoints in careers aid individuals in the first stages of careers.

▼ **A CAREER**

is the sequence of work-related positions occupied throughout a person's life.

▲ **Figure 11–4**

Stages in Mentor/Learner Relationships

STAGE	LENGTH OF TIME	YOUNGER MANAGER	OLDER MANAGER
Initiation	6-12 months	Admires the senior manager's competence; recognizes him or her as source of support and guidance	Realizes younger manager is someone with potential and "is coachable"
Cultivation	2-5 years	Gains self-confidence, new attitudes, values, and styles of operation	Provides challenging work, coaching, visibility, protection, and sponsorship
Separation	6-12 months	Experiences independence and autonomy; has feelings of turmoil, anxiety, and loss at times	Demonstrates his or her success at developing management talent as they move apart
Redefinition	Ongoing	Responds with gratitude for the early years, but is not dependent; relationship becomes a friendship	Relationship becomes a friendship; continues to be a supporter; takes pride in the younger manager's accomplishments

more employers are providing career counseling. Certain common career concerns are frequently expressed by employees in all organizations:

▲ What do I really want to do?
▲ What do I know how to do?
▲ What career opportunities can I expect to be available?
▲ Where do I want to go?
▲ What do I need to do to get there?
▲ How can I tell how well I am doing?

In-house career planning and guidance usually is limited to what the organization has to offer. However, these internal opportunities may not reflect adequately all possibilities, especially those in other organizations.

Organization-Centered vs. Individual-Centered Career Planning

The nature of career planning can be somewhat confusing because two different perspectives exist. Career planning can be organization centered and/or individual centered. **Organization-centered career planning** focuses on jobs and on constructing career paths that provide for the logical progression of people between jobs in one organization. These paths represent ladders that each individual can climb to advance in certain organizational units. For example, a person might enter the sales department as a sales counselor, then be promoted to account director, to sales manager, and finally to vice-president of sales.

Individual-centered career planning, on the other hand, focuses on individuals' careers rather than organizational needs. An individual's goals and skills are the focus of the analysis. Such analyses might consider situations both within and outside the organization that can expand a person's career. The individual perspective has been the major thrust in career research to date.[26] The points of focus for organization- and individual-oriented career planning are compared in Figure 11–5.

Retrenchment and downsizing have changed career plans for many people. Primarily, middle-aged managers and nonmanagerial employees have found themselves in a "career transition" as a result—in other words, in need of finding another job. This unplanned transition points out one of the more recent characteristics of careers—employers can no longer be counted on for long-term employment. In the last ten years the number of people changing occupations

▼ **ORGANIZATION-CENTERED CAREER PLANNING**

focuses on jobs and on constructing career paths that provide for the logical progression of people between jobs in one organization.

▼ **INDIVIDUAL-CENTERED CAREER PLANNING**

focuses on individuals' careers rather than organizational needs.

▲ **Figure 11–5**

Organizational and Individual Career Planning Perspectives

ORGANIZATIONAL CAREER PERSPECTIVE	INDIVIDUAL CAREER PERSPECTIVE
▲ Identify future organizational staffing needs	▲ Identify personal abilities and interests
▲ Plan career ladders	▲ Plan life and work goals
▲ Assess individual potential and training needs	▲ Assess alternative paths inside and outside the organization
▲ Match organizational needs with individual abilities	▲ Note changes in interests and goals as career and life stage change
▲ Audit and develop a career system for the organization	

has almost doubled, from 6.6 million to 10 million a year.[27] Small businesses, some started by early retirees from big companies, provide many of the new career opportunities.

How Do People Choose Careers?

Four general individual characteristics affect how people make career choices.

1. *Interests.* People tend to pursue careers that they believe match their interests.
2. *Self-identity.* A career is an extension of a person's self-image, as well as a molder of it.
3. *Personality.* This factor includes an employee's personal orientation (whether the employee is realistic, enterprising, artistic, etc.) and personal needs (including affiliation, power, and achievement needs).
4. *Social backgrounds.* Socioeconomic status and the education and occupation level of a person's parents are a few factors included in this category.

Less is known about how and why people choose specific organizations than about why they choose a specific career. One obvious factor is the opportunity and availability for a job when the person is looking for work. The amount of information available about alternatives is an important factor as well. Beyond these issues, people seem to pick organizations on the basis of a "fit" between the climate of an organization as they perceive it and their own personal characteristics.

One poll found that 50% of Americans would choose the same career, 45% said they would choose a different career, and the remaining respondents did not know. Blue-collar workers were most likely to wish for another career (62%), while only 36% of executives and professionals would change. Only 18% of those polled said their careers were both personally and financially rewarding. Approximately 50% said there was more personal than financial reward in their jobs.[28]

Tribune Media Services, Inc., September 14, 1992.

Careers and Life Experiences

The typical career today probably will include many different positions, transitions, and organizations—more so than in the past, when employees were less mobile and organizations more stable as long-term employers. Many theorists in adult development would describe the first half of life as the young adult's quest for competence and a way to make a mark in the world. According to this view, happiness would be sought primarily through external achievements, and acquiring skills and goods. The second half of life is different. Once an adult starts to measure time from the expected end of his or her life rather than from the beginning, the need for competence and acquisition changes to the need for integrity, values, and well-being. Internal values take precedence over external scorecards for many.[29] Mature adults already have certain skills, so their focus may shift to other interests.

Contained within this theory is the view that careers and lives are not predictably linear, but cyclical. Periods of high stability are followed by transition, less stability, and inevitable discoveries, disappointments, and triumphs. Therefore, lives and careers must be viewed as cycles of structure and transition, which may be a useful perspective for those suffering the negative results of downsizing and early career plateaus in large organizations. Such a perspective argues for the importance of flexibility in an individual's career and may encourage a willingness to acquire diverse skills.

Retirement

Whether retirement comes at age 50 or 70, it can require a major adjustment for many people. Of course, from the standpoint of the organization, retirement is an orderly way to move people out at the end of their careers. Mindful of the problems that retirement poses for some individuals, however, some organizations are experimenting with *phased retirement* through gradually reduced workweeks and increased vacation time. Some common emotional adjustments faced by all retirees include:

▲ *Self-management*. The person must adjust to being totally self-directed after retirement. There is no longer any supervisor or work agenda dictating what to do.

▲ *Need to belong*. When a person retires, he or she is no longer a member of the work group that took so much time and formed an important social structure for so many years. What takes its place?

▲ *Pride in achievement*. Achievement reinforces self-esteem and is often centered around work. In retirement, past achievements quickly wear thin as a source of self-esteem.

▲ *Territoriality*. Personal "turf," in the form of office, company, and title, are lost in retirement. They must be replaced with other sources to satisfy a person's territoriality needs.

▲ *Goals*. Organizations provide many of a person's goals. Some people may be unprepared to set their own goals when they retire.

Preretirement and postretirement programs aimed at helping employees deal with these problems aid transition to a useful retirement. The phenomenon of "forced" early retirement that began in the 1980s has required thousands of managers and professionals to determine what is important to them while they

HR Perspectives:
Research on Effect of Employment "Gaps" on Careers

Schneer and Reitman examined the effect that breaks in employment had on the subsequent careers of MBAs. As reported in the *Academy of Management Journal,* they surveyed 925 MBAs who had graduated 10 to 15 years previously. Average age was 38; 88% were currently employed full time. The responses were almost equally divided between men and women.

About 24% of the women and 12% of the men had experienced an employment gap. The reason for the gap cited most frequently by men was organizational restructuring. Childrearing was most frequently cited by women. MBAs with employment gaps earned 14% less than those who had been continuously employed. Also, women were more likely to experience gaps, but career satisfaction

was more likely to be reduced for men than for women as a result of those gaps in employment.

The researchers speculate that gender-related career-path stereotypes (men must work straight through a career, but it is acceptable for women to take time out to raise children) affect society's perceptions and therefore what men and women expect in their careers.[34]

---

are still young and healthy and plan accordingly. Because of economic factors, many organizations have used early retirement to reduce their workforces. Some of these young retirees "go fishing," but many begin second careers.

Career Planning: Individual Perspectives

Effective career planning at the individual level first requires self-knowledge. A person must face issues such as, How hard am I really willing to work? What is most important in life to me? What trade-off between work and family or leisure am I willing to make? These questions and others must be confronted honestly before personal goals and objectives can be realistically set in a career plan. Professional counseling may be helpful.

Changing jobs and careers has become an accepted practice in recent years, and it can be financially rewarding; estimates are that individuals average around a 10% increase in salary on a new job.[30] However, "job-hopping" (changing jobs very frequently) can cause problems in retirement, vacation, seniority, and other benefits. Perhaps more important is the perception that job-hopping is a sign of instability, especially in more mature managers.[31]

However, as the baby boom generation reaches midlife, and as large employers cut back on their workforces, increasing numbers of managers will find themselves at a career plateau. Every middle-management opening had about 10 potential candidates in 1975, about 30 in 1995, and will have 50 candidates by the year 2000.[32] Plateauing may seem the result of failure to many people, but for the most part it is simply arithmetic. However, plateaued employees can cause problems for employers if frustrated expectations of promotion affect performance. The effect of "breaks" or "gaps" in employment of the displaced manager is examined in the "HR Perspective." As a result of such gaps, the career path for professionals and managers in the last of this century and the beginning of the next may look like that in Figure 11–6.[33]

Surveys show that middle managers' optimism about opportunity for advancement has declined. But middle managers are not a disappearing breed. In small and middle-sized organizations across the country, the ranks of middle managers actually are growing. Large industrial organizations, on the other hand, finally have been forced to deal with the problem of overstaffing by laying off many middle managers. For those managers left behind, their world has changed. They have additional responsibility and more influence in the decision-making process, making for a leaner, more competitive organization. The result for the small- and middle-sized firms to which the displaced managers go is a bonanza of talent and experience.

Dual-Career Paths for Technical and Professional Workers

Technical and professional workers, such as engineers and scientists, present a challenge for the organization in developing career paths. Many of them want to stay in their labs or at their drawing boards rather than move into management; yet, advancement frequently *requires* a move into management. Most of these people like the idea of the responsibility and opportunity associated with advancement, but they do not want to leave the technical puzzles and problems at which they excel.

▲ **Figure 11–6**

The "New Portable" Career Path

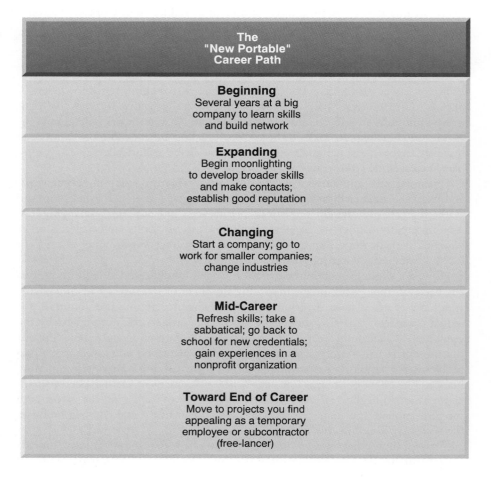

The "New Portable" Career Path

Beginning
Several years at a big company to learn skills and build network

Expanding
Begin moonlighting to develop broader skills and make contacts; establish good reputation

Changing
Start a company; go to work for smaller companies; change industries

Mid-Career
Refresh skills; take a sabbatical; go back to school for new credentials; gain experiences in a nonprofit organization

Toward End of Career
Move to projects you find appealing as a temporary employee or subcontractor (free-lancer)

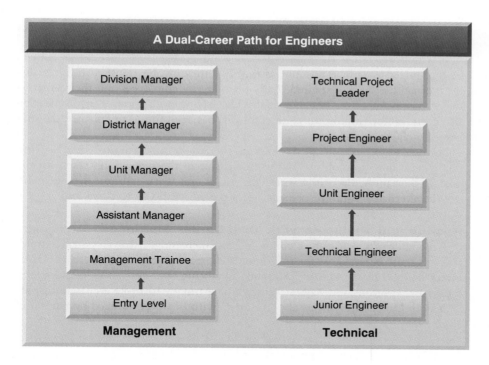

A Dual-Career Path for Engineers

Management	Technical
Division Manager	Technical Project Leader
↑	↑
District Manager	Project Engineer
↑	↑
Unit Manager	Unit Engineer
↑	↑
Assistant Manager	Technical Engineer
↑	↑
Management Trainee	Junior Engineer
↑	
Entry Level	

▲ **Figure 11–7**

Dual-Career Path for Engineers

The *dual-career ladder* is an attempt to solve this problem. As shown in Figure 11–7, a person can advance up either the management ladder or a corresponding ladder on the technical/professional side. Unfortunately, the technical/professional ladder sometimes is viewed as leading to "second-class citizenship" within the organization.

Dual-career paths have been used at IBM, Union Carbide, and AT&T/Bell Labs for years. They are most common in technology-driven industries such as pharmaceuticals, chemicals, computers, and electronics. Pacific Bell has created a dual-career ladder in its data-processing department to reward talented technical people who do not want to move into management. Different tracks, each with attractive job titles and pay opportunities, are provided. But for a second or third career track to be taken seriously, management must apply standards as rigorous as those applied to management promotions. Studies have shown that dual-career paths are ineffective when organizations fail to document and define performance qualifications and standards.[35]

Dual-Career Marriages

The increasing number of women in the workforce, particularly in professional careers, has greatly increased the number of dual-career couples as noted in Chapter 2. The U.S. Bureau of Labor Statistics reports that over 50% of all couples are dual-career couples, and the Bureau of the Census reports 14 million total.[36] Leading areas of growth in the number of dual-career couples are the West Coast, Denver, Chicago, New York, and the Washington, D.C.–Baltimore area.

Marriages in which both mates are managers, professionals, or technicians have doubled since 1970. Dual-career couples traditionally have been subject to transfers as part of the path upward in organizations. However, the dual-career couple is much less mobile because transfer interferes with a spouse's career.

It is important that the career-development problems of dual-career couples be recognized as early as possible, especially if they involve transfer, so that realistic alternatives can be explored. Early planning by employees and their supervisors can prevent crisis. Whenever possible, having both spouses involved, even when one is not employed by the company, has been found to enhance the success of such efforts.[37]

For dual-career couples with children, the family may take precedence. Thus, one spouse may be more willing to be flexible in the type of job taken for the sake of the family. Part-time work, flex-time, and work-at-home arrangements may be alternative solutions, especially for parents with younger children.

Recruitment Problems with Dual-Career Marriages   Recruitment of a member of a dual-career couple means, increasingly, that an equally attractive job must be available for the candidate's spouse at the new location. Dual-career couples have more to lose when relocating, and as a result often exhibit higher expectations and requests for help and money to make a change that affects both careers. Employers also must deal with turnover induced by transfer of a spouse.

Relocation of Dual-Career Couples   Dual-career couples, besides having invested in two careers, have established support networks of friends and neighbors to cope with their transportation and dependent-care needs. These needs, in a single-career couple, would normally be met by the other spouse. Relocation of one spouse in a dual-career couple means upsetting this carefully constructed network or creating a "commuting" relationship.

If a company has no spouse-assistance program, an employee may be hesitant to request such services and may turn down the relocation. The dual-career family has not been the norm for very long, and traditional role expectations remain. Some male employees still fear they will appear "unmanly" should a wife refuse to become a trailing spouse in support of her husband's career, while female employees may feel guilty about violating the traditional concept of male career dominance.

When relocation is the only way to handle a staffing situation, employers increasingly have support services to help the couple adapt to the new location. Some companies go so far as to hire the spouse at the new location or find the spouse a job with another company. At times, companies have agreed to pay part of the salary or benefits when another company hires the spouse and to reciprocate at some future time. When such arrangements cannot be made, professional job search counseling can be obtained for the spouse. It makes sense to take into account the dual-career social trend when revising HR policies on employee relocation assistance. Some approaches that could be considered are:

▲ Paying employment agency fees for the relocating spouse.

▲ Paying for a designated number of trips for the spouse to look for a job in the proposed new location.

▲ Helping the spouse find a job within the same company or in another division or subsidiary of the company.

▲ Developing computerized job banks on spouses who are available for job openings to share with other companies in the area.

Moonlighting

Moonlighting traditionally has been defined as work outside a person's regular employment that takes 12 or more additional hours per week. More recently, the concept of moonlighting has been expanded to include such activities as self-employment, investments, hobbies, and other employee interests for which additional remuneration is received. The perception that moonlighting is a fixed outside commitment is no longer sufficiently broad, since the forms that it may take are varied and sometimes difficult to identify.

A growing number of managers are dividing their work efforts by moonlighting as consultants or self-employed entrepreneurs. Consulting not only increases income but it provides new experiences and diversity to managerial lives as well. Moonlighting is no longer just a second job for the underpaid blue-collar worker but also a career development strategy for some professionals.

Many individuals also view such activities as extra security, especially in these times of layoffs among middle managers. Most of these managers cannot afford to walk away from their corporate salaries, but they are looking elsewhere for fulfillment. An HR manager at a TV network moonlights by working for a training firm that she and a friend set up. An advertising executive at a cosmetics company accepts free-lance assignments from his employer's clients. A computer software expert secretly develops a home computer program to market on his own.

If someone is working for a company and free-lancing in the same field, questions about whose ideas and time are involved are bound to arise. Some organizations threaten to fire employees who are caught moonlighting, mainly to keep them from becoming competitors. But it does not seem to stop the activities. Other organizations permit free-lance work so long as it is not directly competitive. Many believe their staff members should be free to develop their own special interests.

There is evidence that some multiple-job holders work a second job in preparation for a career change. More than 8% of the men and 6% of the women in one study reported working two jobs in order to gain the necessary experience to meet the skill requirements of another job.[38] Whether or not a career change is sought, the concept is "job insurance." Moonlighting can be viewed in the same context as auto, car, home, or life insurance. The second job could serve as a backup in the event the primary job is lost.

Moonlighting is not without its problems. The main argument against moonlighting has been that energy is being used on a second job that should be used on the primary job. This diversion of effort may lead to poor performance, absenteeism, and reduced job commitment. However, these arguments are less valid with ever-shorter average workweeks.

Key for employers in dealing with moonlighting employees is to devise and communicate a policy on the subject. Such a policy should focus on defining those areas where the employer limits employee activities because of business reasons.

▼ **MOONLIGHTING**

is work outside a person's regular employment that takes 12 or more additional hours per week.

▲ **SUMMARY**

▲ Development is different from training because it focuses on less tangible aspects of performance, such as attitudes and values.

▲ Successful development requires top management support and an understanding of its relationship to other HR activities.

▲ Replacement charts are like football depth charts. From them, decisions can be made about developing people internally or going outside for new talent.

▲ On-the-job development methods include coaching, committee assignment, and job rotation.

▲ Off-the-job development methods include classroom courses, special programs, psychological testing, human relations training, case studies, role-playing, simulation, sabbatical leaves, and "outdoor training."

▲ Assessment centers provide valid methods of assessing management talent and development needs.

▲ Mentoring and modeling are two ways for younger managers to acquire the skills and know-how necessary to be successful. Mentoring follows a four-stage progression in most cases.

▲ Career planning may focus on organizational needs, individual needs, or both.

▲ A person chooses a career based on interests, self-image, personality, social background, and other factors.

▲ A person's life is cyclical, as is his or her career. Putting the two together offers a perspective that can be useful in understanding employee problems.

▲ Retirement often requires serious emotional adjustments.

▲ Development of career paths may be done by charting ways of moving up in the organization or by identifying the types of jobs that will provide the desired experience to move up.

▲ Dual-career ladders are used with scientific or technical employees.

▲ Dual-career marriages increasingly require spouse relocation assistance for transferring employees.

▲ Moonlighting is growing in usage by professionals, technical workers, clerical workers, and others.

▲ **REVIEW AND DISCUSSION QUESTIONS**

1. What is HR development, and why is top management support so important?

2. You are the head of a government agency. What two methods of on-the-job development would you use with a promising supervisor? What two off-the-job methods would you use? Why?

3. Why have many large organizations started assessment centers?

4. Discuss whether you would prefer organization-centered or individual-centered career planning.

5. List reasons why dual-career paths for professional and technical workers may grow in importance in the future.

6. Assume you had to develop a company policy to address concerns about dual-career couples. What would you propose for such a policy?

ROHR INDUSTRIES CHANGES MANAGEMENT DEVELOPMENT

Rohr Industries, a California aerospace manufacturer, discovered that its approach to management development was not working, and it turned to the corporate training and development (T&D) department for help. T&D serves as the primary internal source for developing supervisory personnel at Rohr.

The existing supervisory development course was voluntary. Generally, supervisors were promoted from the ranks of the 6,200 employees to serve as liaisons between employees and midlevel managers. Each had 12 to 40 employees reporting to a supervisor.

Corporate T&D decided that the supervisory development course was a good place to upgrade the development of supervisors. A survey found that supervisory skills needed to be more clearly defined. Only 25% of the supervisors had taken the course, there was no incentive to take the course, and there was no follow-up after the course.

First T&D created a checklist of successful supervisory behaviors based upon job descriptions. Then observer sessions were scheduled with the best supervisors wherein T&D observers noted what these supervisors did. The observations led to classifying necessary supervisory skills as the following:

▲ Employee communication
▲ Coaching
▲ Team building
▲ Motivation and performance counseling

Supervisors who already had taken the course were asked to rate the importance of the skills. Generally, the skills were considered of about equal importance. Further evaluation of the previously offered course identified effective and ineffective portions. T&D produced a report of its findings, and during a Saturday meeting of supervisory course graduates presented its report. This session provided an opportunity for T&D and the supervisors to discuss how the course could be made more useful. For instance, revisions led to more sessions utilizing role-playing, case studies, and discussion.

Standard feedback forms are now used at the end of each course. In addition, a schedule for evaluation by supervisors six months after finishing the course provides further information. Using the evaluations to revise and improve course offerings is an ongoing process.[39]

▲ **QUESTIONS**

1. Evaluate the methods corporate T&D used to revise the supervisory development course.
2. Compare the findings of the T&D survey to what is done for supervisory development in organizations for which you have worked.

▲ **NOTES**

1. Adapted from Sue Shellenbarger, "Work and Family," *The Wall Street Journal*, June 24, 1992, B1; Sue Shellenbarger, "Allowing Fast Trackers to Stay in One Place," *The Wall Street Journal*, January 7, 1992, B1; Sue Shellenbarger, "MBA's Hope to Keep Jobs in their Place," *The Wall Street Journal*, January 19, 1993, B1; "Survey: Family Bigger Influence on Career," *Omaha World-Herald*, January 22, 1989, 9G; Cathy Trost, "Labor Letter," *The Wall Street Journal*, May 23, 1989, 1; and "Families Pay Emotional Cost of Relocating," *Omaha World-Herald*, February 19, 1989, 1G; and Joseph McKenna, "A Few Good Heroes," *Industry Week*, October 15, 1990, 16–19.

2. Chris Argyris, "Teaching Smart People How to Learn," *Harvard Business Review,* May–June 1991, 100.

3. P. Evans, "Management Development as Glue Technology," *Human Resource Planning,* 15 (1992), 85.

4. Robert J. Sahl, "Succession Planning Drives Plant Turnaround," *Personnel Journal,* September 1992, 67.

5. *The Wall Street Journal,* November 21, 1989, B1.

6. JoAnn S. Lublin, "Younger Managers Learn Global Skills," *The Wall Street Journal,* March 31, 1992, B1.

7. S. Doyle and G. Roth, "Selling and Sales Management in Action: The Use of Insight Coaching to Improve Relationship Selling," *Journal of Personal Selling and Sales Management,* Winter 1992, 59–64.

8. J. Rigdon, "Using Lateral Moves to Spur Employees," *The Wall Street Journal,* May 26, 1992, B1.

9. J. Byrne, "Back to School," *Business Week,* October 28, 1991, 102–114.

10. B. Thompson, "The Great Road Show of Learning," *Training,* August 1991, 41–44.

11. "Learning More," *The Wall Street Journal,* January 2, 1990, 1.

12. S. Sugar, "A Game Plan," *Training and Development Journal,* July 1990, 98.

13. Bruce Shutan, "Changing Sabbaticals, a Sign of the Times," *Employee Benefit News,* September, 1993, 19-20.

14. "A Few Firms Offer Workers Sabbaticals," *Omaha World-Herald,* June 28, 1992, 16; and D. Summers, "When a Change Is as Good as a Rest," *Financial Times,* March 6, 1992, 1.

15. G. Fuchsberg, "Managing," *The Wall Street Journal,* September 8, 1992, B1.

16. R. Wagner et al., "Outdoor Training: Revolution or Fad?" *Training and Development Journal,* March 1991, 51; and P. Buller et al., "Getting the Most Out of Outdoor Training," *Training and Development Journal,* March 1991, 58.

17. S. J. Yeager, "Use of Assessment Centers by Metropolitan Fire Departments in North America," *Public Personnel Management* 15 (1986), 55.

18. P. Rea et al., "Use Assessment Centers in Skill Development," *Personnel Journal,* April 1990, 126–131.

19. J. Schneider and N. Schmitt, "An Exercise Design Approach to Understanding Assessment Center Dimension and Exercise Constructs," *Journal of Applied Psychology* 77 (1992), 32–41.

20. Paul Miller, "A Strategic Look at Management Development," *Personnel Management,* August 1991, 45.

21. D. Sommer, M. Frohman, "American Management," *Industry Week,* July 20, 1992, 36–37; and Tracy E. Benson, "The New Leadership," *Industry Week,* June 1, 1992, 12–21.

22. M. Rogers, "Educational Models and their Influence on Executive Development," *Performance and Instruction,* April 1992, 14.

23. Adapted from information in K. E. Kram, "Phases of the Mentor Relationship," *Academy of Management Journal* 26 (1983), 608–625.

24. "Mentors Put Women on a Faster Track," *Omaha World-Herald,* September 1, 1991, 12G; A. Karr, "Progress Seen in Breaking Glass Ceilings," *The Wall Street Journal,* August 12, 1992, B1; and Julie H. Lopez, "Study Says Women Face Glass Walls as Well as Glass Ceilings," *The Wall Street Journal,* March 3, 1992, B1.

25. "Racial Differences Discourage Mentors," *The Wall Street Journal,* October 29, 1991, B1 and D. Horgan and R. Simeon, "The Downside of Mentoring," *Performance and Instruction,* January 1991, 34.

26. M. B. Arthur et al., *Handbook of Career Theory* (Cambridge, MA: Cambridge University Press, 1989).

27. P. Mergenbagen, "Doing the Career Shuffle," *American Demographics,* November 1991, 42.

28. "Half Would Pick Same Career Again," *Omaha World-Herald,* September 13, 1992, G-1.

29. J. Schuster, "Beyond the Velcro Approach," *Training and Development Journal,* January 1991, 57–58.

30. "The Right Report," *Right Associates—Management Consultants* 5 (1988).

31. M. Kastre, "The Two-Year Itch," *National Business Employment Weekly,* June 19, 1988, 12.

32. "Job Plateaus Coming Earlier in Career Path," *Omaha World-Herald,* November 11, 1990, G1.

33. B. Nuessbaum, "I'm Worried about my Job!" *Business Week,* October 7, 1991, 94–104.

34. J. A. Schneer and F. Reitman, "Effects of Employment Gaps on Careers of MBAs," *Academy of Management Journal* 33 (1990), 391–406.

35. V. Perro, "The Case for Career Management.," *Perspectives* 11 (1992),5–6.

36. "2 Tracks Can Spell Trouble," *Omaha World-Herald,* March 21, 1992, G1.

37. JoAnn S. Lublin, "Spouses Find Themselves Worlds Apart.," *The Wall Street Journal,* August 19, 1992, B1.

38. R. Half, "Managing Your Career," *Management Accounting,* August 1986, 16.

39. Adapted from Brenda J. Martin et al., "Strategies for Training New Managers," *Personnel Journal,* November 1991, 114–117.

CHAPTER 12

APPRAISAL OF HUMAN RESOURCES

After you have read this chapter, you should be able to:

1. Identify the major uses of appraisals.

2. Discuss three different categories of raters.

3. Give examples of three general types of appraisal methods.

4. Explain several rater errors.

5. Describe how to construct behaviorally anchored rating scales (BARS).

6. Explain the management by objectives (MBO) process.

7. Discuss several concerns about appraisal feedback interviews.

8. List the characteristics of a legal appraisal system.

9. Identify at least two characteristics of an effective appraisal system.

Determining how well an employee is doing his or her job and communicating that information is common in American business. Even in the public sector performance appraisal is common—but not in our public schools for teachers. Teaching presents some special problems for appraisal. What performance standards should be set? How well the teacher gets along with the students or how neat the room appears seem beside the point. Changes in the pupils' abilities or teacher behaviors that can be clearly linked by research to learning seem more appropriate. But the idea that there is a single best method of teaching may prevent an unbiased evaluation of just how good a teacher is.

There are no agreed-upon, measurable standards of what is most important in good teaching. In one study of 60 teachers, trained observers visited the classes for two years and reported on how well the teachers did on 25 abilities often measured in teacher competency tests. When the results were compiled, it became clear that not much was clear. About half the measures had no relationship to either student achievement scores or student self-esteem (the dependent variables used in the study). Skills such as using praise, responding to student questions, and giving students a voice in decision making actually were negatively related to academic achievement. Use of supportive classroom techniques also was negatively related to self-esteem. This is only one study; but the mixed or negative support given to factors thought to be related to good teaching suggests that those who wish to formulate teaching appraisal standards should proceed with caution.

When (or if) proper criteria for teacher evaluation are identified and used, the schools, like any other organization, public or private, will have another hurdle to overcome—acceptance of the performance appraisal process. This concern is magnified because performance appraisal can be used to remove those teachers who are not rated as satisfactory or better. For example, in one school district the teachers themselves helped to draw up the performance appraisal system that was in operation. But they began to fear that the system would be misused by new administrators. The teachers felt that if an administrator wanted to remove a teacher, all the administrator would have to do is rig the performance appraisal system to rank the teacher low and he or she would be gone.

Clearly, teacher evaluation at any level is difficult and controversial. For performance appraisal to be properly applied to this kind of endeavor, the questions of who should do the appraising, and how can accurate and equitable procedures be developed need to be answered.[1]

23

> Let's face reality, sloppy management is easy. That's why we have so much of it.
>
> *Jan Muezyk*

After an employee has been selected for a job, has been trained to do it, and has worked on it for a period of time, his or her performance should be reviewed. **Performance appraisal (PA),** the process of evaluating how well employees do their jobs compared with a set of standards and communicating that information to employees. It also has been called *employee rating, employee evaluation, performance review, performance evaluation,* and *results appraisal.*

That sounds simple enough. Research shows that performance appraisal is widely used for wage/salary administration, performance feedback, and identification of individual employee strengths and weaknesses.[2] Certainly performance appraisal is a common HR activity. Well over 80% of U.S. companies have PA systems for office, professional, technical, supervisory, middle management, and nonunion production workers.[3]

Yet performance appraisal often is management's least favored activity. There may be good reasons for that feeling. Not all performance appraisals are positive, and for that reason discussing ratings with the employee may not be pleasant. It may be difficult to differentiate among employees if good performance data are not available. Further, some supervisors are uncomfortable with the role of "playing God" with employees' raises and careers, which they feel results from some performance appraisals.

In general terms, performance appraisal has two roles in organizations that often are seen as potentially conflicting. One role is to measure performance for the purpose of rewarding or otherwise differentiating among employees. Promotions or layoffs might hinge on these ratings, making discussions of them difficult at times. Another role is development of individual potential. In this case the manager is featured more as a counselor than as a judge, and the atmosphere is often different.

▼ **PERFORMANCE APPRAISAL (PA)**

is the process of determining how well employees do their jobs compared with a set of standards and communicating that information to employees.

▲ USES OF PERFORMANCE APPRAISAL

The three major uses of performance appraisal, as shown in Figure 12–1, are for compensation administration, feedback for development, and various administrative decisions such as layoffs, promotions, and transfers.

Compensation Administration

A performance appraisal system is the link between the reward an employee hopes to receive and his or her productivity. The linkage can be thought of as:

productivity → performance appraisal → rewards

If any link fails, the most productive employees will not receive the larger rewards, resulting in all the problems that come from perceived inequity in the workplace. This approach to compensation is at the heart of the idea that raises

Figure 12–1

Uses of Performance Appraisal

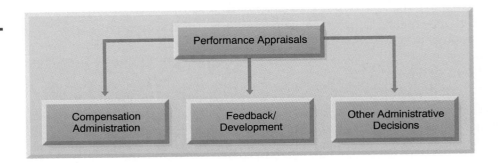

should be given for merit rather than for seniority. Under merit systems, employees receive raises based on performance. The manager's role is as evaluator of a subordinate's performance, and the focus is usually on comparison of performance levels among individuals.

Most American workers perceive little connection between the levels of their efforts and the sizes of their paychecks—according to a survey of 5,000 American employees, only 28% saw a link. Further, only about one-third of the sample rated their supervisors as good at giving performance feedback.[4] Most research indicates that the use of performance appraisal to determine pay is very common. Consequently, the research indicating its failure to be perceived as equitable warrants close attention.

Feedback for Development

Performance appraisal, even if it is not linked to wage/salary treatment, is a primary source of information and feedback, for employees both on areas in which they are doing well and ones where improvement is needed. So performance appraisal has a developmental use. When supervisors identify the weaknesses, potentials, and training needs of employees through PA feedback, they can inform employees about their progress and tell them what skills they need to develop to become eligible for promotions, transfers, and other HR actions.

The manager's role in such a situation is like that of a coach. The "coach's" job is to reward good performance with recognition, explain what improvement is necessary in some areas, and show the employee *how* to improve. People do not always know where they could improve, and managers really cannot expect improvement if they are unwilling to explain where and how improvement can occur. The purpose of performance appraisal feedback is to change or reinforce individual behavior, rather than to compare individuals as is the case in the other uses of performance appraisal. Positive reinforcement for the behaviors the organization wants is an important part of development.

The development function of performance appraisal allows for determination of areas in which the employee might wish to grow. For example, in a performance appraisal interview that was targeted exclusively to development, an employee found out that the only factor keeping her from being considered for a management job in her firm was a working knowledge of cost accounting. Her supervisor suggested that she consider taking such a course at night at the local college.

Other Administrative Decisions

Several other uses of performance appraisal results can be classified as administrative decisions. Promotion, termination, layoff, and transfer assignment decisions often are made on the basis of performance. For example, the order of layoffs can be justified by performance appraisals. However, if an employer claims that the decision was performance based, the performance appraisals must clearly document the differences in employee performance. Similarly, promotion or demotion based on differences in performance must be documented with performance appraisals.

▲ JOB CRITERIA AND PERFORMANCE STANDARDS

Job analysis helps identify the most important duties and tasks of jobs. The **job criteria** are elements of a job to be evaluated during performance appraisal, and they should be specified. For example, one criterion for a typist's job might be typing speed; another might be typing accuracy.

▼ **JOB CRITERIA**

are the elements of a job to be evaluated during performance appraisal.

Each job criterion should be compared with a *performance standard,* which is the expected level of performance. For the typist's job, the standard might be 50 words per minute and no more than two errors. Performance is almost never one-dimensional. In baseball the leading home-run hitter may not be the best fielder or even hit for the highest average. Job performance in this case might include home runs, hitting average, fielding percentage, and on-base performance, to name a few criteria. Multiple job criteria are the rule rather than the exception for all but the simplest jobs.

The various criteria for a given job also should be *weighted* to reflect the relative importance of criteria. For example, in the typist's job speed might be twice as important as accuracy, and accuracy might be equally as important as getting to work on time and being there every day. Thus, the weighting might look like this:

CRITERION	WEIGHT
Typing speed	2
Accuracy	1
Attendance	1
Tardiness	1

Types of Job Performance Criteria

Criteria for evaluating job performance can be classified as trait-based, behavior-based, or results-based criteria. A *trait-based* criterion identifies subjective character traits such as "pleasant personality," "initiative," or "creativity" and has little to do with the specific job. Such traits tend to be ambiguous, and courts have held that evaluations based on traits such as "adaptability" or "general demeanor" are too vague to use as the basis for performance-based HR decisions.[5]

Behavior-based criteria focus on specific behaviors that lead to job success when exhibited. For example, a salesperson who can exhibit the behavior of "verbal persuasion" appropriately has satisfied a behavior-based criterion. Behavioral criteria are more difficult to develop, but have the advantage of clearly specifying the behaviors management wants to see. A potential problem is that there may be several behaviors, all of which can be successful in a given situation.

Results-based criteria look at what the employee has done or accomplished. For some jobs where measurement is easy and appropriate, the results approach works very well. However, that which is measured tends to be emphasized, and equally important nonmeasurable parts of the job may be left out. For example, a car salesman who gets paid only for sales may be unwilling to do any paperwork not directly necessary to sell cars. Further, when only results are emphasized and not *how the results were achieved,* ethical or even legal issues may arise.

Performance Standards

Realistic, measurable, clearly understood performance standards benefit both the organization and the employee. It is important to establish standards *before* the work is performed so that all involved will understand the level of accomplishment expected.

Standards often are established for the following:

▲ Quantity of output
▲ Quality of output
▲ Timeliness of results
▲ Manner of performance
▲ Effectiveness in use of resources

Supervisory ratings of *quantity* of work produced have been found to be accurate, but measuring *quality* against a standard is less precise.[6]

What exactly is "outstanding"? What does "poor" mean? What is "average"? An identification of these terms is useful but it may be difficult. Figure 12–2 shows terms used in evaluating employee success in reaching standards at one company.

▲ **Figure 12–2**

Terms Used In Rating Performance at One Company

Outstanding. The person is so successful at this job criterion that special note should be made. Compared with the usual standards and the rest of the department, this performance ranks in the top 10%.

Very Good. Performance at this level is one of better-than-average performances in the unit, given the common standards and unit results.

Satisfactory. Performance is at or above the minimum standards. This level of performance is what one would expect from most experienced, competent employees.

Marginal. Performance is somewhat below the minimum-level standard on this job dimension. However, there appears to be potential to improve the rating within a reasonable time frame.

Unsatisfactory. Performance on this item in the job is well below standard, and there is serious question as to whether the person can improve to meet minimum standards.

▲ INFORMAL VERSUS SYSTEMATIC APPRAISAL

Performance appraisal may occur in two ways, informally or systematically. An *informal appraisal* is conducted whenever the supervisor feels it is necessary. The day-to-day working relationship between a manager and an employee offers an opportunity for the employee's performance to be judged. This judgment is communicated through conversation on the job, over coffee, or by on-the-spot examination of a particular piece of work. Informal appraisal is especially appropriate when time is an issue. Studies show that the longer feedback is delayed, the less likely it is to motivate behavior change.[7] Frequent informal feedback to employees can avoid surprises (and therefore problems) later when the formal evaluation is communicated.

A *systematic appraisal* is used when the contact between manager and employee is formalized and a system is established to report managerial impressions and observations on employee performance. Informal appraisal is useful, but should not take the place of formal appraisal.[8] When a formalized or systematic appraisal is used, the interface between the HR unit and the appraising manager becomes more important.

Appraisal Responsibilities

The appraisal process can be quite beneficial to the organization and to the individuals involved if done properly. It also can be the source of a great deal of discontent. In situations in which an employer must deal with a strong union, performance appraisals may be conducted only on salaried, nonunion employees. Generally, unions emphasize seniority over merit which precludes the use of performance appraisal. Unions view all members as equal in ability, and therefore, the one with the most experience is considered most qualified.

Figure 12–3 shows that the HR unit typically designs a systematic appraisal system. The manager does the actual appraising of the employee, using the procedures developed by the HR unit. As the formal system is being developed, the manager usually offers input on how the final system will work. Only rarely does an HR specialist actually rate a manager's employees.

Timing of Appraisals

Timing of appraisals is important. Systematic appraisals typically are conducted once or twice a year. One study showed that appraisals most often were conducted once a year, usually near the employee's anniversary date.[9] For new employees, an appraisal 90 days after employment, again at six months, and annually thereafter is common timing.

HR UNIT	MANAGERS
▲ Designs and maintains formal system	▲ Actually rate performance of employees
▲ Establishes formal report system	▲ Make formal reports
▲ Makes sure reports are on time	▲ Review appraisals with employees
▲ Trains raters	

▲ **Figure 12–3**

Typical Appraisal Responsibilities

This regular time interval is a feature of formal or systematic appraisals and distinguishes them from informal appraisals. Both employees and managers are aware that performance will be reviewed on a regular basis, and they can plan for performance discussions. Nevertheless, informal appraisals should also be conducted whenever a manager feels they are desirable.

Appraisals and Pay Discussions

The timing of performance appraisals and pay discussions should be different, some argue, because:

▲ Pay decisions may include factors other than performance. For example, a good performer may get the same raise as a poor employee because raises are granted "across the board" that year.

▲ Performance appraisal can be reinforcing by itself, especially if there are not raises in a given year. The reinforcement value can be lost if pay is brought in at that point.

▲ People may focus more on the pay treatment than on what they have done well or need to improve.

▲ Sometimes managers may manipulate performance appraisal ratings to justify the desired pay treatment for a given individual.

But, not everyone agrees that performance appraisal and pay are best discussed separately.[10] In fact, research provides conflicting evidence. One study found that discussing pay during the performance review did not affect future behavior, and another found mixed results.[11]

▲ WHO DOES THE APPRAISING?

Performance appraisal can be done by anyone familiar with a person's performance including the following:

▲ Supervisors who rate their employees
▲ Employees who rate their superiors
▲ Peers who rate each other
▲ Some combination of raters
▲ The employee himself or herself
▲ Outside sources

The first method is the most common. The immediate superior has the sole responsibility for appraisal in most organizations, although it is common practice to have the appraisal reviewed and approved by the supervisor's boss. Combinations of these methods are possible, too. Any system should include a face-to-face discussion between rater and ratee.

Supervisor Rating of Subordinates

Rating of employees by supervisors is based on the assumption that the manager is the most qualified person to evaluate the employee's performance realistically, objectively, and fairly. The *unity of command* notion—that every subordinate should have only one superior—underlies this approach.

As with any rating system, the supervisor's judgment should be objective and based on actual performance. Toward this end, some managers keep logs of what their employees have done. These logs provide specific examples when rating time arrives. They also serve to jog the memory, because managers cannot be expected to remember every detail of performance over a six-month or one-year period. A manager's appraisal typically is reviewed by the manager's superior to make sure that the manager has done a proper job of appraisal and, if the review and merit discussion is not separated, that the recommended pay increase is justified. Figure 12–4 shows this review process.

One study has shown that managers and employees evaluate performance appraisal systems on different bases. Managers tend to evaluate the system on how well it helps them communicate employee performance to employees. Employees rate the fairness of a performance appraisal on the following factors:[12]

▲ Pay adjustments are related to the ratings.

▲ Ratings are based on actual performance.

▲ Standards are consistently applied.

▲ Input is solicited and used *before* rating.

▲ Two-way communication is allowed during the interview.

Multiple-Rating System   If rating is done by a committee of superiors, more useful information may be available because more people have had a chance to know and observe the individual being rated. With more information, an organization can better pinpoint the appropriate employees for promotions or future job assignments. As with any HR technique there are some disadvantages to a multiple-rating system. More information does not necessarily mean better information. Without using objective data to make appraisals, committees may simply be pooling their collective ignorance.

A variation of the multiple-rating system requires that several superiors fill out separate rating forms on the same employee. The results are then tabulated. For instance, a young loan officer in a bank who is responsible for loan judgments may have her performance reviewed by a group of superiors comprising the bank's loan committee. This method preserves the role of judge for the superiors involved in the rating process.

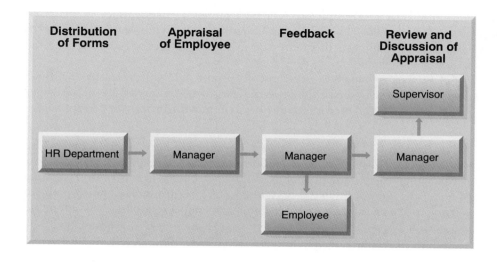

▲ **Figure 12–4**

Appraisal Process

HR Perspectives:
Practicing Performance Appraisal in Reverse

At Photocircuits, a New York company that manufactures printed circuit boards, managers and supervisors get regular reviews by their workers. Employees fill out questionnaires on supervisory attitudes that ask:

▲ Does your manager show interest in you as a person?

▲ Does he or she accept suggestions easily?

▲ Does he or she give criticism in a fair and considerate manner?

Employees summarize strong and weak points, then discuss the appraisals with their supervisors. At first, employees had trouble being critical of the supervisor. Initial appraisals were uncritical, even "glowing."

However, company president John Endee encouraged honest appraisal. "This sort of program doesn't work in a climate of fear," he said. He was told by one employee that he was "too aggressive" and "frightened people." As a result, he made some changes in his management style.

Fear can work on managers too. Some were afraid of being evaluated by employees. But criticism of management occurs all the time. Employees constantly criticize their supervisors. The manager who has a problem—who needs to improve his behavior or attitude—can be made aware of this by the very people who can help him most.[13]

An Indianapolis printing firm, Queen's Group Indiana, Inc., reviews its supervisors with a team of four or five managers who work with them regularly, though not necessarily in the same department. The team goes over a list of criteria that supervisors should meet. Each team member rates the supervisor, and ratings are merged. The rating is then communicated to the supervisor by one or two team members.[14]

Employee Rating of Superiors

The concept of having superiors rated by employees is being used in a number of organizations today (see the "HR Perspective" on practicing performance appraisal in reverse). A prime example of this type of rating takes place in colleges and universities where students evaluate a professor's performance in the classroom. Industry also has used employee ratings for developmental purposes—to help managers improve themselves or to help organizations assess managerial leadership potential.

Subordinate appraisals do serve a useful purpose in HR decision-making. But a combination of subordinate appraisals *and* assessment-center data has proved superior to either method used independently to improve management performance.

Advantages   The advantages of having employees rate superiors are at least three. First, in situations where superior/employee relationships are critical, employee ratings can be quite useful in identifying competent superiors. The rating of leaders by combat soldiers is an example. Second, this type of rating program can help make the superior more responsive to employees, though this advantage can quickly become a disadvantage if it leads to the superior trying to be "nice" rather than trying to manage. Nice people without other qualifications may not be good managers in many situations. Finally, it can be the basis for coaching as part of a career development effort.

Disadvantages   A major disadvantage is the negative reaction many superiors have to being evaluated by employees.[15] Fear of reprisal may be too great for employees to give realistic ratings. The principles of "proper" manager/employee relations may be violated by having workers rate managers. Employees may resist rating their bosses because they do not perceive it as part of their jobs. If this is the case, workers may rate the manager only on the way the manager treats them, and not on critical job requirements.

The problems associated with employees rating managers seem to limit the usefulness of this appraisal approach to certain situations, such as in a university or an engineering research department. The traditional nature of most organizations appears to restrict the applicability of employee rating except for self-improvement purposes.

Peer Ratings

The use of peer groups as raters is a third type of appraisal system, one that can be handled unwisely. For example, if a group of salespersons meets as a committee to talk about one another's ratings, future work relationships might be impaired. Therefore, the peer rating approach is best done if individual ratings are done separately and then summarized.

Peer ratings are especially useful when supervisors do not have the opportunity to observe each employee's performance but other work group members do. Peer evaluations are not widely used, though. One reason groups may resist evaluating members is that, as just mentioned, it can damage relationships. It may be that peer evaluations are best used for developmental purposes rather than for administrative purposes. In fact, some contend that *any* performance appraisal, including peer ratings, can affect teamwork and participative-management efforts negatively.

Appraisal Teamwork and TQM   Total quality management (TQM) and other participative-management approaches emphasize teamwork and team performance rather than individual performance. Effectiveness is viewed as the result of systematic factors rather than the product of individual efforts. Individual accomplishment occurs only by working with others.[16] In this system individual performance appraisal is seen as producing fear and hindering the development of teamwork.

The noted management consultant W. Edwards Deming sees performance appraisal as one of the seven deadly diseases afflicting American management practice. He argues that such appraisals (even peer appraisals) inappropriately attribute variation in performance to individuals rather than to problems in the system. Deming contends that variation in individual performance is generally due to factors outside of individual control.[17]

This approach of not appraising team members is used in high involvement/high commitment groups and focuses on helping those whose performance is "out of system tolerances." But even if formal appraisals seem inappropriate, informal appraisals by peers or team leaders are likely to be occasionally necessary.

Self-Ratings

Self-appraisal works in certain situations. Essentially, it is a self-development tool that forces employees to think about their strengths and weaknesses and set goals for improvement. If an employee is working in isolation or possesses a unique skill, the employee may be the only one qualified to rate his or her own behavior, but employees may not rate themselves as supervisors would rate them; they may use quite different standards. Despite the difficulty in evaluating self-ratings, research suggests the performing individual can be a valuable and credible source of performance information. Some research shows a leniency error in self-ratings, whereas other research does not.[18]

Outside Raters

Rating also may be done by outsiders. Outside experts may be called in to review the work of a college president, for example, or professional assessors at an assessment center might evaluate a person's potential for advancement in an organization. Outsiders may furnish managers with professional assistance in making appraisals, but there are obvious disadvantages. The outsider may not know all the important contingencies within the organization. In addition, outsider appraisals are time consuming and expensive.

The customers or clients of an organization are obvious sources for outside appraisals. For salespeople and other service jobs, customers may provide the only really clear view of certain behaviors. One corporation uses measures of customer satisfaction with service as a way of helping to determine bonuses for top marketing executives.

▲ METHODS FOR APPRAISING PERFORMANCE

Performance actually can be appraised by a number of methods. In Figure 12–5 the various methods are categorized into four major groups.

Figure 12–5

Performance Appraisal Methods

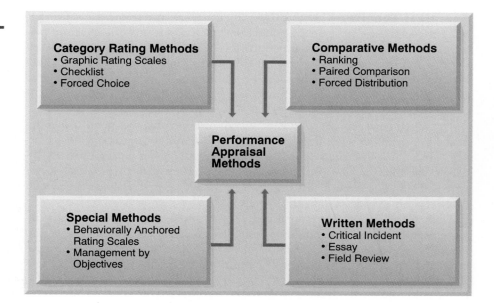

Category-Rating Methods

The simplest methods for appraising performance are those that require a manager to mark an employee's level of performance on a specific form. The graphic rating scale and checklist are common category-rating methods.

Graphic Rating Scale   The **graphic rating scale** allows the rater to mark an employee's performance on a continuum. Because of its simplicity, this method is the most frequently used method. Figure 12–6 shows a graphic rating

▲ **Figure 12–6**   Sample Performance Appraisal Form (Simplified)

APPRAISAL FORM

Date sent ___4-7-94___   Return by ___4-21-94___

Name ___Alicia Williamson___   Job Tilte ___Receiving Clerk___

Department ___Receiving___   Supervisor ___Robert Martinez___

Full-time ☐   Part-time ☐   Date of Hire _____

Appraisal Period: From _____   To _____

Reason for appraisal (check one):   Regular interval ☐   Probationary ☐

Counseling only ☐   Discharge ☐

Major job duties

Job duty 1: ___Recive and check inventory___

Lowest		Satisfactory		Highest
1	2	3	4	5

Explanation for rating _____

Job duty 2: ___Keep accurate records___

Lowest		Satisfactory		Highest
1	2	3	4	5

Explanation for rating: _____

Job duty 3: ___Maintain good vendor relations___

Lowest		Satisfactory		Highest
1	2	3	4	5

Explanation for rating _____

Overall Rating: Consider a general view of the employee's job performance during the rating perio

_____
_____
_____

A study of 52 registered nurses asked which performance appraisal method they preferred, who should do the rating, and how they preferred the ratings to be used.

The nurses generally preferred numerical scales that did not compare individuals to each other. Scales that relied on external criteria and applied to all workers were preferred.

The nurses made little differentiation among ratings being performed by peers, supervisors, or employees themselves, but preferred any of these three options over being rated by subordinates. The nurses preferred that the evaluations be used for promotion or pay decisions, but not for assigning shift work or determining layoffs.[19]

Three general observations can be made from the study that fit with other research results. First, people seem to prefer to be measured objectively against a standard rather than subjectively against other people. Second, subordinate evaluation is not popular. Third, the use of performance appraisal for "negative" outcomes such as layoffs is not popular.

scale form used by managers to rate office employees. The rater checks the appropriate place on the scale for each duty listed. More detail can be added in the space for comments following each factor rated.

There are some obvious drawbacks to the graphic rating scale. Often separate traits or factors are grouped together and the rater is given only one box to check. Another drawback is that the descriptive words sometimes used in such scales may have different meanings to different raters. Factors such as *initiative* and *cooperation* are subject to many interpretations, especially in conjunction with words such as *outstanding, average,* or *poor.* Graphic rating scales in many forms are used widely because they are easy to develop. But for the same reason, they encourage errors on the part of the raters, who may depend too heavily on them.

▼ **A CHECKLIST**

uses a list of statements or words that are checked by raters.

Checklist   The **checklist** uses a list of statements or words that are checked by raters. Raters check statements most representative of the characteristics and performance of employees.

The following are typical checklist statements:

_____ can be expected to finish work on time.

_____ seldom agrees to work overtime.

_____ is cooperative and helpful.

_____ accepts criticism.

_____ strives for self-improvement.

The checklist can be modified so that varying weights are assigned to the statements or words. The results can then be quantified. Usually, the weights are not known by the rating supervisor and are tabulated by someone else, such as a member of the HR unit.

There are several difficulties with the checklist: (1) as with the graphic rating scale, the words or statements may have different meanings to different raters; (2) raters cannot readily discern the rating results if a weighted checklist is used; and (3) raters do not assign the weights to each factor. These difficulties limit the use of the information when a rater discusses the checklist with the employee, placing a barrier to effective developmental counseling.

Comparative Methods

Comparative methods require that managers directly compare the performances of their employees against one another. For example, a data-entry operator's performance would be compared with that of other data-entry operators by the computing supervisor. Comparative techniques include ranking, paired comparisons, and forced distribution.

Ranking   The **ranking** method consists of listing all employees from highest to lowest in performance. The primary drawback of the ranking method is that the size of the differences among individuals is not well defined. For example, there may be little difference in performance between individuals ranked second and third, but a big difference in performance between those ranked third and fourth. This drawback can be overcome to some extent by assigning points to indicate the size of the gaps existing among employees.

Ranking also means that someone must be last. It is possible that the last-ranked individual in one group would be the top employee in a different group. Further, ranking becomes very unwieldy if the group to be ranked is very large.

Paired Comparisons   The rater using the **paired comparison** method formally compares each employee with every other employee in the rating group one at a time. Figure 12–7 illustrates the paired comparison method with three individuals.

▼ **RANKING**

consists of listing all employees from highest to lowest in performance.

▼ **PAIRED COMPARISON**

formally compares each employee with every other employee in the rating group one at a time.

▲ **Figure 12–7**   Paired Comparisons

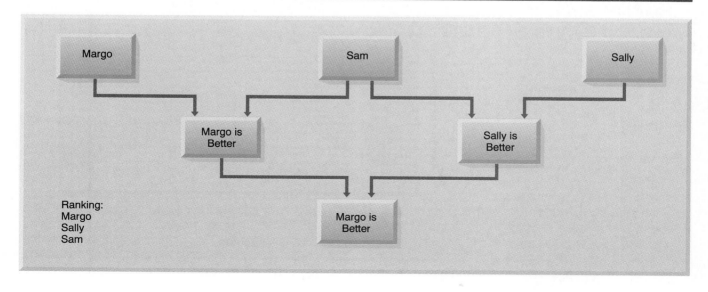

The number of comparisons can be calculated using the following formula:

$$\frac{n(n-1)}{2} \qquad [n = \text{number of people rated}]$$

For example, a manager with 15 employees would compare one person's performance with that of each of the other 14 employees. Each employee, in turn, would be compared in a similar fashion. The manager doing the ratings would have to make 105 different comparisons on each rating factor. Use of the paired comparison method gives more information about individual employees than the straight ranking method does. Obviously, the large number of comparisons that must be made is the major drawback of this method.

FORCED DISTRIBUTION

rates employees from highest to lowest performance and assumes results in a bell-shaped curve.

Forced Distribution   The **forced-distribution** method rates employees from highest to lowest performance and assumes results in a bell-shaped curve. It is also a comparative technique but without the drawback of the large number of comparisons in the paired-comparison method. By using the forced-distribution method, for example, a head nurse can rank nursing personnel along a scale, placing a certain percentage of employees at various performance levels. This method assumes that the widely known "bell-shaped curve" of performance exists in a given group. Figure 12–8 shows a scale used with a forced distribution.

A drawback of forced distribution is that a supervisor may resist placing any individual in the lowest (or the highest) group. Difficulties can arise when the rater must explain to the employee why he or she was placed in one grouping and others were placed in higher groupings. Further, with small groups, there may be no reason to assume that bell-shaped distribution of performance really exists. Finally, in some cases the manager may feel forced to make distinctions among employees that may not exist.

In fact, generally, the distribution of performance appraisal ratings does not approximate the normal distribution of the bell-shaped curve. It is common for 60% to 70% of the organization's workforce to be rated in the top two performance

▲ Figure 12–8

Forced Distribution on a Bell-Shaped Curve

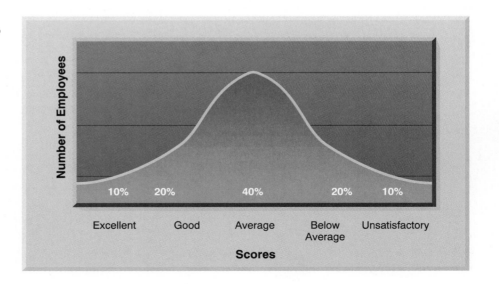

levels. This could reflect outstanding performance by a lot of employees, or it could reflect *leniency bias,*[20] discussed later in this chapter under "Rater Errors."

Narrative Methods

Some managers or HR specialists are required to provide written appraisal information. Documentation and description are the essence of the critical incident, the essay, and the field-review methods. These records describe an employee's actions rather than indicating an actual rating.

Critical Incident In the critical-incident method, the manager keeps a written record of the highly favorable and unfavorable actions in an employee's performance. When something happens (a "critical incident" involving an employee), the manager writes it down. A list of critical incidents is kept during the entire rating period for each employee. The critical-incident method can be used with other methods to document the reasons why an employee was rated in a certain way.

 The critical-incident method also has its unfavorable aspects. First, what constitutes a critical incident is not defined in the same way by all supervisors. Next, producing daily or weekly written remarks about each employee's performance can take considerable time. Further, employees may become overly concerned about what the superior writes and begin to fear the manager's "black book."

Essay The essay, or "free-form," appraisal method requires the manager to write a short essay describing each employee's performance during the rating period. The rater usually is given a few general headings under which to categorize comments. The intent is to allow the rater more flexibility than other methods do. As a result, the essay is often combined with other methods.

Field Review In the field review, the HR unit becomes an active partner in the rating process. A member of the unit interviews the manager about each employee's performance. The HR representative then compiles the notes of each interview into a rating for each employee. Then the rating is reviewed by the supervisor for needed changes. This method assumes that the representative of the HR unit knows enough about the job setting to help supervisors give more accurate and thorough appraisals.

 The major limitation of the field review is that the HR representative has a large amount of control over the rating. Although this control may be desirable from one viewpoint, supervisors may see it as a challenge to their managerial authority. In addition, the field review can be time consuming, particularly if a supervisor has to rate a large number of employees.

Special Appraisal Systems: BARS and MBO

Two special appraisal systems that attempt to overcome some of the difficulties of the methods just described are the behaviorally anchored rating scale (BARS) and management by objectives (MBO). Behaviorally anchored rating scales seem to hold promise for situations in which many people are doing the same job, whereas MBO is useful for management appraisals.

Behaviorally Anchored Rating Scale (BARS)

A BARS system describes examples of good or bad behavior. These examples are "anchored," or measured, against a scale of performance levels. Figure 12–9 shows a BARS that rates a college professor's attitude toward students. What constitutes various levels of performance is clearly defined in the figure. Spelling out the behavior associated with each level of performance helps minimize some of the problems noted earlier.

Constructing BARS   Construction of a BARS begins with identification of important *job dimensions*. The dimensions are the most important performance factors in an employee's description. To continue with the college professor example, assume the major job dimensions associated with teaching are:

▲ Course organization

▲ Attitude toward students

▲ Fair treatment

▲ Competence in subject area

Short statements, similar to critical incidents, are developed that describe both desirable and undesirable behaviors (anchors). Then they are "retranslated" or assigned to one of the job dimensions. This task is usually a group project, and assignment to a dimension usually requires the agreement of 60% to 70% of the group. The group, consisting of people familiar with the job, then assigns each "anchor" a number, which represents how good or bad the behavior is. When numbered, these anchors are fitted to a scale. Figure 12–10 shows a flow diagram of the BARS construction process.

▲ **Figure 12–9**   Behaviorally Anchored Rating Scale for Professor's Attitude toward Students

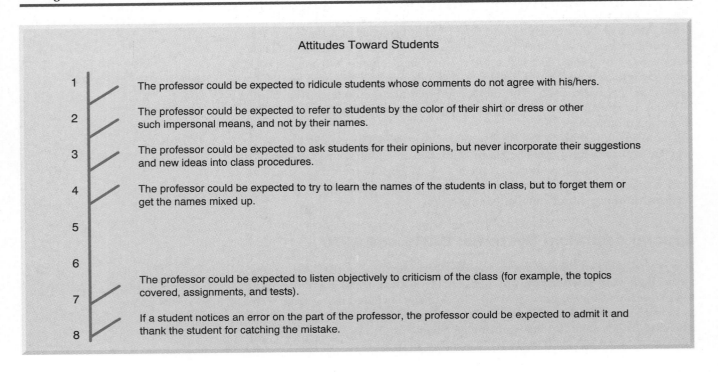

Attitudes Toward Students

1 — The professor could be expected to ridicule students whose comments do not agree with his/hers.

2 — The professor could be expected to refer to students by the color of their shirt or dress or other such impersonal means, and not by their names.

3 — The professor could be expected to ask students for their opinions, but never incorporate their suggestions and new ideas into class procedures.

4 — The professor could be expected to try to learn the names of the students in class, but to forget them or get the names mixed up.

5

6

7 — The professor could be expected to listen objectively to criticism of the class (for example, the topics covered, assignments, and tests).

8 — If a student notices an error on the part of the professor, the professor could be expected to admit it and thank the student for catching the mistake.

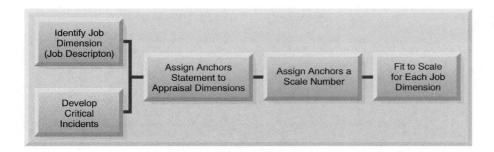

▲ **Figure 12–10**

Flow Diagram of BARS
Construction

Behaviorally anchored rating scales require extensive time and effort to develop and maintain. Several appraisal forms also are necessary to accommodate different types of jobs in an organization. In a hospital, nurses, dieticians, and admission clerks all have different jobs; separate BARS forms would need to be developed for each distinct job.

Management by Objectives (MBO)

A system of "guided self-appraisal" called management by objectives (MBO) is useful in appraising managers' performances. Although not limited to the appraisal of managers, MBO is most often used for this purpose. Disenchantment with previously discussed approaches has increased the popularity of MBO. Other names for MBO include *appraisal by results, targeting-coaching, work planning and review, performance objectives,* and *mutual goal setting.*

MBO specifies the performance goals that an individual hopes to attain within an appropriate length of time. The objectives that each manager sets are derived from the overall goals and objectives of the organization, although MBO should not be a disguised means for a superior to dictate the objectives of individual managers or employees.

Key MBO Ideas   Three key assumptions underlie an MBO appraisal system. First, if an employee is involved in planning and setting the objectives and determining the measure, a higher level of commitment and performance may result.

Second, if what an employee is to accomplish is defined clearly and precisely, the employee will do a better job of achieving the desired results. Ambiguity and confusion—and therefore less effective performance—may result when a superior determines the objectives for an individual. By having the employee set objectives, the individual gains an accurate understanding of what is expected.

Third, performance objectives should be measurable and should define results. Vague generalities, such as "initiative" or "cooperation," which are common in many superior-based appraisals, should be avoided. Objectives are composed of specific actions to be taken or work to be accomplished. Sample objectives might include:

▲ Submit regional sales report by the fifth of every month
▲ Obtain orders from at least five new customers per month
▲ Maintain payroll costs at 10% of sales volume
▲ Have scrap loss less than 5%
▲ Fill all organizational vacancies within 30 days after openings occur

▲ **Figure 12–11**

MBO Process

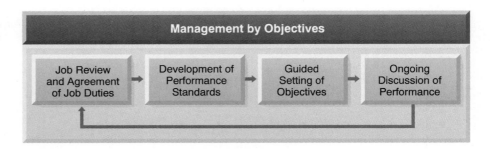

The MBO Process   Implementing a guided self-appraisal system using MBO is a four-stage process. These phases are shown in Figure 12–11 and discussed next.

1. *Job review and agreement.* The employee and the superior review the job description and the key activities that comprise the employee's job. The idea is to agree on the exact makeup of the employee's job.
2. *Development of performance standards.* Specific standards of performance must be mutually developed. This phase specifies a satisfactory level of performance that is specific and measurable. For example, a salesperson's quota of selling five cars per month may be an appropriate performance standard.
3. *Guided objective setting.* Objectives are established by the employee in conjunction with, and guided by, the superior. For the automobile salesperson, an objective might be to improve performance; the salesperson might set a new objective of selling six cars per month. Notice that the objective set may be different from the performance standard. Objectives should be realistically attainable.
4. *Continuing performance discussions.* The employee and the superior use the objectives as bases for continuing discussions about the employee's performance. Although a formal review session may be scheduled, the employee and the manager do not necessarily wait until the appointed time for performance discussion. Objectives are modified mutually, and progress is discussed during the period.

MBO Critique   No management tool is perfect, and certainly MBO is not appropriate for all employees or all organizations. Jobs with little or no flexibility are not compatible with MBO. An assembly-line worker usually has so little job flexibility that performance standards and objectives are already determined. The MBO process seems to be most useful with managerial personnel and employees who have a fairly wide range of flexibility and control over their jobs. When imposed on a rigid and autocratic management system, MBO may fail. Extreme emphasis on penalties for not meeting objectives defeats the development and participative nature of MBO. As Figure 12–12 indicates, MBO is used by supervisors to rate subordinates, for self-rating, or in combination with several raters.

▲ RATER ERRORS

There are many possible sources of error in the performance appraisal process. One of the major sources is mistakes made by the rater. There is no simple way

	METHODS				
	Category Rating Methods	Comparative Methods	Narrative Methods	BARS	MBO
Rater					
Supervisor Rating Subordinates	✓	✓	✓	✓	✓
Employees Rating Superiors	✓		✓	✓	
Peers Rating Each Other	✓	✓	✓	✓	
Combination of Raters	✓	✓	✓	✓	✓
Self-Rating	✓	✓	✓		✓
Outside Sources	✓	✓	✓		

Figure 12–12

Performance Appraisal Methods And Who Uses Them

to eliminate these errors, but making raters aware of them is helpful. A variety of rater errors are discussed next.

Problems of Varying Standards

When appraising employees, a manager should avoid using different standards and expectations for individual employees performing similar jobs, which is certain to incur the anger of employees. More problems are likely to exist when ambiguous criteria and subjective weightings by supervisors are used.

Even if an employee actually has been appraised on the same basis as other employees, the employee's perception is critical. If a student felt a professor had graded his exam harder than another student's exam, he might ask the professor for an explanation. The student's opinion might not be changed by the professor's claim that she had "graded fairly." So it is with performance appraisals in a work situation. If performance appraisal information is to be helpful, the rater must use the same standards and weights for every employee and be able to defend the appraisal.

Recency Effect

The **recency effect** gives greater weight to recent occurrences when appraising an individual's performance. This *recency effect* often occurs. Giving a student a course grade based only on performance in the last week of class or giving a drill press operator a high rating even though he/she made the quota only in the last two weeks of the rating period are examples.

THE RECENCY EFFECT

gives greater weight to recent occurences when appraising an individual's performance.

The recency effect is an understandable rater error because it is difficult to remember performance that may be seven or eight months old. Employees also become more concerned about performance as formal appraisal time approaches. Some employees may attempt to take advantage of the recency factor by currying favor with their supervisors shortly before their appraisals are conducted. The problem can be minimized by using critical-incident recording or some other method of documenting both positive and negative performance occurrences.

Rater Bias

Rater bias occurs when a rater's values or prejudices distort the rating. If a manager has a strong dislike of certain ethnic groups, this bias is likely to result in distorted appraisal information for some people.[21] Age, religion, seniority, sex, appearance, or other arbitrary classifications may be reflected in appraisals if the appraisal process is not properly designed. Examination of ratings by higher-level managers may help correct this problem.

Rater bias may be subconscious or quite intentional. One reason is that *leniency bias,* for example, may exist because supervisors are concerned about damaging a good working relationship by giving an unfavorable rating. Or they may wish to avoid giving negative feedback, which is often unpleasant, so they inflate the ratings. Reasons for a rating biased on the low side might include sending the employee a "message" for several reasons or documenting a case leading to dismissal. Subconscious rater bias is difficult to overcome, especially if a manager is not aware of the bias or will not admit to it.

Rater Patterns

Students are well aware that some professors tend to grade easier or harder than others. Likewise, a manager may develop a *rating pattern.* When appraisers rate all employees within a narrow range (usually the middle or average), this is called a **central tendency error.** For example, Dolores Bressler, office manager, tends to rate all her employees as average. Even the poor performers receive an average rating from Dolores. Jane Carr, the billing supervisor, believes that if employees are poor performers, they should be rated below average. An employee of Jane's who is rated average may well be a better performer than one rated average by Dolores.

Halo Effect

The **halo effect** occurs when a manager rates an employee high or low on all items because of one characteristic. For example, if a worker has few absences, her supervisor might give her a high rating in all other areas of work, including quantity and quality of output, because of her dependability. The manager may not really think about the employee's other characteristics separately.

An appraisal that shows the same rating on all characteristics may be evidence of the halo effect. Clearly specifying the categories to be rated, rating all employees on one characteristic at a time, and training raters to recognize the problem are some means of reducing the halo effect.

Contrast Error

Rating should be done on the basis of standards that are established before the rating. The **contrast error** is the tendency to rate people relative to other people rather than to performance standards. For example, if everyone else in a group is doing a mediocre job, a person performing somewhat better may be rated as excellent because of the contrast effect.

But in a group performing well, the same person might have received only a poor rating. Although it may be appropriate to compare people at times, the rating should reflect performance against job requirements, not against other people.

▲ **CONTRAST ERROR**

is the tendency to rate people relative to other people rather than to performance standards.

▲ THE APPRAISAL FEEDBACK INTERVIEW

Once appraisals have been made, it is important to communicate them so that employees have a clear understanding of how they stand in the eyes of their immediate superiors and the organization. It is fairly common for organizations to require that managers discuss appraisals with employees. The appraisal feedback interview can clear up misunderstandings on both sides. In this interview, the manager should emphasize counseling and development, not just tell the employee, "Here is how you rate and why." Focusing on development gives both parties an opportunity to consider the employee's performance and its potential for improvement.

The appraisal interview presents both an opportunity and a danger. It is an emotional experience for the manager and the employee because the manager must communicate both praise and constructive criticism. A major concern is how to emphasize the positive aspects of the employee's performance while still discussing ways to make needed improvements. If the interview is handled poorly, the employee may feel resentment, and conflict may result, which probably will be reflected in future work.

Employees usually approach an appraisal interview with some concern. They often feel that discussions about performance are very personal and important to their continued job success. At the same time, they want to know how the manager feels they have been doing.[22] Figure 12–13 summarizes hints for an effective appraisal interview.

DO	DON'T
▲ Prepare in advance	▲ Lecture the employee
▲ Focus on performance and development	▲ Mix performance appraisal and salary or promotion issues
▲ Be specific about reasons for ratings	▲ Concentrate only on the negative
▲ Decide on specific steps to be taken for improvement	▲ Do all the talking
▲ Consider supervisor's role in the subordinate's performance	▲ Be overly critical or "harp on" a failing
▲ Reinforce desired behaviors	▲ Feel it is necessary that both parties agree on all areas
▲ Focus on future performance	▲ Compare the employee with others

▲ **Figure 12–13**

Hints for Managers in the Appraisal Interview

Reactions of Managers

Managers and supervisors who must complete appraisals on their employees often resist the appraisal process. As mentioned earlier, the manager may feel he or she is put in the position of "playing God." A major part of the manager's role is to assist, encourage, coach, and counsel employees to improve their performance. However, being a judge on the one hand and a coach and counselor on the other may cause internal conflict and confusion for the manager.

The fact that appraisals may affect an employee's future career may cause raters to alter or bias their rating. This bias is even more likely when managers know that they will have to communicate and defend their ratings to the employees, their bosses, or HR specialists. From the manager's viewpoint, providing negative feedback to an employee in an appraisal interview easily can be avoided by making the employee's ratings positive.

Reactions such as these are attempts to avoid unpleasantness in an interpersonal situation. Avoidance helps no one. A manager *owes* an employee a well-considered appraisal.

Reactions of the Appraised Employee

A common reaction by employees is to view appraising as a zero-sum game in which there must be a winner and a loser. Employees may well see the appraisal process as a threat and feel that the only way to get a higher rating is for someone else to receive a low rating. This win/lose perception is encouraged by comparative methods of rating.

Appraisals can be both zero-sum and non-zero-sum (in which both parties win and no one loses) in nature. Emphasis on the self-improvement and developmental aspects of appraisal appears to be the most effective means to reduce some zero-sum reactions from those participating in the appraisal process.

Another common employee reaction is similar to students' reactions to tests. Because a professor prepares a test he or she feels is fair, it does not necessarily follow that students will feel the test is fair. They simply may see it differently. Likewise, employees being appraised may not necessarily agree with the manager doing the actual appraising. In most cases, however, employees will view appraisals done well for what they are meant to be—constructive feedback.

▲ PERFORMANCE APPRAISAL AND THE LAW

A growing number of court decisions have focused on performance appraisals, particularly in relation to equal employment opportunity (EEO) concerns. In addition, there are ethical issues that have legal consequences associated with them, as the following "HR Perspective" indicates. The Uniform Guidelines issued by the Equal Employment Opportunity Commission (EEOC) and other federal enforcement agencies make it clear that performance appraisals must be job related and nondiscriminatory.

Court Cases and Appraisals

It may seem unnecessary to emphasize that performance appraisals must be job related, because appraisals are supposed to measure how well employees are

HR Perspectives:
Ethics of Dismissing a "Satisfactory" Employee

"We should never have kept him in that job so long. It was a mistake and now we have to bite the bullet." "We were wrong. Fred should have been told years ago that his performance was marginal." "We should have fired Fred ten years ago."

So went the comments just before the decision was made to dismiss Fred Johnson, a supervisor and 20-year employee at a large firm in the telecommunications industry. But, his performance had consistently been rated "satisfactory"—"3" on a five-point scale. No one had ever said anything to him that would cause him to be concerned about his future. There were certainly no rave reviews, but no condemning comments either, and he had received "merit" pay increases over his 20 years with the company. But the ground rules had changed, and suddenly he was out.

If management wants to make employment changes, it clearly has the right to do so. However, is it ethically proper to disregard years of "satisfactory" (by management's own rating) performance? Or, should Fred's boss identify the specific goals to be met and a timetable for meeting them, knowing full will that Fred is likely to fail? Is there an age discrimination issue here as well?

Dentists allegedly extract their mistakes; physicians are said to bury theirs. What is the ethical course of action a company should take when changes must be made, but years of past performance appraisals do not indicate that anything is wrong with an individual's performance?

doing their jobs. Yet in numerous cases, courts have ruled that performance appraisals were discriminatory and not job related.

One court case provides an important illustration. Fort Worth Bank and Trust was a relatively small bank with 80 employees. It hired Clara Watson as a proof operator. Two years later she was promoted to teller. Eight years after going to work for the bank she was promoted to commercial teller. She then applied over the next year-and-a-half for four different promotions. In each case, a white employee was selected over Watson, who is a member of a racial minority group. The bank admitted it had no precise and formal criteria to evaluate good performance for the positions for which Watson had applied. It relied instead on the subjective judgment of supervisors. Watson resigned, sued, and won. In *Watson v. Fort Worth Bank and Trust,* the U.S. Supreme Court ruled a violation of Title VII of the Civil Rights Act could occur when an employer's *subjective* promotion criteria resulted in disproportionately fewer minority employees receiving promotions. The Court noted that an "undisciplined system of subjective decision making" could have the same negative consequences as a process that was intended to discriminate. Performance appraisal systems without formal criteria and standards appear to qualify as subjective.[23]

Elements of a Legal Performance Appraisal System

The elements of a performance appraisal system that can survive court tests can be determined if existing case law is investigated.[24] These elements are:

▲ Performance appraisal criteria based on job analysis
▲ Absence of adverse impact and evidence of validity exists
▲ Formal evaluation criteria that limit managerial discretion in the appraisal process

▲ Formal rating instrument
▲ Personal knowledge and contact with appraised individual
▲ Training of supervisors in conducting appraisals
▲ Review process that prevents one manager acting alone from controlling an employee's career
▲ Counseling to help poor performers improve

It is clear that the courts are interested in fair and nondiscriminatory performance appraisals. Employers must decide how to design their appraisal systems to satisfy the courts, enforcement agencies, and their employees.[25]

▲ AN EFFECTIVE PERFORMANCE APPRAISAL SYSTEM

Regardless of which performance appraisal method is used, an understanding of what an appraisal is supposed to do is critical. When performance appraisals are used to develop employees as resources, they usually work. When management uses it as a punishment or when raters fail to understand its limitations, it fails. The key is not which form or which method of performance appraisal to use, but managers and employees who understand its purposes. In its simplest form, performance appraisal is a manager's statement: "Here are your strengths and weaknesses, and here is a way to shore up the weak areas." It can lead to higher employee motivation and satisfaction if done right.

Unfortunately, many performance appraisal systems have not met their potential. Although most organizations (at least larger ones) have them, appraisal systems often are poorly designed and frequently fail to tie pay to performance or help improve employee motivation.[26] PA systems, however, usually do let employees know where they stand, provide input about their jobs, and help establish and clarify goals.

The effective performance-appraisal system will:

▲ Support the strategic mission of the organization
▲ Have usefulness as a development tool
▲ Have usefulness as an administrative tool
▲ Be legal
▲ Be seen as generally fair by employees

Most appraisal systems can be improved by training the appraising supervisors. Training should focus on minimizing rater errors and providing a common frame of reference on how raters observe and recall information. Feedback on how well a supervisor has rated employees is an excellent method of improving rating effectiveness. In many organizations, managers and supervisors have had little appraisal training. Training appraisers gives them confidence in their ability to make appraisals and handle appraisal interviews. Familiarity with avoiding common rating errors can improve rater performance as well.[27]

Organizationally there is a tendency to distill the performance appraisals into a single number that can be used to support pay raises. Systems based on this concept reduce the complexity of each individual's contribution in order to satisfy compensation-system requirements. They are too simplistic to give employees feedback or help managers pinpoint training and development needs. In fact, a single rating often is a barrier to useful performance discussions, because what is emphasized is attaching a label to a person's performance and defending or attacking that label. Effective performance appraisal systems evolve from a recognition that human behaviors and capabilities collapsed into a single score have limited use in developing human resources.

▲ SUMMARY

▲ Appraising employee performance is useful for compensation, feedback, and administrative purposes.

▲ Performance appraisal can be done either informally or systematically. If done systematically, appraisals usually are done annually.

▲ Appraisals can be done by superiors, employees, peers, subordinates, or a combination of raters.

▲ Superiors' ratings of employees are most frequently used.

▲ Four types of appraisal methods are available: category ratings, comparative ratings, narrative methods, and special rating methods such as behaviorally anchored rating scales and management by objectives.

▲ Category-rating methods, especially graphic rating scales, are widely used methods.

▲ Ranking, paired comparison, and forced distribution are all comparative methods.

▲ Narrative methods of appraisal include the critical incident technique, the essay approach, and the field review.

▲ The behaviorally anchored ratings scale (BARS) and management by objectives (MBO) are two special methods of appraisal.

▲ Construction of a BARS requires a detailed job analysis; the rating criteria and anchors must be job specific.

▲ Management by objectives (MBO) is an approach that requires joint goal setting between a superior and an employee.

▲ Performance appraisal problems include varying standards, recency effect, rater bias such as leniency bias, rater patterns such as central tendency error, halo effect, and contrast error.

▲ The appraisal feedback interview is a vital part of any appraisal system.

▲ Both managers and employees may resist performance appraisals.

▲ Federal employment guidelines and numerous court decisions have scrutinized performance appraisals. The absence of specific job-relatedness and subjectivity can create legal problems.

▲ Training of appraisers and guarding against the tendency to reduce an appraisal to a single number are important for an effective appraisal system.

▲ REVIEW AND DISCUSSION QUESTIONS

1. What are the three major uses of performance appraisals?
2. Identify the advantages and disadvantages of using different rater approaches.
3. What are the three methods of appraisal? Which method would you prefer as an employee? As a manager? Why?

4. Suppose you are a supervisor. What errors might you make when doing an employee's performance appraisal?

5. Describe how to prepare a BARS for a payroll clerk.

6. Explain MBO, and identify some problems associated with it.

7. Construct a plan for a postappraisal interview with an employee who has performed poorly.

8. Discuss the following statement: "Most performance appraisal systems in use today would not pass legal scrutiny."

9. Why is the training of appraisers so vital to an effective performance appraisal system?

 PERFORMANCE APPRAISAL AT XEROX

Xerox's Reprographic Business Group (RBG) develops, designs, engineers, and manufactures the corporation's copiers. Its performance appraisal system had been used for annual appraisals for more than 20 years: managers rated employees' performances and assigned numbers to these performances. In short, the system was typical of those of most employers in the United States.

Atypical, however, was Xerox's willingness to listen to employee and manager complaints about the system and then undertake to make it more useful for all concerned. One major complaint was that 95% of the ratings were "3"s or "4"s (on a five-point scale). Merit increase amounts (tied to the appraisals) were within 1% to 2% of one another. In addition, appraisal discussions had become unpleasant situations for managers and employees alike.

Xerox set up a taskforce to design a new performance appraisal system. The taskforce used surveys of the work force and then developed the new system they labeled PF + D (performance feedback and development). Key features of the system are as follows:

▲ Objectives are set between manager and employee.
▲ A six-month review of progress takes place.
▲ A final written appraisal is done at yearend.
▲ No numerical summary rating is used.
▲ Merit increase discussions are separated by two months from the performance appraisal discussions.
▲ The focus is on coaching and development.

Videotapes of behavioral modeling were used to teach managers how to conduct appraisals. Further, managers and employees were surveyed during the first-year operation of the new system to see how it was working and what changes, if any, were needed.

The results of the surveys were encouraging. Of those surveyed, 81% felt they better understood what their work groups were trying to accomplish; 84% felt their appraisals were fair; 70% met their objectives; and 72% said they understood how merit pay figures were determined. Survey results were slightly more favorable for salaried employees than for hourly ones.[28]

In summary, Xerox feels that these results, combined with the redefinition of the managers as a coach and developer, will help improve teamwork. Doing this is a strategic part of RBG's approach to innovation and productivity.

▲ Questions

1. What are the pertinent elements in the success of Xerox's approach?

2. What potential problems can you identify?

▲ Notes

1. Adapted from M. G. Derven, "The Paradox of Performance Appraisals," *Personnel Journal,* February 1990, 107–111; and J. Plavner, "Performance Appraisals: Sword or Shield?" *SHRM Legal Report,* Fall 1992, 6–8.

2. J. Cleveland, K. Murphy, and R. Williams, "Multiple Uses of Performance Appraisal Prevalence and Correlates," *Journal of Applied Psychology* 74 (1989), 130–135.

3. G. English, "Tuning Up for Performance Management," *Training and Development Journal,* April 1991, 56–60.

4. D. Daley, "Pay for Performance, Performance Appraisal, and TQM," *Public Productivity and Management Review,* Fall 1992, 39–50.

5. J. Plavner, "Performance Appraisals," 6–7.

6. C. Hoffman et al., "A Comparison of Validation Criteria," *Personnel Psychology* 44 (1991), 44.

7. S. L. Bordman and Gerald Melnick, "Keep Productivity Ratings Timely," *Personnel Journal,* March 1990, 50.

8. D. Meyers et al., "The Role of Human Interaction Theory," *SAM Advanced Management Journal,* Summer 1991, 28.

9. Michael A Verespej, "Performance Reviews Get Mixed Reviews," *Industry Week,* August 20, 1990, 49.

10. Julie H. Lopez, "Companies Split Reviews on Performance and Pay," *The Wall Street Journal,* May 10, 1993, B1.

11. R. Bretz, G. Milkovich, and W. Read, "The Current State of Performance Appraisal Research: Concerns, Directions, and Implications," *Journal of Management* 18 (1992), 321–352.

12. J. Greenberg, "Determinants of Perceived Fairness of Performance Evaluations," *Journal of Applied Psychology* 71 (1986), 340–342.

13. "A Rounded Approach to Employee Reviews," *Nation's Business,* February 1992, 10.

14. Adapted from L. Reibstein, "Firms Ask Workers to Rate Their Bosses," *The Wall Street Journal,* June 13, 1988, 1; and "Reversing Performance Reviews," *Psychology Today,* March 1984, 80.

15. "Program Lets Workers Rate their Bosses," *Omaha World-Herald,* April 6, 1992, G1.

16. D. Daley, "Pay for Performance, Performance Appraisal, and Total Quality Management," *Public Productivity and Management Review,* Fall 1992, 43.

17. K. Carson et al., "Performance Appraisal as Effective Management or Deadly Management Disease," *Group and Organizational Studies* 16 (1991), 145–146.

18. M. Somers and D. Birnbaum, "Assessing Self-Appraisal of Job Performance as an Evaluation Device," *Human Relations* 44 (1991), 1081.

19. J. Jordan and D. Nasis, "Preferences for Performance Appraisal Based on Method Used, Type of Rater, and Purpose of Evaluation," *Psychological Reports* 70 (1992), 966–969.

20. R. Bretz et al., "The Current State," 333.

21. Paul R. Sackett et al., "Tokenism in Performance Evaluation: The Effects of Work Group Representation on Male-Female and White-Black Differences in Performance Ratings," *Journal of Applied Psychology* 76 (1991), 263–267.

22. "Persuading Bosses to Revise Reviews," *The Wall Street Journal,* May 22, 1992, B1.

23. G. Mertens, *"Watson v. Fort Worth Bank and Trust:* Unanswered Questions," *Employee Relations Law Journal* 14 (1988), 163–173.

24. R. Nobile, "The Law of Performance Appraisals," *Personnel,* January 1991, 7.

25. D. Martin and K. Bartol, "The Legal Ramifications of Performance Appraisal: An Update," *Employee Relations Law Journal* 17 (1991), 257–286.

26. A. Bennett, "Paying Workers to Meet Goals, Spreads, but Gauging Performance Proves Tough," *The Wall Street Journal,* September 10, 1991, B1; and C. Longenecker and S. Goff, "Performance Appraisal Effectiveness: A Matter of Perspective," *SAM Advanced Management Journal,* Spring 1992, 19.

27. G. Kaupins and M. Johnson, "Keeping Lies Out of the Performance Appraisal," *IM,* January–February 1992, 6.

28. Adapted from N. R. Deets and D. T. Typler, "How Xerox Improved Its Performance Appraisals," *Personnel Journal,* April 1986, 50–52.

Section 5: Compensating Human Resources

Compensation of human resources is often one of the largest costs faced by employers, particularly those in the service industries. Retailers, hotels, computer software companies, nonprofit social agencies, and many others may have labor costs representing over half of all operating expenses. Compensation is more than just direct wages and salaries paid. Additional direct payments in the form of bonuses and other incentives are used extensively. A growing cost for many employers is employee benefits, which represent indirect compensation because employees receive the value of the benefits without getting direct cash payments.

But if compensation, incentive, and benefits programs are not designed well, much of the money spent may not be viewed as worthwhile by employees. Compensation as a reward for organization and job efforts represents both value and status to many employees. People want to be compensated fairly in relation to their peers internally, as well as externally in relation to what they could receive from other employers. However, fairness is complicated because what may seem fair to a manager may not seem equitable to an employee.

The first component of compensation discussed in this section is base pay. Chapter 13 examines various ways that equitable pay systems can be determined, including some based on newer approaches such as skill-based or competency-based pay. Well-designed base pay systems build upon job descriptions and job specifications and jobs internally are rated using job evaluation to ensure internal equity. Then pay survey data is used to ensure equity externally. Finally, because many organizations follow a "pay-for-performance" philosophy, tying pay to performance appraisal results is essential. Throughout the process, awareness of various legal constraints that influence base pay practices must be considered.

People are paid for more than just performing their jobs at satisfactory levels. As Chapter 14 indicates, many organizations compensate some or all of their employees with additional direct compensation in the form of incentives. Different incentive plans can be designed to reward different measures of results. Some incentive programs focus on rewarding individual performance, while others reward group or organizational performance. Gainsharing programs in which employees throughout the organization share "gains" resulting from increases in productivity, quality, and service are particularly popular now.

A special group of employees, top executives, receive significant rewards in many organizations. In fact, the lavish compensation packages for executives at some large corporations have exceeded $20 million per year, when base pay, bonuses, stock options, and perquisites are added together. But with huge payouts has come increasing criticism that executive compensation is not linked closely to organizational performance. Issues associated with executive compensation are examined in the second half of Chapter 14.

Chapter 15 discusses a major expense item for organizations—employee benefits. Currently benefits expenditures average about 38% of payroll for the average U.S. employer. Various benefits can be offered ranging from retirement plans to employer-sponsored bowling teams. But the benefits area receiving the greatest attention, due to the rapidly escalating costs faced by a majority of employers, is health-care coverage for employees. Health-care cost-containment pressures have existed for several years, and yet health-related costs have continued to increase. As a result, pressure for legislative action has grown and federal and state legislators have responded with sweeping changes and proposals up to and including national health insurance for all U.S. workers. But those proposals will take several years to be implemented, and the framework and specifics of them still are not fully known. With the escalating cost of benefits, both employees and managers want well-designed plans that are cost-effective and that distribute benefits equitably.

CHAPTER 13

COMPENSATION ADMINISTRATION

After you have read this chapter, you should be able to:

1. Define the three types of compensation and discuss the bases for determining each type.

2. Describe how organizational justice is related to compensation.

3. Identify the basic provisions of the Fair Labor Standards Act.

4. Briefly explain three federal laws that can affect compensation practices.

5. Define job evaluation and discuss four methods of performing it.

6. Outline the process of building a wage and salary administration system.

7. Discuss how a pay-for-performance system is established.

HR Today and Tomorrow:
Pay for Knowledge and Skills

One innovative approach for compensation that is gaining in popularity pays for the level of knowledge, skills, or competencies that employees have rather than for the tasks or jobs they perform. In these *knowledge-based pay* (KBP) or *skill-based pay* (SBP) systems, employees are paid for their knowledge and skill variety. They start at a base level of pay and receive increases as they learn to do other jobs or gain other skills and therefore become more valuable to the company. For example, a printing firm has two-color, four-color, and six-color presses. The more colors, the more skill is required by the press operators. Consequently, under a KBP or SBP system, press operators increase their pay as they learn how to operate the more complex presses, even though sometimes they may be running only two-color jobs.

At American Steel and Wire, workers can increase their wages up to $6 an hour by acquiring up to ten skills. Other organizations using KBP or SBP systems include Honeywell, General Mills, TRW, Johnson & Johnson, Polaroid, Hughes Aircraft, and Corning. A survey of firms with these programs found that approximately three-fourths of them had higher employee job satisfaction and better product quality and productivity than had been the case under previous systems.

A more detailed survey sponsored by the American Compensation Association (ACA) of 97 firms found that the success of these plans requires managerial commitment to a different philosophy than has existed traditionally in organizations. This approach places far more emphasis on training employees and supervisors. Also, work flow must be adapted to allow workers to move from job to job as needed.

According to the ACA survey, there were significant positive organizational-related and employee-related outcomes, as follows:

Organization-Related

▲ Greater workforce flexibility
▲ Increased effectiveness of work teams
▲ Fewer bottlenecks in work flow
▲ Increased worker output per hour

Employee-Related

▲ Enhanced employee understanding of organizational "big picture"
▲ Greater employee self-management capabilities
▲ Improved employee satisfaction
▲ Greater employee commitment

To move to an SBP or KBP system, considerable time must be spent identifying what the required knowledge or skills are for various jobs. Then each *block* of skills and knowledge must be priced using market data. Progression of employees must be possible, and they must be paid appropriately for all of their knowledge and skills. Any limitations on the numbers of people who can acquire the top knowledge and skills levels should be identified clearly. Training in the appropriate knowledge and skills is critical. Important also to SBP and KBP systems is a system for *certification* of employees who have acquired certain knowledge and skills. Further, a process must exist for verifying that employees maintain their competency.

Because these plans focus on having knowledgeable and skilled employees, those employees who continue to develop their capabilities and competencies to receive pay raises are the real *winners*. As more organizations recognize their employees as valuable human resources, it is likely that SBP and KBP systems will spread.[1]

21

> What is needed in many situations is a new approach to management that includes new pay-system assumptions and practices.
>
> *E. E. Lawler*

Compensation is fundamentally about balancing labor costs with the ability to attract and keep employees by providing fairness of rewards. In addition, the compensation system should support organizational objectives and strategies.

▲ BASIC COMPENSATION CONSIDERATIONS

Compensation serves the function of allocating people among employers based on the attractiveness of jobs and compensation packages. Employers must be reasonably competitive to hire and keep the people they need.

Types of Compensation

The three forms of compensation are *pay, incentives,* and *benefits*. **Pay** is the basic compensation an employee receives, usually as a wage or salary. An **incentive** is compensation that rewards an employee for efforts beyond normal performance expectations. Examples of incentives include bonuses, commissions, and profit-sharing plans. A **benefit** is an indirect reward such as health insurance, vacation pay, or retirement pensions, given to an employee or group of employees as a part of organizational membership.

▽ **PAY**

is the basic compensation an employee receives, usually as a wage or salary.

▽ **AN INCENTIVE**

is compensation that rewards an employee for efforts beyond normal performance expectations.

▽ **A BENEFIT**

is an indirect reward given to an employee or group of employees as a part of organizational membership.

Compensation Responsibilities

Compensation costs are significant expenditures in most organizations. At one large hotel, employee payroll and benefits expenditures comprise about 50% of all business costs. Although compensation costs are relatively easy to calculate, the value derived by employers and employees is much more difficult to identify. To administer these expenditures wisely, HR specialists and other managers must work together.

A typical division of compensation responsibilities is illustrated in Figure 13–1. HR specialists usually guide the overall development and administration

HR UNIT	MANAGERS
▲ Develops and administers compensation system ▲ Conducts job evaluation and wage surveys ▲ Develops wage/salary structures and policies	▲ Attempt to match performance and rewards ▲ Recommend pay rates and pay increases, based upon guidelines from HR unit ▲ Monitor attendance and productivity for compensation purposes

▲ **Figure 13–1**

Typical Compensation Responsibilities

of an organizational compensation system by conducting job evaluations and wage surveys. Also, because of the technical complexity involved, HR specialists typically are the ones who develop the wage and salary structures and policies. On the other hand, operating managers try to match employees' efforts with rewards by using guidelines provided by the HR unit when recommending pay rates and pay increases. Much managerial activity goes into monitoring employee attendance and productivity. Because time and/or productivity are the bases for compensation, this monitoring is a vital part of any manager's job.

▲ COMPENSATION AND ORGANIZATIONAL STRATEGY

For virtually every kind of organization, the objectives of an effective pay system are to:

▲ Identify prevailing market wages and salaries
▲ Pay competitive wages and salaries, considering organizational financial constraints
▲ Administer pay within legal constraints
▲ Minimize turnover, grievances, and perceptions of inequity as a result of dissatisfaction with the compensation package
▲ Control labor costs with carefully designed programs that identify a job's value and an employee's value to the organization
▲ Identify the appropriate frequency and size of raises, and restrain an individual manager's ability to give unwarranted raises
▲ Induce and reward higher levels of performance

Meeting these objectives requires that management view compensation strategically. First, the life-cycle stage of the organization, its business objectives, and its culture must be considered.[2]

Compensation and Organization Life Cycle

Because compensation is such a key activity, compensation philosophies and objectives must reflect the overall culture, life-cycle stages, and strategic plans of the organization. As Figure 13–2 shows, the compensation practices that typically exist in a new organization may be different from those in a mature, bureaucratic organization.[3] For example, if a firm wishes to create an innovative, entrepreneurial culture, it may offer stock equity programs so that employees can participate in the growth and success of the company but keep pay at modest levels. However, for a large stable organization, highly structured pay and benefit programs may be more appropriate.

Bases for Compensation

Another strategic issue is how the compensation philosophy of the organization is to be reflected in the design of compensation systems. Those are: (a) time, and (b) performance and productivity.

Time   Employees may be paid for the amount of time they are on the job. The two pay classes in many organizations are identified according to the way

▲ **Figure 13–2** Compensation and Organization Life-Cycle Stages

COMPENSATION	INTRODUCTORY	GROWTH	MATURITY	DECLINE
Pay	Competitive, but conservative wages/salaries	Moderate wages/salaries	Above-market wages/salaries	High wages and salaries with pressure for reductions
Incentives	Stock/equity possibilities	Bonuses tied to objectives; stock options	Bonuses, incentive plans, stock options	Reduced bonuses; cost-saving incentive plans
Benefits	Core benefits; very basic	Complete benefits at moderate level; limited executive perks	Comprehensive benefits; expanded executive perks	Cost-consciousness to limit benefit costs; "frozen" executive perks

pay is distributed and the nature of the jobs. The classifications are: (1) *hourly* and (2) *salaried.*

The most common means of payment based on time is *hourly* pay; employees who are paid hourly are said to receive **wages,** which are payments directly calculated on the amount of time worked. Another means of paying people is **salary,** which is payment that is consistent from period to period despite the number of hours worked. Being salaried typically has carried higher status for employees than being paid wages. Some organizations have switched to an all-salaried approach with their manufacturing and clerical employees in order to create a greater sense of loyalty and organizational commitment.

Performance and Productivity Another general basis for compensation is to tie pay to performance or productivity. A direct productivity-based system, called a **piece-rate system,** is one in which an employee is paid for each unit of production. For example, an employee who works in a telemarketing firm may be paid one dollar for every sale made.

Merit or *pay-for-performance* systems, discussed later in the chapter, also attempt to link employee performance to pay-increase decisions.[4] Two other main issues must be decided by management:

▲ Should performance be measured and rewarded based on individual, group, or organizational performance?

▲ Should the length of time for measuring performance be short term (less than one year) or long term (more than one year)? The latter issue is particularly important for executive and managerial jobs.[5]

Task or Skill-Based Pay As the opening discussion of the chapter indicates, a growing number of organizations are paying employees, particularly hourly ones, for the skills or competencies they have, rather than for the specific tasks being performed. Paying for skills rewards employees who are more versatile and have continued to develop their skills through cross-functional training.

Usually an organization ends up using a combination of approaches to compensation, depending upon its culture, philosophy, life cycle, and financial constraints. Whatever specific systems and programs used, it is important that the impact of compensation on behavior of employees and managers be recognized.

▼ **WAGES**

are payments directly calculated on the amount of time worked.

▼ **SALARY**

is payment that is consistent from period to period despite the number of hours worked.

▼ **PIECE-RATE SYSTEM**

is a productivity-based compensation system in which an employee is paid for each unit of production.

HR Perspectives:
Global Compensation

Organizations with employees in many different countries face some special compensation pressures. Variations in laws, living costs, tax policies, and other factors all must be considered when establishing the compensation for expatriate managers and professionals. Even fluctuations in the value of the U.S. dollar must be tracked and adjustments made as the dollar rises or falls in relation to currency rates in other countries. Add to all of these concerns compensation for additional costs for housing, schooling for children, and yearly transportation home for family members.

The components of international compensation and how expatriate managers viewed these components were the subject of a survey. The results of that survey, highlighted in the following table, give some indications of how complex designing global compensation plans can become.

EXPATRIATE FINANCIAL INDUCEMENTS	What Companies Provide		How Expatriate Managers View It	
	Percent Providing	*Average★ Rating*	*Percent Providing*	*Average★ Rating*
Tax equalization.	97%	4.53	86%	2.51
Temporary living allowance.	97%	4.30	82%	2.76
Children's education allowance	96%	4.44	84%	2.77
Goods and services differential.	96%	4.46	50%	2.20
Housing differential.	96%	4.49	76%	2.61
Reimbursement for tax return preparation	92%	4.46	89%	2.85
Household furnishing allowance	79%	3.27	48%	2.09
Transportation differential.	70%	3.21	68%	2.45
Hardship premium.	72%	3.06	59%	2.21
Currency protection.	68%	3.08	48%	2.07
Foreign service premium	61%	3.02	50%	2.09
Home-leave allowance	47%	2.29	38%	1.81
Stopover allowance.	46%	2.14	51%	2.10
Mobility premium	41%	2.21	49%	2.06
Subsidized health and fitness facilities	29%	1.54	33%	1.69
Completion bonus.	26%	1.50	47%	1.81
Assignment extension bonus	12%	1.25	40%	1.61
Extended work week payment	5%	1.12	55%	1.97

★Note: the rating is on a 1–5 scale, with 1 = not provide, and 5 = to a great extent.
n = 148 expatriate managers and 66 firms.

Behavioral Aspects of Compensation

People work to gain rewards for their efforts. Because employee motivation is closely related to the rewards received, the behavioral dimensions of compensation must be considered. When people work, they expect to receive fair value (*equity*) for their efforts, and they expect the rewards received to be distributed fairly.[6] This perception of whether or not fair value exists has a significant effect on the satisfaction and performance of employees. As a result, compensation usually has several different meanings to employees: economic, psychosocial, and growth.

Economic   The economic meaning of compensation is the most obvious because pay serves as a way of obtaining the necessities and luxuries people need and want. For most people, employment in an organization is the way to obtain economic resources that can be exchanged for such items as food, rent or house payments, a car, clothes, furniture, vacations, and countless other goods and services. The economic considerations for setting compensation for international employees is discussed in the "HR Perspective."

Psychosocial   Compensation also can have a psychosocial meaning. Pay and other types of compensation offer a symbolic means of "keeping score" and a sense of achievement. If a cost accountant receives a raise, he may see his change in compensation as recognition of his efforts and he may derive a sense of achievement from his work. This internal satisfaction may mean more to him than what he can buy with the additional money. Conversely, the absence of adequate compensation may cause him to become discouraged or dissatisfied.

Psychosocial factors are based on the *equity* perceptions of individuals. For example, a division manager might compare her pay, and therefore her *status* in the organization, with that of other division managers. She may be satisfied with her pay, or she may become dissatisfied because other division managers have higher pay and higher status. Because compensation can symbolize status, it often remains important even after the basic material needs of an employee are satisfied. Consider the case of the professional baseball player whose status needs are unfulfilled by a million-dollar paycheck because of another player's higher paycheck.

Growth   Compensation also is a means for employees to measure their growth in performance and capabilities. Based on *expectancy theory,* increased compensation can serve as a goal for which people will strive if they see that greater effort brings more compensation. However, the amount and type of compensation that serves to motivate one employee to produce more may not motivate another employee.

Procedural and Distributive Justice in Compensation

A growing issue in organization research is organizational *justice.* The two major areas are *procedural justice* and *distributive justice.* **Procedural justice** is the perceived fairness of the process and procedures used to make decisions about em-

▼ **PROCEDURAL JUSTICE**

is the perceived fairness of the process and procedures used to make decisions about employees, including their pay.

ployees, including their pay. The process of determining the base pay for jobs, the allocation of pay increases, and the measurement of performance must be perceived as fair.[7]

Two critical issues are how appropriate and fair the process is that is used to assign jobs to pay grades and how the pay ranges for those jobs are established.[8] If employees believe that managers play favorites, then the credibility of the entire pay system will be viewed suspiciously.

Further, **distributive justice,** which refers to the perceived fairness of the amounts given for performance, must be considered also.[9] For example, one study of U.S. government workers revealed that 90% wanted a pay-for-performance system, but 74% believed that the existing merit system in the government was unfair.[10] The "HR Perspective" describes a related research study.

To address such concerns, some organizations establish *appeals procedures.* In public-sector organizations, the appeals procedures usually are identified formally, whereas in private-sector firms the appeals process is usually more informal. Typically, employees can contact the HR department after they have discussed their concerns with their immediate supervisors and managers.

Secret vs. Open Pay System Another issue concerns the degree of openness or secrecy that the organizations allow regarding their pay systems. Pay information kept secret in "closed" systems includes how much others make, what raises others have received, and even pay grades and ranges in the organization. One reason for secret or closed pay systems is the fear that open pay systems will encourage petty complaints and create discontent and tensions. If an accountant knows for sure that he is paid less than another accountant, he may become dissatisfied at receiving "inequitable" treatment. Also, with a closed pay system, managers do not have to explain and justify pay differences.

Policies that prohibit discussion of individual pay are likely to be violated anyway. Co-workers do share pay information, and an open pay system recognizes this fact. Explaining the pay system might prevent misinformation carried by the grapevine.

Employees generally do not estimate accurately the pay of fellow employees. Consequently, they may act on these misperceptions by leaving the organization or letting dissatisfaction diminish their work performances. Because comparison is such a critical part of how employees view compensation, some theorists advocate the need for *open pay systems* in which employees are informed about the pay of co-workers. By having pay openness, organizations that truly base pay on performance can emphasize the importance of performance leading to higher pay. This approach is particularly useful when objective measures of individual performance exist, such as in some sales jobs.

A growing number of organizations are opening up their pay systems to some degree by informing employees of compensation policies, providing a general description of the basis for the compensation system, and indicating where an individual's pay is within a pay grade. Such pay information allows employees to make more accurate equity comparisons. It is crucial in an open pay system that managers be able to explain satisfactorily any pay differences that exist.

▲ LEGAL CONSTRAINTS ON PAY SYSTEMS

Good pay systems are legal pay systems. A myriad of government constraints on pay practices exists. Minimum wage standards and hours of work are two important areas that are addressed by the laws.

▼ **DISTRIBUTIVE JUSTICE**

refers to the perceived fairness of the amounts given for performance.

HR Perspectives:

Organizational Justice and Pay for Performance

Employee perceptions and reactions to pay systems were the focus of a research study reported in the *Journal of Applied Psychology*. Conducted by Miceli, Jung, Near, and Greenberger, a survey was done of employees in various federal government agencies. Data from approximately 2,000 middle managers and executives was used in this study.

As background to the study, beginning in 1981, the U.S. Merit Systems Protection Board had implemented a program for federal government workers that prohibited seniority increases and allowed only half of the money allocated to make up for market differences between public-sector and private-employer pay rates. Instead, the extra money was collected and allocated using a pay-for-performance approach, including performance bonuses up to 20% of annual salary. The researchers sent questionnaires to the managers and executives that inquired about their views of the competitive levels of salaries, the fairness of the pay system, and the success of the new pay system.

As would be expected, the results revealed that those managers who had received the performance bonuses had a much more positive view of the new pay system. Also, those who viewed the system more favorably were more likely to view their pay as more market competitive.

Regarding the procedural justice, or perceived fairness of the pay administration system, several interesting results were found. For middle managers the fairness of the pay system depended on its link to the formalized performance appraisal standards. However, if there was inadequate funding of the bonuses, then the middle managers perceived that more fairness was needed in the pay system. For executives, results were mixed.

The authors of the study concluded that the managers and executives viewed the pay system more favorably when it operated using formal performance standards and when bonuses were given in accordance with the established distribution procedures. They concluded that employee reactions about pay system fairness are related to organizational justice.[11]

Fair Labor Standards Act (FLSA)

The major law affecting compensation is the Fair Labor Standards Act (FLSA). The act has three major objectives: (1) to establish a minimum wage floor, (2) to encourage limits on the number of weekly hours employees work through over-time provisions, and (3) to discourage oppressive use of child labor. The first two objectives are the most relevant in this chapter. Passed in 1938, the FLSA has been amended several times in order to raise the minimum wage rates and ex-pand the employers covered.

Employers Covered Unless otherwise noted in the discussion that fol-lows, both private- and public-sector employers are affected by the act. Gener-ally, private-sector employers engaged in interstate commerce and retail service firms with two or more employees and gross sales of at least $500,000 per year are covered by the act. Very small, family owned and operated entities, and family farms generally are excluded from coverage. Most federal, state, and local government employers are subject to the provisions of the act also, except for military personnel, volunteer workers, and a few other limited groups. Covered employers must keep accurate time records on all employees subject to the act, and the government can request access to those records.[12]

Enforcement Compliance with the provisions of the FLSA is enforced by the Wage and Hour Division of the U.S. Department of Labor. To meet its require-ments, employers must keep accurate time records and maintain these records for three years. Inspectors from the Wage and Hour Division investigate complaints filed by individuals who believe they have not received the overtime payments due them. Also, certain industries which historically have had a large number of wage and hour violations can be targeted, and firms in those industries can be investigated. Penalties for wage and hour violations often include awards of back pay for affected current and former employees for up to two years.

Exempt and Nonexempt Status   Under the FLSA, employees are classified as exempt or nonexempt. **Exempt employees** are those who hold positions classified as *executive, administrative, professional,* or *outside sales,* for whom employers are not required to pay overtime. **Nonexempt employees** are those who are required to be paid overtime under the Fair Labor Standards Act.

Three major factors are considered in determining whether an individual holds an exempt position:

▲ Discretionary authority for independent action
▲ Percentage of time spent performing routine, manual, or clerical work
▲ Earnings level

Figure 13–3 shows the impact of these factors on each type of exemption.

Under provisions of the FLSA, jobs can be categorized in three groupings:

▲ Hourly
▲ Salaried-nonexempt
▲ Salaried-exempt

Hourly jobs are those that require employers to pay overtime and comply with the FLSA. Each salaried position must be identified as *salaried-exempt* or *salaried-nonexempt*. Employees in positions classified as salaried-nonexempt are covered by the overtime provisions of the FLSA, and therefore must be paid overtime. Salaried-nonexempt positions sometimes include secretarial, clerical, or salaried blue-collar positions.

Minimum Wage   The FLSA sets a minimum wage to be paid to the broad spectrum of covered employees. The actual minimum wage must be changed by congressional action. The lower minimum-wage level is set for "tipped" employees who work in such firms as restaurants, but their payment must at least equal the minimum wage when *average* tips are included.

Overtime Provisions   The FLSA also contains overtime pay requirements. Still in effect under the 1938 version are provisions setting overtime pay at one-and-one-half times the regular pay rate for all hours in excess of 40 per week, except for employees who are not covered by the law.

The work week is defined as a consecutive period of 168 hours (24 hours × 7 days) and does not have to be a calendar week. Hospitals are allowed to use a 14-day period instead of a 7-day week as long as overtime is paid for hours worked beyond 8 in a day or 80 in a 14-day period. Overtime provisions do not apply to farm workers, who also have a lower minimum wage schedule. No daily number of hours requiring overtime is set, except for special provisions relating to hospitals and other specially-designated organizations. Thus, if a manufacturing firm has a 4-day/10-hour schedule, no overtime pay is required by the act.

Compensatory Time-Off   Often called *comp-time,* **compensatory time-off** is given in lieu of payment for time worked. However, unless it is given at the rate of one-and-one-half times the hours worked over a 40-hour week,

▼ **EXEMPT EMPLOYEES**

are those who are not required to be paid overtime under the Fair Labor Standards Act because their positions are classified as executive, administrative, professional, or outside sales.

▼ **NONEXEMPT EMPLOYEES**

are those who are required to be paid overtime under the Fair Labor Standards Act.

▼ **COMPENSATORY TIME-OFF**

is time off given in lieu of payment for time worked.

▲ **Figure 13–3**   Wage/Hour Status under Fair Labor Standards Act

EXEMPTION CATEGORY	A DISCRETIONARY AUTHORITY	B PERCENT OF TIME	C EARNINGS LEVELS
Executive	1. Primary duty is managing 2. Regularly directs work of at least two others 3. Authority to hire/fire or recommend these	1. Must spend 20% or less time doing clerical, manual, routine work (less than 40% in retail or service establishments)	1. Paid salary at $155/wk or $250/wk if meets A1–A2
Administrative	1. Responsible for nonmanual or office work related to management policies 2. Regularly exercises discretion and independent judgment and makes important decisions 3. Regularly assists executives and works under general supervision	1. Must spend 20% or less time doing clerical, manual, routine work (less than 40% in retail or service establishments)	1. Paid salary at $155/wk or $250/wk if meets A1–A2
Professional	1. Performs work requiring knowledge of an advanced field *or* creative and original artistic work *or* works as teacher in educational system 2. Must do work that is predominantly intellectual and varied	1. Must spend less than 20% of time doing nonprofessional work	1. Paid salary at least $170/wk or $250/wk if meets A1
Outside Sales	1. Customarily works away from employer site *and* 2. Sells tangible or intangible items *or* 3. Obtains order or contracts for services	1. Must spend 20% or less time doing work other than outside selling	1. No salary test

Note: For more details, see *Executive, Administrative, Professional, and Outside Sales Exemptions Under the Fair Labor Standards Act,* WH Publication no. 1363 (Washington, DC: U.S. Department of Labor, Employment Standards Administration, Wage and Hour Division).

comp-time is illegal in the private sector. Also, comp-time cannot be carried over from pay one period to another.

The only major exception to those provisions are for public-sector employees, such as fire and police employees, and a limited number of other workers. Because they often are on 24-hour duty, these individuals may receive compensatory time. Police and fire officers can accumulate up to 480 hours; all other covered public-sector employees can accumulate up to 240 hours of comp-time. When those hours are used, the employees must be paid their normal rates of pay, and the comp-time hours used *do not* count as hours worked in the paid week.

Child-Labor Provisions   The child-labor provisions of the FLSA set the minimum age for employment with unlimited hours at 16 years. For hazardous occupations (see Chapter 16), the minimum is 18 years of age. Those aged 14 to 15 years old may work outside school hours with the following limitations:

1. No more than 3 hours on a school day, 18 hours in a school week, and 8 hours on a nonschool day, or 40 hours in a nonschool week.
2. Work may not begin before 7 a.m. nor end after 7 p.m., except between June 1 and Labor Day, when 9 p.m. is the ending time.

Many employers require age certificates for employees because the FLSA places the responsibility on the employer to determine an individual's age. The certificates may be issued by a representative of a state labor department, education department, or local school district.

Beginning in 1990, a concerted effort was made to enforce the child-labor provisions. The fast-food and restaurant industries were the most frequent violators. For example, Burger King paid $500,000 to settle child-labor violations, and as a result, stated its intention to discontinue hiring anyone under age 16.[13]

Walsh-Healey and Service Contracts Act

The Walsh-Healey Public Contracts Act and Service Contracts Act require companies with *federal supply* or *service contracts* exceeding $10,000 to pay a prevailing wage. This act applies only to those working directly on the contract or who substantially affect its performance. The *prevailing wage* is determined by a formula that considers the rate paid for a job by a majority of the employers in the appropriate geographic area.

Davis-Bacon Act of 1931

Still in force with many of the original dollar levels intact, the Davis-Bacon Act of 1931 affects compensation paid by firms engaged in federal construction projects valued in excess of $2,000. It deals only with federal construction projects and requires that the "prevailing wage" rate be paid on all federal construction projects. States also have had their own versions of the Davis-Bacon provisions, but many of them are being dropped.

Equal Pay Act of 1963

Another piece of legislation that was passed as a major amendment to the FLSA in 1963 is the Equal Pay Act. The original act and subsequent amendments focus on wage discrimination on the basis of sex. The act applies to both men and women and prohibits paying different wage scales to men and women performing substantially the same jobs. Except for differences justifiable on the basis of merit (better performance), seniority (longer service), quantity or quality of work, or any factor other than sex based, similar pay must be given for jobs requiring equal skills, equal effort, equal responsibility, or for jobs done under similar working conditions. Comparable worth, as discussed in Chapter 6 and later in this chapter, is a different issue than equal pay for equal work. Most of the equal-pay cases decided in court have been situations in which women were paid less than men for doing similar work, even though different job titles were used. For example, equal-pay violations have been found in health-care institutions in which male "physician assistants" were paid significantly more than females with equal experience and qualifications who were called "nurse practitioners," even though their job duties were the same.

State Laws

Modified versions of federal compensation laws have been enacted by many states and municipal government bodies. These laws tend to cover workers included in intrastate commerce not covered by federal law. If a state has a higher minimum wage than that set under the Fair Labor Standards Act, the higher figure becomes the required minimum wage.

Many states once had laws that limited the number of hours women could work. However, these laws generally have been held to be discriminatory in a variety of court cases. Consequently, most states have dropped such laws.

Garnishment Laws

Garnishment of an employee's wages occurs when a creditor obtains a court order that directs an employer to submit a part of the employee's pay to the creditor for debts owed by the employee. Regulations passed as a part of the Consumer Credit Protection Act established limitations on the amount of wages that can be garnished and restricted the right of employers to discharge employees whose pay is subjected to a single garnishment order. All 50 states have laws that apply to wage garnishments.

▼ **GARNISHMENT**

is a court action in which a portion of an employee's wages is set aside to pay a debt owed a creditor.

▲ WAGE AND SALARY ADMINISTRATION

The development, implementation, and ongoing maintenance of a base pay system usually is described as **wage and salary administration.** The purpose of wage and salary administration is to provide pay that is both competitive and equitable. Underlying the administered activities are pay policies that set the overall direction of pay within the organization.

▼ **WAGE AND SALARY ADMINISTRATION**

is the activity involved in the development, implementation, and maintenance of a base pay system.

Pay Policies

Organizations must develop policies as general guidelines to govern pay systems. Uniform policies are needed for coordination, consistency, and fairness in compensating employees. One specific organizational policy decision defines the relationship between pay expenditures and such factors as productivity, sales, or number of customers. In the retail industry, it is common to have a policy of maintaining payroll expenditures at about 10% of gross sales volume. These policies reflect a major consideration in management decision making: how much an organization can afford to pay employees.

Market Competitiveness A major policy decision must be made about the comparative level of pay the organization wants to maintain. Specifically, an employer must identify how competitive it is and wishes to be in the market for employees. Organizations usually want to "pay market," that is, to *match* the "going rates" paid employees by competitive organizations.[14]

Some organizations choose to *lead* the market by paying above market rates. This policy aids in attracting and retaining employees. One transportation firm that pays about 10% to 15% above local market medians for clerical employees consistently has a waiting list for qualified word-processing and other office workers. By paying above market, the firm feels that it deters efforts to unionize its office workers.

Firms with either monopolies in their markets or that operate in regulated "cost-plus" markets also may have higher-than-market wages. For instance, the electric utility industry generally pays higher-than-local-average rates to clerical employees. These higher wage rates also are included in the cost structure for setting consumer electric rates.

On the other hand, some employers may deliberately choose to *lag* the market by paying below market. If there is an excess of qualified workers in an area, an adequate number of people are willing to work for lower pay. Also, organizations in declining industries and some small businesses may not be able to afford to pay going rates because of financial pressures. However, the impact of paying rates below market can result in higher turnover or in having to hire less qualified employees.

Market Pricing   Some employers do not establish a formal wage and salary system. Smaller employers particularly may assume that the pay set by other employers is an accurate reflection of a job's worth, so they set their pay rates at **market price,** the prevailing wage paid for a job in the immediate job market.

One difficulty with this approach is the assumption that jobs are the same in another organization, which is not necessarily the case. Also, obtaining market information often means calling one or two other firms, which may not give an accurate picture of the true market for the jobs in the firm. Direct market pricing also does not adequately consider the impact of economic conditions, employer size, and other variables. Consequently, more complex methods have been developed.

▼ **MARKET PRICE**

is the prevailing wage rate paid for a job in the immediate job market.

Unions and Compensation

A major variable affecting the pay policies used by an employer is whether any employees are represented by a labor union. In nonunion organizations, employers have significantly more flexibility in determining pay levels and policies. Unionized employees usually have their pay set according to the terms of a collective bargaining contract between their employers and the unions that represent them. Because pay is a visible issue, it is natural for unions to emphasize pay levels.

According to U.S. Bureau of Labor Statistics data, employers having unionized employees generally have higher wage levels than nonunion employers. The strength and extent of unionization in an industry and in an organization also affect wage levels. Firms in heavily unionized industries with highly unionized workforces generally have higher wage levels. However, as union strength and heavily unionized industries have declined, pay increases for nonunion employees have diminished somewhat in recent years.

▲ DEVELOPMENT OF A PAY SYSTEM

Once pay policies have been determined, the actual development of a pay system begins. As Figure 13–4 shows, the development of a wage and salary system assumes that accurate job descriptions and job specifications are available. The job descriptions then are used in two activities: *job evaluation* and *pay surveys.*

Figure 13–4

Compensation Administration
Process

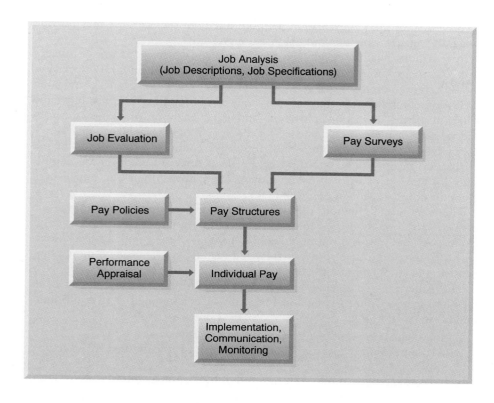

These activities are designed to ensure that the pay system is both internally equitable and externally competitive. The data compiled in those two activities are
used to design *pay structures,* including *pay grades* and minimum-to-maximum *pay
ranges.* After the pay structures have been developed, individual jobs must be
placed in the appropriate pay grades and employees' pay adjusted based upon
length of service and performance. Finally, the pay system must be monitored
and updated.

Job Evaluation

Job evaluation provides a systematic basis for determining the relative worth of
jobs within an organization. It flows from the job analysis process and is based
on job descriptions and job specifications. In a job evaluation, every job within
an organization is examined and ultimately priced by comparing:

▲ Relative importance of the job
▲ Relative skills needed to perform the job
▲ Difficulty of the job compared with other jobs

It is important that employees perceive their pay as appropriate in relation to pay
given for jobs performed by others. Because jobs may vary widely in an organization, it is particularly important to identify **benchmark jobs,** which are those
performed by several individuals with similar duties that are relatively stable, requiring similar KSAs, and found in many other organizations. For example,
benchmark jobs commonly used in clerical/office situations are accounts payable
processor, word-processing operator, and PBX receptionist. Benchmark jobs are

▼ **JOB EVALUATION**

is the systematic determination of the
relative worth of jobs within an
organization.

▼ **A BENCHMARK JOB**

is one performed by several individuals
with similar duties that are relatively
stable, requiring similar KSAs, and found
in many other organizations.

used with all of the job evaluation methods discussed later because they provide "anchors" against which unique jobs can be evaluated.

Systematic evaluation of jobs is a way to reduce favoritism. However, subjective judgments cannot be avoided entirely, so managers and HR specialists should not overemphasize the objectivity of a job evaluation system. Using a job evaluation committee in which several evaluators rate jobs can help improve the reliability of the evaluation. However, unions generally distrust job evaluations and view them as being manipulated for the benefit of management.

For these reasons, firms often bring in outside consultants to perform the job evaluation. In one study, one-third of the firms surveyed used outside consultants to establish pay structures for management people, and one-fourth used them for nonmanagement positions.[15]

There are several methods used to determine internal job worth through job evaluation. All methods have the same general objective, but each differs in its complexity and means of measurement. Regardless of the method used, the intent is to develop a usable, measurable, and realistic system to determine compensation in an organization.

The American Compensation Association (ACA) conducted a survey of its members in the United States, and 1,845 members responded. The results indicated that:[16]

▲ Job evaluation point plans are the most popular.
▲ Market pricing is next in popularity and most usually used for executive jobs.
▲ Job evaluation is most often performed by a compensation analyst (37%), and next most often by a committee (20%).

Ranking Method   The ranking method is one of the simplest methods of job evaluation. It places jobs in order, ranging from highest to lowest in value to the organization. The entire job is considered rather than the individual components. Several different methods of ranking are available, but several problems exist.

Ranking methods are extremely subjective, and managers may have difficulty explaining why one job is ranked higher than another to employees whose pay is affected by these rankings. When there are a large number of jobs, the ranking method also can be awkward and unwieldy. Therefore, the ranking method is more appropriate to a small organization having relatively few jobs.

Classification Method   The classification method of job evaluation was developed under the old U.S. Civil Service system and was widely copied by state and local government entities. A number of classes, or *GS grades,* are defined. Then the various jobs in the organization are put into grades according to common factors found in jobs, such as degree of responsibility, abilities or skills, knowledge, duties, volume of work, and experience needed. The grades are then ranked into an overall system.

The major difficulty with the classification method is that subjective judgments are needed to develop the grade descriptions and to place jobs accurately in them. With a wide variety of jobs and generally written grade descriptions, some jobs may appear to fall into two or three different grades.

Another problem with the classification method is that it relies heavily on job titles and duties and assumes that they are similar from one organization to another. For these reasons many federal, state, and local government entities have shifted to point systems.

Point Method   The point method is the most widely used job evaluation method. It breaks down jobs into various compensable factors and places weights, or *points,* on them. A **compensable factor** is one used to identify a job value that is commonly present throughout a group of jobs. The factors are determined from the job analysis as being ones present in the jobs under study. For example, for jobs in warehouse and manufacturing settings, *physical demands, hazards encountered,* and *working environment* may be weighted heavily. However, in most office and clerical jobs, those factors would be of little importance. Consequently, the compensable factors used and the weights assigned to each degree of each factor must reflect the nature of the job under study.

The point method is more sophisticated than the ranking and classification methods. Because the different job components carry different weights, each is assigned a numerical value. The values of the various components then are added for each job and compared with other jobs.

The individual using the point chart in Figure 13–5 looks at a job description and identifies the degree to which each element is necessary to perform the job satisfactorily. For example, the points assigned for a payroll clerk might be as follows: Education (42 points, 3rd degree); Responsibility for Trust Imposed (50 points, 4th degree); and Work Environment (25 points, 2nd degree). To reduce subjectivity, such determinations often are made by a group of people familiar with the jobs. Once point totals have been determined for all jobs, the jobs are grouped together into pay grades.

A special type of point method used by a consulting firm, Hay and Associates, has received widespread application, although it is most often used with exempt employees. The *Hay plan* uses three factors: *know-how, problem solving,* and *accountability,* and numerically measures the degree to which each of these three elements is required in each job.

The point method has grown in popularity because it is a relatively simple system to use. It considers the components of a job rather than the total job, and is a much more comprehensive system than either the ranking or classification method. Once points have been determined and a job evaluation point manual has been developed, the method can be used easily by people who are not specialists. The system can be understood by managers and employees, which gives it a definite advantage.

Another reason for the widespread use of the point method is that it evaluates the components of a job and determines total points before the current pay structure is considered. In this way, an assessment of relative worth can be made instead of relying on past patterns of worth.

One major drawback to the point method is the time needed to develop a system. For this reason, manuals and systems developed by management consultants or other organizations often are used by employers. Also, point systems have been criticized for reinforcing traditional organizational structures and job rigidity.[17] Although not perfect, the point method of job evaluation generally is better than the classification or ranking methods because it quantifies job elements.[18]

Factor Comparison   The factor-comparison method is a very quantitative and complex combination of the ranking and point methods. It involves first determining the benchmark jobs in an organization, selecting compensable factors, then ranking all benchmark jobs factor by factor. Next, the jobs are compared with market rates for benchmark jobs, and monetary values are assigned to each

A COMPENSABLE FACTOR

is one used to identify a job value that is commonly present throughout a group of jobs.

▲ **Figure 13–5**   Point Chart

CLERICAL GROUP					
SKILL	1ST DEGREE	2ND DEGREE	3RD DEGREE	4TH DEGREE	5TH DEGREE
1. Education	14	28	42	56	
2. Experience	22	44	66	88	110
3. Initiative & ingenuity	14	28	42	56	
4. Contacts with others	14	28	42	56	
Responsibility					
5. Supervision received	10	20	35	50	
6. Latitude & depth	20	40	70	100	
7. Work of others	5	10	15	20	
6. Trust imposed	10	20	35	50	70
9. Performance	7	14	21	28	35
Other					
10. Work environment	10	25	45		
11. Mental or visual demand	10	20	35		
12. Physical effort	28				

The specific degrees and points for Education, Trust Imposed, and Work Environment are as follows:

Education is the basic prerequisite knowledge that is essential to satisfactorily perform the job. This knowledge may have been acquired through formal schooling such as grammar school, high school, college, night school, correspondence courses, company education programs, or through equivalent experience in allied fields. Analyze the minimum requirements of the job and not the formal education of individuals performing it.

 1st Degree—Requires knowledge usually equivalent to a two-year high school education. Requires ability to read, write, and follow simple written or oral instructions; use simple arithmetic processes involving counting, adding, subtracting, dividing, and multiplying whole numbers. May require basic typing ability.

 2nd Degree—Requires knowledge equivalent to a four-year high school education in order to perform work requiring advanced arithmetic processes involving adding, subtracting, dividing, and multiplying, or decimals and fractions; maintain or prepare routine correspondence, records, and reports. May require knowledge of advanced typing and/or basic knowledge of shorthand, bookkeeping, drafting, etc.

 3rd Degree—Requires knowledge equivalent to four-year high school education plus some specialized knowledge in a particular field such as advanced stenographic, secretarial or business training, elementary accounting, or a general knowledge of blueprint reading or engineering practices.

 4th Degree—Requires knowledge equivalent to two years of college education in order to understand and perform work requiring general engineering or accounting theory. Must be able to originate and compile statistics and interpretive reports, and prepare correspondence of a difficult or technical nature.

Responsibility for Trust Imposed   This factor appraises the extent to which the job requires responsibility for safeguarding confidential information and the effect of such disclosure on the Company's relations with employees, customers, or competitors.

 1st Degree—Negligible. Little or no confidential data involved.

 2nd Degree—Some access to confidential information but where responsibility is limited or where the full import is not apparent.

 3rd Degree—Occasional access to confidential information where the full import is apparent and where where disclosure may have an adverse effect on the Company's external or internal affairs.

 4th Degree—Regularly works with and has access to confidential data, which if disclosed could seriously affect the Company's internal or external affairs or undermine its competitive position.

 5th Degree—Full and complete access to reports, policies, records, and plans of Company-wide programs, including financial cost and engineering data. Requires the utmost discretion and integrity to safeguard the Company's interests.

Work Environment   This factor appraises the physical surroundings and the degree to which noise is present at the work location. Consider the extent of distraction and commotion caused by the sounds.

 1st Degree—Normal office conditions. Noise limited to the usual sounds of wordprocessing and other equipment.

 2nd Degree—More than average noise due to the intermittent operation by several employees of adding machines, calculators, wordprocessing equipment, or duplicating machines.

 3rd Degree—Considerable noise generated by constant machine operation such as is present in the Data Processing section.

SOURCE: *Wage and Salary Administration: A Guide to Current Policies and Practices* (Chicago: Dartnell Corp.). Used with permission.

factor. The final step is to evaluate all other jobs in the organization by comparing them with the benchmark jobs.

One of the major advantages of the factor-comparison method is that it is tied specifically to one organization. Each organization must develop its own key jobs and its own factors. For this reason, buying a packaged system may not be appropriate. Finally, factor comparison not only tells which jobs are worth more, it also indicates how much more, so factor values can be more easily converted to monetary wages.

The major disadvantages of the factor-comparison method are its difficulty and complexity. It is not an easy system to explain to employees, and it is time-consuming to establish and develop. Also, a factor-comparison system may not be appropriate for an organization with many similar types of jobs. Managers attempting to use the method should consult a specialist or one of the more detailed compensation books or manuals that discuss the method.

Computerized Job Evaluation   The advent of computerized job analysis programs has led to computerized job evaluation programs. Generally, the computerized processes still must identify the prevalence of compensable factors in jobs. Some of the computerized programs integrate market pricing into the job evaluation ratings as well.[19] However, some experts question whether computer-assisted job evaluation is a different method. Instead, it may be just applying computer techniques and analyses to the point or factor-comparison methods.[20]

Job Evaluation and Comparable Worth

Employers usually view evaluating jobs to determine rates of pay as a separate issue from selecting individuals for those jobs. However, this nation has had a long history of classifying jobs, at least implicitly, as "male" or "female." Although that is changing, there are still far more nurses, elementary school teachers, and secretaries who are female than are male.

As noted previously, **comparable worth** is the concept that all jobs requiring comparable knowledge, skills, and abilities be paid similarly even if actual duties and market rates differ significantly. Growing concerns about comparable worth have been translated into laws. These laws and agreements all focus on public-sector jobs, especially those in state governments. Some of the states with comparable-worth policies include Hawaii, Iowa, Maine, Michigan, Minnesota, Montana, Ohio, Oregon, Washington, and Wisconsin.

Comparable-worth advocates have attacked typical job evaluations as gender biased. Many jobs traditionally held by women are clerical and service, whereas many jobs dominated by men are craft and manual. Critics have charged that traditional job evaluation programs weight knowledge, skills, and working conditions used in many female-dominated jobs less than the same factors in male-dominated jobs. Also, jobs typically are compared only to others in the same job "family."[21]

Many employers base their pay rates heavily on *external equity* comparisons in the labor market, which is their major defense for adopting the pay systems they have. Undoubtedly, with additional court decisions, government actions, and research, job evaluation activities will face more pressures to address comparable worth.

▼ **COMPARABLE WORTH**

requires that jobs with comparable knowledge, skills, and abilities be paid similarly even if actual duties and market rates differ significantly.

Pay Survey

Another part of building a pay system is to survey the pay that other organizations provide for similar jobs. A **pay survey** is a collection of data on compensation rates for workers performing similar jobs in other organizations. An employer may use surveys conducted by other organizations or may decide to conduct its own survey.

Using Prepared Pay Surveys   Many different surveys are available from a variety of sources. National surveys on many jobs and industries are available through the U.S. Department of Labor, the Bureau of Labor Statistics, or through national trade associations. In many communities, employers participate in a wage survey sponsored by the Chamber of Commerce to provide information to new employers interested in locating in the community.

When using surveys from other sources, it is important to use them properly.[22] Some questions that should be addressed before using a survey are:

1. Is the survey a realistic sample of those employers with whom the organization competes for employees?
2. Is the survey "balanced" so that organizations of varying sizes, industries, and locales are included?
3. How current are the data; determined by when the survey was conducted?
4. How established is the survey, and how qualified are those who conducted it?
5. Does it contain job summaries so that appropriate matchups to organizational job descriptions can be made?

Developing a Pay Survey   If needed pay information is not already available, the employer can undertake its own pay survey. Employers with comparable positions should be selected. Also, employers considered to be "representative" should be surveyed. If the employer conducting the survey is not unionized, the pay survey probably should examine unionized as well as nonunionized organizations. Developing pay competitive with union wages may deter employees from joining a union.

The positions to be surveyed also must be decided. Not all jobs in all organizations can be surveyed, and not all jobs with the same titles in all organizations will be the same. An accounting clerk in a city government office might perform a different job from an accounting clerk in a credit billing firm. Therefore, managers should select jobs that can be easily compared, have common job elements, and represent a broad range of jobs. Key or benchmark jobs are especially important ones to include. Also, it is advisable to provide brief job descriptions for jobs surveyed in order to ensure more accurate matches. For executive-level jobs, data on total compensation (base pay and bonuses) often are gathered also.

The next phase of the pay survey is for managers to decide what compensation information is needed for various jobs. Information such as starting pay, base pay, overtime rate, vacation and holiday pay and policies, and bonuses all can be included in a survey. However, requesting too much information may discourage survey returns.

The results of the pay survey usually are made available to those participating in the survey in order to gain their cooperation. Most surveys specify confidentiality, and data are summarized to assure anonymity. Different job levels often are included, and the pay rates are presented both in overall terms and on a city-by-city basis to reflect regional differences in pay.

▲ **Figure 13–6**   Establishing a Pay Structure

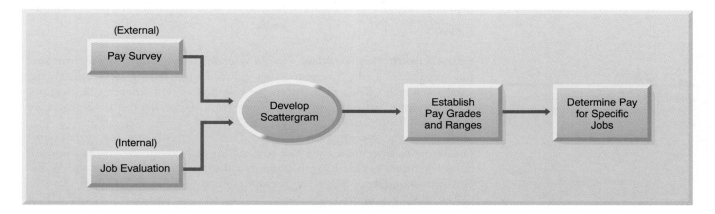

Pay Structure

Once survey data are gathered, the pay structure for the organization can be developed using the process depicted in Figure 13–6. As indicated in that figure, one means of tying pay survey information to job evaluation data is to plot a *wage curve* or *scattergram,* shown in Figure 13–7. This plotting is done by first making a graph that charts job-evaluation points and pay-survey rates for all surveyed jobs. In this way the distribution of pay for surveyed jobs can be shown, and a trend line using the *least squares regression* method can be drawn to plot a *market line.* This line shows the relationship between job value, or points, and wage/salary survey rates. (For details on this method see any basic statistics text.)

Use of pay-survey data links the internal rating of jobs through job evaluation to external market considerations. This linkage ensures that the internal view of jobs can be checked against the external "realities." One study of approximately

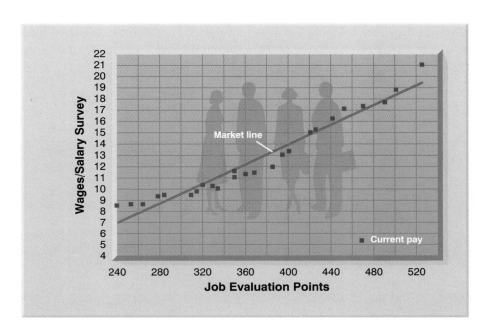

▲ **Figure 13–7**

Pay Scattergram

400 corporate compensation managers found that when differences between job evaluation and pay-survey data existed, these managers gave more emphasis to the market data.[23] Such a market emphasis is even more likely for scarce-skill occupational groups.

Establishing Pay Grades   In the process of establishing a pay structure, **pay grades** are used to group together individual jobs having approximately the same job worth. While there are no set rules to be used when establishing pay grades, some overall suggestions have been made. Generally, 11 to 17 grades are used in small companies.

By using pay grades, management can develop a coordinated pay system without having to determine a separate pay rate for each job in the organization. All the jobs within a grade have the same range of pay regardless of points. As discussed previously, the factor-comparison method uses monetary values. An employer using that method can easily establish and price pay grades. A vital part of the classification method is developing grades, and the ranking method can be converted to pay grades by grouping several ranks together.

Pay Ranges   Using the market line as a starting point (see Figure 13–8), maximum and minimum pay levels for each pay grade can be determined by making the market line the midpoint line of the firm's new pay structure. By calculating values that are the same percentage above and below the midpoint value, the minimums and maximums can be determined.

A smaller minimum-to-maximum range should be used for lower-level jobs than for higher-level jobs, primarily because employees in lower-level jobs tend to stay in them for shorter periods of time and have greater promotion possibilities. For example, a clerk-typist might advance to the position of secretary or word-processing operator. However, a design engineer likely would have fewer possibilities for future upward movement in an organization. At the lower end of a pay structure, the pay range may be 20% (minimum to maximum), whereas upper-level ranges may be as high as 100% (minimum to maximum). This approach recognizes that individual performance can vary more greatly among people in upper-level jobs than in lower-level jobs. However, the same percentage range used at all levels can make administration of a pay system easier in small firms.

Experts recommend having overlap between grades, such as those in Figure 13–8, which allows an experienced employee in a lower grade to be paid more

▼ **PAY GRADES**

are used to group together individual jobs having approximately the same job worth.

▲ **Figure 13–8**

Example of Pay Grades

GRADE	MINIMUM PAY	MIDPOINT PAY	MAXIMUM PAY	POINT RANGE
1	$ 5.92	$ 7.26	$ 8.59	240–269
2	6.94	8.50	10.06	270–299
3	7.96	9.75	11.54	300–329
4	8.98	11.00	13.02	330–359
5	10.00	12.24	14.49	360–389
6	11.01	13.49	15.97	390–419
7	11.79	14.74	17.69	420–449
8	12.79	15.99	19.18	450–479
9	14.51	18.14	21.77	480+

than a less experienced employee in a job in the next pay grade. Overlap between three adjacent grades, but no more than three, is advised.

▲ INDIVIDUAL PAY

Once managers determine pay ranges, they can set the specific pay for individuals. Each of the dots in Figure 13–9 represents an individual employee's current pay in relation to the pay ranges that have been developed. Setting a range for each pay grade gives flexibility by allowing individuals to progress within a grade instead of having to be moved to a new grade each time they receive a raise. Also, a pay range allows managers to reward the better-performing employees while maintaining the integrity of the pay system.

Rates Out Of Range

Regardless of how well-constructed a pay structure is, there usually are a few individuals whose pay is lower than the minimum or higher than the maximum. These situations occur most frequently when firms that previously have had an informal pay system develop a new, more formalized one.

Red-Circle Jobs   A job whose pay is above the range is identified as a **red-circle job.** A red-circle job is noted on the graph in Figure 13–9. For example, assume an employee's current pay is $7.18 per hour, but the pay grade of that

▼ **A RED-CIRCLE JOB**

occurs when the incumbent is paid above the range set for the job.

▲ **Figure 13–9**

Pay Structure Depicted Graphically

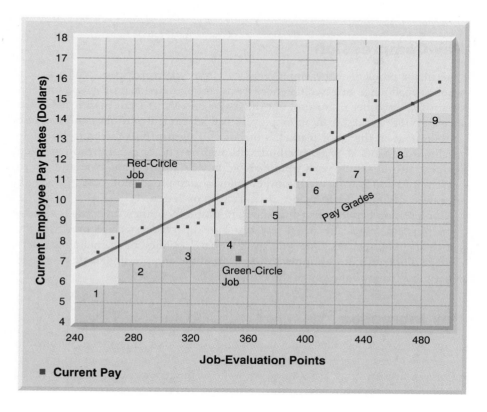

Current Pay

job is between $5.44 and $6.80. The person would be red circled, and attempts would be made over a period of time to bring the employee's rate into grade. Typically, the red-circled job is filled by a longer-service employee who has declined promotions or has been viewed as unpromotable. For instance, a long-service employee, who started as a forklift driver right out of high school and has worked up to warehouse manager probably would not have the formal educational background needed to become Purchasing/Inventory Manager. Yet, the individual might have continued to receive large increases.

Several approaches can be used to bring a red-circled person's pay into line. Although the fastest way would be to cut the employee's pay, that approach is not recommended and is seldom used. Instead, the employee's pay may be frozen until the pay range can be adjusted upward to get the employee's pay rate back into the grade. The employee also can be transferred to a job with a higher grade or have responsibilities added to the red-circled job, which would result in greater job evaluation worth, thus justifying its being upgraded. Another approach is to give the employee a small lump-sum payment but not adjust the pay rate when others are given raises.

Green-Circle Jobs   An individual whose pay is below the range is in a **green-circle job.** Generally, it is recommended that the green-circled individual receive pay increases to get to the pay grade minimum fairly rapidly. More frequent increases can be given if the increase to minimum would be large.

Occasionally, managers may have to deviate from the priced grades to hire scarce skills to respond to competitive market shortages of particular job skills. For example, if the worth of a welder's job is evaluated to be $8 to $10 an hour, but welders are in short supply, the going rate for welders in the community may be $12 an hour. To fill the position, the firm must pay $12 an hour.

Pay Compression

One major problem many employers face is **pay compression,** which occurs when a small range of pay differences exists among individuals. Pay compression occurs for a number of reasons, but the major one is that labor market pay levels increase more rapidly than an employer's pay adjustments. To illustrate, because of a shortage in the labor market, a manufacturing firm was forced to hire new machine operators at $7.00 per hour, although several operators who had been with the firm for three years were making only $7.20 per hour. One solution to pay compression is to have employees follow a step progression based on length of service, assuming performance is satisfactory or better.

Compression between first-line supervisors and those they supervise is a common problem, especially when few first-line supervisors receive overtime pay but their employees do. One strategy is to have a policy of maintaining a percentage differential, for example 15% to 20%, if the compression occurs between supervisors' pay and the pay of those supervised.

Pay Increases

Once pay ranges have been developed and individuals' placements within the range have been identified, managers must look at adjustment to individual pay. Decisions about pay increases often are some of the more critical ones that affect relationships among employees, their managers, and the organization. Individuals

▼ **A GREEN-CIRCLE JOB**

is one in which the incumbent is paid below the range set for the job.

▼ **PAY COMPRESSION**

occurs when pay differences among individuals become small.

have expectations about their pay and about how much increase is "fair," especially in comparison to the increases received by other employees. There are several ways to determine pay increases.

Pay-for-Performance Systems   Many employers profess to having a pay system based on performance. But reliance on performance-appraisal information for making pay adjustments assumes that the appraisals are done well; and this is not always the case, especially for employees whose work cannot be measured easily. Consequently, some system for integrating appraisals and pay changes must be developed and applied equally. Often this integration is done through the use of a *pay adjustment matrix* or *salary guide chart* (see Figure 13–10). These charts base adjustments on a person's **compa-ratio,** which is a pay level divided by the midpoint of the pay range.

Such charts reflect a person's upward movement in an organization. Upward movement depends on the person's performance, as rated on an appraisal, and on where the person is within the pay range, which has some relation to experience as well. A person rated as exceeding standards (#4) whose compa-ratio is 94 would be eligible for a raise of 7% to 9% according to the chart in Figure 13–10.

Notice that as employees move up the pay range, they must exhibit higher performance to obtain the same raise as those lower in the range performing at the "meets performance expectations" (#3) level. This approach is taken because the firm is paying above "the market" midpoint but receiving only satisfactory performance rather than "above-market" performance. Charts can be constructed to reflect the specific pay-for-performance policy and philosophy in an organization.

▼ **COMPA-RATIO**

is a pay level divided by the midpoint of the pay range.

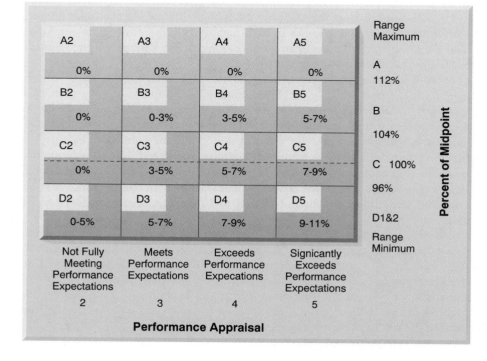

▲ **Figure 13–10**

Pay Adjustment Matrix

A2	A3	A4	A5	Range Maximum
0%	0%	0%	0%	A 112%
B2	B3	B4	B5	
0%	0-3%	3-5%	5-7%	B 104%
C2	C3	C4	C5	
0%	3-5%	5-7%	7-9%	C 100% / 96%
D2	D3	D4	D5	
0-5%	5-7%	7-9%	9-11%	D1&2 Range Minimum
Not Fully Meeting Performance Expectations	Meets Performance Expectations	Exceeds Performance Expecations	Signicantly Exceeds Performance Expectations	Percent of Midpoint
2	3	4	5	

Performance Appraisal

Most employees who receive pay increases, either for merit or seniority, first have their base pay adjusted and then receive an increase in the amount of their regular monthly or weekly paycheck. For example, an employee who makes $1,200 per month, and receives a 6% increase, would get gross pay of $1,272 per month.

In many organizations pay-for-performance systems are becoming a very popular way to change the way pay increases are distributed. For example, Chrysler Corporation's pay-for-performance system eliminated cost-of-living adjustments for 14,000 nonunion white-collar workers and replaced them with pay increases tied to employees' job performances as determined by annual performance appraisals by their supervisors. In the first year of the system, employees whose performances were satisfactory received a pay increase of 3%. Those performing better received increases as high as 15%. Employees whose performances were not satisfactory received no pay increases.

In a truly performance-oriented system, no pay raises are given except for increases in performance. Giving pay increases to people because they have 10 to 15 years' experience, even though they are mediocre employees, defeats the approach. Also, unless the performance-based portion of a pay increase is fairly significant, employees may feel it is not worth the extra effort.[24] Giving an outstanding industrial designer making $40,000 a year the "standard raise" of 6% plus 1% for merit means only $400 for merit versus $2,400 for "hanging around another year."

LUMP-SUM INCREASE (LSI)

is a one-time payment of all or part of a yearly pay increase.

Lump-Sum Pay Increases (LSI)   Sometimes called a *performance bonus,* a **lump-sum increase** (LSI), is a one-time payment of all or part of a yearly pay increase. For example, an employee in an LSI plan would receive a check for $864 (before taxes are deducted), instead of getting $72 per month for 12 months. Some organizations place a limit on how much of a merit increase can be taken as a lump-sum payment. Other organizations split the lump sum into two checks, each representing one-half the year's pay raise.

Organizations that use the LSI often limit eligibility for the plan to employees with longer service who are not in high turnover groups. Also, some employers treat the lump-sum payment as an advance, which must be repaid if the employee leaves the firm before the year is finished.

As with any plan, there are advantages and disadvantages. The major advantage of an LSI plan is that it heightens employees' awareness of what their performance "merited." A lump-sum check also gives employees some flexibility in their spending patterns so that they can buy big-ticket items without having to take out a loan. In addition, the firm can slow down the increase of base pay, so that the compounding effect of succeeding raises is reduced. Unionized employers, such as Boeing and Ford, have negotiated LSI plans as a way to hold down base wages, which also holds down the rates paid for overtime work. Pension costs and some other benefits, often tied to base wages, can be reduced some also.

One disadvantage of an LSI plan is administrative tracking, including a system to handle income tax and Social Security deductions from the lump-sum check. Also, workers who take a lump-sum payment may become discouraged because their base pay has not changed. Unions generally resist LSI programs because of this and because of the impact on pensions and benefits. To some extent, this problem can be reduced if the merit increase is split to include some in the base pay and the rest in the lump-sum payment.

Cost-of-Living Adjustments (COLA)   One common pay-raise practice is the use of a *standard raise* or *cost-of-living adjustment* (COLA). Giving all employees a standard percentage increase enables them to maintain the same real wages in a period of economic inflation. Often these adjustments are tied to changes in the Consumer Price Index (CPI) or some other general economic measure. Unfortunately, some employers give such across-the-board raises and call them *merit raises,* which they are not. If all employees get a pay increase, it is legitimately viewed as a cost-of-living adjustment having little to do with merit and good performance. For this reason, employers should reserve the term *merit* for any amount above the standard raise.

Seniority   Seniority, or time within the organization or on a particular job, also can be used as the basis for giving pay increases. Many employers have policies that require persons to be employed for a certain length of time before they are eligible for pay increases. Pay adjustments based on seniority often are set as automatic steps once a person has been employed the required length of time, although performance must be at least satisfactory in many nonunion systems. One study found that seniority is a major determinant of individual pay growth, even in pay-for-performance and pay-for-knowledge plans.[25]

Maturity Curves   A closely related approach uses a **maturity curve** that depicts the relationship between experience and pay rates. Pay rises as an employee's experience increases, which is especially useful for professionals and skilled craft employees. Unlike a true seniority system in which a pay raise occurs automatically once someone has put in the required time, maturity curves are built on the assumption that as experience increases, proficiency and performance also increase, so pay raises are appropriate. If proficiency does not increase, theoretically pay adjustments are reduced, although that seldom happens in practice. Once a person plateaus in his/her proficiency, then the pay progression is limited to following the overall movement of the pay structure.

▼ **A MATURITY CURVE**

depicts the relationship between experience and pay rates.

 SUMMARY

▲ Compensation provided by an organization can come through pay (base wages and salaries), incentives (performance-based rewards), and benefits (indirect compensation).

▲ Compensation responsibilities of both HR specialists and managers must be performed well because compensation practices are closely related to organizational strategies, life cycles, and culture.

▲ Bases for determining compensation include time, performance and productivity, skills, or a combination of these; the approach chosen should reflect the tasks employees perform.

▲ Behavioral considerations affect compensation because of the economic, psychosocial, and growth meanings that compensation has to employees.

▲ Organizational justice, both procedural and distributive in nature, affects the way that compensation is viewed by employees.

▲ The Fair Labor Standards Act (FLSA), as amended, is the major federal law that affects pay systems. It requires most organizations to pay a minimum wage and to meet the overtime provisions of the act, including appropriately classifying employees as exempt or nonexempt.

▲ Other laws have been passed that place restrictions on employers who have federal supply contracts, federal construction contracts, or who garnish employees' pay.

▲ Administration of a wage/salary system requires the development of pay policies that incorporate internal and external equity considerations.

▲ Job evaluation determines the relative worth of jobs, and several different methods exist, with the point method being the most widely used.

▲ Once the job evaluation process has been completed, wage/salary survey data must be collected and pay structure developed. An effective pay system requires that changes continue to be made as needed.

▲ Individual pay treatment must take into account employees' placement within pay grades and their ranges. Problems of rates above or below range and pay compression must be addressed.

▲ Pay increases can be based on performance, cost-of-living adjustments, seniority, or a combination of approaches.

▲ REVIEW AND DISCUSSION QUESTIONS

1. Give examples of the three types of compensation.
2. Discuss the following statement: "If employees believe that subjectivity and favoritism shape the pay system in an organization, then it does not matter that the system was properly designed and implemented."
3. What factors should be considered to determine if an employee who worked over 40 hours in a week would be due overtime under the FLSA?
4. What is the focus of the following laws?
   a. Walsh-Healey Act
   b. Davis-Bacon Act
   c. Equal Pay Act
5. Considering all methods, why is the point method the most widely used for job evaluation?
6. You have been named compensation manager for a hospital. How would you establish a pay system?
7. Why are pay-for-performance systems growing in importance?

 CHANGING THE PAY SYSTEM

A financial institution headquartered in a major city had assets of approximately $500 million and 115 employees. It also had branches in some smaller suburbs around its headquarters. Until several years ago, the firm had been operating with a compensation system that had been devised by its accounting firm several years earlier. However, because of growth and changes within the firm, the HR Director felt it was time for a complete review of the firm's base compensation program. The review became even more important as the firm, like many other savings and loans, faced earnings declines and losses because of economic and interest rate factors, deregulation of the industry, and declining agricultural economic conditions. Also, the management of the firm wanted to emphasize more clearly a pay-for-performance approach.

To begin the project the HR Director contacted a professional acquaintance with expertise in compensation who had assisted other financial institutions with similar projects as a consultant. After an initial meeting with the consultant, a detailed review of all of the firm's job descriptions was done. Some changes were identified in the loan operations area and revised descriptions were written.

The next stage of the project was a comparison of the firm's existing pay structure to that of other employers in the area and in the industry. A job evaluation committee, composed of several executives, a supervisor in the accounting area, the HR Director, and the consultant, was formed. Using a job evaluation point system, the committee individually assigned points to all jobs in the organization on such factors as *knowledge required, experience required, supervision given and received, interpersonal contacts,* and *working conditions.* Then the committee met several times, compared points assigned for each job, discussed each job, and reached a point total consensus for each job.

Pay survey data that was gathered revealed that the firm was paying below-market for both full-time and part-time entry-level tellers. Also, pay in that geographic area for programmers and systems analysts had increased significantly in the previous two years, primarily due to the growth of a major software design firm in the same city. Otherwise, the firm was relatively close to market rates for virtually all other jobs, especially when the experience and performance of its employees were considered.

Using all this data, the consultant constructed a recommended pay structure containing about 20 separate pay grades and the minimum and maximum pay for each range. Based on the job evaluation points assigned, all jobs were placed into the appropriate grades. Then the pay for all employees was reviewed to determine to what extent they were being paid below, within, or above the recommended pay ranges.

With only a few exceptions, all employees' pay fell within the new ranges. For the programmer and systems analyst jobs, the job evaluation points suggested a pay grade and range that was 15% below the market data. The HR Director knows that a decision to "overpay" may be necessary for the firm to attract and/or retain qualified individuals for those jobs.

Also, one of the key employees in the loan processing area, who had been with the firm for 18 years, had a compa-ratio of 128, which was 8% above the maximum of the pay grade. This employee was a satisfactory performer who had received "automatic" increases every year since she joined the firm.

While the new pay system was being developed, a new performance-appraisal system also was being prepared. Using input from various managers and supervisors, the new performance appraisal system was designed to reinforce management's pay-for-performance orientation. The performance appraisal form was tied directly to job description responsibilities. Managers and supervisors were trained to use the new performance appraisal system.

The firm is now ready to implement the new pay system. Given the economy at the present time and a forecast of a turbulent year ahead, management and the HR Director determined that the total pay increases for the upcoming year could average no more than 5%. The HR Director now must finalize the implementation process and decide how to handle the individual situations described above.

▲   **QUESTIONS**

1. Discuss how developing and implementing a new pay system was tied to changing organizational strategy and culture at the firm.
2. How should the firm deal with the "mismatch" between the job evaluation (internal) and market rates (external) for the programmers and systems analysts?
3. What would you recommend be done with the "green-circle" and "red-circle" employees identified in the case?

▲   **NOTES**

1. The authors acknowledge the assistance provided by Thomas A. Buelt in preparing the discussion of KBP and SBP; adapted from "Skill-Based Pay," *The Wall Street Journal,* June 23, 1991, A1; and Nina Gupta, G. E. Ledford, G. D. Jenkins, and D. H. Doty, "Survey-Based Prescriptions for Skill-Based Pay," *ACA Journal,* Autumn 1992, 48–59.
2. For a discussion, see Edward E. Lawler, III, *Strategic Pay* (San Francisco: Jossey-Bass Publishers, 1990), 13–53.
3. Adapted from Kathryn McKee, First Interstate Bankcorp, 1986; A. C. Hax, "A New Competitive Lesson: The Human Resource Strategy," *Training and Development Journal,* May 1985, 76–82; and Thomas A. Barocci and Thomas A. Kochan, *Human Resource Management and Industrial Relations* (Boston: Little, Brown, 1985), 101–109.
4. Linda Thornburg, "Pay for Performance: What You Should Know," *HR Magazine,* June 1992, 72–78.
5. Luis R. Gomez-Mejia and David B. Balkin, *Compensation, Organizational Strategy, and Firm Performance* (Cincinnati: South-Western Publishing, 1992), 39–49.
6. Boris Kabanoff, "Equity, Equality, Power, and Conflict," *Academy of Management Review* 16 (1991), 416–441.
7. Blair H. Sheppard, Ray J. Lewichi, and John W. Minton, *Organizational Justice* (New York: Lexington Books, 1992), 122–129.
8. Robert J. Greene, "Evaluating Base Pay Programs," *Compensation and Benefits Review,* September–October 1991, 20–31.
9. For a discussion of aspects of procedural and distributive justice, see Robert L. Heneman, *Merit Pay* (Reading, MA: Addison-Wesley, 1992), 187–200.
10. A. C. Hyde, "The New Environment for Compensation and Performance in the Public Sector," *Public Personnel Management* 19 (1988), 351–357.
11. M. P. Miceli, I. Jung, J. P. Near, D. B. Greenberger, "Predictors and Outcomes of Reactions to Pay-for-Performance Plans," *Journal of Applied Psychology* 76 (1991), 508–521.
12. For more specifics, see Employment Standards Administration, Wage and Hour Division, *Handy Reference Guide to the Fair Labor Standards Act,* WH Publication 1282 (Washington, D.C.: U.S. Department of Labor).
13. *The Wall Street Journal,* November 20, 1992, B5.
14. Thomas M. Hestwood, "Setting Fair Pay Policy," *HR Magazine,* January 1992, 75–78.
15. D. J. Mitchell, *Human Resource Management: An Economic Approach* (Boston: PWS-Kent Publishing, 1989), 184.
16. "Survey of Job Evaluation Practices," *American Compensation Association,* August 1989, 1–12.
17. Sandra M. Emerson, "Job Evaluation: A Barrier to Excellence?" *Compensation and Benefits Review,* January–February 1991, 39–51.
18. For research on the point system, see Tom D. Taber and Theodore D. Peters, "Assessing the Completeness of a Job Analysis Procedure," *Journal of Organizational Behavior* 12 (1991), 581–593.
19. Jay R. Schuster, Patricia K. Zingheim, and Marvin G. Dertien, "The Case for Computer-Assisted Market-Based Job Evaluation," *Compensation and Benefits Review,* May–June 1990, 44–54.

20. Laurent Dufetel, "Job Evaluation: Still at the Frontier," *Compensation and Benefits Review,* July–August 1991, 53–66.

21. Steven E. Rhoads, "Pay Equity Won't Go Away," *Across the Board,* July/August, 1993, 37–41.

22. Suggestions for pay survey usage are in L. Kate Beatty, *The Use and Abuse of Salary Surveys* (Deerfield, IL: William M. Mercer, Inc., 1993).

23. Caroline L. Weber and Sara L. Rynes, "Effects of Compensation Strategy on Job Pay Decisions," *Academy of Management Journal* 34 (1991), 86–109.

24. Jerry M. Newman and Daniel J. Fisher, "Strategic Impact Merit Pay," *Compensation and Benefits Review,* July–August 1992, 38–45.

25. Monica L. North and Larry W. Hunter, "Relational Demography in Internal Labor Markets," *Best Paper Proceedings, 52nd Annual Academy of Management,* Las Vegas, NV: August, 1992, 279–283.

CHAPTER 14

INCENTIVES AND EXECUTIVE COMPENSATION

After you have read this chapter, you should be able to:

1. Define incentive and give examples of three categories of incentives.

2. Identify four guidelines for incentive programs.

3. Discuss three types of individual incentives.

4. Define gainsharing and explain several types of gainsharing plans.

5. Discuss why profit-sharing and employee stock ownership plans (ESOPs) are important as organizational incentive plans.

6. Identify the components of executive compensation.

7. Discuss several criticisms of board compensation committees and long-term incentives for executives.

HR Today and Tomorrow:

CEO Compensation: Pay for Performance or Pandering to Greed?

"Out of control," "obscene," "sickening," "outrageous and irresponsible." No, these comments are not being made about toxic waste or organized crime. Instead they are comments made about the compensation given to chief executive officers (CEOs) of corporations during the past few years. Some examples cited by politicians, lawmakers, corporate critics, and news media stories follow:

▲ The five highest-paid CEOs of U.S. corporations received a combined $322 million increase in one year, an average of $64.4 million per CEO.

▲ Almost 400 U.S. CEOs earned over $1 million in pay in one recent year.

▲ Reebok International CEO Paul Fineman received compensation from 1986 to 1990 that averaged $13.84 million per year.

▲ Anthony O'Reilly, CEO of H. J. Heinz Company, received $75 million during 1991 alone with a base salary of $514,000 and he exercised stock options worth $74.5 million.

▲ Coca-Cola Chairman Roberto Goizueta was awarded stock options worth $81 million as a reward for company growth and profitability.

▲ In a year in which IBM had operating losses of $5 billion, John Akers of IBM received a "performance bonus" of $375,000 on top of a salary of over $700,000—even though he was replaced as Chairman because of poor corporate performance.

▲ One small company's CEO made $600,000 in the same year that the company had layoffs, closed some plants, and cut the wages of hourly workers.

These examples illustrate the problems, but a broader study by *Business Week* for a recent year found that:

▲ Salary and bonuses for CEOs of major U.S. firms averaged about $1.2 million per year.

▲ Stock options for the average CEO pay around $2 million a year.

▲ Golden parachutes guarantee CEOs more than three years' annual salaries and bonuses if they lose their jobs.

Many other examples and statistics can be cited as well in regard to both large and small corporations throughout the U.S. The reasons for the compensation levels and reactions to them are multiple and varied. Some of the proposed solutions include the following:

▲ Limiting the deductibility of executive compensation on amounts beyond 20 times that of the lowest paid or average worker in the same firm.

▲ Requiring companies to lower earnings each year by the value that stock options increase each year.

▲ Reducing the "cross breeding" on boards of directors by limiting the numbers of boards upon which individuals can sit.

▲ Requiring that directors whose firms do not receive fees from a firm be on board compensation committees.

▲ Restructuring the number of "insider directors" (who are employees of the company) on boards of directors of firms whose stock is publicly traded.

▲ Placing limits on the use of golden parachutes and other executive severance packages.

The years ahead likely will see continued criticism of the compensation packages of CEOs and other executives. At the same time, the expectations for improving corporate competitiveness are increasing, and executives want to be compensated for improving the performance of their firms. The challenge is to ensure that executive compensation packages truly are based on pay for performance.[1]

66 ————————————————————————

Incentive is the driving force which can improve one's fated course.
                                              A. L. Romanoff ——————— 99

A growing number of employers have found traditional pay systems to be inadequate. They see the need to offer additional pay beyond that needed to
be "market competitive" to reward performance accomplishments. Many of
these plans link pay to performance, as the previous chapter emphasized. But
critics have suggested that CEOs have some nerve adopting such plans for employees when their own often huge salaries are not tied to performance. As the
opening vignette indicates, that too is changing slowly.

The need for new ways of paying people to increase their productivity has resulted in many different approaches, plans, and ideas. But experts say that about
half of the pay-for-performance plans they see *don't work!* Poor design and poor
administration are the culprits.

Many elements must be present for incentive plans to work, but two of the
most important ones sometimes are also the most difficult. Management must be
willing to *share* and to *listen*. Sharing the increased fruits of increased efforts in an
equitable fashion is obviously a key—yet management may have difficulty sharing enough. Listening to employee ideas and concerns and providing information on the budget, business conditions, and the economy are critical as well.

Money and other tangible rewards can motivate. The hard part is using them
to motivate the kind of behavior desired by management. Designing an incentive program is far from easy, but the efforts can be well worth the cost.

HR professionals are under more pressure to design and install variable pay
systems because the feeling is that they provide more incentive, greater rewards,
and lower fixed labor costs. Some employers use performance-based pay systems
to encourage individual effort, teamwork, and better organizational results.[2]

A study of 629 organizations found that their top compensation goals were, in
order: (1) linking pay to performance, (2) controlling costs, (3) linking pay to
quality, and (4) encouraging teamwork. The study also found that one-third of
the organizations had increased the incentive portion as a percent of compensation in the previous two years. Also, incentives are not just being used for top
executives. About 33% of the respondents said that incentives have spread to
lower-level managers, 26% to professional and technical staff members, and 22%
to all administrative, clerical, and hourly employees.[3]

But linking pay to performance is not always successful or even appropriate. For
example, if the output cannot be objectively measured, how can management reward the higher performers with more pay? Managers may not even be able to
identify accurately the higher performers. Requirements for successful incentive
plans and executive compensation programs are discussed in this chapter.

▲ INCENTIVES

The main purpose of incentives is to tie employees' rewards closely to their output. Thus, an **incentive** is compensation that rewards an employee for efforts
beyond normal performance expectations. Whether an individual will strive for
increased productivity and receive rewards that follow higher levels of perfor-

▼ **AN INCENTIVE**

is compensation that rewards an
employee for efforts beyond normal
performance expectations.

mance depends on the individual. Also, some people may prefer some extra time off for higher productivity rather than more money.

Types of Incentives

A variety of incentive systems are available for use in organizations. As Figure 14–1 shows, incentive plans can be individual, group, or organizational. Individual plans work well to tie pay to performance when productivity is being directly measured, but they do not encourage people to cooperate with one another. Either group or organizational plans work better if cooperation or acceptance is important. Organizational-level incentives include both profit-sharing and employee ownership plans.

Guidelines for Incentive Systems

Incentive systems can be complex and take many forms. Managers should consider the following general guidelines when establishing and maintaining such systems.

Recognize Organization Culture and Resources   The most critical factor determining the success of any incentive program is for it to be consistent with both the culture and the financial resources of the organization. For example, if an organization is very autocratic and adheres to traditional rules and procedures, an incentive system that rewards flexibility and teamwork is likely to fail. The incentive plan is being "planted" in the wrong growing environment.

Any incentive system requires a *climate of trust and cooperation* between employees and managers. Figure 14–2 illustrates how the factors of trust and objectivity are related. As the amount of trust between employees and managers increases, the criteria used for determining rewards tied to performance may become less objective. In some situations, trust may be so low that even use of highly objec-

Figure 14–1

Incentive Plans: Focus and
Cooperation Requirements

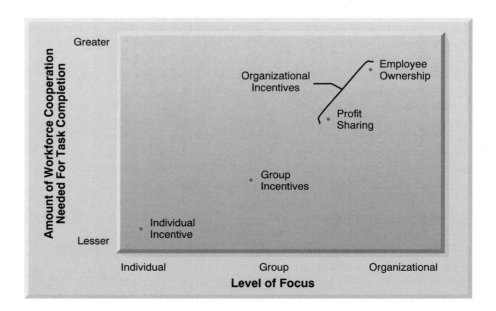

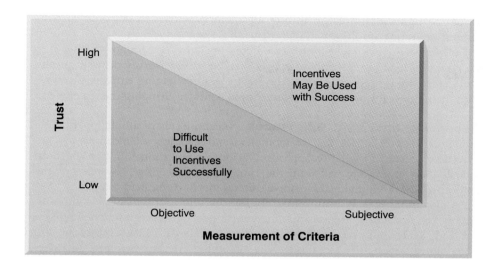

Relationship between Trust and Objectivity in Individual Incentive Systems

tive measures may be unwise. However, if workers have a high level of trust and good working relationships with their superiors, they may accept more subjective performance measures.

Unions may resist incentive systems. Most unions are built on the concepts of security, seniority, and group solidarity instead of individual productivity. Individual incentive systems may favor only the most highly motivated, competent workers and may actually depress the average worker's earnings. For this and other reasons, employers often use group or organizational incentive systems.

Tie Incentives to Desired Performance   Incentive systems should be tied as much as possible to desired performance. Employees must see a direct relationship between their efforts and their rewards. Further, both employees and managers must see the rewards as equitable and desirable. Expectancy theory indicates that incentives are most effective when employees can see clearly that their extra efforts lead to increased performance and desirable rewards. Otherwise, stress can be created.[4]

Because people tend to produce what is measured and rewarded, it is important to make sure that what is being rewarded is *really* what is needed and something important is not being left out.[5] For example, assume a hotel reservation center sets incentives for its employees to lower their time spent per call. That reduction may occur, but customer service and the number of reservations made might drop as employees rush callers to reduce talk time.

Additionally, *employee competition* for incentives may produce undesirable results. Paying salesclerks in a retail store a commission may encourage "fighting" over customers. Some salesclerks may be reluctant to work in departments that sell low-cost items if their commissions are figured on the basis of total sales. For example, clerks in a department store may concentrate on selling major appliances without giving adequate attention to small household appliances.

Keep Incentive Plans Current   An incentive system should consistently reflect current technological and organizational conditions. Offering an incentive for sales clerks to sell outdated merchandise in order to clear it out of stock would be more appropriate than offering them incentives to sell only current-fashion items that are already in high demand.

Incentive systems should be reviewed continually to determine whether they are operating as designed. Follow-up, through an attitude survey or other means, will determine if the incentive system is actually encouraging employees to perform better. If it is not, then managers should consider changing the system.

Recognize Individual Differences   Incentive plans should provide for individual differences. People are complex, and a variety of incentive systems may have to be developed to appeal to various organizational groups and individuals. Not everybody will want the same type of incentive rewards. For this and other reasons, individual incentive systems must be designed carefully.

As illogical as it may seem, informal group pressure and sanctions commonly are used to restrict the amount that individuals produce, even if individual pay is reduced. Those who seek to maximize their earnings by exceeding group-imposed limits are labeled "rate busters" or something even more graphic. Rate restrictors often feel they are being made to suffer by comparison with the higher producers.

Separate Plan Payments from Base Pay   Successful incentive plans separate the incentive payment from base salary. That separation makes a clear connection between performance and pay. It also reinforces the notion that one part of the employee's pay must be "re-earned" in the next performance period. Many employees prefer the security of automatic increases in pay based upon length of service in the organization instead of having incentives paid based on performance as judged by their immediate supervisors.

▲ INDIVIDUAL INCENTIVES

Individual incentive systems attempt to relate individual effort to pay. Conditions that favor the use of individual incentive plans are:[6]

- ▲ Individual performance must be able to be identified and isolated by the nature of the job performed.
- ▲ A substantial amount of independent work must be performed, allowing individual contributions to be identified.
- ▲ The individuals must not cooperate too closely with other workers, or if they do, competition among employees must be desirable for an individual system to work.
- ▲ The organizational culture must emphasize individual achievements and rewards.

Piece-Rate Systems

The most basic individual incentive system is the piece-rate system, whether of the straight or differential type. Under the **straight piece-rate system,** wages are determined by multiplying the number of units produced (such as garments sewn or customers contacted) by the piece rate for one unit. The rate for each piece does not change regardless of the number of pieces produced. Because the cost is the same for each unit, the wage for each employee is easy to figure, and labor costs may be accurately predicted.

▼ **STRAIGHT PIECE-RATE SYSTEM**

is a pay system in which wages are determined by multiplying the number of units produced by the piece-rate for one unit.

A **differential piece-rate system** pays employees one piece-rate wage if they produce less than a standard output and a higher piece-rate wage if they produce more than the standard. Developed by Frederick W. Taylor in the late 1800s, this system is designed to stimulate employees to achieve or exceed established standards of production.

Managers often determine the quotas or standards by using time and motion studies. For example, assume that the standard quota for a worker is set at 300 units per day and the standard rate is 14¢ per unit. For all units over the standard, however, the employee receives 20¢ per unit. Under this system, the worker who produces 400 units in one day would get $62 in wages (300 × 14¢) + (100 × 20¢). There are many other possible combinations of straight and differential piece-rate systems. The specific system used by a firm depends on many situational factors.

Despite their incentive value, piece-rate systems are difficult to use because standards for many types of jobs are difficult and costly to determine.[7] In some instances, the cost of determining and maintaining the standards may be greater than the benefits derived from piecework. Jobs in which individuals have little control over output or in which high standards of quality are necessary also may be unsuited to piecework. Though the system still is widely used in certain industries, such as the garment industry, it seldom is used in white-collar, office, and clerical jobs, in which an individual employee's performance often is affected by factors beyond the employee's control.

Commissions

An individual incentive system widely used in sales jobs is the **commission,** which is compensation computed as a percentage of sales in units or dollars. Commissions are integrated into the pay given to sales workers in three common ways: straight commission, salary-plus-commission, and bonuses.

Straight Commission   In the straight commission system, a sales representative receives a percentage of the value of the sales made. Consider a sales representative working for a consumer products company. She receives no compensation if no sales are made, but for all sales made in her territory she receives a percentage of the total amount. The advantage of this system is that the sales representative must sell to earn. The disadvantage is that it offers no security for the sales staff, even though the product or service sold might be one that requires a long lead time before purchasing decisions are made. One sales representative with a telecommunications firm spent five months working with a large corporation to sell a $1 million phone and communication system, for which the representative received a sizable commission. But during the five months, he received no income; he was paid only when the sale was closed and the equipment installed.

For that reason, some employers use a **draw** system, in which the sales representative can draw advance payments against future commissions. The amount drawn then is deducted from future commission checks. From the employer's side, one of the risks in a draw system is that future commissions may not be large enough to repay the draw, especially for a new or marginally successful salesperson. In addition, arrangements must be made for repayment of drawn amounts if an individual leaves the organization before earning the draw in commission.

▼ **DIFFERENTIAL PIECE-RATE SYSTEM**

pays employees one piece-rate wage if they produce less than a standard output and a higher piece-rate wage if they produce more than the standard.

▼ **COMMISSION**

is compensation computed as a percentage of sales in units or dollars.

▼ **DRAW**

is an amount advanced and repaid from future commissions earned by the employee.

Salary-Plus-Commission   The most frequently used form of sales compensation is the *salary-plus-commission,* which combines the stability of a salary with the performance aspect of a commission. A common split is 80% salary to 20% commission, although that split varies by industry and with other factors.

Consultants criticize many sales commission plans as being too complex to motivate sales representatives. Others are too simple, focusing only on the salesperson's pay, not on organizational objectives. Although a majority of companies use overall sales growth as the only performance measure, performance would be much better if these organizations used a variety of criteria, including new accounts and product mix that reflect marketing plans.[8]

Bonuses

Lump-sum payments or bonuses are less costly than general wage increases since bonuses do not become part of employees' base wages, upon which future percentage increases are figured. One method of determining an employee's annual bonus is to compute it as a percentage of the individual's base salary. Often such programs pay bonuses only if specific individual and organizational objectives are achieved. Though technically this type of bonus is individual, it comes close to being a group or organization incentive system. Because it is based on the profits of the division, management must consider the total performance of the division and its employees. Individual incentive compensation in the form of bonuses often is used at the executive or upper-management levels of an organization, although it is increasingly used at lower levels, too. The "HR Perspective" describes how an incentive program has been used at Taco Bell Corporation.

Special Incentive Programs

Although special incentive programs can be developed for groups and for entire organizations, they focus on rewarding only high-performing individuals. Giving the salesperson who sells the most new cars a trip to Las Vegas is one example of a special incentive program. Sales contests, productivity contests, and other incentive schemes can be conducted so that individual employees receive extra compensation.

Special incentive programs are used widely in sales-related jobs. Cash, merchandise, travel, and combinations of those are the most frequently used rewards. The main reasons for using awards are to achieve immediate sales gains and to focus attention on specific products or obtaining new accounts.[9]

▲ GROUP INCENTIVE SYSTEMS

A group incentive system may be useful in overcoming some problems associated with the individual incentives.

The size of the group is critical. If it becomes too large, employees may feel their individual efforts will have little or no effect on the total performance of the group and the resulting rewards. Incentive plans for small groups are a direct result of the growing number of complex jobs requiring interdependent effort. Small-group plans may encourage teamwork in groups where interdependence is high.[10] They have been used in many service-oriented industries because of a high degree of contact with customers that may require teamwork. When there

HR Perspectives:
Managerial Incentives at Taco Bell

In order to keep pace with the growth in new restaurants, Taco Bell Corporation had to revise its managerial incentive program. During a recent two-year period, Taco Bell added more than 350 new restaurants. As a result, the company implemented a new field organization structure. Because of concerns that Taco Bell would not be able to recruit and retain a sufficient number of managers to have one manager in each restaurant, the firm decided to have existing restaurant managers be responsible for two locations, not just one.

To compensate these managers for the additional responsibilities and demands placed on them, Taco Bell had two choices. The first, which was rejected, was to increase the base salaries for the managers. Instead, a decision was made to institute a new

managerial incentive program. Under the previous bonus program, most managers (whose base salaries averaged about $30,000) received $1,000 bonuses every quarter. However, under the new managerial incentive program, managers who have outstanding performances can earn up to $5,000 twice a year, more than twice the amount possible under the old program. In this way managers with responsibilities for two restaurants receive more than twice as much additional compensation.

The new program instituted for over 1600 restaurant managers uses three measures of performance: (1) targeted profit, (2) customer service, and (3) store sales. Using the performance objectives set under the new program, 60% to 70% of the managers typically meet their

objectives each six months, compared to 85% who met the easier goals set under the old program. But those who do not measure up lose out on up to $10,000 per year, not $4,000, which provides stronger incentives for managers to meet their objectives.

In addition to rewarding performance more, Taco Bell has seen better results in other areas throughout the chain. The first eighteen months after implementing the new managerial incentive program, profit records were broken, customer service scores were higher than ever before, and food costs as a percentage of store sales decreased. These results indicate that the revised managerial incentive program has had the positive impact desired when it was designed and implemented.[11]

---

are no customers, employees are idle. With a team approach, idle employees can perform other tasks until customers arrive. Such flexibility reduces costs. Flexibility in using employees can be a benefit of the team approach in nonservice industries as well.

Figure 14–3 shows the results of a survey of firms reporting the reasons that they established group incentive programs. In summary, group incentives seem to work best when the following criteria are present:[12]

▲ Significant interdependence exists among the work of several individuals, and teamwork and cooperation are essential.
▲ Difficulties exist in identifying exactly who is responsible for differing levels of performance.
▲ Management wants to create or reinforce teamwork and cooperation among employees.

If these conditions cannot be met, then either individual or organizational incentives may be more appropriate.[13]

Problems with Group Incentive Plans

Groups, like individuals, may restrict output, resist revision of standards, and seek to gain at the expense of other groups. Compensating different employee groups

Figure 14–3   Reasons for Establishing Group Incentive Programs

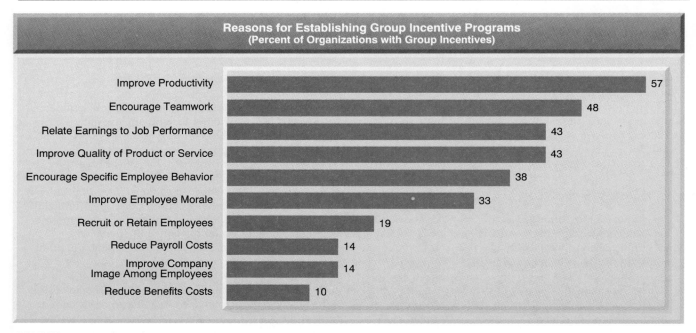

SOURCE: *Non-Traditional Incentive Pay Programs,* Personnel Policies Forum Survey No. 148 (Washington, D.C.: The Bureau of National Affairs, 1991), 13. Used with permission.

with separate incentives may cause them to overemphasize certain efforts to the detriment of the overall organizational good. For example, conflict often arises between the marketing and production functions of organizations because marketing's incentive compensation is based on what is sold, while production's incentive compensation is based on keeping unit production costs as low as possible. Marketing representatives may want to tailor products to customers' needs to increase their sales, but production managers emphasize production of identical items to lower costs. The overall company good therefore may be sidetracked.

Another problem that causes group incentives to fail is if a poorly performing individual influences the group results negatively. For instance, if holding data-entry errors to below 2% is an objective that triggers payment of a group incentive, the presence of one or two poor performers who make numerous errors can result in the group being denied an incentive payment for a month. Unfortunately, even if management retrains or removes poor performers, some incentive already has been lost.

A third problem with group incentives is that union representatives are often skeptical of them. Union leaders frequently charge that the group incentive payments are being used as "union busting" tactics by employers.

▲ ORGANIZATIONAL INCENTIVES

An organizational incentive system compensates all employees in the organization based on how well the organization as a whole does during the year. The basic concept behind organizational incentive plans is that overall efficiency depends on organizational or plantwide cooperation. The purpose of these plans is to produce teamwork. For example, the conflict between marketing and production can be overcome if management uses an incentive that emphasizes organizational profit and productivity. To be effective, an incentive program should include everyone from nonexempt employees to managers and executives. Common organizational incentive systems include gainsharing, profit sharing, and employee stock ownership plans (ESOPs).

Gainsharing

Gainsharing is the sharing with employees of greater-than-expected gains in profits and/or productivity. Gainsharing attempts to increase "discretionary effort," that is, the difference between the maximum amount of effort a person can exert and the minimum amount of effort necessary to keep from being fired. It can be argued that workers currently are not paid for discretionary effort in most organizations. They are paid to meet the minimum acceptable level of effort required. However, when workers do exercise discretionary effort, the organization can afford to pay them more than the going rate, because the extra effort produces financial gains over and above the returns of minimal effort.

To determine when to pay some of the gains generated to employees, a study of gainsharing type plans found that 43% of the surveyed firms used financial measures, 38% used productivity measures, and 36% used quality measures. This study also revealed that employees received about 35% of the gains generated, while organizations retained about 65% of the gains.[14]

Determining Payment and Performance Measures   Gainsharing programs begin with management identifying the ways that increased productivity, quality, and financial performance can occur and deciding that some of the gains should be shared with employees. The most critical step is to involve employees at all levels in the gainsharing process, often by establishing a gainsharing taskforce composed of managers and nonmanagers alike. Once the taskforce meets, then there are two crucial decisions to be made: (1) How much gain is to be shared with employees? (2) What are the performance measures to be used?

Payouts of the gains can be monthly, quarterly, semiannually, or annually, depending upon management philosophy and the performance measure used. The more frequent the payouts, the greater the visibility of the rewards to employees. Therefore, given a choice, most firms with gainsharing plans have chosen to make the payouts more frequent than annually. The rewards can be distributed in four ways:[15]

▲ A flat amount for all employees.
▲ Same percentage of base salary for all employees.
▲ Percentage of the gains by category of employees.
▲ Amount or percentage paid on individual performance against measures.

ꞓ first two methods generally are preferred because they promote and re-
teamwork and cooperation more than the other two payment methods.
ꞏding performance measures, only those measures that employees actually
ffect should be used. Often measures such as labor costs, overtime hours,
uality benchmarks are used. Both organizational measures and departmen-
easures may be used, with the gainsharing weighting being split between
wo categories. Naturally, individual performance must be satisfactory in
to receive the gainsharing payments.[16]

▼ **GAINSHARING**

is the sharing with employees of greater-than-expected gains in profits and/or productivity.

HR Perspectives:

Research on Gainsharing Participation

The growing popularity of gainsharing programs has raised questions about how individual employees respond and participate in these programs. Often, employee participation and involvement is through submitting suggestions for work changes and improvements. To provide insight into why individuals do or do not participate and make suggestions, Hatcher, Ross, and Collins coordinated a research study on supervisors and nonmanagers in five firms with gainsharing plans. The results of that study, published in the *Group & Organization Studies* journal, provided some useful insights for managers considering the development of gainsharing programs.

To conduct the study, the researchers selected five manufacturing firms in the Midwest. Firm size ranged from 100 to 322 employees where gainsharing plans had been in operation for 16 to 72 months. Gainsharing payouts were made monthly in four of the firms and every

two months in the other firm. The average bonus paid as a percentage of annual employee wages/salaries varied from 2.17% to 17.63%.

To select employees to participate in the study, the researchers reviewed company records to determine the number of gainsharing suggestions submitted by employees in each department, and then the employees' names in each unit were segmented according to the number of suggestions submitted. Those who had submitted gainsharing suggestions were grouped separately and interviewed using a structured questionnaire. Approximately 82% of those interviewed had submitted at least one suggestion.

The results revealed that the primary reasons given for submitting suggestions were to: (1) improve individual or company performance, (2) make the individual's work easier; and (3) be more involved in work-related decisions. Supervisors also listed gaining recognition as another

prominent reason. Interestingly, earning the gainsharing payouts was only number five in importance.

Primary reasons for nonparticipation were: (1) negative attitudes or apathy toward the gainsharing plan; (2) ability to circumvent the gainsharing suggestion system; and (3) negative attitudes or apathy toward management and/or the company. Interestingly, nonparticipation because of a negative or apathetic attitude toward the company was cited more frequently by supervisors than nonsupervisors.

In reviewing the results of the study, the authors emphasize that the degree of commitment, interest, and trust employees have in the organization and its managers play a major role in the involvement of individuals in gainsharing plans. Just offering gainsharing payouts may be insufficient to generate participation in gainsharing plans.[18]

The success or failure of incentive programs begins with the culture of the organization, as illustrated in the "HR Perspective." Putting a gainsharing program in autocratically or in desperation to save a badly managed firm virtually guarantees failure. Inadequate financial information systems and severe external competitive conditions and government constraints also inhibit the success of gainsharing programs.[17]

Improshare   Improshare stands for Improved Productivity Through Sharing, and it was created by Mitchell Fein, an industrial engineer. It is similar to a piece-rate plan except that it rewards all workers in the organization. Input is measured in hours and output in physical units. A standard is calculated and weekly bonuses are paid based on the extent to which the standard is exceeded. The impact of Improshare programs was identified in a survey of 112 firms using these programs. The firms had a median productivity increase of 8% during the first year, and productivity gains of 17.5% by the third year.[19]

Scanlon Plan   Since its development in 1927, the Scanlon plan has been implemented in many organizations, especially in smaller unionized industrial firms. The basic concept underlying the Scanlon plan is that efficiency depends on teamwork and plantwide cooperation. The plan has two main features: (1) a system of departmental committees and a plant-screening committee to evaluate all cost-saving suggestions, and (2) direct incentive rewards to all employees to improve efficiency.

The system is activated through departmental employee committees that receive and review cost-saving ideas submitted by employees. Suggestions beyond the departmental committees are passed to the plant-screening committee for review. Savings that result from suggestions are passed on to all members of the organization.

Incentive rewards are paid to employees on the basis of improvements in pre-established ratios. Ratios of "labor costs to total sales value" or "total production" or "total hours to total production" most commonly are used. Savings due to differences between actual and expected ratios are placed in a bonus fund. A predetermined percentage of this fund is then split between employees and the organization.

The Scanlon plan is not a true profit-sharing plan because employees receive incentive compensation for reducing labor costs, regardless of whether the organization ultimately makes a profit. Organizations that have implemented the Scanlon plan have experienced an increase in productivity and a decrease in labor costs. Also, employee attitudes have become more favorable, and cooperation between management and workers has increased.[20]

Rucker Plan   The Rucker plan, almost as old as the Scanlon plan, was developed in the 1930s by economist Allan W. Rucker. The Scanlon formula measures performance against a standard of labor costs in ratio to the dollar value of production, whereas the Rucker formula introduces a third variable: the dollar value of all materials, supplies, and services that the organization uses to make its product. The Rucker formula is:

$$\frac{\$ \text{ Value of Labor Costs}}{\$ \text{ Value of Production} - \$ \text{ Value of Materials, Supplies, Services}}$$

The result is what economists call the "value added" to a product by the organization. The use of value added rather than the dollar value of production builds in an incentive to save on other inputs.

Profit Sharing

As the name implies, a **profit-sharing** program distributes a portion of organizational profits to the employees. Typically, the percentage of the profits distributed to employees is agreed on by the end of the year before distribution. In some profit-sharing plans, employees receive portions of the profits at the end of the year; in others, the profits are deferred, placed in a fund, and made available to employees on retirement or on their leaving the organization. Figure 14–4 describes how profit-sharing plans are set up, according to a study by the U.S. Department of Labor, Bureau of Labor Statistics.

Unions used to be skeptical of profit-sharing plans, because the system only works when there are profits to be shared. Often the level of profits is influenced

▼ **PROFIT SHARING**

distributes a portion of the profits of the organization to employees.

▲ **Figure 14–4**   Profit-Sharing Plans in Medium and Large Firms (in Percentages)

Item	All participants	Professional and administrative participants	Technical and clerical participants	Production and service praticipants
Method of determining employer contributions				
Based on stated formula	60	56	54	65
Fixed percent of profits	10	11	9	9
Sliding percentage based on profits				
sales or return on assets	18	12	10	24
Determined by unit profits	(')	(')	(')	–
Other stated formula	33	33	35	32
No predetermined formula	40	44	46	35
Allocation of profits to individual employees				
Equally to participants				
Based on earnings	1	–	–	1
Based on earnings and service	64	67	71	60
Based on participants' contributions	9	10	8	9
Other..	9	7	7	11
	17	16	14	18
Loans from employees' accounts				
Permitted...				
Not permitted...................................	19	28	28	18
	81	72	72	89
Total	100	100	100	100

[1] Less than 0.5 percent.

[2] Includes participants in plans that based allocation on unit performance or the ratio of employee compensated hours to total compensated hours.

NOTE: Because of rounding sums of individual items may not equal totals. Where applicable dash indictes no employee in category.

SOURCE: Edward M. Coates, III, "Profit Sharing Today: Plans and Provisions," *Monthly Labor Review,* April 1991, 24.

by factors not under the employees' control. However, in recent years, organized labor has supported profit-sharing plans in which employees' pay increases are tied to improved company performance.

Objectives and Drawbacks of Profit-Sharing Plans The primary objectives of profit-sharing plans are to:[21]

▲ Improve productivity
▲ Recruit or retain employees
▲ Improve product/service quality
▲ Improve employee morale

When used throughout an organization, including lower-echelon workers, profit-sharing plans can have some drawbacks. First, management must be willing to disclose financial and profit information to employees.[22] As many people know, both the definition and level of profit can depend upon the accounting system used and decisions made. Therefore, to be credible, management must be willing to disclose sufficient financial and profit information to alleviate the skepticism of employees, particularly if the profit-sharing levels are reduced from previous years. Second, profits may vary a great deal from year to year—resulting in windfalls and losses beyond the employees' control. Third, the payoff may be seen as too far removed from employees' efforts to serve as a strong link between better performance and higher rewards.

Employee Stock Ownership Plan (ESOP)

A common type of profit sharing is the **employee stock ownership plan (ESOP).** An ESOP is designed to give employees stock ownership of the organization for which they work, thereby increasing their commitment, loyalty, and effort. During a 17-year period more than 9,000 ESOP plans were established, with some being used by employees to buy out firms that might otherwise have been closed.[23] Also, organizations that promote employee ownership through grants of stock receive favorable income tax treatment.

EMPLOYEE STOCK OWNERSHIP PLAN (ESOP)

is a plan whereby employees gain stock ownership in the organization for which they work.

Establishing an ESOP
An organization establishes an ESOP by using its stock as collateral to borrow capital from a financial institution. Once the loan repayment begins through the use of company profits, a certain amount of stock is released and allocated to an Employee Stock Ownership Trust (ESOT). Employees are assigned shares of company stock, kept in the trust, based on their lengths of service and pay levels. On retirement, death, or separation from the organization, employees or their beneficiaries can sell the stock back to the trust or on the open market, if the stock is publicly traded.[24]

Employee stock ownership plans are subject to changes in tax laws. Generally, the employers who have treated all employees alike are affected the least. Those that provide different levels of benefits for different groups of employees are affected the most by changes in tax laws.

Advantages and Disadvantages
There are several advantages to an ESOP. The major one is that the firm receives highly favorable tax treatment of the earnings that are earmarked for use in the ESOP. Second, an ESOP gives employees a "piece of the action" so that they can share in the growth and profitability of their firm. Employee ownership may be effective in motivating employees to work harder.[25]

Almost everyone loves the concept of employee ownership as a kind of "people's capitalism." However, the sharing also can be a disadvantage because employees may feel "forced" to join, thus placing their financial fitness at greater risk. Both their wages/salaries and their retirement benefits are dependent on the performance of the organization. This concentration is even riskier for retirees because the value of pension fund assets also depends on how well the company does.

Another drawback is that ESOPs have been used as a management tool to fend off unfriendly takeover attempts. Holders of employee-owned stock often align with management to turn down bids that would benefit outside stockholders but would replace management and restructure operations. Surely, ESOPs were not created to entrench inefficient management. Despite these disadvantages, ESOPs have grown in popularity.

▲ EXECUTIVE COMPENSATION

Many organizations, especially large ones, administer executive compensation somewhat differently than compensation for lower-level employees. An executive typically is someone in the top two levels of an organization, such as President or Senior Vice-President. Executive compensation programs often include incentives, as well as other forms of compensation. Two objectives influence executive compensation: (1) tying the overall performance of the organization over a period of time to the compensation paid executives and (2) ensuring that the total compensation packages for executives are competitive with the compensation packages in other firms that might employ them.

Compensation Committee

▼ **A COMPENSATION COMMITTEE**

usually is a subgroup of the Board of Directors who are not officers of the firm.

A **compensation committee** usually is a subgroup of the Board of Directors composed of directors who are not officers of the firm. Compensation committees generally make recommendations to the Board of Directors on overall pay policies, salaries for top officers, supplemental compensation such as stock options and bonuses, and additional perquisites for executives. As the "HR Perspective" indicates, the "independence" of Board compensation committees increasingly has been criticized.

At the heart of most executive compensation plans is the idea that executives should be rewarded if the organization grows in profitability and value over a period of years. Because many executives are in high tax brackets, their compensation often is provided in ways that offer significant tax savings. Therefore, their total compensation packages are more significant than their base pay. When the base salary is $1 million or more, the executive often is interested in the mix of items in the total package, including current and deferred compensation. Figure 14–5 shows the components of executive compensation, which are *salaries,* annual *bonuses, long-term incentives, benefits,* and *perquisites* ("perks").

▲ **Figure 14–5**

Executive Compensation Components

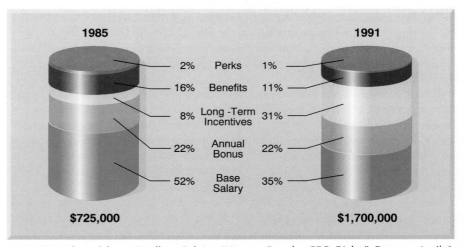

SOURCE: Adapted from Geoffrey Colvin, "How to Pay the CEO Right," *Fortune,* April 6, 1992, 62.

HR Perspectives:
Ethical Issues Regarding the Independence of Board Compensation Committees

Critics point out that many U.S. corporate CEOs make 95 to 150 times more than the average worker in the firm makes, whereas in Japan the ratio is 15 to 1 and in Europe 20 to 1. Also, Japanese CEOs are paid about one-third of what U.S. CEOs of comparable sized firms are paid. Stock options are seldom used in Japan and many other countries, and base salaries and bonuses often are significantly lower as well.

But in the U.S. a major cause for the high total compensation for CEOs is the use of executive stock options, in which executives are given the right to purchase shares of corporate stock at a specific price. For example, a CEO has an option granted in 1989 to purchase 10,000 shares for $20 per share in the future. If the price of the stock rises to $50 per share by 1994, then the executive can exercise the option and make $40 per share, or $400,000. Supporters of stock options point out that the company shareholders also benefit by a $40 per share gain. However, critics say that giving one

person that much credit for improving the performance in a corporation employing 20,000 people is not reasonable.

One major concern voiced by many critics is that the base pay and bonuses of CEOs often are set by board compensation committee members, many of whom are CEOs of other companies with similar compensation packages. Also, the compensation advisors and consultants to the CEOs often collect large fees, and critics charge that those fees distort the objectivity of the advice given. For example, one of the directors on the compensation committee of Coca-Cola heads a firm receiving $24 million in investment fees in six years from Coke. Another example is a law firm of a director at Philip Morris that received almost $25 million in fees over a three-year period.

Situations such as these give the impression of self-serving conflicts-of-interests between outside directors and corporate executives. A related problem exists when the Board compensa-

tion committee in one firm is composed solely of executives of other companies, whose compensation often is compared to each other. Therefore, there obviously may be self-serving reasons for supporting higher compensation for executives so that the director benefits when the compensation committee in his own firm looks at his compensation package. Also, if an executive from Firm A sits on the Board Compensation Committee of Company X, and the CEO of Company X sits on the Compensation Committee of Firm A, how "independent" is each of them likely to be?

To counter criticism, some corporations are changing the composition of the compensation committee and giving it more independence. Some of the changes include prohibiting "insider" company officers and Board members from serving on compensation committees and empowering the compensation committee to hire pay and compensation consultants without executive management involvement.[26]

Executive Salaries

Salaries of executives vary by type of job, size of organization, region of the country, and industry. On average, salaries make up about one third of the typical top executive's annual compensation total. One study found that as the length of time a CEO stays at a firm increases, the CEO pay rises—but that the stock performance decreases.[27] These results reinforce the concerns voiced by critics of executive compensation practices.

Executive Bonus Plans

Because executive performance may be difficult to determine, bonus compensation must reflect some kind of performance measure if it is to be meaningful. As an example, a retail chain with over 250 stores ties annual bonuses for managers to store profitability. The bonuses have amounted to as much as 35% of a store manager's base salary.

Bonuses for executives can be determined in several ways. A discretionary system whereby bonuses are awarded based on the judgments of the chief executive officer and the board of directors is a simple way. However, the absence of formal, measurable targets is a major drawback of this approach. Also, bonuses can be tied to specific measures, such as to return on investment, earnings per share, or net profits before taxes. More complex systems create bonus pools and thresholds above which bonuses are computed. Whatever method is used, it is important to describe it so that executives trying to earn bonuses understand the plan; otherwise the incentive effect will be diminished.

Long-Term Performance Incentives

Performance-based incentives, often in the form of stock options, attempt to tie executive compensation to the long-term growth and success of the organization. As would be expected, supplemental compensation is prevalent in the private sector but rarely used in the public sector and other nonprofit organizations.

▼ A STOCK OPTION

gives an individual the right to buy stock in a company, usually at a fixed price for a period of time.

Stock Options   A stock option gives an individual the right to buy stock in a company, usually at an advantageous price. Different types of stock options have been used depending on the tax laws in effect. Stock options have increased in use as a component of executive compensation during the past ten years, and employers may use a variety of very specialized and technical approaches to them, which are beyond the scope of this discussion. However, the overall trend is toward using stock options as performance-based long-term incentives.

Many privately held companies also have long-term incentive programs. One study found that more than half of the surveyed firms had long-term incentive programs.[28] Even though stock is closely held, the firms grant "stock equivalencies" in the form of *phantom stock* or *share appreciation rights.* These plans pay recipients the cash value of the increased value of the stock in the future, determined by a base valuation given at the time the phantom stock or share appreciation rights are given.[29]

Criticisms of Executive Compensation

One criticism of executive compensation is that it does not offer long-term rewards. Instead, performance within a given year leads to large rewards even though corporate performance over time may be mediocre. This difference is especially apparent if the yearly measures are carefully chosen. Executives can even manipulate earnings per share by selling assets, liquidating inventories, or reducing research and development expenditures. All these actions may make organizational performance look better, but they may impair the long-term growth of the organization.

The opening discussion of the chapter also highlights another major criticism of executive compensation, which is the disparity between total compensation received and corporate performance. Although supplements such as bonuses and stock options are supposed to be tied to the performance of the organization, conflicting research results exist as to whether or not this linkage occurs.[30]

As a result of the criticisms, several provisions on executive compensation were passed in 1993 tax legislation. One provision requires that firms establish pay-for-performance criteria based on financial results or stock price increases if the executive payments are to be considered tax deductible expenses for that firm. Also, requiring shareholder approval for bonus plans and a tighter definition of "outside" director were both included in the legislation.

Executive Benefits and Perquisites

In addition to the regular benefits received by all employees, executives often have other special benefits and perquisites available to them. One frequent benefit is severance protection or pay for executives who lose their jobs.

Golden and Silver Parachutes   A special severance benefit available to some executives, a **golden parachute,** provides protection and security to executives who may be affected if they lose their jobs or if their firms are acquired by another firm. Typically, employment contracts are written to give special compensation to executives if they are negatively affected in an acquisition or merger.

Golden parachutes often are criticized for giving executives protection, while lower- and middle-level managers and other employees are left vulnerable when mergers or acquisitions occur. As a result, some firms have established *silver parachutes* to protect nonexecutives. A **silver parachute** is a severance and benefit plan to protect nonexecutives if their firms are acquired by another firm. For example, Herman Miller, a Zeeland, Michigan, manufacturer of office furniture, has designed a generous severance pay and benefits plan that goes into effect if a hostile takeover threatens any of the 3,500 employees' jobs. All employees with at least two years' service would be protected. They would get at least one full year's salary if they are fired within two years for other than just cause.

Miller says the idea is to protect the employees. Of course, the plan should also serve to deter takeover artists. Whether golden or silver, the parachute phenomenon is a clear response to the takeover strategy that many organizations have faced.[31]

Perquisites

Perquisites ("perks") are special executive benefits that are usually noncash items. Perks and special executive benefits are useful in tying executives to organizations and in demonstrating their importance to the company. It is the "status enhancement" value of perks that is important to many executives. Visible symbols of status allow executives to be seen as "very important people (VIPs)" both inside and outside their organizations. In addition, perks can offer substantial tax savings because many perks may not be taxed as income. Figure 14–6 lists some that are available.

▼ **A GOLDEN PARACHUTE**

is a severance benefit that provides protection and security to executives who may be affected if they lose their jobs or if their firms are acquired by another firm.

▼ **A SILVER PARACHUTE**

is a severance and benefit plan to protect nonexecutives if their firms are acquired by another firm.

▼ **PERQUISITES (PERKS)**

are special benefits for executives that are usually noncash items.

▲ **Figure 14–6**   Executive Perks

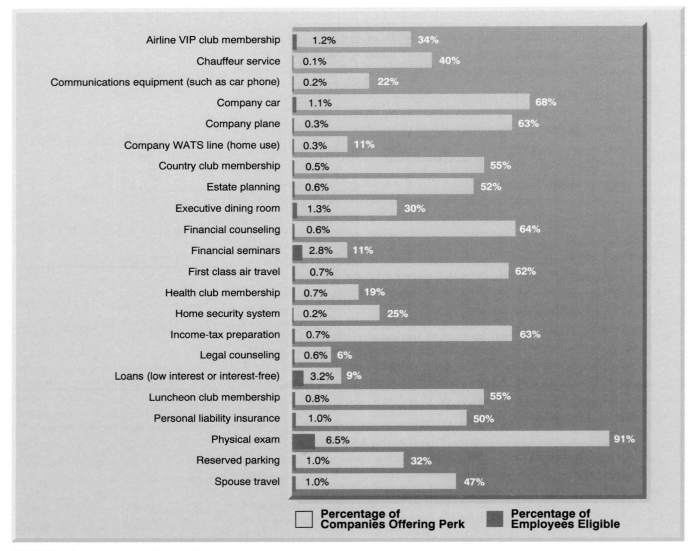

SOURCE: Adapted from Hewitt Associates, 1990.

Unfortunately, the existence of perks also highlights for critics the overall compensation of executives, particularly if the executives continue to receive the perks even when their organizations are performing poorly. In the future, it is likely that even more restrictions will be placed on the tax-deductibility of some perks, just as excessive executive compensation has been attacked. However, the spread of performance-oriented incentives throughout the organization at all levels may help to mute some of the criticism.

▲ SUMMARY

- ▲ An incentive is tangible compensation received for efforts beyond normal performance expectations.
- ▲ Three types of incentive systems are individual, group, and organizational.
- ▲ An effective incentive program should recognize organization culture and resources, tie incentives to performance, be kept current, recognize individual differences, and separate plan payments from base pay.
- ▲ Individual incentives include piece-rate systems, commissions, bonuses, and special incentive programs.
- ▲ To overcome some problems associated with individual incentives, group incentive systems encourage and reward teamwork and group effort.
- ▲ One organizational incentive system is gainsharing, which provides rewards based on greater-than-expected gains in profits and/or productivity.
- ▲ Types of gainsharing plans can include Improshare, Scanlon, or Rucker plans.
- ▲ Profit-sharing plans set aside a portion of the profits earned by organizations for distribution to employees.
- ▲ An employee stock ownership plan (ESOP) is one in which employees gain ownership in the firm for which they work.
- ▲ Executive compensation must be viewed as a total package composed of pay, bonuses, long-term performance-based incentives, and special benefits and perquisites ("perks").
- ▲ A compensation committee, which is a subgroup of the Board of Directors, has authority over executive compensation plans.
- ▲ Performance-based incentives often represent a significant portion of an executive's compensation package. Stock options are widely used.
- ▲ Many different special benefits and perks, all of which provide additional noncash compensation, are available to executives.

▲ REVIEW AND DISCUSSION QUESTIONS

1. Identify what an incentive is and discuss why group and organizational incentives are growing in usage.
2. Give several examples of individual incentives that you have received or that have been used in an organization in which you were employed. What problems did you observe with them?
3. What are the advantages and disadvantages of using a piece-rate incentive plan?
4. Why do you think that increased emphasis on productivity in the U.S. has led to greater interest in gainsharing?
5. Why would an employee stock ownership plan (ESOP) be seen by employees both as an attraction and as a risk?
6. Locate a corporate annual report and review it to identify the components of executive compensation discussed in it.
7. What is your view of criticisms of Board compensation committees and highly paid executives? What changes would you recommend?

INCENTIVES PAY OFF FOR VIKING FREIGHT SYSTEMS

The success of an incentive plan can be measured by a number of different methods. By virtually all measures, the incentive pay program at Viking Freight System has been very successful. Viking Freight is a trucking and shipping carrier based in San Jose, California, with 4,500 employees.

The deregulation of the trucking industry in the early 1980s changed the business environment for most trucking firms, including Viking. To respond to those changes, in 1986 Terry Stambaugh (Vice-President of Human Resources), Ron Pelzel, (Executive Vice-President), and Phil Smith (Vice-President of Corporate Planning) reviewed the incentive compensation programs at Viking. Their review clarified that employee productivity and performance were critical to success in a deregulated industry. To reward employees for superior performance and productivity, they developed the Viking Performance Earnings Plan (VPEP).

In VPEP, all Viking employees except corporate officers receive monthly rewards for achievement of objectives. Once employees complete a 90-day probation program, they are eligible for VPEP. The officers have a separate Management Incentive Compensation Plan (MICP).

Under VPEP, each employee group has its own set of objectives appropriate for its own operating area. For instance, each freight terminal has its own objectives, and appropriate objectives are set for maintenance, sales, claims, and other departments. Performance is measured every four weeks, and payments are made on the accomplishment of objectives for that four-week period. The performance measures and standards are established by Viking's performance engineers and executive committee. For support staff in clerical and other areas where it is difficult to identify specific work standards, the payouts are based on the operating ratio of the firm. This ratio is as follows:

$$\frac{\text{Operating Expenses}}{\text{Revenues before Interest and Taxes}}$$

The ratio is applicable for other areas as well, because the operating ratio for a four-week period must be below 95% (including the cost of VPEP payouts) for there to be any payouts, regardless of group or individual performance. Also, any employee who has an avoidable accident forfeits the VPEP payout for the four-week period.

Incentive payouts are computed as a percentage of the employee's four-week gross pay as follows:

Hourly employees	7.5%
Salaried supervisors	11.25
Salespeople	12.25
Department managers	15.0
Terminal managers	20.0

The criteria for freight terminal performance indicates the use of the performance measures. They are (with weights):

Revenue attainment	30%
Labor performance	30
On-time service	30
Claims ratio	10

This system is communicated clearly to all terminal employees, and they know how important performance in each area is.

When the plan was implemented in 1989, the VPEP payouts averaged less than $50. By 1991 the average payout check had increased to over $125 per period, which represents about 5.5% of the average gross pay. More importantly, corporate performance rose and continues to be at a high level. For example, for a recent year Viking had an on-time ratio of 98.1% and a claims ratio of .9%, both much better than is typical in the trucking industry.[32]

▲ Questions

1. What is the importance of having separate incentive programs for corporate officers and for all other employees?

2. What is the significance of saying that the level for the operating ratio must be below 95% or no payouts occur, regardless of group or individual performance?

3. Discuss why you believe VPEP had a key role in generating the superior corporate performance experienced by Viking.

▲ Notes

1. Sources used included Graef S. Crystal, *In Search of Excess: The Overcompensation of American Executives* (New York: W. W. Norton & Co., 1991); T. McCarroll, "Executive Pay: The Shareholders Strike Back," *Time,* May 4, 1992, 46–48; "Executive Pay," *Business Week,* April 26, 1993, 56–78; "How Much Japanese CEOs Really Make," *Business Week,* January 27, 1992, 31–32; "CEO Pay," *Industry Week,* April 15, 1991, 13–20; and "Boss's Pay," *The Wall Street Journal,* R9–11.

2. C. Cumming and D. Neceda, "Rewards or Incentives: Is There a Difference?" *Perspectives* 1(1989), 4.

3. "Performance-Based Incentives Spreading Through the Ranks," *Employee Benefit News,* February 1993, 45.

4. Jennifer M. George, Arthur P. Brief, and Jane Webster, "Organizational Intended and Unintended Coping: The Case of an Incentive Compensation Plan," *Journal of Occupational Psychology* 64 (1991), 193–205.

5. M. Blessing and S. Mlot, "The Motivation Equation: Quality + Pay," *Perspectives* 4 (1992), 8–14.

6. Luis R. Gomez-Mejia and David B. Balkin, *Compensation, Organizational Strategy, and Firm Performance* (Cincinnati: South-Western Publishing Co., 1992), 260–261.

7. Thomas B. Wilson, "Is It Time to Eliminate the Piece-Rate Incentive System?" *Compensation and Benefits Review,* March–April 1992, 43–49.

8. M. Blessing, "Designing a Sales Strategy that Keeps the Customer in Mind," *Compensation and Benefits Review,* March–April 1992, 30–42.

9. "Sales Incentives," *Incentive,* September 1992, 77–82.

10. J. Huret, "Paying for Team Results," *HR Magazine,* May 1991, 39–41.

11. Adapted from Shari Caudron, "Variable-Pay Program Increases Taco Bell's Profits," *Personnel Journal,* June 1993, 641.

12. James E. Nickel and Sandra O'Neal, "Small-Group Incentives," *Compensation and Benefits Review,* March–April 1990, 22–29.

13. T. Rollins, "Productivity-Based Group Incentive Plans: Powerful, but Use with Caution," *Compensation and Benefits Review,* May–June 1989, 39–50.

14. Jerry L. McAdams and Elizabeth J. Hawk, "Capitalizing on Human Assets Through Performance-Based Rewards," *ACA Journal,* Autumn 1992, 60–72.

15. D. Beck, "Implementing a Gainsharing Plan: What Companies Need to Know," *Compensation and Benefits Review,* January–February 1992, 21–33.

16. For a more detailed discussion of establishing performance measures, see Brian Graham-Moore and Timothy L. Ross, *Gainsharing: Plans for Improving Performance* (Washington, D.C.: The Bureau of National Affairs, 1990), 48–99.

17. Ibid., 100–115.

18. Adapted from L. Hatcher, T. L. Ross, and Denis Collins, "Attributions for Participation and Nonparticipation in Gainsharing Plan Involvement Systems," *Group & Organization Studies* 16 (1991), 25–43.

19. R. T. Kaufman, "The Effects of Improshare on Productivity," *Industrial and Labor Relations Review* 45 (1992), 311–322.

20. For a case example, see S. E. Markham, K. D. Scott, and W. G. Cox, Jr., "The Evolutionary Development of a Scanlon Plan," *Compensation and Benefits Review,* March–April 1992, 50–56.

21. *Non-Traditional Incentive Pay Programs,* Personnel Policies Forum Survey #148 (Washington D.C.:, The Bureau of National Affairs, 1991), 19.

22. S. Ogden, "The Limits to Employee Involvement: Profit Sharing and Disclosure of Information," *Journal of Management Studies* 29 (1992), 230–246.

23. *Employee Benefits News,* June 1993, 3.

24. For a general discussion, see C. Rosen and K. M. Young, editors, *Understanding Employee Ownership* (Ithaca, NY: ILR Press, 1991).

25. For a discussion of research issues, see Jon L. Pierce, Stephen A. Rubenfeld, and Susan Morgan, "Employee Ownership: A Conceptual Model of Process and Effects," *Academy of Management Review* 16 (1991), 121–144.

26. Lawrence M. Baytos, "Board Compensation Committees: Collaboration or Confrontation?" *Compensation and Benefits Review,* May–June 1991, 33–38; Graef S. Crystal, "Why CEO Compensation Is So High," *California Management Review,* Fall 1991, 9–29; and JoAnn S. Lublin, "Compensation Panels Get More Assertive, Hiring Consultants and Sparking Clashes," *The Wall Street Journal,* July 15, 1992, B1.

27. C. Hill and P. Phan, "CEO Tenure as a Determinant of CEO Pay," *Academy of Management Journal* 34 (1991), 707–717.

28. John McMillan, Ken Allen, and Robert Salwen, "Private Companies Offer Long-Term Incentives," *HR Magazine,* June 1991, 63–66.

29. J. D. England, "Don't Be Afraid of Phantom Stock," *Compensation and Benefits Review,* September–October, 1992, 39–46.

30. For a comprehensive review, see Gomez-Mejia and Balkin, *Compensation, Organizational Strategy, and Firm Performance,* 115–221.

31. "New Regulations for Golden Parachutes," *Perspectives* 1, (1989), 2 and "Silver Parachute Protects Work Force," *Resource,* January 1987, 3.

32. Adapted from Terry Stambaugh, "An Incentive Pay Success Story," *Personnel Journal,* April 1992, 48–54.

CHAPTER 15

EMPLOYEE BENEFITS

After you have read this chapter, you should be able to:

1. Define a benefit and identify approximate average benefit costs.

2. Discuss the provisions of the Family and Medical Leave Act of 1993 and tell how it relates to mandated benefits.

3. Explain two security benefits.

4. List and define at least six pension-related terms.

5. Explain why health-care cost management has become important and list some methods of achieving it.

6. Discuss several types of financial and related benefits.

7. Identify typical patterns of time-off benefits.

8. Discuss benefits communication and flexible benefits as considerations in benefits administration.

HR Today and Tomorrow:
Benefits for Domestic Partners and Spousal Equivalents?

As lifestyles have changed in the U.S., employers are being confronted with requests for benefits by employees who are not married but have close personal relationships with others. The lifestyles giving rise to these requests are:

▲ Gay and lesbian employees requesting benefits for their partners

▲ Unmarried employees who have living arrangements with individuals of the opposite sex

The terminology most often used to refer to individuals with such living arrangements are *domestic partners* or *spousal equivalents.*

The argument made by these employees is that if an employer provides benefits for the spouses of married employees, then benefits should be provided for employees with alternative lifestyles and relationships. This view is reinforced by: (1) more gays and lesbians being open about their lifestyles; and (2) data that show a significant percentage of couples of the opposite sex live together before formally marrying. A Protestant minister in the Midwest is quoted as saying, "In 80% to 90% of all first-time marriages, the couples have been living together for at least a year."

Several cities have passed laws requiring that some types of coverage be extended to domestic partners if an employer provides benefits to the spouses of married employees. For instance, in Sacramento, California, a law requires that unpaid leave be given to domestic partners if leave is given to married workers. The governor of Massachusetts signed an Executive Order extending sick and bereavement leave to all workers with domestic partners.

Some employers have offered benefits to eligible domestic partners voluntarily. Some of the firms with such policies are Lotus Development Corporation, Levi Strauss & Company, and Ben & Jerry's Homemade, Inc. At Lotus, both the employee and the "eligible partner" must sign an "Affidavit of Spousal Equivalence."

In this affidavit, the employee and his/her partner are asked to affirm that:

▲ They are each other's only spousal equivalent

▲ They are of the same sex and/or not blood relatives

▲ They are living together and jointly share responsibility for their common welfare and financial obligations

Also, spousal equivalents are required to sign an affidavit if the relationship ends, and a one-year waiting period is imposed before the employee can sign up another eligible partner.

At Levi Strauss, the benefits for the unmarried partner are considered taxable income to the employee. Most of those signing up for these benefits have been heterosexual women, even though the initial thrust of the policy was to serve the needs of gay and lesbian employees.

There are two major hurdles that firms adopting these policies have found. First, getting conservative managers, most of whom are older with more traditional lifestyles, to accept and have the company "endorse" the alternative lifestyles can be a challenge. Once that resistance is overcome, then getting insurance and benefit providers to give coverage at reasonable costs requires considerable effort by HR experts.

The consequence of having such policies extends beyond providing leaves or health benefits. At Krum and Foster, a large insurance company, providing relocation and job-hunting assistance for domestic partners along with spouse assistance, had to be considered. A software computer firm had to revise its sales incentive awards to allow sales representatives to bring "any other person" on company sales incentive cruises and trips because married sales representatives could bring spouses.

In summary, employers today and in the future must evaluate benefits policies in light of widely varying lifestyles. Undoubtedly, these policies will increase benefits costs for organizations and create more HR management challenges.[1]

We used to call them 'fringe benefits,' but we quit using the word 'fringe' when we saw the magnitude of that figure.

James Morris

A **benefit** is an indirect reward given to employees for organizational membership. The benefits given to employees by an employer represent indirect compensation or tangible rewards in a form other than money. As the opening discussion indicates, employers are being pressured to extend benefits to people formerly not covered—that is, to "domestic partners" or "spousal equivalents." Employers also have growing concerns about the increasing costs and complexities associated with employee benefits.

When the management of employee benefits is considered by HR managers, the operational and technical facets often take precedence over strategic considerations in daily management. However, strategic considerations must be examined also. Some of the strategic issues to be addressed concerning employee benefits are as follows:[2]

▲ How much total compensation, including benefits, should be provided?
▲ What part should benefits be of the total compensation of individuals?
▲ What are the purposes for offering each type of benefit?
▲ What expense levels are acceptable for each benefit offered?
▲ Which employees should be given or offered which benefits?

By answering these questions, HR managers and top executives obtain both strategic and operational perspectives on managing employee benefits programs.

> **▼ A BENEFIT**
>
> is an indirect reward given to employees for organizational membership.

▲ BENEFITS OVERVIEW

Effective management of employee benefits is critical because benefits represent significant expenditures from an employer's point of view. The U.S. Chamber of Commerce surveys a large number of industries on a regular basis to determine the extent of benefit payments. In a recent survey, benefits represented an average of 39.2% of organizational total payroll. As a result, the average employee received $13,126 worth of benefits per year. However, the amount of benefits varied significantly in different fields. For example, an employee in the department store industry averaged 30% of salary in benefits, while an employee in public utilities averaged 44.6% of salary in benefits. Figure 15–1 shows some details from the Chamber of Commerce survey about how a benefit dollar is spent.[3]

Benefits and Taxation

Benefits expenditures have grown because employees get the *value* of the money spent without actually receiving money. That is why benefits generally are not taxed as income to employees, in spite of repeated attempts by the U.S. Internal Revenue Service to do so. For this reason, benefits represent a somewhat more valuable reward to employees than an equivalent cash payment. For example, assume that employee Henry Schmidt is in a 25% tax bracket. If Henry earned $400, he would have to pay $100 in taxes. Then if he had to pay $300 for prescription drugs, he would have had to earn $400 in order to have the $300. But

▲ **Figure 15–1**

How the Benefit Dollar Is Spent

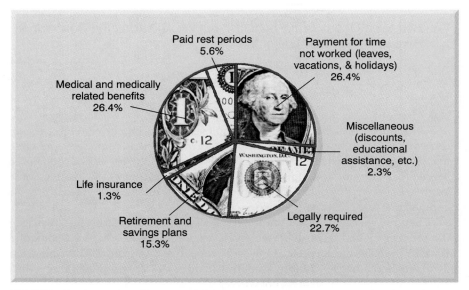

SOURCE: *Employee Benefits, 1992 Edition,* (Washington, D.C.: U.S. Chamber of Commerce, 1992). Used with permission.

if the employer provides prescription drug coverage in a benefit plan, Henry does not claim that amount as income, and therefore doesn't have to pay taxes on it. So benefits are a desirable form of compensation to employees, and more benefits are more desirable. That is a primary reason why the growth in employer benefits costs has been greater than the growth in base pay costs.

Controlling Benefits Costs

Employers, large and small alike, have identified controlling benefits costs as a high priority for HR managers. The greatest cost increases have been those associated with health care. This subject will be discussed in depth later in this chapter under "Health-Care Benefits." Because costs of all types of benefits are projected to rise along with the rising age of the workforce and various other social changes, the management of such costs will increase in importance.

Mandated Benefits

▼ **MANDATED BENEFITS**

are benefits that employers are required by law to provide.

One developing trend is **mandated benefits,** which are benefits that employers are required by law to provide. The concept of mandated employee benefits is not new, because it is reflected in the requirements for Social Security, workers' compensation, and unemployment insurance. Before 1984, employers were required to give few benefits other than these. However, beginning with the Consolidated Omnibus Budget Resolution Act (COBRA) of 1984, federal regulations requiring employers to provide additional benefits began to proliferate.

Some areas in which coverage is mandated or has been proposed include:

▲ Universal health-care benefits provided to all workers
▲ Child-care assistance

▲ Family leave

▲ Pension plan coverage for more workers

▲ Core benefits for part-time employees working at least 500 hours per year

There are several reasons why employers face increasing pressure to provide benefits. A major one is that federal and state governments want to shift many of the social costs for health care and other expenditures to employers. This shift would relieve some of the budgetary pressures facing legislators to raise taxes and cut government spending.

Also, demographic changes in the United States mean that more workers will need child care and older citizens will require more health care. Mandated benefits coverage will force employers to help fund more of these benefits costs.

Employer reactions to efforts to mandate benefits have been swift and vehement. Employers emphasize that small businesses are more heavily burdened because they have smaller staffs to handle the increased work of benefits administration. Fears about the costs of providing the mandated benefits also trigger the reaction. One study estimated that labor costs for businesses would increase at least $40 billion per year if all of the mandated benefits proposed were enacted.[4] As the U.S. workforce ages and becomes more diverse, other benefits issues will arise in which mandatory benefits coverage may be attempted or may occur. Undoubtedly, employers also will continue to resist and lobby against efforts to mandate more benefits.

Family Related Issues

Family related needs include leave to care for family members, child-care assistance, and elder care. They have received increasing attention as a result of workforce and social changes.

Family and Medical Leave Act of 1993 (FMLA)   In 1993, President Clinton signed into law the Family and Medical Leave Act (FMLA), which covers all employers with 50 or more employees within 75 miles of a workplace, and includes federal, state, and private employers. Only employees who have worked at least 12 months or 1,250 hours in the previous year are eligible for leaves under FMLA. The law requires that employers allow eligible employees to take a total of 12 weeks' leave during any 12-month period for one or more of the following situations:

▲ Birth, adoption, or foster-care placement of a child.

▲ Caring for a spouse, child, or parent with a serious health condition.

▲ Serious health condition of the employee.

A **serious health condition** is one requiring inpatient, hospital, hospice, or residential medical care or continuing physician care. Employers may require employees to provide certificates by a doctor verifying such illnesses.

Regarding taking leaves, FMLA provides for the following:

▲ Employees taking family and medical leave must be able to return to the same job or a job of equivalent status or pay.

▲ Health benefits must be continued during the leave at the same level and conditions. If the employee does not return to work for a reason other than serious health problems, the employer may collect the employer-paid portion of the premiums from the nonreturning employee.

▼ **A SERIOUS HEALTH CONDITION**

is one requiring inpatient, hospital, hospice, or residential medical care or continuing physician care.

▲ The leave taken may be intermittent rather than in one block, subject to employee and employer agreements when birth, adoption, or foster-child care is the cause. For serious health conditions, employer approval is not necessary.

▲ Employees can be required to use all paid-up vacation and personal leave before taking unpaid leave.

▲ Employees are required to give 30-day notice, where practical.

All of these provisions will have significant effects on employers and employees alike. Numerous HR policies have had to be revised as a result of this act. It has also required HR managers and other managers to do better staffing, planning, and scheduling.

Child Care   As mentioned in Chapter 2, balancing work and family responsibilities is a major challenge for many workers. Whether single parents or dual-career couples, these employees often experience difficulty in obtaining quality, affordable child care.

Employers are addressing the child-care issue in several ways. Some organizations have established on-site day-care facilities. Costs and concerns about liability and attracting sufficient employee use are major reasons that few on-site facilities have been established. However, at least one study found that on-site child care had a positive impact on employees who used the service. The study found that the greater the use of the care service, the more favorable employees' attitudes toward management.[5]

Other options offered by employers include:

▲ Providing referral services to aid parents in locating child-care providers.

▲ Establishing discounts at day-care centers, which may be subsidized by the employer.

▲ Arranging with hospitals to offer sick-child programs that are partially paid for by employers.

▲ Developing after-school programs for older school-age children, often in conjunction with local public and private school systems.

Elder Care   Another family related issue of growing importance is caring for elderly relatives. Different organizations have surveyed their employees and found that as many as 30% of their employees have had to miss work to care for an aging relative.[6] The responsibilities associated with caring for elderly family members have resulted in reduced work performance, increased absenteeism, and more personal stress for the affected employees. Many more employers will have to respond to this issue as the U.S. population continues to age.

Types of Benefits

Employees are given many different benefits, as shown in Figure 15-2. They are grouped into several types, each of which is discussed in this chapter:

▲ Security benefits
▲ Health-care benefits
▲ Retirement benefits
▲ Financial and other insurance benefits
▲ Social, recreational, and other benefits
▲ Time-off benefits

SECURITY	HEALTH CARE	RETIREMENT
Workers' compensation	Medical	Social Security
Unemployment compensation	Dental	Early retirement
Supplemental unemployment insurance	Vision care	Preretirement counseling
Severance pay	Prescription drugs	Disability retirement benefits
Social Security (retirement, old age, survivor's, and disability insurance)	Psychiatric counseling	Health care for retirees
	HMO or PPO health-care plans	Pension plans
	COBRA provisions	IRA, 401(k), Keogh plans
INSURANCE AND FINANCIAL	**SOCIAL AND RECREATIONAL**	**TIME-OFF**
Life insurance	Tennis courts	Lunch and rest breaks
Disability insurance	Bowling league	Holidays and vacations
Stock plans	Service awards	Family and medical leaves
Financial counseling	Sponsored events (athletic and social)	Military reserve time-off
Company-provided car and expense account	Cafeteria	Election and jury leaves
Educational assistance	Service awards	Funeral and bereavement leaves
Relocation and moving assistance	Recreation program	

▲ **Figure 15–2**

Benefits Classified by Type

▲ SECURITY BENEFITS

Several benefits offer protection and/or security to employees. Some are required by federal and state laws. Others are given voluntarily by management or are made available through provisions in labor/management contracts. *Workers' compensation, unemployment compensation,* and *Social Security* are the most important of the security benefits.

Workers' Compensation

▼ **WORKERS' COMPENSATION**

provides benefits to a person injured on the job.

Workers' compensation provides benefits to a person injured on the job. Starting with the Federal Employees' Compensation Act of 1908 and laws enacted by California, New Jersey, Washington, and Wisconsin in 1911, workers' compensation laws to aid injured employees have spread to all the remaining states. Federal employees are covered under the Federal Employees' Liability Act administered by the Department of Labor.

Workers' compensation requires employers to give cash benefits, medical care, and rehabilitation services to employees for injuries or illnesses occurring within the scope of their employment. Employees are entitled to quick and certain payment from the workers' compensation system without proving that the employer is at fault. In exchange, employees give up the right of legal actions and awards. The employer enjoys limited liability for occupational illnesses and injury.

Employers provide workers' compensation coverage by purchasing insurance from a private carrier or state insurance fund or by providing self-insurance. Employers that self-insure are required to post a bond or deposit securities with the state industrial commission. State laws usually require that employers have a specific number of employees before they are permitted to use self-insurance. Group self-insurance is permitted in some states and is useful for groups of small businesses.[7]

Workers' Compensation and the ADA   Because workers' compensation costs are borne by employers, the types of injuries covered include more than on-the-job physical injuries. Coverage has been expanded in many areas to include emotional impairment that may have resulted from a physical injury, job-related strain, stress, anxiety, or pressure. Some cases of suicide also have been ruled to be job related, with payments due under workers' compensation.[8]

The passage of the Americans with Disabilities Act of 1990 created new problems for employers trying to return injured workers to "light-duty" work in order to reduce workers' compensation costs. However, under the ADA, by making reasonable accommodation through light-duty work, employers may be undercutting what really are *essential job functions.* By making an accommodation for an injured employee, an employer may have to make accommodation for applicants with disabilities.

Criticisms of Workers' Compensation   Costs to employers for workers' compensation have increased dramatically, as shown in Figure 15–3. Costs of workers' compensation claims have risen dramatically also, primarily because of increased litigation expenses and higher medical charges. Another, even more dramatic example is the situation faced by railroads covered by the Federal Employees' Liability Act (FELA). Total payouts under FELA increased about $600 million in ten years.[9]

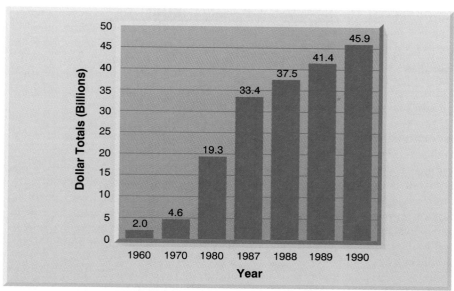

SOURCE: Adapted from information in William H. Miller, "The Costs of Workers' Comp," *Industry Week,* August 17, 1992, 22–28.

Employers with high workers' compensation costs may attempt to reduce them by: (1) improving employee safety through extensive safety training and accident investigation procedures, (2) monitoring employees' rehabilitation to ensure that they are still unable to work, or (3) moving to another state.[10] Consequently, employers continually must watch their workers' compensation expenditures.

Unemployment Compensation

Another benefit required by law is unemployment compensation, established as part of the Social Security Act of 1935. Each state operates its own unemployment compensation system, and provisions differ significantly from state to state.[11]

Employers finance this benefit by paying a tax on the first $7,000 (or more, in 37 states) of annual earnings of each employee. The tax is paid to state and federal unemployment compensation funds. The payment percentages for employers are based upon "experience rates," which reflect the number of claims filed by workers who leave. If an employee is out of work and is actively looking for employment, he or she normally receives up to 26 weeks of pay, at the rate of 50% to 80% of normal pay. Most employees are eligible. However, workers fired for misconduct or those not actively seeking employment generally are ineligible.

Criticism of Unemployment Insurance   Proposed changes in unemployment insurance laws have been introduced in bills at both state and federal levels for two reasons: (1) Abuses are estimated to cost billions each year, and (2) many state unemployment funds are exhausted during economic slowdowns. Some states allow union workers who are on strike to collect unemployment benefits, a provision bitterly opposed by many employers.

Supplemental Unemployment Benefits (SUB)   Supplemental unemployment benefits (SUB) are closely related to unemployment compensation, but they are not required by law. First obtained by the United Steelworkers in 1955, a SUB program is a benefit provision negotiated by a union with an employer as part of the collective bargaining process. The provision requires organizations to contribute to a fund that supplements the unemployment compensation available to employees from federal and/or state sources, or both.

Severance Pay   Severance pay is a security benefit voluntarily offered by employers. Employees who lose their jobs permanently may receive lump-sum payments if they are terminated by the employer. For example, if a facility closes because it is outmoded and no longer economically profitable to operate, the employees who lose their jobs may receive lump-sum payments based on their years of service. Severance pay provisions often appear in union/management agreements and usually provide larger payments for employees with longer service. Many firms also provide *outplacement* assistance in the form of resume writing, interviewing skills workshops, and career counseling.

The Worker Adjustment and Retraining Notification Act (WARN) of 1988 requires that many employers give 60 days' notice if a mass layoff or facility closing is to occur. The act does not require employers to give severance pay.

Social Security

The Social Security Act of 1935, with its later amendments, established a system providing *old age, survivor's, disability,* and *retirement benefits.* Administered by the federal government through the Social Security Administration, this program provides benefits to previously employed individuals. Both employees and employers share in the cost of Social Security by paying a tax on the employee's wages or salaries. Both the percentage of tax paid and the earnings levels covered have increased over time.

Social Security Changes   Because the Social Security system affects a large number of individuals and is government operated, it is a politically sensitive program. Social Security increases are often voted by Congress, and Social Security payments have been tied to the cost of living (through the consumer price index). This action, plus the increasing number of persons covered by the Social Security system, has raised concerns about the availability of future funds from which to pay benefits. An aging population due to increased longevity also may place severe strains on the system. By increasing the payment percentage and the earnings levels against which those percentages apply, congressional representatives hoped to avoid future funding problems. Yet critics believe that future changes will be needed to ensure the viability of the Social Security system after the year 2000.

▲ HEALTH-CARE BENEFITS

Employers provide a variety of health-care and medical benefits. The most common ones cover medical, dental, prescription-drug, and vision-care expenses for employees and their dependents. Basic health-care insurance to cover both normal and major medical expenses is highly desired by employees. Likewise, dental insurance is important to many employees. Many dental plans also have orthodontic coverage, which is usually more costly. Some employer medical insurance plans also cover psychiatric counseling. The rapidly escalating costs of health-care benefits are a major concern for employers.

Rise of Health-Care Costs

Costs for health care in the United States have risen dramatically in the past three decades. In 1960 about $26 billion was spent on health care, representing 5.4% of the nation's gross domestic product (GDP). By the year 1994, health-care costs rose to be $1 trillion, about 16% of the GDP.[12] In a recent year, the cost of health-related benefits rose 10.2% over the previous year, with the average employee receiving $3,465, according to the U.S. Chamber of Commerce survey mentioned earlier.[13] Employers have felt the impact of the increase in costs, as the following examples illustrate:[14]

▲ The costs for health-care benefits add over $900 to every car manufactured by Chrysler, Ford, and General Motors.

▲ DuPont Corporation had health-care costs rise 50% from 1989 to 1993, with a cost of $6,000 per worker being paid each year.

▲ Xerox Corporation has seen health-care costs rise at a rate quadrupling the national inflation rate, despite aggressive cost-management efforts.

▲ Dayton Hudson, a Minneapolis retailer, calculated that it had to sell 39,000 Ninja Turtle toys just to pay for one employee to have an appendectomy, and Goodyear Tire & Rubber had to sell 461 radial passenger car tires to pay for an appendectomy.

▲ A 22-employee firm in Florida spent over $95,000 in health-care benefits costs in one year; a study of small businesses found that health-care costs annually averaged $3,600 per worker for the typical small business.

Health-Care Cost Management

Faced with spiraling costs for health-care benefits, many employers have begun aggressive efforts to manage and control such costs. Instead of offering health insurance to employees and paying all or most of the premiums, employers are using a variety of strategies to contain costs. Figure 15–4 shows some of the

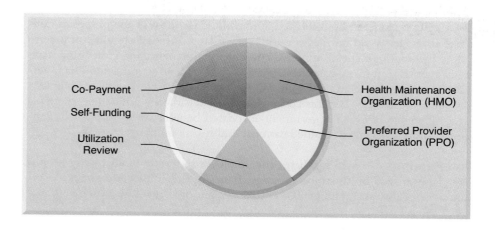

▲ **Figure 15–4**

Health-Care Cost Management Strategies

Co-Payment

Self-Funding

Utilization Review

Health Maintenance Organization (HMO)

Preferred Provider Organization (PPO)

ways employers are attempting to control health-care costs. These strategies are often referred to as *managed care:* co-payment, self-funding, preferred provider organizations (PPOs), health maintenance organizations (HMOs), and utilization review.

Co-payment   In the past, many employers offered what is called *first-dollar coverage.* In this type of coverage, all expenses, from the first dollar of health-care costs, were paid by the employee's insurance, with the exception of costs associated with hospitalized illness covered by major medical plans. Commonly, a small deductible amount was paid by employees for illnesses covered under major medical plans, but many basic coverage plans did not have an employee-paid deductible. Experts say that by having first-dollar coverage in the basic plan, employees may see a doctor for every slight illness, which results in an escalation of the costs of the benefits.

As health insurance costs have risen, employers have attempted to shift some of those costs to employees. The **co-payment** strategy requires employees to pay a portion of costs of both insurance premiums and medical care. Related to this idea is *comprehensive health-care insurance,* which means that employees pay a deductible on all medical-care costs. Many employers also are raising the deductible per person from \$50 to \$200.[15] Such attempts have been met with fierce resistance by unions. Yet, some companies with unionized workforces have used collective-bargaining sessions to demand that workers pay more of the health-benefit costs. As a result, several have experienced strikes by workers who refused to give up health benefits totally paid by their employers. Other employers have required their nonunion employees to pay higher deductibles, obtain second opinions before elective surgery, use designated preferred providers, or pay higher rates.

Some small businesses are dropping their health-care plans to avoid increasing costs. Such action increases the number of uninsured workers in the U.S. It is estimated that about 20% of all workers in the U.S. do not have health-care benefits, which has led to calls for the establishment of national health insurance requirements. Companies and unions endorsing such an approach have included Bethlehem Steel, the United Steelworkers Union, AT&T, the Communications Workers of America, and Chrysler Corporation.

Recognizing the importance of this national health coverage issue, President Clinton in 1993 established a taskforce to develop recommendations and submitted a proposal for universal national health insurance for virtually all people in the U.S. As of the writing of this text, many different counterproposals and provisions were being considered by the U.S. Congress. Under most of the proposals, universal coverage would not begin until 1996 or later. Readers should continue to follow the development of universal coverage requirements and costs using news media reports. But many states have not waited for federal action. Minnesota, Vermont, Florida, and Hawaii are among the states that have passed various laws mandating health-care benefits coverage (discussed earlier).[16] Of course, there is a great difference between government-mandated benefits to be paid for by employers and a government-funded national health-care insurance system.

Self-Funding   In **self-funding,** the employer sets aside funds to pay health-care claims in lieu of insurance coverage. Basically, the employer earmarks a certain amount (for example, \$800,000) to cover normal medical insurance bene-

▼ **CO-PAYMENT**

requires employees to pay a portion of costs of both insurance premiums and medical care.

▼ **SELF-FUNDING**

occurs when an employer sets aside funds to pay health claims in lieu of insurance coverage.

fits. The exact figure is based on an analysis of previous health benefit use patterns. Instead of buying health insurance plans from a firm such as Blue Cross and Blue Shield or Aetna, the employer sets aside funds and also buys an *excess policy*. The employer agrees to pay up to the normal amount ($800,000 in the example) of employees' health-care costs. These plans also are called *stop-loss* plans because the company expenses stop at the set level. The excess policy then provides coverage for all expenses beyond that level.[17] Just as the premium for health-care insurance is much lower for a $1,000 deductible rather than a $100 deductible for an individual, the employer pays significantly less for the excess coverage than it would for a total coverage package.

Furthermore, the employer earns interest on the funds that are set aside because these funds are paid out during the year as employees use their health benefits, rather than at the beginning of the year to pay an insurance premium. Employers can either process the claims themselves or contract with an outside service to administer them. Some large insurance firms even provide this claims administration service for a percentage fee of the value of the claims.

Preferred Provider Organization (PPO)   Another cost-containment strategy is the establishment of a **preferred provider organization (PPO)**, which is a health-care provider that contracts with an employer or an employer group to provide health-care services to employees at a competitive rate. By encouraging employees to use lower-cost providers, employers can reduce their benefit outlays. Hospital-based PPOs and groups of physicians have the assurance of a continuing source of patients, even though employees have the freedom to go to other providers if they want to pay the difference in costs.

> ▼ **A PREFERRED PROVIDER ORGANIZATION (PPO)**
> is a health-care provider that contracts with an employer or an employer group to provide health-care services to employees at a competitive rate.

Utilization Review   Many employers are finding that some of the health care provided by doctors and hospitals is unnecessary, incorrectly billed, and deliberately overcharged. Consequently, both employers and insurance firms are requiring that medical work and charges be audited and reviewed through a **utilization review.** The utilization review process includes the following:[18]

> ▼ **UTILIZATION REVIEW**
> is an audit and review of the services and costs billed by health-care providers.

▲ *Precertification review.* Approval of a second medical opinion is required before employees receive certain elective medical treatments. Such reviews encourage use of outpatient surgery and reduce hospital use.

▲ *Concurrent review.* At the same time that health-care treatment and/or hospitalization begin, the appropriateness of the medical procedures used are reviewed by nurses and doctors hired by the review firm.

▲ *Case management.* Independent medical professionals monitor the treatments given to employees with catastrophic health problems to ensure that they are necessary and that less-costly options are considered.

▲ *Posttreatment bill review.* An independent firm reviews bills submitted by health-care providers to ensure that all charges are appropriate and realistic.

Health Maintenance Organization (HMO)   A unique form of health care is available through a **health maintenance organization (HMO),** which provides services for a fixed period on a prepaid basis. Unlike other health-care benefits, the HMO emphasizes prevention as well as correction. An employer contracts with an HMO, which has doctors and medical personnel on its staff, to furnish complete medical care, except for hospitalization. The employer pays a flat rate per enrolled employee or per family. The covered individuals may then

> ▼ **A HEALTH MAINTENANCE ORGANIZATION (HMO)**
> is a form of health care that provides services for a fixed period on a prepaid basis.

▲   **Figure 15–5**

Increase in Memberships in
HMOs, 1981–1991

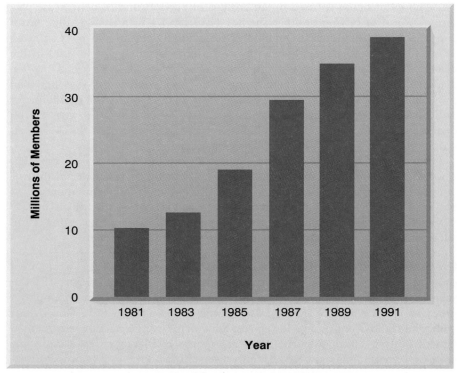

SOURCE: Group Health Association of America, *Employee Benefit News,* July 1992, 3.

go to the HMO for health care as often as they need. Supplemental policies for hospitalization also are used.

The HMO Act of 1973 requires that if employers with 25 or more employees provide other health-care coverage, then they also must offer an HMO as an option to their employees if one is available in the local area. As a result, HMOs have grown in popularity, as shown in Figure 15–5.

Other Cost-Management Efforts   Other means used to contain health-care costs include preventive health and physical *wellness programs, communication efforts,* and *financial incentive programs* to make employees more knowledgeable about health-care costs. Wellness programs try to encourage employees to have more healthy lifestyles. Included in wellness programs are activities such as smoking cessation classes, diet and nutrition counseling, exercise and physical fitness centers and programs, and health education. Wellness programs are discussed in more detail in Chapter 16.

Employers also are educating employees about health-care costs and how to reduce them. Newsletters, formal classes, and many other approaches are used, all of which are designed to make employees more aware about why health-care costs are increasing and what employees can do to control them.

Finally, some employers are offering financial incentives for healthy habits. These programs reward employees who stop smoking, lose weight, wear seat belts, and participate in exercise programs.[19]

Health Insurance

The traditional approach for providing employees health-care benefits has been through health insurance purchased from insurance carriers such as Mutual of Omaha, Aetna, or Blue Cross and Blue Shield.

COBRA Provisions   Legal requirements in the Consolidated Omnibus Budget Reconciliation Act (COBRA) in 1986 increased employer health-care costs. Provisions within the law required that most employers (except churches and the federal government) with 20 or more employees offer *extended health-care coverage* to the following groups:

▲ Employees who voluntarily or involuntarily quit, except those terminated for "gross misconduct."
▲ Widowed or divorced spouses and dependent children of former or current employees.
▲ Retirees and their spouses whose health-care coverage ends.

Employers must notify appropriate employees and/or their spouses within 60 days after the employees quit, die, get divorced, or change their status. The extended coverage must be offered for 18 to 36 months, depending on the qualifying circumstances. The employer may charge no more than 102% of the premium costs to insure a similarly covered employee, but the individual not employed by the organization must pay the premiums.

For most employers, the COBRA requirements mean additional paperwork and related costs. For example, firms must not only track the former employees but also notify their qualified dependents. The 2% premium addition generally does not cover all relevant costs, which often run several percentage points more. Consequently, additional management efforts to reduce overall health benefits costs become even more important.

▲ RETIREMENT-RELATED BENEFITS

A widespread package of benefits offered by most employers attempts to provide income for employees when they retire. Few people have independent reserves to use when they retire. However, financial resources represent only one facet of the broader issue of retirement policies.

Retirement Policies

As a result of a 1986 amendment to the Age Discrimination in Employment Act, most employees can no longer be forced to retire at any age. Employers have developed different policies to comply with these regulations. "Normal retirement" is the age at which employees can retire and collect full pension benefits. Employers must decide whether or not individuals who continue work past age 65 should receive the full benefits package, especially pension credits. As changes in Social Security increase the age for full benefits past 65, these policies likely will be modified.

Despite removing mandatory retirement provisions, the age at which individuals retire has continued to decline in the United States. In 1990, the average retirement age was 62, and it is projected by the U.S. Bureau of Labor Statistics to decline only slightly by the year 2000.[20]

Early Retirement   Provisions for early retirement currently are included in many pension plans. Early retirement gives people an opportunity to get away from a long-term job. Individuals who have spent 25 or 30 years working for the same employer may wish to use their talents in other areas. Phased-in and part-time retirements also are used by some individuals and firms.

Some employers use early retirement buyout programs to cut back their workforce and reduce costs. Care must be taken to make the early retirement programs truly voluntary. Forcing workers to take advantage of an early retirement buyout program has led to age discrimination suits.

Preretirement Counseling

Preretirement counseling is aimed at easing employees' anxieties and preparing them for retirement and the benefits associated with it. The biological changes of aging may be a concern, but suddenly having no job can cause even more anxiety and stress. Preretirement counseling should not begin just before retirement; it should be a systematic process of gradual preparation. Topics most frequently covered are health, housing, Social Security, legal and financial considerations, and use of leisure time.

Health-Care Benefits for Retirees

As people age, their health problems may intensify. Prolonged hospital stays can be extremely costly, and many older persons worry about having sufficient resources to sustain them through serious illnesses—and after. However, the federal government provides some medical assistance to all elderly persons who are covered by Social Security through Medicare, beginning at age 65.

The cost of retiree health benefits has been growing. For example, at B. F. Goodrich in 1993, there were 10,000 retirees and 14,000 active employees covered under health plans. Goodrich spent $25 million to $30 million a year on retiree heath benefits.[21]

Employers have tried to combat rising costs by trying such strategies as:

▲ Cancelling retiree health-care benefits, especially if retirees take other jobs offering benefit coverage. (See the "HR Perspective.")

▲ Restricting retirement benefits for current retirees by raising deductibles, cutting coverage, or reducing employer contributions.

▲ Lobbying for tax law changes to allow employers to tap excess pension benefits to fund retiree health-care costs, resulting in lower pension payments to retirees.

To ensure that firms adequately reflected the liabilities for retiree health benefits, the Financial Accounting Standards Board (FASB) in 1992 issued a rule requiring firms to establish accounting reserves for funding retiree health-care benefits. Prior to 1992, most firms did not set aside funds for these benefits, and most paid those costs out of current yearly income. FASB Rule 106 affected many firms because they have to reflect the liability on financial statements and reduce their current earnings each year to fund the retiree health-care benefits. Huge write-offs against earnings were taken in 1993 by many firms in order to comply with FASB 106. For instance, AT&T took a one-time charge of $7.5 billion, and General Motors charged $23 billion against earnings in 1993.

HR Perspectives:
The Ethics of Cutting Retirees' Health Benefits

For many retirees the pension and health-care benefits provided by their former employers are the core of their retirement security, both financial and emotional. At the same time, pension benefits and retiree health-care costs represent major expenses and/or a source for additional savings for employers, but there is another dimension to this issue: *How ethical is it for a firm to cap or cut the pensions and health-care benefits offered to retired former employees?*

Firms argue that cutting retiree health-care benefits must be done if current employee health-care benefits are being reduced. If a firm puts an 80% reimbursement limit on existing

employees, why shouldn't retirees face the same limit? These cutbacks also may be necessary for some firms to remain cost competitive and preserve jobs for current employees.

On the other hand, retirees argue that having given 20 or more years service to a company, they should continue to receive the same level of benefits that they received as employees. Some retirees, assisted by the American Association of Retired Persons (AARP), have sued their employers for violating the legal terms of benefit plans as described in employee handbooks, retirement planning sessions, and benefit plan descriptions. The court decisions

generally have depended upon the exact language in each firm's plan and what was said to retirees about their health-care benefits. As a result, employers are being advised to make no future promises and to specifically state that the company can change retiree health-care benefits at any time.[22]

This issue raises troubling ethical concerns. Many of the retirees worked for their employers for 20, 30, 40 years, or more. Yet the reward for long and loyal service increasingly is a reduction in health-care benefits for those retirees.

Pensions

A second group of retirement benefits is provided through **pension plans** established and funded by employers and employees. Because organizations are not required to offer pension plans to employees, only 40% to 50% of U.S. workers are covered by them. Smaller firms offer them less often than large ones. Many firms do not offer pension plans primarily because of the costs and administrative burdens imposed by government legislation.

Employee Retirement Income Security Act (ERISA)   Many firms do not offer any benefits, including pensions, to part-time employees who work fewer than 1,000 hours in a year as required by the Employee Retirement Income Security Act (ERISA) for the provision of benefits. It was widespread criticism of pension plans that led to the passage of ERISA in 1974. The purpose of this law and subsequent amendments to it is to regulate private pension plans in order to assure that employees who put money into them or depend on a pension for retirement funds actually will receive the money when they retire.

Pension Contributions   Pension plans can be either contributory or noncontributory. In a **contributory plan** money for pension benefits is paid in by both employees and employers. In a **noncontributory plan,** an employer provides all the funds. As would be expected, the noncontributory plan is preferred by employees and labor unions.

▼ **PENSION PLANS**

are retirement benefits established and funded by employers and employees.

▼ **A CONTRIBUTORY PLAN**

is one in which the money for pension benefits is paid in by both employees and employers.

▼ **A NONCONTRIBUTORY PLAN**

is one in which all the funds for pension benefits are provided by the employer.

▼ **A DEFINED-CONTRIBUTION PLAN**

is one in which the employer makes an annual payment to an employee's pension account.

▼ **A DEFINED-BENEFIT PLAN**

is one in which an employee is promised a pension amount based on age and service.

▼ **PORTABILITY**

is a pension plan feature that allows employees to move their pension benefits from one employer to another.

▼ **VESTING**

is the right of employees to receive benefits from their pension plans.

Pension Benefits   Pension plans can pay benefits based on one of two types of plans. A **defined-contribution plan** is one in which the employer makes an annual payment to an employee's pension account. The key to this plan is the *contribution rate;* employee retirement benefits depend on fixed contributions and employee earnings levels. Profit-sharing plans, employee stock ownership plans (ESOPs), and thrift plans often are defined-contribution plans. Because these plans hinge on the investment returns of the previous contributions, which can vary according to profitability or other factors, employees' retirement benefits are less secure and predictable. But because of their structure, they are preferred by younger, shorter-service employees.

A **defined-benefit plan** is one in which an employee is promised a pension amount based on age and service. In this plan the employer's contributions are determined by actuarial calculations that focus on the *benefits* to be received by employees after retirement and the *methods* used to determine such benefits. The amount of an individual employee's benefits is determined by the person's length of service with the organization and the person's average earnings over a five-year or longer period. A defined-benefit plan gives the employee greater assurance of benefits and greater predictability in the amount of benefits that will be available at retirement. Therefore, it generally is preferred by older workers.

If the funding in a defined-benefit plan is insufficient, the employers may have to make up the shortfall. Therefore, a growing number of employers are dropping defined-benefit plans in favor of defined-contribution plans so that they have a known contribution liability.[23]

Portability   Another feature of some employee pensions is **portability.** In a portable plan, employees can move their pension benefits from one employer to another. A commonly used portable pension system in colleges and universities is the Teacher Insurance Annuity Association (TIAA) system. Under this system, any faculty or staff member who accumulates pension benefits at one university can transfer these benefits to another university within the TIAA system.

If individuals are not in a portable system, they must take a *lump-sum settlement* of money that they contributed to the plan plus accumulated interest on their contributions when they leave. Unless their pensions are vested, they do not receive the employer's contribution. But they can roll the lump sum over into an individual retirement account (IRA) or other retirement plan.

Vesting Rights   Certain rights are attached to employee pension plans. The right of employees to receive benefits from their pension plans is **vesting.** Typically, vesting assures employees of a certain pension, provided they have worked a minimum number of years. If employees resign or are terminated before they are vested (that is, before they have been employed for the required time), no pension rights accrue to them except the funds that they have contributed. If employees stay the allotted time, they retain their pension rights and receive benefits from the funds contributed by both the employer and themselves.

Discrimination in Pension Plans   The pension plan area is like many others in the HR management area—it is constantly changing. The more recent changes highlighted in this section are concerned with making pension plans nondiscriminatory. The term *nondiscriminatory* has two different meanings here: (1) discrimination favoring highly compensated individuals and (2) discrimination against women.

The Tax Reform Act of 1986 contained a provision, referred to as Section 89, to ensure that qualified retirement plans did not unreasonably benefit "highly compensated individuals." The section required that at least 70% of the non-highly compensated employees be covered by the pension plan if one existed. Other stipulations also were included. The proposed rules were extremely complex and would have required significant administrative costs for employers to comply with them. As a result of the number of complaints, Congress repealed Section 89 in November 1989. However, it is likely that simpler regulations will be drafted in order to ensure that pension plans are set up to benefit all employees, not just highly paid individuals.

Statistics have shown that women generally live longer than men. As a result, before 1983 women received lower benefits for the same contributions made by men. However, this kind of discrimination was declared illegal by a U.S. Supreme Court decision against pension plans that required women to contribute greater amounts because they live longer, as a group. The *Arizona Governing Committee v. Norris* ruling forced pension plan administrators to use "unisex" mortality tables that do not reflect the gender differential in mortality.[24] To bring legislation in line with this decision, the Retirement Equity Act was passed in 1984 as an amendment to ERISA and the Internal Revenue Code. It liberalized pension regulations that affect women, guaranteed access to benefits, prohibited pension-related penalties during absences from work, such as maternity leave, and lowered the vesting age.

Pension Plan Terminations and Asset Use   ERISA has provided rules to restrict employers' actions in order to protect those who contributed to pension plans. However, a significant number of firms, especially smaller ones, have terminated their pension plans. ERISA also probably has had the effect of limiting the number of new plans introduced because compliance is seen as too costly. The greatest difficulty in complying with ERISA seems to be the voluminous paperwork required in record keeping and reporting.

A fairly recent and potentially dangerous use of pension funds is as a source of financing for companies acquiring other firms. For example, when a West German company bought Great Atlantic & Pacific Tea (A&P), it borrowed a large amount of the money for the purchase. Once the purchase was completed, the German firm used $200 million in excess A&P pension funds to pay much of the debt of the acquisition. Other corporate raiders also have terminated pension plans and used the excess assets to pay down the debt used to acquire the firm. For retirees, such use of pension assets puts their pension benefits at greater risk and may lead to reduced benefits. It is likely that legislative efforts to restrict practices such as these will be proposed in the future.

Individual Retirement Benefit Options

The availability of retirement benefit options makes the pension area more complex. Three options are individual retirement accounts (IRAs), 401(k) plans, and Keogh plans.

Individual Retirement Account (IRA)   An **individual retirement account (IRA)** allows an employee to set aside funds in a special account, keeping them tax deferred until the employee retires. The major advantages of an IRA are the ability to accumulate extra retirement funds and the shifting of taxable

▼ AN INDIVIDUAL RETIREMENT ACCOUNT (IRA)
allows an employee to set aside funds in a special account, keeping them tax deferred until the employee retires.

income to later years, when total income, and therefore taxable income is likely to be lower. Until 1987 many workers took advantage of IRAs offered by financial institutions, insurance companies, and brokerage firms. However, with the passage of the Tax Reform Act of 1986, IRA use became more limited.

▼ **A 401(k) PLAN**

allows employees to receive cash or to have employer contributions from profit-sharing and stock-bonus plans placed into a tax-deferred account.

401(k) Plan   The **401(k) plan** gets its name from Section 401(k) of the federal tax code. It allows employees to choose whether to receive cash or have employer contributions from profit-sharing and stock-bonus plans placed into tax-deferred accounts. Because of the deferral feature, 401(k) plans also are called *salary reduction plans.* In these plans employees can elect to have their current pay reduced by a certain percentage and that amount paid into a 401(k) plan.

The use of 401(k) plans and the assets in them has grown significantly in the past few years, as is shown in Figure 15–6. By 1995 over $440 billion will be invested in 401(k) plans, up from $290 billion in 1992. The advantage to employees is that they can save up to approximately $8,500 per year (as a ceiling) of pre-tax income toward their retirement. Typically, employers match employee contributions at a 50% rate up to a certain percentage of employee pay, and often employees can contribute additional funds of their own up to the ceiling set by the Internal Revenue Service.[25]

▼ **KEOGH PLAN**

allows self-employed individuals to establish an individualized pension plan.

Keogh Plan   A **Keogh plan** is a special type of retirement plan that allows self-employed persons to establish individualized pension plans. These individuals can set aside a percentage of their incomes into pension accounts. Keogh

▲ **Figure 15–6**

Growth of 401(k) Plans

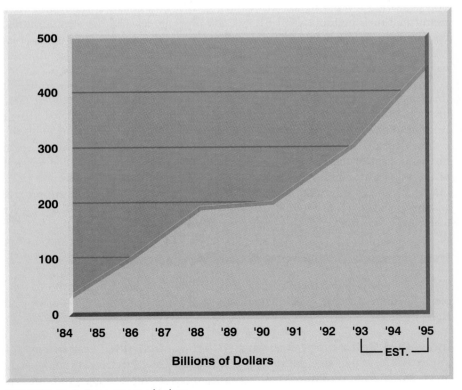

SOURCE: U. S. Department of Labor.

plans can either be defined contributions or defined benefits in nature. Because of the complexity and special regulations covering Keogh plans, it is not unusual that advice from tax specialists must be obtained by self-employed individuals.

▲ FINANCIAL AND RELATED BENEFITS

Employers may offer workers a wide range of special benefits—financial benefits, insurance benefits, educational benefits, social benefits, and recreational benefits. From the point of view of the employer, such benefits can be useful in attracting and retaining employees. Workers like receiving special benefits because they are not taxed as income.

Financial Benefits

Financial benefits can include a wide variety of items. A *credit union* provides savings and lending services for employees. *Purchase discounts* allow employees to buy goods or services from their employers at reduced rates. For example, a furniture manufacturer may allow employees to buy furniture at wholesale cost plus 10% or a bank may offer the use of a safety deposit box and free checking to its employees.

Employee *thrift, saving,* or *stock investment plans* may be made available. Some employers match a portion of the employee's contribution. These plans are especially attractive to executive and managerial personnel. To illustrate, in a stock purchase plan the corporation provides matching funds equal to the amount invested by the employee to purchase stock. In this way, employees can benefit from the future growth of the corporation. Also, it is hoped that employees will develop a greater loyalty and interest in the organization and its success.

Financial planning and counseling are especially valuable to executives who may need information on investments, tax shelters, and comprehensive financial counseling because of their higher levels of compensation. One survey found that 45% of the firms surveyed already offer or plan to offer financial planning to employees.[26] These financial planning benefits likely will grow as a greater percentage of workers approach retirement age.

Numerous other financial-related benefits may be offered, such as the use of a company car, company expense accounts, and relocation assistance in buying or selling a house when an employee is transferred.

Other Insurance Benefits

In addition to health-related insurance, some employers also provide other types of insurance. These benefits have major advantages for employees because many employers pay some or all of the costs. In addition, cheaper insurance rates are available through group programs.

Life Insurance   It is common for employers to provide *life insurance* for employees. Life insurance is bought as a group policy, and the employer pays all or some of the premiums, but the level of coverage is usually low and is tied to an employee's base pay. A typical level of coverage is one-and-a-half or two times an employee's annual salary. Some executives may get higher coverage as part of executive compensation packages.

Disability Insurance   Other insurance benefits frequently tied to employee pay levels are *short-term* or *long-term disability insurance*. This type of insurance provides continuing income protection for employees if they become disabled and unable to work. Long-term disability insurance is much more common because many employers cover short-term disability situations by allowing employees to accrue the sick leave granted annually.

Legal Insurance   As society becomes more complex, more people need legal assistance. However, attorney fees have increased to the point that many who need such assistance with wills, contracts, divorces, and other situations cannot afford legal advice. An insurance plan that pays a portion of legal fees saves the employees money because the fees are paid with pretax dollars, rather than from the employees' take-home pay.

Educational Benefits

Another benefit used by employees comes in the form of *educational assistance* to pay for some or all costs associated with formal education courses and degree programs, including the costs of books and laboratory materials. Some employers pay for schooling on a proportional schedule, depending on the grades received by employees; other simply require a passing grade of C or above.

Tax Status of Educational Benefits   Unless the education paid for by the employer meets certain conditions, the cost of the education aid must be counted as taxable income by employees. To qualify as nontaxable income under Section 127 of the Internal Revenue Code, the education must be:[27]

▲ *Job related,* such that it is used to maintain or improve a person's skills for the current job
▲ *Expressly required,* either to meet specific current job requirements or for the person to maintain required professional standing, such as licenses or continuing education.
▲ *Above minimum standards,* meaning that it is not education that is necessary for the person to qualify for a job initially

Because of U.S. federal budget deficits, repeated attempts have been made to include all educational benefits as taxable income to employees, thereby raising the taxes to be paid by employees using those benefits. Some proposals have attempted to narrow the criteria for deciding if education is job related and expressly required. As of the writing of this text, those efforts have been unsuccessful, so that many of the employer-paid courses under tuition-aid plans remain nontaxable to employees.

Social and Recreational Benefits

Some benefits and services are social and recreational in nature, such as bowling leagues, picnics, parties, employer-sponsored athletic teams, organizationally owned recreational lodges, and other sponsored activities and interest groups. As interest in employee wellness has increased, more firms are providing recreational facilities and activities. But employers should retain control of all events associated with their organizations because of possible legal responsibility. The idea behind social and recreation programs is to promote employee happiness and team

HR Perspectives:
Unusual Benefits

Many employers offer their employees a wide range of benefits other than those normally provided. Food services, counseling services, paid professional memberships, uniforms, and employee discounts are common ones. Often the benefits given are tied to the goods and services provided by the firms.

But other firms offer more unusual benefits as the following examples illustrate:

▲ Employees at Ben and Jerry's, the New England-based ice cream firm, are allowed to have up to three pints of ice cream per day free.

▲ Most airlines allow employees to fly free on a stand-by basis, and immediate family members of airline employees can fly stand-by at significantly reduced rates.

▲ A Livermore, California, employer, Lawrence Livermore National Laboratory, sponsors over 100 clubs for employees. Employees join based upon their interests and the clubs meet after work hours. Karate, chess, and computers are just three clubs that exist.

▲ Numerous firms have "dress-down" or "jeans" days, often on Fridays. Microsoft, the large software firm, has no dress code anytime.

▲ Free breakfast every day is given to employees at Computer Associates International, based in Islandia, N.Y.

▲ The manufacturer of Budweiser and Michelob beer, Anheuser-Busch, allows employees to take home two cases of beer per month at no cost.

▲ Because of unhappiness with the local school system in Moorpark, California, the owner of a 25-employee plumbing company established a school for employees' children in a company warehouse. Operating for more than six years, the school serves 15-20 students each year.

▲ Apple Computer gives each new employee a free personal computer.

▲ On their birthdays each employee at Mary Kay Cosmetics in Dallas, Texas, receives a birthday card and a coupon for a free lunch or movie tickets for two. After five years with the company, employees receive a $100 U.S. Savings Bond.

The reason that organizations offer such benefits is to reward employees in ways not readily available at other organizations. Hopefully, greater employee loyalty will be created, which will enhance employee retention. Also, offering unusual benefits may help differentiate employers when recruiting workers, particularly scarce-skilled professionals and managers.[28]

spirit. Employees *may* appreciate this type of benefit, but managers should not necessarily expect increased job productivity or job satisfaction as a result. Other benefits too numerous to detail here are made available by various employers as well. The "HR Perspective" describes some of them.

▲ TIME-OFF BENEFITS

Employers give employees paid time-off for a variety of circumstances. Paid lunch breaks and rest periods, holidays, and vacations are the most well known. But leaves are given for a number of other purposes as well. A study of time-off benefits for firms with fewer than 100 employees found that those benefits represent a cost of 5% of total compensation or an average of 68 cents per hour for each employee.[29] Some of the more common time-off benefits include holiday pay, vacation pay, and leaves of absence.

Holiday Pay

Most, if not all, employers provide pay for a variety of holidays, as Figure 15–7 shows. Other holidays are offered to some employees through selected laws or

Figure 15–7

Paid Holidays

Rank	Holiday	%Off
1.	Christmas	100%
2.	New Year's Day	99
3.	Thanksgiving	99
4.	Independence Day	99
5.	Labor Day	99
6.	Memorial Day	98
7.	Day after Thanksgiving	63
8.	Presidents Day	45
9.	Good Friday	40
10.	Christmas Eve	38
11.	New Year's Eve	22
12.	Veterans Day	20
13.	Columbus Day	18
14.	Martin Luther King, Jr. Day	17
15.	Employee's Birthday	16

SOURCE: Adapted from *Omaha World-Herald,* January 16, 1992, B18.

union contracts. As an abuse–control measure, employers commonly require employees to work the last scheduled day before the holiday and the first scheduled workday after a holiday to be eligible for holiday pay. Also, some employers pay time-and-a-half to hourly employees who must work holidays. Some exempt employees can take "comp time" (compensatory time-off) and have a different day off with their managers' agreement.

Vacation Pay

Paid vacations are a common benefit. Employees often have graduated vacation-time scales based on length of service. Some organizations also allow employees to accumulate unused vacation.[30] As with holiday pay, employees often are required to work the day before and the day after vacations to prevent abuse.

Leaves of Absence

Leaves of absence as time-off with or without pay are given for a variety of reasons. All of the leaves discussed next add to employer costs even when they are unpaid, because usually the missing employee's work must be covered, sometimes by other employees working overtime or by contracting for temporary employees.

Family Leave   As mentioned earlier in the chapter, the passage of the Family and Medical Leave Act of 1993 helped clarify the rights of employees and the responsibilities of most employers. Even though *paternity leave* for male-workers is available, a relatively low percentage of men take it. The primary reason for the low usage is a perception that it is not as socially acceptable for men to stay home for child-related reasons. That view likely will change as a result of there being more dual-career couples in the workforce.

Medical and Sick Leave   Medical and sick leave are closely related. Many employers allow their employees to miss a limited number of days because of illness without losing pay. Some employers allow employees to accumulate unused sick leave, which may be used in case of catastrophic illnesses. Others pay employees for unused sick leave.

Some organizations have shifted emphasis to reward people who do not use sick leave by giving them **well-pay**—extra pay for not taking sick leave. Other employers have made use of the **earned-time plan,** which is a plan that combines sick leave, vacations, and holidays into a total number of hours or days that employees can take off with pay. One organization found that when it stopped designating a specific number of sick-leave days and an earned-time plan was implemented, absenteeism dropped, time-off was scheduled better, and employee acceptance of the leave policy improved.

Other Leaves Other types of leaves are given for a variety of purposes. Some, such as *military leave, election leave,* and *jury leave,* are required by various state and federal laws, although employers commonly pay the difference between the employee's regular pay and the military, election, or jury pay. Some firms grant employees time-off and give them regular pay while the employees also receive military pay. Federal law prohibits taking discriminatory action against military reservists by requiring them to take vacation time in order to attend summer camp or other training sessions. However, the leave request must be reasonable and truly required by the military.

Funeral or *bereavement leave* is another common leave offered. This leave is usually up to three days for immediate family members, as specifically defined in many employers' policy manuals and employee handbooks. Some policies also give unpaid time-off for the death of more distant relatives or friends.

▼ **WELL-PAY**

is extra pay for not taking sick leave.

▼ **AN EARNED-TIME PLAN**

is one that combines all time-off benefits into a total number of hours or days that employees can take off with pay.

▲ BENEFITS ADMINISTRATION

With the myriad of benefits and regulations, it is easy to see why many organizations must have coordinated efforts to administer a benefits program. Figure 15–8 shows how benefits administration responsibilities can be split between HR specialists and other managers. Notice that the greatest role is played by HR specialists, but managers are responsible for the communication aspects of benefits administration.

Benefits Communication

Employees generally are rather ignorant about the values and costs associated with benefits they receive from employers. Yet, as the "HR Perspective" indi-

HR UNIT	MANAGERS
▲ Develops and administers benefit systems	▲ Answer simple questions on benefits
▲ Answers employees' technical questions on benefits	▲ Maintain liaison with HR specialists on benefits
▲ Assists employees in filing benefit claims	▲ Maintain good communications with employees near retirement
▲ Coordinates special preretirement programs	

▲ **Figure 15–8**

Typical Benefits Administration Responsibilities

HR Perspectives:
Research on Benefits Communications

Researchers have examined the link between benefits communication and how employees view their benefits. As described in *Personnel Psychology,* Dreker, Ash, and Bretz examined how benefit coverage and employee cost sharing affect employees' satisfaction with their total compensation. To conduct the research they examined pay and benefit practices at eight different state highway patrol departments. Before surveying employee satisfaction, the researchers interviewed HR specialists at each organization and reviewed relevant policy and procedure documentation.

Following this internal review, a cover letter and survey were sent to 2,925 persons, of whom 1,433

returned surveys, a 49% response. First, the survey asked for basic demographic data such as state, gender, age, years of service, education level, etc. This was followed by 18 questions on pay satisfaction, in which respondents chose answers on a five-point scale. Finally, participants were asked to compare their benefits with those provided by similar law enforcement agencies by rating each type of benefit on a five-point scale.

The results offered some interesting insights. As would be expected, respondents generally indicated that benefit satisfaction increased with improved benefit coverage and decreased when higher costs were borne by the individuals. Also, the

more accurate the information about actual coverage levels that individuals had, the greater their benefit satisfaction. Little consistent relationship was found between pay level satisfaction and benefit satisfaction.

The authors concluded that improving benefit satisfaction (even when providing additional benefit coverage) is directly linked to the quality and extent of the benefits communications efforts made by employers. As more and more organizations contemplate shifting cost to employees, employers must give greater attention to better benefits communications programs.[31]

cates, benefits communication and benefits satisfaction are linked. Many employers have instituted special benefits communication systems to inform employees about the value of the benefits provided. Explaining benefits during new employee orientation programs, holding periodic meetings, preparing special literature, and using in-house employee publications to heighten awareness of benefits are among the methods used.

Many employers also give employees an annual "personal statement of benefits" that translates benefits into dollar amounts. Federal regulations under ERISA require that employees receive an annual pension-reporting statement, which also can be included in personal statements. By having a personalized statement, each employee can see how much his or her own benefits are worth. Employers are hopeful that by educating employees on benefits costs, expenditures can be managed better and the employees will have a higher appreciation for the employers' payments.

Flexible Benefits

▼ **A FLEXIBLE BENEFITS PLAN**

allows employees to select the benefits they prefer from groups of benefits established by the employer.

A **flexible benefits plan,** sometimes called a *flex* or *cafeteria* plan, allows employees to select the benefits they prefer from groups of benefits established by the employer. By making a variety of "dishes," or benefits, available, the organization allows each employee to select an individual combination of benefits within some overall limits. As a result of the changing composition of the workforce, flexible benefits plans have grown in popularity. These systems recognize that individual employee situations differ because of age, family status, and lifestyles. For instance, individuals in dual-career marriages may not want the same benefits from two different employers. Under a flex plan, one of them can forgo some benefits available in the spouse's plan and take other benefits instead.

Flexible Spending Accounts   Under current tax laws (Section 125 of the Tax Code administered by the Internal Revenue Service), employees can divert some income before taxes into accounts to fund certain benefits. A **flexible spending account** allows employees to contribute pretax dollars to buy additional benefits. An example helps to illustrate the advantage of these accounts to employees. Assume an employee earns $3,000 per month. Further, he has $100 per month deducted to put into flexible spending accounts. That $100 does not count as gross income for tax purposes, thus reducing his amount of taxable income. Then the employee uses the money in his account to purchase additional benefits.

Under tax law at the time of this writing, the funds in the account can be used only to purchase the following: (1) *additional health care* (including offsetting deductibles); (2) *life insurance;* (3) *disability insurance;* or (4) *dependent-care benefits.* However, tax regulations require that if the employees do not spend all of the money in their accounts by the end of the year, they must take the remaining balance as cash and pay income tax on it or forfeit it. Therefore, it is important that employees estimate very closely the additional benefits they will use.

These plans have grown in popularity as more flexible benefits plans have been adopted by more employers. Of course, such plans and their tax advantages can be changed as Congress passes future health-care and tax-related legislation.

▼ **A FLEXIBLE SPENDING ACCOUNT**

allows employees to contribute pre-tax dollars to buy additional benefits.

Advantages of Flexible Benefits Plans   The flexible benefits approach has several advantages. First, this scheme takes into consideration the complexity of people and situations. Because employees in an organization have different desires and needs, they can *tailor benefit packages* to fit their individual life situations within the limits of legal restrictions.

The second advantage, and certainly an important one to most employers, is that flex plans can aid in *benefits cost-control efforts.* The impact of flex plans is seen in a study done over several years that compared flex plans with the more fixed types. The study found that employers without flex plans had medical-care costs rise 41.1% while employers with flex plans experienced an increase of only 22.7%.[32] Although employers without flex plans could take some cost-containment steps, the decision by employers to reduce benefits or increase required employees' co-payments is made easier and is more palatable to employees by integrating these measures into flex plans.

Another advantage of the flexible benefits approach is heightened *employee awareness* of the cost and the value of the benefits. By having to determine the benefits they will receive, employees know what the trade-offs are.

The fourth advantage is that employers with flexible benefits plans can recruit, hire, or retain employees more easily because of the *attractiveness* of flexible plans. By being able to tailor benefits to their needs, employees may not be as interested in shifting to other employers with fixed benefits plans.

Disadvantages of Flexible Benefits Plans   The flexible approach to benefits is not without some drawbacks. The major problem is the *complexity* of keeping track of what each individual chooses, especially if there are a large number of employees. Sophisticated computer software is now available to manage these complexities. Also, the *increase in benefits communications costs* is a concern. As more benefits are made available, employees may not be able to understand the options because the benefits structure and its provisions often become quite complicated.

A third problem is that an *inappropriate benefits package* may be chosen by employees. A young construction worker might not choose disability benefits; however, if he or she is injured, the family may suffer financial hardship. Part of this problem can be overcome by requiring employees to select a core set of benefits (life, health, and disability insurance) and then offering options on other benefits.

A final problem can be **adverse selection,** which means that only higher-risk employees select and use certain benefits. Because many insurance plans are based on a group rate, the employer may face higher rates if insufficient numbers of employees select an insurance option.

Despite these disadvantages, it is likely that flex plans will continue to grow in popularity. The ability to match benefits to differing employee needs, while also controlling some costs, is so attractive that employers will try to find ways to overcome the disadvantages while attuning their benefits plans to the 1990s.

▼ **ADVERSE SELECTION**

means that only higher-risk employees select and use certain benefits.

▲ Summary

▲ Benefits provide additional compensation to employees as a reward for organizational membership.

▲ Because benefits generally are not taxed, they are highly desired by employees. As a result, the average employee now receives an amount equal to about 38% of his or her pay in benefit compensation.

▲ Employers in the 1990s face major benefits issues. Three prominent ones are mandated benefits, health-care cost containment, and family related issues.

▲ Mandatory benefits means that employers are required by law to provide certain benefits previously offered voluntarily.

▲ Family related challenges for the 1990s include complying with the Family and Medical Leave Act of 1993 and offering both child-care and elder-care assistance.

▲ The general types of benefits include those for security, retirement, health care, financial, social and recreational, and time-off.

▲ Workers' compensation, unemployment compensation, and Social Security are three prominent security-oriented benefits.

▲ Health-care benefits are the most costly insurance-related benefits. Employers have become more aggressive in managing their health-care costs through co-payments, self-funding, preferred provider organizations, health maintenance organizations, and utilization review.

▲ Organizations that provide retirement-related benefits should develop policies on early retirement, offer preretirement counseling, and plan how to integrate Social Security benefits into employees' benefit plans.

▲ Retiree health-care costs represent an area of increasing employer concern for employers.

▲ The pension area is a complex area governed by the Employee Retirement Income Security Act (ERISA). There are a number of key terms that must be learned in order to understand ERISA.

▲ Individual Retirement Accounts, 401(k) plans, and Keogh plans are important individual options available for supplementing retirement benefits.

▲ Various types of insurance, financial planning, tuition aid, and other benefits that employers may offer enhance the appeal of benefits to employees.

▲ Holiday pay, vacation pay, and various leaves of absence are means of providing time-off–related benefits to employees.

▲ Because of the variety of benefit options available and the costs involved, employers need to develop systems to communicate these options and costs to their employees.

▲ Flexible benefits systems, which can be tailored to individual needs and situations, have grown in popularity.

▲ REVIEW AND DISCUSSION QUESTIONS

1. Why have benefits grown in strategic importance to employers?
2. Discuss the following statement: "Employers should expect that more benefits issues will become mandatory just as the Family and Medical Leave Act did."
3. Why are workers' compensation, unemployment compensation, and Social Security appropriately classified as security–oriented benefits?
4. Define the following terms: (a) contributory plan, (b) defined–benefit plan, (c) portability, and (d) vesting.
5. Discuss the following statement: "Health-care costs are out of control in the U.S. and it is up to employers to put pressure on the medical system to reduce costs."
6. What types of financial and other benefits would you most prefer? Why?
7. Some experts have forecast that time-off–related benefits will expand in the future. Why?
8. Why are benefits communications and flexible benefits systems so intertwined?

 FLEXIBLE BENEFITS AT UNITED HOSPITALS, INC.

All employers, including health-care providers, are concerned about the escalating costs of employee benefits, especially health-care costs. For hospitals, the need to have benefits tailored to varied workforces of part-timers, full-timers, medical/nursing professionals, and support staff, with all their individual differences, presents special problems. To address these problems, United Hospitals, Inc. (UHI), decided to implement a flexible benefits program, called Flex, for the 3,500 individual employees in its four-hospital system.

A flexible benefits program permits employees to decide which benefits they will receive and how much of them they wish, within some broad limitations placed by the employer on costs and types of benefits offered. To implement Flex at UHI, a taskforce from the finance, HR, and management information systems departments received plans and proposals from consultants, insurance providers, and computer software vendors. The taskforce decided to develop the Flex plan themselves instead of having it done by outsiders.

The implementation of Flex included developing a suitable design, an administrative system that interfaced with existing systems, and a communications program that enabled employees to get the most value from the program. The taskforce worked for almost a year to produce a program that would meet corporate goals and the budget and time constraints set by top management. The key to success seemed to lie in the great amount of advance planning done in all areas.

A significant effort was made to communicate to employees the reasons why changes were necessary. The purpose of the communication was to help employees accustomed to receiving the traditional benefits programs offered by insurance carriers adjust to the new reality. Based on intensive feedback from a group of employees selected from throughout UHI, the taskforce members proceeded to fashion a benefits program.

As a result of all of the input, UHI ended up using a core-plus-options approach. Employees selected from a core set of benefits, including ones such as health and life insurance equal to their annual salaries. Then each full-time employee was allocated a monthly base amount of dollars for use in "purchasing" benefits. Flex contained three base-allowance programs. Each base allowance had different parameters to it which allowed employees to purchase their current benefits packages, trade in some benefits for others, trade vacation time for additional benefits coverage, lower employee contributions, or others.

UHI managers engaged in extensive communication efforts. All employees received a personalized enrollment form along with a workbook containing instructions and a sample form. In addition, employee meetings were held in which a slide-and-tape presentation was followed by a question-and-answer session. The audiovisual program urged employees to think through their decisions, and individual consultations were scheduled at employees' requests.

The result of Flex in just one year indicated that its implementation achieved the primary goal of controlling the escalation in benefits costs. Benefits costs in the first year increased only 3%, resulting in a savings of over $2.5 million when compared with projections under the old benefits program. Also, the Flex plan contributed to the defeat of a unionization effort among 450 employees at one UHI hospital, so it appears that UHI did "Flex for success."[33]

▲ **QUESTIONS**

1. Explain how the success of United Hospitals' flexible benefits program relied on employee communication.
2. If you worked at UHI, which benefits would you select and which ones would you not select? Why?

▲ **NOTES**

1. Adapted from information in "Most Levi's Workers Tapping New Benefit for Unmarried Couples Are Heterosexual," *Employee Benefit News,* August 1992, 7; Jennifer J. Laabs, "Unmarried with Benefits," *Personnel Journal,* December 1991, 62–70; and "Two Leave Measures for Employees Who Have Domestic Partners," *Personnel Journal,* February 1993, 108.

2. David Bowen and Christopher A. Wadley, "Designing a Strategic Benefits Program," *Compensation and Benefits Review,* September–October 1989, 44–57.

3. *Employee Benefits, 1992 Edition,* (Washington D.C.: U.S. Chamber of Commerce, 1992).

4. "How Costly Are Mandated Benefits?" *Nation's Business,* April 1988, 12–14.

5. E. E. Kosseh and V. Nichol, "The Effects of On-Site Child Care on Employee Attitudes and Performance," *Personnel Psychology* 45 (1992), 485–507.

6. J. L. Lefkovich, "Business Responds to Elder-Care Needs," *HR Magazine,* June 1992, 103–108.

7. James A. Swanke, Jr., "Ways to Tame Workers' Comp Premiums," *HR Magazine,* February 1992, 39–41; and Roger Thompson, "Taking Charge of Workers' Comp," *Nation's Business,* October 1993, 18–23.

8. Rodney R. Nordstrom, "Suicide as a Compensable Injury under Workers' Compensation Statutes," *Employee Relations Law Journal* 16 (1990), 37–55.

9. James R. Norman, "Gravy Train," *Forbes,* January 20, 1992, 42–43.

10. Marlene L. Morgenstern, "Workers' Compensation: Managing Costs," *Compensation and Benefits Review,* September–October 1992, 30–38.

11. "Employers May Reap Savings from Improved Unemployment Comp Benefits Administration," *Employee Benefit News,* September 1992, 87.

12. J. S. DeMott, "Health-Care Expenses: Heading for $1 Trillion," *Nation's Business,* February 1993, 12.

13. U.S. Chamber of Commerce, *Employee Benefits.*

14. From a variety of sources, including Michael Clements, "DuPont Shifts Burden onto Employees," *USA Today,* March 12, 1993, 2B; "Xerox Pushed HMOs Hard," *Omaha World-Herald,* February 28, 1993, G1; *Fortune,* June 3, 1991, 12; and Roger Thompson, "States Take Lead in Health Reform," *Nation's Business,* April 1992, 18–26.

15. R. Thompson, "Employers' Costs for Employees Soar," *Nation's Business,* May 1992, 62.

16. Susan B. Garland, "The States Are Fed Up with Diddling on Health Care," *Business Week,* August 17, 1992, 28.

17. Peggy Stuart, "Self-Insurance Cuts Health Care Costs," *Personnel Journal,* July 1992, 51–57.

18. "When You Think Hospital Bills Are Too High: Utilization Review," *Inc.,* December 1989, 147–148.

19. Richard Preister, "Are Financial Incentives for Wellness Fair?" *Employee Benefits Journal,* March 1992, 38–40.

20. Murray Gendell and Jacob S. Siegel, "Trends in Retirement Age by Sex, 1950–2005," *Monthly Labor Review,* July 1992, 22–29.

21. "Costs Shrink Benefit Plans for Retirees," *Omaha World-Herald,* April 5, 1992, 1G.

22. Adapted from a variety of news articles, including "Honest Balance Sheets, Broken Promises," *Business Week,* November 23, 1992, 106–107; Kevin Anderson, "Retirees' Health Plans Get the Ax," *USA Today,* November 14, 1991, 1B–2B.

23. M. Zall, "Understanding the Risks to Pension Benefits," *Personnel Journal,* January 1992, 62–69; and Alan L. Gustman and Thomas L. Steinmeier, "The Stampede Toward Defined Contribution Pension Plans: Fact or Fiction?" *Industrial Relations* 31 (1992), 361–369.

24. *Arizona Governing Committee v. Norris,* 103 S.Ct. 3492, 32FEP Cases 233 (1983).

25. "In Hot Pursuit of Fat Pension Purses," *Business Week,* November 30, 1992, 86–87.

26. "Poll: More Firms Eye Financial Planning," *Employee Benefit News,* May 1992, 56.

27. "When the Deduction Is for Employee Education," *CPA Client Bulletin,* November 1989, 3.

28. Adapted from Julia Lawlor, "Offbeat Perks Can Perk Up Workers," *USA Today* July 20, 1993, B2; and "Perks Can Make the Difference," *Omaha World-Herald,* April 11, 1993, 1G.

29. Michael A. Miller, "Time-off Benefits in Small Establishments," *Monthly Labor Review,* March 1992, 3–8.

30. David G. Schorr and George R. Faulkner, Jr., "Buying and Selling Vacation Time," *Compensation and Benefits Review,* May–June 1992, 15–19.

31. Adapted from George F. Dreker, Ronald A. Ash, and Robert D. Bretz, "Benefit Coverage and Employee Cost: Critical Factors in Explaining Compensation Satisfaction," *Personnel Psychology* 41 (1988), 237–254.

32. "Tough Choices: Extra Vacation or a Free Trip to the Dentist," *Finance Executive,* May 1989, 6–7.

33. Adapted from M. Michael Markowich, "United Hospitals Makes Flex Fly, *Personnel Journal,* December 1989, 40–47.

Employee and Labor Relations

An interesting collection of topics makes up this section on employee and labor relations: health and safety, employee rights and discipline, union/management relations, collective bargaining and grievances, and assessing HR systems. An important part of HR management is to provide employees with safe working environments and to acquire help for those with health problems. Healthy and safe employees are likely to be more productive than those affected by illness or unsafe working conditions. Every year organizations lose money because of illness, accidents, and injuries on the job. Suggestions for dealing with employee health and safety are included in Chapter 16.

Health and safety are much in the everyday news. From the "sick building" syndrome to repetitive stress injuries, employers and employees have concerns about health. Further, criminal prosecution of executives who knowingly endanger employees has added more concerns for management.

The pressures of modern life, including work, can lead to emotional stress. For some people stress is a serious consequence of their jobs. They may react with substance abuse or in any of many other ways. Alcoholism and drug abuse are two serious problems encountered in virtually all work places. Management must realize the magnitude of the problem and how to deal with it. Wellness programs, AIDS, and the federal government's Occupational Safety and Health Act are also important topics covered in Chapter 16.

Employee rights and employer responsibilities have received increasing attention. Chapter 17 outlines the major issues in this area including such aspects as employment-at-will, employee handbooks as contracts, just cause, and employee privacy. Not many years ago, "employee rights" was a phrase not often heard. But wrongful discharge suits, negligent hiring, and an extremely litigious workforce has employers paying close attention to the topic now. Especially when it becomes necessary to discipline and even dismiss an employee, managers simply *must* know the basics of defensible discipline.

Some organizations interact formally with their employees through unions. Chapter 18 provides a synopsis of the evolution of unionism and labor legislation in the United States. Even though union membership in the U.S. has declined, the process of unionization should be understood by all managers and HR staff members. Unions are strong in certain segments of specific industries. The country has established an elaborate federal system to protect the rights of employees to join unions.

If an organization is unionized, a labor contract outlines the relationship between an employer and a union. In Chapter 19 the process of reaching a contract agreement, known as collective bargaining, and typical issues in collective bargaining are discussed. Included in all labor contracts is a grievance procedure that identifies how employee/employer problems are to be resolved. The grievance procedure is a valuable tool whether there is a union present or not. It is a way of resolving disputes and feelings of injustice employees may have.

Finally, an assessment of human resources in every organization is needed from time to time to make sure it continues to be effective. Chapter 20 considers some of the major areas to look at when assessing the effectiveness of HR activities in an organization.

CHAPTER 16

HEALTH AND SAFETY

After you have read this chapter, you should be able to:

1. Define health and safety and explain their importance in an organization.

2. Discuss three issues affecting organizational safety.

3. Describe the impact of four health problems on organizations.

4. Explain how organizations can respond to employee alcoholism, drug abuse, and other health problems.

5. Identify basic provisions of the Occupational Safety and Health Act of 1970.

6. Describe OSHA record-keeping and inspection requirements, and identify five types of OSHA citations.

7. Discuss both positive and negative aspects of OSHA regulations.

8. Identify and briefly explain the basic components of a systems approach to safety.

HR Today and Tomorrow:
Office Health Hazards—RSI, the Occupational Injury of the 1990s

Repetitive stress injuries, repetitive motion injuries, cumulative trauma disorders, carpal tunnel syndrome, ergonomic hazards—this listing of serious-sounding problems applies to the kind of workplace once thought to be free of injuries except for paper cuts and occasional stapler punctures. Today office work is definitely the source of some primary health and safety issues. Most are a variation or a result of repetitive stress injuries (RSI), sustained from repeated strain such as typing on a poorly positioned keyboard, lifting heavy objects again and again, or reaching for objects from an awkward positions. Such repetitive stress on the hand and wrist has led to a 25% increase in this category of occupational injuries in the last decade. RSIs now constitute 56% of all occupational injuries, according to the U.S. Labor Department.

Carpal tunnel syndrome has existed for years, but its incidence appears to be increasing as a result of so much RSI. It is an injury common to people who put their hands through repetitive motions such as typing, playing some musical instruments, cutting, or sewing. The motion irritates the tendons in the "carpal tunnel" area of the wrist. As the tendons swell, they squeeze the median nerve. The result is pain and numbness in the thumb, index finger, and middle finger. The hands of victims become clumsy and weak. Pain at night increases, and at advanced stages not even surgery can cure the problem. Victims eventually lose feeling in their hands without timely treatment.

Ergonomics is a term used to describe the study of workplace design as it relates to the physical needs of people. Designing the places where people work and the jobs they do so they do not hurt themselves seems to be among the solutions to RSI. For example, State Farm Insurance found that an ergonomically designed chair helped reduce injuries and increase efficiency. Also, Citibank found that encouraging employees to take more frequent work breaks to walk around and focus on objects other than the computer screen helped with eyestrain.

Use of ergonomics has helped in a variety of situations. Georgia Tech scientists analyzed workstations and videotaped employees at work in the apparel industry. They found the height of the sewing machines was a culprit in a surprising 55% of the cases of employees who complained of pain in the upper back and neck. Another example is the Sara Lee Bakery that solved persistent carpal tunnel syndrome problems by having a hand surgeon come to the plant and evaluate its work procedures.

The Occupational Safety and Health Administration (OSHA) is in the process of drafting rules to eliminate exposure to "ergonomic hazards." Also the first lawsuits are finding their way to court. A Seattle woman won a $1.2 million settlement from Boeing for RSI that left her unable to work. In San Francisco the city government passed a controversial ordinance setting standards for office and video display terminal ergonomics. However, it was repealed one month after it was enacted.

Office health hazards bring to mind the old TV commercial selling oil filters—"You can pay me now, or you can pay me later!" Currently the focus has been more on fixing the physical problems *after* they have happened. But it's much easier and cheaper to prevent the problems with some common sense and a little expert help.[1]

If only it weren't for the people always getting tangled up with the machinery . . . Earth would be an engineer's paradise.

Kurt Vonnegut

E mployers are obligated to provide employees with safe and healthy work environments. Requiring them to work with unsafe equipment or in areas where hazards are not controlled is a highly questionable practice that has led to the passage of workplace safety laws. Managers also must ensure that employees are safety conscious and are encouraged to maintain good health. Both managers and HR specialists have responsibilities for health and safety in organizations.

▲ HEALTH AND SAFETY DEFINED

The terms *health* and *safety* are closely related. The broader and somewhat more nebulous term is **health,** which refers to a general state of physical, mental, and emotional well-being. A healthy person is one who is free of illness, injury, or mental and emotional problems that impair normal human activity. However, the question of exactly what is healthy or normal behavior is open to interpretation. Health management practices in organizations strive to maintain the overall well-being of individuals.

Typically, **safety** refers to protection of the physical well-being of people. The main purpose of effective safety programs in organizations is to prevent work-related injuries and accidents.

Health and safety policies focus on the safe interaction between people and the work environment. Because many employers' efforts in the past were inadequate in providing healthy and safe work environments, Congress passed the Occupational Safety and Health Act in 1970. This act has had a tremendous impact on the workplace; therefore, any person interested in HR management must develop a knowledge of the act's provisions and implications. The Occupational Safety and Health Administration (OSHA) administers the act.

▼ **HEALTH**

refers to a general state of physical, mental, and emotional well-being.

▼ **SAFETY**

refers to protection of the physical well-being of people.

Health and Safety Responsibilities

As Figure 16–1 indicates, the primary health and safety responsibilities in an organization usually fall on supervisors and managers. An HR manager or safety specialist can help coordinate health and safety programs, investigate accidents,

HR UNIT	MANAGERS
▲ Coordinates health and safety programs ▲ Develops safety reporting system ▲ Provides accident investigation expertise ▲ Provides technical expertise on accident prevention	▲ Monitor health and safety of employees daily ▲ Coach employees to be safety conscious ▲ Investigate accidents ▲ Observe health and safety behavior of employees

▲ **Figure 16–1**

Typical Health and Safety Responsibilities

produce safety program materials, and conduct formal safety training. However, department supervisors and managers play key roles in maintaining safe working conditions and a healthy workforce. A supervisor in a ball bearing plant has several health and safety responsibilities: reminding employees to wear safety glasses; checking on the cleanliness of the work area; observing employees for any alcohol, drug, or emotional problems that may affect their work behavior; and recommending equipment changes (such as screens, railings, or other safety devices) to specialists in the organization.

An HR safety specialist in the same plant has other safety responsibilities: maintaining government-required health and safety records; coordinating a safety training class for new employees; assisting the supervisor in investigating an accident in which an employee was injured; and developing a plantwide safety communication program and informational materials. The interface between managers and HR specialists is crucial to a coordinated health and safety maintenance effort.

A Changing View of Safety

Before the passage of workers' compensation laws, an employee could not recover damages for an injury, even if it happened because of hazards inherent in the job or because of the negligence of a fellow worker. Workers who died or became disabled as a result of occupational injury or disease received no financial compensation for their families. Employers (and society) assumed that safety was the employee's responsibility.

However, in 1911, with the passage of the first workers' compensation law in Wisconsin, the attitude of society began to change. Soon workers' compensation laws passed in all states. Then the Occupational Safety and Health Act was passed at the national level in 1970. Employers once thought that accidents and occupational diseases were unavoidable by-products of work. This idea was replaced with prevention and control concepts to minimize or eliminate health and safety risks in the workplace.

▲ ACCIDENT RATES AND COSTS

Occupational health and safety experts say that workplace safety recently has become less urgent to employers. Changes in accident trends seem to run in cycles and lag by three to five years behind changes in federal safety policy. The industries where safety conditions appear to have deteriorated most seem to be those that have been depressed or in which severe competition exists.

Recently, job-related injuries and illnesses hit 6.8 million, an annual increase of about 200,000 from the year before. It was the highest number since the U.S. Department of Labor began tracking figures in 1972. Also, 2,900 work-related deaths were reported, but the Labor Department believes that number is probably understated. Other estimates range from 7,000 to 10,000.[2]

Figure 16–2 shows the industries that report the most injuries and illnesses. Bear in mind that the figures are not weighted for the seriousness of the injuries. Certain jobs and industries are more hazardous in terms of fatal accidents than others. Farming, mining, construction, and transportation are the industries with the highest fatality rates.

▲ **Figure 16–2**

Industries with Most Injuries

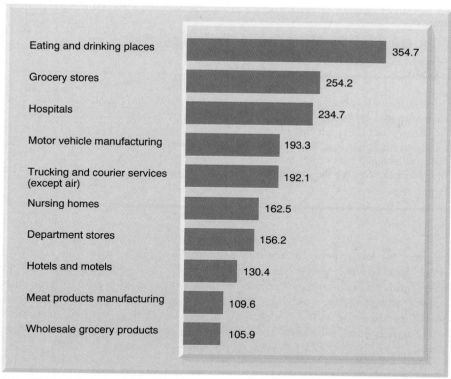

Eating and drinking places — 354.7
Grocery stores — 254.2
Hospitals — 234.7
Motor vehicle manufacturing — 193.3
Trucking and courier services (except air) — 192.1
Nursing homes — 162.5
Department stores — 156.2
Hotels and motels — 130.4
Meat products manufacturing — 109.6
Wholesale grocery products — 105.9

SOURCE: U.S. Bureau of Labor Statistics

The most dangerous single jobs are as follows:

▲ Timber logger
▲ Airline pilot
▲ Asbestos and insulation worker
▲ Structural metal worker
▲ Electrical power-line/cable installer

▲ Firefighter
▲ Garbage collector
▲ Truck driver
▲ Bulldozer operator
▲ Earth driller

Accident Costs

Workers' compensation cost increases are a major issue in many states. There are many reasons for the increase—one of which is the increase in accident rates, although that may not be the major cost factor. Accidents are often preventable. One study concluded that two-thirds of the disabilities suffered from accidents annually could have been prevented.[3] Employee Assistance Programs (EAPs) (discussed later in this chapter) can reduce the number of mental health problems and substance abuse problems. Also, "wellness" programs can reduce the incidence of other physical disabilities, and safety programs and workplace engineering can help reduce accidents.

Industrial accidents cost more than $32 billion each year in direct and indirect costs to employers. Calculating the cost of accidents for each employer is desirable because top management can easily understand such data, and expenditures for improving worker health and safety are justified more easily.

Tangible benefits of a well-managed safety program include: (1) reduction in insurance premiums, (2) savings of litigation costs, (3) fewer wages paid for

HR Perspectives:

The Ethics of Suing Yourself For Safety Negligence

The part owner of a California manufacturer was working in the factory when he snagged his sweater and was pulled into the machinery. He hired a lawyer (in his role as an employee) to sue himself (in his role as owner). Then he hired *another* lawyer to defend himself as owner.

The two attorneys felt the owner had been negligent in allowing the bolt that snagged his sweater to stick out. Further, they felt he should pay the "employee" compensation. The "employee" got the money, $122,500 *tax free,* and the "owner" got to deduct the amount as a business expense.

Yes, this is a true story.[4]

---

lost time, (4) less expense in training new workers, (5) less overtime, and (6) greater productivity. Every year employers lose an astounding amount of money and other resources because of accidents, and the figures have increased. Safety and labor officials tie the rate of injury increase to competition and the pressure for more productivity. Smaller work crews, more overtime, faster assembly lines, all equate to more *speed* in working and less concern for safety.

▲ ISSUES IN OCCUPATIONAL SAFETY

Before discussing ways to deal with health and safety challenges, there are some issues to be considered that (in some cases) are controversial. Several of the most prominent issues are discussed next.

Criminal Prosecution of Executives

In an effort to assign individual responsibility for corporate practices, several legal cases across the country have taken aim at executives in companies that have had serious workplace injuries. At Chicago Magnet Wire, five senior executives in the firm were charged with aggravated battery, reckless conduct, and conspiracy. They were accused of allowing more than 40 workers to become ill and suffer nerve and lung damage through exposure to hazardous chemicals at the company's plant. Murder charges were filed against three senior executives of Film Recovery Systems, Inc., after a worker died from inhaling cyanide fumes. In New York, PYMM Thermometer Company owners were convicted on charges of assault and reckless endangerment for exposing workers to mercury. In Austin, Texas, the president of Sabine Consolidated, Inc., was convicted of criminally negligent homicide when two employees died in the collapse of a trench in which they were working.[5]

There is another side of the issue, of course. Employer groups contend that it is unfair for companies that comply with OSHA regulations to be prosecuted for criminal conduct.

Child Labor

Another safety concern is reflected in restrictions affecting younger workers, especially those under the age of 18. Child-labor laws, found in Section XII of the Fair Labor Standards Act, set the minimum age for most employment at 16 years. For "hazardous" occupations, 18 years is the minimum. Figure 16–3 presents a list of 17 occupations considered by the government to be hazardous for children.

The law is quite strict for those aged 14 to 16, who may hold only clerical, office, and retail food service jobs, pump gas, or do errand and delivery work. They can work only between 7 A.M. and 7 P.M. during the school year, three hours per day on school days, and they are restricted to an eight-hour day on weekends. These provisions do not apply to newspaper delivery, theater performances, and children working for their parents in farming and similar occupations.

Many employers require age certificates for employees, because the Fair Labor Standards Act places the responsibility on the employer to determine an individual's age. These certificates may be issued by a representative of a state labor department, education department, or by a local school official. In various states they are referred to as *age certificates, employment certificates, work permits,* or *working papers.*

Recently, child-labor law violations have increased. About 500 federal agents conducted more than 3,400 investigations of child-labor violations during a nationwide three-day probe. About 43% of the employers were found to be in apparent violation. The major violations were with 14- and 15-year-olds working

 Figure 16–3

Child Labor and Hazardous Occupations (18 is Minimum Age)

1. Manufacturing or storing explosives
2. Driving a motor vehicle and being an outside helper
3. Coal mining
4. Logging and sawmilling
5. Using power-driven woodworking machines*
6. Exposure to radioactive substances and to ionizing radiations
7. Operating power-driven hoisting apparatus
8. Operating power-driven, metal-forming, punching, and shearing machines*
9. Mining, other than coal mining
10. Slaughtering, or meat packing, processing, or rendering*
11. Using power-driven bakery machines
12. Operating power-driven paper-products machines*
13. Manufacturing brick, tile, and related products
14. Using power-driven circular saws, band saws, and guillotine shears*
15. Wrecking, demolition, and shipbreaking operations
16. Roofing operations*
17. Excavation operations*

*In certain cases, the law provides exemptions for apprentices and student learners in these occupations.

SOURCE: Employment Standards Administration, Wage and Hour Division, U.S. Department of Labor, *Child Labor Requirements in Nonagricultural Occupations.* WH Publication No. 1330 (Washington D.C.: U.S. Government Printing Office).

too many hours and 16- and 17-year-olds working hazardous jobs. The fast-food industry and New York's garment industry were those industries most frequently cited for violations.[6]

Causes of Accidents: The Workplace or the People?

If accidents are caused by *dangerous work,* one obvious solution is to reengineer that work and the workplace to eliminate the accidents. This approach suggests a different approach to the problem of accidents than if one believes that *people* and their carelessness, reduced awareness, or limited capacities are the causes of accidents.

Logic and reason suggests that both factors—work design and human nature—contribute to accidents. Yet some approaches to reducing accidents focus on one or the other exclusively. Both approaches are valuable, so they tend to be most effective when considered together.

Engineering Approach to Safety   Employers can prevent some accidents by designing machines, equipment, and work areas so that workers who daydream periodically or who perform potentially dangerous jobs cannot injure themselves or others. Providing safety equipment and guards on machinery and installing emergency switches often forestall accidents. To prevent a punch-press operator from mashing her finger, a safety guard is attached to a machine so her hand cannot accidentally slip into the machine. Actions such as installing safety rails, keeping aisles clear, and installing adequate ventilation, lighting, or heating and air conditioning can all help make work environments safer.

A **safety hierarchy** represents the order in which actions should be taken to eliminate danger effectively:[7]

▲ *First priority:* To eliminate hazard completely
▲ *Second priority:* To use safeguards
▲ *Third priority:* To use warning signs
▲ *Fourth priority:* To train and instruct
▲ *Fifth priority:* To prescribe personal protection

Notice that three of the five methods are engineering approaches to safety.

Ergonomic Approach to Safety   **Ergonomics** is the proper design of the work environment to address the physical demands experienced by people. The term comes from the Greek *ergon,* meaning "work," and the suffix *-omics,* meaning "management of." An ergonomist studies physiological, psychological, and engineering design aspects of a job, including such factors as fatigue, lighting, tools, equipment layout, and placement of controls. Human factors engineering is a related field.

Most recently attention has focused on the application of ergonomic principles to the design of workstations where computer operators work with personal computers and video display terminals (VDTs) for long periods of time. Workstations, tools, and jobs must "fit" a person just as a pair of shoes must "fit" or injuries can occur.

As noted in the opening discussion of this chapter, repetitive stress injuries (RSIs) can occur from poorly designed workstations. Further, the American Optometric Association reports handling more than 8,000,000 VDT-related

---

▼ **A SAFETY HIERARCHY**

is the order in which actions should be taken to eliminate work safety problems.

▼ **ERGONOMICS**

is the proper design of the work environment to address the physical demands experienced by people.

eyestrain cases annually. Many are related to glare and poor lighting or poor resolution. In San Francisco the local government has attempted to legislate ergonomically correct workstations focusing on some design problems: chair adjustment and support, VDT area and quality, station height, lighting, glare, noise levels, document placement, screen flicker, rest breaks, and employee ergonomics training.[8] Figure 16–4 shows an ergonomically correct PC/VDT workstation.

Behavioral Approach to Safety   Engineers approach safety from the perspective of redesigning the machinery or the work area. Industrial psychologists see safety differently. They are concerned with the proper match of people to jobs and emphasize employee training in safety methods, fatigue reduction, and health awareness.

Industrial psychologists have conducted numerous field studies with thousands of employees looking at the "human factors" in accidents. The results show a definite relationship between emotional factors, such as stress, and accidents. Other studies point to the importance of individual differences, motivation, attitudes, and learning as key factors in controlling the human element in safety.

Attitudinal variables, as well as equipment and work design, affect accident rates. Attitudes toward working conditions, accidents, and safe work practices are very important because more problems are caused by careless employees than by machines or employer negligence. At one time, workers who were dissatisfied with their jobs were thought to have higher accident rates. However,

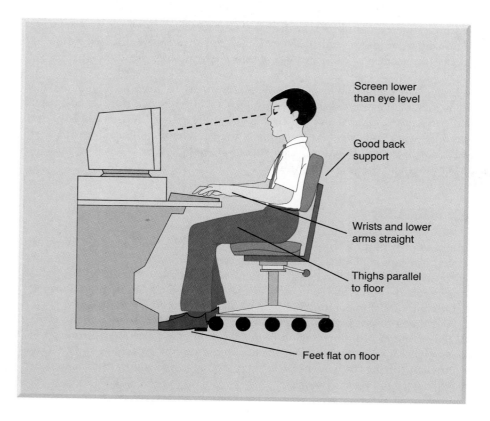

▲ **Figure 16–4**

An Ergonomically Correct Workstation

HR Perspectives:

Research Correlates Overtime Work and Accidents

Researchers Michael Schuster and Susan Rhodes of Syracuse University examined the records at three New York manufacturing firms to see if there was a relationship between overtime and accidents.

The logic of a relationship between overtime and accidents is as follows: Fatigue based on physical factors rarely exists in today's industrial workplace. But fatigue, which is defined as boredom, occurs when a person is required to do the same tasks for a long period of time, and boredom is rather common. As fatigue of this kind increases, motivation is reduced; along with decreased motivation, workers' attention wanders, and the likelihood of accidents increases.

The researchers examined 462 accidents and the amount of overtime preceding each in the three firms. As reported in *Industrial Relations,* the study results tentatively support the hypothesis that overtime work *is* related to accident incidence. Further, the more overtime worked, the more severe the accident appeared to be. In conclusion, the authors caution that this study is not the final word, although it is the first one using an individual level of analysis *and* looking at the overtime that preceded accidents.[9]

this assumption has been questioned in recent years. One study of accident-proneness found that younger and less-experienced employees were involved in more injuries and accidents. This same study suggested that there were some differences in personality and emotional characteristics between people who had no accidents and those who had repeated accidents.[10] Although employees' personalities, attitudes, and individual characteristics apparently have some influence on accidents, exact cause-and-effect relationships are difficult to establish.

Employees doing the same job repeatedly tend to become bored. At that point they may begin to pay less attention to their tasks and develop bad habits that can cause accidents and injuries, as the study in the "HR Perspective" on overtime work indicates. Redesigning a job to relieve monotony is a way of dealing with worker boredom. Elements of job design such as job scope and job depth should be assessed continually.

▲ HEALTH

Employee health problems are somewhat inevitable—and varied. They can range from minor illnesses such as a cold to serious illnesses related to the jobs performed. Some employees have emotional problems; others have alcohol or drug problems. Some problems are chronic; others are transitory. But all may affect organizational operations and individual employee productivity.

Four major health problems have direct relevance to HR management: physical illness, emotional illness, alcoholism, and drug abuse (see Figure 16–5). Employers who are concerned about maintaining a healthy workforce must engage in problem solving in these areas. In the paragraphs that follow, these and other health-related issues are discussed.

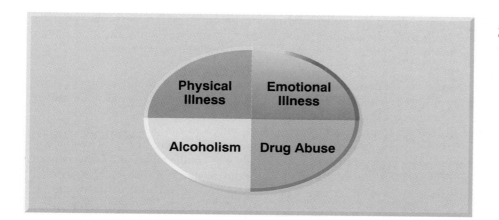

Health and the Work Environment

Because physical illnesses often reduce employees' abilities to perform a job, most employers help employees who have physical illnesses and health problems by providing hospitalization and health insurance. But sound health programs focus on prevention as well as on treatment of illness.

Many people have heard of the health problems developed by asbestos workers, coal miners, and some chemical workers. Cancer, black lung disease, and radiation poisoning are among the many physical health concerns of employers and employees. For example, it has been estimated that over 150,000 U.S. workers in 56 different occupations are exposed to mercury on the job.[11]

Other health problems can be caused by an environment that exposes workers to excessive noise or harmful lighting. New technology has created its own hazards—as indicated by the VDT-related injuries discussed earlier.

Sick Building Syndrome   The Environmental Protection Agency (EPA) defines sick building syndrome as a situation in which occupants experience acute health problems and discomfort that appear to be linked to time spent in a building, but no specific illness or cause can be identified. There are between 800,000 and 1.2 million such buildings in the U.S. according to one study. An example is the new DuPage County Courthouse in Wheaton, Illinois, which cost $53 million to build and will cost millions more to fix. People complained of headaches and flu-like symptoms that would improve when they left the workplace. Sick days have soared, lawsuits have been filed, and county officials have left the building.[12]

There are many pollutants that contribute to the poor quality of indoor air. The problem became an issue in the 1970s when a national push to save energy resulted in more tightly sealed buildings (often with windows that cannot be opened) and poor indoor-air quality. Inadequate ventilation as well as airborne contamination from carpets, molds, copy machines, adhesives, and fungi can be at the root of the problem.

Studies suggest that in a very high percentage of cases of sick building syndrome the problems result because the controls are too sophisticated for the people who maintain them or because operators try to cut corners to save energy.

Often the building is poorly maintained or overcrowded.[13] Consequently, architects seem to be approaching new building design with more attention to the function of the interior and less to the "statement" the exterior makes.[14]

Threats to Reproductive Health　A very recent health concern is the threat to unborn children and a person's ability to reproduce that may be caused by exposure to certain chemical hazards in the workplace. In so-called "clean rooms," where computer chips are etched with acid and gases at Digital Equipment Corporation, miscarriage rates among women were nearly twice the national average. As a result, a four-year study was conducted by the University of California at Davis, funded by the semiconductor industry. The study confirmed that women who work at chip manufacturing plants run a 20% to 40% greater risk of miscarriage than women in nonmanufacturing jobs.[15] Chip makers reacted swiftly to the research. Intel guaranteed nonproduction jobs for pregnant employees who wanted to switch. It and other companies began eliminating the suspected chemical from the process. At present, about 21,000 women work in microchip plants across the country.[16]

In another reproductive health situation, the Supreme Court held that Johnson Controls' policy of keeping women of childbearing capacity out of jobs that might lead to lead exposure violated the Civil Rights Act and the Pregnancy Discrimination Act. To protect unborn children from the toxic effects of lead, Johnson Controls (which made lead batteries) barred women from jobs working around the lead. The Court said, "Decisions about the welfare of future children must be left to the parents who conceive, bear, support, and raise them rather than to the employers who hire those parents."[17]

There is very little research focusing on reproductive health hazards. Yet employers need to protect themselves from liability for the effects of workers' exposure to threats to reproductive health. One attorney suggests the following:[18]

▲ Maintain a safe workplace for all by seeking the safest methods.
▲ Comply with all state and federal safety laws.
▲ Inform employees of any known risks.
▲ Document employee acceptance of any risks.

However, it should be noted that there is no *absolute* protection from liability for employers.

Stress

The pressures of modern life, coupled with the demands of a job, can lead to emotional imbalances that are collectively labeled *stress*. Not all stress is unpleasant. To be alive means to respond to the stimulation of achievement and the excitement of a challenge. In fact, there is evidence that people *need* a certain amount of stimulation and that monotony can bring on some of the same problems as overwork. What is usually meant by the term *stress* is excessive stress, or distress.

Evidence of stress can be seen everywhere, from the 35-year-old executive who dies of a sudden heart attack to the dependable older worker who unexpectedly commits suicide. One indicator of stress is hypertension (high blood pressure). Twenty-five million U.S. workers suffer from hypertension, resulting in a $20 billion loss in wages and productivity every year.[19] Many experts believe that some people who abuse alcohol and drugs do so to help reduce stress.

Until recently, most companies reasoned that if their managers could not handle stress, they were not tough enough for the job. But now many companies offer counseling programs aimed at stress reduction.[20]

What Is Stressful?   Many factors determine what a person will find stressful. Those who have a hard time adjusting to change are more susceptible. Other factors, including biochemistry, physical strength, psychological makeup, values, and habits, affect individual reactions. Other major contributors to stress have been found to be:

▲ Lack of control
▲ Inability to predict
▲ Inaccurate perceptions of events
▲ Intense responsibility or demands
▲ Lack of social support

Two recent cases have found that stress, including mental depression resulting in suicide, may be an "occupational illness" and compensable under workers' compensation statutes.[21] In a Maine case, a police officer, an 18-year veteran of the municipal police force, became depressed over his failure to be promoted, and committed suicide. Evidence introduced before the state Workers' Compensation Appeal Board confirmed that the officer had become severely depressed over this failure and that this disappointment was a major factor in his resultant suicide. The court found suicide to be a compensable claim where the claimant establishes a causal connection between the work-related activity and the resulting death.

A Nebraska case also allowed compensation benefits to be awarded to an employee who suffered severe anxiety and mental depression following a work-related injury. The Supreme Court agreed with the workers' compensation court's finding that the mental depression was either caused by or aggravated by the accident. The decision relied on several earlier Nebraska cases that allowed the compensation court to consider all factors, both mental and physical, in determining the amount of compensation due the employee.

Stress: A Survey   A survey done for *The Wall Street Journal* uncovered several interesting facts about stress and business.[22] Of executives who do complain of stress, a large percentage are young, suggesting that as people grow older they may learn to handle stress better (or perhaps people who do not handle stress well do not grow older).

Executives in the survey attributed more stress to certain industries. Commodity trading, advertising, and investment banking were considered by many to be stressful industries. Figure 16–6 lists some more stressful and less stressful occupations. Executives cited employees under their direction as the biggest cause of stress in large and middle-sized organizations. At smaller firms, financial problems were the main source. Strategies used by executives to cope with stress can include physical exercise (golf, tennis, hunting or fishing, aerobics, and running), a change of scene, reading, and hobbies. More work-related strategies may include rational, task-oriented behavior such as working harder, emotional release, distraction, and social support.[23]

Research on stress suggests that high workload alone does not prove out as a significant stressor.[24] Yet in Japan, *Karoshi,* or "overwork," is being implicated in

▲ **Figure 16–6**

Most and Least Stressful Jobs
(no rank order implied)

MOST STRESSFUL	LEAST STRESSFUL
Inner-city schoolteacher	Forest ranger
Security trader	Craftsman
Air traffic controller	Natural scientist
Medical intern	Architect
Newspaper editor	Actuary
Assembly-line worker	Librarian
Firefighter	Barber
Police officer	

SOURCE: Adapted from "In Search of Workplace Serenity," *Denver Post,* July 22, 1991, 8B.

sudden death by heart attack of some Japanese males, and their survivors have been compensated by the Japanese government.[25]

Management's Role   When an emotional problem (stress related or otherwise) becomes so severe that it disrupts an employee's ability to function normally, the employee should be directed to appropriate professionals for help. Because emotional problems are difficult to diagnose, supervisors and managers should not become deeply involved. If a worker is emotionally upset because of marital difficulties, for example, a supervisor should not give advice but should realize that appropriate professionals are better qualified to help.

Employee Assistance Programs (EAPs)

AN EMPLOYEE ASSISTANCE
PROGRAM (EAP)

provides counseling and other help to employees having emotional, physical, or other personal problems.

One method that organizations are using to respond to employee problems is an **employee assistance program (EAP)** which provides counseling and other help to employees having emotional, physical, or other personal problems. In such a program, an employer establishes a liaison relationship with a social service counseling agency. Employees who have problems may then contact the agency, either voluntarily or by employer referral, for assistance with a broad range of problems (see Figure 16–7). Counseling costs are paid for by the employer in total or up to a preestablished limit.

EAPs are attempts to help employees with their most difficult problems. Some HR managers feel that EAPs make their other HR programs more effective. For example, in one large company the Vice-President of Human Resources found that much of his department's time was being consumed by such problems as employee anxiety reactions, suicide attempts, alcohol- and drug-related absences, and family disturbances. Further, the medical department was not able to provide accurate information on whether affected employees could successfully return to work. The Vice-President decided an EAP might save a great deal of time and money.

Evaluating EAPs   Currently, many employers have EAPs. However, it is very hard to find an objective assessment of how effective EAPs have been. On one hand, the Employee Assistance Professionals Association contends that for every $1 employers invest in EAPs, they recover an estimated $3 to $5 in reduction of other costs or increased productivity.[26] On the other side of the issue are those who contend that EAPs cause health-care costs to go up, not down, because of difficulty in measuring effectiveness.[27] Further, there are many areas of potential

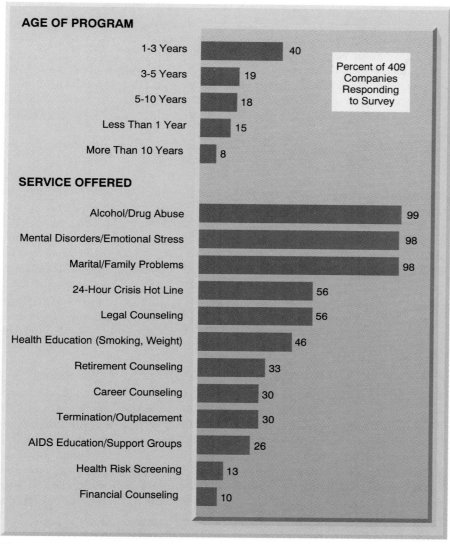

AGE OF PROGRAM

1-3 Years	40
3-5 Years	19
5-10 Years	18
Less Than 1 Year	15
More Than 10 Years	8

Percent of 409 Companies Responding to Survey

SERVICE OFFERED

Alcohol/Drug Abuse	99
Mental Disorders/Emotional Stress	98
Marital/Family Problems	98
24-Hour Crisis Hot Line	56
Legal Counseling	56
Health Education (Smoking, Weight)	46
Retirement Counseling	33
Career Counseling	30
Termination/Outplacement	30
AIDS Education/Support Groups	26
Health Risk Screening	13
Financial Counseling	10

SOURCE: SHRM-BNA survey, 1990.

▲ Figure 16–7

Problems Addressed by Employee Assistance Programs

liability arising out of EAPs for employers that must be considered.[28] One study of the effectiveness of EAP drug interventions found only about 8% of employers rating them very effective and 26% as fairly effective.[29] This is not to say that EAPs are ineffective, but simply that they have entered a period where good solid management evaluation is necessary to help them reach their potential.

Substance Abuse

Substance abuse is defined as the use of illicit substances or the misuse of controlled substances, alcohol or other drugs. There are currently (conservatively) about 13 million substance abusers in the work force and they cost the U.S. economy about $230 billion annually.[30]

▼ SUBSTANCE ABUSE

is the use of illicit substances or the misuse of controlled substances, alcohol, or other drugs.

The incidence of substance abuse is greatest among white men aged 19 to 23. It is higher among men than women and higher among whites than minority-group members at work. Blue-collar workers are more likely to abuse substances than white-collar workers.[31]

Employers are concerned with substance abuse because of altered work behaviors. The effects may be subtle, like tardiness, increased absenteeism, slower work pace, higher rate of mistakes, and less time spent at the workstation. Or changes in behavior may be more obvious, such as personality changes, abusive behavior, assaults, and on-the-job accidents.[32] Research has shown that substance abuse has altered behaviors at work such that more withdrawal (physical and psychological) and antagonistic behaviors were present.[33]

Substance Abuse and the ADA   The Americans with Disabilities Act (ADA) determines the way management can handle substance-abuse cases. The practicing illegal drug abuser specifically is excluded from the definition of "disabled" under the act. However, addiction to legal substances (alcohol, for example) is *not* excluded. Previous legislation and various government agencies have defined "disabled" differently, but the medical community seems to be in accord that both alcohol and drug abuse are mental disorders. Therefore, addiction is generally regarded as a disease, similar to mental disorders. Further, the regulations promulgated to administer ADA define both alcoholism and drug addiction that has been treated as disabilities.[34] Therefore, the prudent employer would probably be wise to consider recovering substance abusers as disabled under the ADA and proceed accordingly.

Substance Abuse and Supervisor's Responsibility   To encourage employees to seek help for their substance-abuse problems, a *firm-choice* option is usually recommended and has been endorsed legally. In this procedure the employee is privately confronted by a supervisor or manager about unsatisfactory work-related behaviors. Then, in keeping with the disciplinary system, he or she is offered a choice between treatment and discipline. Treatment options and consequences of further unsatisfactory performance are *clearly* discussed. What the company will do is made clear. Confidentiality and follow-up are critical when the firm-choice option is used by employers.

Many companies have established formal and mandatory orientation programs for their supervisors, since the supervisor or manager is usually the person who observes and deals with substance-abuse problems. These programs teach supervisors and managers to recognize at-risk employees and make EAP or other referrals as appropriate. A firm-choice conversation between the supervisor and employee might begin something like this:

"Susan, you've been a great salesperson. You've brought us some of our best accounts. Lately, though, your sales have been slipping and we've noticed that you're having some other problems. We know this may be related to some substance abuse and we want to help you. You're important to us and we would hate to lose you, because you really are valuable. Not only do we care about you as a colleague, but as a friend, too. It upsets us to watch what you're doing to yourself, and you need to get help, if you wish to stay employed here."

Alcoholism   The economic costs of alcoholism are growing. The National Center for Health Statistics projects that the costs to employers will be up about 17% over the preceding ten years by 1995.[35] Alcohol is implicated in 47% of industrial accidents and half of all auto fatalities. Alcoholic workers were found to miss 113 days more than the average employee and file $23,000 more in medical claims over a five-year period in a study done for McDonnel Douglas Corporation.[36]

Psychologically, alcoholism is marked by denying that there are any problems, and alcoholics tend to blame others for their problems. There is no cure for alcoholism. People who have stopped drinking are called "recovering alcoholics" in recognition of the fact that the potential to relapse is still there. But recovering alcoholics can lead full healthy lives. Recovery rates differ from program to program but Kimberly-Clark Corporation reports a recovery rate of about 65% through its EAP. The Dupont Company reports a rate of 70%. The highest recovery rate noted was among airline pilots (a highly motivated group) which is somewhere around 90%.[37]

Drug Abuse   Drug abuse is pervasive throughout society, from the inner-city ghetto to the affluent suburb. It involves legal drugs, such as barbiturates and tranquilizers, as well as illegal "hard" drugs, such as heroin and crack cocaine. Some organizations have found employees selling drugs to other employees at work. Management at one computer firm discovered a drug ring in which employees grossed $10,000 a week. In a California firm some employees were observed drying cocaine in a microwave oven in the company cafeteria. Initially many employers assumed drug-abuse problems were confined to the loading dock, or its equivalent, and would not be found in the front office. After contacts with EAPs, it became obvious that abusers existed throughout the organization.

The success rate for drug rehabilitation has not been very good. It may be about half the rate for recovery for alcoholics.[38] In addition to drug testing, which will be covered in more detail in the next chapter, some companies are using peer pressure to curb drug use. Burlington Northern Railroad found that while 19% of railroad employees had a drug- or alcohol-abuse problem, the majority of the employees had no such problem and would rather not have substances abused by co-workers on the job. In some programs, employees are given options to express their concerns about a peer's substance abuse.[39]

The Drug Free Workplace Act of 1988 was passed and it says any employer who has contracts with the U.S. government must maintain a drug-free environment for its workers. Failure to do so can lead to contract termination. Tobacco and alcohol are not considered controlled substances under the act, and off-the-job drug use is not included. To be in conformance with the act employers must do the following:

▲ Inform employees of drug-free requirements
▲ Outline actions to be taken for violations
▲ Establish awareness programs and supervisory training

AIDS

Employers are increasingly confronted by the problems associated with employees having AIDS. First, there is the eventual decline in productivity and attendance brought on by the inevitable diseases that follow in an employee with AIDS. Then there are the problems associated with the fear and panic in the workplace born of misunderstanding and misinformation.

Some firms have policies to deal with AIDS. The firms that have lost an employee are more likely to have a policy than those who have not, by 35% to 8% according to another survey. Nearly 56% said they did not believe a uniform policy to be possible.[40]

Many companies are unwilling to deal with the HR management problems involved with an AIDS-infected staff member. No matter what information experts might offer to assuage fear, an employee with AIDS, whether on the shop floor or in the executive offices, creates feelings of anxiety and unrest among other employees, suppliers, and customers. To meet this problem and yet address the needs of afflicted employees, some companies are electing to continue to pay the employees full salary, medical, and retirement benefits on the stipulation they not return to work.

Many companies feel that it is unnecessary to adopt specific policies that deal solely with AIDS for the following reasons:[41]

1. They do not want to draw attention to the problem and unnecessarily alarm employees.
2. Current company policy on life-threatening illnesses probably covers the situation, so there is no reason to treat AIDS differently from any other illness.
3. A specific AIDS policy may prove too restrictive, since flexibility is needed as changes in scientific knowledge and the law occur.

Wellness Programs

▼ **WELLNESS PROGRAMS**

are programs designed to maintain or improve employee health before problems arise.

Unlike EAPs that deal with employee health problems after they have occurred, **wellness programs** are designed to maintain or improve employee health before problems arise. Employer desires to improve productivity, decrease absenteeism, and put a lid on health-care costs have come together in the "wellness" movement. Wellness programs encourage self-directed lifestyle changes. Early wellness programs were aimed primarily at reducing the risk of disease. The newer programs have emphasized healthy lifestyles and environment. Typical programs may include the following:

▲ Screenings (risk factors, blood pressure, cardiovascular disease, cancer, etc.)
▲ Exercise programs (endurance, aerobics, strength, etc.)
▲ Education/awareness programs (stress reduction, weight control, preventing back pain, etc.)
▲ Skills programs (CPR, first aid, etc.)

Organizations have entered the "wellness business," not because they have suddenly developed a more active social conscience, but because in each year employers spend billions of dollars on group life and health insurance premiums. Much of that money goes to finance care after emergencies (like heart attacks) that are, at least to some degree, preventable.

Although the percentage of companies that are still paying the full cost of medical insurance for retirees is dropping rapidly, many of those are considering wellness plans as a way of cutting medical costs for retirees as well. When viewing the effectiveness of wellness plans and their costs, the results are mixed. Advocates eagerly point to the successful plan that Adolph Coors Company has initiated (discussed in the "HR Perspective").

HR Perspectives:

Research Shows Wellness Pays at Adolph Coors Company

The Adolph Coors Company in Golden, Colorado, has offered a wellness program to its employees for more than ten years. The very comprehensive program stems from the philosophy of President Bill Coors that wellness programs are "the right thing to do" for employees. The program is widely viewed as a successful model for wellness programs. It has also been rigorously studied by other employers interested in implementing wellness programs.

The Colorado facility employs 6,500 persons, working different shifts. The plant is open 24 hours and 7 days per week. The Wellness Center is open from 5 A.M. to 1:30 A.M. 6 days a week to accommodate the employees' varying schedules. The center offers hazard appraisals and screenings, physical-fitness and exercise equipment, smoking-cessation programs, nutrition and weight-loss counseling, physical and cardiovascular rehabilitation, and stress management.

The Wellness Center has been evaluated in terms of economic cost impact using a cost-avoidance approach. It shows a return on investment of $3.37 for each dollar invested using this approach. A break-even analysis showed that the operating costs of the program annually (fixed and variable) can be covered with participation in the range of 130 to 580 participants. Thus, the results of the analysis suggests this program is cost beneficial.[44]

One study of about 200 wellness programs found that:[42]

▲ Absenteeism decreased
▲ Blood pressure decreased
▲ Medical costs went down, but the number of claims went up
▲ Cholesterol went down
▲ Smoking was reduced

Another three-year study found that addition of a physical fitness facility produced no incremental benefits in reducing risks over simply concentrating on health-education classes. Health education, follow-up counseling, and health promotion were most cost effective in dealing with cardiovascular disease.[43]

Smoking at Work

Arguments and rebuttals characterize the smoking-at-work controversy, and statistics are rampant. On one hand, scientific studies (over 33,000 at last count) and health organizations contend that one-third of all cancer deaths, one-fourth of all heart disease, and 80% of all emphysema cases are attributable to smoking. Further, 50% of all cancer deaths among males in their working years are smoking related. Tobacco companies, on the other hand, still argue that scientific evidence does not support a link between smoking and cancer or heart disease.

A multitude of state and local laws have been passed that deal with smoking in the workplace and public places. Passage of these laws has been viewed by many employers positively, as they relieve employers of the responsibility for making decisions on smoking issues. But the courts have been hesitant to address the smoking-at-work issue. They clearly prefer to let employers and employees resolve their differences rather than prohibiting or supporting the right to smoke. Although many smoking employees complain initially when a smoking ban is instituted, they seem to have relatively little difficulty adjusting within a few weeks.

▲ OCCUPATIONAL SAFETY AND HEALTH ACT (OSHA)

The Occupational Safety and Health Act of 1970 was passed "to assure so far as possible every working man or woman in the Nation safe and healthful working conditions and to preserve our human resources." Every employer engaged in commerce who has one or more employees is covered by the act. Farmers having fewer than ten employees are exempt from the act. Covered under other health and safety acts are employers in specific industries such as coal mining. Federal, state, and local government employees are covered by separate provisions or statutes.

Basic Provisions

The act established the Occupational Safety and Health Administration, known as OSHA. The act also established the National Institute of Occupational Safety and Health (NIOSH) as a supporting body to do research and develop standards.

Enforcement Standards   To implement the act, specific standards were established regulating equipment and working environments. OSHA often uses national standards developed by engineering and quality control groups. Figure 16–8 gives examples of some specific standards.

▲ **Figure 16–8**

Sample OSHA Standards

> **§ 1910.151 Medical services and first aid.**
> (a) The employer shall ensure the ready availability of medical personnel for advice and consultation on matters of plant health.
> (b) In the absence of an infirmary, clinic, or hospital in near proximity to the workplace which is used for the treatment of all injured employees, a person or persons shall be adequately trained to render first aid. First aid supplies approved by the consulting physician shall be readily available.
> (c) Where the eyes or body of any person may be exposed to injurious corrosive material, suitable facilities for quick drenching or flushing of the eyes and body shall be provided within the work area for immediate emergency use.

> **§ 1910.157 Portable fire extinguishers.**
> (a) *General requirements*—(1) *Operable condition.* Portable extinguishers shall be maintained in a fully charged and operable condition, and kept in their designated places at all times when they are not being used.
> (2) *Location.* Extinguishers shall be conspicuously located where they will be readily accessible and immediately available in the event of fire. They shall be located along normal paths of travel.
> (3) *Marking of location.* Extinguishers shall not be obstructed or obscured from view. In large rooms, and in certain locations where visual obstruction cannot be completely avoided, means shall be provided to indicate the location and intended use of extinguishers conspicuously.
> (4) *Marking of extinguishers.* If extinguishers intended for different classes of fire are grouped, their intended use shall be marked conspicuously to insure choice of the proper extinguisher at the time of a fire.
> (5) *Temperature range.* Extinguishers shall be suitable for use within a temperature range of at least 40° to 120° Fahrenheit.

SOURCE: General Industry Standards. USDOL Pamphlet OSHA No NO. 2206, OSHA Safety & Health STDS (29CFR 1910).

"General Duty" Clause   Section 5a(1) of the act is known as the "general duty" clause. This section requires that in areas in which no standards have been adopted, the employer has a *general duty* to provide safe and healthy working conditions. Employers who know of, or who should reasonably know of, unsafe or unhealthy conditions can be cited for violating this clause. The existence of standard practices or of a trade association code, which is not included in OSHA standards, often is used as the basis for citations under the general-duty clause. Employers are responsible for knowing about and informing their employees of safety and health standards established by OSHA and for displaying OSHA posters in prominent places. In addition, they are required to enforce the use of personal protective equipment and to provide safety communications to make employees aware of safety considerations. The act also states that employees who report safety violations to OSHA cannot be punished or discharged by their employers.

Hazard Communication   The federal Hazard Communication Standard requires manufacturers, importers, distributors, and users of hazardous chemicals to evaluate, classify, and label these substances. Employers must also make available to employees, their representatives, and health professionals information about hazardous substances. "Right to know" regulations have survived legal challenges from some industry and union groups and they have been held to be a "standard" within the meaning of the Occupational Safety and Health Act. The right to know of hazards is covered in more detail with employee rights in the next chapter.

Refusing Unsafe Work   Both union and nonunion workers have refused to work when they considered the work unsafe. Although such actions may appear to be insubordination, in many cases they are not. Two important Supreme Court cases have shed light on this issue. In *Whirlpool v. Marshall* (1980), employees and unions won a major victory. The U.S. Supreme Court unanimously ruled that workers have the right to walk off a job without fear of reprisal from the employer if they believe it is hazardous. The Court ruled that "employees have the right not to perform an assigned task because of a reasonable apprehension of health or serious injury coupled with a reasonable belief that no less drastic alternative is available."[45] *Gateway Coal v. the United Mine Workers* clarified the necessary requirements by which employees could refuse unsafe work.[46] Current legal conditions for refusing work because of safety concerns are:

▲ The employee's fear is objectively reasonable.
▲ The employee tried to get the dangerous condition corrected.
▲ Using normal procedures to solve the problem has not worked.

Record-Keeping Requirements

OSHA established a standard national system for recording occupational injuries, accidents, and fatalities. Employers are generally required to maintain an annual detailed record of the various types of accidents for inspection by OSHA representatives and for submission to the agency.

Employers who have had good safety records in the previous years and who have fewer than ten employees are not required to keep detailed records. Only those small organizations meeting the following conditions must complete OSHA form 200 (shown in Figure 16–9), the basic reporting document:

▲ Firms having frequent hospitalization, injuries, or illnesses
▲ Firms having work-related deaths
▲ Firms included in OSHA's annual labor statistics survey

No one knows how many industrial accidents go unreported. It may be many more than anyone suspects, despite the fact that OSHA has increased its surveillance of accident-reporting records. OSHA guidelines state that facilities whose accident record is less than the national average rarely need to be inspected, which gives organizations an incentive to become lax with safety standards.

Accident Frequency Rate   Accident frequency and severity rates must be calculated. Regulations from OSHA require organizations to calculate injury frequency rates per 100 full-time employees on an annual basis. The accident frequency rate is figured as follows:

$$\frac{N}{EH} \times 200,000$$

where N = number of occupational injuries and illnesses
     EH = total hours worked by all employees during reference year
200,000 = base for 100 full-time equivalent workers (working 40 hours per week 50 weeks per year)

Employers compute accident severity rates by figuring the number of lost-time cases, the number of lost workdays, and the number of deaths. These figures are then related to total work hours per 100 full-time employees and compared with industrywide rates and other employers' rates.

Reporting Injuries/Illnesses   There are four types of injuries or illnesses defined by the act:

1. *Injury- or illness-related deaths.*
2. *Lost-time or disability injuries.* Disabling or job-related injuries that cause an employee to miss his or her regularly scheduled work on the day following the accident.
3. *Medical care injuries.* Injuries that require treatment by a physician but do not cause an employee to miss a regularly scheduled work turn.
4. *Minor injuries.* Injuries that require first-aid treatment and do not cause an employee to miss the next regularly scheduled work turn.

The record-keeping requirements under OSHA are summarized in Figure 16–10. Notice that only minor injuries do not have to be recorded for OSHA. Managers may attempt to avoid reporting lost-time or medical care injuries. For example, if several managers are trained in first aid, some injuries can be treated on the worksite. In one questionable situation, an employee's back injuries were treated with heat packs by the plant HR manager to avoid counting the accident as a medical care injury.

Employers sometimes move injured employees to other jobs to avoid counting an injury as a lost-time injury. For example, if a seamstress in a clothing factory injured her hand on the job so that she could not operate her sewing machine, her employer might ask her to carry thread to other operators and perform other "make-work" jobs so that she did not miss work, and the injury would not have to be reported. Current regulations attempt to control this kind of subterfuge by requiring employees to perform the same type of jobs they performed before being injured.

▲ **Figure 16–9**   OSHA Form 200

U.S. Department of Labor

For Calendar Year 19 _____   Page ____ of____

Company Name		
Establishment Name		Form Approved O.M.B. No. 1220-0029
Establishment Address		

Extent of and Outcome of INJURY						Type, Extent of, and Outcome of ILLNESS								

| Fatalities | Nonfatal Injuries | | | | | Type of Illness | | | | | | | | | | Fatalities | Nonfatal Illnesses | | | | |

| Injury Related | Injuries With Lost Workdays | | | | Injuries Without Lost Workdays | CHECK Only One Column for Each Illness *(See other side of form for terminations or permanent transfers.)* | | | | | | | Illness Related | Illnesses With Lost Workdays | | | | Illnesses Without Lost Workdays |

| Enter **DATE** of death. | Enter a **CHECK** if injury involves days away from work, or days of restricted work activity, or both. | Enter a **CHECK** if injury involves days away from work. | Enter number of **DAYS** away *from work.* | Enter number of **DAYS** of *restricted work activity.* | Enter a **CHECK** if no entry was made in columns 1 or 2 but the injury is recordable as defined above. | Occupational skin diseases or disorders | Dust diseases of the lungs | Respiratory conditions due to toxic agents | Poisoning (systemic effects of toxic materials) | Disorders due to physical agents | Disorders associated with repeated trauma | All other occupational illnesses | Enter **DATE** of death. | Enter a **CHECK** if illness involves days away from work, or days of restricted work activity, or both. | Enter a **CHECK** if illness involves days away from work. | Enter number of **DAYS** away *from work.* | Enter number of **DAYS** of *restricted work activity.* | Enter a **CHECK** if no entry was made in columns 8 or 9. |

| Mo./day/yr. | | | | | | | | | | | | | Mo./day/yr. | | | | | |

(1)	(2)	(3)	(4)	(5)	(6)	(7)							(8)	(9)	(10)	(11)	(12)	(13)
						(a)	(b)	(c)	(d)	(e)	(f)	(g)						

Certification of Annual Summary Totals By _____ Title _____ Date _____

OSHA No. 200   **POST ONLY THIS PORTION OF THE LAST PAGE NO LATER THAN FEBRUARY 1.**

▲ **Figure 16–10**   Guide to Recordability of Cases Under the Occupational Safety and Health Act

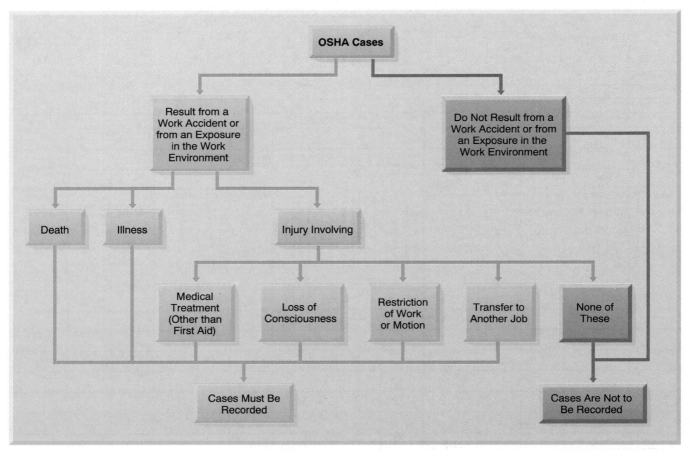

SOURCE: U.S. Department of Labor Statistics. *What Every Employee Needs to Know About OSHA Record Keeping* (Washington D.C.: U.S. Government Printing Office).

Inspection Requirements

The act provides for on-the-spot inspection by OSHA agents, known as *compliance officers* or *inspectors*. Under the original act, an employer could not refuse entry to an OSHA inspector. Further, the original act prohibited a compliance officer from notifying an organization before an inspection. Instead of allowing an employer to "tidy up," this *no-knock provision* permits inspection of normal operations. The provision was challenged in numerous court suits. Finally, in 1978, the U.S. Supreme Court ruled on the issue.

Marshall v. Barlow's, Inc.   An Idaho plumbing and air conditioning firm, Barlow's, refused entry to an OSHA inspector. The employer argued that the no-knock provision violated the Fourth Amendment of the U.S. Constitution, which deals with "unreasonable search and seizure." The government argued that the no-knock provision was necessary for enforcement of the act and that the Fourth Amendment did not apply to a business situation in which employees and customers have access to the firm.

The Supreme Court rejected the government's arguments and held that safety inspectors must produce a search warrant if an employer refuses to allow an inspector into the plant voluntarily. However, the Court ruled that an inspector does not have to prove probable cause to obtain a search warrant. A warrant can be obtained if a search is part of a general enforcement plan.[47]

Conduct of Inspection   When the compliance officer arrives, the manager should request to see the inspector's credentials. After entering, the OSHA officer typically requests a meeting with the top representative or manager in the organization. The officer also may request that a union representative, an employee, and a company representative be present as the inspection is conducted. The OSHA inspector checks organizational records to see if they are being maintained and the number of accidents that have occurred. Following this review of the safety records, the inspector conducts an on-the-spot inspection and may use a wide variety of equipment to test compliance with the standards. After the inspection, the compliance officer can issue citations for violations of standards and provisions of the act.

Safety Consultation   In conjunction with state and local governments, OSHA has established a safety consultation service. An employer can contact the state agency and have an authorized safety consultant conduct an advisory inspection. The consultant cannot issue citations or penalties and generally is prohibited from providing OSHA with any information obtained during the consultation visit. Such a visit provides an employer with safety information to help prevent future difficulties when OSHA does conduct an inspection.

Citations and Violations

The OSHA violation and citation notices issued depend on the severity and extent of the problems and on the employer's knowledge of them. There are basically five types ranging from severe to minimal:

- ▲ Imminent danger
- ▲ Serious
- ▲ Other than serious
- ▲ *De minimis*
- ▲ Willful and repeated

Imminent Danger   If there is reasonable certainty that the condition will cause death or serious physical harm if it is not corrected immediately, an imminent-danger citation is issued and a notice posted by an inspector. Imminent danger situations are handled on the highest priority basis. They are reviewed by a regional OSHA director and must be corrected immediately. If the condition is serious enough and the employer does not cooperate, a representative of OSHA may go to a federal judge and obtain an injunction to close the company until the condition is corrected. The absence of any guard railings to prevent an employee from falling three stories into heavy machinery could be classified as an imminent-danger violation.

Serious   When a condition could probably cause death or serious physical harm, and the employer should know of the condition, a serious-violation citation is issued. Examples are the absence of a protective screen on a lathe (which could easily allow an employee to mangle a hand) or the lack of a blade guard on an electric saw.

Other Than Serious   Other-than-serious violations could have an impact on employees' health or safety but probably would not cause death or serious harm. Having loose ropes in a work area on which people could trip and hurt themselves might be classified as an other-than-serious violation.

De Minimis   A *de minimis* condition is one that does not have a direct and immediate relationship to the employees' safety or health. A citation is not issued, but the condition is mentioned to the employer. Lack of doors on toilet stalls is an example of a *de minimis* violation.

Willful and Repeated   Citations for willful-and-repeated violations are issued to employers who have been previously cited for violations. If an employer knows about a safety violation or has been warned of a violation and does not correct the problem, a second citation is issued. The penalty for a willful-and-repeated violation can be very high. If death results from an accident in which there is a safety violation, a jail term of six months can be imposed on responsible executives or managers.

Penalties

OSHA has recently changed its penalties. The Congressional Budget Office estimates the fines will provide $70 million per year for the federal coffers. Figure 16–11 shows the new penalty maximums compared with the old ones. Failure to abate refers to lack of action to correct a problem, and posting refers to placing written material in public view.

Effects of OSHA

By making employers and employees more aware of safety and health considerations, OSHA has had a significant impact on organizations. But how effective

▲ **Figure 16–11**

New OSHA Penalties

TYPE OF VIOLATION	OLD PENALTY MAXIMUM	NEW PENALTY MAXIMUM
Willful and repeated violations ($5,000 minimum penalty for willful violations)	$10,000	$70,000
Serious and other-than-serious violations	1,000	7,000
Failure-to-abate violations	1,000	7,000
Posting requirements	1,000	7,000

Figure 16–12   OSHA Success Over Time

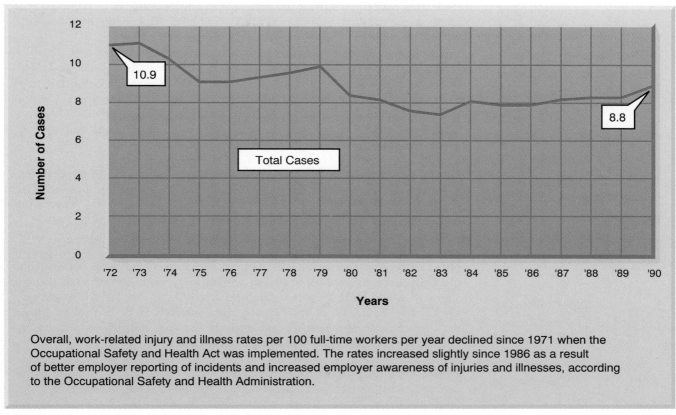

Overall, work-related injury and illness rates per 100 full-time workers per year declined since 1971 when the Occupational Safety and Health Act was implemented. The rates increased slightly since 1986 as a result of better employer reporting of incidents and increased employer awareness of injuries and illnesses, according to the Occupational Safety and Health Administration.

SOURCE: U.S. Department of Labor, Bureau of Labor Statistics.

the act has been is not clear. It does appear that OSHA regulations have been able to reduce the number of accidents and injuries in some cases. Some studies have shown that OSHA has had a positive impact; others have shown that OSHA has had no impact. Figure 16–12 tracks OSHA success over time.

Criticisms of OSHA

Most employers agree with the act's intent to provide healthy and safe working conditions for all employees. However, criticism of OSHA has emerged for several reasons.

Vague Standards   Some OSHA standards are vague, especially the "general duty" clause. It is difficult for an employer to know whether or not it is complying. In one case, a standard required that plants with a certain number of workers have qualified medical personnel "in near proximity" to the work area. This standard has been the subject of several OSHA violations and cases. What is meant by "near proximity"? Is it in the work area? In the plant? Is it a hospital ten minutes away?

Highly Technical Rules   OSHA rules often are very complicated and technical. Small business owners and managers who do not have specialists on their staffs find the standards difficult to read and understand. The presence of many minor standards also hurts OSHA's credibility. To counter such criticism, OSHA has revoked about 900 minor or confusing standards.

Need for Safety Counseling   Another major criticism is that an OSHA inspector cannot serve as a safety counselor. However, with the establishment of the consultation program this criticism has lost some of its strength. Officials from OSHA also can meet with employers who are designing and building new facilities to review blueprints and plans. This review enables the employers to design their facilities to comply with OSHA regulations.

Costs of Compliance   An additional concern is that the cost of correcting violations may be prohibitive for many employers. For a small company to make major structural changes in a building may be financially impossible. The cost of compliance may not be realistic given the cost of the violation.

In one case, the U.S. Supreme Court indicated that OSHA regulations limiting the exposure of workers to cotton dust do not have to meet a cost/benefit test. The decision in the case indicated that the congressional intent of establishing OSHA was to provide maximum worker protection. Use of a cost/benefit approach would lead to less protection because of high costs, which would violate the law. As a result of this decision, some efforts have been made to amend the act to include cost/benefit considerations. But such efforts have been strongly resisted by the AFL-CIO and other labor organizations.[48]

Probability of Inspection   Because OSHA has so many worksites to inspect, many employers have only a relatively small probability of being inspected. Some suggest that many employers pay little attention to OSHA enforcement efforts for this reason. Labor unions and others have criticized OSHA and Congress for not providing enough inspectors.

▲   A SYSTEMS APPROACH TO SAFETY

Effective safety management considers the types of safety problems, accidents, employees, and technology in the organizational setting. Furthermore, the systems approach to safety recognizes the importance of the human element in safety. Simply attempting to engineer machines, without dealing with the behavioral reactions of employees and without encouraging safe behavior, compartmentalizes the safety effort. Several basic components are involved in a systematic approach to safety.

Organizational Commitment

Any systematic approach to safety begins with organizational commitment to a comprehensive safety effort. This effort should be coordinated from the top to include all members of the organization. It should also be reflected in management's actions and work. One study of five plants that won safety awards showed that "active management involvement in occupational safety makes the major difference between success and failure."[49] If the president of a small electrical manufacturing firm does not wear a hard hat in the manufacturing shop, he can hardly expect to enforce a requirement that all employees wear hard hats in the shop. Unfortunately, sincere support by top management often is missing from many safety programs.

Coordinated Safety Efforts

Once a commitment is made to safety, planning efforts must be coordinated, with duties assigned to supervisors, managers, safety specialists, and HR specialists. Naturally, duties vary according to the size of the organization and the industry. For this reason, it is impossible to suggest a single proper mixture of responsibilities. The focus of any systematic approach to safety is the continued diligence of workers, managers, and other personnel. Employees who are not reminded of safety violations, who are not encouraged to be safety conscious, or who violate company safety rules and policies are not likely to be safe.

Safety Committees   Workers frequently are involved in safety planning through safety committees, often composed of workers from a variety of levels and departments. At least one member of the committee is usually from the HR unit. A safety committee generally has regularly scheduled meetings, has specific responsibilities for conducting safety reviews, and makes recommendations for changes necessary to avoid future accidents.

The safety emphasis must be consistently made and enforced. Properly coordinated efforts between HR units and managers will aid in developing safety-conscious and safety-motivated employees. Self-directed workforces and other types of participation seem to increase compliance and interest in safety issues.[50]

Employee Safety Motivation   Encouraging employees to keep safety standards continuously in mind while performing their jobs is difficult. Often, employees think that safety measures are bothersome and unnecessary until an injury occurs. For example, requiring employees to wear safety glasses in a laboratory may be necessary most of the time. But if the glasses are awkward, employees may resist using them, even when they know they should have protection. Some employees may have worked for years without them and think this new requirement is a nuisance.

Safety Discipline   Enforcing safety rules and disciplining violators are important components of safety efforts. Frequent reinforcement of the need for safe behavior and feedback on positive safety practices are extremely effective in improving worker safety.

Consistent enforcement has been used by employers as a defense against OSHA citations. In one situation, a utility foreman was electrocuted while operating an overhead crane. However, the company was exonerated because it had consistently enforced safety rules and penalized violators. The employee who was killed violated a safety rule for grounding equipment even though the company had given him regular safety training, had posted signs prominently, and had warned all employees about grounding equipment. The OSHA district director ruled that the employee's action was an isolated incident and management was not to blame.

Safety Incentives　Some organizations have used safety contests and given incentives to employees for safe work behavior. Jewelry, clocks, watches, and even vacation trips have been given as rewards to employees for good safety records. For example, safe driving awards for drivers in trucking firms have been quite successful in generating safety consciousness. Belt buckles and lapel pins are especially popular with the drivers.

Safety Training and Communications　One way to encourage employee safety is to involve all employees at various times in safety training sessions and committee meetings and to have these meetings frequently. In addition to safety training, continuous communication programs to develop safety consciousness are necessary. Merely sending safety memos is not enough. Posting safety policies and rules is part of this effort. Contests, incentives, and posters are all ways employers can heighten safety awareness. Changing safety posters, continually updating bulletin boards, and posting safety information in visible areas also are recommended. Safety films and videotapes are additional ways to communicate safety ideas.

Safety Inspection and Accident Investigation　It is not necessary to wait for an OSHA inspector to inspect the work area for safety hazards. Such inspections may be done by a safety committee or by the safety coordinator. They should be done on a regular basis because OSHA may inspect organizations with above-average lost workday rates more frequently.

In investigating the *scene* of an accident, it is important to determine the physical and environmental conditions that contributed to the accident. Poor lighting, poor ventilation, and wet floors are all possible considerations at the scene. Investigation at the scene should be done as soon as possible after the accident to ensure that conditions under which the accident occurred have not changed significantly. One way to obtain an accurate view of the accident scene is with photographs or videotapes.

The second phase of the investigation is the *interview* of the injured employee, his or her supervisor, and witnesses to the accident. The interviewer attempts to determine what happened and how the accident was caused. These interviews may also generate some suggestions on how to prevent similar accidents in the future. Based upon observations of the scene and interviews, the third phase is completion of an *accident investigation report*. This report form provides the necessary data required by OSHA.

Finally, recommendations should be made on how the accident could have been prevented and what changes could prevent further similar accidents. Identifying why an accident occurred is useful, but taking steps to prevent similar accidents from occurring again is important also.

Accident Research　Closely related to accident investigation is research to determine ways to prevent accidents. Employing safety engineers or having outside experts evaluate the safety of working conditions is useful. If a large number of similar accidents seem to occur in an organizational unit, a safety education training program may be necessary to emphasize safe working practices. As an example, a publishing company reported a greater than average number of back injuries caused by employees lifting boxes. Safety training on the proper way to lift heavy objects was then initiated to prevent back injuries.

Evaluation of Safety Efforts

Organizations need to monitor their safety efforts. Just as organizational accounting records are audited, periodic audits of a firm's safety efforts should be made also. Accident and injury statistics should be compared with previous accident patterns to determine if any significant changes have occurred. This analysis should be designed to measure progress in safety management. A manager at a hospital might measure its safety efforts by comparing the hospital's accident rate with hospital industry figures and with rates at other hospitals of the same size in the area.

Another part of safety evaluation is updating safety materials and safety training aids. The accident-investigation procedures and accident-reporting methods also should be evaluated continually to make sure these are actually generating ideas useful in reducing accidents. Safety policies and regulations should be reviewed and made to comply with both existing and new standards set up by OSHA, state, and professional agencies.

 SUMMARY

- ▲ Health is a general state of physical, mental, and emotional well-being.
- ▲ Safety is protection of the physical well-being of people.
- ▲ Accidents and industrial health concerns are major problems both from cost and personal standpoints.
- ▲ Worker attitudes play a major role in accidents and accident prevention.
- ▲ Accident prevention can be approached from an engineering or behavioral perspective, but both should be considered.
- ▲ The work environment has been found to contain some health problems such as sick building syndrome and fetal protection concerns.
- ▲ Stress is a major concern today because of its relationship to physical illness. However, not all stress is bad.
- ▲ People find that situations in which they cannot control, accurately predict, accurately perceive, or escape intense responsibility are very stressful.
- ▲ Employee Assistance Programs (EAPs) provide counseling and other help to employees having emotional, physical, or other health problems.
- ▲ Alcoholism and drug abuse are extremely expensive to industry.
- ▲ AIDS and smoking at work are two issues growing in importance.
- ▲ Employer policies against substance abuse will be affected by the Americans With Disabilities Act.
- ▲ Many employers are reacting to substance abuse by workers by getting tough or by increasing use of EAPs.
- ▲ The Occupational Health and Safety Act (OSHA) is designed to help improve the accident-prevention and health situation in business and industry.
- ▲ OSHA requires record keeping, reporting of injuries, and inspection of worksites.
- ▲ Criticisms of OSHA range from charges of vague standards to a lack of effectiveness.

▲ A good safety program that considers accident prevention from a systems perspective includes organizational commitment, coordination, employee motivation, accident investigation, accident research, and evaluation of safety efforts.

▲ REVIEW AND DISCUSSION QUESTIONS

1. Differentiate between health and safety as HR activities. Then identify some factors that affect health and safety.
2. Discuss the following statement by a supervisor: "I feel it is my duty to get involved with my employees and their personal problems to show that I truly care about them."
3. Why should an employer be concerned about employee substance abuse?
4. Describe the Occupational Safety and Health Act (OSHA) and some of its key provisions regarding standards, record keeping, and inspection requirements.
5. Discuss the following comment: "OSHA should be abolished because it just serves to harass small businesses."
6. Why is a systems approach to safety important?

 ESTABLISHING AN EAP

A medium-sized company in Dayton, Ohio manufactures premium pet food. It has done well by carefully and methodically growing at the expense of competitive brands of pet food. The IAMS Company showed the same methodical approach in establishing an employee assistance program (EAP) for its employees and their families.

"We had several discussions with a consultant. He recommended several providers, and we interviewed them over several months," says Richard Liette, Director of Employee Relations. "Most important were the references from other [employers] we contacted, asking what kind of services they used, what kind of reports they got, what complaints they'd heard, and were they happy."

IAMS' EAP covers everything from substance abuse to financial counseling for a cost of $32 per person/per year. A year into it, Liette says IAMS is "extremely happy" with the program. "It takes us out of the middle," he explains. "If there are emotional problems, there's a way to get at them."

And that's the nub of it. Companies don't want to be in the middle of employees' emotional problems. They don't deal well with them, even glancingly. But by using a contract provider, companies can enjoy the benefits of mentally healthier and happier employees. Steady performance, employee retention and more stable insurance costs are the benefits to the employer, without having to do the social work themselves.

It sounds simple, but a paradox remains. Despite not wanting to be directly involved, somebody has to hire the contractor and assess the value of the services provided. And the services involve no ordinary business consulting.

Instead, they can relate to addiction, sexual abuse, and the arcane areas of psychiatry and therapeutic counseling. Rare is the company that has a staff person with credentials to evaluate providers in this sector.[51]

▲ **Questions**

1. How could a company set up a system to evaluate EAP contract services provided?

2. Do you think IAMS' reluctance to "do the social work themselves" is appropriate in an employee/employer relationship?

▲ **Notes**

1. Adapted from "Costs Prod Firms to Combat Repetitive-Stress Injuries," *Omaha World-Herald,* August 16, 1992, G1; "With Computers Comes Pain," *Omaha World-Herald,* January 3, 1993, 62R; "Safeguard Operator's Health," *Nation's Business,* April 1991, 22; "Ergonomics Research," *HR Magazine,* July 1990, 20; Albert R. Karr, "Labor Agency Begins Move to Set Rules on 'Ergonomic Hazards' in Workplace," *The Wall Street Journal,* August 5, 1992, A8; Julia Lawlor, "Jury Gives RSI Award," *USA Today,* August 24, 1992, B1; and J. Rigdon, "The Wrist Watch," *The Wall Street Journal,* September 28, 1992, 1.

2. "Workplace Injuries, Illnesses Surge to New Record," *The Lincoln Star,* November 20, 1991, 9.

3. J. Mishizen, "In the Eye of the Health Care Storm," *HR Magazine,* September 1991, 49.

4. "True Tales from the Workplace," *Training and Development,* May 1991, 93.

5. Michael A. Verespej, "Execs Could Be Tried for Murder," *Industry Week,* March 6, 1989, 61; Milo Geyelin, "Verdict Upheld for Workers in Personal Injury Case," *Wall Street Journal,* June 2, 1989, B1; and Susan B. Garland, "Safety Ruling Could Be Hazardous to Employer's Health," *Business Week,* February 20, 1989, 34.

6. "Investigation of Child Labor Hits Thousands," *Omaha World-Herald,* March 15, 1990, 1; and "Child Labor Violations on the Rise," *Omaha World-Herald,* February 11, 1990, 8G.

7. R. L. Barnett and D. B. Brickman, "Safety Hierarchy," *Journal of Safety Research* 17 (1986), 50.

8. P. Fernberg, "Laying Down the Law on Ergonomics," *Modern Office,* October 1992, 74–76.

9. Adapted from Michael Schuster and Susan Rhodes, "The Impact of Overtime Work on Industrial Accident Rates," *Industrial Relations* 26 (1985), 234–246.

10. John B. Miner and Mary G. Miner, *Personnel and Industrial Relations,* 4th ed. (New York: Macmillan, 1985), 485–487.

11. U.S. Department of Labor, Occupational Safety and Health Administration, *Mercury,* OSHA Pamphlet No. 2234 (Washington, D.C.: U.S. Government Printing Office).

12. "Sick Buildings Affect Workers, Puzzle Scientists, Scare Firms!", *Omaha World-Herald,* October 11, 1992, G1.

13. Stephanie Overman, "Prescriptions for Healthier Offices," *HR Magazine,* February 1990, 30–31.

14. M. Alpert, "Office Buildings for the 1990's," *Fortune,* November 18, 1991, 140.

15. J. Carlton, "Study of Computer Chip Plants Finds Worker Miscarriage Risk," *The Wall Street Journal,* December 14, 1992, B1.

16. J. Burgess, "Miscarriages High at Microchip Plants," *Denver Post,* December 5, 1992, 12A.

17. *United Autoworkers v. Johnson Controls, Inc.* 111S.Ct. 1196 (1991).

18. Howard A. Simon, "Mixed Signals: The Supreme Court's Title VII Decisions," *Employee Relations Law Journal* 7 (1991), 214.

19. M. Osborn, "Workers Stretched to Limits," *USA Today,* September 8, 1992, 1.

20. M. Malik, "All Stressed Up and No Place to Go," *Modern Office Technology,* February 1993, 27.

21. *HRAM Newsletter,* February 1990, 2.

22. R. Ricklefs, "Many Executives Complain of Stress," *The Wall Street Journal,* September 29, 1989, 27.

23. P. Dewe and D. Guest, "Methods of Coping with Stress at Work: A Conceptual Analysis and Empirical Study of Measurement Issues," *Journal of Organizational Behavior* 11 (1990), 135–150.

24. Daniel Ganster and John Schaubroeck, "Work Stress and Employee Health," *Journal of Management* 17 (1991), 235–271.

25. K. Miller, "Now Japan Is Admitting It: Work Kills Executives," *Business Week,* August 3, 1992, 35.

26. D. Kirrane, "EAPs: Dawning of a New Age," *HR Magazine,* January 1990, 34.

27. See the following for a discussion of evaluating EAPs and some of the problems: W. Afield, "Running Amok," *Business Insurance,* May 29, 1989; E. Settineri, "Effectively Measuring Costs of EAPs," *HR Magazine,* April 1991, 53; and R. Stolz (ed.), "A Closer Look at EAPs," *Employee Benefit News,* March 1992, 4–15.

28. G. Parliman and E. Edwards, "Employee Assistance Programs: Am Employer's Guide to Emerging Liability Issues," *Employee Relations Law Journal* 7 (1991), 593–601.

29. "HRM Update," *HR Magazine,* August 1990, 23.

30. M. Kronson, "Substance Abuse Coverage Provided by Employer Medical Plans," *Monthly Labor Review,* April 1991, 3.

31. P. Gleason et al., "Drug and Alcohol Use at Work: A Survey of Young Workers," *Monthly Labor Review,* August 1991, 3–7.

32. J. Yu et al., "An Analysis of Substance Abuse Patterns, Medical Expenses and Effectiveness of Treatment in the Workplace," *Employee Benefit Journal,* September 1991, 26.

33. W. Lehman and D. Simpson, "Employee Substance Use and On-the-Job Behaviors," *Journal of Applied Psychology* 77 (1992), 309.

34. 45 CFR 84-3 (J)(2)(i).

35. G. Koretz, "Alcoholism's Drain on the Economy May Be Deeper Than Ever," *Business Week,* December 30, 1991, 26.

36. W. Symonds and Peter Coy, "Is Business Bungling Its Battle with Booze?", *Business Week,* March 25, 1991, 76–77.

37. J. Castelli, "Employer-Provided Programs Pay Off," *HR Magazine,* April 1990, 55.

38. S. Bergeman, "Addiction," *HR Magazine,* April 1990, 48.

39. E. Wiseman, "Peer Pressure Curbs Drug Use," *Personnel Journal,* November 1990, 29.

40. T. Tyrer, "AIDS, AA Survey Shows Workplace Concern," *Advertising Age,* April 3, 1989, 1, 22, 27; J. Mello, "AIDS Education for the Workplace," *Training and Development Journal,* December 1990, 65; and R. Tedlow and M. Marram, "A Case of AIDS," *Harvard Business Review,* November–December 1991, 14.

41. Jonathan A. Segal, "AIDS Education Is a Necessary High-Risk Activity," *HR Magazine,* February 1991, 82.

42. Jack Kondrasuk and C. Carl, "Wellness Programs: Present and Future," *Employee Services Management,* December–January 1991–1992, 10.

43. J. Erfurt et al., "The Cost-Effectiveness of Worksite Wellness Programs" *Personnel Psychology* 45 (1992), 5.

44. D. Bunch, "Coors Wellness Center—Helping the Bottom Line," *Employee Benefits Journal,* March 1992, 14; and Shari Caudron, "The Wellness Payoff," *Personnel Journal,* July 1990, 55.

45. *Whirlpool v. Marshall,* 78–1870 (1980).

46. *Gateway Coal Co. v. the United Mine Workers of America,* 94 S. Ct. 641 (1981).

47. *Marshall v. Barlow's, Inc.,* 76–1143 (1978)

48. "Union Claims OSHA Fails U.S. Workers," *HR Executive,* June 1992, 15.

49. L. Broadwell, "The Wheels Are Turning," *Safety Incentives,* September 1992, 84–89; and D. Warner, "Ways to Make Safety Work," *Nation's Business,* December 1991, 25.

50. J. Jenkins, "Self-Directed Work Force Promotes Safety," *HR Magazine,* February 1990, 54; and D. Pillsbury, "Worker Safety," *Forbes,* October 19, 1992, 399.

51. Adapted from Katherine G. Hauck, "Examining Effectiveness," *Human Resource Executive,* June 1992, 63.

CHAPTER 17

EMPLOYEE RIGHTS AND DISCIPLINE

After you have read this chapter, you should be able to:

1. Explain how employee rights and HR policies are interrelated.

2. Identify three exceptions to employment-at-will used by the courts.

3. List elements necessary to maintain an employee handbook as part of an implied employment contract.

4. Explain the concept of just cause and how it is determined.

5. Discuss the issues and problems associated with drug tests.

6. Identify the major concerns about polygraph and honesty testing.

7. Outline a progressive discipline sequence.

HR Today and Tomorrow:
Computerized "Spying": An Employee Rights Issue?

When Andy Hopper leaves his Olivetti Research Lab Office, within 15 seconds anyone who wants to know about it will be informed. Andy wears an "active badge" that signals his whereabouts by sending infrared signals to a computer. Andy wears his badge voluntarily, but as the use of such systems spreads, the balance between corporate desires for efficiency and control and employees' rights to privacy will surely be tested.

Eavesdropping is on the rise, both on and off the job, thanks to advances in surveillance technology. On the job, employers are using sensitive instruments to check on supermarket checkers, bank tellers, stockbrokers, IRS agents, hotel reservation agents, hospital workers, and airline pilots. This surveillance is called *monitoring,* and is usually aimed at measuring the performance of service workers. Although monitoring has been used in the past, it has been made much easier by the advent of computer technology. It may take many forms, from counting the number of keystrokes a secretary makes per hour, to tallying the lines of copy a programmer writes per day.

Monitoring of employees has resulted in some real cost savings. Equitable Life Assurance Society uses a computer to check on how much work each employee is producing and it has cut its claims-processing force significantly and is paying 20% more claims with 30% fewer people. Also, in the financial industry, Kidder Peabody and Company says it monitors bond-trading conversations between brokers and customers to safeguard order accuracy. In most states a company *legally* can eavesdrop on its employees' telephone calls as long as it tells employees that is what it is going to do.

Despite success stories, the negative effects of monitoring are a growing concern. Some people simply do not like it, including some lawmakers and privacy-rights advocates. The issue is becoming a power pull, and the strong undoubtedly will win. Through collective bargaining, airline pilots won the right not to be monitored. Monitoring has become an issue for Equitable too, as claims processors bargain for a say in the monitoring standards used.

Another technology, electronic mail (E-mail) has led to cases of disputes. Over 12.5 million people currently use electronic messaging at work. People are exchanging messages over E-mail networks that previously would have been communicated by phone or in the hallway. While many civil libertarians believe such communication should not be subject to Big Brothers looking over people's shoulders, others feel it should be public.

Electronic eavesdropping works both ways, of course. *The Wall Street Journal* reported an increase in secret tapings of supervisors by their employees. Such taping is often done to buttress legal claims. One lawyer said, "If Anita Hill had had a tape recorder, we wouldn't have had that hearing." Incidently, federal law currently allows such taping as long as *one* of the people being recorded knows about it. In 14 other states, all parties to conversations being recorded must know.

There *are* sound, business-related arguments for using monitoring of employees of some kind. For example, a Michigan Bell spokesman notes that the company monitors a random sampling of calls to operators and customer service representatives. He says the practice is "essentially the only quality control tool we have. We don't have a product like a car that rolls off the assembly line and can be inspected." Indeed, in many kinds of service industries the only way to make sure of service quality and training needs employees may have is to monitor their work, and this may necessarily include electronic conversations.[1]

One factor is certain. More will be heard about employee privacy rights clashing with technology in the future.

" ━━━━━━━━━━━━━━━━━━━━

The right to be left alone—the most comprehensive of rights and the most valued by civilized men.

Louis Brandeis ━━━━━━━━━━ "

This chapter considers three related and important issues in the management of human resources: employee rights, HR policies and rules, and discipline. At first consideration these may seem separate issues, but in truth they are not. The policies and rules that an organization enacts define employee rights to a certain extent and also constrain those same rights (sometimes inappropriately or illegally). Similarly, discipline of those who fail to follow policies and rules often is seen as a fundamental right of employers.

The three concepts are interconnected and constantly changing as laws and societal values change. Although the U.S. Constitution grants citizens rights to freedom and due process, all such rights are not necessarily present in the workplace. Federal, state, and local laws or labor/management contracts have been necessary to grant employees such rights at work. Without these constraints, the right of management to run organizations as it chooses was at one time so strong that employee rights were practically nonexistent. Laws involving such areas as equal employment opportunity, collective bargaining, and safety have changed traditional management prerogatives. These laws and their recent interpretations have been the subjects of considerable dispute.

▲ EMPLOYEE RIGHTS AND RESPONSIBILITIES

Generally rights do not exist in the abstract. They exist only when someone is successful in demanding their practical applications. A **right** is that which belongs to a person by law, nature, or tradition. Of course, there is considerable potential for disagreement as to what really is a right. Employer pressures on employees with "different" lifestyles illustrate one area in which conflicts can occur. Moreover, *legal* rights may or may not correspond to certain *moral* rights, and the reverse is true as well.

Rights are offset by **responsibilities** which are duties or obligations to be accountable for actions. Jeremy Bentham, the European reformer, observed that when one party is given a "right," there is a certain behavior that another party is obligated to maintain for the exercise of that right by the first party. Put another way, when a person has a "moral right" to do or have something, then some other person has corresponding obligations.[2] For example, if an employee has the right to work in a safe working environment, the employer has an obligation to provide a safe workplace. However, because rights and responsibilities are reciprocal, the employer also has a right to expect uninterrupted, high-quality work from the employee, meaning that the worker has the responsibility to be on the job and do it carefully. Employment is a reciprocal relationship (both sides have obligations), and employee rights arise in exchange for reciprocal employee actions such as loyalty and service.

This reciprocal nature of rights and responsibilities suggests that each party to an employment relationship should regard the other as having equal rights and treat the other party accordingly, with respect.[3] Discussing rights without an

▼ **A RIGHT**

is that which belongs to a person by law, nature, or tradition.

▼ **A RESPONSIBILITY**

is a duty or obligation to be accountable for an action.

awareness of corresponding responsibilities shows knowledge of only part of the issue.

Rights at Home and at Work

Some rights have applications both on and off the job. Health and safety rights, free speech, and the right to due process are three examples. Other rights might apply in the workplace, but not the home, or vice versa. A restriction on employees smoking at work versus smoking at home is an example. Sometimes management and employees do not have a clear agreement as to which rights exist in the workplace. Unions have tried over the years to define employer-employee rights, often through confrontation. Unionism has declined, but increased legal restrictions on employer HR practices through state legislation and court decisions have increased employee rights.

The proliferation of court-backed employee rights mirrors a change in society's attitude toward work. To live within the new employee-rights environment, employers must ensure that the HR procedures are fair and not applied arbitrarily or capriciously. Figure 17–1 shows a possible division of responsibilities between the HR unit and operating managers over employee rights and discipline issues. Rights and responsibilities of the employee to the employer may be spelled out in a job description, in an employment contract, or in HR policies, but many are not. They may exist only as unwritten employer expectations about what is acceptable behavior or performance on the part of the employee.

Employee Rights Currently

Workplace litigation has reached epidemic proportions as employees who feel their rights have been violated sue their employers. Advocates for expanding employee rights warn that management policies abridging free speech, privacy, or due process will lead to national legislation to regulate the relationship.[4] At the same time, management is under pressure to maintain a lean, efficient, flexible, drug-free workforce. HR professionals argue that to remain competitive they must protect management's traditional employment-at-will prerogatives (discussed later in this chapter) to hire and fire and promote and demote employees as they see fit. To maintain efficiency and quality, poor performers cannot be tolerated.[5]

As employees increasingly regard themselves as free agents in the workplace—and the power of unions declines—the struggle between employee and employer

▲ **Figure 17–1**

Typical Division of Responsibilities for Employee Rights and Discipline

HR UNIT	MANAGERS
▲ Designs HR procedures that incorporate employee legal and moral rights ▲ Designs progressive discipline process if nonunion ▲ Trains managers on the protection and limits of employee rights and discipline process	▲ Keep informed of employee-rights concerns ▲ Operate under the discipline system—make disciplinary decisions and dismiss employees who violate policies and rules ▲ Provide feedback to HR to process on situations not covered by the disciplinary process

HR Perspectives:
Research on Policies to Protect Employees and Employers

Ben Rosen and Catherine Schwoerer reported in *HR Magazine* on a survey of 785 Society for Human Resource Management members on policies in effect to protect employee and employer rights. About 44% of those responding characterized their companies' policies as striking a balance between employee and employer rights. Thirty-seven percent said the policies emphasized employer rights, and 19% said employee rights were emphasized.

The following chart shows typical employee rights protection policies, the percentage of firms who have such a policy, and the percent that deem it successful.[6]

HR Activity	*Have a Policy*	*Feel the Policy is Successful*
Access to records	89.8%	93%
Privacy protection	83.2	96
Health/safety information	79.0	91
Disciplinary policy	71.7	95
Company ombudsman	39.8	91
Free-speech protection	26.3	85
Impartial arbitrators	23.3	87
Background investigation	80.9	89
Avoid "implied contract"	79.7	95
Termination at will	51.1	93
Medical screening	40.6	88
Drug testing	37.0	93
Psychological/polygraph testing	10.5	74
Electronic surveillance	7.4	73

"rights" is heightening. Employers have not fared very well in many cases. One study of claims of wrongful discharge found the employee had a 86% chance of winning a case brought against a private employer and a 33% chance against a government entity.[7] Another study showed that workers who sued for invasion of privacy, sexual harassment, or slander won an average jury award of $375,000. The invasion-of-privacy verdicts included cases of drug and alcohol abuse, unlawful surveillance, and use of polygraph tests. As in the previous study, a high percentage (72%) of the cases were won by employees.[8]

Further, it is not only the company that is liable in many cases. Individual managers and supervisors have been found liable when hiring or promotion decisions are based on discriminatory factors or when they have knowledge of such conduct and do not take steps to stop it. The "HR Perspective" shows the extent of policies designed to protect employees and employers in the U.S.

Employee rights defined in various state laws are divided here into three major categories:

1. Rights affecting the employment agreement
   - ▲ Employment-at-will
   - ▲ Implied employment contracts (employee handbooks)
   - ▲ Due process
   - ▲ Dismissal for just cause

2. Employee privacy rights
   ▲ Employee right to review records
   ▲ Substance abuse and drug testing
   ▲ Polygraph and honesty testing
3. Other employee rights
   ▲ Rights of workplace investigation
   ▲ Rights to know of potential hazards and unsafe working conditions
   ▲ Employee free speech and whistle-blowing
   ▲ Notification of plant closings
   ▲ Security at work

▲ RIGHTS AFFECTING THE EMPLOYMENT AGREEMENT

Although it can be argued that all the employee-rights issues affect the employment relationship, four basic issues predominate: employment-at-will, implied contracts, due process, and dismissal for just cause.

Employment-at-Will (EAW)

▼ **EMPLOYMENT-AT-WILL (EAW)**

is a common-law doctrine stating that employers have the right to hire, fire, demote, or promote whomever they choose, unless there is a law or contract to the contrary.

Employment-at-will (EAW) is a common-law doctrine stating that employers have the right to hire, fire, demote, or promote whomever they choose, unless there is a law or contract to the contrary. Employers often defend EAW for one or more of the following reasons:

1. The right of private ownership of a business guarantees EAW.
2. EAW defends employees' rights to change jobs, as well as employers' rights to hire and fire.
3. Interfering with EAW reduces productivity in our economy.

History of EAW   EAW is a by-product of the nineteenth-century Industrial Revolution. Laissez-faire social thought encouraged rapid economic expansion and granted business complete flexibility in the way employees were handled. Very little changed until the twentieth century, when unionized labor gained protection from arbitrary and capricious discharge through grievance-arbitration procedures in most union contracts. In disputed cases, a neutral arbitrator ruled whether or not there were adequate grounds for dismissal. Over time, both management and unions generally became familiar with restraints placed on employers who discharged employees. Many public-sector employees are granted due process protection under civil service regulations, whether or not employees are represented by a union. Nonunion employees remained under the EAW doctrine. In the 1960s, however, an increasing number of state courts began to create exceptions to EAW ideas. Courts questioned the *fairness* of an employer's decision to fire an employee without just cause and due process. The suits imply that employees have job rights that must be balanced against EAW.

The courts in California and New York have taken two very different approaches to EAW. These positions represent the extreme ends of a continuum of approaches being taken nationwide. In New York, courts have refused to take EAW cases, saying that EAW is a legislative concern, not one for the courts to decide. On the other hand, in California, courts will take EAW cases almost without exception.

Wrongful Discharge   The courts have recognized three different rationales for hearing EAW cases and concluding wrongful discharge:[9]

1. *Public policy exception.* This exception to EAW holds that an employee can sue if he or she is fired for action against public policy. For example, if an employee refused to commit perjury and was fired, he could sue. Or, if an employee refused to engage in a price-fixing arrangement and was fired, she could sue the employer.
2. *Implied employment contract.* This approach holds that the employee will not be fired as long as he or she does the job. Long service, promises of continued employment, lack of criticism of job performance, and how the employer has handled similar cases imply continuing employment.
3. *Good faith and fair dealing.* This approach suggests that a covenant of good faith and fair dealing exists between the employer and at-will employees. If the employer has broken this covenant by unreasonable behavior, the employee has legal recourse.

A landmark court case in this area is *Fortune v. National Cash Register Company.* The case involved the firing of a salesman (Fortune) who had been with National Cash Register (NCR) for 25 years.[10] Fortune was fired shortly after winning a large order that would have earned him a big commission. From the evidence, the court concluded that he was fired because NCR wanted to avoid paying him the commission, which violated the covenant of good faith.

The courts generally have conceded that unionized workers cannot pursue EAW actions as at-will employees because they are covered by an alternative remedy: the grievance-arbitration process.[11] Nearly all states have adopted one or more statutes that limit an employer's right to discharge. The universal restrictions include race, age, sex, national origin, religion, and handicap. Restrictions on other areas vary from state to state

Figure 17–2 shows a distribution of wrongful-discharge suits by tenure, sex, job, and race. The lesson of wrongful-discharge suits is that employers should take care to see that dismissals are handled properly, that all HR management systems are in order, and that due process and fair play are followed. Suggestions for preparing for the defense of any such lawsuits follow:

▲ Put grounds for dismissal in writing and distribute them to all employees.
▲ Keep good written records on all termination actions.
▲ Make sure performance appraisals give an honest picture of a person's performance.
▲ Warn employees of problems that possibly could lead to termination in writing before someone is dismissed.
▲ Involve more than one person in termination decisions.

Wrongful-discharge lawsuits have become a major concern for many firms. Such lawsuits (based on one study) cost an average of $80,000 to defend. Further, a Rand Corporation study found that "firms can avoid the legal threat [only] by not firing workers even when justified by economic conditions or poor job performance . . . trading off production efficiency for diminished exposure to legal liability."[12] In addition, companies are hiring fewer full-time employees and using more temporary workers and overtime to reduce the threat of wrongful-discharge lawsuits.[13]

Indeed, wrongful discharge has become a dilemma for even well-intentioned firms, as the following example of conflicting considerations relative to sexual harassment and wrongful discharge illustrates. Federal law requires employers to

▲ **Figure 17–2**   Wrongful-Discharge Suits

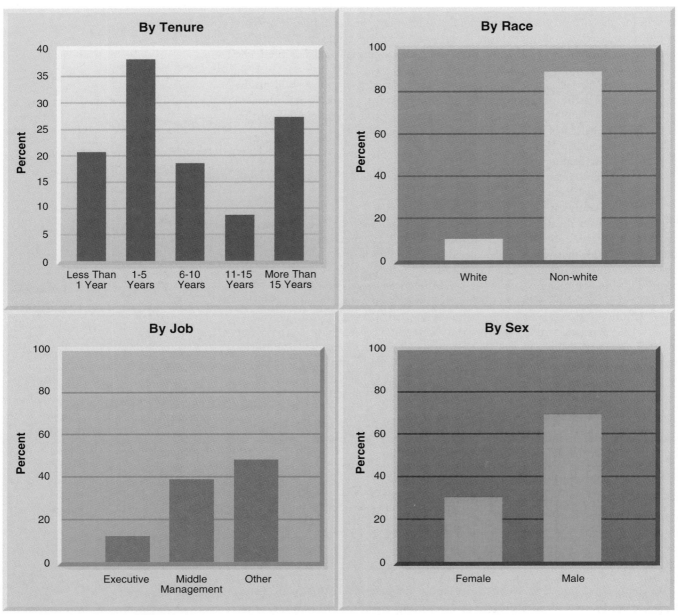

SOURCE: *The Wall Street Journal,* September 7, 1989, B1.

maintain a workplace free of sexual harassment. But some states allow workers to sue if they are discharged without good reason. The fired sexual harasser frequently sues the company, contesting the "good reason." When the court hears the case, the legal question becomes whether EEOC guidelines requiring "immediate and appropriate corrective action" when an employee complains of sexual harassment take precedent over state law and employment agreements that say the employer must have "just cause" before firing.[14]

Rights in the Employment Contract (Employee Handbooks)

Like employment-at-will, the idea that a contract (even an implied, unwritten one) exists between workers and their employer affects the employment relationship. Several courts have held that if an employer hires someone for an indefinite period, and promises job security, or gives specific procedures for discharge, the employer has lost the right to terminate at will. These actions establish employee expectations. When the employer fails to follow up on them, employees have recourse in court. In essence, the courts have held that such promises, especially when contained in an employee handbook, constitute a contract between an employer and its employees, even though there is no signed document. A landmark case is *Pine River State Bank v. Mettile,* but many other cases have led to similar conclusions: that handbooks are implied contracts. The legal remedy for a broken contract requires the party breaking the contract to perform and keep its contracted obligation. However, courts have also imposed compensatory and punitive damages for breaking such implied contracts.[15]

Due Process

Due process is the opportunity to defend oneself against charges. For unionized employees, due process usually refers to rights to use the grievance procedure specified in the union contract. It may include specific steps in the grievance process, time limits, arbitration procedures, and knowledge of disciplinary penalties.

▼ **DUE PROCESS**

gives one the opportunity to defend oneself against charges.

Compared with due process procedures specified in union contracts, at-will employee procedures are more varied and may address a broader range of issues. Attempts by at-will employees to use their rights of due process often run into difficulties for the following reasons:

1. Employees do not get enough help in preparing their defenses.
2. There is little protection for the employees who use the procedure against management.
3. The final decision maker may not be entirely independent from management.

These three issues must be addressed by management if due process procedures are to be perceived as fair by the courts. Employees certainly must be given the opportunity to present their sides of the story during the disciplinary process.

Nonunion organizations are well advised to have a grievance procedure providing due process for their employees. Just the presence of an equitable procedure can be a positive indication that an employee has been given due process. Further, if the due process procedure is seen as fair, discharged employees are less likely to sue.[16] The design of grievance procedures is covered in Chapter 19.

Organizational Ombudsman   An **ombudsman** is a person outside the normal chain of command who acts as a problem solver for management and employees. For example, one firm uses an ombudsman to resolve complaints from employees that cannot be settled through the employee's supervisor or the HR department. The ombudsman first reviews the employee's information and complaint. After the problems are discussed with other individuals, such as the employee's supervisor or a representative of the HR department, the ombudsman recommends a solution to the problem. Making such an individual available

▼ **AN OMBUDSMAN**

is a person outside the normal chain of command who acts as a problem solver for management and employees.

Figure 17–3

Criteria for Determination of Just Cause

▲ Was the employee warned of the consequences of his/her conduct?
▲ Was the company's rule reasonable?
▲ Did management investigate before disciplining?
▲ Was the investigation fair and impartial?
▲ Was there evidence of guilt?
▲ Were the rules and penalties applied in an evenhanded fashion?
▲ Was the penalty reasonable, given the offense?

gives employees the opportunity to talk freely about complaints and frustrations that may not otherwise surface until they become serious problems. Using an ombudsman also can be a way to make sure that employees are given a fair hearing and due process in attempting to address their problems. The idea has caught on with a number of medium and large companies, doubling in recent years.[17]

Dismissal for Just Cause

▼ **JUST CAUSE**

includes reasons for dismissal usually spelled out in a union contract.

▼ **CONSTRUCTIVE DISCHARGE**

is most often found when an employer deliberately makes conditions intolerable in an attempt to get the employee to quit.

Like due process, dismissal for **just cause** usually is spelled out in a union contract, but often is not as clear in an at-will situation.[18] While the definition of just cause varies from case to case, the criteria used by courts have become well-defined over time from arbitration awards. They appear in Figure 17–3.

Related to just cause is the concept of **constructive discharge** which occurs when an employer deliberately makes conditions intolerable in an attempt to get the employee to quit. Under normal circumstances, an employee who resigns rather than being dismissed cannot later collect damages for violation of legal rights. An exception to this rule occurs when the courts find that the working conditions are so intolerable as to *force* a reasonable employee to resign. Then, the resignation is considered a discharge. For example, an employee had been told he should resign but refused. He was then given lesser assignments, publicly ridiculed by his supervisor, and threatened each day with dismissal. He finally resigned, sued his employer, and the judge held that he had been "constructively discharged." His employer owed unemployment benefits because it had forced him to resign.

Discharge for "just cause" is especially difficult to establish when the case involves an employee's off-the-job behavior. The basic premise is that an employer should not control the lives of its employees off the job.

Behavior off the Job   Taking disciplinary action for off-the-job behavior of employees is unsettling to both employers and employees. In one case, the Baltimore Transit Company fired the Acting Grand Dragon of the Ku Klux Klan. The arbitrator upheld the dismissal and said that there was a clear danger of physical violence and an economic boycott to the company if the man were retained. In another case, Southern California Edison Company fired an employee because he lied about his arrest for possession of marijuana. The arbitrator upheld the dismissal because the company's need for accurate information from the employee was important in his job.[19]

However, the general public is leery of employers investigating off-the-job behavior of their workers. For example, one poll found that the vast majority of people feel the boss has no right to ask about private lives, lifestyles, and off-work activities. Close to 80% surveyed felt that recreational, political, or factors such as smoking should not be considered in employment decisions. However, close to the same proportion felt it was all right to differentiate in employee health-care premiums for off-the-job smokers.[20] Other polls have shown that a similar number feel that employers do not have the right to monitor personal telephone conversations, forbid dating a rival firm's employee, or require an employee to diet.[21] Twenty-three states have laws that prohibit firing workers for their private use of legal products (like tobacco or alcohol) or engagement in legal activities when away from the job.[22]

▲ EMPLOYEE PRIVACY RIGHTS

Three categories of employee privacy rights are considered: (1) employee rights to review records, (2) substance abuse and drug testing, and (3) polygraph and honesty testing.

Employee Rights to Review Records

As a result of concerns about the protection of individual's privacy rights, the Privacy Act of 1974 was passed. It includes provisions affecting HR record systems. This law applies *only* to federal agencies and organizations supplying services to the federal government, but similar state laws, somewhat broader in scope, also have been passed. Regulation of private employers on this issue for the most part is a matter of state rather than federal law. Public-sector employees have greater access to their files in most states than do private-sector employees.

The following legal issues are involved in employee rights to privacy and HR records:

- ▲ Right to access personal information
- ▲ Opportunity to respond to unfavorable information
- ▲ Right to correct erroneous information
- ▲ Right to be notified when information is given to a third party
- ▲ Right to know how the information is being used internally
- ▲ Right to reasonable precautions, assuring the individual that the information will not be misused

Probably the most frequent way for an employer to run afoul of laws on employee records is when another employer asks for information about a former employee. Lawyers recommend that only the most basic employment history such as job title, dates of employment, and ending salary data be given. Although that information may be safe, it probably is not especially helpful to the employer seeking the reference, since such information doesn't answer questions a potential employer may have about an employee's suitability.[23] Access to HR records is discussed further in Chapter 20. Figure 17–4 shows some guidelines for maintaining privacy in employee records.

Substance Abuse and Drug Testing

The issue of substance abuse and drug testing at work has received a great deal of attention. Drug testing now occurs at 85% of major companies. Results of the test show that 2.5% of workers on the job and 4.3% of job applicants test positive on average.[24]

▲ **Figure 17–4**

Guidelines for Privacy in
Employee Records

> ▲ Disclose to employees the records kept on them and the company's policy on records.
> ▲ Have a policy that limits record usage and allows employees to see their files.
> ▲ Review contents regularly and destroy outdated items as appropriate.
> ▲ Designate a file custodian.
> ▲ Restrict separate files.
> ▲ Train managers on liability-free documentation.

There are difficult issues regarding the trade-off between a safe workplace and rights to privacy, but the importance of the problem to HR management is clear. In one study substance abuse resulted in sixteen times the normal absenteeism rate, four times the accident rates, one-third more illness benefits, and five times as many workers' compensation claims.[25] Another study followed 5,465 job applicants who were tested for drugs and then hired. After an average of 1.3 years on the job, those who had tested positive had a 59% greater absenteeism rate and 47% higher voluntary turnover.[26] It is easy to see why management is in favor of drug testing.

Despite the examples above, there are several arguments against drug testing: (1) It violates employees' rights. (2) Drugs may not affect job performance in every case. (3) Employers abuse the results of tests. (4) Such tests are often inaccurate or the results are misinterpreted.

Employee Attitudes toward Drug Testing   Surveys show that employee attitudes toward drug testing have changed. Apparently experience with workplace drug problems has made managers and employees less tolerant of drug users.[27] Drug testing appears to be most acceptable to employees when they see the procedures used as *fair*[28] and when characteristics of the job (such as danger to other people) require that the employee be alert and fully functioning.[29]

Drug Testing and the Law   Two misconceptions about privacy in the workplace should be clarified. First, federal constitutional rights, such as unreasonable search and seizure, protect an individual only against the activities of the government. Thus, employees can be searched at work by representatives of the employer. This principle was reaffirmed by a U.S. Supreme Court decision that even employers in government workplaces may search desks and files without search warrants if they believe that a work rule was violated.[30]

Second, employer due process need not include the criminal standard of "beyond a reasonable doubt." Termination of an employee because of substance-abuse problems must be in keeping only with the due process described in an employer's policy. Unless state or local law prohibits testing, employers have a right to require employees to submit to a blood test or urinalysis. But court decisions generally have indicated that random drug testing may be unconstitutional and that public agencies must have "probable cause" to test.

Drug testing can be done before and/or after hiring. If done afterwards, three different methods may be used: (1) random testing of everyone at periodic intervals; (2) testing only when there is probable cause; or (3) after accidents. Each method raises its own set of problems.[31] However, from a policy standpoint, it is most appropriate to test for drugs when the following conditions exist:

HR Perspectives:
Fitness for Duty and "The Smiling Sailor"

A smiling sailor pops onto the computer screen. He has a row of diamonds in one hand and hearts in the other. Do the hearts (or diamonds) at his feet match those in his hands? It gets tougher when the sailor is turned upside down or backwards, especially for someone who is impaired by substance abuse or fatigue. When Robert Anguay and his fellow delivery-truck drivers come to work, they "play" a similar video game—with serious consequences. Unless the machine presents a receipt saying they "passed" the test, they cannot get behind the wheels of their trucks.

Known as *fitness-for-duty testing,* these video games measure whether employees have the hand/eye coordination to perform their jobs on a given day. Interestingly most failures are *not* drug- or alcohol-related. Initial results suggest that fatigue, illness, or personal problems render a person unfit to perform a sensitive job more frequently. Whatever the reason, for one company accidents fell 67%, errors declined 92%, and workers' comp claims dropped 64% after one year of using the fitness-for-duty tests.

The computer calculates a baseline for each employee after he or she has performed the test several times, then employees are measured against their averages. At Domino's Pizza Distribution, truck drivers, warehouse workers, and dough makers are tested. Plant workers need to be alert when using machinery, or they can get caught in it. If some workers flunk the test, they spend the day doing paperwork or painting—jobs where they cannot hurt themselves or others.

Not everyone likes the idea. One federal drug official questions the reliability of such tests in detecting impairment. And a union official opposes the tests on the principle that management could come in and establish a company baseline to get rid of older members. But another union president notes, "It's a hell of a lot better than asking our people to urinate in a jar." And indeed it may be—a common saying is that in some dangerous jobs the urinalysis results always arrive just in time for the funeral.[32]

▲ Job consequences of abuse are so severe they outweigh privacy concerns.

▲ Accurate test procedures are available.

▲ Consent of the employee in writing is obtained.

▲ Results are treated confidentially, as any medical record.

▲ Employers have a complete drug program including counseling assistance to drug users.

The U.S. Supreme Court has ruled that certain drug-test plans do not violate the Constitution. But private employer programs are governed mainly by state laws which currently are a confusing hodgepodge. Federal agencies are moving ahead rapidly despite legal challenges. Passage of the Drug-Free Workplace Act in 1988 placed requirements on government contractors to take steps to eliminate employee drug usage. The Transportation Department is testing truck and bus drivers, train crews, mass transit employees, airline pilots and mechanics, pipeline workers, and licensed seamen. Up to 30% of truck driver tests have proved positive. On the other hand, out of 35,000 air traffic controllers' tests, only 161 were positive. Thirty-four were fired and the rest were reassigned or returned to duty after rehabilitation.[33]

Both NASA and the U.S. Air Force have used a simple test of critical tracking ability to detect impairment due to drug use. The test is easier and quicker than urinalysis. It can be used to assess a worker's fitness on the spot before he or she goes to work. The test operates much like a video game. It measures the ability to use fine hand/eye coordination and reaction time and takes less than a minute to administer. The "HR Perspective" details fitness-for-duty tests.

Polygraph and Honesty Testing

The late senator Sam Ervin called them "twentieth-century witchcraft," but until recently some employers continued to use polygraph or "lie-detector" tests. The theory behind a polygraph is that the act of lying produces stress that in turn causes observable physical changes. The examiner can then interpret those physical responses to specific questions and make a judgment as to whether the person being tested is practicing deception.

However, the Office of Technology Assessment determined that the validity of lie detector tests could not be established. The American Psychological Association contends that an "unacceptable number of false positives" occur.[34] For these reasons, few U.S. courts will admit polygraph data as evidence. In addition, Congress has passed the Polygraph Protection Act, which prohibits the use of polygraphs for most preemployment screening and judging a person's honesty.

Honesty Tests   "Pencil-and-paper" honesty tests have gained popularity recently. They are not restricted by the polygraph law nor by most states. Many organizations are using this alternative to polygraph testing, and over two dozen variations of such tests are being sold.

Like personality tests, honesty tests were developed from test items that differentiated between people known to be honest and those known to be dishonest. But it is not always easy to determine who is honest for the purpose of validating the tests, and serious questions have been raised about the validity of the tests. Honesty tests do not violate any legal rights of employees if private-sector employers adhere to state laws. The Fifth Amendment (which prohibits self-incrimination) may be a basis for prohibiting such tests in public-sector employment.

▲ MISCELLANEOUS EMPLOYEE RIGHTS

Four other areas of employee rights should be mentioned briefly: (1) employee rights in workplace investigations, (2) employee rights to know of potential hazards, (3) employee free speech, and (4) employee notification of plant closing.

Workplace Investigations of Employees

Employers have increased their attempts to investigate employee theft and substance abuse in their organizations. For example, General Motors operated a "sting" operation to identify drug users in some of its plants. As a result, some 200 persons were arrested. Drug abuse, dishonesty, and unethical behavior are the focus of such investigations.

Public-sector employees are protected by the Constitution in the areas of due process, searches and seizure, and privacy. But employees in the private sector have raised the following major concerns about such investigations:

▲ *Defamation* can occur when remarks about an employee are made during an investigation. For example, if an employee is referred to as a thief, the employer may be sued for slander and defamation of character.

▲ *Invasion of privacy* results when private facts about an employee discovered in an investigation are disclosed publicly. Physically entering another's personal property (home, purse, or shopping bag) may also constitute invasion of privacy.

▲ *Emotional distress* can occur when one person knowingly engages in "outrageous conduct" that results in severe emotional distress to another person. For example, one employer announced it would fire people, one by one, until the thief confessed. This tactic produced several successful "emotional distress" lawsuits.

▲ *False imprisonment* occurs when an individual is wrongfully restrained physically. Denying an employee permission to leave the room when an interview is being conducted may qualify.

▲ *Assault and battery* results if a person is touched or fears being touched without permission. Physical detention may violate assault-and-battery restrictions.

Employee Rights and Knowledge of Hazards

The public's increased awareness of hazards associated with workplace chemicals has been reflected in legislation designed to inform and train employees in the use of hazardous materials. The Hazard Communications Standard, an OSHA regulation (29 CFR 1910.1200), places specific responsibilities on employers to inform employees about the hazards of chemicals with which they work. The standard was first issued in 1983 and targeted the manufacturing sector; later it was expanded to cover *all* employers engaged in the handling and use of hazardous materials. Over the years it has become known as the "worker's right-to-know" law.

Chemical manufacturers must provide a material safety data sheet for every hazardous substance. Employer hazard communication programs have several requirements: (1) Employers are required to evaluate chemicals that employees are exposed to and inform them of any hazardous properties. (2) Employers also are required to post a list of all hazardous chemicals in the workplace. Examples include welding fumes, wood dust, paints, solvents, sterilizing chemicals and cleaners, and carbon monoxide from vehicles. (3) Hazardous chemicals must bear identifying labels that state the hazard and employees must be trained in the recognition of hazards and the safe handling and use of chemicals.

Free Speech (Whistle-Blowing)

A person who reports a real or perceived wrong done by his or her employer is called a "**whistle-blower.**" Two key questions are: (1) When do employees have the right to speak out with protection from retribution? (2) When do employees violate the confidentiality of their jobs? Often the answers are difficult to determine. A widely publicized case involved an employee in the U.S. Defense Department who revealed that significant cost overruns on an airplane contract were being concealed from the U.S. Congress. Attempts were made by his superiors to transfer him, demote him, or fire him. The whistle-blower ultimately left the Defense Department, but not before Congress held a series of public hearings and investigations.

Whistle-blowing is an important right, although one that can be abused. But whistle-blowers are less likely to lose their jobs in public employment than in private employment because most civil service systems have rules protecting whistle-blowers. However, rights to free speech are not protected by a comprehensive whistle-blowing law that applies to both public and private employees. If an individual is fired or made miserable for reporting a perceived wrongdoing, that person may not receive proper redress.[35]

▼ **A WHISTLE-BLOWER**

is a person who reports a real or perceived wrong done by his or her employer.

Employee Rights to Know of Plant Closings

When an employer chooses to close a facility, the employees usually experience severe economic and psychological problems. The federal government requires a 60-day notice before a "massive layoff" or "plant closing" involving more than 50 people. The WARN Act (Worker Adjustment and Retraining Notification) imposes stiff fines on employers who do not give such notice.[36]

Employee Rights and Security at Work

The traditional idea of workplace security emphasized an employer's ability to control employees' conduct during working hours and on company property. Yet security at work is increasingly a concern for some. Homicide on the job has become the fastest growing kind of murder, and violence of all kinds is increasing as frustrated or unstable workers have resorted to threats and intimidation of co-workers and supervisors.[37]

The following methods used by employers to maintain workplace security have been covered in this chapter or others. Each has obvious limitations:

▲ Testing for substance abuse
▲ Surveillance and monitoring
▲ Applicant screening
▲ Honesty testing/polygraph
▲ Background checks
▲ Considering off-job conduct

Concerns about workplace security often challenge employee privacy. Yet an employer may be compelled to provide security at work not only by its own economic interests, but by laws such as the Drug-Free Workplace Act .[38]

▲ HR POLICIES, PROCEDURES, AND RULES

It is useful at this point to consider some guidelines for HR policies, procedures, and rules. They greatly affect employee rights (just discussed) and discipline (discussed next). Where there is a choice among actions, **policies** act as general guidelines that regulate organizational actions. Policies are general in nature, while procedures and rules are specific to the situation. The important role of policies in guiding organizational decision making requires that they be reviewed regularly, because obsolete policies can result in poor decisions and poor coordination. Policy proliferation also must be carefully monitored. Failure to review, add to, or delete policies as situations change may lead to problems.

Procedures are customary methods of handling activities and are more specific than policies. For example, a policy may grant that an employee will be given a vacation. Procedures will establish a specific method for authorizing vacation time without disrupting work.

Rules are specific guidelines that regulate and restrict the behavior of individuals. They are similar to procedures in that they guide action and typically allow no discretion in their application. Rules reflect a management decision that action be taken—or not taken—in a given situation and provide more specific behavioral guidelines than policies. For example, one welding company has a policy stating that management intends to provide the highest quality welding service in the area. The rule that a welder with fewer than five years of welding

▼ **POLICIES**

are general guidelines that regulate organizational actions.

▼ **PROCEDURES**

are customary methods of handling activities.

▼ **RULES**

are specific guidelines that regulate and restrict the behavior of individuals.

experience will not be hired carries out this policy. This rule constrains HR selection decisions.

HR Policy Coordination Responsibilities

For policies, procedures, and rules to be effective, coordination between the HR unit and other managers is vital. As Figure 17–5 shows, managers are the main users and enforcers of rules, procedures, and policies and should receive some training and explanation in how to carry them out. The HR unit supports managers, reviews the disciplinary rules, and trains managers to use them. It is critical that any conflict between the two entities be resolved so employees receive a fair and coordinated treatment.

Guidelines for HR Policies and Rules

The following guidelines suggest that well-designed HR policies and rules should be consistent, necessary, applicable, understandable, reasonable, and distributed and communicated. A discussion of each characteristic follows.

Consistent Rules should be consistent with organizational policies, and policies should be consistent with organizational goals. The principal intent of policies is to provide written guidelines and to specify actions. If some policies and rules are enforced and others are not, then all tend to lose their effectiveness.

Necessary HR policies and rules should reflect organizational philosophy and directions. To this end, managers should confirm the intent and necessity of proposed rules and eliminate obsolete ones. Policies and rules should be reviewed whenever there is a major organizational change. Unfortunately, this review is not always done, and outdated rules are still on the books in many organizations.

Applicable Because HR policies are general guidelines for action, they should be applicable to a large group of employees. If they are not, then the appropriate areas or people must be identified. For instance, if a sick-leave policy is applicable only to nonexempt employees, that should be specified in the company handbook. Policies and rules that apply only to one unit or type of job should be developed as part of specific guidelines for that unit or job.

HR UNIT	MANAGERS
▲ Designs formal mechanisms for coordinating HR policies ▲ Provides advice in development of organizationwide HR policies, procedures, and rules ▲ Provides information on application of HR policies, procedures, and rules ▲ Explains HR rules to managers ▲ Trains managers to administer policies, procedures, and rules	▲ Help in developing HR policies and rules ▲ Review policies and rules with employees ▲ Apply HR policies, procedures, and rules ▲ Explain rules and policies to employees

▲ **Figure 17–5**

Typical Responsibilities for HR Policies and Rules

Understandable   HR policies and rules should be written so employees can clearly understand them. One way to determine if policies and rules are understandable is to ask a cross section of employees with various positions, education levels, and job responsibilities to explain the intent and meaning of a rule. If the answers are extremely varied, the rule should be rewritten.

Reasonable   Ideally, employees should see policies as fair and realistic. Policies and rules that are perceived as being inflexible or penalizing individuals unfairly should be reevaluated. For example, a rule forbidding workers to use the company telephone for personal calls may be unreasonable if emergency phone calls are occasionally necessary. Limiting the amount of time the telephone can be used for personal business and the number of calls might be more reasonable.

Some of the most ticklish policies and rules involve employee behavior. Dress codes are frequently controversial, and organizations that have them should be able to justify them to the satisfaction of both employees and outside sources that might question them.

Distributed and Communicated   In order to be effective, HR policies must be distributed and communicated to employees. Employee handbooks can be creatively designed to explain detailed policies and rules so that people can refer to them at times when no one is available to answer a question. Supervisors and managers can maintain discipline by reminding their employees about policies and rules. Because employee handbooks are used so widely, guidelines for their preparation are discussed next.

Guidelines for an Employee Handbook

An employee handbook gives employees a reference source for company policies and rules and can be a positive tool for effective management of human resources. Even smaller organizations can prepare handbooks relatively easily using computer software such as *Personnel Policies Expert* or others. However, management should consider several factors when preparing handbooks.

Readability   Specialists who prepare employee handbooks may not write on the same level as those who will read them. One review of some company handbooks revealed that the average reading level of most handbooks was the third year of college, which is much higher than the typical reading level of employees in most organizations. One solution is to test the readability of the handbook on a sample of employees before it is published.

Use   Another important factor to be considered in preparing an employee handbook is its method of use. Simply giving an employee a handbook and saying, "Here's all the information you need to know," is not sufficient. In one study, employee handbooks ranked third behind a supervisor and "the grapevine" as sources of information about the organization.

Some organizations distribute handbooks as part of their orientation processes. One company periodically gives all employees a written test on the company handbook. In this company the HR managers use questions that are consistently missed to focus their communication efforts. These tests also are used to update the handbook.

HR Perspectives:
Ethical Issues and Protection of Trade Secrets

Peter Bogyhand was one of IBM's star engineers when Seagate Technology hired him away. IBM contends Seagate lured him to steal its secrets. There would be no way, said IBM, for him to do his new job at Seagate without disclosing IBM confidential trade secrets.[39]

Many employers use employment agreements (often called *noncompete agreements*) to block workers from going to competitors with trade secrets. But these agreements can pose some ethical and legal concerns as

well. Noncompete agreements are signed by employees promising not to work for a rival firm for a limited period of time after they resign or are fired. However, some companies have drawn such agreements so broadly that they may preclude the employee's right to change jobs. For example, a scientist for Baxter International left to go to work for Biomerieux Vitek as director of biosciences. He had signed an agreement not to work for a rival firm for one year. But these firms were the only two in the field both selling

diagnostic equipment for microbiological labs. *Where else could he work?* The court held the non-compete agreement was too broad, and the scientist could keep his new job but for one year could not discuss certain issues.[40]

Ethically and legally, companies will have to analyze what is a protectable interest and what is not. Relationships between companies and employees are constantly changing, and a straitjacket agreement may not be right or even legally defensible.

Legal Review of Language   The current legal trend to use employee handbooks against employers in lawsuits charging a broken "implied" contract is no reason to abandon employee handbooks as a way to communicate policies to employees. Not having an employee handbook with HR policies spelled out can also leave an organization open to costly litigation and out-of-court settlements. Policies may be difficult to specify in the handbook or may present ethical problems such as the "noncompete" clause some companies use. The "HR Perspective" on ethical issues and protecting trade secrets illustrates the problem.

A more sensible approach is to develop sound HR policies and employee handbooks to communicate them, then have legal counsel review the language contained in them. Some recommendations include the following:

▲ *Eliminate controversial phrases.* For example, the phrase "permanent employee" often is used to describe those people who have passed a probationary period. This wording can lead to disagreement over what the parties meant by "permanent." A more appropriate phrase is "regular employee."

▲ *Use disclaimers.* Contract disclaimers have been upheld in court. However, there is a trade-off between disclaimers and the image presented by the handbook, so disclaimers should not be overused. A disclaimer also should appear on application forms. A disclaimer in the handbook can read as follows:

> This employee handbook is not intended to be a contract or part of a contractual agreement between the employer and the employee. The employer reserves the right to modify, delete, or add to any policies set forth herein without notice and reserves the right to terminate an employee at any time with or without cause.

▲ *Keep the handbook current.* Many employers simply add new material to handbooks rather than delete old inapplicable rules. Those old rules can become the bases for new lawsuits. Consequently, handbooks and HR policies should be reviewed periodically and revised every few years.

▲ **Figure 17–6** The Disciplinary System

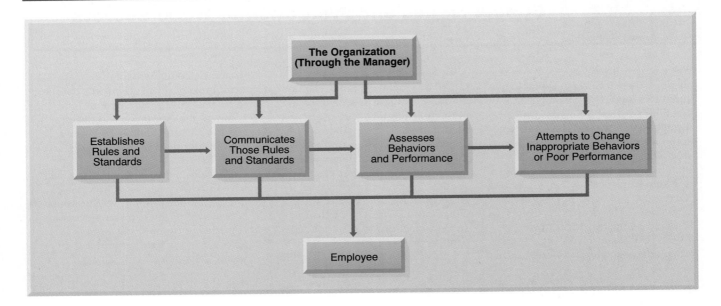

▲ EMPLOYEE DISCIPLINE

Employee rights are an appropriate introduction to the topic of employee discipline because employee rights are often an issue in disciplinary cases. **Discipline** is a form of training that enforces organizational rules. The goal of preventive discipline is to heighten employee awareness of organizational policies and rules. Knowledge of disciplinary actions may prevent violations. The emphasis on preventive discipline is similar to the emphasis on preventing accidents. Counseling by a supervisor in the work unit can have positive effects. Many times people simply need to be made aware of rules.

The disciplinary system (see Figure 17–6) also can be viewed as an application of behavior modification to marginal or unproductive employees. The best discipline is clearly self-discipline. Once most people understand what is required at work, they can usually be counted on to do their jobs effectively. Yet some find that the prospect of external discipline helps their self-discipline. Even though an employer's description of discipline is purposely upbeat and nonnegative in tone, there are times when discipline involves the use of punishment. Under such circumstances, managers must see to it that punishment is *corrective* in nature and not purely punitive.[41]

Marginal Employees

The marginal employee is typically one of a small number of employees who cause the most problems. If the employer fails to deal with marginal employees, they can have adverse effects on the entire work group. Disciplinary problems caused by marginal employees include absenteeism, tardiness, productivity deficiencies, alcoholism, and insubordination.

▼ **DISCIPLINE**

is a form of training that enforces organizational rules.

Counseling and Discipline

Counseling can be an important part of the discipline process. The focus should be on fact-finding and guidance to encourage desirable behavior, instead of using penalties to discourage undesirable behavior. The philosophy is that violations are actions that usually can be constructively corrected without penalty.

Typically, there is a sequence of events in counseling and discipline. Often, an employee's first violation results in a meeting with the immediate supervisor. A second violation brings another discussion with the supervisor on how this kind of behavior can be avoided in the future. The next violation leads to counseling with the same manager and that manager's immediate superior. A fourth infraction results in "final counseling" with top management. The offender is typically sent home for the rest of the day without pay and told that any further violation will result in termination. If the employee has no further violations for a year, his or her personnel file is wiped clean. Any new violations start the process all over again. Certain serious offenses are exempted from the procedure and may result in immediate termination. Stealing or coming to work intoxicated are common offenses leading to immediate termination. Certain offenses typically carry more severe penalties than others, as can be seen in Figure 17–7.

Progressive Discipline

Progressive discipline incorporates a sequence of steps into the shaping of employee behaviors. Progressive discipline suggests that actions to modify behavior become progressively more severe as the employee continues to show improper behavior. Figure 17–8 shows a typical progressive discipline system. At one manufacturing firm, failure to call in when a employee is to be absent from work may lead to a suspension after the third offense in a year.

An employee is given every opportunity and help, as appropriate, to correct deficiencies before being dismissed. Following the progressive sequence ensures that both the nature and the seriousness of the problem have been clearly communicated to the employee. Not all steps in the progressive discipline procedure have to be followed in every case. The idea is to impress on the offender the seriousness of the problem and the manager's determination to see that the behav-

PROBLEM	TYPICAL HANDLING		
	Warnings	Suspension	Discharge
Attendance	X	XX	XXX
Intoxication at work		XX	XXX
Fighting		O	XXX
Failure to use safety devices	X	O	XXX
Sleeping on the job	X		XXX
Possession of weapons			XXX
Theft			XXX
Drug use at work			XXX
Falsifying employment application			XXX
Outside criminal activities			XXX

Note: O means this step *may* be omitted

 Figure 17–7

Offenses and Penalty Patterns

▲ **Figure 17–8**

Progressive Discipline Procedures

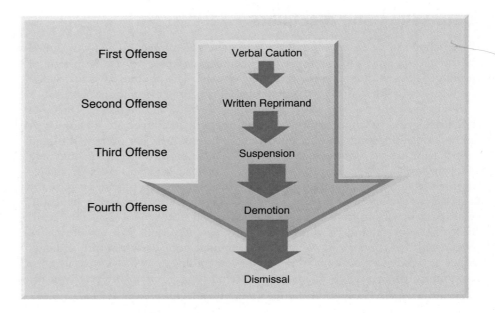

ior is changed. Most progressive discipline procedures include verbal and written reprimands and suspension before dismissal occurs.

The Use of Threat

Changes in society have made it increasingly difficult to make employees fear failure and punishment. Many limitations on negative sanctions have been imposed during the last century. Management's ability to use punishment has not disappeared, but it is less subject to control by the individual manager. However, under certain circumstances, threats and discipline can work.

Threats appear to be most effective when individuals have a strong fear of failure and low personal standards of conduct or productivity. Threats are ineffective, however, when inappropriate behavior is caused by intellectual or physical factors. In fact, under those circumstances, punishment can cause considerable harm and should not be used.

One area in which threats have been used with positive results is in controlling absenteeism. Threats and discipline do not work as direct solutions to alcohol- and drug-related problems, but they might be used to motivate employees to seek assistance and treatment.

For discipline to work, it must focus on a specific problem and indicate how employees can change or improve their behavior to avoid further discipline. In addition, the manager must make it clear that threats will be carried out (bluffing will not work), time limits will be adhered to, and that administration of discipline is a legitimate part of a manager's responsibility. This kind of communication requires coolness under emotionally tense conditions, as well as management expertise in diagnosing and resolving the situation.

Reasons Why Discipline Might Not Be Used

Sometimes managers are reluctant to use discipline. There are a number of reasons why discipline may not be used:

1. *Lack of training.* Many managers have little background in using discipline and have no idea how to administer it effectively. As a result, they should avoid using discipline or be trained on its use.

2. *Lack of support.* Many managers do not want to use discipline because they fear that their decisions will not be backed by higher management.

3. *Fear of acting alone.* A manager may feel that he or she is the only one who is enforcing a rule. For example, an employee protests discipline by saying, "You are the *only manager* that makes us arrive at eight o'clock."

4. *Guilt.* Some managers feel that before they became managers, they committed the same violations as their employees, so they cannot discipline others for doing something they used to do.

5. *Loss of friendship.* If managers allow themselves to become too friendly with employees, they might fear losing that friendship if they use discipline.

6. *Time loss.* Discipline, when done properly, does require a lot of time. There are many steps involved and many interviews with the employee. Sometimes it is easier for managers not to spend the time disciplining, especially if their actions may be overturned by higher management.

7. *Loss of temper.* Managers may be afraid that they will lose their tempers when talking about a rule violation with the employee.

8. *Rationalization.* Many managers rationalize that employees know when they have done something wrong so managers do not really need to talk to the offenders because the employees realize that they did wrong.

9. *Lack of appropriate policies.* Absence of appropriate policies within the organization for disciplinary action may dissuade managers from taking action otherwise deserved.

10. *Fear of lawsuits.* Managers are increasingly concerned about being *sued* for disciplining someone, particularly for taking the ultimate disciplinary step of dismissal (see the "HR Perspective").

If managers do not take disciplinary action when gross infractions occur, there is a chance that some individuals who usually would *not* get into trouble will do so. Some organizations take a lenient attitude toward theft of company property. A major felony may result in nothing more than a reprimand or disciplinary suspension. The drastic step of calling in the police is almost never taken unless a sizable permanent cash loss is involved. Yet it is clear that anything short of drastic action tends to encourage some people to steal.

Effective Discipline

Because of the legal aspects, managers must understand discipline and know how to administer it properly. Good discipline always should be aimed at the behavior, not at the employee personally. The reason for discipline is to improve performance.

The manager administering discipline must consider the effect of actions taken by other managers and actions taken in the past.[42] *Consistency and precedent* are important if employees are to perceive discipline as equitable. For example, if two people commit the same offense, but one person is more severely disciplined, he may rightfully complain about differential treatment and favoritism. Consistent discipline helps to set limits and informs people about what they can and cannot do. Inconsistent discipline leads to confusion and uncertainty. The purpose of discipline is not to get revenge or satisfaction for wrongs that have been committed; rather, it is to change undesirable behavior.

Effective discipline requires *accurate written record-keeping* and written notifica-

HR Perspectives:
Researching the Risks of Firing

In the comics, Mr. Dithers always shakes a finger at Dagwood Bumstead and fires him on the spot, but the funny papers no longer follow real life. Firing is not that easy anymore. The right to fire employees, a manager's ultimate weapon, is coming under unprecedented legal attack. A number of lawsuits have been settled *for the complainant,* and these cases usually are based on the court's assessment that the complainant has been *unfairly treated.*

Some organizations are pressing managers to be more truthful when they give employees performance appraisals. These employers insist that managers use progressive discipline and document reasons for dismissals more thoroughly. One management lawyer cautions that managers may have *personal liability* if they do not give honest appraisals.

In a recent case involving Bissell, Incorporated, an executive's performance began to slip after he was passed over for promotion to Vice-President. He received neither dismissal warnings nor an opportunity to improve before he was fired. He accused Bissell of negligence and a federal judge partially agreed, saying that Bissell had a duty to inform the executive more fully about the reasons for the termination decision. The judge ultimately awarded the man over $60,000. The decision has led Bissell to put greater emphasis on tough, honest performance appraisals. Now, before dismissals can occur, the general manager says he asks the supervisor, "Has he been warned properly and notified and does the person's personnel file reflect the justification?"[43]

tion to the employee. In many cases the lack of written notification has been evidence for an employee's argument that he or she "did not know."[44]

Effective discipline in our society requires that *people know the rules.* When people perceive discipline as unfair, it is often on the basis that they did not realize they had broken a rule. This situation is different from the legal system in which "ignorance of the law is no excuse." Where employee discipline is concerned, honest ignorance is indeed an acceptable excuse, which puts the pressure on management to see to it that employees have been informed of all rules as well as of any changes that might have occurred.

Good discipline is *immediate.* The longer the time that transpires between the offense and the disciplinary action, the less effective the discipline will be. For example, an employee who has a poor record for wearing safety gear fails to wear his goggles one day. His supervisor notices it, but is busy with another problem so he does not confront the employee about it. Just before quitting time, the supervisor calls the employee into the office to give him a two-day suspension without pay. This tactic is a poor way to handle discipline.

Good discipline is handled *impersonally.* Although the person being disciplined may often feel resentful, managers can help minimize these feelings by being as objective as possible. Managers cannot make discipline an enjoyable experience, but they can minimize the unpleasant effects somewhat by presenting it impersonally and by focusing on behaviors, not on the person. Effective discipline also must be clearly linked to job-related behavior or performance.

Discharge: The Final Alternative

The manager may feel guilty when dismissing an employee. Sometimes guilt is justified. If an employee fails, it may be because the manager was not able to create an appropriate working environment. Perhaps the employee was not adequately trained, or management failed to establish effective policies. Managers are responsible for their people, and to an extent they share the blame for failures.

General Electric, Union Carbide, and S. C. Johnson and Sons have adopted systems that require employees who have been warned about deficiencies to create their own improvement plans. Firing workers because they do not keep their own promises is more likely to appear equitable and defensible to a jury. Also, such a system seems to reduce the emotional reactions that lead fired workers to sue in the first place.

Federal Express allows employees to appeal discharge to a five-member board of their peers. "Equity Committees" have heard such cases for 20 years at Donnelly Corporation and have never been challenged in court.[45] Such *peer review* panels are really the last part of a formal grievance procedure for nonunion employees. They have worked well to settle contested dismissals and to keep the process out of court.[46]

Discipline and Productivity

That discipline and sanctions are positively related to performance surprises some who feel that punishment can only harm behavior. Yet employees look to other people to learn appropriate behaviors and attitudes (the process of *modeling*). In work organizations, standards become institutionalized through roles, operating procedures, and group norms. A work group may feel uncertain or perceive that an inequity has taken place if one individual violates these standards. Those individuals who violate organizational rules may violate group norms as well, so lack of discipline can cause problems for the group in addition to the manager.

If a manager tolerates unacceptable behavior, the group may feel further threatened. Although employees may understandably resist unjustified discipline from a manager, actions taken to maintain legitimate standards actually may reinforce productive group norms and result in increased performance.

▲ SUMMARY

- ▲ Ideas about employee rights, HR policies, and rules have continued to change and evolve.
- ▲ The employment relationship is viewed as a reciprocal one in which the employee, in return for loyalty and service, has moral rights.
- ▲ Employee rights affecting the employment agreement include employment-at-will, implied employment contracts, due process, and dismissal for cause.
- ▲ Employment-at-will relationships are changing in the courts which have found public policy exceptions, implied contract exceptions, and good faith/fair dealing exceptions.
- ▲ Although due process is not guaranteed for at-will employees, the courts expect to see evidence of due process in employee discipline cases. It is good management to do so anyway.
- ▲ Dismissal for just cause has been tested through arbitration and court cases.
- ▲ Employee rights to review records vary considerably from state to state. Government employees have consistent rights and guarantees in this regard.

▲ Drug testing generally is legal and thus is widely used as employers try to deal with increasing drug problems at work.

▲ Polygraph testing appears to be relatively inaccurate, and its use has declined. Pencil-and-paper honesty tests are being used in its place.

▲ Miscellaneous employee rights include rights during workplace investigations, the right to know of hazards, whistle-blowing, the right to know of plant closings, and the right to security at work.

▲ In order to be effective, HR policies and rules should be consistent, necessary, applicable, understandable, reasonable, and distributed and communicated.

▲ Employee handbooks have been viewed as contracts by the courts, which presents no problem as long as the handbook conforms to certain standards. HR policies that are expressed verbally also have been viewed as unwritten contracts, so it is best to have all policies clearly written in a handbook.

▲ Facts to be considered when preparing an employee handbook include readability, use, and legal review of language.

▲ Discipline is best thought of as a form of training. Although self-discipline is the goal, sometimes counseling or progressive discipline is necessary to encourage self-discipline.

▲ Threat works to change behavior in certain situations. In others, it does not.

▲ Managers may fail to discipline when they should for a variety of reasons. The end point in the discipline process—termination—has been drastically changed as a result of redefinition of employee rights.

▲ Good discipline can have a positive effect on productivity.

▲ REVIEW AND DISCUSSION QUESTIONS

1. From where do employee rights originate?
2. Explain the public policy exception to employment-at-will.
3. Discuss the differences and similarities between the issues of due process and just cause.
4. What are the pros and cons of giving a prospective employer honest information on a former employee of yours who stole from the company?
5. Design a checklist of items to remember when doing an investigation of an employee suspected of drug usage in your company.
6. What does it mean for discipline to be internal as opposed to external? Which is best?

 YOU CAN'T FIRE ME!

Paul Zimmerman went to work for H. E. Butt Grocery, a Texas grocery chain, and was a *fine* employee. In fact, the company president told him, "You've done a really good job; you've earned your way and you have a contract for life." Zimmerman was sacked six years later for stealing inventory and trying to hide it.

He sued for breach of contract. Contract employees *can* be fired, of course, but the employer must prove that there was just cause. Zimmerman argued that he had not stolen and had not falsified records and was therefore fired without cause.

The company countered that Zimmerman did not have a contract, but that he was an "at-will" employee. Zimmerman was awarded $391,000 in damages. The judge found that he did have a contract because he had signed an employee handbook that his boss had told him was a contract. Further, the company had treated the handbook like a contract.

A three-judge panel of the Fifth Circuit Court reversed every aspect of the judge's finding. They held that there was no language in the handbook that said employees only could be fired for cause. They also held that lifetime contracts must be in writing to be enforceable. The moral to the story—Employers: Watch what you say. Employees: Get it in writing.[47]

▲ QUESTIONS

1. Under what circumstances is it realistic to think of "employment for life" in any business?
2. Explain "just cause" and "at-will employee" in the context of this case.

▲ NOTES

1. Adapted from Peter Coy, "Big Brother Pinned to Your Chest," *Business Week,* August 17, 1992, 38; M. Kapor, "Computer Spies," *Forbes,* November 2, 1992, 288; "Silicon Valley Case May Set E-Mail Precedent," *Omaha World-Herald,* January 19, 1992, 9G; L. Flynn, "E-Mail Privacy," *Omaha World-Herald,* April 4, 1993, 1G; and Junda Woo, "Secret Taping of Supervisors Is on the Rise, Lawyer Says," *The Wall Street Journal,* November 3, 1992, B1.

2. Yg Chimezie, A. B. Osigweh, "Elements of an Employee Responsibilities and Rights Paradigm," *Journal of Management* 16 (1990), 835–850.

3. Ibid., 839.

4. G. Gomes and J. Morgan, "Managing the Future Employment Relationship: the Legislative Alternative," *SAM Advanced Management Journal,* Summer 1991, 41–46.

5. Benson Rosen and Catherine Schwoerer, "Balanced Protection Policies," *HR Magazine,* February 1990, 59.

6. Rosen and Schwoerer, "Balanced Protection," 61.

7. Donald C. Bacon, "See You in Court," *Nation's Business,* July 1989, 17.

8. "50 State Survey," *Omaha World-Herald,* September 17, 1989, 16.

9. Adapted from Mark A. Player, *Federal Law of Employment Discrimination* (St. Paul: West Publishing, 1991).

10. *Fortune v. National Cash Register Co.,* 373 Mass. 96, 36 NE 2d 1251, 1977.

11. Dan Lacey, "Your Legal Rights when Being Fired," *National Business Employment Weekly,* November 5, 1992, 5.

12. D. Frum, "The Right to Fire," *Forbes,* October 26, 1992, 76–77.

13. Milo Geyelin, "Rulings on Wrongful Firing Curb Hiring," *The Wall Street Journal,* April 7, 1992, B3.

14. G. Kang, "Laws Covering Sex Harassment and Wrongful Discharge Collide," *The Wall Street Journal,* September 24, 1992, B1.

15. J. Lyons, "You Can't Fire Me!" *Forbes,* September 16, 1991, 164.

16. "Employee Termination," *Ideas and Trends in Personnel,* August 5, 1992, 122.

17. Junda Woo, "Ombudsmen Proliferate in the Workplace," *The Wall Street Journal,* February 19, 1993, B2.

18. David Levine, "Just Cause Employment Policies in the Presence of Worker Adverse Selection," *Journal of Labor Economics,* 9 (1991), 294.

19. C. Skrzycki, "Just Who Is In Charge Here, Anyway? *Washington Post,* January 29, 1989, H1.

20. Michael R. Losey, "Workplace Privacy," *Modern Office Technology,* May 1993, 56–58.

21. B. Tarrant, "Alaskans Believe Off-Duty Time Is Off-Limits to Bosses," *Anchorage Times,* January 17, 1992, C1.

22. M. Schaefer, "Two States Pass Privacy Rights Laws," *Human Resource Executive,* June 1992, 14.

23. Barry A. Hartstein, "Rules of the Road in Dealing with Personnel Records," *Employee Relations Law Journal* 17 (1992), 673–692.

24. "Drug Testing Grows," *USA Today,* April 2, 1993, B1.

25. B. Murphy, "Drug Testing in the Utility Industry," *Management Quarterly,* Summer 1989, 16–30.

26. J. Normand et al., "An Evaluation of Preemployment Drug Testing," *Journal of Applied Psychology* 75 (1990), 629–639.

27. Michael A. Verespej, "Drug Users—Not Testing—Angers Workers," *Industry Week,* February 17, 1992, 33.

28. M. Konovsky and R. Cropanzano, "Perceived Fairness of Employee Drug Testing. . . .", *Journal of Applied Psychology* 76, (1991), 698.

29. K. Murphy et al., "Influence of Job Characteristics on the Acceptability of Employee Drug Testing," *Journal of Applied Psychology* 76 (1991), 447.

30. M. Zigarelli, "Random Drug Testing in the Public Sector: the Legal Parameters," *Employee Relations Law Journal* 17, (1991–1992), 459.

31. Michael Carrell and Christina Heavrin, "Before You Drug Test," *HR Magazine,* June 1990, 66–68.

32. J. Hamilton, "A Video Game That Tells If Employees Are Fit for Work," *Business Week,* June 3, 1991, 36; and L. McGinley, "Fitness Exams Help to Measure Worker Activity," *The Wall Street Journal,* April 21, 1992, B1.

33. "Labor Letter," *The Wall Street Journal,* May 8, 1990, 1.

34. S. Dentzer et al., "Can You Pass the Job Test?" *Newsweek,* May 5, 1990, 47.

35. D. Fiesher and T. Buttross, "Whistle-Blowing Hotlines," *Internal Auditor,* August 1992, 54; and E. Callahan and J. Collins, "Employee Attitudes toward Whistleblowing: Management and Public Policy Implications," *Journal of Business Ethics* 11 (1992), 939–948.

36. R. S. Savage and T. M. Kollmorgen, "Limitations on Applicability of the WARN Act: A Defendant's Strategy," *Employee Relations Law Journal* 16 (1991), 453.

37. T. F. O'Boyle, "Disgruntled Workers Intent on Revenge Increasingly Harm Colleagues and Bosses," *The Wall Street Journal,* September 15, 1992, B1.

38. M. Rosenblum, "Security vs. Privacy: An Emerging Employment Dilemma," *Employee Relations Law Journal* 17 (1991), 81–101.

39. M. Miller, "IBM Sues to Silence Former Employee," *The Wall Street Journal,* July 15, 1992, B1.

40. Junda Woo, "Trade Secrets vs. Workers Rights in Court," *The Wall Street Journal,* October 13, 1992, B8.

41. Brian S. Klaas, "The Determinants of Disciplinary Decisions," *Personnel Psychology* 44 (Winter 1991), 813.

42. Brain S. Klaas and H. Wheeler, "Managerial Decision Making about Employee Discipline," *Personnel Psychology* 43 (1990), 117–133.

43. S. Alexander, "Firms Get Plenty of Practice at Layoffs, but They Often Bungle the Firing Process," *The Wall Street Journal,* October 14, 1991, B1; and Dan Lacey, "Common Ingredients of an Illegal Firing," *National Business Employment Weekly,* November 12, 1992, 9.

44. M. Ralfs and J. Mosley, "Turning Employee Problems into Triumphs," *Training and Development Journal,* November 1990, 73.

45. "Who Fires?" *The Wall Street Journal,* May 2, 1992, A1.

46. R. C. Grote, "Peer Review May Keep You Out of Court," *The Wall Street Journal,* August 4, 1992, A14.

47. J. Lyons, "You Can't Fire Me!" *Forbes,* Sept 16, 1991, 164.

CHAPTER 18

UNION/MANAGEMENT RELATIONS

After you have read this chapter, you should be able to:

1. Describe what a union is and identify the two major roles of unions in the U.S.

2. Discuss how unions generally affect productivity.

3. Explain the acts that compose the "National Labor Code."

4. Describe the different structure levels of unions.

5. Identify and discuss the stages in the unionization process.

6. Explain reasons for the decline in the percentage of U.S. workers represented by unions.

Since the 1930s when unions were provided the protection necessary to exist, the union/management relationship has been a stormy one. However, with many employers facing international competition on costs and prices and unions losing membership and representation elections, the relationship seems to be changing. The benefits of cooperative relations have never loomed larger.

An interesting example is provided by Arizona's Magma Copper Company and its President, J. Burgess Winter. Magma Copper was on a downhill road to bankruptcy, carrying its ten contentious unions with it. The firm was deeply in debt and living with an "ill-advised" labor contract negotiated several years before. In return for previous wage givebacks, the company had tied employee bonuses to the price of copper. When the prices increased, Magma was forced to borrow money at high interest rates to pay $56 million in employee bonuses, adding to the debt that was quickly driving it out of business.

The labor agreement was up for renegotiation, and both sides braced for a strike. The company planned for replacement workers, violence erupted, bombs were planted in the company's mines, and shots were fired at President Winter's home. Although a contract was eventually signed, Winter said, "We got nowhere with our labor force after that. We couldn't conduct our daily business properly." The unions agreed that relations with the company were at an all-time low.

But Winter wanted to end the "them versus us" attitude that existed and find a way to get the employees' help in turning the company around. The first step came when 17 senior management and union representatives met for two days with a facilitator. The first day was spent venting years of frustrations, but on the second day the adversaries were able to focus on mutual interests. The result was a document outlining basic principles of cooperation that was handed out to the employees. During the next year all employees attended two-day team-building workshops in groups of 50. President Winter usually opened these sessions with a presentation on the company and its problems. Further, all supervisors received training on changing their supervisory styles.

Union/management problem-solving teams tackled a number of problems. But none was more important than a breakthrough in methods that allowed the company to cut costs by 12.5% and made it possible to develop an ore body (a mass of valuable mineral) that will keep people at work. All the problems were not solved, but the company's bond ratings were upgraded and productivity increased 43%.

In summary, Burgess Winter says, "If you can work within the framework of a union, you can accomplish a lot. There's a structure there for communications."[1]

> The labor union is an elemental response to the human instinct for group action in dealing with group problems.
>
> *William Green*

A **union** is a formal association of workers that promotes the interests of its members through collective action. In different countries the status of unions varies depending on the culture and the laws that define union/management relationships. This chapter takes a broad look at union/management relations. Specific information on how unions become employee representatives is also presented.

When employees choose a union to represent them, management and union representatives enter into formal collective bargaining over certain issues such as pay scales, benefits, and working conditions. Once these issues are resolved in a labor contract, management and union representatives must work together to manage the contract and deal with grievances. Grievances are formal complaints filed by workers with management. Collective bargaining and grievance procedures are two important interfaces that occur between management and labor unions once a union has gained recognition as a legal representative of employee interests. Both areas are examined in Chapter 19.

▼ **A UNION**

is a formal association of workers that promotes the interests of its members through collective action.

▲ UNIONS IN THE WORLD

Theories of labor in capitalist economies have emphasized that over time, similar labor relations situations will evolve among countries. That has not happened.[2] Union influence during the 1970s and 1980s dropped abruptly in the U.S. It also dropped (but much less) in Japan, the Netherlands, the United Kingdom, and France. But in most other European countries, Canada, and Australia, it increased or maintained high levels.

The different bargaining arrangements existing in various countries are quite noticeable. In the U.S., local unions bargain with individual employers to set wages and working conditions. In Australia, unions argue their cases before arbitration tribunals. In Scandinavia, national agreements with associations of employers are the norm. In France and Germany, industrywide or regionwide agreements are common. In Japan, local unions do the bargaining but combine at some point to determine national wage patterns.

However, unions appear to have somewhat similar effects internationally in most situations regarding employment, provision of benefits, turnover, change, and profits. The presence of unions results in less employment in the private sector, increased benefits costs, and less turnover. Unions appear not to affect the speed of adaptation to new technology, but heavily unionized industries appear to engage in less research and development (R&D) and have markedly lower profitability.[3]

Unions and Productivity

Controversy over the extent that unions affect productivity continues. Some argue that unionized firms are more productive. Others contend that studies coming to that conclusion are flawed.[4] Training, work redesign, employee ownership, and the new workforce are emphasized as points where unions can increase productive efforts in the organization.[5] Perhaps the effect of unions on productivity depends more on the state of labor relations in the company than on the presence of a union per se—witness the Magna Copper case that opened this chapter.

▲ UNIONISM IN THE UNITED STATES

Figure 18–1 shows a typical division of responsibilities between the HR unit and operating managers in dealing with unions. This pattern may vary in different organizations. In some organizations, HR is not involved with labor relations because the operating management handles them. In other organizations, the HR unit is almost completely in charge of labor relations. The typical division of responsibilities shown in Figure 18–1 is a midpoint between these extremes.

Unionism in the U.S. has followed a somewhat different pattern than unionism in other countries. In such countries as Italy, England, and Japan, the union movement has been at the forefront of nationwide political trends. For the most part, this politicalization has not occurred in the U.S. Perhaps workers here tend to identify with the American free enterprise system. Further, class consciousness and conflict between the working class and the management class is less in the U.S. than in many other countries. Ownership of private property by both management and workers is a further mediating influence.

Unions' Roles

Unions in the U.S. serve two major roles. The first centers around employees' job interests; the second serves as a general balance to management.

Job-Centered Role   The primary role of unionism in the U.S. has been the collective pursuit of "bread-and-butter" economic gains. Unions have emphasized helping workers obtain higher wages, shorter working hours, job security, and safe working conditions from their employers.

Achieving their goals has meant that unions have had to be politically active in order to get supportive laws passed. Such political activity traditionally was oriented more toward specific workplace issues such as health and safety, mini-

▲ **Figure 18–1**

Typical Labor Relations
Responsibilities

HR UNIT	MANAGERS
▲ Deals with union organizing attempts at the company level ▲ Monitors "climate" for unionization and union relationships ▲ Helps negotiate labor agreements ▲ Provides detailed knowledge of labor legislation as needed	▲ Provide conditions conducive for positive relationships with employees ▲ Avoid unfair labor practices during organizing efforts ▲ Administer the labor agreement on a daily basis ▲ Resolve grievances and problems between management and employees

mum wage increases, and pension protection. But, increasingly, unions have taken positions on broad social and economic issues. For example, unions have been in the forefront of those pushing for mandatory parental leave, universal health insurance for most workers, and child-care tax credits for working parents. In a period of economic and demographic change, unions likely will continue to press for broader worker-oriented laws.

Unions have been active in other ways as well in achieving job-oriented goals. For example, one study found that unionized establishments are more likely to receive OSHA inspections, face greater scrutiny in those inspections, and pay higher penalties for violations than nonunion firms.[6]

Countervailing-Force Role   Another role unions fill is as a countervailing force that keeps management "honest" and makes management consider the impact of its policies on its employees. However, a rather delicate balance exists between management power and union power in an organization. It is easy for this balance to be tipped one way or the other.

Unions have chosen to use federal regulations in nonlabor areas recently to "countervail" against management. For example, in Dixon, California, a union used an environmental impact statement to close down a project being built with nonunion labor.[7] BASF Corporation ended a five-year union lockout in Louisiana after a union filed environmental objections to the company's expansion in the state.[8]

Through their respective representatives, management and unions spend a great deal of time and effort disagreeing with each other. Because of their built-in adversarial roles, some disagreement is to be expected. Yet it is naive to suppose that either position or group is right all the time or to assume that there are many disagreements that lead to strikes. Work lost because of strikes or lockouts has constituted a relatively small percentage of total work time. The U.S. figures are considerably lower than those of many other countries.

▲   MILESTONES IN UNION HISTORY

These two philosophical roles of unions, focusing on jobs and serving as a countervailing force, can be seen throughout the evolution of the union movement in the U.S. An overview of major milestones in that evolution follows.

Early Union Circumstances

As early as 1794, shoemakers organized a union, picketed, and conducted strikes. However, in those days, unions in the U.S. received very little support from the courts. In 1806, when the shoemaker's union struck for higher wages, a Philadelphia court found union members guilty of engaging in a "criminal conspiracy" to raise wages.

In 1842, the Massachusetts Supreme Court handed down a decision in the case of *Commonwealth v. Hunt* that became an important legal landmark. The court ruled, "For a union to be guilty of conspiracy, either its objective or the means used to reach it must be criminal or unlawful."[9] As a result of this decision, unions were no longer seen as illegal conspiracies in the eyes of the courts, the conspiracy idea lost favor, and employees were no longer legally precluded from forming unions.

Labor Organizations

The end of the Civil War in 1865 was followed by rapid industrial expansion and a growth of giant business trusts. The 1870s were characterized by industrial unrest, low wages, long hours, and considerable unemployment. In 1877, great railroad strikes spread through the major U.S. railroad companies as union members protested against the practices of railroad management. Eight years later, a group of workers formed the Knights of Labor. The goals of the Knights of Labor were: (1) to establish one large union embracing all workers, and (2) to establish a cooperative economic system to replace capitalism. The leaders of the Knights of Labor believed that a large, national union was necessary to counterbalance the huge business trusts of that time. They emphasized political reform and establishment of work cooperatives. But after their peak in 1885, the Knights soon faded from the labor scene.

American Federation of Labor (AFL)   In 1886, the American Federation of Labor (AFL) was formed as a federation of independent national unions. Its aims were to organize skilled craft workers, like carpenters and plumbers, and to emphasize such bread-and-butter issues as wages and working conditions. Samuel Gompers was the AFL's chief spokesman and served as president until his death in 1924. At first the AFL grew slowly. Six years after its formation, its total membership amounted to only 250,000. However, it managed to survive in the face of adversity while other labor groups withered and died.

Congress of Industrial Organizations (CIO)   Earlier, the Civil War had given factories a big boost. Factory mass-production methods using semiskilled or unskilled workers were necessary to supply the armies. Though factories provided a potential area of expansion for unions, they were hard to organize. Unions found that they could not control the semiskilled workers entering factory jobs because such workers had no tradition of unionism. It was not until 1938, when the Congress of Industrial Organizations (CIO) was founded that a labor union organization focused on semiskilled and unskilled workers. Years later the AFL and the CIO merged to form one coordinating federation, the AFL-CIO.

Early Labor Legislation

The right to organize workers and engage in collective bargaining is of little value if workers are not free to exercise it. Historical evidence shows that management developed practices calculated to prevent workers from using this right. The federal government has taken action to both hamper unions and protect them.

Sherman and Clayton Acts   The passage of the Sherman Antitrust Act in 1890 forbade monopolies and certain efforts to restrain trade. Later, as a result of a 1908 Supreme Court case (*Loewe v. Lawlor*), union boycott efforts were classed as attempts to restrain trade.

In 1914 the Clayton Act, which limited management's use of legal injunctions to stop labor disputes, was passed. But it had little effect because of a Supreme Court interpretation of the act. As a result, union strength declined throughout the 1920s.

Railway Labor Act The Railway Labor Act (1926) represented a shift in government regulation of unions. As a result of a joint effort between railroad management and unions to reduce transportation strikes, this act gave railroad employees "the right to organize and bargain collectively through representatives of their own choosing." In 1936, airlines and their employees were added to those covered by the act. Both these industries are still covered by this act instead of by others passed later.

▲ "NATIONAL LABOR CODE"

Union progress from the 1930s to the mid-1950s provided the basis for the development and passage of several acts: (1) the Wagner Act, (2) the Taft-Hartley Act, and (3) the Landrum-Griffin Act. These acts have had the most direct and continuing impact on employers and unions and form the "National Labor Code," the legal basis for today's labor relations in the private sector. Each of the acts was passed to protect some entity in the union/management relationship. Figure 18–2 shows each segment of the code and which entity receives the greatest protection. The nature of this protection will become clearer as each act is discussed.

A fourth law, the Federal Service Labor-Management Statute of 1978, applies only to U.S. government employees and unions representing them. That act became the model for labor codes covering state government workers. Also, the act used many provisions from the "National Labor Code" to tailor a law specifically for federal workers.

Wagner Act (National Labor Relations Act)

The Wagner Act has been called the Magna Carta of labor and was, by anyone's standards, *pro-union*. Passed in 1935, the Wagner Act was an outgrowth of the Great Depression. With employers having to close or cut back their operations, workers were left with little job security. Unions stepped in to provide a feeling of solidarity and strength for many workers. Their success in organizing workers for common goals dramatically increased union membership during the period

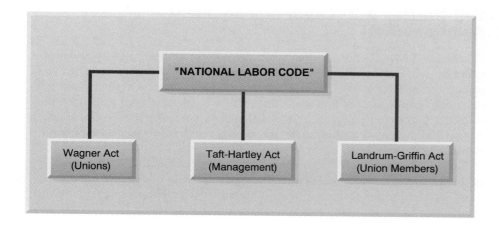

▲ **Figure 18–2**

National Labor Code

from 1935 to 1947 to 14 million members, an approximately fourfold increase. Close to 35% of the workforce was unionized.

The Wagner Act declared, in effect, that the official policy of the U.S. government was to encourage collective bargaining. It helped union growth in three ways:

1. It established workers' right to organize, unhampered by management interference.
2. It defined unfair labor practices on the part of management.
3. It established the National Labor Relations Board (NLRB) to see that the rules were followed.

The NLRB, although set up as an impartial umpire of the organizing process, has changed its emphasis depending on which political party is in power to appoint members. This body administers all of the provisions of the Wagner and subsequent labor relations acts.

The Wagner Act established the principle that employees would be protected in their rights to form a union and to bargain collectively. To protect union rights, the act prohibited employers from undertaking the following five unfair labor practices:[10]

1. Interfere with, restrain, or coerce employees in the exercise of their rights to organize, bargain collectively, and engage in other concerted activities for their mutual aid or protection. (Examples would be threatening or spying on employees.)
2. Dominate or interfere with the formation or administration of any labor organization or contribute financial or other support to it. (An example would be encouraging employees to select one union over another.)
3. Encourage or discourage membership in any labor organization by discrimination with regard to hiring or tenure or conditions of employment, subject to an exception for a valid union security agreement. (An example would be firing someone for being prounion.)
4. Discharge or otherwise discriminate against an employee because he or she filed charges or gave testimony under the act. (Examples would be discharging or denying promotion to someone who filed a complaint with the NLRB.)
5. Refuse to bargain collectively with representatives of the employees. (Examples would be refusing to meet with the union representative or not bargaining "in good faith.")

Taft-Hartley Act (Labor-Management Relations Act)

When World War II ended, the pent-up demand for consumer goods was frustrated by numerous strikes—about three times as many as before the war. The passage of the Taft-Hartley Act in 1947 answered the concerns of many who felt that union power had become too strong. This act was an attempt to balance the collective bargaining equation. It was designed to offset the pro-union Wagner Act by limiting union actions; therefore, it was considered to be *pro-management*. It became the second part of the "National Labor Code."

The new law amended or qualified in some respect all of the major provisions of the Wagner Act and established an entirely new code of conduct for unions. The Taft-Hartley Act forbade a series of unfair labor practices by unions. It became unlawful for a union to take the following actions:[11]

1. Restrain or coerce employees in the exercise of their rights under the act; restrain or coerce any employer in the selection of his bargaining or grievance representative.
2. Cause or attempt to cause an employer to discriminate against an employee on account of membership or nonmembership in a labor organization, subject to an exception for a valid union security agreement.
3. Refuse to bargain collectively in good faith with an employer if the union has been designated as bargaining agent by a majority of the employees.
4. Induce or encourage employees to stop work for the object of forcing an employee or self-employed person to join a union or forcing an employer or other person to stop doing business with any other persons (boycott provisions).
5. Induce or encourage employees to stop work for the object of forcing an employee to assign particular work to members of a union instead of to members of another union (jurisdictional strike).
6. Charge an excessive or discriminatory fee as a condition of becoming a member of the union.
7. Cause or attempt to cause an employer to pay for services that are not performed or not to be performed (featherbedding).

National Emergency Strikes   The Taft-Hartley Act also allows the president of the U.S. to declare a national emergency exists in a strike. A **national emergency strike** is one that affects an industry or a major part of it such that the national health or safety would be impeded. Under the Taft-Hartley Act, such strikes can be delayed up to 80 days by the action of the President. The national emergency provisions of the act require: (1) the appointment of a fact-finding board, (2) resumption of bargaining by the parties, (3) obtaining an injunction against the strike from federal courts, and (4) a report to Congress. These provisions were upheld following a challenge by the United Steel Workers in 1959.[12]

▼ **A NATIONAL EMERGENCY STRIKE**

is one that affects an industry or a major part of it such that the national health or safety would be impeded.

"Right to Work"   One specific provision (Section 14b) in the Taft-Hartley Act deserves special explanation. The so-called right-to-work provision outlaws the closed shop, except in construction-related occupations, and allows states to pass right-to-work laws. A **closed shop** requires individuals to join a union before they can be hired.

The act did allow the **union shop,** which requires that an employee join the union, usually 30 to 60 days after being hired. **Right-to-work laws** are *state* laws that prohibit both the closed shop and the union shop. They were so named because they allow a person the "right to work" without having to join a union. The states that have enacted these laws are shown in Figure 18–3.

▼ **A CLOSED SHOP**

requires individuals to join a union before they can be hired.

▼ **A UNION SHOP**

requires that an employee join a union, usually 30 to 60 days after being hired.

▼ **RIGHT-TO-WORK LAWS**

are state laws that prohibit both the closed shop and the union shop.

Landrum-Griffin Act (Labor-Management Reporting and Disclosure Act)

In 1959 the third segment of the "National Labor Code," the Landrum-Griffin Act, was passed as a result of a congressional committee's finding of union corruption. The Teamsters Union, headed by Dave Beck and James Hoffa, was investigated by the committee, and the law was aimed at protecting the rights of individual union members.

▲ **Figure 18–3**   Right-to-Work States

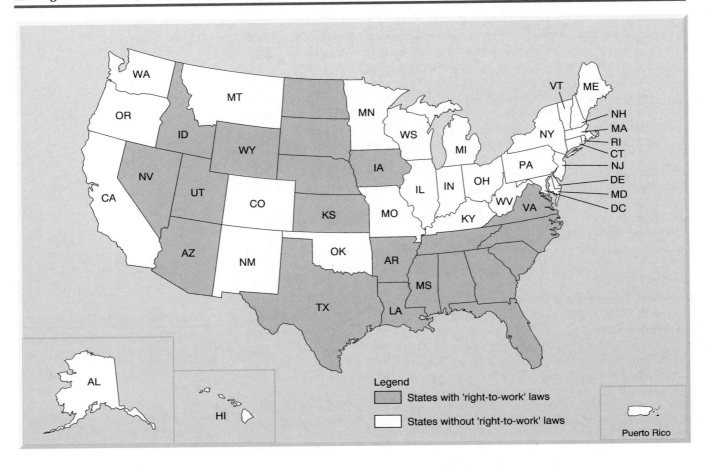

Among the provisions of the Landrum–Griffin Act are that:[13]

1. Every labor organization is required to have a constitution and bylaws containing certain minimum standards and safeguards.
2. Reports on the union's policies and procedures, as well as an annual financial report, must be filed with the Secretary of Labor and must be disclosed to the union's members.
3. Union members must have a bill of rights to protect their rights.
4. Standards are established for union trusteeship and union elections.
5. Reports on trusteeships must be made to the Secretary of Labor.
6. A fiduciary relationship is imposed upon union officers.
7. Union leaders are required to file reports with the Secretary of Labor on conflict-of-interest transactions.
8. The Secretary of Labor is made a watchdog of union conduct, is a custodian of reports from unions and their officers, and is given the power to investigate and prosecute violations of many of the provisions of the act.

Union Member Rights   A union is a democratic institution in which union members vote on and elect officers and approve labor contracts. The Landrum–Griffin Act was also passed to ensure that the federal government protects those democratic rights. Some important rights guaranteed to individual union members are as follows:

▲ Right to nominate and vote on officers.

▲ Right to attend and participate in union meetings.

▲ Right to have pension funds properly managed.

In a few instances, union officers have attempted to maintain their jobs by physically harassing or attacking individuals who try to oust them from office. In other cases, union officials have "milked" pension fund monies for their own use. Such instances are not typical of most unions, but illustrate the need for legislative oversight to protect individual union members.

Federal Service Labor-Management Relations Statute

Passed as Title VII of the Civil Service Reform Act of 1978, the Federal Service Labor-Management Relations statute made major changes in how the federal government dealt with unions. The act also identified areas that are and are not subject to bargaining.

The act established the Federal Labor Relations Authority (FLRA) as an independent agency similar to the NLRB. The FLRA was given authority to oversee and administer union/management relations in the federal government and to investigate unfair practices during union organizing efforts. The FLRA is a three-member body appointed on a bipartisan basis and each member is appointed for five years. In addition, the act gave the Federal Service Impasse Panel (FSIP) the authority to investigate situations in which union/management negotiations reach an impasse.

▲ UNION STRUCTURE

American labor is represented by many different kinds of unions. Some of them represent workers who do the same kind of job, whereas others represent all employees in a particular industry. Some are small, others are large. Some are national, others international.

Regardless of size and geographic scope, there are two basic types of unions that have developed over time. A **craft union** is one in which its members do one type of work, often using specialized skills and training. Examples include the International Association of Bridge, Structural, and Ornamental Iron Workers and the American Federation of Television and Radio Artists. An **industrial union** is one that includes many persons working in the same industry or company, regardless of jobs held. Examples are the United Food and Commercial Workers, United Auto Workers, and the American Federation of State, County, and Municipal Employees.

Union Hierarchy

Labor organizations have developed complex organizational structures with multiple levels. The broadest level is a **federation,** which is a group of autonomous national and international unions. The federation allows for individual unions to work together and present a more unified front to the public, legislators, and their members.

▼ **A CRAFT UNION**

is one in which its members do one type of work, often using specialized skills and training.

▼ **AN INDUSTRIAL UNION**

is one that includes many persons working in the same industry or company, regardless of jobs held.

▼ **A FEDERATION**

is a group of autonomous national and international unions.

▲ **Figure 18–4**   Structure of the AFL-CIO

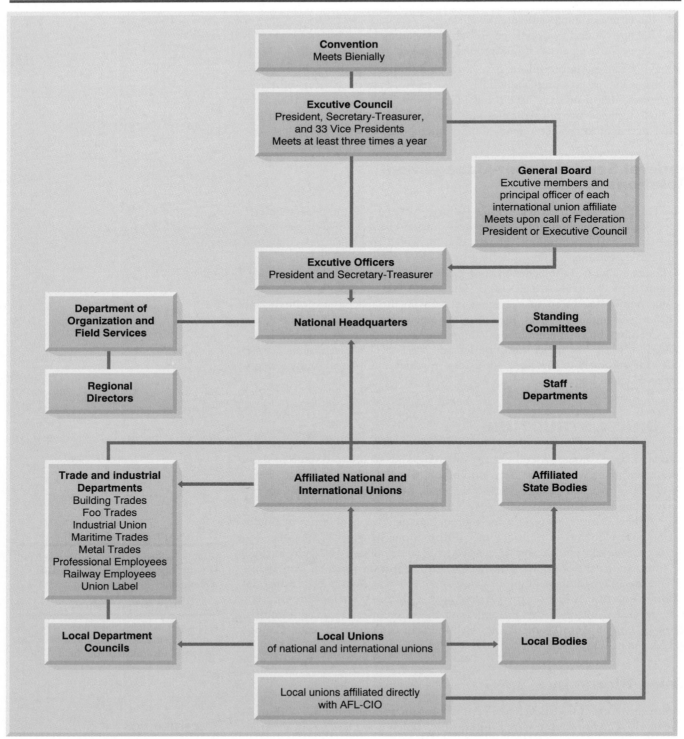

SOURCE: U.S. Department of Labor, Bureau of Labor Statistics, *Directory of National Unions and Employee Associations,* published annually.

The most prominent federation in the U.S. is the AFL-CIO which is a rather loose confederation of national and international unions. Altogether, the labor organizations in the AFL-CIO represent about 14 million workers. The structure of the AFL-CIO is shown in Figure 18–4.

National Unions

National or international unions are autonomous from the federation though they often are affiliated with it. They collect dues and have their own boards, specialized publications, and separate constitutions and bylaws. Such national-international unions as the United Steel Workers or the American Federation of State, County, and Municipal Employees determine broad union policy and offer services to local union units. They also help maintain financial records, provide a base from which additional organization drives may take place, and control the money for strike funds.

Intermediate union organizational units coordinate the activities of a number of local unions. All local unions in a state, or in several states, may be grouped together with some type of joint governing board. Such organizations may be citywide, statewide, or multistatewide.

Local Unions

Local unions may be centered around a particular employer organization or around a particular geographic location. For example, the Communication Workers of America local in Dallas, Texas, might include all the nonexempt Southwestern Bell telephone company employees in Dallas. (Nonexempt employees are subject to the overtime provisions of federal wage and hour laws.)

The policymaking process of the local union is generally democratic in form. Members vote on suggestions by either the membership or the officers. Normally, secret ballots are used. Officers in local unions are elected by the membership and are subject to removal if they do not perform satisfactorily. For this reason, local union officers tend to be concerned with the effect of their actions on the perceptions of the membership. They tend to react to situations as politicians do because they, too, are concerned about obtaining votes. The importance of preserving union democracy was the reason for the passage of the Landrum-Griffin Act.

Business Agents and Union Stewards   Local unions typically have *business agents,* who are full-time union officials. The agents run the local headquarters, help negotiate contracts with management, and become involved in attempts to unionize employees in other organizations.

Union stewards are usually elected by local union members and represent the lowest elected officer in the union. Stewards negotiate grievances with supervisors and generally represent employees at the worksite. The union steward is the "first-line" union representative for employees.

▲   THE UNIONIZATION PROCESS

A group of employees might begin the process to gain union representation for one of two primary reasons: (1) union targeting of an industry or company or

▲   **Figure 18–5**   Typical Unionization Process

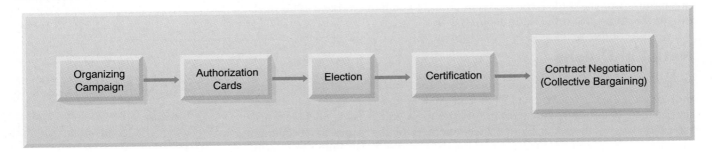

(2) employee requests. In the former case, the local or national union identifies a firm or industry in which it believes unionization can succeed. Usually the industry has a significant number of employees who may be amenable to organizing. For example, the insurance industry in several midwestern cities was targeted because many of its workers were women in lower-paying clerical jobs, almost all of whom were not represented by a union. The logic for targeting is that if the union is successful in one firm or a portion of the industry, then many other workers in the industry will be more willing to consider unionizing.

The second type of impetus for union organizing is when individual workers in an organization contact a union and express a desire to unionize. The employees themselves or the union then may begin a campaign to win support among the other employees. Whether a union pursues the unionization effort is determined by such factors as the size of the potential employee unit, how expensive it will be to campaign for support, and whether the requesting employees' complaints are an accurate gauge of employee feelings.

Once the unionization efforts begin, all activities must conform to the requirements established by labor laws and the National Labor Relations Board for private-sector employees or the appropriate federal or state governmental agency for public-sector employees. Both management and the unions must adhere to those requirements or the results of the effort can be appealed to the NLRB and overturned. With those requirements in mind, the union can embark on the first stage of the typical union organizing effort, shown in Figure 18–5.

Organizing Campaign

Like other entities seeking members, a union usually mounts an organized campaign to persuade individuals to support the union's efforts. This persuasion takes many forms, ranging from personal contacts with employees outside of work, mailing materials to employees' homes, inviting employees to attend special meetings away from the company, or publicizing the advantages of union membership.

▼ **HANDBILLING**

is written publicity given to employees by unions to convince the employees to sign authorization cards.

Handbilling is written publicity given to employees by unions to convince them to sign authorization cards. Brochures, leaflets, and circulars are all handbills. These items can be passed out to employees as they leave work, mailed to their homes, or even attached to their vehicles, as long as they comply with the rules established by laws and the NLRB. Their purpose is to convince employees to sign authorization cards.

HR Perspectives:
Free Medical Screening Tests—An Ethical Practice?

The care that unions and management must take to avoid committing an "unfair practice" during a union representation election can be seen in the experience of the United Food and Commercial Workers (UFCW), in its attempt to organize a union at Mailing Services, Inc., in Hillside, New Jersey. The UFCW won a representation election by a 151 to 113 margin. However, the firm filed an unfair-practices charge against the UFCW.

It seems that three days before the election, the union sent out a handbill to publicize what it labeled as the "first union benefit"—free medical screening tests for cholesterol, blood pressure, etc. The handbill said, "Please take advantage of your first union benefit. It's for your health." Eighty employees did so.

The National Labor Relations Board (NLRB) ruled that offering such a benefit was an improper inducement to vote for the union and ordered a new election to be held. The NLRB decision indicated that it would have ruled against the employer if a similar program had been offered by the company. The NLRB decision said, "It is reasonable to conclude . . . that the recipient of this gift would likely have felt a sense of obligation to the donor, the union . . . Therefore, we find the union's announcement and subsequent provision of free medical screening within three days of the representation election to be objectionable conduct that impaired the employees' exercise of free choice."[14]

Authorization

An **authorization card** is signed by an employee to designate a union as his/her collective bargaining agent. At least 30% of the employees in the targeted group must sign authorization cards before an election can be called. If at least 50% of the targeted employees sign authorization cards, the union can request that the employer recognize the union as the official bargaining agent for all of the employees, meaning that no election need be held. However, as would be expected, most employers refuse this request. Consequently, the union must petition the NLRB to hold a representation election.

In reality, the fact that an employee signs an authorization card does not mean that the employee is in favor of a union, but that he or she would like the opportunity to vote on having one. Employees who do not want a union still might sign authorization cards to attract management's attention to the fact that employees are disgruntled.

▼ **AN AUTHORIZATION CARD**

is signed by an employee to designate a union as his/her collective bargaining agent.

Representation Election

An election to determine if a union will represent the employees is supervised by the NLRB for private-sector or another legal body for public-sector organizations. If two unions are attempting to represent employees, the employees will have three choices: union A, union B, or no union.

Bargaining Unit   Before the election is held, the appropriate bargaining unit must be determined. A **bargaining unit** is composed of all employees eligible to select a single union to represent and bargain collectively for them. If management and the union do not agree on who is and who is not included in the unit, then the NLRB must make a determination.

▼ **A BARGAINING UNIT**

is composed of all employees eligible to select a single union to represent and bargain collectively for them.

One of the major criteria used in deciding the composition of a bargaining unit is what the NLRB has called a "community of interest." This concept means that there is a mutuality of interests of employees in the following areas:

▲ Wages, hours, and working conditions
▲ Traditional industry groupings for bargaining purposes
▲ Physical location of employees and the amount of interaction and working relationships among employee groups
▲ Supervision by similar levels of management

Unfair Labor Practices   Both the Wagner and Taft-Hartley Acts place restrictions on employer and union actions in this process before the election, when authorization cards are being solicited, and after an election has been requested. The "HR Perspective" describes how a union had a successful election overturned due to an unfair practice.

A number of tactics may be used by management representatives to try to defeat a unionization effort. Such tactics often begin when handbills appear or when authorization cards are being distributed. Figure 18–6 contains a list of some common tactics that management can and cannot legally use.

Unions have constraints on their activities as well. For example, the Supreme Court has held that union organizers who were not company employees did not have to be allowed into the parking lot to distribute handbills. This ruling addressed the balance between employer property rights and employee rights to organize.[15]

▲ **Figure 18–6**

Legal Do's and Don'ts for Managers During the Unionization Process

DO (LEGAL)	DON'T (ILLEGAL)
▲ Tell employees about current wages and benefits and how they compare with other firms	▲ Promise employees pay increases or promotions if they vote against the union
▲ Tell employees that the employer opposes unionization	▲ Threaten employees with termination or discriminate when disciplining employees
▲ Tell employees the disadvantages of having a union (especially cost of dues, assessments, and requirements of membership)	▲ Threaten to close down or move the company if a union is voted in
▲ Show employees articles about unions and negative experiences others have had elsewhere	▲ Spy on or have someone spy on union meetings
▲ Explain the unionization process to employees accurately	▲ Make a speech to employees or groups at work within 24 hours of the election (before that, it is allowed)
▲ Forbid distribution of union literature during work hours in work areas	▲ Ask employees how they plan to vote or if they have signed authorization cards
▲ Enforce disciplinary policies and rules in a consistent and fair manner	▲ Urge employees to persuade others to vote against the union (such a vote must be initiated solely by the employee)

Some organizations have experts who specialize in helping management combat unionization efforts. They have had a measure of success. One study found that unions had won only 48% of the elections in which management consultants were used compared with 65% of those in which consultants had not been used.[16]

Election Process   Assuming an election is held, the union needs to receive only the votes of a *majority of those voting* in the election. For example, if a group of 200 employees is the identified unit, and only 50 people vote, only 26 employees would need to vote "yes" in order for a union to be named as the representative of all 200. If either side believes that unfair labor practices have been used by the other side, the election results can be appealed to the NLRB. If the NLRB finds that unfair practices were used, it can order a new election. Assuming that no unfair practices have been used and the union obtains a majority in the election, the union then petitions the NLRB for certification.

Over the years unions have won representation elections about 45% to 50% of the time. Statistics from the NLRB consistently indicate that the smaller the number of employees in the bargaining unit, the higher the percentage of elections won by unions.[17] Recently in the manufacturing sector unions won 40% of the elections, but mining unions won only 32% of theirs.[18] An AFL-CIO study found that win rates were higher when the campaign focused on working conditions, grievance procedures, and dignity on the job. When unions focused only on wages, they won about half as frequently.[19]

Certification and Decertification

Official certification of a union as the legal representative for employees is given by the NLRB, or the relevant body for public-sector organizations. Once certified, the union attempts to negotiate a contract with the employer. The employer *must* bargain, as it is an unfair labor practice to refuse to bargain with a certified union.

Employees who have a union and no longer wish to be represented by it can use the election process called **decertification.** The decertification process is similar to the unionization process. Employees attempting to oust a union must obtain decertification authorization cards signed by at least 30% of the employees in the bargaining unit before an election is called. If a majority of those voting in the election want to remove the union, the decertification effort succeeds. One caution: Management may not assist the decertification effort in any way by providing assistance or funding.

▼ **DECERTIFICATION**

is a process whereby a union is removed as the representative of a group of employees.

Decertification elections generally result in the union losing. According to data from the NLRB, unions have lost about three-fourths of all decertification elections in recent years. Some of the reasons that employees decide to vote out a union include the following:[20]

▲ Better treatment by employers, so employees no longer feel they need a union to protect their interests.

▲ Efforts by employers to discredit the union, resulting in employees initiating decertification.

▲ The inability of some unions to address the changing needs of a firm's workforce.

▲ Declining image of unions, coupled with the lack of confidence in aging labor leaders by younger, more educated workers.

After election and certification of the union comes negotiation of a labor contract, one of the most important methods that unions use to obtain their major goals. A general discussion of collective bargaining is contained in Chapter 19.

▲ TRENDS IN UNION MEMBERSHIP

For organized labor in the United States, the statistics tell a disheartening story. As shown in Figure 18-7, union membership had been as high as 40% prior to 1960. But in the 1990s, unions represent less than 16% of all workers.

Why Employees Unionize

Whether the union targets a group of employees or the employees themselves request union assistance, the union still must win sufficient support from the employees. Research studies consistently reveal that employees join unions for one primary reason: They are dissatisfied with their employers and how they are treated by their employers and feel the union can improve the situation. Important factors seem to be wages and benefits, job security, and supervisory treat-

▲ **Figure 18–7**

Union Membership as Percentage of U.S. Workforce

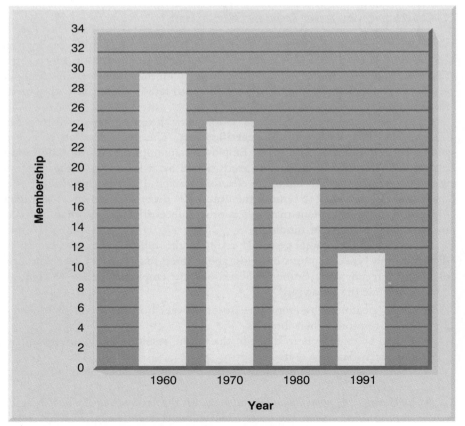

SOURCE: Bureau of Labor Statistics, U.S. Department of Labor, 1992.

HR Perspectives:
Research on Commitment to Unions

The degree to which employees are committed to their unions is of interest to many academic researchers. One study found that predictors of commitment to the union were different than predictors of commitment to the company. In this research, length of time in the union was found to be a main predictor of commitment to the union.[21]

Another study found that commitment was related to whether the union was accomplishing its goals and the accessibility of the officers.[22]

Still another study by some of the same researchers found as many differences in commitment to unions between blue- and white-collar workers as between workers from different countries.[23]

A final study looked at 71 apprentices in a union/management training program. Each apprentice was assigned to a journeyman who was also a union member. The variables that most influenced the apprentice's loyalty to the union were the attitudes the apprentice brought with him

about unions and the satisfaction he had with the training.[24]

Clearly more research on the topic is necessary if we are to understand why some people are loyal and committed to the union and others are not. But the research done to date suggests that how well the union is succeeding in providing services to members may be the most important factor in fostering union commitment today.

---

ment. The type of work done does not seem to be as great a factor in unionization as working conditions.[25]

The primary determinant of whether or not employees unionize is management. If management treats employees like valuable human resources, then employees generally feel no need for outside representation. That is why providing good working conditions, fair treatment by supervisors, responsiveness to worker complaints and concerns, and reasonably competitive wages and benefits are antidotes to unionization efforts. As would be expected, individuals who tend to be more independent or who generally view unions negatively are the most likely to oppose unionization efforts.

One study found that the pressures and views of co-workers, family members, and others in their job categories influence an individual's intention to vote for or against union representation. Another study found that cultural background may make a difference in enthusiasm for joining a union. African Americans were found to have the most favorable attitude toward joining a union; Hispanics the least.[26] The "HR Perspective" discusses research on variables affecting commitment to unions.

Declining Union Membership

Economists speculate on the issues that have sparked union decline: deregulation, foreign competition, a larger number of people looking for jobs, and a general perception by firms that dealing with unions is expensive compared with the nonunion alternative. Also, management took a much more activist stance against unions during the 1980s than during the previous years of union growth.

The decline in union representation of the labor force also can be attributed to many of the workforce changes discussed earlier. The decline of manufacturing jobs has occurred in the industries that traditionally had the highest percentage of union members. Consequently, the number of union jobs has declined, even though the overall number of jobs in all industries has grown. Furthermore, the primary growth in jobs in the U.S. has been in service industries having large numbers of white-collar jobs.[27] Also, the influx of more women into the workforce and the growth in part-time workers indicate the changing mix of jobs. But unions traditionally have had the greatest difficulty convincing white-collar workers and women to join unions. The only area where unions have had some measure of success is with public-sector employees.

White-Collar Unionism

White-collar workers include clerical workers, insurance agents, keypunchers, nurses, teachers, mental health aides, computer technicians, loan officers, auditors, and salespeople. Efforts to organize white-collar workers are increasing because advances in technology have boosted their numbers in the workforce. With the proportion of such employees increasing relative to employees in manufacturing jobs, unions have had to focus on white-collar workers in order to obtain new members.

Union leaders feel that white-collar workers and professionals have the same employment concerns as manufacturing workers—pay, job security, and working conditions. However, one major difficulty that unions face in organizing these workers is that many of them see unions as resistant to change and not in touch with the concerns of the more educated workers in technical and professional jobs. In addition, many white-collar workers exhibit quite a different mentality and set of preferences than those held by blue-collar union members. Professionals define fairness in pay differently than do blue-collar workers. They view fairness as pay based on individual performance, while the blue-collar workers always have preferred pay based on equality of job title and seniority, two basic tenets of traditional unionism. However even with these difficulties, 37% of government workers, and 22% of professionals currently belong to unions, and both figures are higher than the overall workforce union density.[28]

Unions and Women Workers

Unions generally have not been as successful in organizing women workers as they have men. Figure 18–8 indicates that the percentage of women who are union members did not decline as much as that for men workers but the actual number of women workers represented by unions changed little despite there being many more women in the workforce.

There are some indications that unions are trying to focus on recruiting women members. Unions have been in the forefront in the push for legislation on such family related goals as childcare, maternity and paternity leave, pay equity, and flexible work arrangements. Unions in the garment and service industries, which have a high concentration of female workers, generally emphasize the conflicting demands of work and family and the inequality of women's wages compared with men's.

Unionism in the Public Sector

Unions have been somewhat more successful in finding members in the public sector than in the private sector. State and local government workers particularly have been joining unions.

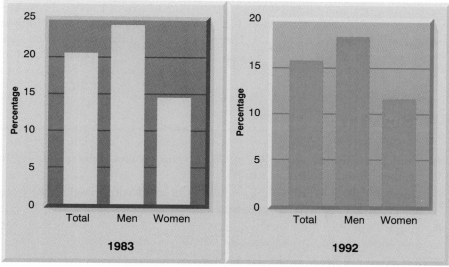

SOURCE: Bureau of Labor Statistics, U.S. Department of Labor, 1992.

▲ **Figure 18–8**

Percentages of Men and Women in Unions

State and Local Government Unionism   Unionization of state and local government employees presents some unique problems and challenges. First, many unionized local government employees are in exclusive and critical service areas. Allowing police officers, firefighters, and sanitation workers to strike endangers public health and safety. Consequently, over 30 states have laws prohibiting public employee work stoppages. These laws also identify a variety of ways to resolve negotiation impasses, including arbitration.

Public employee wage increases are another concern, because the taxpaying general public is increasingly critical of state and local government expenditures. Thus, wage demands by public employees often become political issues. One study of 700 cities found that collective bargaining increased expenditures in the departments covered by union contracts but did not affect the total expenditures, total revenues, or property taxes of the cities.[29] A possible explanation for these results is that even though the departments represented by unions had increasing labor costs, the cities adjusted other expenditures to keep total costs in line. Also, the study examined only property taxes, whereas many cities have raised their sales taxes to generate additional revenues.

State and local government unions operate under laws and hiring policies that vary widely from city to city and state to state. Civil service and so-called merit systems make the public sector vastly different from the private sector. State and local laws, not federal labor laws, take precedence, so unique legal situations often occur. Local and state officials who lack experience with unions and collective bargaining processes may hamper union/management relations. Consider a farmer and a dentist serving on a county board; their limited knowledge of union-related activities and processes might easily stand in the way of effective union/management decisions.

Unionism and the Federal Government   Although unions in the federal government hold the same basic philosophy as unions in the private sector, they do differ somewhat. Through past executive orders and laws, methods of labor/management relations that consider the special circumstances present in the federal government have been established. The Office of Personnel Management has considerable control over HR policies and regulations. For example, because of limitations on collective bargaining, federal government unions cannot bargain over wages.

▲ SUMMARY

- ▲ A union is a formal association of workers that promotes the interests of its members through collective action.
- ▲ Unions in the U.S. primarily have been concerned with job-centered issues and acting as a countervailing force to management.
- ▲ Unions in the U.S. have survived many ups and downs but saw their greatest growth in earlier days and have seen declining numbers lately.
- ▲ The "National Labor Code" is composed of three laws that provide the legal basis for labor relations today. The three laws are the Wagner Act, Taft-Hartley Act, and Landrum-Griffin Act.
- ▲ The Wagner Act was designed to protect the unions and workers. The Taft-Hartley Act restores some powers to management, and the Landrum-Griffin Act protects individual union members.
- ▲ The Federal Service Labor-Management Relations statute, passed in 1978, made major revisions in the union/management relations process in the federal government.
- ▲ The structural levels of a union include a federation, the national or international union, the local union, business agents, and union stewards.
- ▲ Workers join unions primarily because of management's failure to address major job-related concerns.
- ▲ The process of organizing includes an organizing campaign, authorization, a representation election, NLRB certification, and collective bargaining.
- ▲ The process can be reversed through decertification.
- ▲ Union membership as a percentage of the workforce is down from approximately 25% in 1970 to below 16% currently.
- ▲ For unions to reverse this decline in membership, they must organize more white-collar, women, and government workers.

▲ REVIEW AND DISCUSSION QUESTIONS

1. How effectively are U.S. unions fulfilling their two self-identified roles: a job-centered role and a countervailing-force role?
2. How could unions have a positive effect on productivity and a negative effect on profitability?
3. Identify the three parts of the "National Labor Code" and the key elements of each act.
4. What is the meaning of a "confederation" of unions? What are the levels within a union confederation?

5. A co-worker has just brought you a union leaflet that urges employees to sign an authorization card. What events would you expect to occur from this point on?

6. Discuss the following comment by an internationally known management consultant: "I think anybody who anticipates that unions will exist in any major role or in major quantities as bargaining units in the U.S. in the year 2000 is dreaming."

| CASE | NISSAN WORKERS REJECT UNIONIZATION |

One of the most widely publicized efforts by a union to represent a group of employees took place in 1989 at the Nissan Motor Manufacturing Corporation Plant in Smyrna, Tennessee. The union election received extensive media coverage for several reasons.

First, this effort by the United Auto Workers (UAW) was the first union election conducted by the National Labor Relations Board at a Japanese-owned auto plant in the U.S. Second, more and more Japanese automobile firms have established plants in the U.S., and the Nissan election was seen by many as a test of some of the Japanese management strategies used in those plants. The only previous effort by the UAW to organize a Japanese automobile plant was at the Honda plant in Marysville, Ohio, in 1985. However, the union withdrew its request for an election shortly before voting was to occur. The UAW did win representation at some plants that are jointly owned by U.S. and Japanese firms, such as the Mazda/Ford plant in Flat Rock, Michigan, and the Toyota/General Motors plant in Fremont, California. But the Nissan election vote was the first one in which no U.S. partner was involved. A third reason for the attention given to the Nissan election was that the plant was the first of a number of new Japanese-owned plants to open in the southern United States, which traditionally has been hostile to unions.

The results of the election represented a major setback to efforts to unionize Japanese-owned auto plants. By more than a two-to-one margin, Nissan workers rejected the union. The vote was 1,622 against and 711 for the union. The reasons for the decisive rejection of the union provide some interesting insights on why unions in the U.S. have had increasing difficulty recruiting members in the 1980s and how an employer's style of management can affect workers' views of the need for union representation.

The primary reason that the union lost the election can be summarized in remarks by Nissan members such as Dotty Lachert, a production technician, who said, "The UAW can't give us anything we don't already have." Bucky Kahl, the director of human resources at Nissan, said, "We pride ourselves in being a company that functions in a participatory way. . . . The vote was a statement of support for strongly participative management."

In the effort to persuade workers to vote one way or the other, the company and the union used different appeals. The UAW campaigned on the issues of workplace safety and the fast pace of the assembly line at Nissan. To convey its message, the UAW president, Owen Bieber, led the organizing campaign, aided by thirty professional organizers.

The company countered the union campaign by emphasizing the good benefits, pay levels, and participative-management climate. During the last few weeks before the election, Nissan management held small-group meetings with workers at which managers stated that the teamwork atmosphere in the plant would be threatened if the union won. Also, management showed videos on strike violence at union-represented plants in other industries. The company also emphasized that in the six years since the plant had been open, no workers had been laid off and that it expected continued expansion and addition of jobs.

Following the election, the Nissan plant manager, Jerry Berefield, said, "I'm more convinced than I ever have been that the UAW is never going to organize this plant." Whether that prediction holds true depends on a number of factors, not the least of which is the continued economic strength of Nissan.[30]

▲ **QUESTIONS**

1. Describe the Nissan vote in terms of the reasons why employees do or do not join unions.
2. How might the UAW have approached this campaign differently?

▲ **NOTES**

1. Adapted from W. J. Miller, "Metamorphosis in the Desert," *Industry Week,* March 16, 1992, 27–34.
2. D. G. Blanchflower and R. B. Freeman, "Unionism in the United States and Other Advanced OECD Countries," *Industrial Relations* 31 (1992), 56–79.
3. S. Bronars and D. Deere, "Union Representation Elections and Firm Profitability", *Industrial Relations* 29 (1990), 15.
4. J. Arthur and J. Dworkin, "Current Topics in Industrial and Labor Relations Research and Practice," *Journal of Management* 17 (1991), 515–551.
5. John Hoerr, "What Should Unions Do?" *Harvard Business Review,* May–June 1991, 42.
6. D. Weil, "Enforcing OSHA: The Role of Labor Unions," *Industrial Relations* 30 (1991), 20.
7. "Unions Use Earth as Weapon", *Omaha World-Herald,* September 13, 1992, G1.
8. R. Tomsho, "Unions Search for Regulatory Violations," *The Wall Street Journal,* February 28, 1992, B1.
9. *Commonwealth of Massachusetts v. Hunt,* Massachusetts, 4 Metcalf 3 (1842).
10. "National Labor Relations Act," *United States Statutes at Large* 49, 449.
11. "Labor-Management Relations Act, 1947" (PL 101, 23 June 1947), *United States Statutes at Large* 61, 136–162.
12. *United Steel Workers v. United States,* 45 LRRM 2066 (1959).
13. "Labor-Management Reporting and Disclosure Act of 1959" (PL 86-257, 14 September 1959), *United States Statutes at Large* 73, 519–546.
14. Adapted from *Resource,* May 1989, 61; and *Mailing Services, Inc.* 293 NLRB N. 58 (March 31, 1989).
15. Paul Barrett, "Employers Win Supreme Court Ruling," *The Wall Street Journal,* January 28, 1992, A4.
16. J. J. Lawler, "The Influence of Management Consultants on the Outcome of Union Certification Elections," *Industrial and Labor Relations Review* 40 (1984), 38–51.
17. "Unions Won 48.6 Percent of 1988 Elections," *Resource,* May 1989, 16.
18. "Union Organizers Fall on Hard Times," *The Wall Street Journal,* January 29, 1991, 1.
19. Stephanie Overman, "The Union Pitch Has Changed," *HR Magazine,* December 1991, 46.
20. Marvin J. Levine, "Double-Digit Decertification Activity: Union Organizational Weakness in the 1980s," *Labor Law Journal* 40 (1989), 311–315.
21. J. Barling et al., "Predicting Employee Commitment to Company and Union: Divergent Models," *Journal of Occupational Psychology* 63 (1990), 49–61.

22. J. Thacker et al., "Union Commitment: An Examinations of Antecedent and Outcome Factors," *Journal of Occupational Psychology* 63 (1990), 33–48.

23. J. Thacker et al., "Commitment to the Union: A Comparison of United States and Canadian Workers," *Journal of Organizational Behavior* 12 (1991), 63–71.

24. C. Fullagar et al., "The Socialization of Union Loyalty," *Journal of Organizational Behavior* 13, (1992), 13–26; also see a related study, J. Barling et al., "Pre-employment Predictors of Union Attitudes: The Role of Family Socialization and Work Beliefs," *Journal of Applied Psychology* 76, (1991), 725–731.

25. Jeanne M. Brett, "Why Employees Want Unions," *Organizational Dynamics,* Spring 1980, 47–59.

26. R. S. Iverblatt and R. J. Amann, "Race, Ethnicity, Union Attitudes, and Voting Predictions," *Industrial Relations* 30, (1991), 271–285.

27. D. Milbank, "On the Ropes," *The Wall Street Journal,* May 5, 1992, 1.

28. J. Moskal, "Unions Stem Member Losses," *USA Today,* February 21, 1992, 2B.

29. Robert G. Valleta, "The Impact of Unionism on Municipal Expenditures and Reviews," *Industrial and Labor Relations Review* 42 (1989), 430–442.

30. Adapted from a variety of news stories, including David Landis, "Union Again Fails to Make Gain in South," *USA Today,* July 28, 1989, B1–2; "The UAW vs. Japan," *Business Week,* July 24, 1989, 64–65; Gregory A. Patterson, "Nissan Workers Reject UAW Bid to Organize Plant in Tennessee," *The Wall Street Journal,* July 28, 1989, A3; Stephanie Overman, "Nissan Sees Union's Loss as Management Style's Win," *Resource,* September 1989, A12; and Sal Vittolino, "Nissan Drives 'Em Away," *Human Resource Executive,* October 1989, 1, 24–27.

CHAPTER 19

COLLECTIVE BARGAINING AND GRIEVANCE MANAGEMENT

After you have read this chapter, you should be able to:

1. Define collective bargaining and identify at least four bargaining relationships and structures.

2. Explain the three categories of collective bargaining issues.

3. Identify and describe a typical collective bargaining process.

4. Define and explain the differences among conciliation, mediation, and arbitration.

5. Discuss two major collective bargaining trends.

6. Define a grievance and describe the importance and extent of grievance procedures.

7. Explain the basic steps in a grievance procedure.

8. Discuss arbitration as the final phase of a grievance procedure.

HR Today and Tomorrow:
Arbitration Rather Than a Lawsuit?

Collective bargaining agreements between unions and management typically have required that grievances and disputes be resolved by a neutral third party through arbitration. Legal precedent holds that when two parties agree to have disputes settled in such a way, the decision is "insulated" from review by the courts. That means that the arbitrator can make a binding final resolution of the problem, and neither one of the parties can then sue to try (once again) to win the point. Generally speaking, the arbitration process has worked very well.

Recently the U.S. Supreme Court cleared the way for the use of a similar remedy in nonunion settings, the *predispute arbitration agreement.* In the precedent-setting case, a New York stockbroker and his company had both signed a form stating "any dispute, claim, or controversy . . . arising out of the employment or termination of employment . . . is required to be arbitrated." The Supreme Court held that the stockbroker's later claim of dismissal because of age discrimination therefore belonged before an arbitrator, not in federal court. A week later the Court in a similar case extended the ruling to most race, sex, and age discrimination claims under Title VII of the Civil Rights Act.

At almost the same time, the National Conference of Commissioners on Uniform State Laws suggested that the states adopt a uniform state employment statute that would let most fired employees take their cases to a neutral arbitrator. The commission says its plan would cover 60 million workers and estimates that 10% of the 2 million workers who are fired each year would have valid claims.

Why all the interest in arbitration? The simple answer is that lawsuits over employment-related matters have exploded! The courts are bogged down in employment litigation. Especially in the states where employers have been hardest hit (California, Michigan, and Illinois), this arbitration approach seems to make sense. In California the employee wins 70% of the jury trials and collects awards averaging $300,000 to $500,000—before legal costs. Companies' legal fees on such cases average $75,000, workers' $40,000. In contrast, arbitration costs a total of about $15,000 per case. Arbitration is much quicker as well as less expensive.

Whether the future holds the adoption by the various states of a uniform law requiring arbitration, or whether arbitration simply will evolve as a result of the Supreme Court decisions, we are likely to see more of it. However, trial lawyers dislike the idea. Judith Vladeck, a New York plaintiff's attorney, complained that under arbitration agreements employees are essentially told, "If you come here to work, you give up your right to enforce your public right to be free of discrimination." A director of the American Civil Liberties Union says that the arbitration agreements could be beneficial if arbitration processes are conducted fairly. Indeed, if arbitration is to succeed it must be seen as fair and noncoercive.

But if the problems can be worked out, a system that parallels what has worked in union contracts for years could fairly and rapidly solve employment disputes. In fact, the trend in the federal courts (as they have gotten further swamped) is to favor arbitration rather than lawsuits for employment disputes.[1]

Collective bargaining should be more than a fistfight, more than rulemaking. It must be more than merely adversarial. And there is ample evidence that it can be.

D. Quinn Mills

Collective bargaining takes center stage in an organization following a successful unionization attempt. This final stage of the unionization process is the negotiation and signing of a contractual agreement between a union and an employer. In this chapter, the process of contract negotiation through collective bargaining is discussed. Also, day-to-day union/management relations through grievance management is examined.

▲ COLLECTIVE BARGAINING

In the U.S. collective bargaining is somewhat different than in other countries because of different philosophical and political origins. Different legal frameworks for collective bargaining also exist in various countries.

Collective bargaining is the process whereby representatives of management and workers negotiate over wages, hours, and other terms and conditions of employment. It is a give-and-take process between representatives of two organizations for the benefit of both. It is also a power relationship. The power relationship in collective bargaining involves conflict, and the threat of conflict seems necessary to maintain the relationship.[2] But perhaps the most significant aspect of collective bargaining is that it is an ongoing relationship that does not end immediately after agreement is reached.

▼ **COLLECTIVE BARGAINING**

is the process whereby representatives of management and workers negotiate over wages, hours, and other terms and conditions of employment.

Types of Bargaining Relationships

The attitude of management toward unions is one major factor in determining the relationship between union and management. This attitude plays a crucial role in management's strategic approach to collective bargaining. Management/union relationships in collective bargaining can follow one of several patterns. Figure 19–1 shows the relationship as a continuum, ranging from conflict to col-

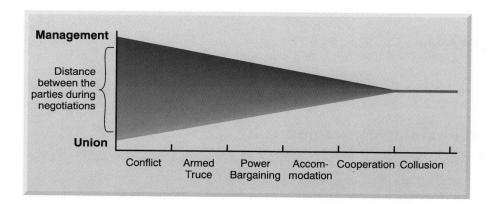

▲ **Figure 19–1**

Collective Bargaining Relationship Continuum

lusion. On the left side of the continuum, management and union see each other as enemies. On the right side, the two entities join together illegally. There are a number of positions in between, and a discussion of six strategies follows.[3]

Conflict   In the conflict strategy, management takes a totally uncompromising view. A desire to "bust the union" may underlie the use of the conflict strategy. To paraphrase a saying from old western movies, management's attitude is that "the only good union is a dead union!"

Armed Truce   Management representatives who practice the armed-truce strategy take the position that they are well aware of the vital interests of the organization, while the union is poles away and always will be. However, management realizes that forcing head-on conflict is not in the best interests of either party and that the union is not likely to disappear. Consequently, management is willing to negotiate a basic agreement. Many union/management relationships, especially in smaller businesses, have not progressed beyond this armed-truce stage.

Power Bargaining   Managers engaged in a power bargaining relationship can accept the union; many even pride themselves on the sense of "realism" that forces them to acknowledge the union's power. Managerial philosophy here assumes that management's task is to increase its power, then use it whenever possible to offset the power of the union. The union engages in power bargaining, using tactics that have an impact on the employer's pocketbook such as lawsuits, public hearings, demonstrations, and appeals to legislators.

Accommodation   In accommodation, management and the union learn to tolerate each other and attempt to minimize conflict and to conciliate whenever necessary. The accommodation strategy in no way suggests that management goes out of its way to help organized labor but merely that it recognizes the need to reduce confrontation in dealing with common problems often caused by external forces, such as imports and government regulations.

Cooperation   The cooperation strategy involves full acceptance of the union as an active partner in a formal plan. In this strategy management supports both the right and the desire of unions to participate in certain areas of decision making. The two parties jointly resolve human resource and production problems as they occur. Labor/management committees and quality-improvement groups are examples of cooperation.

Collusion   Collusion, relatively rare in American labor history, is illegal. In the collusion strategy, union and management engage in labor price fixing designed to inflate wages and profits at the expense of the general public. Or they may institute "sweetheart" deals that benefit management and union officials at the expense of the employees.

Bargaining Structures

Collective bargaining can be structured in several different ways:

▲ One employer, one union
▲ One employer, multiplant

▲ One employer, multiunion
▲ Multiemployer, one union
▲ Multiemployer, multiunion

The *one-employer, one-union* structure is the simplest and most common. It occurs when an employer has just one unionized operating facility. If the union represents employees at other facilities of the firm, then the collective bargaining structure is *one employer, multiplant*. For example, if a printing company has three facilities, each located in a different state, then a collective bargaining contract can be negotiated for all plants at the same time. The *one-employer, multiunion* structure may be used when a large employer has employees represented by different unions, and contracts with each union are negotiated at the same time. This model is common in the construction industry, where one employer may face several different building trade unions representing a number of different crafts.

Another variation, *multiemployer, one union,* was developed in the coal-mining industry. This structure also has been used extensively in the steel industry in the form of a *master contract* that applies to all companies. This master agreement then is supplemented by a *local contract* dealing with individual company and/or plant issues.

The final bargaining structure is the *multiemployer, multiunion* one. It has been used in the construction industry in which a group of unions negotiates with a contractor's association representing all of the unionized construction companies in a geographic area.

Some unions favor negotiating with one company, and then using the contract gained as a model for other firms in the same industry. This approach has been labeled *pattern bargaining*. It has been used by the United Auto Workers with General Motors, Ford, and Chrysler.

Employers may prefer different structures for different reasons. If an employer has multiple unions with which to bargain, the company may spend less time and get more consistent contracts by negotiating with all unions at once. Or an employer may prefer a one-employer, multiplant structure to get similar contracts at widely diverse plants, which also may put pressure on individual locals to agree to similar concessions.

In summary, the choice of a bargaining structure is made for a variety of reasons, many of which reflect the bargaining power and pressures that each party believes it can exert. The structure may change over time as both parties attempt to stay up to date with industry changes.

Issues for Bargaining

The Wagner Act clearly expects management and the union to bargain over "wages, hours, and other terms and conditions of employment." However, what specifically are included in those categories has been defined over the years by the National Labor Relations Board (NLRB) and Supreme Court rulings. They have defined the expectations through three groupings: mandatory, permissive, and illegal issues.

Mandatory Issues   Those issues that are identified specifically by labor laws or court decisions as being subject to bargaining are **mandatory issues.** If either party demands that issues in this category be bargained over, then bargain-

▼ **MANDATORY ISSUES**

are those issues that are identified specifically by labor laws or court decisions as being subject to bargaining.

ing must occur. Generally, mandatory issues relate to wages, benefits, nature of jobs, and other work-related subjects. That broad view means that the following issues have been ruled to be mandatory subjects for bargaining:[4]

- ▲ Discharge of employees
- ▲ Job security
- ▲ Grievances
- ▲ Work schedules
- ▲ Union security and dues checkoff
- ▲ Retirement and pension coverage
- ▲ Vacations

- ▲ Individual merit raise plans
- ▲ Christmas bonuses
- ▲ Rest- and lunch-break rules
- ▲ Safety rules
- ▲ Profit-sharing plans
- ▲ Required employee physical exams

▼ **PERMISSIVE ISSUES**

are those issues that are not mandatory but relate to jobs.

Permissive Issues   Those issues that are not mandatory but relate to jobs are **permissive issues.** They can be bargained over if both parties agree. Some examples are:

- ▲ Benefits for retired employees
- ▲ Product prices
- ▲ Performance bonds
- ▲ A union label

▼ **ILLEGAL ISSUES**

are those issues that require either party to take illegal action.

Illegal Issues   A final category is **illegal issues,** those that require either party to take illegal action, such as giving preference to individuals who have been union members when hiring employees. If one side wants to bargain over an illegal issue, the other can refuse. Outside of these illegal issues, typical items in a formal labor contract are shown in Figure 19–2. Two areas of common concern in contract bargaining are management rights and union security agreements.

▼ **MANAGEMENT RIGHTS**

are those rights reserved to the employer to manage, direct, and control its business.

Management Rights   Virtually all labor contracts include **management rights** which are those rights reserved to the employer to manage, direct, and control its business. Such a provision often reads as follows:

> The employer retains all rights to manage, direct, and control its business in all particulars, except as such rights are expressly and specifically modified by the terms of this or any subsequent agreement.[5]

By including such a provision, management is attempting to preserve its unilateral right to decide or make changes in any areas not identified in a labor contract. Some labor contracts spell out in more detail the issues that fall under management rights, while others use the general language just quoted. As would

▲ **Figure 19–2**

Typical Items in a Labor Contract

1. Purpose of agreement	11. Separation allowance
2. Nondiscrimination clause	12. Seniority
3. Management rights	13. Bulletin boards
4. Recognition of the union	14. Pension and insurance
5. Wages	15. Safety
6. Incentives	16. Grievance procedure
7. Hours of work	17. No-strike or lockout clause
8. Vacations	18. Definitions
9. Sick leave and leaves of absence	19. Terms of the contract (dates)
10. Discipline	20. Appendices

be expected, management representatives want to have as many issues defined as "management rights" as they can.

Union Security A major concern of the union representatives when bargaining is to negotiate **union security** provisions to aid the union in obtaining and retaining members. One major union security agreement is the *dues checkoff*, which is a provision that union dues will be deducted automatically from the payroll checks of members. This provision makes it much easier for the union to collect its funds, which otherwise must be collected by billing each individual member.

Another form of union security is *requiring union membership* of all employees, subject to state right–to–work laws (see Chapter 18). The following types of union security agreements can be negotiated in states without right–to–work laws:

▲ *Union shop.* Employee must join the union after a waiting period or be terminated.

▲ *Modified union shop.* After a waiting period all new employees must join the union. Present union members must maintain their memberships, but present employees who are not members do not have to join the union.

▲ *Maintenance of membership.* Workers joining a union must maintain their memberships or be terminated.

▲ *Agency shop.* Employees who are not union members must pay dues and fees equivalent to those paid by union members. All workers in the unit are covered by provisions of the contract that is negotiated.

Union security agreements are very common in labor contracts. For example, over 80% of all labor contracts surveyed contained some union security provisions. Dues checkoff and union shop agreements were the most common.[6]

▲ PROCESS OF COLLECTIVE BARGAINING

The collective bargaining process has a number of stages. Over time, each union and management situation develops slight modifications which are necessary for effective bargaining. The process shown in Figure 19–3 is typical.

▼ **UNION SECURITY**

refers to provisions to aid the union in obtaining and retaining members.

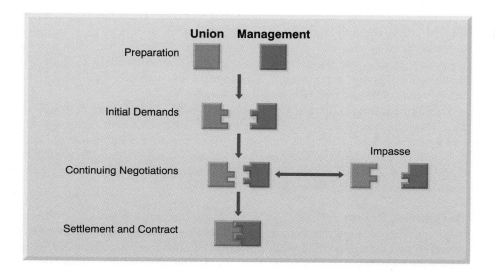

▲ **Figure 19–3**

Typical Collective Bargaining Process

Preparation

Especially after a bitter organizing campaign, a union may take months to win an initial contract. Some unions never reach contract agreement and voluntarily relinquish their certification. Both labor and management representatives spend much time preparing for negotiations. If a previous contract is expiring, the grievances filed under the old contract will be reviewed to identify contract language changes to be negotiated. Employer and industry data concerning wages, benefits, working conditions, management and union rights, productivity, and absenteeism are gathered. Once the data are analyzed, each side identifies what its priorities are and what strategies and tactics it will use to obtain what it wants. Each tries to allow itself some flexibility in order to trade off less important demands for more critical ones.

The courts have stated that unions cannot represent workers in a competent manner if they do not have necessary company information. Therefore, management must provide the necessary data. If the organization argues that it cannot afford to pay what the union is asking, the employer's financial situation and accompanying data are all the more relevant. However, the union must request such information before the employer is obligated to provide it.[7]

Initial Demands

Typical bargaining includes an initial proposal of expectations by both sides. The amount of rancor or calmness exhibited will set the tone for future negotiations between the parties. Union and management representatives who have been part of previous negotiations may adopt a pattern that has evolved over time. In negotiations for the first contract between an employer and a union, the process can be much more difficult. Management representatives must adjust to dealing with a union, and employees who are leaders in the union must adapt to their new roles.[8]

Continuing Negotiations

After opening positions have been taken, each side attempts to determine what the other values highly so the best bargain can be struck. For example, the union may be asking the employer to pay for dental benefits as part of a package that also includes wage demands and retirement benefits. However, the union may be most interested in the wages and retirement benefits and willing to trade the dental payments for more wages. Management has to determine which the union wants more and decide exactly what to give up.

During negotiations, both management and union must evaluate cost proposals concerning changes in wages, benefits, and other economic items quickly and accurately. A mathematical modeling system tied to a computer spreadsheet will perform the calculations and produce a total cost figure almost immediately. Such issues as an extra day off or a 10-cent-an-hour pay raise can be converted easily to annual cost figures for comparison.

Bargaining Power   The factors affecting the outcomes when collective bargaining occurs are shown in Figure 19–4. As that model shows, there are four sets of factors that determine the bargaining power of management and a union, all of which must be considered by the negotiators in their give-and-take discussions.

▲ **Figure 19–4**   Determinants of Collective Bargaining Actions

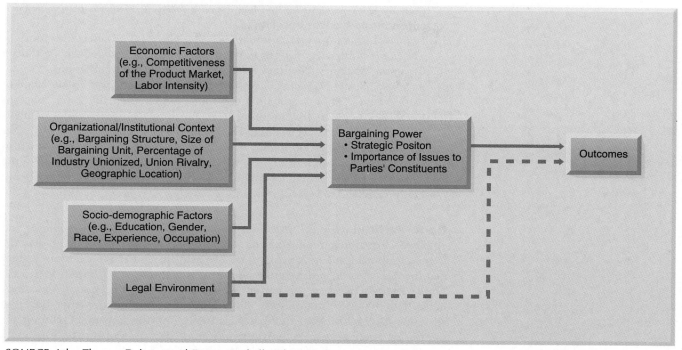

SOURCE: John Thomas Delaney and Donna Sochell, "The Mandatory-Permissive Distinction and Collective Bargaining Outcomes," *Industrial and Labor Relations Review 42* (1989), 571 © 1989 Cornell University. Used with permission.

Obviously, *economic factors* are important. What a firm can afford without jeopardizing its economic health is important to both the management and the union. The various *organizational factors* reflect the relative strength or weaknesses of the union. The *sociodemographic factors* will affect the types of proposals made by management and union. For example, if the workers represented by the union are older and predominately male, then certain benefits such as maternity coverage or child-care assistance may not be desired as much as additional pension contributions. Both parties must comply with all *legal restraints and regulations* on bargaining procedure and outcomes. Depending on the analyses of those factors, the parties make use of their bargaining power to obtain concessions from the other party. Ultimately, the outcomes are represented as provisions in the labor contract.

Bargaining Behavior   Collective bargaining is not always a strictly logical, rational process. The behavior of the negotiators is critical. Representatives can exhibit any of four behavior subprocesses in collective bargaining:[9]

1. *Distributive bargaining* occurs when one party must win and the other must lose over a conflicting issue. If a union wants a dues checkoff, and the employer does not want a checkoff, only one side can win. Either there will or will not be a checkoff.

2. *Integrative bargaining* occurs when both management and union face a common problem and must work together for a solution. For example, the two

parties might negotiate a joint program for handling alcoholism, both agreeing to provide some funds to pay for alcoholic treatment activities, because there are joint gains to be had from such a program in terms of reduced absenteeism and discipline problems.

3. *Attitudinal structuring* occurs when each side attempts to affect the tone, or "climate," of the negotiations. The result will determine which of the six bargaining strategies identified earlier is adopted during negotiations.

4. *Intraorganizational bargaining* occurs when disagreements exist *within* labor or management. Union negotiators may not be addressing the same concerns that union members have in some areas. For instance, some union members feel that dental insurance should be included in a union proposal and other union members feel that higher retirement benefits are more important than dental insurance. Some consensus will have to be reached before going to the bargaining table. Sometimes union negotiators will have the members rank their preferences for specific benefits.

Good Faith   Provisions in federal labor law require that both employer and employee bargaining representatives negotiate in *good faith,* meaning that the parties agree to send negotiators who can bargain and make decisions, rather than people who do not have the authority to commit either group to a decision. Meetings between the parties cannot be scheduled at absurdly inconvenient hours. Some give-and-take discussions also must occur. After decisions are made in good faith, neither party can renege on the agreement. Blatant antiunion or antimanagement propaganda cannot be used during the bargaining process. The specifics of the good faith relationship for collective bargaining are defined by a series of National Labor Relations Board (NLRB) and court rulings.[10]

Settlement and Contract Agreement

After an initial agreement has been made, the two sides usually return to their respective constituencies to determine if what they have informally agreed on is acceptable. A particularly crucial stage is **ratification** of the labor agreement, which occurs when union members vote to accept the terms of a negotiated labor agreement. Prior to the ratification vote, the union negotiating team explains the agreement to the union members and presents it for a vote. If approval is voted, the agreement is then formalized into a contract. The agreement also contains language on the duration of the contract.[11]

Bargaining Impasse

Regardless of the structure of the bargaining process, labor and management do not always reach agreement on the issues. In such cases, a deadlock may lead to union strikes or management lockouts. During a **strike,** union members refuse to work in order to put pressure on an employer. Often the striking union members picket or demonstrate against the employer outside the place of business by carrying placards and signs. In a **lockout,** management shuts down company operations to prevent union members from working. This action also may avoid possible damage or sabotage to company facilities or injury to employees who continue to work.

▼ **RATIFICATION**

occurs when union members vote to accept the terms of a negotiated labor agreement.

▼ **A STRIKE**

occurs when workers refuse to work in order to put pressure on an employer.

▼ **A LOCKOUT**

occurs when management shuts down company operations to prevent union members from working.

Both strikes and lockouts are forms of pressure on the other party. By striking, the union attempts to pressure management into making some concessions and signing a contract. However, management may respond by hiring replacement workers or may operate the company by using supervisors and managers to fill in for striking workers. By locking out workers, an employer puts economic pressure on union members in the hope that they will make concessions and support a contract agreement.

Types of Strikes   Workers' rights vary depending on the type of strike that occurs. For example, in an economic strike an employer is free to replace the striking workers. But during unfair-labor-practice strikes, workers who want their jobs back at the end of the strike must be reinstated. The types of strikes include the following:

▲ *Economic strikes* occur when the parties fail to reach agreement during collective bargaining.

▲ *Unfair-labor-practice strikes* occur when union members walk away from their jobs over what they feel are illegal employer actions, such as refusal to bargain.

▲ *Wildcat strikes* occur during the life of the collective bargaining agreement without approval of union leadership and violate a no-strike clause in a labor contract. Strikers can be discharged or disciplined.

▲ *Jurisdictional strikes* occur when one union's members walk out to force an employer to assign work to them instead of to another union.

▲ *Sympathy strikes* express one union's support for another involved in a dispute, even though the first union has no disagreement with the employer.

Generally, work stoppages due to strikes and lockouts are relatively rare. Figure 19–5 shows that during the 1980s the number of strikes each year actually declined, except for a slight rise in 1986. In the early 1990s the average had dropped to below 40 from 300 in the 1960s.[12] The decline in number can be traced to many factors.[13] Overall, there has been a decline in union power, paralleling the decline of heavy industry in the United States and decreased public support of unions. Thus, many unions are reluctant to go on strike because of the financial losses their members would incur or the fear that the financial losses would cause the employer to go bankrupt. In addition, management has shown its willingness to hire replacements, and some strikes have ended with union workers losing their jobs. Efforts to forestall such drastic actions on the part of either party can take the form of conciliation, mediation, or arbitration.

Conciliation or Mediation   Conciliation or mediation occurs when an outside individual attempts to help two deadlocked parties continue negotiations and arrive at a solution. In **conciliation** a third party attempts to keep the union and management negotiators talking so that they voluntarily can reach a settlement. In **mediation** a third party assists the negotiators in their discussions and also suggests settlement proposals. In neither conciliation nor mediation does the third party attempt to impose a solution.

Conciliators and mediators usually are experienced neutrals who act as counselors to reopen communication, clarify problems, and try to find areas in which the two parties can agree. The success of mediators often is linked to their having significant previous experience, being flexible, and taking an active role in keeping the parties negotiating.[14]

▼ **CONCILIATION**

occurs when a third party attempts to keep the union and management negotiators talking so that they

▼ **MEDIATION**

occurs when a third party assists the negotiators in their discussions and also suggests settlement proposals.

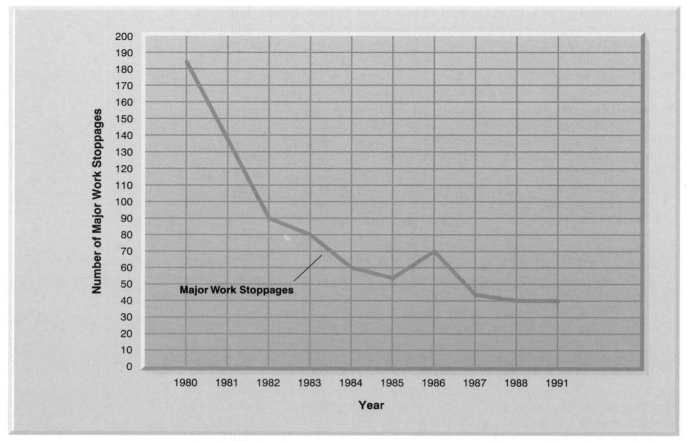

▲ **Figure 19–5**   Number of Major Work Stoppages, 1980–1991

SOURCE: U.S. Department of Labor, Bureau of Labor Statistics.

Often, mediators and conciliators are provided by the Federal Mediation and Conciliation Services (FMCS). This agency assists union and management negotiations when impasses arise. The FMCS has offices in most major U.S. cities and employs several hundred trained labor experts. Employees of the FMCS sit down with the negotiators from both union and management and attempt to forestall strikes or lockouts.

▼ **ARBITRATION**

is a means of deciding a dispute in which negotiating parties submit the dispute to a third party to make a decision.

Arbitration   The process of **arbitration** is a means of deciding a dispute in which negotiating parties submit the dispute to a third party to make a decision. Arbitration can be conducted either by an individual or a panel of individuals. It is a major interest today, as the chapter opening discussion suggested. Arbitration can be used to solve bargaining impasses primarily in the public sector. This "interest" arbitration is not frequently used in the private sector because companies generally do not want an outside party making decisions about their rights, wages, benefits, and other issues. However, grievance, or "rights," arbitration is used extensively in the private sector. Arbitration will be discussed in more detail when the grievance process is presented later in this chapter.

▲ TRENDS IN COLLECTIVE BARGAINING

During the 1980s and early 1990s many organizations in virtually all economic sectors felt an immediate need to reduce costs. Labor costs represented significant expenses in many of these organizations, so they were often the first to be cut. This put management on a collision course with the status quo and the unions. The resulting change in the environment of labor/management negotiations has changed the collective bargaining process itself. Rather than simply being concerned with wages and benefits, unions have had to add plant closings, workforce reduction, and productivity concerns to the agenda. One observer suggests, "Part of the union membership would like to go back to the days of 30 years ago when there were no partnerships or jointness between labor and management and each side played adversarial roles."[15] But both sides realize that without changes there will be no company and thus no jobs. The more notable trends evolving from this situation are: union/management cooperation, concessionary bargaining, bankruptcy and plant closings, and striker replacement.

HR Perspectives:

Labor/Management Cooperation at A. O. Smith

The benefits of labor/management cooperative efforts on productivity are illustrated at A. O. Smith, a Milwaukee-based automotive parts manufacturing firm. Beginning in the early 1980s, both management and union leaders recognized that major problems existed at Smith. Bored workers doing repetitive tasks were directed by dictatorial supervisors. Grievances over work rules were common, and the piece-rate wage system was based on quantity, not quality. For instance, about 20% of the truck frames produced for Ford had to be repaired before shipment to Ford.

Skip ahead six or seven years, and the defect rate on the Ford truck frames was about 3% and productivity had doubled. What happened to turn around the situation at Smith can be tied to joint labor/management efforts to involve workers in improving productivity, to change work rules, and to transform the management practices used.

Smith formed "employment-involvement" (EI) groups to discuss

ways of improving quality and lowering costs. But those EI groups were set up by management without union input. Therefore, the unions representing Smith workers refused to support the efforts, and little productivity or quality enhancement resulted.

However, when General Motors, one of Smith's larger customers, began reducing its purchases, both union representatives and management knew radical steps were needed to prevent loss of jobs and company revenues. Thus, the seven unions representing Smith employees and management agreed to participate in new EI efforts.

Problem-solving groups were established at all levels, beginning with the plant floor, at which both management and union officials participated along with workers. EI groups made some progress, but further reductions in orders from automakers forced Smith to lay off 1,300 workers. The company also threatened to close the Milwaukee plant unless major work-rule changes were made.

During contract negotiations both

sides agreed to drop the piece-rate pay system and to make many work-rule changes. The company also agreed to freeze worker pay rates at existing levels instead of cutting workers' pay $3 per hour.

The work-rule changes allowed the installation of the work-team approach. These teams are composed of five to seven workers who perform a group of jobs on a rotating basis. The teams designate their own leaders, who can request maintenance as needed, schedule production and overtime, and stop production to fix quality problems. Using teams in this way meant that Smith could reduce the number of first-line supervisors. For the remaining supervisors and managers, management training programs were instituted.

The unions and management continue to discuss changes in seniority rules and job security guarantees for workers. But no longer do workers or managers worry about the plant closing because of low productivity or quality problems.[16]

Union/Management Cooperation

Union/management cooperation has taken many forms, from union participation in certain management decisions to outright union ownership of the company in others. One survey of large firms found that 57.5% of firms had some type of group discussion about production or quality problems with unionized employees. The "HR Perspective" on A. O. Smith provides more detail on a successful cooperative program.

Several examples illustrate how such union/management cooperation has worked:[17]

▲ At Xerox, the joint management/union team identified ways to save $3.7 million and keep the unionized workers employed.

▲ National Steel saw productivity rise by 11% and costs cut by $100 million without any layoffs. The company president credit members and their ideas for the turnaround.

▲ The New Castle, Indiana, Chrysler plant went from running a deficit of $5 million a year to saving $1.5 million a year and making money with shared information and teamwork.

▲ Thomson Consumer Electronics worked with the International Brotherhood of Electrical Workers to cut absenteeism 26% after a union/management steering committee produced a "competitiveness plan."

▲ Saturn's "co-managed" facility run jointly by management and workers has produced a car and system that is widely viewed as successful.

There are many more examples of course. Some hail these successes as a new era in bargaining where labor has begun to focus on the *process* of change, not just the results.[18] Other research suggests the process of change is far from complete and quite varied.[19] Even the commitment to joint programs is quite variable.

Many in the labor movement (and some academics) fear that these programs may lead to an undermining of union support by creating a closer identification with the company's concerns and goals.[20] In fact, for a while it was unclear whether the NLRB would continue to allow such cooperation or outlaw it (see the "HR in Perspective" on cooperation.)

Union Ownership   Unions have become active participants in the restructuring of American industry by encouraging workers to become partial or complete owners of their employers. These efforts were spurred by concerns that firms were preparing to shut down or to be merged or bought out by financial investors who the unions feared would cut union jobs.

Unions have been active in assisting members to put together *employee stock ownership plans (ESOPs)* to purchase all or part of some firms. For example, in 1983, when closure of Weirton Steel in West Virginia was announced, the unionized employees purchased the firm through an ESOP, and the firm has continued to operate satisfactorily since then. However, not all union-led ESOPs have been successful, as illustrated by the collapse of the Hyatt Clark Industries' ESOP takeover of a General Motors plant which was led by the United Auto Workers union.[21]

Unions also have made offers to purchase firms to head off financially leveraged takeovers by other investors. For example, the unions representing United

HR Perspectives:
Is Employee Involvement Illegal?

Suggesting that cooperation could ever be bad seems a little like arguing against motherhood, the flag, and apple pie. Yet some historical perspective is required to understand the issues that surrounded an NLRB decision that has caught the attention of American business. The decision dealt with "worker involvement" or "employee participation" committees.

In the 1930s, when the Wagner Act was written, certain employers would form sham "company unions" and threaten workers into joining them in order to keep legitimate unions from making organizing attempts with the company's employees. As a result, the Wagner Act contained prohibitions against employer-dominated labor organizations. These prohibitions were enforced, and company unions disappeared.

However, 60 years later, because of this 1930s law, some or all of the 30,000 employee-involvement programs set up in recent years are illegal. The American Postal Union's attorney says, "A timeless evil lurks behind this new fashionable trend called employee involvement." Business lawyers argue that modern worker-involvement committees are a far cry from the company unions the law prohibits. Union attorneys counter that the committees are a challenge to their right to be exclusive representatives of the workers. Unions would be agreeable to such worker-involvement programs only if they had control over the workers' side of the discussions when dealing with working conditions, wages or benefits.

The National Labor Relations Board has ruled that employee involvement groups *can be* illegal. Electromation, an Elkhart, Indiana, firm used teams of employees to solicit other employees' views dealing with issues such as wages and working conditions. The Board labeled them "labor organizations" as defined by the NLRB in 1935. It further found they were "dominated" by management which had formed them, set their goals, and decided how they would operate. The long-term effect of this decision remains to be seen but it could stifle employee involvement efforts.

Are employee-involvement committees "company dominated labor organizations"? Apparently, the answer depends on where one's interests lie. For the union, such committees offer no benefit. For the company, they are often very beneficial, motivating employees to work harder and better, providing valuable feedback to management. Also, the committees may encourage employee creativity and innovation that leads to new product ideas and solutions to operating problems. The question remains whether such committees are in the employees' best interests as well. Many say yes, most unions say no.[22]

Airlines employees made a counteroffer to a takeover attempt of that firm. In conjunction with the top management group at United Airlines, the pilots' union also persuaded the unions representing flight attendants and machinists to back the buyout offer, but it failed at that time.[23]

Some firms also have union representatives on their board of directors. The best known example is Chrysler Corporation, in which a representative of the United Auto Workers was given a seat on the board in exchange for assistance in getting federal government financial help in the late 1970s. Such a practice is very common in European countries, where it is called **co-determination.**

Most situations in which unions become involved in ownership either occur with troubled firms or are defensive in nature to prevent some other party from buying the firm. However, the AFL-CIO has now created a union-backed fund to finance employee buyouts of their companies.[30]

▼ **CO-DETERMINATION**

is a practice whereby union or worker representatives are given positions on a company's board of directors.

Concessionary Bargaining

▼ **CONCESSIONARY BARGAINING**

occurs when the union agrees to reduce wages, benefits, or other factors during collective bargaining.

In many industries, unions have engaged in **concessionary bargaining,** which occurs when the union agrees to reduce wages, benefits, or other factors during collective bargaining. Unions have agreed to concessions in such industries as auto, airline, rubber, meat processing, steel, and trucking. When the unions have refused to grant concessions, companies have simply shut down or hired replacement nonunion workers at lower wage and benefit levels.

Economic survival and/or competitiveness have been the driving forces behind employers' demands for concessions from unions. The willingness of a union to negotiate cutbacks depends on pressures from the public as well as from management. Also, the package of concessions must appear to provide a legitimate solution to a company's problem and to give some job security guarantees in exchange for giving up previous bargaining gains. However, when unions engage in concessionary bargaining, union solidarity, credibility of union leaders, and union effectiveness all may be affected negatively.

▼ **A TWO-TIER WAGE STRUCTURE**

is one in which new union members receive lower wages and fewer benefits than existing members performing similar jobs.

Two-Tier Bargaining   Another approach taken both to reduce labor costs yet provide job security for union members is a **two-tier wage structure** in which new union members receive lower wages and fewer benefits than existing members performing similar jobs. As unionized firms negotiated two-tier contracts, they brushed aside the prediction by some that such plans would inevitably cause friction on the job. Significant problems did arise in many cases. For instance, Hughes Aircraft Company, a military contractor, used such a plan in Tucson, Arizona. Raises were given to Hughes workers at its missile factory, but the wages for new hires were frozen so much lower that pay scales for the newly hired would never match the current employee pay rates. The plan flopped! New workers did not stay, and workmanship became so sloppy that the U.S. Air Force suspended contract payments. As a result, Hughes backed away from the plan by raising starting wages 24% and removing the cap on new workers' future wages.[24]

There is little comfort in being in the top tier of a two-tier plan because top-tier workers are always concerned about a "backlash." The plans are not popular with the new employees, and the longer-service workers fear that their high wages give management an incentive to get rid of them.

Formal studies on the phenomenon suggest that newly hired employees may be less productive. Also, the programs are seen quite differently by new employees, managers, unions, and senior workers. In summary, two-tier wage schemes, which may have been a triumph of collective bargaining when they were negotiated, now seem to have lost some of their appeal.[25]

Bankruptcy and Closings as Bargaining Tactics

One management tactic affecting collective bargaining is filing for bankruptcy. For example, Continental Airlines declared bankruptcy and then continued to operate in reorganization, having voided an expensive union contract. Unions argued that this tactic took away their abilities to negotiate with Continental. The airline, on the other hand, felt that it was necessary for its survival in a deregulated industry that permits open competition and often engages in price-cutting wars.

Congress decided the issue when it passed a new bankruptcy law. The law basically represents a compromise between the positions of employers and labor unions. Under the law, an employer must petition the courts for a hearing on proposed changes in a labor contract and must provide financial data to the union. If the court finds that the union rejected the proposal without good cause and evidence clearly supports the employer's plea for relief, the employer has the right to reject the labor contract.[26]

Other firms less well known also have used bankruptcy or closing a plant as the ultimate bargaining threat. Also, the NLRB has expanded the law so that organizations are now relatively free to move to another location. Unions contend that such decisions will lead to a wave of plant closings in order to escape union influence; but management feels such steps are part of management rights. However, employers must comply with the provisions of the Worker Adjustment and Retraining Notification Act (WARN).

Replacement of Strikers

Management has always had the ability to simply replace workers who struck, but the option was not widely used. A strike by the United Auto Workers (UAW) against Caterpillar in 1992 changed that. The UAW brought an $800 million strike fund to the situation, but in the end it did not mean much to 12,600 employees with an average seniority of 26 years when they were told they would be replaced. The unemployment rate was high at the time, and replacement workers were widely available.

Many employers appear willing to hire replacement workers. A survey showed that four out of five employers were willing to at least consider replacing their workforce to keep operating.[27] In response, organized labor has proposed strike-replacement legislation prohibiting employers from hiring permanent replacement workers. The union movement argues that such legislation is necessary to restore balance to the collective bargaining process. However, others contend that such legislation would do just the opposite by tilting the balance too far in favor of striking employees.[28]

▲ GRIEVANCE MANAGEMENT

Alert management knows that dissatisfaction is a potential source of trouble whether or not it is expressed. Hidden dissatisfaction grows and creates reactions that may be completely out of proportion to the original complaint. Before long, workers' attitudes can be seriously affected. Therefore, it is important that dissatisfaction be given an outlet. The **grievance,** a specific, formal notice of employee dissatisfaction expressed through an identified procedure, provides one outlet. A **complaint,** which is merely an indication of employee dissatisfaction that has not taken the formal grievance-settlement route, is another outlet. Management should be concerned with both grievances and complaints because many complaints can become grievances. Complaints are good indicators of potential problems within the workforce.

▼ **A GRIEVANCE**

is a specific, formal notice of employee dissatisfaction expressed through an identified procedure.

▼ **A COMPLAINT**

is an indication of employee dissatisfaction that has not taken the formal grievance settlement route.

Union vs. Nonunion Grievance Management

There are differences in how grievances are handled between union and nonunion firms. In an organization with a union, grievances might occur over interpretation of the contract, disputes not covered in the contract, and grievances of individual employees. In nonunionized organizations, complaints cover a variety of concerns that for a unionized organization would be covered in the contract: wages, benefits, working conditions, and equity. Grievance procedures almost always are specified in labor/management contracts. One review found that 99% of labor contracts in all industries specified grievance procedures.[29] Relatively few nonunion firms have grievance procedures, although more and more are beginning to have them.

Grievance Management at Unionized Organizations The reason that virtually all labor contracts specify grievance procedures is that such procedures are extremely important for effective employee/employer relations in unionized firms. From the standpoint of the union, grievance systems allow employees a way to dispute management's implementation of the collective bargaining agreement. Management benefits from a grievance system, too. Without a grievance procedure, management may be unable to respond to employee concerns because managers are unaware of them. Such information does not always come to the attention of top management automatically. A great deal of discontent is dismissed at lower levels and never rises to the managers who have the authority to make decisions to solve the problems. For these reasons, a formal grievance procedure is a valuable communication tool for the organization.

A crucial measure of the performance of a grievance system is the rate of grievance resolution. Those grievances that have been resolved then become feedback to help resolve future grievances at an earlier stage.

Dispute-Resolution Process at Nonunion Organizations Many managers insist that they have an *open-door policy:* if anything is bothering employees, all they have to do is come in and talk. However, employees are often skeptical of this approach, feeling that their complaints might be viewed as unnecessary "rocking the boat." An open-door policy is not sufficient as a grievance procedure. It would require a "super manager" to maintain such open channels of communication that he or she could quickly spot and rectify any troubles that might become grievances. Managers with this degree of communication ability are relatively rare.

A growing number of nonunion firms have established formal grievance procedures because of the legal issues raised in Chapter 17. Increasingly, court decisions reflect concerns about protecting employee rights and providing them with due process. These nonunion grievance procedures often are called *dispute-resolution.*

Many organizations, dissatisfied with little-used open-door policies, are instituting *peer review boards* to resolve disciplinary and promotion disputes. The technique is also becoming a way to reduce lawsuits, especially frivolous ones. The typical peer review panel consists of five members: three employees and two managers. The peer review comes into play as the last step in a grievance procedure, when all other avenues have been exhausted.

It is estimated that employees win grievance cases about 40% of the time in both union and nonunion grievance procedures. But nonunion employees are less likely to file grievances.[30]

Grievance Responsibilities

The typical division of responsibilities between the HR unit and line managers for handling grievances is shown in Figure 19–6. These responsibilities vary con-

HR UNIT	MANAGERS
▲ Assists in designing the grievance procedure ▲ Monitors trends in grievance rates for the organization ▲ May assist preparation of grievance cases for arbitration ▲ May have responsibility for settling grievances	▲ Operate within the grievance procedure ▲ Attempt to resolve grievances where possible as "person closest to the problems" ▲ Document grievance cases at own level for the grievance procedure ▲ Have responsibility for grievance prevention

▲ **Figure 19–6**

Typical Grievance Responsibilities

siderably from one organization to another, even between unionized firms. But the HR unit usually has a more general responsibility. Managers must accept the grievance procedure as a possible constraint on some of their decisions.

Approaches to Grievances

A formal grievance procedure sometimes leads management to conclude that the proper way to handle grievances is to abide by the "letter of the law." Therefore, management does no more nor less than what is called for in the contract. Such an approach can be labeled the *legalistic approach* to the resolution of grievances. A much more realistic approach, the *behavioral approach*, recognizes that a grievance may be a symptom of an underlying problem that management should investigate and rectify.

It is important to consider the behavioral aspects of grievances in order to understand why grievances are filed and how employees perceive them. Management should recognize that a grievance is a behavioral expression of some underlying problem. This statement does not mean that every grievance is symptomatic of something radically wrong. Employees do file grievances over petty matters as well as over important concerns, and management must be able to differentiate between the two. However, to ignore a repeated problem by taking a legalistic approach to grievance resolution is to miss much of what the grievance procedure can do for management.

▲ GRIEVANCE PROCEDURE

Grievance procedures are formal communications channels designed to settle a grievance as soon as possible after the problem arises. First-line supervisors are usually closest to a problem; however, the supervisor is concerned with many other matters besides one employee's grievance and may even be the subject of an employee's grievance.

Supervisory involvement presents some problems in solving a grievance at this level. For example, William Dunn, a 27-year-old lathe operator at a machine shop, was approached by his supervisor, Joe Bass, one Monday morning and told that his production was lower than his quota. Bass advised him to catch up. Dunn reported that there was a part on his lathe needing repair. Bass suggested that Dunn should repair it himself to maintain his production because the mechanics were busy. Dunn refused, and a heated argument ensued, which resulted in Bass ordering Dunn home for the day.

▼ **THE GRIEVANCE PROCEDURE**

is a formal channel of communication used to resolve formal complaints (grievances).

This illustration shows the ease with which an encounter between an employee and a supervisor can lead to a breakdown in the relationship. This breakdown, or failure to communicate effectively, could be costly to Dunn if he lost his job, a day's wages, or his pride. It also could be costly to Bass, who represents management, and to the owner of the machine shop if production were to be delayed or halted. Grievance procedures can resolve such conflicts.

In this particular case, however, the machine shop had a contract with the International Brotherhood of Lathe Operators, of which Dunn was a member. The contract specifically stated that company plant mechanics were to repair all manufacturing equipment. Therefore, Bass appears to have violated the union contract. What is Dunn's next step? He may use the grievance procedure provided for him in the contract. The actual grievance procedure is different in each organization. It depends on what the employer and the union have agreed on and what is written into the labor contract.

Individual Rights in a Grievance

A unionized employee generally has a right to union representation if he or she is being questioned by management and if discipline may result. If these so-called *Weingarten rights* (named after the court case that established them) are violated and the employee is dismissed, he or she usually will be reinstated with back pay.

However, individual union members do not always feel that their best interests are properly served by the union. Workers and unions may not agree on the interpretation of a contract clause. For example, a worker might feel strongly that his suspension for drinking was not sufficiently represented by the union because the shop steward (his union representative) is a teetotaler.

If an individual does not feel the union has properly and vigorously pursued the grievance, he or she may have recourse to the federal court system. Such cases attempt to pinpoint individual rights inside the bargaining unit and determine what those rights are if a person has been denied due process through the grievance procedure. In fact, an individual can pursue a grievance against an employer on his or her own if a union does not back the claim.

Steps in a Grievance Procedure

As Figure 19–7 shows, several steps exist in most grievance procedures. The grievance can be settled at any stage.
1. The employee discusses the grievance with the immediate supervisor.
2. The employee then discusses the grievance with the union steward (the union's representative on the job) and the supervisor.
3. The union steward discusses it with the supervisor's manager.
4. The union grievance committee discusses the grievance with the unit plant manager or the employer's HR department.
5. The representative of the national union discusses it with the company general manager.
6. The final step may be use of an impartial umpire or arbitrator for ultimate disposition of the grievance.

Employee and Supervisor   In our example, Dunn has already discussed his grievance with the supervisor. The first step should eliminate the majority of gripes and complaints that employees may view as legitimate grievances.

▲ **Figure 19–7**   Steps in a Grievance Procedure

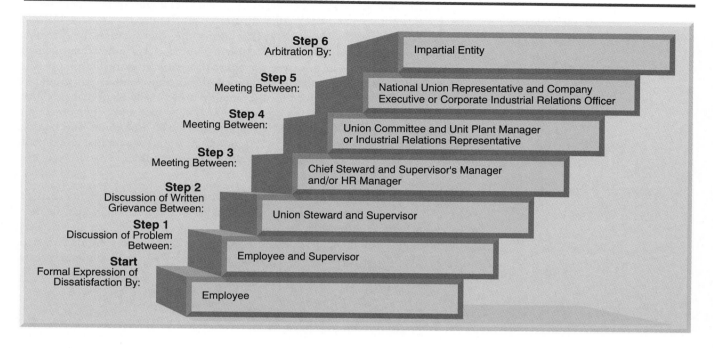

Supervisors are generally responsible for understanding the contract so that they can administer it fairly on a day-to-day basis. They must be accessible to employees for grievance investigation and must gather all the pertinent facts and carefully investigate the causes, symptoms, and results. But the filing of grievances does create some risks for employees. The reactions of supervisors to employees who file grievances may affect the employees' performance ratings. This reaction may be even more pronounced if the supervisor is the target of the grievance.[31]

Union Steward and Supervisor   The second step involves the union steward, whose main task is to present the grievance of a union member to management. However, the responsibility rests not only with the individual steward, but also, to a large degree, with the union membership as a whole. The effect of this grievance on the relationship between a union and management must be determined.

Assume that Dunn's grievance remains unsettled after the second step. The steward contacts Bass's boss and/or the unit's HR manager. In most grievance procedures, the grievance is documented and, until it is settled, much of the communication between management and the union is in writing. This written communication is important because it provides a record of each step in the procedure and constitutes a history for review at each subsequent step.

One study found that an employee's previous work history with an organization influences managerial decisions on grievances at the second and third stages. An employee whose work history shows that he or she has been disciplined less, has more tenure on the job, and has compiled a better performance record is more likely to have a grievance upheld by management. This study underscores the impact of behavioral factors on the grievance process.[32]

Union Grievance Committee and Unit Manager   Pressure tends to build with each successive step because grievances that are not precedent setting or difficult are screened out earlier in the process. If the department manager (who is supervisor Bass's boss) backs Bass against the chief steward, the grievance goes to the next step. The fourth step brings in the local union management grievance committee. In our case, the grievance committee of the union convinces the plant manager that Bass violated the contract and Dunn should be brought back to work and paid for the time he missed. The plant manager gives in, partly because he thinks the company has a weak case and partly because, if the grievance continues past him, it will probably go to arbitration, and he does not feel the issue is worth the cost. Although in Dunn's case a grievance committee was used, not all grievance procedures use committees.

National Representatives and Arbitrators   If the grievance had remained unsettled, representatives for both sides would have continued to meet to resolve the conflict. On rare occasions, a representative from the national union might join the process. Or a corporate executive from headquarters (if the firm is a large corporation) might be called in to help resolve the grievance. If not solved at this stage, it goes to arbitration.

▲   GRIEVANCE ARBITRATION

Arbitration is flexible and can be applied to almost any kind of controversy except those involving criminal matters. Advisory or voluntary arbitration may be used in the negotiation of agreements, in the interpretation of clauses in existing agreements, or in both. Because labor and management generally agree that disputes over the negotiation of a new contract should not be arbitrated in the private sector, the most important role in labor relations played by arbitration is as the final step in the grievance procedure.

▼ **GRIEVANCE ARBITRATION**

is a means of settling disputes arising from different interpretations of a labor contract by using a third party.

Grievance arbitration is a means of settling disputes arising from different interpretations of a labor contract by using a third party. This should not be confused with contract arbitration, discussed earlier, which is arbitration to determine how a contract will be written. Grievance arbitration is a deeply ingrained part of the collective bargaining system, although it was not always so. In earlier times, arbitration was not considered useful in settling labor disputes.

However, in 1957 a court decision that established the right of unions to sue for specific performance arbitration awards gave arbitration new strength.[33] Later court cases added more powers to the arbitration process. The legal standing of grievance arbitration was clarified in a series of cases involving the United Steelworkers union, called the "Steelworkers Trilogy." The cases involved are *United Steelworkers of America v. American Manufacturing Co.,* 363 US 564 (1960); *United Steelworkers of America v. Warrior and Gulf Navigation Co.,* 363 US 574 (1960); and *United Steelworkers of America v. Enterprise Wheel and Car Corp.,* 363 US 593 (1960). To summarize the results of these three cases, it was ruled that a company had to arbitrate all issues not specifically excluded in the contract. Courts were directed not to rule on the appropriateness of an arbitration award unless misinformation, fraud, or negligence was involved.

Grievance Arbitration Process

The wording of the contract clause to express accurately each party's intent relative to arbitration is a common arbitration issue. It is important to spell out the types of disputes that may be taken to arbitration. Most collective bargaining contracts suggest that either party may start arbitration proceedings. Others state that only the union can initiate arbitration proceedings. Still others permit arbitration only when both parties agree.

Assuming that a grievance has not been resolved and the labor contract calls for arbitration, that the arbitration process begins with the selection of a single arbitrator or a panel of arbitrators, usually three in number. The manner of selecting arbitrators varies, but usually each party eliminates names from a list of potential arbitrator candidates until only one name remains. If a panel is used, then the union selects one name, the management selects one name, and the "neutral" is selected in the manner just noted. Most contracts call for union and management to share equally in the cost of arbitration.

Some parties may have a permanent arbitrator, but more typically the arbitrator is selected from a list supplied by either the Federal Mediation and Conciliation Service or the American Arbitration Association.

Arbitration Hearing

There is no single way to conduct an arbitration hearing. The purpose is to gather the information necessary for the arbitrator to make a decision. A formal hearing may resemble a courtroom trial. A less formal hearing has little of the courtroom atmosphere—witnesses make presentations and are questioned by the opposition. The style depends on the arbitrator, but most hearings have the following parts:

▲ Opening the hearing
▲ Defining the issue
▲ Making opening statements
▲ Swearing in witnesses
▲ Presenting the case
▲ Making closing arguments

Following the hearing, each side may be asked to submit a post-hearing brief. The arbitrator then reviews all the evidence, including the applicable section of the labor contract, and makes a decision. This decision also is called an *award* and is enforceable in federal court if the labor contract indicates that arbitration decisions are binding on both parties.

Grievance arbitration presents several problems. It has been criticized as being too costly, too legalistic, and too time-consuming. Also, one study found that arbitrators generally treated women more leniently than men in disciplinary grievance situations.[34] In addition, many feel that there are too few qualified and experienced arbitrators. Nevertheless, as was noted at the beginning of this chapter, it has been successful and is currently very much seen as a potentially superior solution to traditional approaches to union/management problems.

Preventive Arbitration

Labor and management sometimes tend to ignore potential problem areas in a relationship until it is too late. The result can be an explosive dispute that does a great degree of harm. Preventive arbitration can minimize this sort of difficulty. It is the duty of a preventive arbitrator to meet periodically (at least monthly) with union and management representatives to discuss areas of potential trouble between the parties. Although the use of a preventive arbitrator is not a panacea for resolving difficulties in labor/management relations, it can be a useful tool. The plan calls for adherence by both parties to the arbitrator's recommendations during a 60-day period, during which time the problem can be solved in a calm and considered manner.

▲ SUMMARY

- ▲ Collective bargaining occurs when management negotiates with representatives of workers over wages, hours, and working conditions.
- ▲ Different collective bargaining relationships exist. Conflict, armed truce, power bargaining, accommodation, cooperation, and collusion are recognized as special relationships.
- ▲ Different collective bargaining structures are used, ranging from one employer and one union to multiple employers bargaining with multiple unions.
- ▲ The issues subject to collective bargaining fall into three categories: mandatory, permissive, and illegal.
- ▲ Provisions on management rights and union security typically appear in labor contracts.
- ▲ The collective bargaining process includes preparation, initial demands, negotiations, and settlement.
- ▲ Once an agreement (contract) is signed between labor and management, it becomes the document governing what each party can and cannot do.
- ▲ Bargaining power of both management and a union is determined by economic, organizational, sociodemographic, and legal factors.
- ▲ During bargaining, different types of behavior can be used, including distributive, integrative, attitudinal structuring, and intraorganizational.
- ▲ When impasse occurs, work stoppages through strikes or lockouts can be used to pressure the other party.
- ▲ Efforts to resolve impasses can include conciliation, mediation, or arbitration.
- ▲ One major trend in collective bargaining has been union-management cooperation, either through union ownership or productivity assistance.
- ▲ Concessionary bargaining occurs when the union agrees to reductions in wages, benefits, or other reductions during the bargaining process.
- ▲ Grievances express worker dissatisfaction or differences in contract interpretations. Grievances follow a formal path to resolution.
- ▲ A formal grievance procedure is usually specified in a union contract, but it should exist in any organization to provide a system for handling problems. Nonunion organizations often term these procedures "dispute-resolution."
- ▲ Grievances can be approached by management from either a behavioral or a legalistic viewpoint; however, the behavioral approach is recommended.
- ▲ A grievance procedure begins with the first-level supervisor—and ends (if it is not resolved along the way) with arbitration.

▲ Arbitration has worked well in settling union–management grievances. Consequently, it is being considered for a larger role in settling employment disputes.

▲ REVIEW AND DISCUSSION QUESTIONS

1. Why do collective bargaining relationships and structures differ?
2. Give several examples of mandatory, permissive and illegal bargaining issues.
3. What are the stages in a typical collective bargaining process?
4. Assume that a bargaining impasse has occurred. What would be the differences between using mediation and arbitration to resolve the impasse?
5. Discuss why union/management cooperation and concessionary bargaining has led to a backlash from some unionized workers.
6. Give an example of a grievance and how both unionized and nonunion firms might handle it.
7. What steps would be followed in a typical grievance process? Why is arbitration, as the final step of a grievance process, important and useful?

 CASE   THE "STOLEN" ORANGE JUICE

Grievances can be filed on actions on large or small matters. The following case represents a grievance that was decided by an arbitrator hired by Greyhound Food Management (Warren, Michigan) and the United Catering Restaurant, Bar, & Hotel Workers, Local 1064.[35]

The grievance was filed by the union on behalf of Tom, a union member working as a fast-food attendant at a Greyhound-operated cafeteria. The Greyhound Food Service provided food service management on a contract basis for many firms, including Hydra Matic, a manufacturing company located in Warren, Michigan.

Tom had been working for Greyhound for almost a year, and was working the 1 P.M.–8:30 P.M. shift making $5.25 an hour at the time of his discharge from the company. The company justified Tom's employment termination by asserting that he had attempted to steal a six-ounce container of orange juice, which normally sold for 58 cents. Tom's supervisor testified that from his office he observed Tom attempting to leave the premises with the container of orange juice hidden under his jacket. After stopping Tom, the supervisor accused him of attempting to steal the orange juice. Then the supervisor telephoned the assistant manager for instructions. The assistant manager told the supervisor to document the incident and stated that he (the assistant manager) would take care of the matter the next morning. The supervisor's written report stated that he had heard the refrigerator door slam, followed by Tom's walking toward the door. The supervisor asked Tom twice what Tom had in his coat, after which Tom pulled the juice out of his coat, dropping and spilling it over the floor.

The following morning the assistant manager called Tom and the union steward into his office and confronted them with the supervisor's written description of the incident. Tom denied that he attempted to steal the orange juice, saying that the supervisor just saw some orange juice on the floor. At a meeting later that morning, the assistant manager terminated Tom's employment. Tom filed a grievance, which was immediately denied. Tom and the union then requested arbitration, as was allowed under the company/union labor contract.

The arbitrator reviewed several documents, including statements from the supervisor, the assistant manager, a former employee, and the union steward. Also, he had to review the relevant sections of the labor contract on management rights, seniority, and the grievance procedure. Finally, the arbitrator reviewed the list of company rules and regulations that were posted by the time clock, one of which said that disciplinary action ranging from reprimand to immediate discharge could result from rule violation. The first rule prohibited "stealing private, company, or client's property."

Company Position

The company's position was that Tom had knowledge of the posted work rules, the first of which clearly prohibited theft. The company also had a policy that no company property was to leave the restaurant. The testimony of the supervisor established that Tom attempted to steal and remove company property. It was not relevant that Tom's impermissible act did not succeed. The detection by management of the theft before Tom left the premises did not excuse the act. Also, the company said that the size or dollar amount of the theft was immaterial. Therefore, because the company followed the terms of the union contract that provided for dismissal of employees for "just cause," and because Tom knew, or should have known, of the rule against stealing, the arbitrator should rule for the company.

Union Position

The union's position was that the act of attempting to steal a container of orange juice valued at 58 cents does involve moral turpitude and therefore requires the application of a "high degree of proof." In addition, the employer carries the burden of convincing the arbitrator beyond a reasonable doubt through the witnesses that Tom did attempt to steal the orange juice. The union contended that even though Tom had been subject to some other minor disciplinary actions in the past, termination was too harsh a penalty and therefore the arbitrator should rule for Tom and the union.

▲ Questions

1. How important is the value of the item in comparison to the alleged act of stealing?
2. Because Tom never actually left the company premises with the juice, did he actually steal it?
3. How would you rule in this case? (Your instructor can give you the actual decision by the arbitrator, which is contained in the instructor's manual that accompanies this text.)

▲ Notes

1. Adapted from Michael A. Verespej, "Arbitration: The Newest Legal Option," *Industry Week*, July 15, 1991, 56–58; Aaron Bernstein and Z. Schiller, "Tell It to the Arbitrator," *Business Week*, November 4, 1991, 109; and Wade Lambert, "Employer Pacts to Arbitrate Sought by Firms," *The Wall Street Journal*, October 22, 1992, B1.
2. T. L. Leap and D. W. Grigsby, "A Conceptualization of Collective Bargaining Power," *Industrial and Labor Relations Review* 39 (1986), 202–212.

3. The six strategies are adapted from R. E. Allen and T. B. Keavany, *Contemporary Labor Relations* (Reading, MA: Addison-Wesley, 1988), 126.

4. John J. Kenney, *Primer of Labor Relations,* 23d ed. (Washington, DC: Bureau of National Affairs, 1986), 46–47.

5. Adapted from William H. Holley and Kenneth M. Jennings, *The Labor Relations Process,* 3d ed., (Chicago, Dryden Press, 1988), 395.

6. *Basic Patterns in Union Contracts* (Washington, DC: Bureau of National Affairs, 1986), 101.

7. C. Martin, "Current Developments in Labor-Management Relations," *Employee Relations Law Journal* 17 (1991), 139–144.

8. J. Wall and M. Blum, "Negotiations", *Journal of Management* 17 (1991), 273–303.

9. Richard E. Walton and Robert B. McKersie, *A Behavioral Theory of Labor Negotiations* (New York: McGraw-Hill, 1965).

10. D. Cantrell, "Spontaneous Strike Notice: Who Is Responsible?" *Personnel Journal,* July 1990, 38–39.

11. K. Murphy, "Determinants of Contract Duration in Collective Bargaining Agreements," *Industrial and Labor Relations Review* 45 (1992), 352.

12. F. Swoboda, "An Artifact of History," *Minneapolis Star Tribune,* November 17, 1992, 10.

13. E. Wasilewski, "Collective Bargaining in 1992," *Monthly Labor Review,* January 1992, 5.

14. M. E. McLaughlin and P. Carnevale, "Professional Mediators' Judgements of Mediation Tactics," *Journal of Applied Psychology,* 76 (1991), 465; and J. Wall and D. Rude, "The Judge as Mediator," *Journal of Applied Psychology* 76 (1991), 54.

15. B. S. Moskal, "Auto Talks Require Enlightenment," *Industry Week,* July 2, 1990, 50.

16. Adapted from John Hoerr, "The Cultural Revolution at A. O. Smith," *Business Week,* May 29, 1989, 66–68.

17. John G. Belcher, Jr., "The Role of Unions in Productivity Management," *Personnel,* January 1988, 54–58; D. Milbank, "National Steel Claims Strength in Its Labor-Management Alloy," *The Wall Street Journal,* April 20, 1992, B1; P. Tobia and S. Johnson, "Chrysler Harnesses Brainpower," *Industry Week,* September 21, 1992, 16–19; L. Hazzard, "A Union Says Yes to Attendance," *Personnel Journal,* November 1990, 47–49; and Stephanie Overman, "Workers, Management Unite," *HR Magazine,* May 1990, 38–41.

18. R. Thomas, "Technological Choice and Union Management Cooperation," *Industrial Relations* 30, (1991), 167.

19. A. Eaton, "The Role of the Local Union in a Participation Program," *Labor Studies Journal,* Spring 1990, 33.

20. J. Arthur and J. Dworkin, "Current Topics in Industrial Relations Research and Practice," *Journal of Management* 17, (1991), 527, 529.

21. Everett M. Kasalow, "Concessions Bargaining: Towards New Roles for American Unions and Managers," *International Labour Review* 127 (1988), 573–592.

22. Aaron Bernstein, "Making Teamwork Work—And Appeasing Uncle Sam," *Business Week,* January 25, 1993, 101; J. McGuiness, "Blunting America's Competitive Edge," *Industry Week,* October 21, 1991, 63; J. Novack, "Make Them All Form Unions," *Forbes,* May 11, 1992, 174; Michael A. Verespej, "New Rules on Employee Involvement," *Industry Week,* February 1, 1993, 55; "Unions, Employee-Participation Movement Await Key Ruling," *Omaha World-Herald,* September 13, 1992, 11–16; and Aaron Bernstein "The Workplace" *Business Week* Jan 25, 1992 p 101.

23. "Labor Deals That Offer A Break from 'Us Vs. Them'," *Business Week,* August 2, 1993, 30.

24. Marvin J. Levine, "The Evolution of Two-Tier Wage Agreements," *Labor Law Journal* 40 (1989), 12–20.

25. S. Thomas and M. Kleiner, "The Effect of Two-Tier Collective Bargaining Agreements on Shareholder Equity," *Industrial and Labor Relations Review* 45 (1992), 339–351; and D. McFarland and M. Frone, "A Two-Tiered Wage Structure in a Non-Union Firm," *Industrial Relations,* 29 (1990), 145.

26. J. Wren and K. Marrmann, "Chapter 11 and Collective Bargaining Agreements," *Employee Relations Law Journal* 16 (1990), 17–28.

27. R. Rose, "Caterpillar's Success in Ending Strike May Curtail Union's Use of Walkouts," *The Wall Street Journal,* April 20, 1992, A3.

28. P. Nash and J. Mook, "Strike Replacement Legislation: If It Ain't Broke Don't Fix It", *Employee Relations Law Journal* 16 (1990), 317.

29. Douglas M. McCabe, "Corporate Nonunion Grievance Arbitration Systems: A Procedural Analysis," *Labor Law Journal* 40 (1989), 432–437.

30. Los Angeles Times, "Non-Union Shops Settling Gripes in Own 'Courts,'" *Omaha World-Herald,* December 9, 1990, IG.

31. Brian S. Klaas and Angelo D. DeNisi, "Managerial Reactions to Employee Dissent: The Impact of Grievance Activity on Performance Ratings," *Academy of Management Journal* 32 (1989), 705–717.

32. Brian S. Klaas, "Managerial Decision Making About Employee Grievances: The Impact of the Grievant's Work History," *Personnel Psychology* 42 (1989), 53–68.

33. *Textile Workers Union of America v. Lincoln Mills of Alabama* 353 U.S. 448 (1957).

34. Brian Bemmels, "Gender Effects in Grievance Arbitration," *Industrial Relations* 30 (1991), 150.

35. 89 LA 1138 (1987).

CHAPTER 20

HUMAN RESOURCE ASSESSMENT SYSTEMS

After you have read this chapter, you should be able to:

1. Identify what an HR audit is and describe how one is conducted.

2. Discuss three major reasons why HR records and record keeping are necessary.

3. Identify several uses of a human resource information system (HRIS) and list its components.

4. Describe two types of formal HR communication, and explain why they are important.

5. Differentiate between primary and secondary research, and identify four methods for researching HR problems.

6. Discuss why assessing HR effectiveness is important, and identify two approaches for doing so.

HR Today and Tomorrow:
IdeAAs at American Airlines

The competitive pressures and changing nature of the airline industry have led to flight overcapacity, fare wars, and airline bankruptcies. Survival in that environment means that greater productivity is needed, and American Airlines turned to its employees to help. HR communication was greatly expanded to involve employees in efforts to reduce costs and increase efficiency without reducing the customer service necessary to be competitive. One prime example of employee involvement and communication is IdeAAs in Action, the employee suggestion system at American Airlines.

When the program began in 1987, about 6% of the approximately 100,000 employees participated, submitting 8,700 suggestions. But that rate increased to about 20% by 1992, representing approximately 50,000 suggestions. To handle and evaluate all of these ideas takes 80 full-time workers supervised by Robert Stoltz, IdeAAs in Action program manager.

The value of the suggestions is seen in perspective when in 1991 the $58.5 million savings produced by the program generated enough to pay for a new Boeing 757. To celebrate the accomplishment, employees submitting the top 200 suggestions received a special trip on the first flight of a new 757 and special awards, in addition to other rewards already received. Under the IdeAAs program, employees receive points for their suggestions, with each point valued as one-half cent. Award amounts are based on 15% of the first-year savings generated by a suggestion. For over $20,000 in credits, cash can be obtained, but most employees redeem their points for travel and merchandise available through the AAchievers Book of Awards. That catalog includes a grand piano among 3,000-plus items.

About 25% of the suggestions submitted are accepted, but even those rejected earn employees $5 (1,000 credits) in order to reward participation and encourage continuing involvement. Each suggestion also triggers a personalized letter to the employee submitting the suggestion explaining why it was rejected or how it will be implemented.

Often, simple ideas result in big savings. Some examples of IdeAAs submitted include:

▲ Buying larger bottles of water for flight attendants to use on flights resulted in $55,000 savings per year because the larger bottles are cheaper per ounce. The flight attendant making the suggestion received IdeAAs credits for that idea.

▲ A suggestion by two maintenance workers to repair scratched window covers in American's own shop instead of sending them to an outside contractor saved $170,000 per year.

▲ A suggestion from a group of 29 flight attendants and food service employees on the redesign and usage of in-flight food and beverage carts saved $2.6 million per year.

As the emphasis on total quality management (TQM) and customer service grows in many organizations, the use of such HR activities as suggestion systems is likely to grow. There is plenty of evidence that they can and do contribute to organizational productivity and performance.[1]

66————————————————————

We are as we find out we are.

Charles Olsen ——————————*99*

It is important that the HR units of organizations assess the effectiveness of their own activities. Certainly the American Airlines suggestion system appears to be effective. In order to assess HR effectiveness properly, sophisticated record keeping, information generation, applied research, and formal communications systems all are necessary. These areas are discussed in this chapter.

▲ ASSESSING HR EFFECTIVENESS

This text began by emphasizing that effective HR management is integral to productivity and performance of individuals and the organizations in which they work. The various challenges that have been discussed require that HR professionals, as well as all managers in organizations, continually assess the effectiveness of their HR activities if those who work in the organization truly are to be human resources.

HR Audit

One general means for assessing HR effectiveness is through the use of an HR audit, similar to a financial audit. An **HR audit** is a formal research effort that evaluates the current status of HR management in an organization. Through the development and use of statistical reports and research data, HR audits attempt to evaluate how well HR activities have been performed, so that management can identify what needs to be improved.

A HR audit begins with management determining the objectives it wants to achieve in the HR area. The audit compares the actual state of HR activities with the objectives. Often a checklist is used such as the one in Figure 20-1.

A variety of research sources may be used to assess HR effectiveness during an HR audit. Review of all relevant HR documents is helpful. Common documents to be reviewed include employee handbooks, organization charts, job descriptions, and many of the forms used such as performance appraisals, benefit statements, and labor union contracts. Also, interviews are conducted with a cross section of executives, managers, supervisors, and HR staff members to obtain information about HR practices and problems. In some organizations, the HR staff members conduct the HR audit. However, a more objective assessment may be achieved if the organization uses external consultants for this task. Regardless of who conducts the HR audit, it is important to prepare a written report. This report should identify the methods used, the specific observations on the state of HR activities, and recommendations for improvements. The report should go to top management, as well as HR staff members, to obtain greater commitment to implementing the recommendations.

▼ **AN HR AUDIT**

is a formal research effort that evaluates the current state of HR management in an organization

▲ **Figure 20–1** Sample HR Audit Checklist

HR Audit

This HR management audit allows you to rate the extent that an organization has basic HR activities in place and how well they are being performed. In deciding upon your rating, consider also how other managers and employees would rate the activities. The total score provides a guide for actions that will improve HR activities in your organization.

Instructions: For each of the items listed below, rate your organization using the following scale:

VERY GOOD (complete, current, and done well)	3 points
ADEQUATE (needs only some updating)	2 points
WEAK (needs major improvements/changes)	1 point
BASICALLY NONEXISTENT	0 points

I. LEGAL COMPLIANCE

____ 1. Equal Employment Opportunity (EEO) requirements
____ 2. Immigration reform
____ 3. Safety (OSHA)
____ 4. Wage and hour laws (FLSA)
____ 5. Employment-at-will statements
____ 6. Privacy protection
____ 7. ERISA reporting/compliance

II. OBTAINING HUMAN RESOURCES

____ 8. Current job descriptions and specifications
____ 9. HR supply-and-demand estimates (for three years)
____ 10. Recruiting process and procedures
____ 11. Job-related selection interviews
____ 12. Physical exam procedures

III. MAINTAINING HUMAN RESOURCES

____ 13. Formal wages/salary system
____ 14. Current benefits programs/options
____ 15. Benefit-cost control management
____ 16. Employee-recognition programs
____ 17. Employee handbook/personnel policy manual
____ 18. Absenteeism and turnover control
____ 19. Grievance resolution process
____ 20. HR record-keeping/information systems

IV. DEVELOPING HUMAN RESOURCES

____ 21. New employee orientation program
____ 22. Job skills training programs
____ 23. Employee development programs
____ 24. Job-related performance appraisal
____ 25. Appraisal feedback training of managers

_____ **TOTAL POINTS**

HR Audit Scoring

Evaluate the score on the HR audit as follows:

60-75 HR activities are complete, effective, and meeting legal compliance requirements.

45-59 HR activities are being performed adequately, but they are not as complete or effective as they should be. Also, it is likely that some potential legal risks exist.

30-44 Major HR problems exist and significant attention needs to be devoted to adding to and changing the HR activities in the organization.

Below 30 Serious potential legal liabilities exist, and it is likely that significant HR problems are not being addressed.

▲ HUMAN RESOURCE RECORDS AND RECORD KEEPING

Many organizations, regardless of size, are addressing the need for more detailed and timely data and information on which to base HR decisions. Gathering and maintaining records on a variety of HR activities are necessary for three reasons:

▲ Government compliance
▲ Documentation
▲ Assessment of HR actions

Government Requirements and HR Records

Federal, state, and local laws require that organizations keep numerous records on employees. The requirements are so varied that it is difficult to identify exactly what should be kept and for how long. Each specific case must be dealt with separately.[2] Generally, records relating to employment, work schedules, wages, performance appraisals, merit and seniority systems, and affirmative action programs should be kept by all employers who are subject to provisions of the Fair Labor Standards Act. Other records may be required on issues related to EEO, OSHA, or the Age Discrimination Act. The most commonly required retention time for such records is three years. Figure 20–2 shows some HR records and data sources that can be maintained in an HR department.

Americans with Disabilities Act (ADA) and Medical Records

Record-keeping and retention practices have been affected by the following provision in the Americans with Disabilities Act (ADA):

> Information from all medical examinations and inquiries must be kept apart from general personnel files as a separate confidential medical record available only under limited conditions specified in the ADA.[3]

As interpreted by attorneys and HR practitioners, this provision requires that all medical-related information be maintained separately from all other confidential files. Also, specific access restrictions and security procedures must be

Accidents	Terminations
Employment requisition	Job specifications
Promotion inventories	Job descriptions
Applicant tracking	Salary increases
Interview results	Training programs
Turnover	Personal history
Job transfers	Affirmative action
Payroll	Medical records
Work schedules	Insurance usage
Test scores	Employee benefit choices
Performance appraisals	Committee meetings
Grievances	Recruiting expenses
Occupational health	Attitude/morale survey results
Job bidding	Open jobs
Exit interviews	Labor market data

 Figure 20–2

Examples of HR Records and Data Sources

HR Perspectives:
Ethical Issues and Employee Records

One ethical issue that HR professionals must address regularly is the right of an employee to inspect the information kept by the employer in the employee's HR file. Related concerns are the types of information kept in those files and the methods used to acquire that information.

In other business-related areas, federal laws have been passed that allows access by individuals to their own files, such as credit records or medical records. But only in some states have such laws been passed to require employers to give employees access to their HR records—or parts of them. Many of these state laws allow employers to exclude certain types of information from inspection, such as reference letters written by former employers. Some employers in states without access laws nevertheless allow employees access to certain records.

The most common records kept include performance appraisals, salary history, and disciplinary actions. However, maintenance of individual medical records and background investigation reports in separate confidential files is common.

Most employers require that an HR staff member be present while employees view their files. Some firms allow access, but limit or restrict the photocopying of certain items. It is recommended that firms allow employees to provide additional statements or dispute the accuracy of details in their files.

It appears that maintaining records on individuals to which access is limited is crucial. And enabling individuals to comment on or correct details in their files insures that HR records are accurate.[4]

adopted for medical records of all types, including employee medical benefit claims and treatment records.

Employee Access to HR Records

One concern that has been addressed in various court decisions and laws is the right of employees to have access to their own files. As mentioned in Chapter 17, many employees have little knowledge of what information is contained in their own HR files. The "HR Perspective" discusses the ethical issues involved.

Establishment of Several Employee Files   The result of all the legal restrictions is that many employers are establishing several separate files on each employee. The following files may be established:

1. Current file containing only the last few years of employee-related information
2. Confidential file containing such items as reference letters and promotability assessments
3. Confidential medical file as required by the ADA
4. Individual personnel file containing older information and nonconfidential, nonmedical benefits documents

Assessing HR Using Documentation and Records

Managers who must cope with the additional paperwork have not accepted such record-keeping requirements easily.[5] Also, many managers feel that HR records can be a source of trouble because they can be used to question past managerial actions.

The other side of the coin is that HR records serve as important documentation should legal challenges occur. Disciplinary actions, past performance appraisals, and other documents may provide the necessary "proof" that employers need in order to defend their actions as job related and nondiscriminatory.

Assessing HR Using Research

Records and data can provide an excellent source of information when organizations audit or assess the effectiveness of any unit. They also provide the basis for research into possible causes of HR problems. However, the usefulness of HR records depends on the records being kept current and properly organized. With the proliferation of government regulations, the number of required records has expanded.

The problem organizations often face with HR record keeping is the inability to retrieve needed information without major difficulties. Better HR decisions can be made if managers have good information on such matters as the causes, and severity of accidents; the reasons for absenteeism; and the distribution of performance appraisals. But in many organizations such information is not readily available. There probably is a point beyond which it costs more to keep records than the records are worth. A solution is a well-designed human resource information system (HRIS).

▲   HUMAN RESOURCE INFORMATION SYSTEM (HRIS)

Computers have simplified the task of analyzing vast amounts of data, and they can be invaluable aids in HR management, from payroll processing to record retention. With computer hardware, software, and databases, organizations can keep records and information better, as well as retrieve them with greater ease. A **human resource information system (HRIS)** is an integrated system designed to provide information used in HR decision making. Although an HRIS does not have to be computerized, most are.

A HUMAN RESOURCE
▼ **INFORMATION SYSTEM (HRIS)**

is an integrated system designed to provide information used in HR decision making.

Purposes of HRIS

There are several reasons why an organization establishes an HRIS. First, many HR activities can be performed more efficiently and with less paperwork if automated. Through on-line data input, fewer forms must be stored and less manual record keeping is necessary. Second, information that management requires for making decisions can be provided faster and easier. For example, instead of manually doing a turnover analysis by department, length of service with the company, and educational background, a specialist can compile such a report quickly by using an HRIS and various sorting and analysis functions. Third, because HR management has grown in strategic value in many organizations, it has emphasized obtaining and using HRIS data for strategic planning and human resource forecasting.

Uses of HRIS

There are many uses for an HRIS in an organization. A survey of 434 HR practitioners revealed that the three most common uses were: payroll (78%), benefits administration (70%), and EEO/affirmative action tracking (69%).[6]

The most basic use of HRIS is the automation of payroll and benefits activities. Instead of having to compute the payroll manually, an HRIS allows employees' time records to be entered into the system. Then the appropriate deductions and other individual adjustments are reflected in the final paychecks. As a result of HRIS development and implementation in many organizations, a number of payroll functions are being transferred from accounting departments to HR departments.[7] Beyond those basic activities, many other HR activities can be affected by the use of an HRIS,[8] as Figure 20–3 notes.

Components of an HRIS

At the heart of an HRIS is a *database* that is accessed using *software* programs that operate on *computer hardware*. Each of these components is discussed briefly as they relate to HRIS.

▼ DATABASE

is the stored data used by the computer.

Database   Central to any HRIS is the **database,** which is stored data used by the computer. All the various records and pieces of data on employees and

▲ **Figure 20–3**   Uses of HRIS

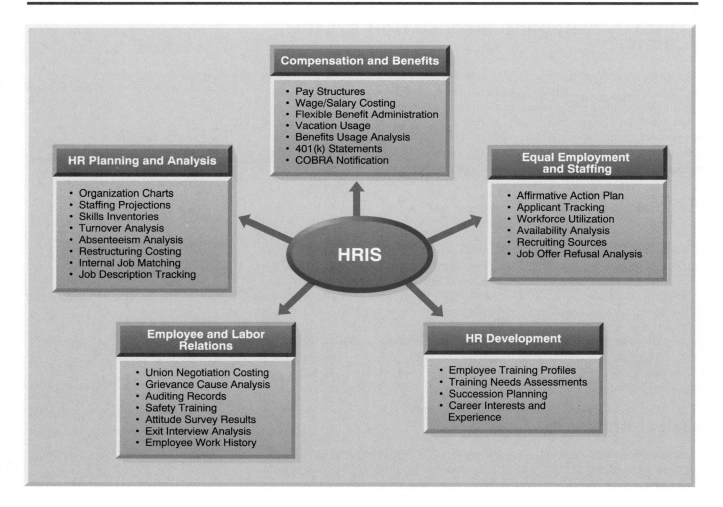

applicants are converted to forms that can be used by the computer, thus creating the organizational database. The amount of data to be stored determines whether disks, magnetic tapes, or other computer storage devices are used. This database can be accessed for a variety of purposes, and data need not be repeated in separate files, such as in both payroll and HR. That way information on an employee's base pay, address, or number of dependents is changed only once. The HR manager can access the up-to-date database for compensation budgeting; the benefits administrator can access it for relevant benefits details; and a payroll coordinator can use it to generate paychecks for the employee.

Often in medium- and larger-sized organizations, the main database is on a large *mainframe* computer, and then the various users *download* (transfer) the relevant data for their uses onto a personal computer (PC).[9] The ability to download (transfer) data this way is an increasingly desirable feature of an HRIS. The PC user in the HR department does not have to create a separate database for some HRIS uses but can download only the information needed, such as the following:

▲ Current jobs and the tasks associated with them
▲ Anticipated jobs and the tasks associated with them
▲ Employee skills needed for all current and future jobs
▲ Skills inventory of current employees, including performance appraisals, interests and training/development needs
▲ Training/development programs attended and available

Hardware   The actual equipment used, such as computers, disk drives, monitors, printers, and optiscanners is the **computer hardware.** An employer has a variety of options for hardware to use for an HRIS. A *mainframe* computer is a large computer that has an extensive memory and performs many different organizational computing functions, including accounting, inventory, and maintaining customer records and other data records. *Minicomputers* are smaller computers, often integrated with one another so a network of users in various locations and departments can access data simultaneously.

A growing trend is to establish *local area networks* (LANs), so that even employees can access selected HR records and make changes in their own files on personal information, such as address changes. Also, some firms have systems that allow employees to obtain benefit information without having to call and talk with a benefits specialist. **Microcomputers** are the smallest computers and often are referred to as *personal computers (PCs).* The growth of PC-based HRIS has been rapid because of the increasing sophistication of information gathering and analysis in HR departments.

Software   The **computer software** contains the program instructions that tell the computer how to process the data. Each kind of hardware system requires different software to operate it. Many different software packages are available for an HRIS. An integrated HRIS software package for a large mainframe computer can cost from $50,000 to $500,000, depending on the scope and sophistication needed. For microcomputers, there are many different software packages available, ranging from single-use programs that can track applicants or maintain organization charts to multiple-function integrated programs. Prices for micro-based software programs can range from less than $100 to $10,000 or more, depending on the capabilities desired.

More software programs are being developed every month, so an exhaustive listing is difficult to maintain. However, listings and summaries of HRIS soft-

▼ **COMPUTER HARDWARE**

is the actual equipment used, such as computers, disk drives, monitors, printers, and optiscanners.

▼ **MICROCOMPUTERS**

are the smallest computers and often are referred to as personal computers (PCs).

▼ **COMPUTER SOFTWARE**

contains the program instructions that tell the computer how to process the data.

ware are published at least once a year in such publications as *HR Magazine* and *Personnel Journal.* Those publications also provide reviews and critiques of some HRIS software.

Establishing an HRIS

To design an effective HRIS, experts advise starting from the standpoint of the data. A manager should ask the following questions:

- ▲ What information is available, and what information will be needed about people in the organization?
- ▲ To what uses will the information be put?
- ▲ In what format should the output be presented to fit with other company records?
- ▲ Who needs the information?
- ▲ When and how often is it needed?

Answers to these questions help pinpoint the necessary hardware and software. Experts recommend that a *project team* be established and extensive planning be done.[10] This team often contains representatives from several departments in the organization, including the HR and management information/data-processing areas. The team serves as a steering committee to review user needs, identify desired capabilities of the system, solicit and examine bids from software and hardware vendors, and identify the implementation process required to install the system. By involving a cross section of managers and others, the organization attempts to ensure that the HRIS fulfills its potential, is accepted by users, and is implemented in an organized manner.[11]

Training   Training those who will be using the system is critical to the successful implementation of an HRIS.[12] This training is at several levels. First, everyone within the organization concerned with data on employees has to be trained to use new recording forms compatible with the input requirements of the system. In addition, in the HR department, staff members, including the executive in that area, must be trained on the system. For many HR professionals, this training may be their first exposure to computers, yet they must learn how to use them. Support and instruction from hardware and software vendors also are important in order for the organization to realize the full benefits of the system.

Security and Privacy   Two other issues of concern are security and privacy. Controls must be built into the system to restrict indiscriminate access to the HRIS data on employees. For example, health insurance claims information might identify someone who has undergone psychiatric counseling or treatment for alcoholism. Likewise, performance appraisal ratings on employees must be guarded. Often, data disks are kept in specially locked cabinets. In addition, restricted passwords are used to access different parts of the HRIS database.

▲ HR ORGANIZATIONAL COMMUNICATION

At the heart of organizational communication is information transfer. Communication affects the management of people as much as, or more than, any other process over which management has influence. Many people think of communication primarily as interpersonal in nature. However, communication throughout organizations in just as important. HR management plays a key role in organizational communication. Through HR communications, new policies are explained, changes are implemented, and employee feedback is given.

Communications Throughout Organizations

Just as an HRIS is built on data and information, HR communication focuses on dissemination of HR data and information throughout the organization. *Downward communication* flows from top management to the rest of the organization and is essential so that employees know what is and will be happening in the organization and what top management expectations and goals are. *Upward communication* also is important so that managers know what the ideas, concerns, and information needs of employees are. Both formal means to encourage upward communication, such as suggestion systems and grievance procedures, and informal means such as the grapevine are used. The communications process is built on transmittal of information downward, upward, and laterally in organizations.

The Grapevine   As anyone who has ever worked in any organization knows, an important part of organizational communication is carried out through informal information channels, referred to as the *grapevine*. Just as jungle drums in old Tarzan movies indicated trouble, activity along the grapevine may reflect employee concerns and organizational problems. Managers should be aware of current grapevine messages and listen for major distortions. Activity in the grapevine depends on how important a topic is and on the presence (or absence) of official communication about it.

It is impossible to eliminate the grapevine. Absence of a grapevine in an organization might indicate that employees are either too scared to talk or that they care so little about the organization that they do not want to talk about it. Because the grapevine is a fact of organization life, it is important that managers share information and communicate details to reduce the need for inaccurate rumors and gossip.

Electronic Mail (E-Mail)   The growth of information systems in organizations has led to the widespread usage of **electronic mail (E-mail),** a computerized system of sending and receiving messages for individuals and organizations. With the advent of E-mail systems, communication throughout organizations can be almost immediate. Also, E-mail often results in bypassing the formal organizational structure and channels.

These systems can operate worldwide through networks such as Compuserve or MCI-Mail and within individual firms. Replies can be returned in a day rather than a week or more. Most E-mail systems can be accessed through various telecommunication devices and laptop computers. According to estimates by the Electronic Mail Association, there will be 27 million users of E-mail by 1995, and each of them will send an average of 500 messages a year.[13] E-mail also is being used to conduct attitude surveys and do HR research, as the "HR Perspective" describes.

▼ **ELECTRONIC MAIL (E-MAIL)**

is a computerized system of sending and receiving messages for individuals and organizations.

Employee Publications and Media

Organizations communicate with employees through internal publications and media, including newspapers, company magazines, organizational newsletters,

HR Perspectives:
Electronic Mail Research

With the evolution of new technologies, additional ways of conducting HR research are available. One of the most intriguing uses of an electronic mail system (E-mail) is to obtain survey information from employees.

Large- and medium-sized organizations increasingly are turning to E-mail. These systems allow anyone with a computer account to compose and send memos, leave messages, and otherwise communicate with others in the organization.

Electronic mail is a feasible way to conduct employee surveys because a researcher can electronically transmit a questionnaire to all or selected E-mail addresses. The respondents then provide their answers and "send" them back to the researcher. The responses can be made in an anonymous manner. As E-mail systems become more widespread, this method of gathering employee survey data is likely to expand.

videotapes, and intensive computer technology. Other formal communication methods include bulletin boards, posters, movies, and slides.

Whatever the formal means used, managers should make an honest attempt to communicate information employees need to know. Communication should not be solely a public relations tool to build the image of the organization. Bad news, as well as good news, should be reported objectively in readable style.[14] For example, an airline publication has a question-and-answer section in which employees anonymously can submit tough questions to management. Management's answers are printed with the question in every issue. Because every effort is made to give completely honest answers, this section has been very useful. The same idea fizzled in another large company because the questions were answered with "the company line" and employees soon lost interest in the less-than-candid replies.

Publications   Various newsletters, magazines, and other internal publications are produced to aid formal HR communications. Some elaborate publications in larger organizations require full-time public relations staff. In smaller organizations, a secretary in the HR department may prepare a newsletter using desktop publishing software.

A survey of the publications in 65 larger organizations revealed the most common topics to be details on current organizational programs and activities, personal news, industry issues, and reduction of labor and production costs.[15] In smaller organizations such publications frequently contain feature stories about employees and their families, promotions, retirements, awards, and organizational operations.

Audiovisual Media   As audiovisual technology has developed, many employers have added audiovisual methods of communication with employees. Some employers produce *audiotapes* or *videotapes* explaining benefit programs, corporate reorganizations, and revised HR policies and programs, which are shipped to each organizational branch. At those locations, the tapes are presented to employees in groups, then questions are addressed by a manager or someone from headquarters. Other organizations have used *teleconferencing*, in which satellite technology links facilities and groups in various locations. In this way, the same message can be delivered simultaneously. For example, Domino's Pizza uses a satellite network to communicate information on new products, store operations, ideas, and other information. Others using satellites are J. C. Penney's, Texas Instruments, and Federal Express.

Suggestion Systems and Total Quality Management

A **suggestion system** is a formal method of obtaining employee input and upward communication. These programs are becoming even more important as they are integrated with gainsharing or total quality management (TQM) efforts.[16] Giving the employees the opportunity to suggest changes or ways in which operations could be improved can encourage loyalty and commitment to the organization. Often an employee in the work unit knows more about how waste can be eliminated, how hazards can be controlled, or how improvements can be made than do managers who are not as close to the actual tasks performed. Many suggestion systems give financial rewards to employees for cost-saving suggestions, and often payments to employees are tied to a percentage of savings, up to some maximum level.

▼ **A SUGGESTION SYSTEM**

is a formal method of obtaining employee input and upward communication.

Suggestion systems have been saving money for employers for almost 100 years. Beginning in 1898, at Eastman Kodak Corporation, the first suggestion award was a $2 payment to a worker who pointed out the advantages of washing windows in the production department in order to improve the light available. For those companies that use suggestion systems effectively, the payoffs can be significant, as the opening discussion about American Airlines indicates.

According to the Employee Involvement Association (formerly the National Association of Suggestion Systems), more than $2 billion was saved as a result of suggestions submitted by employees in one year. The average net savings was $7,102 per suggestion. But suggestion participation and adoption is much greater in Japan. The typical employee in Japanese companies submits 32 suggestions per year, and 28 are adopted, while the typical U.S. employee submits fewer than one suggestion per year and only one is adopted for every 20 submitted.[17]

Making Suggestion Systems Work   Suggestions seldom appear as fully developed plans. They are usually ideas that need some work before they can be implemented. But, as examples cited in this chapter show, good ideas are well worth the work involved in developing them. To be successful, a suggestion system should be publicized. Suggestions should be collected often and evaluated by a committee, usually composed of both managers and nonmanagers. The committee passes on the suggestions it approves to upper management, who accepts or rejects them and determines the rewards to be given.

One major reason that suggestion programs fail is the inattention of management to feedback. Prompt feedback is important to all employees submitting suggestions. If employees are not told if or why their suggestions are accepted or rejected, underlying momentum will be lost. Also, suggestion systems can fail if the employees see the suggestion programs as a waste of time because they believe that little will change, or if they distrust management who may view suggestions as criticisms. Overall, then, the success of a suggestion system is linked to the amount of trust and communication associated with management, particularly top management.

▲ HR RESEARCH IN ORGANIZATIONS

▼ HR RESEARCH

analyzes past and present HR practices by using information from HR records.

HR research analyzes past and present HR practices by using information from HR records. HR research data can be used in four main ways:[18]

- ▲ Monitoring current HR activities
- ▲ Identifying HR problem areas and possible solutions to these problems
- ▲ Forecasting trends and their impact on HR management
- ▲ Projecting the costs and benefits of future HR activities

Conducting research is often crucial to solving HR problems because it is difficult to make good decisions without accurate information. Just as a physician must make a diagnosis before treating an illness, current HR practices must be researched and analyzed to ensure that future HR programs and activities are more effective. Many managers are intimidated by the word *research* and its academic connotations. But research can be quite simple and straightforward, such as using a questionnaire to ask employees about work-scheduling options. For example, employees in a state education agency completed such a survey in their unit. This survey pointed out problem areas that would otherwise not have been discovered, so that the revised work schedules offered were made compatible with the desires of employees.

Types of Research

Research in many fields can be categorized as primary or secondary. Some of the most important methods of conducting HR research are experiments, employee questionnaires, research interviews (all forms of primary research), and using research done by other organizations (secondary research).[19] Each of these methods is discussed briefly.

▼ PRIMARY RESEARCH

is the method by which data are gathered directly on specific problems and issues.

▼ SECONDARY RESEARCH

uses research done by others and reported in articles in professional journals or books.

Primary and Secondary Research   In **primary research,** data are gathered directly on specific problems and issues. Attitude surveys, questionnaires, interviews, and experiments are all primary research methods. When conducting **secondary research,** research is done by others and reported in articles in professional journals or books is used.

Individuals who plan to do primary research should decide first what phenomenon they wish to study. Examples of primary research topics are causes of nursing employee turnover, employee attitudes about flextime, extent of flexible benefits plans, and the relationship of a preemployment physical exam to workers' compensation claims.

HR practitioners do primary research when they conduct a pay survey on computer systems jobs in other companies in their geographic area, or a study of turnover costs and reasons that employees in technical jobs leave more frequently during the first 24- to 30-month period of employment. Thus, primary research has very specific application to researching and resolving actual HR problems in a particular organization.

Examples of research presented on HR topics and issues can be found in the *Academy of Management Journal, Personnel Psychology,* or other research-oriented journals listed in Appendix A. The primary research studies presented in these journals can offer guidance on factors affecting HR problems, the impact of various management approaches to HR issues, or other topics beneficial to HR academicians and practitioners.

In contrast, secondary research uses the primary research done by others. Several different computerized literature databases are available to HR researchers. Pay and benefits surveys prepared by government agencies or management consulting firms illustrate another common type of secondary research on HR activities.

Experiments and Pilot Projects

Experiments and pilot projects can provide useful HR insights. An **experiment** involves studying how something responds when changes are made in one or more variables or conditions. For instance, to test the impact of flextime scheduling on employee turnover, a firm might allow flexible scheduling in one department on a pilot basis. If the turnover rate of the employees in that department drops in comparison with the turnover in other departments still working set schedules, then the experiment may indicate that flexible scheduling can reduce turnover. Then the firm might try flexible scheduling in other departments.

The biggest problem with experiments and pilot projects in HR research is that HR management is practiced in the "real world." Unlike chemistry or other pure sciences, HR management is an applied science, and in real organizations it may be very difficult to control outside factors. Using the flexible scheduling example, other factors may be influencing turnover in the firm. But by having another department as a *control group* (a similar population to that of the experimental group but in which no changes were introduced), the effects of the flexible scheduling change in the pilot department can be compared with those in the control departments, and it is reasonable to assume that any differences are the result of the experimental group variable (flextime).

▼ **EXPERIMENT**

involves studying how something responds when changes are made in one or more variables or conditions.

Employee Questionnaires

One type of research uses questionnaires to give employees opportunities to voice their opinions about specific HR activities. Employee opinion questionnaires can be used to diagnose specific problem areas, identify employee needs or preferences, and reveal areas in which HR activities are well received or are viewed negatively. The "HR Perspective" describes how one small firm uses an employee questionnaire.

Questionnaires may be sent to employees to collect ideas for revising a performance-appraisal system. Or employees may be asked to evaluate specific organizational communication methods, such as the employee handbook or the company suggestion system. One common use of a questionnaire is to determine if employees are satisfied with their benefits programs. In addition, some organizations survey employees before granting new benefits to see if they are desired.

Questionnaires can be distributed and collected by supervisors, given out with employee paychecks, or mailed to employees' homes. More accurate information usually is obtained if employees can return information anonymously. New ways to obtain employee survey information involve E-mail (discussed earlier) and interactive telephone surveys using touch-tone responses.[20]

HR Perspectives:
Small Firm Benefits from Employee Survey

Organizations of all sizes can use employee feedback on questionnaires to improve their HR practices. One small firm that did is Reliable Cartage Company, a trucking company based in Bedford Park, Illinois. The president of the company, George Enguita, believes that surveying employees allows the firm to identify employee communication problems before they become serious.

The firm annually solicits employee input on wages, benefits, policies, and other areas. The surveys can be completed anonymously, but only three were returned unsigned in a recent administration. Employees rate the firm on a five-point scale on the various areas, as well as overall. For one year the firm got a 4.83 rating (5 is high) average from employees.

Using the results to address employee concerns is what makes employee questionnaires valuable. On one annual survey, the Reliable employees expressed concern about how pay scales were tied to performance. Enguita and his management staff responded by developing an employee incentive bonus program based upon attendance, safety, and complying with company policies and rules.[21]

▼ **AN ATTITUDE SURVEY**

is a special type of questionnaire that focuses on employees' feelings and beliefs about their jobs and the organization.

Attitude Surveys A special type of questionnaire is an **attitude survey,** which focuses on employees' feelings and beliefs about their jobs and the organization. By serving as a sounding board for employees to air their feelings about their jobs, supervisors, co-workers, and organizational policies and practices, these surveys can be starting points for improving productivity. Some employers conduct attitude surveys on a regularly scheduled basis (such as every year), while others do it intermittently. A study of 200 employers with more than 10 employees found that 45% of them had conducted an attitude survey in the previous three years. Another 11% of the firms had an attitude survey planned for the upcoming year. However, 18% said that they would not consider doing an attitude survey.[22]

Attitude surveys can be custom designed to address specific issues and concerns in an organization. But only surveys that are valid and reliable can measure attitudes accurately. Often a "research" survey that is developed in-house is poorly structured, asks questions in a confusing manner, or leads employees to respond in a manner that will give the desired results. For these reasons, consultants often are hired to develop and conduct customized attitude surveys.

Prepared attitude surveys also are available from a wide variety of vendors. One drawback to the use of standardized surveys is that they may not cover special concerns. If HR managers choose a standardized survey, they should check published reliability and validity statistics before using it. Figure 20–4 shows sample questions from an attitude survey.

When undertaking an attitude survey, HR management must get the support of top management. Prior to conducting an attitude survey, the specific purposes and objectives of the survey should be identified.[23] By asking employees to respond candidly to an attitude survey, management is building up employee's expectations that action will be taken to do something about the concerns identified. Therefore, a crucial part of conducting an attitude survey is to provide feedback to those who participated in it. It is especially important that negative survey results be communicated so as not to foster the appearance of hiding the results or placing blame. Generally, it is recommended that employee feedback

> **Questions in an attitude survey conducted for an insurance company asked employees to identify how much they agreed or disagreed with the following statements (among others):**
>
> ▲ My immediate supervisor seeks out the thoughts and feelings of others.
> ▲ I find real enjoyment in my job.
> ▲ I would not consider taking another job with another firm.
> ▲ In this firm, high standards for performance are set.
> ▲ If you do good work, you will receive rewards and recognition.
> ▲ Unnecessary requirements and rules are kept to a minimum.
> ▲ I am rewarded fairly for the experience I have.
> ▲ I have little control over how I carry out my daily tasks.
> ▲ I think top management makes an effort to get opinions from the employees.
> ▲ Staying with this organization is a matter of necessity as much as desire.

 Figure 20–4

Sample Questions from an Attitude Survey

be done through meetings with managers, supervisors, and employees, often in small groups to encourage interaction and discussion. That approach is consistent with the most common reason for conducting an attitude survey—to diagnose strengths and weaknesses so that actions can be taken to improve the HR activities in an organization.

Research Interviews

A research interview is an alternative to a survey and may focus on a variety of problems. One widely used type of interview is the **exit interview,** in which those who are leaving the organization are asked to identify the reasons for their departure. This information can be used to correct problems so that others will not leave. HR specialists rather than supervisors usually conduct exit interviews, and a skillful interviewer can gain useful information. A wide range of issues can be examined in exit interviews, including reasons for leaving, supervision, pay, training, and the best-liked and least-liked aspects of the job.

▼ **AN EXIT INTERVIEW**

asks those leaving the organization to identify the reasons for their departure.

Departing employees may be reluctant to divulge their real reasons for leaving because they may wish to return to their jobs some day. They may also fear that candid responses will hinder their chances of receiving favorable references. One major reason an employee commonly gives for leaving a job is an offer for more pay elsewhere. Although this reason is acceptable, the pay increases may not be the only factor. Consequently, to uncover other reasons it may be more useful to contact the departing employee a week or so later. Former employees may be more willing to provide information on questionnaires mailed to their homes or in telephone conversations conducted some time after they leave the organization.[24]

Research Using Other Organizations

HR specialists can gain insights from managers and specialists in other organizations by participating in professional groups. The most prominent professional organizations are the Society for Human Resource Management (SHRM) and the International Personnel Management Association (IPMA). These organizations publish professional journals and newsletters, conduct annual meetings and conferences, and offer many other services, often through local chapters. SHRM is composed primarily of private-sector HR professionals, whereas members of IPMA are HR managers from local, state, and federal government agencies.

Private management consulting firms and local colleges and universities also can assist in HR research. These outside researchers may be more knowledgeable and unbiased than people inside the organization. Consultants skilled in questionnaire design and data analysis can give expert advice on HR research. Appendix B contains a list of organizations and agencies having information useful to HR specialists and other managers.

National or Area Surveys   Surveys by other organizations can provide useful perspectives for an organization. Some organizations, such as the Bureau of National Affairs and the Conference Board, sponsor surveys on HR practices in various communities, states, and regions. The results are distributed to participating organizations. An organization also may conduct its own comparative outside surveys, such as wage surveys.

Current Literature   Professional HR journals and publications are a useful communication link among managers, HR specialists, researchers, and other practitioners. Appendix A contains a list of journals that often publish HR management information. Such publications help professionals learn about current changes in the field and what other organizations are doing.

Importance of HR Research

HR decisions can be improved through research because better information leads to better solutions. Effective management comes through analyzing problems and applying experience and knowledge to particular situations. A manager who just "supposes" that a certain result may occur is not likely to be effective. In some organizations, systematic programs of HR research are used to assess the overall effectiveness of HR activities.

▲ ASSESSING HR ACTIVITIES

Top management increasingly is recognizing that expenditures on HR activities can enhance productivity and the overall effectiveness of an organization. The concern of *effectiveness* is how well an organization reaches its objectives over time. *Efficiency* is concerned with the time and cost involved in doing so. Efficiency is determined through cost/benefit analyses, while effectiveness is determined by comparing HR results to the objectives set for HR activities as a part of the strategic HR planning and organizational planning efforts.

HR Assessment and Measurement

Assessment of HR effectiveness and efficiency is just as necessary as it is in other areas of an organization. These assessment efforts should look both inside and outside the HR department. Inside the HR department, the HR staff must be efficient and productive in handling the internal workings of the department.

HR Perspectives:

Research on the Effectiveness of Public-Sector HR Departments

Organizations of all types and in all industries need to evaluate the effectiveness of their HR departments and activities. As described in the *Review of Public Administration,* Stephen Straus developed a framework to conduct such an evaluation called the Multiple Constituencies Activities and Standards Model (MCAS). The MCAS relies on evaluation of public-sector HR departments by managers and employees. Quantitative data from the different constituencies is compiled, and comparisons are established with other public HR departments.

To conduct the evaluations, Straus used a two-stage process. First, he conducted preliminary interviews with some county HR directors and county managers and employees, totaling 111 persons in all. Each group was asked the same questions that formed an identification of the important activities performed by county HR departments. A total of 29 activities were identified. The questionnaires were sent to managers and employees in 26 counties, and a total of 2,150 people responded.

The results showed that the county HR departments were more effective at administering benefits and maintaining records, but less effective at helping departments improve performance and at soliciting employee opinions. Lower-level supervisors rated the HR departments lower in effectiveness than employees or mid-managers did. Results of this assessment confirm the need for HR staff members to evaluate the effectiveness of their departmental efforts. Also, it appears that more emphasis needs to be placed on areas beyond the administration of internal "processing" activities.[25]

Outside the department, HR staff members must serve their "clients" effectively and efficiently. The HR clients are the employees and managers in the organization, as well as those outside the organization who deal with the HR staff. The "HR Perspective" describes research on how managers and employees viewed the effectiveness of public-sector HR departments.

Extent of HR Assessment   The assessment of HR activities varies from nonexistent to very systematic methods used on an annual basis. However, in many organizations HR efforts are viewed solely as costs. The extent of HR assessment was studied in a survey done of 72 organizations.[26] The organizations studied varied in size and by industry, but neither of those factors was significant in identifying how HR activities are evaluated. Of the 72 surveyed organizations, 32% evaluate HR departments annually, but 29% seldom or never conduct assessments of HR departments and their activities. One key finding was that organizations that have a stated HR mission statement evaluate HR activities more frequently than organizations without such statements. Because HR mission statements often indicate a more formalized planning process, this finding suggests that evaluation and assessment is a logical extension of planning efforts.

The most frequent reasons why evaluating HR effectiveness has been deficient in many settings are:

▲ There is the belief that it is difficult to conduct scientific evaluation.
▲ The amount of HR efforts are difficult to quantify.
▲ It is difficult to identify of when HR objectives are and are not met.
▲ HR staff people do not have sufficient time or may not want to have their effectiveness and efficiency assessed.
▲ There is little interest in evaluating HR effectiveness and efficiency.

Direct and Indirect Measure   Measurement of HR activities can be classified as either direct or indirect. *Direct measures* deal with dollar costs that are spent by the organizations. For instance, recruiting costs will include direct expenditures such as advertising, recruiter travel, and other expenses. *Indirect measures* rely on measurement of time, quality, or quantity. For example, what is the value of reducing the time spent recruiting a key technical employee, such as a biochemistry researcher for a pharmaceutical firm? Or if selection interviewers are able to reduce the number and time of interviews by using a structured interview, what is the value of developing that interview? In this case, the indirect measures can be changed to direct measures by converting the interviewer's pay per hour and the number of interviews conducted.

Absenteeism and turnover costs are two areas that are commonly measured. As mentioned in Chapter 4, the absence of a clerical worker for one day costs up to $100 in reduced productivity and additional management efforts. Turnover also is costly. In one midwestern city, having a data-entry operator leave within the first six months of employment was estimated to cost the firm approximately $1,100, when hiring, training, benefits, and lost productivity were all considered. For specialized professionals and executive positions, turnover can cost over $50,000. Such calculations require consideration of a number of variables, including employment advertising costs, relocation expenses, and recruiting and interviewing time.

Methods of Assessing HR Effectiveness

A variety of methods can be used to assess the effectiveness and efficiency of HR activities. Where appropriate, data can be gathered on specific facets of HR management. These data can be obtained more easily if the organization has an HRIS in place. Attitude survey data also can provide valuable insights. A discussion follows of some methods of assessing HR effectiveness including benchmarking and utility and cost/benefit analyses.

▼ BENCHMARKING

is comparing specific measures of performance against data on those measures in "best practice" organizations.

Benchmarking   One approach to assessing HR effectiveness that uses both indirect and direct measures is **benchmarking,** which compares specific measures of performance against data on those measures in "best practice" organizations. As applied to HR activities, the comparisons let the HR staff know how their activities and accomplishments compare to those in other organizations. HR benchmarking can lead to:[27]

▲ Identifying areas where performance-improvement opportunities exist
▲ Evaluating HR policies and practices
▲ Comparing practices to "best practices and results"
▲ Setting performance goals to narrow the gap between current practices and the best practices

To do benchmarking, planning is required, evaluation methods must be established, best practices must be identified, and changes implemented based upon the gaps that are identified.[28] Benchmark data can be self-developed by contacting organizations identified by the HR staff as "best practice" organizations.

One study found that some of the HR data most frequently used as indicators of HR performance include the following:[29]

▲ Total compensation as a percentage of firm income (net before taxes)
▲ Percentage of workforce unionized
▲ Number or percentage of management positions filled internally
▲ Firm dollar sales per employee
▲ Benefits as a percentage of payroll costs

However, other more general data are available as well. For instance, the Society for Human Resource Management (SHRM) and the Saratoga Institute have developed benchmarks based on data from over 500 companies, presented by industry and by organizational size.[30]

Utility and Cost/Benefit Analyses In **utility analysis,** economic or other statistical models are built to identify the costs and benefits associated with specific HR activities.[32] These models generally contain equations that identify the relevant factors influencing the HR activity under study. According to Jac Fitz-Enz, a pioneer in measuring HR effectiveness, formulas and measures should be derived from a listing of activities and the variables associated with those activities. Figure 20–5 contains an example that quantifies selection interviewing costs.

Two examples illustrate how cost/benefit analyses have been beneficial, one at Union Bank in Los Angeles, and one at AT&T.[33] At Union Bank in Los Angeles, a child-care facility was established at its operations center. By using a cost/benefit analysis, the day-care center was estimated to save the bank approximate-

▼ **UTILITY ANALYSIS**

builds economic or other statistical models to identify the costs and benefits associated with specific HR activities.

Here is an example of how HR costing models can be developed.[31] The following equations show how to compute interviewing costs.

$$C/I = \frac{ST + MT}{I}$$

C/I = *cost of interviewing*

ST = total *staff time* spent interviewing
(interviewer's hourly rate × hours)

MT = *management time* spent interviewing
(manager's hourly rate × hours)

I = number of applicants interviewed

An example helps to illustrate the formula. Assume that an employment interview specialist is paid $12 an hour and interviews eight applicants for a job an hour each. Following the personal interview, the applicants are interviewed by a department manager paid $20 an hour for 30 minutes each. The interview costs would be:

$$\underline{ST} \qquad \underline{MT}$$

$$\frac{(\$12 \times 8 \text{ hours}) + (20 \times 4 \text{ hours})}{8 \text{ interviews}} = \frac{96 + 80}{80} = \frac{176}{8} = \$22 \text{ per applicant}$$

What this equation might indicate is the benefit of reducing the number of applicants interviewed by using better employment screening devices. Obviously, the costs of those screening items, such as a paper-and-pencil test, would have to be included when calculating the total selection costs.

 Figure 20–5

Selection Interviewing Costs

ly $200,000, compared with the cost of about $105,000. The costs identified were the subsidies paid by the bank to cover the additional expenditures that exceeded the fees paid by parents. Most of the savings were attributed to a reduction in employee turnover and absenteeism. The data collected indicated that turnover by employees who had used the child-care center was 2.2%, whereas turnover by employees using other day-care options was 9.5% and the total bank turnover was 18% during the first year that the bank's day-care facility operated. By including the costs of turnover, savings as high as $157,000 were identified.

Regarding absenteeism, those employees using the bank's day-care facility were absent about two days less per year and had one week shorter maternity leaves than those not using the facility. The savings attributed to the lower absenteeism were calculated to be about $35,000. In addition, the bank received significant publicity, news stories, and other media exposures that would have cost an estimated $40,000 to purchase.

The second example involves AT&T's assessment measures for identifying the costs and benefits associated with an employee wellness program. For the four-year program in which over 75,000 employees participated, the firm is comparing the medical claims of participants and nonparticipants. Preliminary results of the study indicate that the program cost of $175 per person will be offset by lower medical benefits costs to AT&T.

Continuing efforts to cost-justify expenditures will require HR professionals to be versed in research and assessment approaches and methods. To face the challenges outlined throughout this text, effective HR management will be essential in organizations both in the U.S. and globally.

▲ SUMMARY

- ▲ HR audits can be used to gather comprehensive information on how well HR activities in an organization are being performed.
- ▲ HR records provide a basis for government compliance, documentation, and research on HR actions.
- ▲ An HRIS is an integrated system designed to make records more useful to management as a source of information.
- ▲ A typical HRIS is composed of a database, computer software, and hardware.
- ▲ An HRIS offers a wide range of HR uses, with payroll, benefits administration, and general record keeping and administration being the most prevalent.
- ▲ Establishment of an HRIS generally is done by a project team. Once the key components are identified, training must be done and security and privacy issues must be addressed.
- ▲ A variety of employee publications and audiovisual media can be used to enhance formal HR communication efforts.
- ▲ Suggestion systems can be a good source of new ideas if employee suggestions are handled properly.
- ▲ Research on HR activities answers questions with facts, not guesswork.
- ▲ Primary researchers gather data directly on issues, whereas secondary researchers use research done by others and reported elsewhere.

▲ Research information can be gathered from several sources: questionnaires, attitude surveys, and exit interviews.

▲ HR activities typically have not been assessed because of a perceived inability to measure their effectiveness and/or a lack of desire to have them assessed.

▲ Measurement of HR activities can include direct and indirect costs.

▲ Benchmarking allows comparisons against "best practices" in other organizations.

▲ REVIEW AND DISCUSSION QUESTIONS

1. Using the HR audit checklist in Figure 20–1, how would you rate an organization where you have worked?
2. Discuss the following statement: "Record keeping is a necessary but mundane part of HR management."
3. If you had to establish an HRIS for a firm with 500 employees, how would you proceed?
4. Give some examples of how you would communicate with and receive communication from employees about implementing a flextime scheduling system in a firm with 200 employees.
5. How would you conduct HR research on turnover and absenteeism problems in a bank?
6. Why is assessing and measuring the effectiveness and efficiency of HR programs so important?

 CASE | **CHEVRON DECENTRALIZES ITS HRIS**

The increasing challenges faced by HR management, as well as the business pressures of the global oil industry, forced Chevron Corporation to decentralize more decision making. As a result, the San Francisco-based international firm had to decentralize both access to its HRIS and what could be input into the system. These changes were necessary to provide greater flexibility and provide instant accessibility to HR professionals, operating managers, and employees around the world.

Prior to beginning its decentralization, the HRIS at Chevron consisted of a central computer system with numerous "dumb" terminals. Highly trained computer technicians and specialists were needed and control of the system was highly concentrated.

The first stage of evolution for Chevron's HRIS meant moving to a series of personal computers (PCs) linked to a central processor. Unlike the earlier system, HR generalists throughout the various Chevron locations could perform some distributed processing. For instance, changes in an individual employee's address or status could be made at workstations in the facility where the employee works by HR specialists in each Chevron location.

The next phase of evolution of the HRIS at Chevron, currently underway, is the establishment of a client server network using local area network (LAN) hardware and software. This phase pushes even more system operations out to the various Chevron locations. Each location, in a sense, controls and operates the HRIS according to locational needs.

What Chevron's experience and planning illustrate are that an HRIS must be updated continually. But such updating pays off. According to a Chevron HRIS manager, the potential saving for decentralizing HRIS operations is $2000 per year per employee. Because Chevron has about 50,000 employees, the gross saving should be over $100 million per year. Just as important, decentralizing the HRIS is necessary to align HR activities with Chevron's mission and strategic plans and objectives.[34]

▲ **Questions:**

1. Discuss how an HRIS can contribute to organizational effectiveness.
2. Why is decentralization of decision making linked to decentralizing the HRIS?

▲ **NOTES**

1. Adapted from "Airline's Employees Flying High on Suggestion-Box Recognition," *Employee Benefit News,* April 1992, 72; and Michael A. Verespej, "Suggestion Systems Gain New Lustre," *Industry Week,* November 16, 1992, 11–18.

2. Barry A. Hartstein, "Rules of the Road in Dealing with Personnel Records," *Employee Relations Law Journal* 17 (1992), 673–692.

3. Equal Employment Opportunity Commission, *Technical Assistance Manual of the Employment Provisions (Title I) of the Americans with Disabilities Act,* presented in *HR News, ADA Special Supplement,* April 1992, C32.

4. Harold P. Coxson, "The Double-Edged Sword of Personnel Files and Employee Records," *SHRM Legal Report,* Fall 1992, 1–5.

5. S. D. Lieber, "Make Sure Personnel Files Help (Not Hurt) in Lawsuit," *Labor Watch,* November 1992, 1.

6. H. Eugene Baker and Sally A. Coltrin, "Computerization of HR Functions," *HR News,* December 1992, A4.

7. Sandra E. O'Connell, "Payroll and HRIS on a PC?" *HR Magazine,* November 1991, 31–34.

8. For extensive overviews of HRIS issues, see Alfred J. Walker, *Handbook of Human Resource Information Systems* (New York: McGraw-Hill, 1992); and Vincent R. Ceriello, *Human Resource Management Systems* (New York: Lexington Books, 1991).

9. F. Silverman, "Stepping Onto the Right Platform," *HR Magazine,* December 1991, 31–34.

10. Larry Dunivan, "Implementing a User-Driven Human Resource Information System," *Journal of Systems Management,* October 1991, 13–15.

11. Ren Nardoni, "Planning Promotes HRIS Success," *Personnel Journal,* January 1991, 61–65.

12. Sandra E. O'Connell, "Implementation Is the Key to Automation," *HR Magazine,* December 1992, 25–26.

13. "For Office Conversation, E-Mail Is Becoming the Water Cooler," *Omaha World-Herald,* December 27, 1992, G1.

14. J. R. Lamb, "Tell Employees the Bad News, Too," *Industry Week,* December 2, 1991, 70–72.

15. G. W. Kemper, "The Real Scoop," *Industry Week,* June 17, 1991, 68–69.

16. M. E. Trunk, "Open to Suggestions," *HR Magazine,* February 1993, 85–89.

17. Michael A. Verespej, "Suggestion Systems Gain New Lustre," *Industry Week,* November 16, 1992, 11–18.

18. Jac Fitz-Enz, *Human Value Management* (San Francisco: Jossey-Bass Publishers, 1990), chap. 9.

19. For a detailed discussion of HR research issues and methods, see Neal W. Schmitt and Richard J. Klimoski, *Research Methods in Human Resource Management* (Cincinnati: South-Western Publishing, 1991).

20. William E. Wymer and Jeanne M. Carsten, "Alternative Ways to Gather Opinion," *HR Magazine,* April 1992, 71–78.

21. "Those Little Things Have to Be Heard," *Nation's Business,* July 1992, 17.

22. William E. Wymer and Joseph A. Parente, "Employee Surveys: What Employers Are Doing and What Works," *Employment Relations Today* 18 (1991–1992), 447–484.

23. Vicki S. Kaman and Jodie Barr, "Employee Attitude Surveys for Strategic Compensation Management," *Compensation and Benefits Review,* January–February 1991, 52–65.

24. "Exit Interviews Handy If Used with Care, Researcher Says," *Omaha World-Herald,* April 18, 1993, 11G.

25. Adapted from Stephen K. Straus, "Multiple Constituencies Activities and Standards: A Framework for Evaluating the Effectiveness of Public Personnel Departments, *Review of Public Administration* 11 (1991), 55–70.

26. Margaret E. Cashman and James C. McElroy, "Evaluating the HR Function," *HR Magazine,* January 1991, 70–73.

27. John Hooper, "Borrowing from the Best," *Human Resource Executive,* June 1992, 38–40.

28. J. D. Weatherly, "Dare to Compare for Better Productivity," *HR Magazine,* September 1992, 42–46.

29. Robert O. Hansson, Nancy D. Smith, and Pamela Mancinelli, "Monitoring the HR Job Function," *HR Magazine,* February 1990, 76–78.

30. For details, request *SHRM/SI Human Resource Effectiveness Report,* which is published annually by the Society for Human Resource Management (see Appendix B).

31. Adapted from Jac Fitz-Enz, *How to Measure Human Resources Management* (New York: McGraw-Hill, 1984), 64–65.

32. Brian D. Steffy and Steven D. Maurer, "Conceptualizing and Measuring the Economic Effectiveness of Human Resource Activities," *Academy of Management Review* 13 (1988), 271–286.

33. Adapted from Julie Soloman, "Companies Try Measuring Cost Savings from New Types of Corporate Benefits," *The Wall Street Journal,* December 29, 1988, B1.

34. Adapted from Jay F. Stright, "Strategic Goals Guide HRIS Development," *Personnel Journal,* September 1993, 68–78.

Students are expected to be familiar with the professional literature in their fields of study. The professional journals are the most immediate and direct communication link between the researcher and the practicing manager. Two groups of publications are listed below:

A. *Research-Oriented Journals.* These journals contain articles that report on original research. Normally these journals contain either sophisticated writing and quantitative verifications of the author's findings or conceptual models and literature reviews of previous research.

Academy of Management Journal
Academy of Management Review
Administrative Science Quarterly
American Journal of Psychology
American Behavioral Scientist
American Journal of Sociology
American Psychologist
American Sociological Review
Annual Review of Psychology
Applied Psychology: An International Review
Behavioral Science
Behavioral Science Research
British Journal of Industrial Relations
Cognitive Studies
Decision Sciences
Group and Organization Studies
Human Organization
Human Relations
Industrial & Labor Relations Review
Industrial Relations
Interfaces
Journal of Abnormal Psychology
Journal of Applied Behavior Analysis
Journal of Applied Business Research
Journal of Applied Psychology
Journal of Business
Journal of Business and Industrial Marketing
Journal of Business and Psychology
Journal of Business Communications
Journal of Business Research
Journal of Communications
Journal of Counseling Psychology
Journal of Experimental Social Psychology
Journal of Human Resources

Journal of Industrial Relations
Journal of International Business Studies
Journal of Labor Economics
Journal of Management
Journal of Management Studies
Journal of Occupational and Organizational Psychology
Journal of Organizational Behavior
Journal of Personality and Social Psychology
Journal of Social Policy
Journal of Social Psychology
Journal of Vocational Behavior
Labor History
Labor Relations Yearbook
Management Science
Occupational Psychology
Organizational Behavior and Human Decision Processes
Personnel Psychology
Psychological Monographs
Psychological Review
Social Forces
Social Science Research
Sociology Perspective
Sociometry
Work and Occupations

B. *Management-Oriented Journals.* These journals generally cover a wide range of subjects. Articles in these publications normally are aimed at the practitioner and are written to interpret, summarize, or discuss past, present, and future research and administrative applications. Not all the articles in these publications are management-oriented.

ACA Journal
Academy of Management Executive
Administrative Management
Arbitration Journal
Australian Journal of Management
Benefits and Compensation Solution
Business
Business Horizons
Business Management
Business Monthly
Business Quarterly
Business and Society Review
California Management Review

Canadian Manager
Columbia Journal of World Business
Compensation and Benefits Review
Directors and Boards
Employee Benefits News
Employee Relations Law Journal
Employment Decisions Practices
Employment Relations
Employment Relations Today
Entrepeneurship Theory and Practice
Forbes
Fortune
Harvard Business Review
Hospital and Health Services Administration
HR Magazine
Human Resource Executive
Human Resource Management
Human Resource Planning
Human Behavior
INC.
Incentive
Industrial Management
Industry Week
International Management
Journal of Business Strategy
Journal of Pension Planning
Journal of Systems Management
Labor Law Journal
Long-Range Planning
Manage
Management Consulting
Management Planning
Management Review
Management Solutions
Management Today
Management World
Managers Magazine
Michigan State University Business Topics
Monthly Labor Review

Nation's Business
Organizational Dynamics
Pension World
Personnel Journal
Personnel Management
Psychology Today
Public Administration Review
Public Opinion Quarterly
Public Personnel Management
Recruiting Today
Research Management
SAM Advanced Management Journal
Security Management
Sloan Management Review
Supervision
Supervisory Management
Training
Training and Development Journal
Working Woman

C.   *Abstracts & Indices.*   For assistance in locating articles, students should check some of the following indices
and abstracts that often contain subjects of interest.

Applied Science and Technology Index
Business Periodicals
Dissertation Abstracts
Employee Relations Index
Human Resources Abstracts
Index to Legal Periodicals
Index to Social Sciences and Humanities
Management Abstracts
Management Contents
Management Research Abstracts
Personnel Management Abstracts
Psychological Abstracts
Reader's Guide to Periodical Literature
Sociological Abstracts
Work-Related Abstracts

Important Organizations in HR Management

Administrative Management Society
4622 Street Rd
Trevose, PA 19047
(215) 953-1040

AFL-CIO
815 - 16th St., N.W.
Washington, DC 20006
(202) 637-5000

American Arbitration Association
140 W. 51st St.
New York, NY 10020
(212) 484-4800

American Compensation Association
14040 N. Northsight Blvd.
Scottsdale, AZ 85260
(602) 951-9191

American Management Association
135 W. 50th St.
New York, NY 10020
(212) 586-8100

American Society for Healthcare
Human Resources Administration
840 N. Lakeshore Dr.
Chicago, IL 60611
(312) 280-6111

American Society for Industrial Security
1655 N. Fort Meyer Dr., Suite 1200
Arlington, VA 22209
(703) 522-5800

American Society for Public Administration
1120 "G" St., NW, Suite 500
Washington, DC 20005
(205) 393-7878

American Society for Training and Development
1630 Duke St.
Alexandria, VA 22312
(703) 683-8100

American Society of Pension Actuaries
1700 K St., NW, Suite 404
Washington, DC 20006
(202) 659-3620

American Society of Safety Engineers
1800 East Oakton
Des Plaines, IL 60018
(312) 692-4121

Association of Executive Search
Consultants, Inc.
151 Railroad Ave.
Greenwich, CT 06830
(203) 661-6606

Association of Human Resource Systems Professionals
P. O. Box 801646
Dallas, TX 75380
(214) 661-3727

Association for Health and Fitness
965 Hope St.
Stamford, CT 06902
(203) 359-2188

Bureau of Industrial Relations
University of Michigan
Ann Arbor, MI 48104

Bureau of Labor Statistics (BLS)
Department of Labor
3rd Street & Constitution Ave., NW
Washington, DC 20210

Bureau of National Affairs (BNA)
1231 - 25th St., NW
Washington, DC 20037

Canadian Public Personnel Management Association
220 Laurier Ave., West, Suite 720
Ottawa, Ontario
Canada K1P 5Z9
(613) 233-1742

Employee Benefit Research Institute
2121 K St., NW, Suite 860
Washington, DC 20037
(202) 659-0670

Employee Relocation Council
1627 K St., NW
Washington, DC 20006
(202) 857-0857

Employee Management Association
5 West Hargett, Suite 1100
Raleigh, NC 27601
(919) 828-6614

Equal Employment Opportunity Commission (EEOC)
2401 E St., NW
Washington, DC 20506

Human Resource Certification Institute (HRCI)
606 N. Washington
Alexandria, VA 22314

Human Resource Planning Society
P. O. Box 2553
Grand Central Station
New York, NY 10163
(212) 837-0632

Industrial Relations Research Association
7726 Social Science Blvd.
Madison, WI 53706
(608)262-2762

Institute of Personnel Management
IPM House
Camp Road, Wimbleton
London, SW19 4UX, England

Internal Revenue Service (IRS)
1111 Constitution Ave., NW
Washington, DC 20224
(202) 566-3171

International Association for Personnel Women
194-A Harvard St.
Medford, MA 02155
(617) 391-7436

International Foundation of Employee Benefit Plans
18700 Blue Mound Rd
Brookfield, WI 53005
(414) 786-6700

International Personnel Management Association
1617 Duke St.
Alexandria, VA 22314
(703) 549-7100

International Society of Pre-Retirement Planners
2400 South Downing St.
Westchester, IL 60153
(617) 495-4895

Labor Management Mediation Service
1620 I St., NW, Suite 616
Washington, DC 20006

National Association for the Advancement of Colored People (NAACP)
4805 Mt. Hope Dr.
Baltimore, MD 21215
(212) 481-4800

National Association of Manufacturers (NAM)
1331 Pennsylvania Ave., NW, Suite 1500N
Washington, DC
(202) 637-3000

National Association of Personnel Consultants
3133 Mt. Vernon Ave.
Alexandria, VA 22305
(703) 684-0180

National Association of Temporary Services
119 South St. Asaph
Alexandria, VA 22314
(703) 549-6287

National Employee Services & Recreation Association
2400 S. Downing Ave.
Westchester, IL 60153
(312) 562-8130

National Public Employer Labor Relations Association
1620 I Street, NW, 4th Floor
Washington, DC 20006
(202) 296-2230

Occupational Safety and Health Administration (OSHA)
200 Constitution Ave., NW
Washington, DC 20210
(202) 523-8045

Office of Federal Contract Compliance Programs
(OFCCP)
200 Constitution Ave., NW
Washington, DC 20210

Pension Benefit Guaranty Corporation
P. O. Box 7119
Washington, DC 20044

Profit Sharing Council of America
200 N. Wacker Drive, Suite 1722
Chicago, IL 60606
(312) 372-3411

Society for Human Resource Management (SHRM)
606 N. Washington
Alexandria, VA 22314
(703) 548-3440

U.S. Chamber of Commerce
1615 H St., NW
Washington, DC 20062

U.S. Department of Labor
200 Constitution Ave., NW
Washington, DC 20210

Questions asked by students in HR management classes often reflect their concerns about getting a job. This appendix, prepared with the assistance of a senior student, provides an overview of some of the activities involved in getting a job. Throughout this section, specific tips and suggestions are made. No attempt has been made to direct you to specific references, as similar points are made in many sources. Instead, you should conduct your own research to identify readings on specific ideas highlighted in the following discussion.

▲ KNOW THYSELF

Before you can tell anyone what your knowledge, skills, and abilities are, you have to understand them yourself. Prior to writing your resumé, you should sit down and identify your strengths. There are four primary areas that you need to explore: the skills you possess; activities that interest you; your personal attributes; and past job and activity results

Your Skills. In defining your skills, you should make a list of what you do well. Keep the list basic and do not leave out the obvious; reading and writing well do count. Now go back and check off those skills that you are willing to use in your work. For example, if you are good at research, would you be willing to take a job that required you to spend time sorting through information to prepare a report? Next get specific. Pick 10 or 12 of the skills that you have checked and define them in more detail. Describe how you have applied or could apply these skills in either work or non-work activities. Finally, pick out the skills that are most valuable to you, write them down, and set that list aside. The next step is to identify your areas of interest.

Your Interests. What do you like to do? What would you like to do if you have the chance? What kind of people do you like? These items do not have to be work-related because this listing is meant to identify activities that give you pleasure. Be honest and do not include items just to make your list "look better." Now narrow the list down to the 10-12 interests you would like to have included in your job. Then, put this list with

your list of skills and move on to an exploration of your personal attributes.

Your Attributes. "I am _____." Now fill in the blank. This is how to identify your attributes. You try to identify who are you, not just the you that people think you are, or the you that you let other people see. The "you" that must be identified here is how you see yourself. Are you hard-working, temperamental, creative, energetic, honest, shy? If so, put all of them down, but be honest with yourself. If you think you are intelligent, then write it down. Be careful not to list "labels" you've been given by others if you do not think they are true.

The next step is the same as in the first two areas: narrowing your list down. You should identify your 5 strongest and most positive attributes. Now put this list (you guessed it) with the others and move on to the final area: your results.

Your Results. What important accomplishments have you had? What have you done of which you are proud? Did you work part-time while you were in school? Did you write a paper or build something? Did you organize and lead some project? If the results are there, then write them down. You may need to use your list of skills and interests to get started. Do not leave any area out. Work, school, military service, community service, hobbies are all areas from which you may show the results of your activities.

Now you should identify the 10 accomplishments you consider to be most relevant to the type of work you want to do in the future. By writing them down and putting that list with the other three, you now have the foundation for your resume and you are about ready to prepare it. There is just one more bit of background work to do: Find out about your targetted job.

▲ RESEARCH THE EMPLOYER

By now you have a good idea of what you want to do, but you must identify what a future employer will expect you to do. The best way to find out is to ask. Contact some organizations in the area that employ people in the fields or jobs in which you would like to work. Talk to a wide range of people, including supervisors or managers, and individuals who are working in those areas. Also, you should talk to the career counselors and professors at your college or university and read books and articles about your field of interest. Make a special effort to find out what kinds of tasks you will be expected to perform and what types of responsibilities you will have. You may think you know all there is to know about the job you want, but you might be wrong. If you are wrong, then your resume also may be wrong (and useless). While you are asking all of these questions, do not forget to find out what kind of person most employers are interested in hiring.

Then, take the information you have gathered and compare it with the lists you have already prepared. The items that match should go on your resume.

▲ THE RESUME

Preparation of a resume starts you on the road to employment. A resume is a summary of your academic accomplishments, your work experiences, and your expectations for employment. It is the first "picture" that most employers will have of you. Because those doing the hiring do not have the time to try to understand what you are trying to say in your resume, you must ensure that your resume shows them, simply and precisely, what contributions you would make to their operations.

As with everything else in life, there are hard and fast rules governing the preparation of a resume—except for the exceptions.

Rule #1: Your resume should be concise; many experts recommend no more than one page. Two pages at the absolute maximum.

Rule #2: Your name, address, and phone number are printed at the top, 1½ inches down, and they are centered on the page.

Rule #3: Your resume should be typed on a high-quality typewriter or laser printer. If you do not have one, find one. If you cannot find one, hire someone who has one to type your resume.

Rule #4: NO MISTAKES! Have two or three people critique it. If there is an error, retype it. A sloppy resume will lose you jobs.

Rule #5: Use action verbs. "Supervised 5-member work crew" looks and sounds much better than "I was in charge of the supervision of the day-to-day workings of a 5-person crew."

Rule #6: Keep your resume simple and uncluttered. If your resume is direct and to the point and the sections are separated with plenty of white space, it stands a much better chance of being read seriously.

Rule #7: No personal data. Your personal description, any references to your age, sex, national origin, religion, material status, or a photograph have no place on your resume. In addition, requests for information in these areas are not legal and should be tactfully denied. No exceptions.

Rule #8: No references. You should have a separate sheet listing your references. Often that sheet is presented later. The last line of your resume should read: "References available upon request." No exceptions.

By now you must be thinking that if you follow these rules, your resume will look just like everyone else's. While this may be possible, it is not very probable.

A resume can follow several forms: chronological, functional, targeted, the resume alternative, or the creative resume. The choice of form depends upon the specific situation, but for the majority of newly graduated college students the chronological or functional formats are the most appropriate. Examples of both are shown in Figure D-1 and D-2. While the spacing between sections depends upon the individual resume, some specific guidelines for preparing your resume follow:

First, below your name and address, along the left margin (one inch from the left edge of the paper), type the word "OBJECTIVE:" followed by a one-or two sentence description of the job (or career field) for which you are applying. It should be single-spaced and no more than two-three lines.

The next area presented is your educational background. The word "EDUCATION:" should appear along the left margin, followed by the degree or degrees you earned, your major, the school you attended (if more than one, list them in chronological order starting from the most recent, one to a line) and the year of your graduation. For people with more experience, education probably should follow the skills section discussed next.

The center sections of your resume are where you tell the employer what you will bring to his/her company. You should get your preparatory lists from before. Can the skills required by the employer for this job be grouped into two or three major categories? If·so, then group your skills and accomplishments under these categories and list them from most important to less important (the least important does not belong in your resume). If not, then list your skills under the heading "CAPABILITIES:" and your accomplishments under "ACHIEVEMENTS:". Start with the items that best match the requirements listed by your outside sources. In either case, remember Rule #5: Use action verbs. These sections can be single- or double-spaced, depending on the room you have. The word "I" should not appear anywhere on your resume.

The last two sections of your resume should be your WORK HISTORY and REFERENCES. As with the other sections, these headings should appear in capital letters at the left margin. Start the work history section with your most recent job and go back in time for four or five jobs. If you had a job more than five years ago but it is extremely relevant to this job, include it also. Start with the dates that you worked at that job. Next list the job title and the name of the company or organization for which you worked. If you performed any duties that are relevant to the job you are applying for, list them on separate lines. The reference section was covered by Rule #8. If employers want your references, they can ask for them later.

You should always remember that your resume is your

```
DEBRA JAMES
5421 Dodge Avenue
Omaha, Nebraska 68104
(402) 221-9908
```

▲ **Figure C-1**

Chronological Resume

```
* OBJECTIVE

     Entry-level management position in marketing/sales.

* EDUCATION

     University of Nebraska at Omaha
     Bachelor of Science in Business Administration, May, 1995
     Specializing in Marketing, Cumulative GPA: 3.4 (4.00)

     Participated in two special research projects with Small
     Business Administration: 1) to assist Boardwalk Shopping
     Center, Omaha, to become more visible to the public and
     increase sales, 2) to study the feasibility of opening an
     interior designer showcase in the Omaha area.

* EXPERIENCE

     Corral Western Wear, Omaha, Nebraska, 7/92 - present (part-time).
     Salesperson. Average twenty-five hours per week involving
     customer contact. Formulated a marketing research proposal
     relating to different lines of western clothing not currently
     in stock.

     University of Nebraska at Omaha, 5/90-7/92 (part-time). Student
     Programming Organization (SPO). Student Director. Planned and
     implemented 10 educational and cultural programs. Selected
     programs for presentation, negotiated contracts with booking
     agents, managed ticket sales based on budgeted expenses.

     Clothing, Inc., Omaha, Nebraska. 10/88-11/89 (full-time). Sales
     Associate. Originated, planned and supervised new fashion show
     presentations. Identified, selected, and assisted in training
     campaigns that were implemented.

*ACTIVITIES

     President, Phi Chi Theta, professional women's business
     fraternity, Spring, 1995; Vice President, Fall, 1994
     Student Orientation Leader (3 semesters)
     Member, American Marketing Association
     Member, Moving Company, modern dance group.

* REFERENCES

     Available upon request.
```

Figure C-2

Functional Resume

William Smith
2020 Jackson Blvd.
Omaha, NE 68111
(402) 664-9496

EDUCATION:

   B.S. Journalism, University of Nebraska at Omaha, 1995

WRITING:

   * Wrote articles for the sports section of college newspaper.
   * Had three articles published in Omaha Sun Newspaper.
   * Served as assistant editor of the sports section of college newspaper.
   * Editor of high school student newspaper.

SPORTS:

   * Played collegiate basketball four years.
   * Captain and starting center for UNO's defending North Central Conference champion basketball team.
   * Voted most improved player by teammates as a junior and chosen to All-Conference tournament team during senior year.
   * Nominated to the NCC All-Academic squad.
   * Coached high school basketball players at summer clinic.

COMMUNICATION/RADIO/VIDEO:

   * Announced live broadcasts of football games on college radio.
   * Wrote and delivered nightly sports news for radio on football weekends.
   * Assisted in developing basketball training via video.
   * Delivered sports promotional spots on local college radio station.

WORK HISTORY:

   1993-95   KVNO, Campus Radio, University of Nebraska at
                  Omaha. Reporter
   Summer 1994   Smietrews Restaurant, Omaha, Nebraska. Night
                  Manager.
   Summer 1992-
      1993   Mutual of Omaha, Omaha, Nebraska. Pressman

REFERENCES:

   * Available upon request.

"paper picture." Taking the time to insure that it looks good, and experimenting with layout and spacing may force you to revise your draft resume. A third draft will almost always be better than the first.

Now you are ready to use your "perfect" resume. The cover letter transmitting the resume may be as important as the resume itself.

▲ THE COVER LETTER

Whenever you send your resume to a company, you should include a cover letter. The cover letter is your personalized introduction to the company and is just as important as your resume. Sending a resume without a cover letter is like sending a piece of junk mail and will almost guarantee that your resume will not be read.

The letter should be addressed to a specific person, by name and position. In general, it is better if you send your letter and resume to the director or supervisor of the department or section for which you would expect to be working. HR departments receive countless resumes every week and many of them can become "lost in the shuffle." In addition, it is usually the department head that has the final decision on whether or not you get the job.

Rules for the preparation of the cover letter are similar to those for the resume. Use a quality (20-lb.) bond paper. You should include the date at the top, along the right margin and the complete address of the recipient along the left margin. As with any standard business letter, never, never, never send a generic cover letter with the name and address of the individual filled in at the top. This innocent shortcut only succeeds in giving the impression that the recipient is just another name on your list.

The body of the letter should be about half a page long. It should point out two or three facts from the resume and expand upon them. The letter should state your reason for sending it, but it should contain something more than "I think I would like to work for your company."

You should always include some personal comment directed specifically to the individual and the company. For example, you might mention a problem that you are aware they are having, and a possible solution that you have. Or, if the individual's name appeared in a news article and that is where you got the idea to contact him or her, say that.

You should always close your cover letter with the suggestion of a meeting but do not just say "I would like to talk to you about this further." Include a time frame. If the company is out of town, you should tell the individual when you will be in that area. In any case, give a date when you will be in contact with her or him again. A statement like "I will be interviewing in your area on May 14 and 15 and would appreciate the opportunity to speak with you further on this subject. I will call the week before I am there to set up a time that is convenient for you" is a very good closing for a cover letter. Then end your letter with an appropriate closing and your signature. Also, it is a good idea to include your address and telephone number above the date, in case the letter and resume are separated.

▲ THE APPLICATION

Some college graduates will not be required to complete an application form when they apply for a job. Most college placement offices supply the companies who will be interviewing their graduates with data sheets that contain all of the relevant information on the candidate. Nevertheless, many graduates will be required at some time to complete a standard application form for a job. The most frequent concern voiced by students is how to handle one problem: illegal questions.

As was mentioned in the text of this book, many of the job application forms in use today contain questions that, by law, do not have to be completed by the appli-

cant. These questions are ones that concern race, sex, age, national origin, religion, and mental and physical limitations not relevant to the performance of the job. In addition, application forms should not ask questions concerning arrests, as people are not judged guilty of a crime solely on the basis of arrests. Questions concerning criminal convictions should be asked only insofar as they pertain to the performance of the job. Questions concerning credit ratings or current financial situation may not be asked unless they have a direct relationship to the job (i.e., if the job will place you in a situation of being unsupervised and around sums of money). Questions about any political or ideological affiliations may not be asked. It is also illegal to ask questions about physical descriptions unless they can be shown to be Bona Fide Occupational Qualifications (BFOQ). Also questions concerning marital status and family may not be asked.

As a general rule, it is best if you as the applicant, leave blank or put a dash (-) for any of these illegal questions on application forms. If the employers are asking questions for the purpose of maintaining EEO compliance records, they should have a separate form or obtain appropriate information after you have been hired.

▲ THE INTERVIEW

You have submitted your resume, contacted the company, and have been invited in for an interview, or you have made an appointment with one of the recruiters who will be visiting your campus. Either way, there are four areas of knowledge that may help you have a better interview: preparation for the interview; behavior during the interview; your rights in the interview; and following up on the interview.

▲ PREPARATION FOR THE INTERVIEW

Once you know that you have an interview, you need to begin preparing for it. As with your resume, a little preparation can set you far above the other applicants in the race for the job. First, find out all the information you can about the company with which you will be interviewing. Questions include: What do they do? What are their markets? Who are their competitors? How are they doing financially? Most of this information is available from the company itself, especially if the company is large enough and publicly-traded. Quite often you will be able to find articles concerning the company in newspapers and magazines. If nothing else, you can call and ask questions of someone working for the company. In addition, you should also try to gather as much information as possible concerning the job for which you are applying. Find out what the duties are for that position, what the salary range is (if possible), why the position is open, and what happened to the last person who had the job.

As the day of the interview draws near, you need to begin preparing yourself for the interview. The appropriate clothing often is a vested suit for men and a skirted suit for women. Your clothing makes a statement about yourself and it should say what you want it to say (for a detailed discussion of the proper clothing, see *Dress for Success or The Woman's Dress for Success Book* both by John T. Molloy). Your personal appearance—whether your hair is neatly groomed, whether you are clean-shaven (men) or statefully made-up (women)—is also critical. You should make sure you look as sharp and crisp as you can before arriving for the interview.

▲ BEHAVIOR DURING THE INTERVIEW

On the day of the interview, it is vital for you to arrive on time. If necessary, give yourself a half-hour head start, just in case. By arriving at the site of the interview, 10 minutes or so before your appointment, you give yourself time to relax. Arriving just in the nick of time, out of breath and flushed, is almost as bad as arriving late. Also, it is generally recommended that you curb your desire for a cigarette and spit out your gum before you walk in the door.

When the person with whom you will be interviewing comes to get you (being called in the office usually is not done), stand, smile, and extend your hand. At that point, the interview has just begun and you can lose the job before the first question is even asked. You should exude confidence and your handshake should be firm, but not a crusher. Also you may wish to take along a small note card with questions you want to ask printed on it.

During the interview you should sit in an erect but comfortable manner. As much as possible, try to avoid any unnecessary body movement such as drumming your fingers, swinging your legs, or squirming in your seat. All of these actions will be distracting to the interviewer and may be the first and major fact that is remembered about you. You should maintain eye contact with the interviewer, but not to the point that you are staring. When asked a question, answer it in an even voice at a conversational level. Above all, remember that an interview is a two-way experience. The interviewer is checking you out and you are checking out the company.

It is important for you to assert yourself during the interview. If the company does offer you a position, you want to be sure that it will suit you as much as you will suit it. By asking questions, you can put the information you gathered prior to the interview to use. Avoid emphasizing questions about benefit plans for employees. Instead focus on questions concerning the job. You should try to answer all questions precisely, but if you feel that the wrong impression has been given from your response, do not hesitate to add to your answer. Never forget that you too have rights in the interviewing process.

▲ YOUR RIGHTS

At some point in the interview, a question may be asked of you that you do not feel is job-related and that may be illegal. However, you should not let yourself be intimidated. If the interviewer asks if you have ever been arrested, you can decline to answer. You should explain that you have never been convicted of any crime and that you have never missed any work time as a result of an involvement with the authorities (provided that it is true). You can, answer any question that you wish, but remember, the interviewer is not legally authorized to ask those types of questions and he or she should know that. However, the interview is not the time to try to correct any illegal practices on the part of the interviewer.

▲ FOLLOWING UP THE INTERVIEW

At the close of the interview, you should be sure to thank the interviewer and shake hands once again. When you return home, make a note or two about the facts discussed during the interview. Then, a day or two after the interview, write a brief thank-you note. The note should thank the interviewer once again for the time spent and should mention something of importance that was brought up in the interview, especially if it was favorable to you.

In summary, remember that you are an equal partner in any interview and you have rights. Prepare in advance for the interview. Focus on your positive attributes during the interview and know your rights. Then, follow the interview up with a brief thank-you note. The tips in this appendix should help you to get many second interviews and job offers. Good luck.

▲ SECTION CASES ▲

CASE | Section 1: Celebrating Workforce Diversity at Motorola's SPS*

Motorola is one of the world's leading providers of electronic equipment, systems components, and services, with more than 100,000 employees worldwide. It is also among the largest industrial companies in the United States ranked by total sales. An indication of the company's commitment to quality and customer satisfaction and service is the fact that Motorola was one of the first winners of the Malcolm Baldrige National Quality Award (in 1988).

Both Motorola's workforce and customer base are global in nature, which challenges its worldwide leadership to tap the talents of many diverse backgrounds and cultures. Founded on the principle that "each employee will be treated with dignity as an individual," management style has changed in various ways. Managing and developing a diverse workforce meant taking a critical look at traditional values, systems, behaviors, and attitudes.

Motorola's Semiconductor Products Sector (SPS) headquartered in Phoenix, Arizona, and led by Jim Norling, Motorola Vice President, President, and Sector General Manager, Motorola, SPS, accepted the challenge to use diversity as a strength in 1988. First a change was initiated to revitalize the Equal Employment Department with a more symbolic name: The Workforce Diversity Department.

By refocusing on a revitalized vision and mission statement, the department emerged newly energized, and quickly set about to investigate how to begin their "cultural revolution." An extended team, the Workforce Diversity Task Force, was identified to assist in the process. In order for the Department and its taskforce to know the challenges facing it, a series of small focus group meetings were held. Over 400 employees grouped according to race, culture, gender, job functions, shift, and subsequently grouped with mixed cul-

tural characteristics provided the base for the emerging roadmap. In the sessions, frustrations were aired, ideas kicked around, subtleties extracted, and observations compiled. In the final analysis, the consensus of opinion was that each of the diverse groups had similar apprehensions and dreams. It was no longer just racial or gender issues, but one of career planning, family issues, and empowerment for all employees, including white males.

Simultaneously, a benchmark study of 75 companies across the U.S. was conducted with the intent to understand and learn from the experiences of other organizations. The resulting matrix that was developed included the following concerns: flexible scheduling, school partnering, community involvement, gender issue training, and on-site day care.

The internal analysis was compared to the external benchmark data from the 75 companies to develop a multiphase organizational change strategy aimed at surfacing diversity as a competitive strength. The key strategies that were identified included:

1. The development of diversity as a critical business issue reflecting sponsorship and leadership by senior managers.
2. Creation of a network and infrastructure capable of sustaining cultural diversity.
3. Enhanced external image to attract individuals from diverse backgrounds.
4. A focus on schools and the community as workforce suppliers.
5. Significant progress toward parity representations in management.

The SPS Workforce Diversity Task Force, armed with these strategies, addressed these issues by forming teams from all areas of SPS. Membership was initially

*Contributed by Gail Majors, SPHR, Motorola Personnel Manager, Workforce Diversity Programs, Motorola Semiconductor Products Sector, Phoenix, Arizona. Used with permission.

small but it quickly swelled with volunteers who wanted to "make a difference." Five teams were established as follows:

1. *Phased Organizational Change* which created energy around management commitment, sponsorship communications, and measurements.
2. *The Emerging Workforce* which looked to the schools as suppliers of our continued need for the "best in class" workforce.
3. *Work / Family* which set out to find ways to assist employees to balance their careers and family life.
4. *Mentoring* which set out to establish methodologies for existing employees to take charge of their careers with the assistance of other professionals.
5. *Training* which sought to create a core group of workshops and experiences around diversity issues, including the "white male" as a cultural theme.

Five years later, the ranks of internal supporters has grown tremendously, especially within senior management. To date, there have been significant contributions made by all of the initial teams, many of which have received community and national recognition. The task force that developed the plan and examples of programs include:

The Emerging Workforce: Partnerships have been formed with numerous schools in the Phoenix and Austin areas. These partnerships include career discussions with students, capital equipment donations, tutoring, temporary job placement for teachers, and invitations to attend special Motorola courses. Partnerships span K-12, in addition to the partnerships which continue to thrive with universities throughout the U.S.

Work and Family: Perhaps the most notable accomplishment has been the initiation of flex-time and job sharing, which was pioneered in non–traditional areas of engineering and manufacturing. Coupled with enhanced parental leave policies, parents are able to participate more freely in the care and lives of their extended families.

Training: This team has sought out courses which have enhanced the understanding of cultural and gender roles in an attempt to foster improved working relationships for all employees. Courses, such as "White Men, Women and Minorities: Power and Culture," by Anthony Ipsaro, provided excellent awareness and a new language around the diversity issue. On the heels of this course, another was developed which addressed the issue of "Intercultural Diversity: Insights into Pat-

terns of Behavior," taught by Dr. Edwin Nichols. The focus of these courses continue to challenge the thinking of Motorola employees.

Efforts are now being made to create real links from the training to applied skills in the workplace. Both management and employees continue to comment on the efforts and the impact of the new knowledge base on their careers.

The most recent undertaking for the Workforce Diversity team has been to combine the concepts of diversity with organizational effectiveness. One wafer manufacturing organization set out to integrate diversity throughout the structure of its work. Faced with many organizational challenges, new product lines, seven day, 24–hour rotating shifts, an "established" workforce which would soon swell with new hires, and long–service managers and supervisors, they chose to embark upon a journey of discovery.

The results of this "discovery" continue to unfold as of this writing. One year into the phased organizational change, no one could have predicted how this organization of over 450 employees would evolve. Employees at all levels of the organization have a personal understanding of customer needs and the business plans. They both speak of and demonstrate the need to work together, capitalizing on their diverse backgrounds which illustrates that communication about diversity is an effective means to improve the productivity of the organization. By looking at the organization as an entire system, diversity can be designed into the systems and processes to create a balanced work environment.

The diversity efforts in the wafer manufacturing organization continue to experience tremendous support from both managers and employees as the change process unfolds. The diverse values and perspectives which previously have not been reflected in the organization are now perceived as organizational strengths. By connecting the values of the employees to the values of the work, diversity has become a dynamic component of the competitive process and not just another program.

At various intervals SPS managers have been asked to provide feedback on their leadership roles in the cultural change process. Their responses reflect significant depth and commitment, listing personal success stories of mentorships, community and educational sponsorships, and involvement in recruitment and retention efforts. One key manager, responding to the challenge stated, "The first step toward embracing diversity is the realization that fairness does not always exist, justice does not always prevail, and all people are not always treated as having equal human value and human dignity. At times my own personal journey is beautiful and exciting; at times it is painful ... nonetheless ... I am committed to this pilgrimage..." That eloquent statement characterizes the diversity quest at Motorola SPS, as the journey continues.

▲ QUESTIONS:

1. How do you suppose that addressing diversity issues has aided Motorola SPS in improving its quality and customer service and improving employee motivation?
2. Discuss how the variety of diversity-related actions have affected various HR activities?
3. Why must diversity actions be seen as an outcome of strategic HR planning?

 ## Section 2: Warehousing EEO Problems?

When Frances Miles looks at her desk after completing her first month at Lynch Warehousing Company (LWC), she knows why she was hired to be the firm's first corporate coordinator of employment and affirmative action. Several interesting situations with equal employment implications she has learned about in the past few weeks stare up at her.

Her new employer is a Dallas-based warehouse and distribution company which manages such facilities throughout the South and Southwest. LWC owns the warehouses and rents or leases space to various firms who need warehouse and distribution space, but who prefer not to own their own facilities. As part of its revenue, the firm also manages and staffs the warehouses where about 300 employees work. During the past year, LWC has sought contracts with several federal and state agencies, which in turn have contracted with LWC for warehouse storage services. As a result, LWC has an affirmative action plan, written six months ago by a consultant with expertise in the area. The consultant and Richard Castro, LWC's HR Director, recommended that an employment coordinator be hired to be affirmative action compliance officer. In that role, Frances is now dealing with one EEO problem in the company.

The firm has received notice that the state equal employment agency of Texas had selected one LWC location to be audited as part of a compliance review. During her second week with LWC she visited the location and its manager, Larry Jensen, to help him prepare for the audit. She performed an adverse impact analysis on employees at the location and on the selection ratio for applicants according to minority status and gender. The worst case of adverse impact was in the warehouse technician job, a second level job which requires some special equipment operations skills and experience. Over the past two years non-minorities were promoted

or hired in the job at a rate of 20% per number of applicants, whereas minority individuals were hired at a rate of 5%. Frances recognized that this disparity definitely constituted adverse impact. She then checked on the selection process for warehouse technician to ensure that all criteria used were related specifically to the job.

Frances had to search through several filing cabinets in order to locate all of the application blanks and selection interview documentation (if it existed) for each rejected minority applicant. Based on her review, Frances concluded that in eight separate instances, minority candidates were equally or more qualified than the non-minority individuals selected. She then met with Jensen, or his assistant manager who had conducted some of the interviews, to discuss those selection decisions which Frances knew the state agency investigator might examine. If, when the investigator conducts an analysis, there is inadequate justification, the firm could be liable for back pay with interest, and have to offer employment to some of the minority applicants not selected.

Much to Frances' dismay, she found out that another selection criterion was being used only with minority applicants—a credit check. According to Jensen, he had experienced several problems with minority employees having financial problems, having wages garnished, or being sued for non-payment of debts. Consequently, for any minority applicant, Jensen was obtaining credit reports. However, no credit checks were run on non-minority applicants. Frances knew that the credit check could not be considered a job-related and business necessity, because the warehouse technicians had no contact with financial affairs, except to check merchandise for proper receiving and shipping of correct quantities. Larry argued that the credit check was a business necessity because personal financial problems of employees led to absenteeism and took additional managerial time. But, when Frances asked him if non-minority employees had experienced financial problems, Larry said, "Well, maybe one or two, but not nearly as often and as many of them caused problems as the minorities. Therefore, I didn't see any need to waste the company's money getting credit reports on everyone because of one or two problems, when 20 or 30 of the minority workers have had financial problems."

Frances then asked Jensen if he used any other criteria to select warehouse technicians. Jensen told her that during the interview he always asked about lifting objects up to 70 pounds and if they had any previous back injuries. The firm also required all warehouse workers to get a physical exam prior to official hiring. If an applicant seemed to be acceptable after an interview, the applicant was taken to the warehouse and asked to maneuver a fork-lift truck through several aisles, off-load some pallets of merchandise to an upper shelf, and back the forklift truck to the starting point. Frances learned that if the forklift "test" could not be completed in five minutes, or if the applicant ran into a shelf or dropped the merchandise pallets, then he/she was rejected.

Frances, back at her office, is trying to decide how she and LWC should prepare for the upcoming EEO investigation. She meets with Castro and the corporate legal counsel tomorrow, so she does not have much time to develop her recommendations.

▲ QUESTIONS:

1. What EEO compliance strategies are highlighted in the case?
2. What approaches should be used to validate and/or defend the various selection "tests" that Jensen is using?
3. What course of action should Frances Miles, Richard Castro, and Larry Jensen follow in planning for the investigator's visit?

 Section 3: Solving a "Hiring Problem"

The hiring at Textel Company was not going well even though high unemployment in the area brought in many candidates. Mr. Simpson, the president of the 175-employee company, had always done the hiring himself. He had started the company 23 years ago and, in fact, had done very well selecting people over the years. Lately things seemed to have changed.

The turnover rate among new hires was too high. Out of the 20 hired in the last year only four were still with the company. Most of the people had been hired for a new job classification that required some knowledge of microcomputers and typical software packages. This was the first time the company had hired outside the traditional blue collar assembly jobs that had been the mainstay of the business for 23 years.

In fact, part of the problem was that Mr. Simpson was not entirely clear on all the specific duties in the new job classification. His production manager had made a convincing argument that this job would help the efficiency of the production operation, but Mr. Simpson didn't use a computer himself and wasn't conversant with either the software or hardware used on the new jobs.

Finally, in a move he had considered for some time, Mr. Simpson hired a Human Resources Manager and placed her in charge of all hiring (with concurrence by the department managers of the final hire). There were plenty of "people" related issues to attend to, he reasoned.

Marcia Lopez had previously been a personnel director at a small manufacturing company. The job at Textel was a move up for her in salary and a challenge as well. But there was *a lot of work to do.* The company had clearly gotten a bit too big to operate without someone who had some expertise in HR. Take the turnover problem among the people hired for the new job classification. That seemed like a problem that just needed some time and attention to fix. By calling several of those who had quit, Marcia discovered some of the reasons: they felt the job had been misrepresented to them initially, the computer equipment had not been as advertised, and they had other job opportunities even in the tight job market.

Marcia knew she had to start with the production manager—after all the new jobs had been his idea and were in his department. In a discussion with Jim Johnson, the production manager, she found that the people who had been hired were not well qualified for what they were being asked to do. She worked with Jim to get a clear description and specification for the job—something that had been lacking previously.

The next step was targeting recruiting efforts. She met with the two instructors of Business Computing at the community college in town. Both agreed to give her names of good students who planned to stay in town when they completed their AA degrees. She wrote to each person who was recommended inviting them to interview with Textel upon graduation. Further, she designed a newspaper ad that clearly described the qualifications necessary for a person to be a successful candidate. The ad would run as long as there was an unfilled position.

Marcia again worked with Jim Johnson (and Mr. Simpson added some ideas) in developing a structured interview format. The same predictive questions would be used with all candidates to allow comparison. Finally, a simple computing test was developed to screen those who did not know how to use the equipment or software. Over time this test screened out 50% of those who claimed to have the required expertise.

The final change was that Marcia began to check previous employment references on all those who made it to the final part of the selection process. She ran into the expected reluctance on the part of some previous employers, but most were willing to provide information on the applicant's performance in the previous job. Mr. Simpson typically had not had the time to check on previous employment references.

The results of these changes were favorable. In the next 12 months, Marcia hired 16 employees for the difficult–to–keep position and 13 of them were still employed.

▲ **Questions:**

1. What were the key actions Marcia took that differed from what Mr. Simpson had done?
2. Comment on the statement that "A lot of success in selection is simply doing your homework".
3. Why weren't the efforts 100% successful so that Marcia would have retained all 16 people she had hired?
4. Why did Mr. Simpson have so little luck hiring for the new job classification?

CASE Section 4: Competency Testing at General Dynamics*

The Land Systems Division of General Dynamics began a new, division–wide program for planning and organizing its manufacturing process. This new computer–based operating system, called Manufacturing Resource Planning (MRP II), integrates all major manufacturing functions. MRP II is a new way of directing the distribution and use of resources to meet General Dynamics Land Systems's manufacturing requirements.

Successful implementation of MRP II requires function–specific users to be thoroughly trained and competent before they are allowed to go on line and access the database. Indeed, MRP II experts cite inadequate training as the number–one reason for system failure.

A special division–wide taskforce representing key functions and plants was created to implement MRP II throughout the Land Systems Division. The taskforce included a Training and Education Coordinator who had responsibility for coordinating all training development, user qualification, and education activities that support MRP II implementation. More than 20 training courses were developed for hundreds of employees. The taskforce and top management mandated that no employee would be allowed access to the database without proper training. Employees would have to demonstrate that they could meet requirements for the appropriate function–specific training courses. As a result, competency exams were constructed to demonstrate user qualification.

Here is how General Dynamics conducted its competency testing:

1. General Dynamics contacted a consultant expert in competency testing to ensure the systematic validation of all written and practical exams.
2. An internal, division–wide MRP II Training and Education Coordinator coordinated the validation efforts and ensured consistency in approach and content.

---

*(Adapted from J.E. Smith and S. Merchant, "Using Competency Exams for Evaluating Training," *Training and Development Journal*, August 1990, pp. 68–69.)

3. The MRP II training and testing target group included some union–represented employees. The consultant and the Training and Education Coordinator met with union officials to explain the user–qualification process, the justification for using competency exams, and how the exams would be used. This session also addressed various issues and concerns raised by union representatives, including re-testing, failure in training, and seniority. Union officials were assured that employees would have an opportunity to retest and that failure would result in reassignment with no reduction in pay or loss of seniority.

4. A content validity manual, *MRP II Qualification Testing: A Manual for Trainers,* was developed and given to each trainer and subject matter expert. This manual was the basis for a workshop on content and validity and served as a reference document during the validation process.

5. Subject matter experts and designated trainers for each of the functional areas attended a one–day workshop on content validation. Before the training, experts were asked to read the content validity manual. During the workshop session, the experts engaged in a series of exercises that took them step by step through the content validation process.

6. The external consultant and the MRP II Training and Education Coordinator held individual meetings with the subject matter experts for each of the functional areas. The purpose of the meeting was to clarify roles, schedule sessions, and reinforce material covered in the manual and in the training.

7. Work sessions were held with subject matter experts to systematically develop and validate written and practical exams for each of the functional areas. Work sessions began with a review of training, content, and learning objectives. They continued through the seven steps of the content validity

process until the exam had been administered and analyzed and appropriate feedback given to the trainer. Whenever possible the development of competency exams were integrated with the development of the training material and content.

▲ THE RESULTS

The use of competency testing at General Dynamics has had positive side effects. First, the validation process helped many subject matter experts to systematically examine their training. Because the experts had little or no background in training or testing, developing content–valid exams helped them verify that their training was relevant and that only essential information was included in training.

Second, competency testing kept trainers on their toes during the actual training process. Success on a competency exam is as much a reflection of trainers as it is of trainees.

Thus, trainers were careful to prepare for and cover all relevant information during training and to avoid the common temptation to say to trainees, "Don't worry if you don't understand it now, you'll pick it up back on the job." When trainers knew they were being judged by exam results, they were more determined to deliver successful training. Finally, preliminary results indicate that competency testing has helped maintain training and testing competency and integrity regardless of plant location.

▲ QUESTIONS:

1. Would competency testing after training (as handled by General Dynamics) meet EEO requirements for promoting those who passed the exams?
2. What would be the objections to using a system like this with public school seniors?
3. Explain the role that job analyses must play in a system like this.

 ## Section 5: New Project Compensation Blues

Robles Company is the second largest wholesaler of office supplies in the area. Julie Phillips has been working for the Robles company as a sales trainer for exactly one year. She was responsible for training all of the sales people on procedures, quotas, and sales techniques.

Recently Julie's boss, Joe Dumars, Director of Sales, and his boss, Gerald Hawes, Vice President of Sales, have been discussing a new project, Officelink. The project has the potential to create a great amount of revenue for the organization. Officelink could be a factor in positioning Robles Company as number one in the area of sales. The project would allow area retailers to link up with Robles' mainframe computer system through personal computers from their offices, which would give them the ability to order supplies online. Officelink would simplify the ordering process, encourage repeat business, give immediate feedback concerning supply availability and restock inventory levels directly into the retailer's records kept on the personal computer.

Joe and Gerald knew that all the retailers would need to be trained on Officelink, and Julie was viewed as the logical choice to do the training. Because Julie had the experience and education to lead the project, the two upper managers asked her to help with the business plan and to research different aspects of Officelink. Julie, always willing to take on new responsibilities and try new challenges, jumped at the change to help. Even though this assignment would be in addition to her training duties, Julie felt that it presented a great opportunity. Gerald and Joe assured Julie that if the project was approved, she would fill the position of Officelink Director.

After two months of working on the project, Julie and the two managers presented the business plan to the Robles Board of Directors. The Board approved the project, and Joe and Julie began to work on the job description for the Officelink Director. Gerald checked with the Human Resources Department about posting the job. He explained that the person he wanted to fill the position had been doing the job of researching and working on the project from the beginning. However, Human Resources indicated that the position should be posted within the division. Gerald therefore posted a description of the job, pay grade, location, education, and skills required. Everyone in the division wondered why the job had been posted since Julie had already been working on the project.

There was also concern among some employees within the division because of the pay garde offered. This pay grade, a 14, was well above what many employees in the division were currently earning. Two employees in the division voiced their concerns about the pay grade to Human Resources. The pay grade listed was what Gerald felt the job was worth, given the revenue potential of Officelink and the responsibility and experience required. The pay grade had not been formally assigned or agreed upon by the Human Resources department.

At the Robles Company, pay grades are assigned by a committee of employees which evaluates job descriptions and determines which pay grade a position

will receive. This is done by looking at the responsibility, experience, and skills required for the position. When the committee met concerning the Officelink Director, they assigned a pay grade four grade levels lower (10) than that posted with the position. Gerald contacted the Vice President of Human Resources to discuss the pay grade and position decision. The Vice President of Human Resources asked him why the position had been posted in the first place, since a person had already been selected for the job. Gerald explained that he was instructed to post the position by someone in Human Resources. The Vice President agreed to reevaluate the position if some market comparison would show the position warranted a higher salary.

Market research in Chicago, and the surrounding areas was done to determine the current market salary for a comparable position. Results indicated that many positions were at the pay level proposed and above. No comparable positions paid less than what had been proposed. The committee met again with the benefit of this new information, and this time awarded a pay grade of eleven.

Gerald Hawes was not satisfied. He scheduled another meeting with the Vice President of Human Resources, but she was not willing to override the committee. The President of Robles was finally asked to make a decision on the proper salary level. The President decided to leave the pay grade at an 11, but to pay Julie the difference between her current pay grade, a 9, and pay grade 14. The net impact was to put her in a red-circled position.

The process took over 5 months. During this time, Julie worked at her regular job, as well as working on the new project. She was aware of all the controversy surrounding the new position and was very disappointed with the final pay grade assigned. She also discovered some jealous co-workers who believed Julie was overpaid. When the final decision was made, Julie agreed to take the job at an increase retroactive to the date the Board approved the position.

▲ QUESTIONS:

1. Discuss whether or not Julie should have begun to work on the project before she was hired for the position?

2. Discuss whether or not Gerald should have posted the position?

3. What is the purpose of using pay grades and did the system get in the way of the objective in this case?

Section 6: Success vs. Failure to Follow Rules

Owning a business had been a dream of Bob and Sue Rowlands. After several years of planning, the time was right to open their own computer store. The loans were in place, suppliers had been arranged and a list of potential clients had been drawn up. As expected, business began slowly. The primary market for this "mom and pop" operation was small industrial firms, but retail sales also played a part. After two years of hard work, they were in the black.

Bob and Sue investigated the possibility of buying into a franchise, after several years of mediocre profits. They thought better earnings could be expected because of lower wholesale costs and improved marketing techniques that came with being a part of a franchises. They deliberated several months before they decided to buy into a successful national franchise.

In the beginning, the husband and wife team were the only company employees. Bob ordered and solicited business sales, while Sue took care of the books and helped with retail sales when needed. As a result of buying into the franchise, their business grew and so did their need for additional sales help. Recruiting was very difficult. Advertisements in the paper went unanswered for months, and leads at the area's technical schools dried up, and they were becoming desperate.

Their daughter knew a young man named Rick Smithson. He had a background as a sales representative for a herbicide manufacturer and experience with computers; he seemed to be a likely candidate. Although he was not qualified exactly as they would have preferred for the sales position, Rick was hired. Bob and Sue felt they probably wouldn't find a better candidate in the area, given their recruiting results, and that with some intense training, Rick should be able to learn the computer business without too much trouble. Rick was sent to several conferences that gave in-depth training on personal computers, software packages, and computer repair. The training came easily to him because of his interest in the subject.

Initially, the pay scale was structured to allow Rick a base salary while he was training. After training was over and he began selling, a base salary plus a commission on his total sales was to be the compensation method. Rick seemed pleased with the arrangement because he could affect his paycheck by the amount of effort he was willing to put into it.

By contacting acquaintances from his previous job, Rick established an impressive network of clients. Many of these clients referred other customers which further increased sales. The owners were delighted with how well Rick was working out and because he was having so much success with the business market, they decided to let him take over the entire segment, only stepping in when requested. Bob set to work on improving the retail side of the business. He developed new marketing strategies specific to the demographics of the area and offered free informational meetings that were well attended by the public. Slowly, the retail segment began to see an improvement in sales.

The owners did not forsee their market expanding greatly in this area because potential was somewhat limited, but they expected business to remain steady as their clients upgraded their systems. They were generally content with the way the business was progressing. As part of their strategy to keep costs low, Bob and Sue avoided hiring anyone else. When necessary, other family members would work at the store to help out.

Business went along as usual for several years with profits remaining relatively constant which was acceptable to the owners. Bob used a hands-off approach with Rick, as he had proven himself to be an exceptional employee. Rick's schedule kept him out of the office most of the time. He stopped by only to turn in orders to pick up equipment that was ready to be installed.

Upon arriving at the office one morning, there was a message for Bob to call one of Rick's clients, Mr. Barrett from Crystal Plastics, because Rick was on a two-week vacation. Mr. Barrett was inquiring about the software package and printer he was supposed to have received with the delivery of his local area network system. Bob thought this sounded odd, so he told Mr. Barret he would check and then call him back.

Bob referred to his copy of the bill of sale and found no mention of a printer or software package. He couldn't understand how Rick could have forgotten to record these items on the bill of sale. To find out specifically what should have been delivered, he called Mr. Barrett again. Bob told Mr. Barrett that Rick must have all the documentation with him, so he needed some clarification as to what was missing from the delivery. Mr. Barrett stated that a dot matrix printer and the Column Pro accounting software package were missing. These had been promised as an incentive to buy the network.

Bob was shocked because the company did not offer "incentives" to buy. He wondered how long this practice had been going on. He and his wife had always prided themselves on low prices with no gimmicks and Rick knew that. Sales incentives were simply not a part of their business policy. Nor did the owners want it to be. With their current inventory/ordering system, however, he saw how easily this practice could be hidden. Software was bought in large quantities and kept in the storeroom. Restocking occurred only when the shelf was low. A similar situation existed with the inexpensive printers. More expensive equipment was brought in only when orders had been placed. No tracking of inventory was done because Bob and Sue trusted the integrity of the only non-family member of the firm.

To determine the extent of the practice, Sue compared actual sales quantities to inventory ordered the past year. Because this comparison had never been done before, it took several days. During that time, Bob

called several other accounts to inquire if incentives had been offered as a part of the sales package. He found out that it was occurring frequently. Sue quantified the sales losses to be in excess of $10,000, but Rick had generated over $250,000 in sales. He had been giving away, at minimum, a software package per purchase.

Rick was to arrive back from vacation the following day. The owners had to make an important HR decision overnight.

▲ **QUESTIONS:**

1. What caused Rick to deviate from the established policy?
2. Why did it take so long to discover Rick's use of incentives?
3. Discuss whether or not a valuable employee should be lost by enforcing appropriate policies.
4. What alternatives are available?
5. If you were Bob and Sue, which alternative would you choose and why?

1. PSP = TQM

ABSOLUTELY, POSITIVELY, INTO THE 1990s:
A CASE STUDY OF THE HUMAN RESOURCE DIVISION AT FEDERAL EXPRESS

Federal Express saw the 1980s drawing to a close as it assimilated the Flying Tiger organization and continued to pursue its goal of building a global express transportation network. Confident that its People-Service-Profit philosophy would be up to the challenges of the 1990s, the company made an auspicious entry into the new decade. In 1990, it was named the first winner of the Malcolm Baldrige National Quality Award in the service category. Chairman Frederick W. Smith observed that this prestigious award was not the realization of a goal but a "license to practice."

A primary principle of the quality process is continuous improvement. This has been the case with Human Resource programs at Federal Express as the company has moved into the early 1990s. Constant review and adjustments to the Guaranteed Fair Treatment Procedure (GFTP), Survey Feedback Action (SFA), disability programs, the Leadership Institute, PRISM, and the Leadership Evaluation Awareness Program (LEAP) have been pivotal to the company's success.

Two years after winning the Malcolm Baldrige National Quality Award, Federal Express found itself facing one of the key challenges for which its human resource policies and practices had prepared it: the restructuring of its European organization. Despite challenges of this type, Chairman and CEO Frederick W. Smith and Chief Personnel Officer James A. Perkins were determined that the company's "people-first" philosophy would remain paramount.

To meet this goal, HR programs, plans, and processes had to be reviewed, evaluated, and optimized. New systems had to be developed to address the changing workforce and regulatory environment and to enhance the effectiveness of organizational structures. Quality improvement principles were incorporated into all planning and development activities as a means to get closer to customers (both internal and external) and to provide better value at lower cost.

▲ THE QUALITY COMMITMENT

The sound business philosophy and the HR strategies that were put into place in the early years at Federal Ex-

press continue to thrive in the 1990s. When he founded Federal Express in 1973, Smith coined the three-word corporate philosophy "People-Service-Profit," or P-S-P.

The company celebrated its twentieth anniversary in 1993 and this P-S-P philosophy still provides the foundation for everything done at Federal Express. The company's leaders believe that if you meet the needs of employees, they will, in turn, feel empowered to deliver the impeccable service demanded by the customers who provide the profitability necessary to secure the future.

Federal Express earned the 1991 Malcolm Baldrige National Quality Award – the first service company to receive this honor in the service category. Winning this award reinforced HR policies at Federal Express because it showed that others also realized that commitment to P-S-P had paid off. The Baldrige examiners cited a number of HR programs as worthy of recognition: excellent in-house training programs, promotion from within, incentive programs, reward and recognition programs, internal grievance procedures, and the attitude survey called Survey-Feedback Action. They noted that employees are empowered to make decisions and to take appropriate risks to serve customers, even if it means going beyond the usual procedures. Because employee satisfaction is such a critical part of quality, employees are encouraged to be the best they can be, to do things right the first time, and to demonstrate a people-first attitude in everything they do.

Quality has been a pivotal component at FedEx for many years. In 1984, Quality Equals Productivity, or Q=P became the new management paradigm. This meant that managers and employees had to constantly examine all processes to simultaneously improve service and lower costs. Starting in 1988, corporate-wide quality training was implemented from the top down. Initially, FedEx's management received QIP (Quality Improvement Process) training; they, in turn, trained 85,000 employees in quality terminology and methods.

In 1988, the Human Resource Development department created Federal Express's Quality Academy. Its curriculum includes TQA (The Quality Advantage) and QAT (Quality Action Teams) courses for managers and quality professionals, team-leading and facilitation skills, quality management skills, and Statistical Process Control (SPC). Today, interactive video instruction (IVI) is available to all employees for basic quality courses. In addition, more than 75 quality professionals work in both staff and operating divisions, teaching courses in quality methodology. These specialists also assist quality team activity, promote success stories and serve as consultants for special corporate-wide quality initiatives. It is their mission to customize quality training, communication, measurement and reward approaches according to the needs of their respective divisions. The quality effort is paying off. More than 700 ongoing QAT's focus on everything from matters as local as re-organizing a warehouse to those as global as creating a major software environment for the company's on-line COSMOS package tracking system.

To ensure customer satisfaction, teams work to streamline processes. A cross-divisional team based in the Finance Department revised the procedure for re-funding customer overpayments, reducing the process from 32 steps, requiring eight employees, to three steps requiring one employee. Customer phone calls concerning refunds decreased by 70%.

To increase customer satisfaction a customer/supplier alignment process was designed and implemented. Its purpose is to build effective working relationships and encourage clear communication of needs and expectations between internal suppliers and their customers within the organization. The process is built around three key questions posed by suppliers to customers:

▲ What do you need from me?
▲ What do you do with what I give you?
▲ What are the gaps between what I give you and what you need?

Chairman Smith continues to emphasize ongoing quality improvement as an unequivocal priority. "At Federal Express, we believe that the key to survival in the globally competitive '90s and beyond is a total focus on quality, and on value-added, customer-driven service," he says.

As part of its effort to measure quality performance, executive management decided to implement a Service Quality Indicator (SQI) report. Before implementation of the SQI, service had been measured in percentages. With the SQI, service is measured in absolutes.

Produced daily, this report measures twelve categories of service failure, assigning weighted values to them of one through ten. As an indicator of customer satisfaction, SQI supports two quality goals: 100% customer satisfaction after every transaction and 100% service performance on every package handled. CEO Smith has repeatedly stated: "Our service standard is 100% plus. Ninety-eight or ninety-nine percent may be fine for other human endeavors. Our chosen profession is not among them. Our customers expect faultless service . . . all the time!"

Service Quality Indicator failure points are compiled daily and each week the results are posted for review. Many departments and divisions have borrowed the SQI concept, developing their own measurement systems which are used to improve service to their internal and external customers (See Exhibit I.)

▲ APPLYING QUALITY PRINCIPLES TO HUMAN RESOURCE PRACTICES

Merger of EEO Investigative Procedure With Guaranteed Fair Treatment Procedure

In February 1993, the Employee Relations and EEO departments of the Human Resource Division announced the merger of two employee complaint processes for U.S. employees: the internal process for

Exhibit I

Service Quality Indicator Categories and Their Weights

Lost Packages	10
Damaged Packages	10
Missed Pick Up	10
Wrong Day Late	5
Overgoods	5
Complaints Reopened	5
Right Day Late	1
Abandoned Calls	1
Missing POD's	1
Inv. Adj. Requested	1
International	1
Traces	1

EEO complaints (Equal Employment Opportunity) and GFTP (Guaranteed Fair Treatment Procedure). The internal EEO complaint process deals with employee complaints regarding allegations of discrimination due to race, color, sex, religion, national origin, age, disability/handicap, or veteran status.

Previously, when an employee filed an EEO complaint, an EEO specialist working in concert with the legal department conducted an investigation, recommending what actions, if any, were appropriate for management to take. This was a lengthy process with the average case taking 120 days to resolve.

Under the new combined system, once a complaint is identified as alleging a discrimination complaint, the employee's managing director conducts the investigation and, within 30 days, makes recommendations in accordance with guidelines of the GFTP/EEO Combined Process Policy (See Exhibit II.) The Employee Relations department consults with the managing director in all phases of the process and reviews the final decision, as does the legal department. If the complainant's managing director and representatives from Employee Relations and Legal do not agree on an appropriate recommendation, the Chief Personnel Officer and the General Counsel make the final decision regarding resolution. For other complaints related to fair treatment issues (selection, disciplinary actions, terminations, etc.), the GFTP has remained essentially the same three-step process as outlined in the previous study with final adjudication by the Appeals Board.

Major considerations in merging the GFTP and the EEO procedures were the time it was taking to resolve cases; the anticipated benefits of the new system; a dramatic change in the legal environment due to the recent enactment of the Americans with Disabilities Act and the Civil Rights Act of 1991; and the need to better position the company to respond to demographic changes in the workforce, as well as the overall need to control general and administrative costs.

The benefits of the combined system include: (a) quicker resolution of the cases, approximately 30 days versus 120 days under the old system and (b) increased management involvement at the director level leading to reductions in the systemic causes of such complaints. In the short time the processes have been combined, fewer EEO complaints have been filed. Involving managing directors in the process has focused attention on the root causes of discrimination and a more conscientious approach has developed to elimi-

nate the underlying behaviors or attitudes which caused the problem in the first place.

Jim Perkins, Chief Personnel Officer, recently stated: "One of the major reasons Federal Express is so highly thought of in American business is its innovative people policies. Perhaps the most notable of all is the GFTP. For years other businesses and business scholars have come to FedEx to study and/or replicate this system for handling employee complaints. Fusing the EEO investigative process into the structure of the GFTP is a stroke of innovation in the area of employee relations. The GFTP has always delivered what it claimed, the expeditious resolution of employee complaints. The new combined process will extend this tradition to the area of discrimination issues." By combining these two processes, Federal Express again has established precedent by reformulating its complaint resolution policies and procedures to adjust to changes in the larger business and legal environment.

Survey Feedback Action Process Goes On-Line

Evidence of the HR Division's efforts to continuously improve its service to its internal customers is also apparent from changes made to its Survey-Feedback-Action (SFA) program. In March of 1992, after being tested the previous fall, an on-line survey was made available to more than 73,000 U.S.-based employees. The on-line system has been well received by employees. Faster and more economical than the paper and pencil SFA, its saves the company approximately $500,000 a year in administrative expenses.

The On-Line SFA System is a user-friendly computerized version of the "old" SFA system. Employees all over the U.S. can enter their responses to the SFA items via over 118,000 terminals connected to the Information Management System (IMS). Also, employees take the SFA individually at a time convenient to their own schedules rather than in scheduled group meetings.

Another advantage of the On-Line SFA System is quicker turn-around time for the feedback reports to managers. Reports are now available in two weeks, rather than the previous 59 days. Managers can now meet with their employees while their responses are still fresh in their minds and develop action plans to address any areas of concern. On-line SFA contains the same 29 questions questions as did the original paper and pencil version.

Exhibit II

GFTP/EEO Complaint Process Policy

GFTP/EEO COMPLAINT PROCESS POLICY

The GFTP/EEO policy affirms your right to appeal fair treatment issues through a process of systematic review by progressively higher levels of management. However, employment discrimination issues will be resolved at the first level of the GFTP/EEO, with review by the Employee Relations, Personnel, and Legal departments. The GFTP/EEO Manual contains procedures to follow when employment discrimination allegations are raised at any level of the GFTP.

An employee's right to participate within the guidelines of the GFTP/EEO process is guaranteed, although the outcome is not assured to be in the employee's favor.

Fair Treatment Issues

1 MANAGEMENT REVIEW

- **COMPLAINANT**
  - Submits written complaint to management with a copy to Personnel within 7 calendar days of the occurrence.
- **MANAGER, SENIOR MANAGER, MANAGING DIRECTOR**
  - Review all relevant information.
  - Hold a telephone conference and/or meeting with the complainant.
  - Make decision to either uphold, modify, or overturn management's action.
  - Communicate their decision in writing to complainant and Personnel matrix.

NOTE: When multiple levels of management exist, a consensus decision will be rendered. All of the above should occur within 10 calendar days of receipt of the complaint, unless written notice of time extension is provided to the complainant, Employee Relations, and Personnel.

2 OFFICER REVIEW

- **COMPLAINANT**
  - Submits written complaint to an officer (vice president or senior vice president) of the division within 7 calendar days of the Step 1 decision.
- **VICE PRESIDENT AND SENIOR VICE PRESIDENT**
  - Review all relevant information.
  - Conduct additional investigation, when necessary.
  - Make decision to either uphold, overturn, modify management's action, or initiate a Board of Review.
  - Communicate their decision in writing to complainant with copy to Personnel matrix and the complainant's management.

NOTE: When multiple levels of management exist, a consensus decision will be rendered. All of the above should occur within 10 calendar days of receipt of the complaint, unless written notice of time extension is provided to the complainant, Employee Relations, and Personnel.

3 EXECUTIVE REVIEW

- **COMPLAINANT**
  - Submits written complaint within 7 calendar days of the Step 2 decision to the Employee Relations Department who investigates and prepares the GFTP case file for Appeals Board review.
- **APPEALS BOARD**
  - Reviews all relevant information.
  - Makes decision to either uphold, overturn, initiate a Board of review, or take other appropriate action.
  - All of the above should occur within 14 calendar days of the complaint, unless written notice of time extensions are provided to the complainant and Personnel.
  - Responds in writing to complainant within 3 calendar days of the decision with copy to Personnel matrix and the complainant's chain of command.

Discrimination Issues

1 MANAGEMENT REVIEW

- **COMPLAINANT**
  - Submits Employee Information Packet to management, Personnel, or Employee Relations with a copy to Personnel matrix within 7 days of the alleged discrimination or consistent with applicable law.
- **MANAGING DIRECTOR**
  - Upon receipt of employee information packet from manager, senior manager, or Personnel, notifies Employee Relations of complaint.
  - Holds a telephone conference and/or meeting with the complainant.
  - Conducts investigation under the direction of the Legal Department.
  - Obtains technical support, advice, and counsel from Employee Relations, Personnel, and Legal throughout the investigation.
  - Prepares EEO Investigative Report.
  - Obtains approval from appropriate supporting staff groups regarding resolution of the complaint.
  - Communicates decision in writing to complainant with copy to Employee Relations, Personnel, and Legal.
  - All of the above should occur within 30 calendar days from the start of the investigation unless written notice of time extension is provided to the complainant, Employee Relations, and Personnel.

NOTE: This decision cannot be appealed.

FOR MORE DETAILS CONTACT YOUR PERSONNEL REPRESENTATIVE OR EMPLOYEE RELATIONS.

Continuing emphasis on quality called for the addition of the following quality-related questions:

30. My manager provides leadership/support to the Quality Improvement Process.

31. My manager emphasizes quality improvement and customer satisfaction.

32. My manager uses quality tools and measurements in my workgroup (brainstorming, Pareto charts, force-field analysis, etc.).

In addition, up to seven local questions may be included to cover areas of concern specific to a local work group.

Human Capital Management Program (HCMP)

With increasing concern about worker injuries and rising health care costs, management throughout Federal Express saw a need for a better and formal process for managing employees who were on medical leaves of absence. A cross-divisional task force was formed and,

in March 1992, the Human Capital Management Program (HCMP) was adopted. The HCMP involves front-line managers in the monitoring of employees who have become ill or injured on- or off-the-job, while utilizing the various benefits associated with medical leave. HR policies covering medical leaves of absence were extensively revised, detailing steps that management should take at the onset of an employee's illness and/or injury. Particular attention was given to compliance with the Americans with Disabilities Act (ADA).

Based on the study of the first six month's activities, a cost saving resulting from process improvements of nearly $1.6 million was realized. Additional benefits include improved employee morale through enhanced communication during medical leave, improved productivity through earlier return of employees from leave, reduced risk of employees developing "disability mentality," and better coordination of workers' compensation benefits. All management has been trained in the administration of this program.

Exhibit III

Orion - Image Station

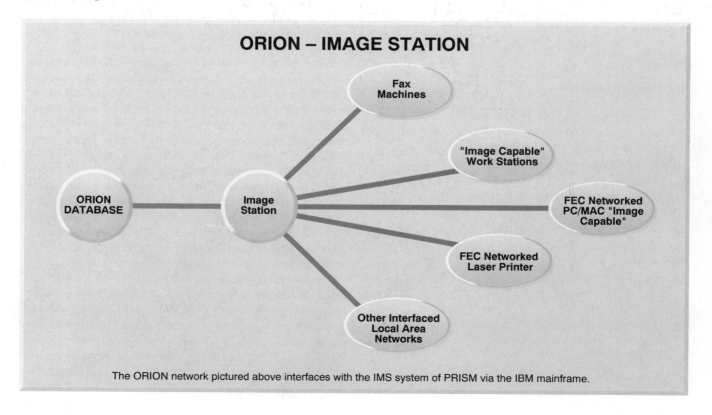

The ORION network pictured above interfaces with the IMS system of PRISM via the IBM mainframe.

ORION System Improves Personnel Information Management

Perhaps the most significant enhancement to PRISM, the on-line personnel information and management system, is the recently-developed ORION (Optically Recorded Information On-Line Network). This new technology reads and copies information from any format, such as computer text, books, newspapers and reports, stores it and, through its compatibility with a variety of information systems, renders it readily available. ORION was developed utilizing a Wang Imaging System platform coupled with an application program interface (API) residing in an IMS (Information Management Systems) region on Federal Express's mainframe. (See Exhibit III.) ORION's paperless operation greatly expedites the processing of corporate information required by government agencies, such as the Department of Transportation (DOT), the Federal Aviation Administration (FAA) and the Office of Federal Contract Compliance (OFCCP), as well as all personnel records and enters it into PRISM by allowing the bi-directional transfer of traditional hard copy documents to and from an optically recorded image data base. It also provides Federal Express management and HR professionals a secured access to personnel records worldwide via 118,000 terminals dispersed throughout the system. With ORION, an employee's personnel file —(performance reviews, résumés, training, etc.)—has become easily accessible without the necessity of key data entry (See Exhibit IV.)

LEAP

As part of the quality assessment of HR programs at Federal Express, a recent study was conducted of the Leadership Evaluation and Awareness Program (LEAP), a case discussed in the sixth edition. The program's effectiveness compared the turnover percentage of LEAP endorsed managers entering and leaving management within 20 months to the percentage of managers entering and leaving management in the 20 months prior to implementation of LEAP. There was a significant reduction in management turnover — 10.7% for non-LEAP managers 20 months prior to LEAP vs. 1.7% for LEAP endorsed managers.

Case Study: European Restructuring Puts P-S-P Philosophy to the Test

In March 1992, Federal Express realized it was facing one of the most difficult periods in its history. A company which prides itself on its strong People-Service-Profit philosophy and its "No Layoff Philosophy" found itself faced with a difficult decision. Discontinuing its intra-European service would cause approximately 6,600 well-qualified and well-trained employees in Continental Europe and the U.K. to be declared redundant.

What were the reasons behind the decision to downsize in Europe? The company's aggressive international expansion in the Eighties was based on anticipation of an exploding European market in 1992. Instead, many of Europe's major economies found themselves in a deepening recession, and Federal Express was experiencing continued international losses. Intra-country and intra-European systems modeled after the U.S. domestic network, were responsible for a disproportionate share of expenses in Europe. The market in Europe for express traffic had not developed as quickly as FedEx had hoped. In fact the focus on shipping packages around Europe was drawing attention away from the development of an intercontinental system.

Continued international losses put a strain on the value of Federal Express stock. Stockholders were disappointed in the return on their investment, something they had come to expect based on past increases in the market value of their shares. Continued international losses could also affect the company's bond or credit rating, which would in turn affect Federal Express's

Exhibit IV

Orion Support Features

ORION is capable of supporting the overall needs of the business in the following ways:

▲ Quantifiable time saver because of immediate, on-line access

▲ Ability of other systems to mesh into it to support company operations

▲ Enhanced efforts to "paperless" concept

▲ Provides employees automated, user-friendly system

▲ Automatically updates and cues management after entry allowing timely processing of necessary changes

▲ Enables the corporation to focus on better service to its customers through training and testing features

ability to borrow money to finance the company's operation and continued growth.

The business requirement to attain profitability, however, did not make the decision to restructure the European organization an easy one for FedEx. Smith and Chief Personnel Officer Perkins were determined to assist all redundant employees in their transition to other employment.

To achieve this, while abiding by the labor laws of each country, Federal Express's human resource staff undertook a unique course. Advertisements were placed in the news and trade media inviting other employers to contact Federal Express to take advantage of the availability of this pool of experienced and highly-trained personnel. It also worked closely with job centers (similar to U.S.-based state employment agencies) in searching for vacancies in other companies for these employees.

This effort was conducted jointly by line management and the HR function. After redundancies were announced, an employment opportunities bulletin was sent out twice a week. Job clubs, managed by a senior manager and a personnel manager, met one day a week to counsel with staff and to demonstrate the company's continuing commitment.

The FedEx experiment, possibly the first of its kind, was a success. Once advertisements were placed, offices were set up to handle calls from prospective employers. The advertising campaign was well received with many HR managers notifying Federal Express of vacancies. In the Belgian headquarters, more than 80 companies responded to the ad, offering a total of 600 jobs.

The entire downsizing process was accomplished, remarkably, in less than two months. Since parts of the company's operation were not being completely closed, Federal Express developed a selection grid to assist in the placement of employees into those areas remaining open. The selection grid took into account length of service, skills experience, disciplinary record, and the employee's score in a recent performance appraisal. Employees were also given an opportunity to appeal if they felt the selection criteria had been unfairly applied.

For employees selected for redundancy, their redundancy payments were calculated and efforts made to secure jobs for as many as possible. Also, training programs were offered which covered resumé preparation, writing application letters, interview techniques and information on dealing with the financial implications of unemployment.

Federal Express's efforts in handling redundancies received widespread recognition. The media, for ex-

ample the *London Sunday Times,* praised the company for the way in which it dealt with a complex situation.

FedEx has cut international losses nearly in half, from $359 million in 1992 to $182 million in fiscal 1993. This was the first decrease in international losses since international service began in June of 1985. European operations were restructured at the end of fiscal 1992, and to date the focus on intercontinental traffic has produced better than expected results, with International Priority Service volumes exceeding monthly plans. This European network, along with extensive operations in Asia and the Pacific, Canada, Latin America, and the Caribbean, is the perfect partner for U.S. domestic operations. Together they provide Federal Express with an intercontinental express delivery system unparalleled in the world.

TOWARD THE 21st CENTURY

In its first twenty years, Federal Express has achieved a staggering record of growth. It has also overcome notable setbacks along the way, most recently its European restructuring. Through it all, the company has been anchored by its ongoing commitment to the People-Service-Profit philosophy.

As it looks to the 21st century, the company's approach to Human Resources is best reflected in the mission statement of the Personnel division:

> The Personnel Division is dedicated to maintaining a global environment consistent with P–S–P, quality standards, local culture, and relevant laws and regulations in which employees are motivated to high levels of achievement of corporate goals, attainment of career objectives, and 100% customer satisfaction.

▲ **Questions:**

1. Discuss how integrated corporate culture at Federal Express is integrated into the various HR activities.

2. How do the activities of the Personnel/HR division at Federal Express include both the administrative/operational role and the strategic HR role?

3. Identify how the various programs at Federal Express reinforce the importance of employees rights and relations in HR management.

4. Identify how each of the six major HR activities listed in figure 1-5 (page 13) appear as part of the case.

5. Discuss why Federal Express HR policies and practices had to be adapted to reflect additional factors present when operating internationally.

6. Compare and contrast the various HR activities at Federal Express with those of an organization at which you have worked.

7. How would you go about evaluating the effectiveness of the various HR activities at Federal Express? What do you think the results would show?

FEDERAL EXPRESS CORPORATION FACT SHEET

Description:	World's largest express transportation company
Began Operations:	April 1973
Worldwide Headquarters:	Memphis Tennessee
Principal Officer:	Frederick W. Smith
	Chairman, President, and CEO
Revenues:	$7.8 billion (Fiscal 1993)
Countries Served:	186
Worldwide Aircraft Fleet:	Total of 465
	McDonnel Douglas MD-11s –11 (5 on order)
	Boeing 747s–6
	McDonnell Douglas DC-10s –30
	Boeing 727s–170
	Cessna 208s–216
	Fokker F-27s–32
	Airbus A300–25 on order
Daily Global Lift Capacity:	Approximately 12.8 Million lbs.
Worldwide Service Centers:	Approximately 1,400
Worldwide Drop Boxes:	Approximately 29,500
Average Daily Pkg Volume:	1.7 million worldwide
Average Call Volume:	More than 325,000 calls daily
Worldwide Vehicle Fleet:	Approximately 28,000
Miles Driven Per Day (U.S.):	More than 2.5 million miles

(090193)

Published with the permission of Federal Express Corporation, 1993. All reprint rights remain with Federal Express Corporation. No reproduction of the case may be made except with the written consent of Federal Express Corporation, Memphis, TN.
Author Background: Carolyn B. Freeman currently works as a Senior Specialist in the Public Relations Department of Federal Express Corporation. With Federal Express since 1980, she has a B.S. in Education, M.A. in Sociology, and J.D.
Special thanks for support in the development of this case are expressed to James A. Perkins, Kathy H. Starkey, Patricia B. Dhority, and Celia A. Strang of Federal Express Corporation.

GLOSSARY

Ability Tests assess the skills that individuals have learned.

Active Practice occurs when trainees perform job-related tasks and duties during training.

Adverse Selection means that only higher-risk employees select and use certain benefits.

Affirmative Action occurs when employees identify problem areas, set goals, and take positive steps to guarantee equal employment opportunities for people within a protected class.

Affirmative Action Plan (AAP) is a formal document that the organization makes available for review by employees and enforcement officers.

Applicant Pool consists of all persons who are actually evaluated for selection.

Applicant Population is a subset of the labor force population that is available for selection using a particular recruiting approach.

Aptitude Tests measure general ability to learn or acquire a skill.

Arbitration is a means of deciding a dispute in which negotiating parties submit the dispute to a third party to make a decision.

Assessment Centers are collections of instruments and exercises designed to diagnose a person's development needs.

Attitude Survey is a special type of questionnaire that focuses on employees' feelings and beliefs about their jobs and the organization.

Authorization Card is signed by an employee to designate a union as his/her collective bargaining agent.

Availability Analysis identifies the number of protected-class members available to work in the appropriate labor market in given jobs.

Bargaining Unit is composed of all employees eligible to select a single union to represent and bargain collectively for them.

Behavior Modeling is copying someone else's behavior.

Behavioral Description Interviews require applicants to give specific examples of how they have performed or handled a problem in the past.

Benchmark Job is one performed by several individuals with similar duties that are relatively stable, requiring similar KSAs, and found in many other organizations.

Benchmarking is comparing specific measures of performance against data on those measures in "best practice" organizations.

Benefit is an indirect reward given to an employee or group of employees as a part of organizational membership.

Bona Fide Occupational Qualification (BFOQ) is a legitimate reason why an employer can exclude persons on otherwise illegal bases of consideration.

Business Necessity is a practice necessary for safe and efficient organizational operations.

Career is the sequence of work-related positions occupied throughout a person's life.

Central Tendency Error is rating persons in a narrow band in the middle of the rating scale.

Checklist uses a list of statements or words that are checked by raters.

Closed Shop requires individuals to join a union before they can be hired.

Co-Determination is a practice whereby union or worker representatives are given positions on a company's board of directors.

Co-Payment requires employees to pay a portion of costs of both insurance premiums and medical care.

Coaching is the daily training and feedback given to employees by immediate supervisors.

Collective Bargaining is the process whereby representatives of management and workers negotiate over wages, hours, and other terms and conditions of employment.

Commission is compensation computed as a percentage of sales in units or dollars.

Compra-Ratio is a pay level divided by the midpoint of the pay range.

Comparable Worth requires that jobs with comparable knowledge, skills, and abilities be paid similarly even if actual duties differ significantly.

Comparable Worth requires that jobs with comparable levels of knowledge, skill, and ability should be paid similarly even if actual duties differ significantly.

Compensable Factor is one used to identify a job value that is commonly present throughout a group of jobs.

Compensation Committee usually is a subgroup of the Board of Directors who are not officers of the firm.

Compensatory Time-Off is time off given in lieu of payment for time worked.

Complaint is an indication of employee dissatisfaction that has not taken the formal grievance settlement route.

Compressed Workweek is one in which a full week's work is accomplished in fewer than five days.

Computer Hardware is the actual equipment used, such as computers, disk drives, monitors, printers, and optiscanners.

Computer Software contains the program instructions that tell the computer how to process the data.

Concessionary Bargaining occurs when the union agrees to reduce wages, benefits, or other factors during collective bargaining.

Conciliation occurs when a third party attempts to keep the union and management negotiators talking so that they voluntarily can reach a settlement.

Concurrent Validity tests current employees and correlates the scores with their performance ratings.

Construct Validity involves the relationship between an abstract characteristic and job performance.

Constructive Discharge occurs when an employer deliberately makes conditions intolerable in an attempt to get the employee to quit.

Content Validity is a logical, nonstatistical method used to identify the KSAs and other characteristics necessary to perform a job.

Contingent Workers are employed on a temporary or part-time basis.

Contrast Error is the tendency to rate people relative to other people rather than to performance standards.

Contributory Plan is one in which the money for pension benefits is paid in by both employees and employers.

Correlation Coefficient is an index number giving the relationship between a predictor and a criterion variable.

Cost/Benefit Analysis is comparing costs of training with the benefits received to see which is greater.

Craft Union is one in which its members do one type of work, often using specialized skills and training.

Criterion-Related Validity assumes that a test is the predictor of how well an individual will perform on the job.

Database is the stored data used by the computer.

Decertification is a process whereby a union is removed as the representative of a group of employees.

Defined-Benefit Plan is one in which an employee is promised a pension amount based on age and service.

Defined-Contribution Plan is one in which the employer makes an annual payment to an employee's pension account.

Differential Piece-Rate System pays employees one piece-rate wage if they produce less than a standard output and a higher piece-rate wage if they produce more than the standard.

Disabled Person is someone who has a physical or mental impairment that substantially limits that person in some major life activities, has a record of, or is regarded as having, such an impairment.

Discipline is a form of training that enforces organizational rules.

Discrimination (EEOC Definition) is the use of any test that adversely affects hiring, promotion, transfer or any other employment or membership opportunity of classes unless the test has been validated and is job related, and/or an employer can demonstrate that alternative hiring, transfer, or promotion procedures are unavailable.

Disparate Impact occurs when there is a substantial underrepresentation of protected-class members as a result of employment decisions that work to their disadvantages.

Disparate Treatment occurs when protected-class members are treated differently from others.

Distributive Justice refers to the perceived fairness of the amounts given for performance.

Downsizing is reducing the size of an organizational workforce.

Draw is an amount advanced and repaid from future commissions earned by the employee.

Due Process gives one the opportunity to defend oneself against charges.

Duty is a work segment composed of several tasks that are performed by an individual.

Earned-Time Plan is one that combines all time-off benefits into a total number of hours or days that employees can take off with pay.

Electronic Mail (E-MAIL) is a computerized system of sending and receiving messages for individuals and organizations.

Employee Assistance Program (EAP) provides counseling and other help to employees having emotional, physical, or other personal problems.

Employee Skills Inventory is a compilation of data on the skills and characteristics of employees.

Employee Stock Ownership Plan (ESOP) is a plan whereby employees gain stock ownership in the organization for which they work.

Employment-At-Will (EAW) is a common-law doctrine stating that employers have the right to hire, fire, demote, or promote whomever they choose, unless there is a law or contract to the contrary.

Encapsulated Development occurs when an individual learns new methods and ideas in a development course and returns to a work unit that is still bound by old attitudes and methods.

Environmental Scanning is the process of studying the environment of the organization to pinpoint opportunities and threats.

Equal Employment Opportunity (EEO) states that individuals should have equal treatment in all employment-related actions.

Equity is the perceived fairness of what the person does (inputs) compared with what the person receives (outcomes).

Ergonomics is the proper design of the work environment to address the physical demands experienced by people.

Essential Job Functions are the fundamental job duties of the employment position that an individual with a disability holds or desires, but they do not include marginal functions of the position.

Executive Order is an order issued by the President of the U.S. to provide direction to government departments on a specific issue or area.

Exempt Employees are those who are not required to be paid overtime under the Fair Labor Standards Act because their positions are classified as executive, administrative, professional, or outside sales.

Exit Interview asks those leaving the organization to identify the reasons for their departure.

Expatriate is a person working in a country who is not a citizen of that country.

Experiment involves studying how something responds when changes are made in one or more variables or conditions.

Extinction is the absence of a response to a situation.

Federation is a group of autonomous national and international unions.

Flexible Benefits Plan allows employees to select the benefits they prefer from groups of benefits established by the employer.

Flexible Spending Account allows employees to contribute pre-tax dollars to buy additional benefits.

Flextime occurs when employees work a set number of hours per day but vary starting and ending times.

Forecasting uses information from the past and present to identify expected future conditions.

Forced Distribution rates employees from highest to lowest performance and assumes results in a bell-shaped curve.

4/5ths Rule states that discrimination generally occurs if the selection rate for a protected group is less than 80% of their representation in the relevant labor market or 80% less than the majority group.

401(k) Plan allows employees to receive cash or to have employer contributions from profit-sharing and stock-bonus plans placed into a tax-deferred account.

Gainsharing is the sharing with employees of greater-than-expected gains in profits and/or productivity.

Garnishment is a court action in which a portion of an employee's wages is set aside to pay a debt owed a creditor.

Glass Ceiling refers to discriminatory practices that have prevented women and other protected-class members from advancing to executive-level jobs.

Golden Parachute is a severance benefit that provides protection and security to executives who may be affected if they lose their jobs or if their firms are acquired by another firm.

Graphic Rating Scale allows the rater to mark an employee's performance on a continuum.

Green-Circle Job is one in which the incumbent is paid below the range set for the job.

Grievance is a specific, formal notice of employee dissatisfaction expressed through an identified procedure.

Grievance Arbitration is a means of settling disputes arising from different interpretations of a labor contract by using a third party.

Grievance Procedure is a formal channel of communication used to resolve formal complaints (grievances).

Halo Effect is rating a person high or low on all items because of one characteristic.

Handbilling is written publicity given to employees by unions to convince the employees to sign authorization cards.

Health refers to a general state of physical, mental, and emotional well-being.

Health Maintenance Organization (HMO) is a form of health care that provides services for a fixed period on a prepaid basis.

HR Audit is a formal research effort that evaluates the current state of HR management in an organization

HR Generalist is a person with responsibility for performing a variety of HR activities.

HR Research analyzes past and present HR practices by using collected data and records.

HR Specialist is a person with in-depth knowledge and expertise in a limited area of HR.

Human Resource (HR) Development focuses on increasing the capabilities of employees for continuing growth and advancement.

Human Resource (HR) Management is the strategic and operational management of activities related to the performance of the human resources in an organization.

Human Resource (HR) Planning consists of analyzing and identifying the need for and availability of human resources required for an organization to meet its objectives.

Human Resource Information System (HRIS) is an integrated system designed to provide information used in HR decision making.

Illegal Issues are those issues that require either party to take illegal action.

Immediate Confirmation indicates that people learn best if reinforcement is given as soon as possible after training.

Incentive is compensation that rewards an employee for efforts beyond normal performance expectations.

Independent Contractors perform specific services on a contract basis.

An Individual Retirement Account (IRA) allows an employee to set aside funds in a special account keeping them tax deferred until the employee retires.

Individual-Centered Career Planning focuses on individuals' careers rather than organizational needs.

Industrial Union is one that includes many persons working in the same industry or company, regardless of jobs held.

Innovation is the introduction of new or creative methods, products, or services

Interfaces are areas of contact between the HR unit and managers within the organization.

Involuntary Part-Time Workers are individuals who work less than 35 hours per week, but would be working full time if they could.

Job is a grouping of similar positions having common tasks, duties, and responsibilities.

Job Analysis is a systematic way to gather and analyze information about the content of jobs, human requirements, and the context in which jobs are performed.

Job Criteria are the elements of a job to be evaluated during performance appraisal.

Job Depth refers to the amount of influence and control that employees have over their jobs.

Job Description specifies in written form the tasks, duties, and responsibilities of a job.

Job Design refers to organizing tasks, duties, and responsibilities into a unit of work.

Job Enlargement is broadening the scope of a job by expanding the number of different tasks to be performed.

Job Enrichment is increasing the depth of a job by adding employee responsibility for planning, organizing, controlling, and evaluating the job.

Job Evaluation is the systematic determination of the relative worth of jobs within an organization.

Job Rotation is the process of shifting a person from job to job.

Job Satisfaction is a positive emotional state resulting from the appraisal of one's job experiences.

Job Scope refers to the number of similar operations of a job.

Job Sharing is where two part-timers share one full-time job by choice.

Job Specifications list the knowledge, skills, and abilities an individual needs to do the job satisfactorily.

Just Cause includes reasons for dismissal usually spelled out in a union contract.

Keogh Plan allows self-employed individuals to establish an individualized pension plan.

Knowledge, Skills and Abilities (KSAs) include education, experience, work skill requirements, personal requirements, mental and physical requirements, and working conditions and hazards.

Labor Force Population includes all individuals who are available for selection if all possible recruitment strategies are used.

Lockout occurs when management shuts down company operations to prevent union members from working.

Loyalty is commitment to and allegiance with an organization.

Lump-Sum Increase is a one-time payment of all or part of a yearly pay increase.

Management Rights are those rights reserved to the employer to manage, direct, and control its business.

Mandated Benefits are benefits that employers are required by law to provide.

Mandatory Issues are those issues that are identified specifically by labor laws or court decisions as being subject to bargaining.

Market Price is the prevailing wage rate paid for a job in the immediate job market.

Massed Practice occurs when a person does all of the practice at once.

Maturity Curve depicts the relationship between experience and pay rates.

Mediation occurs when a third party assists the negotiators in their discussions and also suggests settlement proposals.

Mental Ability Tests measure reasoning capabilities of applicants.

Mentoring is a relationship in which managers at midpoints in careers aid individuals in the first stages of careers.

Microcomputers are the smallest computers and often are referred to as personal computers (PCs).

Moonlighting is work outside a person's regular employment that takes 12 or more additional hours per week.

Motivation is derived from the word motive and is an emotion or desire causing a person to act.

National Emergency Strike is one that affects an industry or a major part of it such that the national health or safety would be impeded.

Negative Reinforcement occurs when an individual works to avoid an undesirable consequence.

Noncontributory Plan is one in which all the funds for pension benefits are provided by the employer.

Nondirective Interview uses general questions, from which other questions are developed.

Nonexempt Employees are those who are required to be paid overtime under the Fair Labor Standards Act.

Ombudsman is a person outside the normal chain of command who acts as a problem solver for management and employees.

Organization-Centered Career Planning focuses on jobs and on constructing career paths that provide for the logical progression of people between jobs in one organization.

Organizational Culture is a pattern of shared values and beliefs giving members of an organization meaning and providing them with rules for behavior.

Orientation is the planned introduction of new employees to their jobs, co-workers, and the organization.

Outplacement is a group of services provided to displaced employees to give them support and assistance.

Paired Comparison formally compares each employee with every other employee in the rating group one at a time.

Pay is the basic compensation an employee receives, usually as a wage or salary.

Pay Compression occurs when pay differences among individuals become small.

Pay Grades are used to group together individual jobs having approximately the same job worth.

Pay Survey is a collection of data on existing compensation rates for workers performing similar jobs in other organizations.

Pension Plans are retirement benefits established and funded by employers and employees.

Performance Appraisal (PA) is the process of determining how well employees do their jobs compared with a set of standards and communicating that information to employees.

Performance Standards tell what the job accomplishes and what performance is considered satisfactory in each area of the job description.

Permissive Issues are those issues that are not mandatory but relate to the jobs.

Perquisites (PERKS) are special benefits for executives that are usually noncash items.

Piece-Rate System is a productivity-based compensation system in which an employee is paid for each unit of production.

Policies are general guidelines that regulate organizational actions.

Portability is a pension plan feature that allows employees to move their pension benefits from one employer to another.

Position is a collection of tasks, duties, and responsibilities performed by one person.

Positive Reinforcement occurs when a person receives a desired reward.

Predictive Validity uses test results of applicants to compare subsequent performance.

Preferred Provider Organization (PPO) is a health-care provider that contracts with an employer or an employer group to provide health-care services to employees at a competitive rate.

Primary Research is the method by which data are gathered directly on specific problems and issues.

Privatization occurs when services formerly performed by public employees are contracted to private-sector firms.

Procedural Justice is the perceived fairness of the process and procedures used to make decisions about employees, including their pay.

Procedures are customary methods of handling activities.

Productivity is a measure of the quantity and quality of work done, considering the cost of the resources it took to do the work.

Profit Sharing distributes a portion of the profits of the organization to employees.

Protected Class is composed of individuals who fall within a group identified for protection under equal employment laws and regulations.

Punishment is action taken to repel the person from the undesired action.

Quality Circles are small groups of employees who monitor productivity and quality and suggest solutions to problems

Ranking consists of listing all employees from highest to lowest in performances.

Rater BIAs occurs when a rater's values or prejudices distort the rating.

Ratification occurs when union members vote to accept the terms of a negotiated labor agreement.

Realistic Job Preview (RJP) is the process through which an interviewer provides a job applicant with an accurate picture of a job.

Reasonable Accommodation is a modification or adjustment to a job or work environment that enables a qualified individual with a disability to enjoy equal employment opportunity.

Recency Effect gives greater weight to recent occurences when appraising an individual's performance.

Recruiting is the process of generating a pool of qualified applicants for organizational jobs.

Red-Circle Job occurs when the incumbent is paid above the range set for the job.

Reinforcement is based on the law of effect that states that people tend to repeat responses that give them some type of positive reward and avoid actions that are associated with negative consequences.

Reliability refers to the consistency with which a test measures an item.

Responsibilities are obligations to perform certain tasks and duties.

Responsibility is a duty or obligation to be accountable for an action.

Retaliation occurs when an employer takes punitive actions against individuals who exercise their legal rights.

Reverse Discrimination may exist when a person is denied an opportunity because of preferences given to protected-class individuals who may be less qualified.

A Right is that which belongs to a person by law, nature, or tradition.

Right-to-Sue Letter is a letter issued by the EEOC that notifies a complainant that he/she has 90 days in which to file a personal suit in federal court.

Right-to-Work Laws are state laws that prohibit both the closed shop and the union shop.

Role-Playing is a development technique requiring the trainee to assume a role in a given situation and act out behaviors associated with that role.

Rules are specific guidelines that regulate and restrict the behavior of individuals.

Sabbatical Leave is paid time off the job to develop and rejuvenate oneself.

Safety refers to protection of the physical well-being of people.

Safety Hierarchy is the order in which actions should be taken to eliminate work safety problems.

Salary is payment that is consistent from period to period despite the number of hours worked.

Secondary Research uses research done by others and reported in articles in professional journals or books.

Selection is the process of choosing individuals who have relevant qualifications to fill jobs in an organization.

Selection Interview is designed to assess job-related knowledge, skills, and abilities (KSAs) and clarify information from other sources.

Self-Funding occurs when an employer sets aside funds to pay health claims in lieu of insurance coverage.

Serious Health Condition is one requiring inpatient, hospital, hospice, or residential medical care or continuing physician care.

Sexual Harassment refers to actions that are sexually directed, unwanted, and subject the worker to adverse employment conditions or that create a hostile work environment.

Silver Parachute is a severance and benefit plan to protect nonexecutives if their firms are acquired by another firm.

Simulation requires the participant to analyze a situation and decide the best course of action based on the data given.

Situational Interview is a highly structured interview limited strictly to job-related questions.

Spaced Practice occurs when several practice sessions are spaced over a period of hours or days.

Stock Option gives an individual the right to buy stock in a company, usually at a fixed price for a period of time.

Straight Piece-Rate System is a pay system in which wages are determined by multiplying the number of units produced by the piece-rate for one unit.

Strategic Planning is the process of identifying organizational objectives and the actions needed to achieve those objectives.

Stress Interview is used to create pressure and stress on an applicant to see how the person responds.

Strike occurs when workers refuse to work in order to put pressure on an employer.

Structured Interview uses a set of standardized questions that are asked of all job applicants.

Substance Abuse is the use of illicit substances or the misuse of controlled substances, alcohol, or other drugs.

Suggestion System is a formal method of obtaining employee input and upward communication.

Task is a distinct identifiable work activity composed of motions.

Tax Equalization Plan is used to protect expatriates from negative tax consequences.

Telecommuting is the process of going to work via electronic computing and telecommunications equipment.

Telecommuting is the process of going to work via electronic computing and telecommunications equipment.

Tester is a protected-class member who poses as an applicant to determine if employers discriminate in their hiring practices.

Testers are protected-class members who pose as applicants to determine if employers discriminate in their hiring practices.

Title VII is that portion of the 1964 Civil Rights Act prohibiting discrimination in employment.

Total Quality Management (TQM) is a comprehensive mangement process focusing on the continuous improvement of organizational activities to enhance the quality of the goods and services supplied

Training is a learning process whereby people acquire skills or knowledge to aid in the achievement of goals.

Turnover occurs when employees leave the organization and have to be replaced.

Two-Tier Wage Structure is one in which new union members receive lower wages and fewer benefits than existing members performing similar jobs.

Undue Hardship means an action requiring significant difficulty or expense for an employer in making "reasonable accommodation" for disabled individuals.

Union is a formal association of workers that promotes the interests of its members through collective action.

Union Security refers to provisions in bargaining to aid the union in obtaining and retaining members.

Union Shop requires that an employee join a union, usually 30 to 60 days after being hired.

Unit Labor Cost is the total labor cost per unit of output which is the average wages of workers divided by their levels of productivity.

Utility Analysis builds economic or other statistical models to identify the costs and benefits associated with specific HR activities.

Utilization Analysis identifies the number of protected-class members employed and the types of jobs they hold in an organization.

Utilization Review is an audit of the services and costs billed by health-care providers.

Validity means that a "test" actually measures what it says it measures.

Validity Generalization means that the validity of a test extends to different groups, similar jobs, and in other organizations.

Vesting is the right of employees to receive benefits from their pension plans.

Voluntary Part-Time Workers are individuals who by choice work less than 35 hours per week.

Wage and Salary Administration is the activity involved in the development, implementation, and maintenance of a base pay system.

Wages are payments directly calculated on the amount of time worked.

Well-Pay is extra pay for not taking sick leave.

Wellness Programs are programs designed to maintain or improve employee health before problems arise.

Whistle-Blower is a person who reports a real or perceived wrong done by his or her employer.

Work Sample Tests require an applicant to perform a simulated job task.

Work Sharing occurs when an employer reduces work hours and total pay for all or a segment of the employees.

Workers' Compensation provides benefits to a person injured on the job.

NAME INDEX

SUBJECT INDEX